What the critics said about
THE TRANSFER AGREEMENT

"Black...has meticulously documented this obscure but important slice of world history...makes an essential contribution to an understanding of Israeli politics and the strife in the Middle East today."

Gladwyn Hill, **Los Angeles Times**

"Black reconstructs in depressing detail the (Jewish world's) strident debates and acrimonious struggles...while pursuing the increasingly unrealistic goal of bringing the Third Reich to its knees."

A.J. Sherman, **The New York Times**

"A struggle to write a painful chapter in Jewish history. What Black began uncovering was a tangled account of an anguished moment in history, one that he at the center had to piece together from...forgotten archives, newspapers from the pre-WWII era and government records."

Jan Cawley, **Chicago Tribune Magazine**

"A fascinating book creating controversy all across the country. Edwin Black applied his established investigative journalism techniques to history. The result is an extraordinary book, *The Transfer Agreement*."

Bill Kurtis, **CBS Morning News**

"Meticulously researched...Black took five years to research and write this incredible volume...Black poses the controversial question: 'Was it madness or was it genius?' The many fascinated readers will have to decide for themselves."

Booklist, American Library Association

"Black brings an incredible amount of material together. With uncanny skill, he keeps it all under control. Five stars."

The Cincinnati Enquirer

"A passionate book certain to be controversial...(an) incredible job."

Chicago Sun-Times

"Black...gives particulars on...the great dilemma of 1933—whether to concentrate on toppling the Nazi regime through boycott or the extrication of German Jews before it was too late."

Publishers Weekly

THE
TRANSFER
AGREEMENT

THE DRAMATIC STORY OF THE
PACT BETWEEN THE
THIRD REICH AND
JEWISH PALESTINE

EDWIN BLACK

CARROLL & GRAF PUBLISHERS, INC.
NEW YORK

First Carroll & Graf edition 2001

Carroll & Graf Publishers, Inc.
A Division of Avalon Publishing Group
19 West 21st Street
New York, NY 10010-6805

Library of Congress Cataloging-in-Publication Data is available.
ISBN: 0-7867-0841-7

Manufactured in the United States of America

To the six million . . .
to my parents who survived . . .
to my grandparents
who didn't.

CONTENTS

PART VII **Decision at Geneva**

Introduction to the 2001 Edition
by Edwin Black

On August 7, 1933, leaders of the Zionist movement concluded a secret and controversial pact with the Third Reich which, in its various
forms, transferred some 60,000 Jews and $100 million to Jewish Pales-
tine. In return, Zionists would halt the worldwide Jewish-led anti-Nazi
boycott that threatened to topple the Hitler regime in its first year. Ultimately, the Transfer Agreement saved lives, rescued assets, and seeded
the infrastructure of the Jewish State.

Fiery debates instantly ignited throughout the pre-War Jewish world as
rumors of the pact leaked out. The acrimony was rekindled in 1984 with
the original publication of *The Transfer Agreement*—and has never stopped.
Understanding the painful process and the agonizing decisions taken by
Jewish leadership requires a journey. This journey will not be a comfortable one. It offers few clear-cut concepts and landmarks. The facts, as
they unfold, will challenge your sense of the period, break your heart, and
try your ethics . . . just as it did for those in 1933 who struggled to identify
the correct path through a Fascist minefield and away from the conflagration that awaited European Jewry.

Why? Simply put, *The Transfer Agreement* came out a decade ahead of
its time. When the book first appeared, in 1984, the world was still preoccupied with the enormity of Nazi genocide. The world's emphasis was on
the murderous events of the war years. The Jewish community's rallying
cry was "Never Forget." Organized remembrance was collectively fighting
an anti-Semitic revisionist movement that was trying to deny or minimize
the Holocaust with rabid pseudo-history.

For perspective, consider that the very first television attempt to treat
the Holocaust was a TV series called "The Holocaust," which aired in
1978, the same year neo-Nazis marched through Skokie. The Second
Generation movement of children of survivors was just forming. The
First World Gathering of Holocaust Survivors was only in the planning
stage. The U.S. Holocaust Memorial Museum, which received its charter
in 1980, was several years and many controversies away from opening.
Organized Holocaust education was essentially nonexistent. For society
and for survivors, the dominant priority was coming to grips with the
genocide.

Nearly seventeen years ago, the world was not ready to comprehend
the notion of Zionists and Nazis negotiating in Reich economic offices
over commercial pacts involving blocked Jewish bank accounts and

German merchandise sales volume. The wounds of destruction were too fresh, too exposed, too unhealed.

Understandably, *The Transfer Agreement* battered readers who struggled to reconcile its implications. Despite my scores of speaking engagements and explanatory articles, too many were not prepared for the details. Years later, the Transfer Agreement is still continuously debated, still the source of conflict and emotion. On the Web, in articles, in books, and in personal exchanges, few are neutral about this extraordinary pact.

In 1998, I was honored in a special ceremony at Chicago's Spertus Institute for *The Transfer Agreement*'s contribution to a better understanding of the Holocaust. The event commemorated my donation of 30,000 documents I had acquired during the book research. A woman in the audience tried to introduce herself, but was frozen in tears. I understood her emotions, emotions I have experienced every day since I began to write *The Transfer Agreement*, emotions I am experiencing this moment as I type these words. Some are vocal, some are silent, but most are visible in their reactions.

Just last year, on the anniversary of *Kristallnacht*, I was speaking on the subject at a synagogue in Roslyn, New York. Several in the congregation were survivors from Germany. One elderly survivor approached me after my remarks. She smiled. "I was there, just a girl—but never understood," she began. Trembling slightly, she took a deep breath, ready to say something more—much more—ready to defend or condemn, as people always do when encountering this topic. However, she stopped herself, regained her smile and simply said, "Thank you for explaining it." As she walked away, she was shaking her head.

I know her anguish.

When, as a young journalist in Chicago, I first learned of the agreement, the possibility of a Zionist-Nazi arrangement for the sake of Israel was inconceivable for a person of my background. My mother, as a girl, had been pushed by her mother through the vent of a boxcar on the way to the Treblinka death camp. She was shot by Nazi soldiers and buried in a shallow mass grave. My father had stepped out of line during a long march to a death camp train. While hiding in the woods, he came upon a leg protruding from the snow. This was my mother. Together, by night and by courage, these two Polish teenagers survived in the forest for two years. When the war was over, they cautiously emerged from the woods believing that all Jews had been exterminated—except them. The question for them was whether there was still any use being "Jewish." And yet—believing themselves to be the last of their people—they decided to live on, as Jews, and never forget.

Quickly, my parents learned that others had survived, although almost no one from their families. They resettled in the United States. I was born in Chicago, raised ordinarily in Jewish neighborhoods. Like many others, my parents tried never to speak of their experience. Like the other children of Holocaust survivors, my life was overshadowed by my family's tragedy. And, like other Jews, I saw the State of Israel as the salvation and redemption of the remnant of the Jewish people. My honeymoon was spent on an Israeli kibbutz. I had returned several times since then, and had long considered emigrating to Israel. The very meaning of Israel was a deep motivation in my life.

Yet there were incongruities I could never understand. Everywhere I looked in Israel, I saw German equipment. The icons of Nazi commerce—Mercedes, Grundig, Siemens, Krupp—were thriving in the Jewish State, even as the ban on Wagner's music was strictly enforced.

Rabbi Byron Sherwin of Spertus Institute had reminded me many times that the most important rule in approaching the Holocaust is that nothing makes sense. And yet I needed to make sense out of it. If I could, then perhaps there was a reason my mother and father had lived, while six million had died.

I spent the next several years traveling through Germany, Israel, England, and the United States, locating forgotten files in archives, scouring newspapers of the era, interviewing principals, and surveying government papers. Millions of microfilm frames of captured Nazi documents had never been analyzed. Boxes of boycott papers had never been organized. Worse, I found that precious little had been written about Hitler's first year—1933. For months, the information confounded me. Nothing made sense. There were so many contradictions. Nazis promoting Jewish nationalism. American Jewish leaders refusing even to criticize the Third Reich. Principal players who said one thing in public and did the opposite in private. Everything was upside down. And historians of the period told me they were equally confused about what had really occurred.

Finally I was able to piece the information together and reconstruct events. To do so, I had to clear my mind of preconceived notions and stare at the situation through the eyes of those who had survived it. And yet, after all the researching and reading and writing, my intense inner attachment to the Zionist concept and Jewish nationalism and the State of Israel had only deepened. That's because I had finally made sense of it. And anyone who does will understand Zionism for what it is: a national movement, with the rights and wrongs, the ethics and expediencies, found in any other national movement.

The Jews were the first to recognize the Hitler threat, and the first to react to that threat. The fact that they were foiled by their own disunity merely puts them in the company of all mankind. Who did not confront the Hitler menace with indecision? Who did not seal pacts of expediency with the Third Reich? The Catholic Church, the Lutheran Church, and the Supreme Moslem Council all endorsed the Hitler regime. The United States, England, France, Italy, Russia, Argentina, Japan, Ireland, and dozens of other nations all signed friendship and trade treaties with the

Reich and knowingly contributed to German economic and military recovery. The international banking and commercial community—no less
than the Zionists—saw Germany as indispensable to its salvation. The
Zionists were indeed in the company of all mankind—with this exception:
The Jews were the only ones with a gun to their heads.

Hitler was not unique; he was organized. But among Hitler's enemies,
none were organized—except the Zionists. The world recognized the
Hitler threat and hoped it would not arrive. The Zionists recognized
the Hitler threat and always expected it. The events of the Hitler era
and the Transfer Agreement were ultimately determined by those factors.

My belief in the Jewish people, in American Jewish organizations, in
Zionism, and in the State of Israel and its founding mothers and fathers
was never shaken. Those who sense outrage or anger in my words are
hearing but the echo of the agony of my discovery.

Now, seventeen years after the book's original publication, things have
changed. The Jewish community has succeeded in spotlighting for the
world the bloody horrors of the Holocaust. The U.S. Holocaust Memorial
Museum is America's most visited museum, annually attracting millions
of Americans and foreign visitors. Stirring memorials have been erected
in many other cities as well. Holocaust education has taken root throughout America. Holocaust Remembrance Day is solemnly observed. Movies
such as *Schindler's List* have made the ghastly nightmare of the Holocaust
a dramatic imperative for people worldwide. Even Hitler's chief American
propagandist, the Ford Motor Company, felt constrained to sponsor
Schindler's List on network television without commercials.

Most importantly, beginning in the 1990s, Holocaust-era asset concerns have leapt to the stage. Hard questions—hard fiscal questions—are
now being asked about the confiscations, exploitations, and expropriations
that victimized the Jews. Swiss banks stealing accounts, German companies
employing slave labor, art dealers trafficking in stolen masterpieces—all
this has prompted governments and the giants of commerce to begin peering into their distant past, fessing up to financial crimes committed against
Jews. These crimes made the Holocaust so economically acceptable, so
profitable, that it was easy to look away or even participate.

Now that the world has confronted the issue of pilfered Holocaust-era
assets—Jewish gold, Jewish art, Jewish insurance, and Jewish slave labor—the Transfer Agreement stands out as the sole example of a Jewish
asset rescue that occurred before the genocidal period. It was the sole success—and daring in its scope. The terrible choices its negotiators undertook can now be viewed in a new light. And that is why this new edition
has been released.

The final leg of my journey is not complete. Not yet.

I assure the world, the ultimate bastion of commercial collusion will be
exposed during the next five years. America's business giants wait across

the final frontier of Holocaust accountability. Holocaust organizations have long been compiling triple-digit lists of suspect American corporations that knowingly cooperated with the Hitler regime, helping it rearm, fortifying its anti-Semitic campaigns, catering to its lucrative plans of conquest and subjugation. It was these powerful corporations that joined the ranks of Nazism, frequently through overseas subsidiaries and special foreign partnerships. These American corporations were the grand economic and technologic wizards of Germany's meteoric recovery and her high-velocity destruction of the Jews. Only supported by the underpinnings of America's economic might was Hitler able to squeeze the Jews, confronting the Zionists with the painful necessity of engineering heartbreaking trade mechanisms with the Devil. The day of hiding behind corporate archivists, highly-paid publicists, and the distant haze of Nazi-era global commerce will soon come to an end.

People today—even more so in this new century—can understand what too many in the past found bewildering. We have all made a collective journey in confronting the Holocaust and its constellation of incomprehensible acts. Now take one more personal journey, back beyond the genocide, before the territorial expansion, to the first days of the twelve-year Hitler regime. I promise that your travels will bring tears and confusion, and they may rewrite everything you know about the period. But at the end of the journey, you too will understand that while the boycott against Hitler did not succeed, it did not fail. For without the worldwide effort to topple the Third Reich, Hitler would have never agreed to the Transfer Agreement. And without the Transfer Agreement, a precious human and financial remnant would not have been saved—a remnant indispensable to building the Jewish State.

The message of *The Transfer Agreement* was in fact the chronicle of the anguish of choice—itself the quintessential notion of Zionism's historical imperative. This book and its documentation posits one question: when will the Jewish people not be compelled to make such choices? Indeed, when will all people similarly confronted be freed from the desperation of such choices?

Perhaps the answer extends beyond the inherent evil of men, reaching also to the complicit greed of corporations. Only when the last nickel and *pfennig* of confession and accountability has been recorded—from the smokestacks of Germany to the stately boardrooms of the United States—will powerful global enterprises realize that the worst instincts of humanity cannot be the best investments for mankind. Only then will the mission of *The Transfer Agreement* be complete. Then I can stop.

Edwin Black
Washington D.C.
February 2001

Acknowledgements

to the 1984 Edition

Great projects are dependent upon two factors: money and people. I didn't have money, but I was blessed with wonderful, giving people. And so many of them became dear friends.

First, my translators and researchers: Gerald Bichunsky, who labored at my side in New York, Chicago, and Jerusalem, working in Hebrew, Yiddish and English; George Zinnemann, who worked in French, German, and English in Washington, Boston, New York, Miami, and London, and who accompanied me to Munich, Bonn, Koblenz, and Berlin; Danuta Dombrowska, who handled German, English, and Polish documents in Jerusalem; Gali Gur, who assisted in interviews, pored over the Hebrew and German documents newspapers, and managed a team of twelve in Israel; Dan Niederland in Munich and Manfred Seyfried in Frankfurt, who worked with German materials; and Nathan Snyder of Austin, Texas, who translated hundreds of pages of Hebrew and German books.

Special thanks to my research assistants: Kathy Maass and Bradley Kliewer in Chicago.

A most vital part of the project was tracing back sources and checking details. That monumental task fell to Beryl Satter and others, who single-handedly triple-checked the accuracy of thousands of sources. This took fourteen grueling months of working full time for little pay.

In addition to those whom I recruited, there were many others who acted above and beyond, and without whose generous and sensitive cooperation the project would have been an impossible task. I speak now of archivists and librarians: Fannie Zelcer and Abraham Peck of the American Jewish Archives in Cincinnati; Richard Marcus of the Asher Library at Spertus College in Chicago; Robert Wolfe and George Wagner of the National Archives in Washington; Sybil Milton of the Leo Baeck Institute in New York; Sylvia Landress of the Zionist Archives in New York; Feiga Zilberminc of the Library of Congress in Washington; Helen Ritter and Ruth Rauch of the American Jewish Committee Archives in New York; Martha Katz-Hyman of the American Historical Society in Waltham; David Massel of the Board of Deputies Archives in London; Klaus Weinandy of the German Foreign Office and the Politische Archiv in Bonn; Shmuel Krakovsky at Yad Vashem Archives in Jerusalem; and Michael Heymann at the Central Zionist Archives in Jerusalem. These people reached out to assist me, and many of them gave me personal inspiration and understanding.

Of course, there were many other generous archivists too numerous to list here, but they as well have my special thanks. Libraries were also vital to my work because each library is distinguished by its own special collections and its own unique selection of publications from the period. Moreover, without the interlibrary loan program, I could not have worked with forgotten volumes suddenly discovered in distant cities but needed urgently. And so I give sincere thanks to the library staffs of Spertus College; Northwestern, Harvard, Columbia, and Roosevelt universities; Hebrew Union College; the University of Bonn; the University of Frankfurt; the Israel National Library at Hebrew University; the University of Texas at Austin; the public libraries of Chicago, Boston, and New York; the American Jewish Periodical Center in Cincinnati; the Center for Library Research in Chicago; and the British Library in London.

Doors throughout the world were opened for me through the gracious help of many people. At the top of the list of those who helped is Rosemary Krensky, followed by Byron Sherwin, Sybil Milton, Robert Wolfe, Fannie Zelcer, David Kahn, Maynard Wishner, Carl Voss, and friends in the Israeli government. Once inside the doors, I needed guidance, and it was granted by many who gave me their time and expertise, including those mentioned above as well as Shaul Arlosoroff, Yehuda Bauer, Jack Boas, Ehud Evriel, Werner Feilchenfeld, Morris Frommer, Yoav Gelber, Moshe Gottlieb, Ben Halpern, John L. Heineman, Yehiel Kudaschai, Abraham Margoliot, Dolf Michaelis, Justine Wise Polier, Arthur Schweitzer, David Yisraeli, and many others.

The monumental challenge of this book would have been impossible to face without the support of my friends, including Robert Tamarkin, Max Pastin, Richard Kimmel, members of my research team, my loving parents Harry and Ethel Black, and the one man who pressed me endlessly but without whom this book would never have come to pass: Edward T. Chase.

Edwin Black
Chicago
1984

Acknowledgements

to the 2001 Edition

The impetus for this updated edition has etched its own list of special names. More than a few are the same as in 1984, precisely because the original *Transfer Agreement* project created so many enduring friendships. Some are new because the book launched many new relationships.

Publishing encouragement came from many quarters, but chief among them was Lynne Rabinoff, who carried *The Transfer Agreement*'s message to the publishers of the world. She worked tirelessly to preserve the book's integrity and encouraged me to produce this special edition. As a result of her efforts, additional generations will continue to explore the anguished events of that era, and my struggle to bring the story to light. The edition's editor, Philip Turner, experienced the original release in 1984. Philip is more to me than the editor on this re-release. He is a person who created a special impact in my own career, and in the public's understanding of the Holocaust. Without these two indefatigable and committed professionals, the ink and paper of the new edition could never have come together.

Academic and communal support again came from the recently-deceased Sybil Milton, and from Spertus Institute of Chicago, including its president Howard Sulkin and its academic dean, Byron Sherwin. Rabbi Sherwin's wisdom and insight has inspired many, but has inspired me especially. It was only right that all the papers, documentation, and research materials associated with the book have been donated to Spertus Institute's Chicago Jewish Archives.

Towering above all the defenders of Jewish rights and liberty anywhere in the world today is Abraham H. Foxman, who wrote the new Afterword. Abe Foxman's understanding of hard choices in the face of jeopardy is a precious asset for all mankind.

In my original acknowledgements, I thanked my parents, and wife Elizabeth, who has earned my enduring gratitude. During the first tour, fifteen years ago, my wife gave birth to our daughter, Rachel. Several years ago, at Rachel's Bat Mitzvah, I gave her my personal copy of the original version of *The Transfer Agreement*. I am happy to say that she will be the first member of the Third Generation to read the new edition. How much more thankful and indebted can one person be for the opportunities my parents gave me in surviving, my wife gave me in helping me tell this story, and my daughter in carrying its message into the new Millennium.

Edwin Black
Washington, D.C.
February 2001

Introduction to the 1984 Edition
by Edwin Black

On August 7, 1933, leaders of the Zionist movement concluded a secret and controversial pact with the Third Reich which in its various forms transferred some 60,000 Jews and $100 million to Jewish Palestine. In return, Zionists would halt the worldwide Jewish-led anti-Nazi boycott that threatened to topple the Hitler regime in its first year. Ultimately, the Transfer Agreement saved lives, rescued assets, and seeded the infrastructure of the Jewish State.

Fiery debates instantly ignited throughout the pre-War Jewish world as rumors of the pact leaked out. The acrimony was rekindled in 1984 with the original publication of *The Transfer Agreement* and has never stopped. Understanding this painful process and the agonizing decisions taken by Jewish leadership requires a journey. This journey will not be a comfortable one with clear-cut concepts and landmarks. The facts, as they unfold, will challenge your sense of the period, break your heart and try your ethics... just as it did for those in 1933 who tried to find the correct path through a Fascist minefield and away from the conflagration that awaited European Jewry.

To discover *The Transfer Agreement*, I took that journey.

It began in 1978 when a small band of misfits preaching Nazism and waving swastikas decided to march through the predominantly Jewish Chicago suburb of Skokie. Suddenly an unimportant group of bigots provoked an important controversy. The outraged community was determined either to prevent the march or to confront the neo-Nazis on the parade route. Many Skokie residents were Holocaust survivors and remembered well that only fifty years before, Hitler's circle had also started as a small band of social misfits. The Jewish community would not ignore an attempt to reintroduce the Nazi concept—no matter how feeble the source.

But establishment Jewish leaders counseled Jews to shutter their windows and pay no attention. And a Jewish attorney from the American Civil Liberties Union rose reluctantly to champion the neo-Nazis' right to freedom of expression— over the survivors' right to be left alone. In covering the issue as a young journalist, and reacting to the crisis as a Jew and the son of Holocaust survivors, I was confused by the response of Jewish leaders.

To prepare for a *Chicago Reader* interview with the Jewish ACLU attorney representing the neo-Nazis, I spoke with Jewish scholar Rabbi Byron Sherwin. He told me there were many enigmas about the Jewish response to Nazism, one of which was a long-rumored arrangement between the Third Reich and the Zionist Organization involving the transfer of German Jewish assets to Palestine. He added that little was known about the arrangement, if it indeed existed.

I couldn't believe what I had heard. The possibility of a Zionist-Nazi arrangement for the sake of Israel was inconceivable for a person of my background. My mother as a girl had been pushed by her mother through the vent of a boxcar on the way to the Treblinka death camp. She was shot by Nazi soldiers and buried in a shallow mass grave. My father had stepped out of line during a long march to a death camp train. While hiding in the woods, he came upon a leg protruding from the snow. This was my mother. Together, by night and by courage, these two Polish teenagers survived in the forest for two years. When the war was over, they cautiously emerged from the woods believing that all Jews had been exterminated—except them. The question for them was whether there was still any use being "Jewish." And yet—believing themselves to be the last of their people—they decided to live on, as Jews, and never forget.

Quickly, my parents learned that others had survived, although almost none from their families. They resettled in the United States. I was born in Chicago, raised in Jewish neighborhoods, and my parents tried never to speak of their experience. Like the other children of Holocaust survivors, my life was overshadowed by my family's tragedy. And, like other Jews, I saw the State of Israel as the salvation and redemption of the remnant of the Jewish people. My honeymoon had been spent on an Israeli kibbutz. I had returned several times since then, and had long considered emigrating to Israel. The very meaning of Israel was a deep motivation in my life.

Yet there were incongruities I could never understand. Everywhere I looked in Israel, I saw German equipment. The names of Nazi commerce—Mercedes, Grundig, Siemens, Krupp—were thriving in the Jewish State, even as the ban on Wagner's music was strictly enforced. And so many families were German Jews who had come to Israel during the Hitler era.

For a year I filed Rabbi Sherwin's rumor in a mental box of imponderables. He had said many times that the most important rule in approaching the Holocaust is that nothing makes sense. And yet I needed to make sense out of it. If I could, then perhaps there was a reason my mother and father had lived, while six million had died.

Working through the staff and resources of Spertus College of Judaica, I was able to obtain some rare Hebrew and German materials that documented in skeletal form that the arrangement indeed existed. After a great deal of personal anguish, I made my decision.

When I told my parents, my mother threatened to disown me and my father threatened personally to strangle me if I would dare lend any credence to the notion of Nazi-Zionist cooperation. This was done against a background of anti-Semitic and anti-Israeli attempts to somehow link the Nazi regime with Zionists.

When I later showed my parents a hundred-page summary of my proposed book, my mother cried and said, "Now I understand what I could never understand. Write the book." My father, who fought in the war as a Zionist Betar partisan, also gave me his blessing with the simple words: "Go write the book."

My agent said he thought there was only one editor with the stamina to take on this book. That man was Edward T. Chase, editor-in-chief of New York Times Books, a man with preeminent credentials in WWII and Holocaust books. Chase read the proposal and said yes.

I spent the next several years traveling through Germany, Israel, England, and the United States, locating forgotten files in archives, scouring newspapers of the era, interviewing principals, and surveying government papers. Millions of microfilm frames of captured Nazi documents had never been analyzed. Boxes of boycott papers had never been organized. Worse, I found that little had been written about Hitler's first year—1933. For months, the information confounded me. Nothing made sense. There were so many contradictions. Nazis promoting Jewish nationalism. American Jewish leaders refusing even to criticize the Third Reich. Principal players who said one thing in public and did the opposite in private. Everything was upside down. And historians of the period told me they were equally confused about what had really occurred.

Finally I was able to piece the information together and reconstruct events. To do so, I had to clear my mind of preconceived notions and stare at the situation through the eyes of those who lived through it. And yet, after all the researching and reading and writing, my intense inner attachment to the Zionist concept and Jewish nationalism and the State of Israel had only deepened. That's because I had finally made *sense* of it. And anyone who does will understand Zionism for what it is: a national movement, with the rights and wrongs, the ethics and expediencies found in any other national movement.

The Jews were the first to recognize the Hitler threat, and the first to react to that threat. The fact that they were foiled by their own disunity merely puts them in the company of all mankind. Who did not confront the Hitler menace with indecision? Who did not seal pacts of expediency with the Third Reich? The Catholic Church, the Lutheran Church, and the Supreme Moslem Council all endorsed the Hitler regime. The United States, England, France, Italy, Russia, Argentina, Japan, Ireland, Poland, and dozens of other nations all signed friendship and trade treaties and knowingly contributed to German economic and military recovery. The international banking and commercial community—no less than the Zionists—saw Germany as indispensable to its salvation. The Zionists were indeed in the company of all mankind—with this exception: the Jews were the only ones with a gun to their heads.

Hitler was not unique; he was organized. But among Hitler's enemies, none were organized—except the Zionists. The world recognized the Hitler threat and hoped it would not arrive. The Zionists recognized the Hitler threat and always expected it. The events of the Hitler era and the Transfer Agreement were ultimately determined by those factors.

My belief in the Jewish people, in American Jewish organizations, in Zionism, and in the State of Israel and its founding mothers and fathers was never shaken. Those who sense outrage or anger in my words are hearing but the echo of their agony.

But many have been unable to take the journey as I did. Put simply, *The Transfer Agreement* came out fifteen years ahead of its time. Some context may help. When the book first appeared, in 1984, the world was still preoccupied with the enormity of Nazi genocide. The Jewish community's emphasis was on the murderous events of the War years. The rallying cry of the Jewish community was "Never Forget." They were fighting the anti-Semitic revisionist movement that was trying to deny or minimize the Holocaust with its brand of rabid pseudo-history. For perspective, consider that the very first television attempt to treat the Holocaust was a TV series called "The Holocaust," which aired in 1978, the year of that Skokie march. The Second Generation movement of children of survivors was just forming. The First World Gathering of Holocaust Survivors was only in the planning stage. The U.S. Holocaust Museum, which received its charter in 1980, was several years and many controversies away from opening. Organized Holocaust education was essentially nonexistent. For society and for survivors, the dominant priority was coming to grips with the genocide.

The world was not ready to comprehend the notion of Zionists and Nazis negotiating in Reich economic offices over commercial pacts involving blocked Jewish bank accounts and German merchandise trade levels. The wounds of destruction were too fresh, too exposed, too unhealed. *The Transfer Agreement* battered readers who struggled to reconcile its implications. Despite scores of speaking engagements and explanatory articles, too many were not prepared for the details. Only last year, in 1998, I was honored in a special ceremony at Chicago's Spertus Institute for *The Transfer Agreement's* contribution to a better understanding of the Holocaust. The event was on the occasion of my donation of the 30,000 documents I acquired during the book research. A woman tried to introduce herself, but was frozen in tears. I understood her emotions, emotions I have experienced every day since I began to write *The Transfer Agreement*, emotions I am experiencing this moment as I type these words.

But things have changed. In the fifteen years since the book's original publication, the Jewish community succeeded in spotlighting for the world the bloody horrors of the Holocaust. The U.S. Holocaust Memorial is Washington D.C.'s most visited museum, annually attracting millions of Americans and foreign visitors. Stirring memorials have been erected in many other cities as well. Holocaust education is beginning to take root throughout America. Holocaust Remembrance Day is solemnly observed. Movies such as *Schindler's List* have made the ghastly nightmare of the Holocaust a dramatic imperative for people worldwide. Even Hitler's greatest American ally, the Ford Motor Company, felt constrained to sponsor *Schindler's List* on network television without commercials.

Most importantly, in the nineties, Holocaust-era asset concerns leapt to the stage. Hard questions—hard fiscal questions—are now being asked about the confiscations, exploitations, and expropriations that victimized the Jews. Swiss banks stealing accounts, German companies employing slave labor, art dealers trafficking in stolen masterpieces, and many others in European government and commerce are now peering into their distant past, fessing up to financial crimes committed against Jews. These crimes made the Holocaust so economically acceptable, so profitable, that it was easy to look away or even participate.

Now that the world has confronted the issue of pilfered Holocaust-era assets—Jewish gold, Jewish art, Jewish insurance, and Jewish slave labor—the Transfer Agreement stands out as the sole example of a Jewish asset rescue that occurred before the genocidal period. It was the sole success—and daring in its scope. The terrible choices its negotiators undertook can now be viewed in a new light. And that is why this new edition has been released.

The final leg of my journey is now complete.

People today can understand what too many in the past found bewildering. We have all made a journey in confronting the Holocaust and its constellation of incomprehensible acts. Now take one more journey, back beyond the genocide, before the territorial expansion, to the first days of the twelve-year Hitler regime. I promise that your travels will bring tears and confusion, and they may rewrite everything you know about the period. But at the end of the journey, you too will understand that while the boycott against Hitler did not succeed, it did not fail. For without the worldwide effort to topple the Third Reich, Hitler would have never agreed to the Transfer Agreement. And without the Transfer Agreement a precious human and financial remnant would have never been saved—a remnant indispensable to building the Jewish State.

PART I

·

Approaching Day One

1. The Powers That Were

SHOCK WAVES rumbled through the world on January 30, 1933. The leader of a band of political hooligans had suddenly become chief of a European state. Before January 30, 1933, the repressive ideology of the National Socialist German Workers Party—NSDAP—had been resisted by the German government. That would all change now.

Hitler had become chancellor of Germany—a shock, but no surprise. The November 1932 general elections were held amid public hysteria over Germany's economic depression. Despite expensive emergency makework programs, more than 5 million people were still unemployed on election eve. In some areas the jobless rate was 75 percent. More than 17 million persons—about a third of the entire population—were dependent upon a welfare stipend equivalent to a few dollars per family per month. Such families knew hungry nights once or twice weekly. Destitute people slept in the streets. The memory of closed or defaulted banks was fresh. The Nazis blamed the Jews and sought voter support through street violence against Jewish members of Germany's urban middle class.

But the November 1932 election was indecisive. Hitler's party received only a third of the vote, about 12 million ballots. Then a coalition government was blocked by Hitler's refusal to share power with the Socialists, who controlled 20 percent of the vote, and the Communists, who controlled 17 percent. Finally, in exasperation, on January 30, 1933, President Paul von Hindenburg exercised his emergency powers, appointing Herr Adolf Hitler interim chancellor.

The Nazis had promised that upon assuming power they would rebuild Germany's economy, dismantle its democracy, destroy German Jewry, and establish Aryans as the master race—in that order. Yet many Western leaders saw only the economic value of Nazism. Hitler seemed the only alternative to a Communist state, a man who might rebuild the German economy and pay Germany's debts. That would be good for all Western economies. As for the threat to Germany's Jews, that was a domestic German affair.[1]

Therefore, if the world's governments would not act, it would fall to the influential Jews of America to save their brethren in Germany. With the ability to be heard, the Jews of America, especially in New York, could mobilize economic and political pressure against Germany that would make war against the Jews a campaign of national suicide.

American Jewish muscle was not a sudden imagined power. For nearly a century, American Jews had been using economic pressure and protest to beat back anti-Semitic outrages throughout the world. But this time the American Jewish community would fail. That failure was tied to the so-called Big Three defense groups: the American Jewish Committee, B'nai B'rith, and the American Jewish Congress.

Both the American Jewish Committee and B'nai B'rith were founded by well-to-do German Jews with a special outlook. Like other European Jews, the Germans immigrated en masse following the political upheavals of the mid-nineteenth century. But unlike their East European counterparts, the Germans clung to their original national identity, and were economically more established. Moreover, many German Jews believed they were so-called *Hoffuden*, or courtly Jews, and that coreligionists from Poland and Russia were "uncivilized" and embarrassing. The bias was best summarized in a June 1894 German-American Jewish newspaper, the *Hebrew Standard*, which declared that the totally acclimated American Jew is closer to "Christian sentiment around him than to the Judaism of these miserable darkened Hebrews."[2]

Having achieved a secure standing in America, the German Jews organized essentially to protect their position from any "Jewish problems" that might appear. In 1843, in a small café on New York's Lower East Side, twelve German Jewish leaders founded B'nai B'rith as a benevolent fraternal organization. By aiding the Jewish poor, they hoped to remove any Jewish welfare burden that could arouse Christian anti-Semitism. In the 1880s, after hordes of impoverished East European Jews flooded America, B'nai B'rith accepted these newcomers as lodge members, but largely to "manage" the East European Jewish presence in the United States.[3]

In 1906, as Czar Nicholas continued his anti-Semitic pogroms, men like Jacob Schiff, Louis Marshall, and Cyrus Adler went beyond philanthropy and constituted the American Jewish Committee. These powerful men would now function as a special lobby concerned with political problems important to Jews. The Committee initially limited its membership to roughly sixty prominent men, led by about a dozen central personalities from the realms of publishing, finance, diplomacy, and the law.[4] As individuals, they had already proven themselves combating hotels and other institutions that discriminated against Jews. Once united as the American Jewish Committee, they waged effective private economic war against the Russian monarchy. Their motives were not based on concern for East European Jews, but rather on a solid opposition to organized Jew hatred anywhere in the world.

But in 1933 things would be different. Quick as they were to oppose anti-Semitism in foreign lands, Germany held a special place in the hearts of Committee leaders. A foreshadowing of just how emotionally paralyzed the Committee would become in a crisis involving their ancestral home was amply displayed during the early years of World War I. Committee stalwarts were torn between their loyalties to the German Fatherland and America's popular allegiance to France and Britain. In 1915, Committee cofounder Jacob Schiff articulated his conflict in a note to German banker Max Warburg: "I still cherish the feeling of filial devotion for the country in which my fathers and forefathers lived, and in which my own cradle stood—a devotion which imbues me with the hope that Germany shall not be defeated in this fearful struggle."[5] Committee members' open support for Germany against Russia did not alter until the United States actually entered the war.

Popular Jewish disenchantment over Committee policies and the known *Hofjuden* prejudice against the Jewish multitudes had long alienated America's East European Jewish community. Increasingly, the Jewish majority saw the gentlemen of the American Jewish Committee as benevolent despots, not entitled to speak for them.[6] In response, a number of national and regional Jewish organizations gathered in Philadelphia in June 1917 and affiliated into the American Jewish Congress. Proving their democratic character, 335,000 Jewish ballots from across the nation were cast. Three hundred delegates were elected and an additional one hundred appointed, representing thirty national Jewish organizations.[7]

After the war, the question of who would represent Jewish interests at the Peace Conference was bitterly contested. A delegation cutting across Committee and Congress lines finally did assemble at Versailles. But the Committee split off from other American Jewish groups negotiating Jewish rights when—in the Committee view—the proposed rights went "too far." Specifically, when Versailles mapmakers were redrawing boundaries based on religious, linguistic, and other ethnic affinities, popular Jewish sentiment demanded to be counted among the minority groups targeted for self-determination. That meant a Jewish homeland in Palestine—Zionism.[8]

Committee leaders were repulsed by Zionism. In their view, a refuge in Palestine would promote Jewish expulsions from countries where Jews lived and enjoyed roots. Anti-Semitic regimes could point to Palestine and claim, "You belong *there* in your own nation."[9] However, majority Jewish sentiments won out at Versailles, assuring a Jewish homeland in Palestine, with stipulations preserving Jewish rights in other countries.

American Jewish Congress leaders returned from Versailles in triumph. They had helped create a Jewish homeland, as well as secure international guarantees for minorities in Europe. In the early 1920s, the Congress solidified its popular Jewish support, thereby becoming the third of the so-called Big Three.

By 1933, the Congress stood as the most representative and outspoken Jewish defense organization. In contrast, B'nai B'rith functioned as little more than a fraternal order (except for its autonomous Anti-Defamation League). And the Committee, in 1933, basically represented the interests of about three hundred and fifty prominent Jewish members. Nonetheless, the Committee and B'nai B'rith—which often acted as a binary lobby—were respected, influential, and adequately financed, with access to the most powerful circles of American government and business. By comparison, the Congress, despite its vast membership, constantly struggled for funds and for recognition. While the Committee and B'nai B'rith generally chose quiet, behind-the-scenes methods, Congress people—predominantly East Europeans—were accustomed to attention-getting protests.[10]

Yet, all were Jews, drawn from a common heritage. And as of January 30, 1933, there arose a clear need to unify to combat the greatest single anti-Jewish threat ever posed. Hitler promised not only to rid Germany of its Jews, but to cleanse the world as well. Action by America's Jews was required—fast action.

As Adolf Hitler's Nazi party was taking over Germany, as the German Jews of New York were dominating the American Jewish political scene, so too, would Germans and Germany now determine the realities in a small, undeveloped stretch of desert by the sea known as Palestine. For hundreds of years, the area had been the kingdom of the Jews. After the Israelites' dispersion in the second century A.D., the Romans changed the region's name to Syria Palaestina to wipe away the Jewish nation forever. Small groups of Jews had remained through the centuries in what became known simply as Palestine, but not until the late nineteenth century, following waves of European anti-Semitism, did large numbers of Jews begin an experimental return to their ancestral home. Agricultural settlements repeatedly failed in Palestine as Jewish idealists and dreamers tried to force the sandy and swampy wasteland to bloom. But with the steady help of European and American Jewish philanthropists, the Jewish agricultural revival finally began to triumph over the neglected Palestinian terrain.[11]

By the time airplanes were flying over the Mideast, the future of Jews in Palestine could be seen as green patches against a bleached beige backdrop. The green patches marked orange groves, the economic basis for Jewish survival in the Holy Land. When the young workers came from Russia, Poland, and even the United States, they were frequently settled on groves to grow oranges and other citrus for export.[12] Orange crates became the building blocks of Zionism.

Promising as those orange groves were, Jewish Palestine in 1933 was still little more than a collection of unconnected enclaves between the Jordan River and the Mediterranean Sea. The nearly 200,000 Jews living in Palestine accounted for only 19 percent of the population. If the enclaves were to grow into an actual homeland and fulfill the promise of God, Abraham, and Balfour, the orange groves would have to prosper. For that, more hands and more lands were needed.

But in 1933, Jewish prosperity in Palestine was in danger of shutting down. In a tense world, the British were once again making strategic plans for the Middle East. These plans were dependent upon the Arab potentates

England had been stringing along for a decade with conflicting promises of Arab nationalism in Palestine. So Palestinian immigration regulations had been pointedly revised a few years earlier. Severe quotas now applied to all Jewish immigrant categories, except the so-called *capitalist* settler with proof of £1,000 (about $5,000) in hand.[13]

Few Palestine-bound Jews possessed that much money. Most were poor European workers. Moreover, the "worker immigrant" quota itself was limited by "absorptive capacity" or the ability of the Palestinian economy to expand and provide new jobs. In this way, existing Arab jobs theoretically would no longer be threatened by new Jewish arrivals. The British didn't really expect the Palestinian economy to grow, because quotas restricted immigration for all but the wealthier Jews, and the great majority of wealthy Jews were uninterested in emigrating to Palestine. With little or no new capital, the Jewish economy in Palestine would stagnate.

At the same time, the message to the world was clear. What began as a private campaign of violence against Jews was now, under Hitler, the unofficial policy of the day. Jews were murdered in their homes, daughters were raped before parents' eyes, rabbis were humiliated in the street, prominent leaders were found floating in the canals and rivers. As early as the first days after Hitler's surprise appointment as interim chancellor, the message was indeed clear to those who would pay attention: The Jews of Germany were facing an hourglass, and time was slipping away.

2. The Ideological Struggle

REACTIONS to Nazi anti-Semitism were immediate, especially in America, reflecting the cross-sectional anger of ordinary people. Naturally, Jewish Americans were at the vanguard. That was a problem for many in Jewish leadership who considered Jewish protest their private province.

On February 22, 1933, B'nai B'rith president Alfred Cohen convened a special conference of fifteen Jewish leaders, five from each of the Big Three. Meeting in New York, the leaders reviewed the situation.[1] Thus far, Hitler was nothing more than an interim chancellor appointed until the next general elections scheduled for March 5. By March 5, Hitler might be gone. But if the election increased Hitler's voter support from a minority 33 percent to an actual majority, he would control the entire German government.

The conference was divided. Two of the American Jewish Congress representatives had discussed a series of public protests, here and abroad, to show the German people that the world was indeed watching and that Brownshirt violence against Jews must stop. The men of B'nai B'rith and the American Jewish Committee rejected this. B'nai B'rith didn't want to endanger its 13,000-member German organization or its 103 fraternal lodges in Germany by publicly antagonizing Hitler and the Nazis. The Committee leadership had close friends and relatives in Germany who had advised that public protest would surely provoke a far stronger Nazi counterreaction. Finally, the leaders agreed to establish a "Joint Conference Committee" merely to "watch developments in Germany very carefully" and hope for the best.[2]

But as the gathering broke up with an apparent trilateral agreement to keep mum, the Congress people planned otherwise. They hadn't told the B'nai B'rith or the Committee representatives, but two weeks earlier the Congress had secretly decided to pursue the path of protest.[3]

On February 27, 1933, the Hitler takeover began. Hitler himself was attending a party at Propaganda Minister Paul Joseph Goebbels' Berlin apartment. A frantic telephone call to Goebbels relayed the news: "The Reichstag is burning!" The Nazis snapped into action. During that night Hitler and Goebbels prepared a propaganda campaign. By the next morning, the German public was convinced that the fire—which Hitler's own people probably ignited—was in fact the beginning of a Jewish-backed Communist uprising. Hitler demanded and received temporary powers suspending all constitutional liberties.

The Nazis were riding a wave of anti-Jewish, anti-Communist hysteria. In the name of defending the nation from a Communist revolution, Hitler's private militia—the Storm Troopers, or SA, together with rank-and-file party Brownshirts—destroyed editorial offices, brutalized political opponents, and increased atrocities against Jews. Through it all, Nazi-dominated local police forces looked the other way. The apparatus of law and order in Germany had been suddenly switched off.

One week before the Reichstag fire, Hitler had met with over a dozen leading industrialists to assure them that nothing was as important to the Nazis as rebuilding the German economy. This was to be the foundation of a strong, rearmed Germany, which, under Hitler, would prepare for war and racial domination. All Hitler wanted from the gathered industrialists was their financial support in the days preceding the March 5 general election. Before the meeting was over, roughly $1 million was pledged to establish an unparalleled propaganda war chest, all to be spent over the next two weeks. With that prodigious sum, the Nazis were able to saturate every newspaper and radio station, dispatch pamphleteers to every city, and flood the streets of Germany with sound trucks blaring election propaganda. Under Hitler's emergency powers, only Nazis were permitted to rally voter support.

Yet when the March 5 votes were counted, the Nazis were still unable to muster a majority. Despite the biggest campaign blitz in history, Hitler polled only 43.9 percent of the vote. Only after sealing alliances with other right-wing parties did Hitler achieve a slim majority. Nevertheless, he called it a "mandate" and promised to quickly eradicate the enemies of Germany: Communism, democracy, and the Jews.

As the polls were opening March 5, the largest Jewish organization in Germany, the Central Verein in Berlin, issued a statement: "In meetings and certain newspapers, violence against Jews is propagated. . . . The spirit of hatred now directed against the Jews will not halt there. It will spread and poison the soul of the German people." When local Nazi party activists learned of the statement, Storm Troopers vandalized the Central Verein office. Worried about the impact of such news among anti-Nazi circles in New York, Nazi leader Hermann Goering summoned Central Verein leaders to his office for a formal apology and assurances that the incident would be the last.[4]

But within days, Germany's dark future became clear. On March 8 and 9, Hitler's Storm Troopers smashed into the provinces and towns. Within forty-eight hours, provincial authority was virtually disassembled and replaced with Hitler's hand-chosen people. At the same time, the Nazis began attaching party observers or *kommissars* to all major newspapers, companies, and organizations. Carefully orchestrated anti-Jewish actions in Essen, Magdeburg, and Berlin accompanied the takeover. In some cases, Nazi flags were merely raised over Jewish store entrances as owners "voluntarily" closed. In other cases, windows were shattered, stench bombs rolled in, customers escorted out, and proprietors manhandled.[5]

The Nazis now controlled not only the federal government, but state and local governments as well. Virtually every institution was now subject to Nazi party dicta and brought into readiness for the achievement of Nazi social, political, and economic aspirations—including the elimination of German Jewry. On March 9, Central Verein leaders returned to Goering's Berlin office. He again used reassuring words to downplay the anti-Jewish incidents.[6] And the Central Verein wanted to believe.

In New York City, however, the Jews were more realistic. On March 12, the American Jewish Congress leadership convened a three-hour session and voted to commence a national program of highly visible protests, parades, and demonstrations. The centerpiece of the protest would be a giant anti-Nazi rally March 27, at Madison Square Garden. An emergency meeting of regional and national Jewish organizations was set for March 19 to work out the details.[7]

Before the group adjourned, Dr. Joseph Tenenbaum, a Congress vice-president, spoke a few words of warning to Germany for the newsmen present. Threatening a bitter boycott, Tenenbaum said, "Germany is not a speck on Mars. It is a civilized country, located in the heart of Europe, relying on friendly cooperation and commercial intercourse with the nations of the world. . . . A *bellum judaicum*—war against the Jews—means boycott, ruin, disaster, the end of German resources, and the end of all hope for the re-habilitation of Germany, whose friends we have not ceased to be." Measuring his final words carefully, Tenenbaum spoke sternly, "May God save Germany from such a national calamity."[8] The protest would begin—American Jewish Committee or no American Jewish Committee.

The next day, March 13, American Jewish Committee leaders were startled to learn of the Congress' protest decision. The Committee called an urgent meeting of the Big Three for the following day under the aegis of the "Joint Conference Committee." The top leadership of the Congress attended, led by Rabbi Stephen S. Wise, the Congress' founder, currently serving as its honorary president. The hierarchy of the Committee and B'nai B'rith were at the meeting as well. The Committee's intent was to abort any Congress protest and forestall Congress attempts to contact "Washington circles."[9]

As the conference began, the Congress people defended their decision to rally at Madison Square Garden. They saw Hitler's bold provincial takeover and the accompanying violence against Jews as a threat that could no longer be ignored. Nazi rhetoric was turning into action at a frightening rate. And the Congress' national affiliates were demanding an immediate response, including a comprehensive boycott of all German goods and services.[10]

Wise added that he had been in touch with Supreme Court Justice Louis Brandeis, a leading American Zionist and one of Wise's close personal friends. The advice was to delay a direct appeal to newly sworn-in President Franklin Delano Roosevelt, who was preoccupied with America's Depression and a calamitous banking crisis. But Brandeis did feel that ultimately the matter should be brought to the ear of FDR personally.[11]

Those Congress leaders most favoring the path of protest and even boy-cott pleaded that only economic retaliation frightened the Nazis. Even Nazi party leaders had admitted Hitler's strength rested on the German public's expectation of economic improvement.[12]

Committee leader David Bressler scorned all protest ideas, insisting that any such moves would only instigate more harm than help for the German Jews. The Committee's reluctance was based upon urgent communications from prominent Jewish families to kill any anti-German protest or boycott. German Jewish leaders were convinced that the German public would aban-don the Nazis once the economy improved. And even if Hitler remained in power, German Jewish leaders felt some compromise would be struck to provide Jewish cooperation for economic convalescence. Hitler might then quietly modify, or set aside, his anti-Semitic campaign.[13]

Wise was also reluctant to move on a boycott, but insisted that a joint protest statement be issued and efforts commence with the new administra-tion in Washington. There could be no more delay. Bressler rejected this and castigated the Congress for even releasing its March 12 protest decision to the press. A conservative Congress leader, Nathan Perlman, tried to assure the Committee people that the protest policy would be overruled or delayed at a meeting of the Congress' Administrative Committee later that night. But Wise advised against second-guessing the Administrative Committee, suggesting instead that for now, the three major organizations agree on a joint statement and a Washington plan. American Jewish Committee Secretary Morris Waldman interrupted and declared that any trilateral action would hinge on the Congress's protest decision. Wise accepted that proviso.[14]

The Committee delegates were cautiously reassured. Immediately following the meeting they dispatched a telegram to B'nai B'rith president Alfred Cohen, in Cincinnati: "CONFERENCE THREE ORGANIZATIONS GERMAN SITUATION . . . DISCOURAGING INDEPENDENT ACTION JEWISH GROUPS THROUGHOUT COUNTRY."[15]

But within hours, the Committee learned that its efforts had failed. The Congress' Administrative Committee had rejected the conservative position and by a vast majority opted for visible, vocal protest highlighted by the March 27 Madison Square Garden rally. The next morning, March 15, American Jewish Committee secretary Morris Waldman telephoned Congress vice-president W. W. Cohen to inform him that the Committee–B'nai B'rith binary would disassociate itself from the Congress—indeed from any anti-Nazi protest. Waldman then sent a telegram to Alfred Cohen in Cincinnati telling him to fly to New York to help plan countermoves to any organized Jewish protest against Hitler.[16] In that moment, the "Joint Conference Committee" was dissolved.

While the Big Three were arguing over whether to protest Hitlerism, smaller Jewish organizations were already committed to action. For these smaller organizations, closer to the Jewish masses, the debate was whether or not the Jews should unleash a comprehensive boycott against Germany as the best means of protest. In pursuit of that answer, the militant Jewish War Veterans held a fiery session in New York the evening of March 18.[17]

Shouts for and against a boycott bounced back and forth as the delegates debated how far the protest against Hitler should actually go. Speeches, interruptions, calls to order, and sporadic applause stretched the meeting well past midnight with no decision. Unable to make their deadlines, the press went home. Finally, to break the deadlock, Benjamin Sperling of Brooklyn, formally moved that the Jewish War Veterans organize a vigorous national boycott of all German goods, services, and shipping lines. The yells in favor were abundant, but the presiding officer insisted on a formal vote, and with a flurry of excitement the boycott was unanimously adopted.[18] It was done so in accordance with the JWV's charter: "To combat the sources of bigotry and darkness; wherever originating and whatever their target; to uphold the fair name of the Jew and fight his battle wherever unjustly assailed."

History thus records that in an era distinguished by appeasement, the Jewish War Veterans were the very first, anywhere in the world, to declare openly their organized resistance to the Nazi regime. They had fought Germany once and would fight again. This small association of ex-warriors, mostly men of little finesse and even less pretense, would no longer be bound by the Jewish hierarchy.

The gentlemen of the JWV felt especially obligated to persevere that night. They wanted to present their boycott movement as a "fact" that would inspire the other 1,500 representatives of Jewish organizations meeting the following day to consider the dimensions of the American Jewish Congress' call to protest. Indeed, a JWV protest march was already planned, as was a boycott office, a publicity campaign, and a fund-raising effort.[19] The Veterans wanted to be sure that when the March 19 emergency conference convened, the word *boycott* would be an established term in the language of confrontation with the Nazis.

But that same day, Nazi, Jewish, and Zionist interests were anxious to stillbirth the protest movement before it could breathe life. A Paris conference, called by a group of European Jewish organizations analogous to the American Jewish Committee and B'nai B'rith, tried to stifle the growing protest movement on the Continent inspired by the American Jewish Congress. The Committee was unable to attend the sudden conference, but did telephone their concerns to the meeting. The Parisian conference unanimously decided that public protest by Jews was "not only premature but likely to be useless and even harmful."[20] Committee people in New York could now tell the Congress that Jewish organizations closest to the trouble in Europe agreed that there should be no public agitation against Hitler.

March 19, 1933, was also the day that the swastika was unfurled over German consulates in Jerusalem and Jaffa. Germany maintained the two consulates in Palestine as part of its normal diplomatic relations with Great Britain. Angry Tel Aviv Jews prepared to storm the consulates and burn the new German flag. But Zionist leaders were afraid to provoke the Nazis, lest Berlin suddenly clamp down on Zionist organizing and fund-raising activities in Germany. In Jerusalem, Jewish Agency Executive Committee member Dr. Werner Senator dispatched a letter about the flag-raising to the Zionist Organization in London. Senator explained that Zionist leaders were working with British Mandatory authorities to defuse the problem "to avoid hostile encounters, which would cause unpleasant repercussions for our people in Germany."[21]

In Berlin, the Hitler regime was clearly worried. Atrocity reports covered the front pages of newspapers on both sides of the Atlantic. *Der Forverts* correspondent Jacob Leschinsky's report from Berlin was typical: "One can find no words to describe the fear and despair, the tragedy that envelops the German Jews. They are being beaten, terrorized, murdered, and . . . compelled to keep quiet. The Hitler regime flames up with anger because it has been forced through fear of foreign public opinion to forego a mass slaughter. . . . It threatens, however, to execute big pogroms if Jews in other countries make too much fuss about the pogroms it has hitherto indulged in." The dispatch was carried by *The New York Times* and many other newspapers. Leschinsky, immediately after the dispatch, was arrested and expelled.[22]

Atrocity scandals were complicating almost every attempt at the German economic and diplomatic recovery Hitler desperately needed to stay in power. The Jews of New York would have to be stopped. Within a few days, the reconvened Reichstag was scheduled to approve sweeping dictatorial powers enabling Hitler to circumvent the legislature and rule by decree. But this talk of an international Jewish-led boycott was frightening Germany's legislators. Such a boycott could disable German export industries, affecting every German family. Goebbels expressed the Nazi fear in his diary: "The horrors propaganda abroad gives us much trouble. The many Jews who have left Germany have set all foreign countries against us. . . . We are defenselessly exposed to the attacks of our adversaries."[23] But as Nazi newspapers castigated German Jewry for the protests of their landsmen overseas, German Jews themselves responded with letters, transatlantic calls, and cables to stifle American Jewish objections to Hitler.

When the Congress' emergency protest planning conference convened on March 19 at New York's Astor Hotel, Committee representatives arrived with a prepared statement. It read: "It is only natural for decent and liberal-minded men and women to feel outraged at these occurrences and . . . to give public expression to their indignation and abhorrence, [but] the American Jewish Committee and the B'nai B'rith are convinced that the wisest and the most effective policy for the Jews of America to pursue is to exercise the same fine patience, fortitude and exemplary conduct that have been shown by the Jews of Germany. This is not a time further to inflame already overwrought feelings, but to act wisely, judiciously and deliberately."[24]

These words of caution were emphatically rejected by the delegates who well knew that the Committee had become a megaphone—via friends and family relations—for Nazi pressure on the American anti-German protest movement. Bernard S. Deutsch, Congress president, set the meeting's defiant tone: "The offices of the American Jewish Congress are being flooded with messages from all over the country demanding protest. . . . We are met here to translate this popular mandate into responsible, vigorous, orderly and effective action." Cries of approval bellowed from the crowd. The protest motion was formally introduced: "This tragic hour in Jewish history calls imperatively for the solidarity of the Jewish people. And we American Jews are resolved to stand shoulder to shoulder with our brother Jews in Germany in defense of their rights, which are being greviously violated, and of their lives, which are imperiled."[25]

The audience cheered. But from among the cheering delegates stood up J. George Fredman, commander in chief of the Jewish War Veterans, who proudly announced his organization had already—on its own initiative—commenced the national anti-Nazi boycott. He urged fellow Jewish organizations to join and formally called for a boycott amendment to the protest resolution.[26]

Judge Joseph M. Proskauer, the American Jewish Committee's representative at the rally, became livid. He stood up and insisted that marches and meetings were improper and unproductive. He advised quiet, behind-the-scenes diplomacy—as the Committee had always done. The crowd booed and hissed. Undaunted, Proskauer turned toward Fredman and condemned his boycott amendment as "causing more trouble for the Jews in Germany by unintelligent action." Over waving hands and hostile jeering, he insisted on placing into the record a message from another Committee stalwart, Judge Irving Lehman, the brother of the governor of New York. In a voice struggling to be heard, Proskauer read Lehman's letter: "I feel that the [Madison Square Garden protest] meeting may add to the dangers of the Jews in Germany. . . . I implore you in the name of humanity, don't let anger pass a resolution which will kill Jews in Germany." At this the crowd stormed their disapproval in English, Yiddish, and Russian. The hotel meeting room became so unruly that police had to be called to restore order.[27]

Stephen Wise stepped in to avoid total humiliation for the Committee, which he still hoped would use its influence in Washington. He offered to redraft the protest resolution, but the final wording was virtually the same and still anathema to the Committee. The date March 27 was approved, and Madison Square Garden was ratified as the epicenter of a day of global anti-German protest that would signal the beginning of mass Jewish resistance to Hitler. But through Wise's counsel, the Congress did not declare a boycott. He felt the big inter-organizational boycott the Congress could mount would be indeed the final nonviolent weapon. The time had not yet come.[28]

Fredman and his Veterans had other plans. Even if they could not persuade a single other group to join them, the JWV would organize the national boycott. Many in the Congress leadership supported the Veterans' decision, but in deference to the Committee, withheld official endorsement. They were waiting for the influential German Jewish families of New York to use their connections, waiting for Committee "methods" to deliver. And waiting for proof that the German Jewish leaders of the Committee were not merely unwitting tools of the Third Reich.

But official Congress hesitation did not rule out outspoken unofficial support for the boycott movement. The very next day, March 20, Congress vice-president W. W. Cohen became inspired while lunching at a fine German restaurant. When the waiter came by and offered Cohen an imported Bavarian beer, Cohen suddenly became enraged, and shouted "No!" The entire restaurant turned to Cohen, who then pointedly asked for the check.[29]

Cohen left the restaurant and went directly to a Jewish War Veterans' boycott rally, where he proclaimed to an excited crowd, "Any Jew buying one penny's worth of merchandise made in Germany is a traitor to his people. I doubt that the American government can officially take any notice of what the German government is doing to its own citizens. So our only line of resistance is to touch German pocketbooks."[30]

As W. W. Cohen was exhorting his fellow Americans to fight back economically, the Jews of Vilna, Poland, were proposing the identical tactic. Poland contained Europe's most concentrated Jewish population, nearly 3.5 million, mainly residing in closely knit urban communities. They were economically and politically cohesive, often militant. Bordering Hitler's Germany, Polish Jewry could organize an anti-Nazi boycott that would not only be financially irritating to the Reich, but highly visible in central Europe. The Jews of Vilna held a boycott rally on March 20, 1933. To recruit added interpolitical and interfaith support, they incorporated their boycott movement into the larger national furor over the Polish Corridor. Hitler, in his first days as chancellor, had hinted strongly that Germany might occupy the Corridor to ensure the Reich's access to the free city of Danzig. German access via a corridor traversing Poland and controlled by Poland was part of the Versailles Treaty. Poland, unwilling to relinquish its Versailles territorial rights, reacted defensively, and rumors of a preemptive Polish invasion of Germany were rampant.[31]

By identifying their anti-Nazi boycott as national rather than sectarian retaliation, the Vilna Jews sought to construct the model for other worried Europeans. Vilna's March 20 mass anti-Hitler rally urged all Polish patriots and Jews throughout the world to battle for Polish territorial defense by not buying or selling German goods. The Jewish War Veterans were no longer alone.[32]

•

As the former governor of New York, President Roosevelt was attuned to the pulse of the Jewish constituency. The legends of FDR's strong friendship with Stephen Wise of the American Jewish Congress were feared in Berlin. In truth, however, the Wise-Roosevelt relationship by 1933 was strained. Two years earlier, in his last face-to-face meeting with FDR, Rabbi Wise had presented Governor Roosevelt with written charges against then New York City Mayor Jimmy Walker. Roosevelt objected to Wise's pejorative manner that day and then lectured the rabbi about an earlier protest on an unrelated issue. That was to be their last private conversation for five years. Wise openly broke with Roosevelt in 1932 by backing Democratic primary loser Alfred E. Smith for the presidential nomination.[33] Berlin did not know it, but in March 1933, Wise was reluctant to test his access to the White House.

Roosevelt himself had shown little official concern for the plight of Germany's Jews. Shortly before the inauguration in the first week of March, one of Wise's friends, Lewis Strauss, tried to convince outgoing President Hoover and President-elect Roosevelt to send a joint message of alarm to the German government. Although Hoover sent word of his concern through the American ambassador in Berlin, FDR refused to get involved.[34]

Yet Nazi atrocities intensified, as bannered each day in the press: Midnight home invasions by Brownshirts forcing Jewish landlords and employers at gunpoint to sign papers relenting in tenant or employee disputes. Leading Jewish physicians kidnapped from their hospitals, driven to the outskirts of town and threatened with death if they did not resign and leave Germany. Dignified Jewish businessmen dragged from their favorite cafés, savagely beaten and sometimes forced to wash the streets.

Wise felt he could wait no longer and on March 21, 1933, he led a delegation of American Jewish Congress leaders to Washington. To set the tone of his Washington efforts, Rabbi Wise released a statement that effectively burned the last thread of hoped-for cooperation with the Committee–B'nai B'rith binary. "The time for caution and prudence is past," Wise said. "We must speak up like men. How can we ask our Christian friends to lift their voices in protest against the wrongs suffered by Jews if we keep silent?"[35]

Seeking an audience with the president, Rabbi Wise telephoned the White House and spoke with FDR's executive assistant, Col. Louis Howe. Howe remembered Wise unfavorably from the 1932 primary campaign, but was nonetheless cordial. Wise mentioned that he had delayed his visit for several weeks on the advice of Supreme Court Justice Brandeis, whom he had checked with again that very day. Howe answered that with Roosevelt preoccupied with the nation's catastrophic banking crisis, the time still wasn't right. Howe did promise, however, to have the president telephone the U.S. delegate to the Geneva Disarmament Conference, who would raise the subject with the Germans there.[36]

Wise and his group also testified before the House Immigration Committee, urging a halt to restrictive procedures at U.S. visa offices in Germany. German relatives of American Jews might then be granted refuge in the United States. Obstructing that succor was a so-called Executive Order issued by Herbert Hoover in 1930 at the height of Depression woes. Actually, the order itself was only a press release circulated to consular officials. Quite reasonably, the presidential memo directed visa sections to stringently enforce a paragraph of the 1924 Immigration Act barring indigent immigrants who might become "public charges." The paragraph was intended to be waived for political refugees. However, consular officials, some of them openly anti-Semitic, used the Hoover order to deny visas to those legitimately entitled. In the past, the wrong enforcement of the order had been of no grave consequence because Germany's immigration quota had been grossly under-filled.[37] But now the need was urgent, especially for German Jewish leaders targeted by Nazi activists. For them, procuring a visa was in fact a matter of life or death.

Chairing the House Immigration Committee was New York Representative Samuel Dickstein, a close friend of Rabbi Wise. Dickstein responded to Wise's testimony by introducing a House resolution to nullify Hoover's Executive Order. Dickstein also set about the longer process of introducing a congressional bill revising immigration procedures in view of the new emergency.[38]

Rabbi Wise also met with Undersecretary of State William Phillips. Wise and the Congress people vividly described the brutalities suffered by German Jews—many of them relatives of American citizens, some of them actual U.S. citizens residing in Germany. Wise made it clear that the Congress was leading a national anti-Nazi movement to be launched by a countrywide day of protest, March 27, focusing on a mass rally at Madison Square Garden. But then Wise assured the State Department that he would not demand American diplomatic countermeasures until the department could verify the atrocity reports. Phillips felt this was reasonable. In his press announcement, Phillips said, "Following the visit of Rabbi Stephen S. Wise, the Department has informed the American Embassy at Berlin of the press report of mistreatment of Jews in Germany . . . [and] the deep concern these reports are causing in this country. The Department has instructed the Embassy to make . . . a complete report of the situation."[39]

Rabbi Wise's maneuver won him a triple achievement: First, he appeared reasonable to the State Department; second, he instigated an on-the-spot State Department investigation putting the Reich on notice that the American government was studying her anti-Semitic campaign; third, the State Department's investigation would provide independent, official confirmation that could not be ignored. This would obligate the U.S. government to follow up diplomatically. The U.S. government was now involved in a conflict it had sought to avoid.

Across the Atlantic, the Reich took notice of Wise's visit to Washington. Goebbels and other party leaders were convinced that Rabbi Wise was the archetypal powerbrokering Jew who could manipulate the U.S. Congress, the State Department, and even the president.[40] Even as Wise was finishing his round of Washington meetings, the Reich Foreign Office in Berlin dispatched a cable to its consulate in New York denying "exaggerated [press] reports" about "brutal mistreatments." The cable denounced "opponents of the present national government" who are hoping that "well-organized atrocity propaganda may undermine the reputation and authority of the national government." The statement added Hitler's personal assurance that future violence would be averted by tough new police efforts.[41]

By 11:30 A.M. the next day, March 22, German Ambassador Friedrich von Prittwitz called on the State Department. Offering a Goering press statement as evidence, von Prittwitz declared that there would be law and order in Hitler's Germany, that Jews would be protected, and that crimes would be punished.[42] The State Department was becoming aware of the escalating Nazi-Jewish conflict. Within twenty-four hours of the German ambassador's visit, an American Jewish Committee–B'nai B'rith delegation called on Secretary of State Cordell Hull. The Committee knew that Hull deplored public protests such as the American Jewish Congress was organizing. Even more importantly, they knew he would oppose any boycott of the Reich. Hull's expressed view was that "the friendly and willing cooperation of Germany is necessary to the program of world [economic] recovery."[43]

Hull received the Committee–B'nai B'rith representatives cordially in his office. The delegation did their best to impugn the methods and the organization of Rabbi Stephen Wise. They wanted no misunderstanding. Their anxiety over the German situation was just as great as that of the Congress, but their tactics differed. The Committee–B'nai B'rith group made clear to Hull that they favored quiet, behind-the-scenes action.[44]

Their argument to the secretary probably added little to the joint Committee–B'nai B'rith communiqué issued after the Congress' March 19 emergency protest organizing meeting. To salve the angry demands of rank-and-file B'nai B'rith members, and to show quotable concern in the light of the Congress' public rallying, that joint communiqué declared: "The American Jewish Committee and the B'nai B'rith express their horror at anti-Jewish action in Germany, which is denying to German Jews the fundamental rights of every human being. . . . The events of the past few weeks in Germany have filled with indignation not only American Jews, but also Americans of every other faith. . . . We shall take every possible measure to discharge the solemn responsibility which rests on our organization to marshall the forces of public opinion among Americans of every faith to right the wrongs against the Jews of Germany and for the vindication of the fundamental principles of human liberty."[45]

From Hull's point of view, listening to a distinguished Committee and B'nai B'rith delegation was an obligation to fulfill, not an inspiration to action. The March 23 visit therefore did not accomplish any amelioration for the Jews in Germany. Worse, the visit confused the State Department. One Jewish group was bent on loud and vigorous protest. Another was calling for quiet, discreet diplomacy. But the Committee–B'nai B'rith people were the influential and prominent leaders of the Jewish community. So Hull concluded that their voice was representative of Jewish sentiment.[46]

In one sense, then, the Committee's "methods" had worked. Despite a tiny constituency that numbered about 300, the Committee's pronouncements were still more potent than those of the half-million-strong American

Jewish Congress.[47] The delegation had effectively discredited the Congress as naïve rabblerousers.

Shortly after the Committee–B'nai B'rith mission left Washington, Hull dispatched a cable to George A. Gordon, America's chargé d'affaires in Germany: "Public opinion in this country continues alarmed at the persistent press reports of mistreatment of Jews in Germany. . . . I am of the opinion that outside intercession has rarely produced the results desired and has frequently aggravated the situation. Nevertheless, if you perceive any way in which this government could usefully be of assistance, I should appreciate your frank and confidential advice. On Monday next [March 27] there is to be held in New York a monster mass meeting. If prior to that date an amelioration in the situation has taken place, which you could report [for] . . . release to the press, together with public assurances by Hitler and other leaders, it would have a calming effect."[48] In essence, Hull was asking for an encouraging report—justified or not—to soothe angry Jewish groups. Thus, he could cooperate with the Committee request as well.

Within twenty-four hours, Gordon composed a response to Hull: "I entirely agree with your view . . . [of] the present situation of outside intercession. . . . There is . . . one suggestion I venture to make in case you have already not thought of it. . . . [T]he general tenor of communications between foreigners and the . . . government here has necessarily been one of complaint and protest, and it is possible that if . . . confidence [were expressed] in Hitler's determination to restore peaceful and normal conditions, emphasizing what a great place he will achieve in the estimation of the world if he is able to bring it about, it might have a helpful effect. . . . Hitler now represents the element of moderation in the Nazi Party and I believe that if in any way you can strengthen his hand, even indirectly, he would welcome it."[49]

Gordon then held meetings with several of his counterparts in the Berlin diplomatic community, obtaining a consensus against any efforts in their countries to use diplomatic channels as a medium of protest against Adolf Hitler. He wired news of his achievement to Hull.[50]

An unwitting alliance of groups now saw their mission as obstructing anti-Nazi protest in America and Europe, especially an economic boycott. The members of this alliance included B'nai B'rith, the American Jewish Committee, and even the Jewish Agency for Palestine, each preoccupied with its own vested interests, each driven by its own ideological imperatives, and each wishing that conditions for German Jews would improve in the quieter climate they hoped to establish.

A fourth member of this alliance was now the United States government, which was pursuing what it thought was America's vital interests. As for the fate of Germany's Jews? Officially, the U.S. government simply wasn't concerned.

3. The Weapon Hitler Feared

CORDELL HULL and the American Jewish Committee soon learned that their efforts to contain the anti-Nazi movement would be seriously challenged. Page-one headlines of the March 23, 1933, *New York Times* portrayed the new public mood.

"PROTEST ON HITLER GROWING IN NATION. Christian and Non-Sectarian Groups Voice Indignation Over Anti-Jewish Drive. URGE WASHINGTON TO ACT."[1]

"BOYCOTT MOVE SPREADS. Merchants Cancelling Orders for German Goods."[2]

The movement was spreading spontaneously, along interreligious lines. Spurred on by the Jewish War Veterans, the nation's emotions were mobilized. *Boycott* was finally a word lifted out of the whispers and into the headlines. Under the direction of Col. Morris J. Mendelsohn, chairman of the JWV's Boycott Committee, a veterans' protest march was organized. In solidarity, W. W. Cohen, vice-president of the American Jewish Congress, accepted the position of parade marshal. He participated at his own initiative, since Stephen Wise was still reluctant to commit the Congress to a boycott per se, and Congress leaders didn't want to detract from their own upcoming Madison Square Garden protest.[3] Cohen's visibility nevertheless associated the powerful Congress with the JWV's banners and placards declaring economic war on Germany.

Without the active support of the Congress, Mendelsohn was uncertain how many marchers would participate and how many prominent figures would actually show up to endorse the boycott. The day before the parade, Mendelsohn tried to cheer up JWV leader J. George Fredman by telling him, "George, if we have nobody else, you and I will march the full line of the parade and call on the mayor." But in truth Mendelsohn doubted whether even Mayor John O'Brien would attend, since he was known to be saving his first anti-Nazi appearance for the Congress rally.[4]

Everyone was surprised, therefore, when the Jewish War Veterans' boycott parade received an enthusiastic reception. Many thousands of cheering sympathetic watchers encouraged the thousands of Jewish and non-Jewish vets as the parade moved through the East Side to City Hall where Mayor O'Brien was waiting on the reviewing stand. With much fanfare and applause, resolutions were presented demanding diplomatic measures and an economic protest against the Reich. Dovetailing with the JWV protest parade was a variety of sympathetic conferences, petitions, and resolutions by interfaith and nonsectarian groups, including the American Federation of Labor, which pledged its 3 million members to fighting Nazism here and in Germany.[5]

March 23 was a success for the Jewish War Veterans. Their boycott kickoff generated maximum publicity. One radio station covered the day with updates every fifteen minutes. Extensive support was offered by those in prominence and power—as well as by the anonymous faces in the crowd, outraged and merely waiting for a raised hand to lead the protest against Adolf Hitler.

German legations around the United States reported the anti-Nazi developments to the fifty-one-day-old Reich. Jewish protest was not merely a nuisance; it preyed upon the minds of the Nazis as they braced for their first big fight against their avowed enemies, the Jews.[6] How effective any anti-German boycott and protest movement would be was the question. Could mere popular protest in Europe and America influence the Third Reich? Could a boycott—an economic war—topple the Hitler regime or force Germany to abandon its anti-Jewish program? At the time, some Jewish leaders either doubted the power of the anti-Nazi movement or were unwilling to participate. This failure to participate worked to Hitler's advantage, because the Jewish-led, worldwide anti-Nazi boycott was indeed the one weapon Hitler feared.

To understand why, one must examine Germany's economic precariousness in 1933, the Nazi mentality, and the historic power of Jewish-led boycotts. To do so requires a dual perspective: statistical and perceptual. Of equal weight in history is *reality* and the *perception of reality*, because the two ignite each other in a continual chain reaction that ultimately shapes events and destinies among men and nations.

The deterioration of the once powerful German economy really began in World War I, when German military and political leaders simply did not calculate the economic effects of a prolonged war. The Allied blockade cut off Germany's harbors and most of her land trade routes. Trade was decimated. Industry couldn't export. War materiel and civilian necessities, including food, could not be imported.

Before the blockade was lifted, 800,000 malnourished German civilians perished. Actually, the blockade created less of a food shortage for Germany, which was 80 percent food self-sufficient before the war, than did the shortsighted policy of pulling Germans off the farms to fight without compensating for reduced food production. But the popular perception among Germans was that they had been starved into submission, defeated not on the battlefield but by political and economic warfare and connivance, by what became known as the "stab in the back."

The Treaty of Versailles' nonnegotiable terms demanded the forfeiture of German colonies as well as a number of conquered or traditionally German lands; the dismemberment of the German military machine; the seizure of key German waterways; the arrest of hundreds of German militarists and leaders as war criminals, including the German emperor Kaiser Wilhelm II; the granting of most-favored, nonreciprocal foreign commercial rights in Germany; and a certain amount of interim foreign occupation. The German leadership was to sign a hated statement of total war guilt. Additionally, Germany was to pay war reparations over the next two years of 5 billion gold marks, and approximately 15 billion marks' worth in cattle, timber, and other barterable items. The Allies allowed no negotiation of Versailles' oppressive terms and refused to lift the economic and material blockade until German leaders accepted what later German generations would call the *Diktat*.

Two years later, the Allied Reparations Commission levied additional reparations of 132 billion gold marks. Such a monumental sum, payable in cash and goods, would be a garnishment for generations, a commercial enslavement that would hold Germany captive for fifty to a hundred years.

Germany's population, and indeed world leaders and historians, would later brand the Versailles Treaty as merciless and intolerable. But the Allies were following in the tradition of previous German victories, which vanquished losers. For example, in February 1918, when Russia, beset by revolution, tried to disengage from the war, German generals issued an ultimatum to surrender within five days or suffer unlimited destruction. At the same time, a renewed German offensive began. Lenin was forced to submit his new nation to the humiliating Treaty of Brest-Litovsk. Its terms defrocked Russia of a third of her farmland, 56 million people—or a third of her population—a third of her railroads, more than 5,000 factories comprising half her industrial capability, almost 90 percent of her coal, and beyond that a cash indemnity of 6 billion gold marks. The treaty was nullified after the Allied victory.

So Germany in 1919 was forced to recover from war under conditions similar to those she had previously imposed on her own enemies. However, the German people did not blame the precedents they themselves had established, but rather the political and economic weapons wielded against them at the Peace Conference. They blamed the blockade and their own civilian leaders for acceding to Allied demands and forfeiting German glory.

And, some Germans, such as the Nazis, blamed a Jewish conspiracy. In their minds it was Jewish bankers who would prosper from Germany's economic tragedy, since massive loans would be necessary both to recover from the war and to pay war indemnity. In Nazi minds, it was Jewish Bolshevism that would gain by undermining the German Empire and replacing it with a Weimar Republic where Marxism could flourish. In their minds it was Jews who at the Treaty of Versailles gained rights of minority citizenship throughout war-reconstructed Europe.[7]

Hitler's own words expressed the scapegoat rationale. Preaching to frantic, impoverished Germans, the Nazi leader cried: "Not so long ago, Germany was prosperous, strong, and respected by all. It is not your fault Germany was defeated in the war and has suffered so much since. You were betrayed in 1918 by Marxists, international Jewish bankers, and corrupt politicians."[8]

Hitler attributed the stories of Germany's wartime atrocities to an international Jewish conspiracy, using newspapers Jews secretly controlled. And so the Nazis held a special fear of what they called *Greuelpropaganda*, or atrocity tales. In Nazi thought, it was *Greuelpropaganda* that distorted German valor into Hun-like savagery. *Greuelpropaganda* was a mighty weapon the Jews knew how to use to harness the German nation into bondage.

The lasting economic agonies of Versailles were soon apparent. Inflation wracked postwar Germany, as the Weimar Republic struggled to keep pace with Allied reparation demands and domestic recovery. German currency was printed—so fast that it was inked on one side only. In 1919, the value of the mark was around 9 to a U.S. dollar; in 1921, 75 marks to a dollar; in 1922, 400 to a dollar; and in early January 1923, 7,000 marks equaled a dollar.

For reparations, France of course preferred commodities, such as timber, and coal, to valueless German currency. But German production was unable and unwilling to satisfy the payment schedule. When the Weimar Republic defaulted on the delivery of 100,000 telephone poles, France exercised her treaty option and in mid-January 1923 invaded Germany's industrial heartland, the Ruhr. Thousands of French troops took charge of mines, mills, and manufacturing plants. Germans were outraged that so petty an infraction could warrant a full-fledged French occupation. Workers throughout the Ruhr went on general strike with the full backing of the Weimar government. To support the strikers, the government cranked out millions upon millions of worthless marks as special welfare assistance. By late January 1923, the mark had jumped to 18,000 to the dollar and began inflating astronomically, until by 1924, it was about 5 trillion to the dollar.

In 1924, German currency could be used for virtually nothing except lighting stoves. People's savings were wiped away, their livelihood ruined. An international commisssion intervened and the Dawes Plan emerged, whereby France would withdraw from the Ruhr and scheduled reparations—mostly in goods—would be resumed. The goods would be manufactured after a national retooling financed by large foreign loans, mostly from America.

Within a few years, billions of U.S. dollars and other foreign currencies flowed into Germany, reequipping and overindustrializing that nation on an unparalleled basis in order to produce merchandise and other barterable items to repay the Dawes loans and war reparations. By the late 1920s, America owned and controlled billions of dollars of German industry. And the entire German economy—which was becoming somewhat stable and prosperous—was now also dependent upon export. Millions of jobs were wholly tied to the foreign market. Export was the oxygen, the bread, and the salt of the German work force. Without it, there would be economic death.[9]

Just before the decade closed, on October 24, 1929, Wall Street crashed. America's economy toppled and foreign economies fell with it. For Germany, intricately tied to all the economies of the Allied powers, the fall was brutal. Thousands of businesses failed. Millions were left jobless. Violence over food was commonplace. Germany was taught the painful lesson that economic survival was tied to international trading partners and exports.

During each economic crisis the Nazis scored electoral triumphs among the disadvantaged. In the boomlike year 1928, the Nazis could poll no more than 810,000 votes nationally. But two years later, well into the Depression, the Nazis' support leaped to about 6.5 million. In July of 1932, at the height of the crisis, oppressed by 6 million unemployed, the nation delivered 13.5 million votes for Hitler, most of it from the young, unemployed middle class.[10]

Shortly after the July 1932 election, the economy improved somewhat, due more to psychological than true financial factors. A bumper wheat and potato harvest made Germany temporarily independent of imported grain and starch related foodstuffs. Public makework gave short-term relief to the most severely hardshipped in big cities. More than 74,000 gardens and 26,000 settlement houses were erected to help feed and shelter the jobless in small towns. Seasonal unemployment came a bit later and less severely that autumn than in previous years. Total acknowledged unemployment was under these circumstances down to just more than 5 million. In certain segments of German society, confidence began to take hold.[11]

As the bankrupt Nazis approached the November 1932 contest, they were unable to pay for a last-minute voter drive. In the aura of stability and with reduced Nazi campaigning, the electorate backed away from the radical program of National Socialism, casting 2 million fewer votes for the NSDAP. But after the November election, with the Nazis nevertheless assured of a leading role in the government, the brief improvement in the economy vanished.[12] The moderate moment had been lost.

Commercial recovery was Adolf Hitler's prime mission when he came to power in January 1933. But Hitler and his circle's conception of their problem and the twisted explanations they ascribed to real and perceived trends became the new determining economic factors. The greatest obstacles to recovery now were, in fact, political instability and bizarre economic policies, including import restrictions that provoked retaliatory bans on German exports.

Economic policies and the worldwide economic depression combined to deprive Germany of her place among the world's trading nations. Without exports, Germany was denied foreign currency—the essential ingredient to her survival. Without foreign exchange, she could not pay for the imported raw materials she needed to continue manufacturing nor for imported foodstuffs to compensate for recurring shortages. Worse, Germany couldn't even borrow money to pay for raw materials and food because without foreign exchange to pay her war reparations and other foreign obligations, her credit was once again unreliable.[13]

In late 1932, the president of the Reichsbank warned the cabinet that further deterioration in foreign exchange would force Germany into another fiscal default. What's more, if there was a sudden run on Germany's banks, it would trigger another total crash of the economy.[14]

But when Hitler and his circle saw Germany deadlocked in depression, they did not blame the world depression and the failures of German economic policy. They blamed Bolshevik, Communist, and Marxist conspiracies, all entangled somehow in the awesome imaginary international Jewish conspiracy. The Jews were not just a handy scapegoat. The paranoid Nazis *believed* in the legendary, almost supernatural economic power of the Jews. When they promulgated the motto "The Jews are our bad luck," they meant it.[15]

Complicating the Reich's response to economic developments was Hitler's impatience for economic details. A British embassy report compiled in early 1933 explained: "Hitler is a pure visionary who probably does not understand the practical problems he is up against." In fact, Hitler saw only the superficial aspects of any economic problem. He was well known for exhorting his followers: "If economic experts say this or that is impossible, then to hell with economics. . . . if our will is strong enough we can do anything![16] Therefore, when problems persisted, the Nazi response was to scream "conspiracy" and make snap decisions to plug holes rather than rebuild the dike.

In the Nazi mind, the Jewish-led, anti-Nazi boycott would reduce exports and foreign currency below the viable threshold. By Nazi thinking, a second prong of the Jewish offensive would be publicizing German atrocities to undermine confidence in the new regime and turn the non-Jewish world against Germany. In this instance, Nazi fears approximated the reality. As an overindustrialized nation dependent upon exports, Germany was especially prone to boycott. Therefore, as the American Jewish War Veterans escalated their anti-Reich agitation in late March 1933, a primary order of Nazi business would now be to end the atrocity claims and stop the boycott.[17]

Nazi preoccupation with the anti-German boycott was not merely a fear of Jewish power. The Nazis dogmatically believed in the power of boycotts in general. Boycott had long been a prime tactic of the German anti-Semitic movement. When in 1873 an economic depression followed a stock market fall, the German Conservative party falsely blamed Jewish speculators and organized anti-Semitic campaigns, including boycotts. A few years later, the Catholic party joined the movement, coining the motto "Don't buy from

Jews." By 1880, Berlin women's organizations had formed housewife boycott committees.[18]

During the years prior to 1933, Hitler, Goebbels, Goering, and other Nazi leaders regularly struggled to attract public support by advocating the anti-Jewish boycott. Brownshirt pickets around a store with signs reading DON'T BUY FROM JEWS served to remind Germans of the Jews' secure economic status and warn Jews of what was in store should National Socialism come to power. The Nazis were convinced that an official countrywide boycott would totally destroy the commercial viability of the Jews in Germany.[19]

But during the first years of the Nazi party, German anti-Semites also became painfully aware of the Jewish power of boycott and backlash. The lesson came in a confrontation waged not in Germany but in the United States, pitting the Jewish community against the American anti-Semite most revered by the Nazis: Henry Ford.

The richest man in America, whose name was stamped on every Model T, quickly catapulted to the forefront of political anti-Semitism after he became convinced of the Jewish conspiracy cliché. Henry Ford's nineteenth-century rural mentality didn't adapt well to the complexities of the twentieth-century world. He did things in his own peculiar way, regardless of the cost. Shortly after the Great War began in Europe, Ford claimed he had discovered "proof" that Jews were behind the world's troubles. In 1918, Ford purchased the weekly *Dearborn Independent* and soon thereafter changed its editorial thrust to virulent anti-Semitism.[20]

Ford also employed agents to seek out more anti-Jewish "evidence." One such agent acquired a typescript entitled *The Protocols of the Elders of Zion*, the fabricated secret minutes of an imaginary Jewish conspiracy to topple governments, dominate economies, pervert morals, and defeat noble bloodlines by intermarriage. The fake *Protocols* were laughed off by many. But a few, including Henry Ford, took them to be a veracious revelation of the most sinister plot of modern times. In May 1920, a series of *Dearborn Independent* articles and editorials publicized the *Protocols* and a host of slanders and accusations under the general heading "The International Jew." Ford's articles accused American Jewish leaders such as Louis Marshall and Louis Brandeis of using Presidents Taft and Wilson as their puppets. Other prominent Jews were accused of perpetrating World War I for the benefit of Jewish bankers and fomenting the Russian Revolution for racial imperialism. The defamations continued weekly, as Ford's paper denounced the Jewish conspiracy for corruption on Wall Street, in labor, and on the ball field—Jews were even behind the Black Sox baseball gambling scandal. Jews were also allegedly responsible for Benedict Arnold, the Civil War, and the assassination of Abraham Lincoln. What Jews could not achieve by money, media, or manipulation, they would achieve by pandering to the sexual perversions of the powerful and prominent.[21]

These accusations were not just the ramblings of *The Dearborn Independent*. They were in fact a product of the Ford Motor Company. Henry Ford listed his name at the top of every front page. Ford motorcar dealers were compelled to buy and sell subscriptions. Dealers who filled their subscription quotas received Ford cars as prizes. Those falling short were assured that *The Dearborn Independent* was "just as much of a Ford product as the car or tractor." Many reluctant dealers received threatening legalistic letters insisting they sell the tabloid. Reprints were bound into booklets and distributed to libraries and YMCAs throughout the nation.[22]

Devoting the national sales force and the assets of Ford Motor Company to spreading Jew hatred made Henry Ford the first to organize anti-Semitism in America. Indeed, he was the hero of anti-Semites the world over. In Germany, thousands of copies of Ford's teachings were published under the title *The Eternal Jew*, by Heinrich Ford.[23]

Ford's book quickly became the bible of the German anti-Semites, including Adolf Hitler—this at least two years before *Mein Kampf* was written. Hitler was so entranced with Ford's struggle against Jewish economic power that he hung a large portrait of Ford beside his desk and spoke of him incessantly.[34] When Hitler was interviewed by a *Chicago Tribune* reporter in 1923 about Ford's chances of winning the U.S. presidency, der Führer enthusiastically declared, "I wish that I could send some of my shock troops to Chicago and other big American cities to help in the elections. We look on Heinrich Ford as the leader of the growing Fascist Party in America."[24]

A year later, in 1924, Hitler wrote his own anti-Jewish epistle, *Mein Kampf*, his blueprint for the destruction of the Jewish people. Many of the ramblings in *Mein Kampf* were identical to passages in "The International Jew." Hitler lionized Ford even after the Nazis became a leading factor on the German political scene. Just before Christmas 1931, der Führer admitted to a *Detroit News* reporter, "I regard Henry Ford as my inspiration." Once the Third Reich came to power, millions of Ford's books were circulated to every school and party office in the nation, many featuring the names Hitler and Ford side by side on the cover.[25]

American Jewish reaction to the Henry Ford threat was swift. Within a few months of the *Dearborn Independent*'s inaugural anti-Semitic issue, a spontaneous Jewish boycott movement erupted. Libel suits were launched against Ford personally. A Jewish-led campaign to legally ban the sale or distribution of the publication began in Chicago, Boston, St. Louis, and other cities. Where legislated bans were overturned by court action, angry mobs often greeted *Dearborn Independent* street vendors.[26]

The backlash campaign started hurting Ford in late 1920, when Jews began refusing en masse to purchase any vehicle bearing a Ford emblem. Typical was a Connecticut Jewish community's 400-car parade in early 1921 honoring Albert Einstein and Chaim Weizmann—parade rules included the proviso "Positively no Ford machines permitted in line." Ford himself couldn't even *give* one away to his Jewish neighbor, Rabbi Leo M. Franklin of Detroit. Each year Ford gave the rabbi a custom-built car as a gift. But the rabbi emphatically refused Ford's gift after the *Dearborn Independent*'s articles began.[27]

Even the American Jewish Committee encouraged the boycott. The Committee opposed proclaiming an "official" boycott, reluctant to openly answer Ford's charges of an economic conspiracy with a coordinated economic weapon. But Committee leader Louis Marshall felt a "silent boycott" would be equally effective, maintaining that any self-respecting Jew would know what to do without being told when purchasing an automobile.[28]

Ford's steepest sales declines first appeared in the Northeast, where Jews comprised a substantial segment of the car-buying market. Within five years, a leading dealer in the Southwest was painfully aware that wealthy Jews in Texas and neighboring states hadn't purchased a Lincoln in years. And company inquiries about low sales in Missouri revealed that Jews wouldn't take a Ford if it was handed to them free.[29]

In reality, the Jewish boycott of Ford products was probably not statistically effective. While Ford's sales in urban centers did decrease significantly, equally important sales in small towns and rural areas either remained constant or increased. And the recorded urban sales slumps were only partially due to the Jewish-led boycott. General economic conditions and the declining popularity of the Model T were equally potent factors. But in the early and mid-1920s, Ford people were convinced that the Jewish-led boycott was in large part responsible.[30]

The precise figures were guarded by Ford's corporate sales hierarchy even as dealers and regional sales managers continually pleaded for Ford's campaign to cease. For example, New York sales manager Gaston Plaintiff, a personal friend of Ford, wrote numerous letters bemoaning the boycott. Ford would typically reply, "If they want our product, they'll buy it."[31]

In 1927, the advent of a competitive Chevrolet made the Jewish boycott an unacceptable liability for Ford Motor Company. Any lost product loyalty would now be lost forever to the competition. The Model T was obsolete, and the company's future was precariously stacked on a new Model A. At the same time, Ford desperately sought to avoid humiliating public trials with libeled Jews who had sued.[32]

In the summer of 1927, Ford's representatives approached Nathan Perlman, a vice-president of the American Jewish Congress, seeking a truce. Stephen Wise was in Europe, so Perlman referred Ford's people to the Committee. Louis Marshall prepared an embarrassing retraction *cum* apology for Ford to sign and publish. Close advisers cautioned the car maker that the humiliating apology might be too much for Ford's pride. But the global leader of anti-Semites had endured boycotts, legal actions, and political abrasions long enough.[33] It was time to make money, secure the future, and fight Chevrolet.

On July 7, 1927, in the last year of the outmoded Model T, as Ford acknowledged a decline of about a half million fewer cars sold, and as he prepared for a major financial effort to introduce his new Model A, the proud gladiator of anti-Semites released to the press his contrite plea for forgiveness for wronging the Jews and misleading mankind.[34]

I have given consideration to the series of articles concerning Jews which have since 1920 appeared in *The Dearborn Independent* . . . and in pamphlet form under the title "The International Jew." . . . To my great regret I have learned that Jews generally, and particularly those of this country, not only resent these publications as promoting anti-Semitism, but regard me as their enemy. . . . I am deeply mortified. . . . I deem it to be my duty as an honorable man to make amends for the wrong done to the Jews as fellowmen and brothers, by asking their forgiveness for the harm that I have unintentionally committed, by retracting so far as lies within my power the offensive charges laid at their door by these publications, and by giving them the unqualified assurance that henceforth they may look to me for friendship and good-will.[35]

Within weeks the retraction appeared in *The Dearborn Independent* itself. Shortly thereafter, Ford's advertising agencies were instructed to spend about 12 percent of the Model A's $1.3 million introductory advertising in Yiddish and Anglo-Jewish newspapers—the only minority press included in the campaign. Ford also directed that five truckloads of "The International Jew" be burned, and ordered overseas publishers to cease publication as well.[36]

Ford's capitulation was taken hardest in Germany among Nazi circles. Nazi boycotter Theodor Fritsch wrote to Ford lamenting the loss of both book sales and "the inestimable mental goods" Ford had bestowed upon civilization. "The publication of this book remains the most important action of your life." Yet now, as Fritsch put it, Ford was capitulating to the financial might of the Jews.[37]

Adolf Hitler, when informed of the retraction, tried to avoid comment. Henry Ford was the man the Nazi party and der Führer himself had lionized as the quintessential fighter of the so-called Jewish economic conspiracy. Hitler had once told reporters in Germany that "the struggle of international Jewish finance against Ford . . . has only strengthened [Nazi] sympathies . . . for Ford." In *Mein Kampf*, Hitler had declared that "only a single great man, Ford," was able to stand up to Jewish economic power.[38]

Ford's unexpected surrender was so powerful a loss to Hitler's movement that the Nazis preferred to ignore the retraction as a mere expediency. Fritsch continued printing "The International Jew." Nonetheless, the tribute to Ford in *Mein Kampf* was changed in its second edition. The words "only a single great man, Ford," were replaced with the phrase "only a very few."[39]

A lesson had been learned by Hitler and the Nazis. Jewish boycotts and economic influence, in the Nazi view, held the power not only to subvert governments, but to silence the most indomitable challengers.

Presidential candidate Norman Thomas declared, "Ford's backdown was good evidence of what a consumers' boycott and a lawyer's million-dollar libel suit can do in the way of educating a man who has heretofore been impervious to history." *The New York Telegram* editorialized, "If one of the richest men in the world cannot get away with an anti-Semitic movement in this country, nobody else will have the nerve to try it, and of that we can all be thankful, gentiles as well as Jews." But perhaps the most poignant summing up was uttered by Will Rogers: "Ford used to have it in for Jewish people—until he saw them in Chevrolets."[40]

Jews also believed in the power of Jewish boycotts. It mattered little whether the real might of the boycott was the statistical business harm or simply the *perception* of it. Boycott was a weapon the Jews were ready and willing to use in emergencies to dissuade the forces of anti-Semitism.

The anti-Ford boycott was but a commercial skirmish compared to the international financial war waged against Russian Czar Nicholas II by Jewish banker Jacob Schiff and the American Jewish Committee. The war began when Jews were blamed for Russia's social and economic chaos in the 1880s. The classic scapegoat scenario developed. Quotas for Jews were decreed in academia and commerce. Jews were physically restricted to the smallest hamlets. Bloody pogroms followed as mounted Cossacks swept through the hamlets pillaging and ravaging defenseless Jews.[41]

Although America's German Jews detested the unkempt Russian Jews, they were nevertheless infuriated by the barbarism of the czar's persecution. Among the *Hofjuden* who considered themselves the custodians of Jewish defense, Jacob Schiff stood out as a central figure. A major factor in international finance, Schiff's greatest weapon was money: giving it, denying it. After the notorious Kishinev pogrom of Passover 1903, Schiff decided to personally lead a crusade to force Czar Nicholas to abandon his anti-Semitic campaign.[42]

Schiff used his influence with friends and family in Europe to commit major Jewish and even non-Jewish financial houses to a banking boycott of Russia.[43] And before long, Russia's loan requests were in fact systematically denied in most French, English, and U.S. money markets. In 1904, after war broke out between Russia and Japan, Schiff lobbied tirelessly among commercial adversaries and cohorts alike to grant high-risk war loans to the Japanese. About $100 million, suddenly infused, quickly armed the underequipped Japanese, allowing them to score a series of humiliating victories.[44] Schiff's loans were officially recognized as the pivotal factor in Japan's victory, and the Jewish leader was commemorated in Japanese newspapers and history books as a new national hero.[45]

The banking boycott and the financing of Japan's victory were only the first rounds. In 1906, Schiff and other influential *Hofjuden* formed the American Jewish Committee. Their first major objective was abrogation of the

Russo-American commercial treaty, the legal basis of all friendly relations with Russia. The Committee asserted that the czar's denial of Russian visas to Jewish American citizens was an affront not just to America's Jewish citizens but to the United States itself.[46]

Although William Taft had issued a presidential campaign promise of abrogation, he refused to honor his pledge once elected. During a February 1911 White House luncheon for Committee leaders, when Taft rendered his final refusal to abrogate, Schiff warned, "We had hoped you would see that justice be done us. You have decided otherwise. We shall now go to the American people." Schiff then stalked from the room, refusing to even shake the president's hand. On the way out, Schiff whispered to fellow Committee leaders, "This means war!"[47]

Calling upon all friends and resources, the Committee began a widespread public appeal to have Congress force the president to end commercial relations with Russia. Within weeks, House and Senate abrogation resolutions—each personally approved by the Committee—were prepared. On December 13, 1911, after the House voted 300 to 1 to abrogate, Taft capitulated, and two days later issued instructions to terminate the treaty.[48]

Despite abrogation, the czar would not yield. Massacres continued, and the Jewish death toll rose. So the banking boycott was tightened. Its effects became most destructive, however, during World War I, when the czar needed multimillion-dollar military loans. Committee members were widely criticized for the stubborn continuation of their boycott even as it threatened the Allied war effort. But the boycott remained in effect until the monarchy was toppled in 1917.[49]

Throughout the nearly fifteen years of anti-czar boycott and backlash, threats of retaliation against Russian Jewry never deterred the men of the Committee. And in fact, during the anti-czar crusade, thousands of Russian lives *were* lost and hundreds of thousands more were devastated in pogroms. But the Committee held that the anti-Semitic outrages of one regime could spread infectiously if not quarantined.

Jacob Schiff addressed the issue in a 1905 cable to Russian premier Count Sergei Witte: "No doubt . . . your local authorities, seeing the coming of the end of the old regime, . . . have in their rage . . . instigated the populace against the Jews. . . . Jewry in general will have at least this consolation; that the present awful sufferings of their co-religionists will not have been for naught, nor their blood spilled in vain." A year later, President Theodore Roosevelt warned Schiff that U.S. protests against pogroms might only provoke more harm from an indignant czar. Schiff ignored the warning, determined that such genocidal actions could not go unprotested.[50]

And in early 1911, Schiff acknowledged in a letter to Taft that as a result of "action on our part, pogroms and massacres of Russian Jews, such as shocked the world in 1905, might be repeated." But he assured the president that the world Jewish community and even the Russian Jews themselves knew such risks were unavoidable. The responsibility for bloody reprisals would be taken "upon our own shoulders," said Schiff. He added, "it was recognized by our co-religionists that in such a situation, as in war, each and every man, wherever placed, must be ready to suffer, and if need be to sacrifice his life."[51]

The art of economic and political confrontation—public and private— was thus a tested and endorsed tradition of the American Jewish Committee. In 1929, Committee president Cyrus Adler wrote an authorized biography of the great economic warrior of the Jews, entitled *Jacob H. Schiff, His Life and Letters*. The book detailed Schiff's and the Committee's tradition of unrelenting economic and political retaliation—regardless of the short-term risks— against those who would threaten Jewish rights. The book's foreword hoped its accounts of staunch Jewish defense would "prove of some value in guiding and inspiring others.[52]

For the three and a half decades before Hitler's rise to power in 1933, the Jews of America were actively engaged in international and domestic boycotts to fight anti-Semitism. They used the backlash weapon to fill newspapers and congressional hearing rooms with the gruesome truths of Jewish oppression. The Jews of America could lead public opinion and marshal government action. They had this power and they used it continuously.

Wielding this power inspired the conspiracy stories. And so Jewish leaders were often reluctant. But what choices did they have? After its expulsion from Israel in the second century, Judaism became a religion without a state and thus without an army.

Papal legions could crush rebellions. Crusaders could invade lands. Islamic armies could conquer and convert. To survive, Jews could only use what they had. And what they had was what they were allowed to have. For centuries, denied lands, denied access to the professions, denied military rank, Jews were forced to deal with money, with trade, with middlemanship, with bargains, with influence, with the portable professions. And so Jews fought fire not with fire but with money, with the media, with access to high position, not in some imaginary conspiracy to dominate the world but in an ongoing effort to stay one step ahead of the blade, the noose, and the burning stake.

Yet the Jewish leaders most skilled in wielding the boycott and backlash weapon would in 1933 refuse, in part because the enemy was now Germany, Fatherland of the Committee. It was now German Jewish blood that would be spilled—not Russian Jewish. It was now their own uncles and lifetime friends whose lives would be subject to reprisal in any war for Jewish rights.

Those skilled in using Jewish weapons would also refuse because a wholly new tactic would now be used to shape Jewish destiny. Palestine would be the new solution. Hence, the question was now whether to use or not to use the one weapon Jews had, the one weapon they knew how to use: boycott and protest.

Yet the one weapon Jews had was the one weapon Hitler feared.

4. The Lonely Decision

BY NAZI DOCTRINE and their facade of self-confidence, National Socialism should have been unbothered by the Jews of New York parading up and down, waving resolutions and condemnatory posters on March 23. Adolf Hitler had declared long ago that the Nazis would never negotiate with the Jews—their opinions, their demands, their fury was meaningless in his program of destiny for Germany.[1] On March 23, the Reichstag granted Hitler legal dictatorial powers. It was a moment of long-awaited triumph for the Nazis. But in fact, March 23, 1933, was a day that frightened the Reich.

A boycott was being organized by the Jewish War Veterans to enthusiastic approval from a gamut of political and social groups. Dr. Stephen Wise would lead an international day of anti-German protest on March 27. Thousands were scheduled to rally at Madison Square Garden. Supportive rallies would be held simultaneously in eighty other American cities. And the New York rally would be broadcast throughout the United States.[2]

European Jewish circles would broadcast the New York rally into Germany itself from stations in neighboring Poland, Austria, and Czechoslovakia. English was widely spoken among the commercially oriented German families owning Germany's more than 5 million radios—approximately one in every four German households.

In Warsaw, a coalition of political, commercial, and religious organizations was debating whether all Poland should follow the lead of the Vilna Jews and the American Jewish War Veterans. Poland's final deliberations on the boycott question were timed to coincide with the Madison Square Garden rally. Boycott movements were also fast developing in Lithuania, France, Holland, Great Britain, and Egypt.[3]

Early results were beginning to show. German steamship lines in New York, which were valuable foreign-currency earners, reported a rash of canceled bookings. One German vessel, the *Europa*, lost twenty-five passengers just before sailing; all of them transferred to the U.S.-owned *Manhattan*, citing their displeasure with the Hitler regime. British trade unionists and

Labour party leaders began posting BOYCOTT GERMAN GOODS notices throughout London, especially the East End. One Jewish-owned firm immediately cancelled orders for £14,000 of German goods, and publicly resubmitted the orders to American suppliers.[4]

As the first anti-Nazi boycott rumblings were heard in Germany, Adolf Hitler was trying to emphasize Germany's desire for unhampered trade relations. In a major speech to the Reichstag that March 23, upon receiving his dictatorial powers, der Führer declared: "We need contact with the outside world, and our foreign markets furnish a livelihood for millions of our fellow citizens." The German government followed up Hitler's speech with an immediate appeal to foreign correspondents whose newspapers were publicizing boycott activities. If the economic boycott against Germany is executed, "as is agitated by certain American circles," the Reich statement asked, how "is the question of private debts to be regulated properly?"[5]

By the next day, March 24, Reich leaders realized that boycott agitation was accelerating, especially in Great Britain. Placards proclaiming BOYCOTT GERMAN GOODS spread infectiously throughout London, and were now in the windows of the most exclusive West End shops. Automobiles bannering boycott placards slowly cruised through the retail districts alerting shoppers. Everywhere store signs warned German salesmen not to enter. British Catholics had been urged by the Archbishop of Liverpool to join the protest. London's *Daily Herald* carried an interview with a prominent Jewish leader who admitted, "The [Jewish] leaders are hanging back," but the Jewish people are "forcing its leaders on." Already the boycott had damaged "hundreds of thousands of pounds' worth of German trade."[6]

The volume of German goods sold abroad was already dangerously low. Germany simply could not stand further export reductions.[7] By March 24, enough consular dispatches had been received in Berlin to paint a clear picture. The rudimentary boycott was indeed snowballing, apparently building to a climax when it would be globally proclaimed by Dr. Stephen Wise. Nazi leadership reacted with paranoia and militancy. Hermann Goering, Prussian minister of the interior and president of the Reichstag, summoned the heads of Germany's three major Jewish organizations: Julius Brodnitz, chairman of the Central Verein; Dr. Max Naumann of the fiercely patriotic Union of National German Jews; and Heinrich Stahl, president of the Berlin Jewish Community. They were to appear in Goering's office at noon the next day, Saturday, March 25.[8]

The Zionists had not been invited. Goering despised the Zionists, as did most Nazis. True, the National Socialists hoped to use Zionism to rid Germany—indeed Europe—of its Jews. But they also distrusted it as one of the three serpentine heads of international Jewry. According to Nazi philosophers, capitalism and Bolshevism were both creations of the so-called Jewish conspiracy. The twisted rationale accused Jews of using either method to topple governments in their quest for world domination. Zionism, in the Nazi view, was the ultimate goal of Jewish international efforts.[9] Moreover, the Nazis knew that the German Zionist movement did not really represent German Jewry. Zionist groups themselves estimated their own strength at only 1 or 2 percent of the country's Jews.[10] The Zionist concept was anathema to the overwhelming majority, who considered themselves assimilated, loyal Germans. Zionism was equally repugnant to orthodox German Jews, who spurned Jewish sovereignty in the Holy Land on religious grounds (e.g., that only the Jewish Messiah could reinstate the Kingdom of the Jews). In 1933, then, Zionism in Germany was a mere Jewish fringe movement.

Though not invited, the German Zionist Federation (ZVfD) did learn of the summit just a few hours before the meeting. ZVfD official Martin Rosenbluth and Federation president Kurt Blumenfeld were mystified about the purpose of the conference, but both men concluded that German Zionism must be present. After frantic telephoning, a Reich contact succeeded in adding Blumenfeld's name to the invitation list.[11]

At about noon, the two Zionists entered the anteroom outside Goering's private office. The three other Jewish leaders were surprised to see them. Brodnitz, of the Central Verein, tried to be cordial and make small talk. But staunchly anti-Zionist Naumann, of the Union of National German Jews, angrily lashed out at Rosenbluth. Why, demanded Naumann, should Zionists have any right to attend a meeting between the government and "the legitimate representatives of the German Jews"? Rosenbluth reacted with his own barbed rhetoric, and within moments the two leaders were trading denigrations. The verbal fight ended only when a uniformed Goering aide entered the room.[12]

Hermann Goering was ready to see them, announced the aide, if they would follow him. All five Jewish leaders began walking into the inner office, but the aide stopped Rosenbluth, asserting that Blumenfeld was the only Zionist on the official list.[13]

As Naumann, Brodnitz, Stahl, and Blumenfeld entered the minister's office, they saw Goering standing in the middle of the room dressed in his Storm Trooper's uniform, thus making clear his dual capacity as government minister and Nazi party leader. In the beginning, decorum was observed. The uniformed aide formally introduced each Jewish leader by name and organization. But the formalities ended there. The men were not invited to be seated.[14] It was plain that, unlike the two previous Jewish conferences in which Goering had politely apologized for transgressions of Nazi zealots, this would not be a friendly encounter.

Goering immediately ripped into the Jewish leaders, accusing them of responsibility for the malicious and treasonable atrocity headlines in the English and American press. The Jewish leaders, trying to hold their ground, denied any knowledge of the newspaper articles.[15] Goering snapped his fingers. The uniformed aide appeared. He was instructed to fetch the clippings. Once Goering had them in hand, he began reading them aloud, growing angrier with each paragraph. In a frenzied shout he warned, "Unless you put a stop to these libelous accusations immediately, I shall no longer be able to vouch for the safety of the German Jews!"[16]

The Jewish leaders attempted to downplay the newspaper accounts. But Goering would not hear any explanations. He ordered them to go to London immediately to convince the British Jews, and from there the American Jews, that Jews in Germany were *not* experiencing physical mistreatment, that the newspaper stories were despicable lies.[17]

Goering then turned to his main worry, the upcoming day of protest and the giant Madison Square Garden rally. Goering cited the dangers of such a rally to Germany's position. With deadly seriousness, he gave the Jewish leaders his prime directive: "The most important thing is for you to make sure that the protest meeting called in New York by Dr. Stephen S. Wise is canceled. That assembly must not take place. Dr. Wise is one of our most dangerous and unscrupulous enemies."[18]

The three Jewish leaders, desperate to disown any supposed influence over Jewish actions in Great Britain or America, denied there would be any usefulness to their visiting London. Brodnitz assured Goering that the Central Verein maintained absolutely no connections with overseas Jewish organizations.[19] Brodnitz dared not mention that Central Verein vice-president Ernest Wallach was already in America trying to dissuade the Congress. It was important for the Jewish leaders to explicitly deny any relationship with Jews in other countries—if only to refute the Nazi accusation of an international Jewish conspiracy.

But then Blumenfeld stepped forward on behalf of the Zionists, declaring that the German Zionist Federation was uniquely capable of conferring with Jewish leaders in other countries, since German Zionists were affiliated with a worldwide organization.[20] Once uttered, the words forever changed the relationship between the Nazis and the Zionists. It was suddenly clear that the Jewish group the Reich had been ignoring was, in fact, the one it should be negotiating with in its efforts to combat the Jewish presence in Germany. After all, both Nazis and Zionists agreed that Jews did not belong in Germany.

Blumenfeld quickly added that even if a Zionist representative did journey to London, there was no chance of exerting any influence over American or British Jewry unless the Zionists had permission to tell "the full truth."[21] Goering exploded, shouting "What is there to tell? You know perfectly well there has been no change in the situation of the Jews, and that nothing untoward has happened to them." Naumann bravely contradicted the shouting Goering, declaring that Goering "must not be well informed" if he was unaware of the radical change in the physical safety of Jews in Germany. Naumann boldly recited case after case of violence against Jews, ranging from manhandling to vicious beatings and death. He then produced a clipping of his own from a Nazi newspaper including a photograph of Jews being forced to wash the streets in Chemnitz. Goering's tirade was abruptly halted by the clip. He passed over the Jewish evidence almost in embarrassment. Then, in a complete about-face, Goering declared he did not object to the facts being told to American and British Jewish organizations, as long as those foreign Jewish organizations would immediately call a halt to the "vicious atrocity propaganda."[22] Tiring of the meeting, Goering demanded that whichever of them went to London was unimportant to him—so long as a delegation left Berlin by the next day.

Each of the four Jewish organizations immediately set about fulfilling its obligation as best it could. Brodnitz, Naumann, and Stahl beseeched their friends and associates to flood U.S. and British government offices and Jewish organizations with every form of denial and disclaimer. Doctors, lawyers, professors, bankers, prominent journalists and their newspapers, professional and civic organizations of every category—they all tried by cable, phone, and letter to convince Jewish organizations to call off the Madison Square Garden rally.[23]

"SHOCKED AT GROSS MISINTERPRETATION OF RECENT GERMAN EVENTS STOP SAVE FOR FEW MOLESTATIONS BY INDIVIDUAL TOUGHS NO HARM DONE TO JEWS STOP LATTER CONTINUE UNDISTURBED IN BUSINESS AND OFFICE STOP NO LEADING JEWISH PAPERS SUPPRESSED STOP GERMANY HAS POSITION WELL IN HAND STOP STRICT DISCIPLINE IS MAINTAINED SIGNED AMERIKA INSTITUT BERLIN."[24]

"WE CAN ASSURE THAT ANY ALARMING RUMOURS REGARDING PUBLIC DISTURBANCES AND ACTS OF VIOLENCE ARE EXTREMELY EXAGGERATED STOP . . . NO ORGANIZED ACTS OF THIS KIND HAVE TAKEN PLACE STOP . . . CALM VIEWS ABROAD WOULD SUPPORT AND ASSIST MAINTENANCE OF NORMAL POLITICAL AND ECONOMIC CONDITIONS SIGNED GERMAN AMERICAN CHAMBER OF COMMERCE HAMBURG."[25]

Central Verein vice-president Ernest Wallach was already traveling through America (ostensibly on business) to help restrain Jewish American protest fervor. Upon hearing of the Goering order, he also wired Stephen Wise, pleading that if the rally could not be canceled, at least would Wise direct the speakers to "refrain from stirring the emotions of the audience against Germany."[26]

The German Jewish protests were transparent attempts to mollify the threatening Nazis, who believed that German Jewry was orchestrating the international anti-Hitler movement. Typical was the official denial of the Central Verein, directed principally at American Jews. Claiming that media stories of Germany's anti-Semitism were "inexcusable distortions," the Central Verein demanded that the foreign press and foreign Jewish groups leave the Reich's internal politics to the Reich.[27]

Yet hundreds of word-of-mouth reports, courageous letters—some mere scraps of paper smuggled out of Germany—argued forcibly for the truth. One eloquent message delivered to Rabbi Wise said simply, "Do not believe the denials. Nor the Jewish denials."[28]

"Pitifully unconvincing," declared American Jewish Congress president Bernard Deutsch in a public reaction to the Central Verein's statement. "The denial does not deny, as indeed it would be futile to deny in the teeth of overwhelming evidence . . . the tales of persecution and horror which thousands are telling."[29]

Rabbi Wise was equally undeterred by the German Jewish protests under duress. "We have no quarrel with our Jewish brothers in Germany and their leaders," Wise declared, "but their policy of uncomplaining assent and of supercautious silence has borne evil fruit."[30]

When in 1932 the Nazi ascent to power became a distinct possibility, Stephen Wise summoned Jewish leaders from many nations to Geneva, Switzerland, for a World Jewish Conference—the first of its kind. The conference was intended as the first step in forming a World Jewish Congress to deal with the welfare of Jews outside Palestine. As such it would be a counterbalance to the Zionist Organization, which was strictly concerned with Jews emigrating to and prospering in Palestine. But German Jewish leaders in Germany and America refused to cooperate with Wise's warning to Germany against installing Adolf Hitler. The Central Verein leadership, seconded by the American Jewish Committee, insisted Hitler was no real threat to German Jewry, and demanded that foreign Jewish groups keep out of Germany's domestic affairs.[31]

Now as the hour of protest approached, only one man had the power to stop the rally—Rabbi Stephen S. Wise. But he was holding fast. When the Committee realized they couldn't actually stop the rally, they tried to convince eminent scheduled speakers to cancel their appearances. New York Governor Herbert Lehman, whose older brother was a Committee vice-president, was persuaded to honor another commitment in Albany. New York City Mayor John O'Brien, a visible supporter of the Jewish War Veteran boycott, was almost talked out of appearing at Madison Square Garden.[32]

When simple arguments failed, the Committee resorted to personal attacks against Wise himself. Distinguished Baltimore Rabbi William Rosenau, a lifelong and cherished friend of Rabbi Wise, forfeited his relationship with Wise when he tried to keep people from the rally by saying, "Dr. Wise will kill the Jews of Germany." Wise wrote his friend, "You have borne false witness against a man, a colleague, and a friend. I can nevermore have any word with you or see you again. Men like you are responsible in part for what is happening in Germany. If counsels of expediency and timidity such as your own had not prevailed in Jewish life in Germany during the last ten years, this great disaster might have been averted."[33]

Last-minute pressure on Rabbi Wise continued that Sunday. Secretary of State Cordell Hull tried to lull Wise into procrastination with false reports of amelioration. On March 26, Hull sent a telegram to the presidents of the Big Three pretending to show State Department action. Hull's telegram, which he released to the press, began, "You will remember . . . I informed you that, in view of numerous press statements indicating widespread mistreatment of the Jews in Germany, I would request the American Embassy at Berlin . . . to investigate the situation and submit a report. A reply indicates "that whereas there was for a short time considerable physical mistreatment of Jews, this phase may be considered virtually terminated."[34]

In truth, no investigation took place. No real report was submitted. After Wise moved the State Department to announce an investigation on March 21, Hull had cabled U.S. chargé d'affaires George Gordon in Berlin, saying, "We are under heavy pressure to make representations on their [the Jew's] behalf to the German government." Hull had added that he didn't want to make any such protests, but if some assuasive statement could be issued to the press, it might help cancel the "monster mass meeting" Wise had scheduled for March 27.[35]

Within a few hours of receiving the cable on March 25, Gordon dictated a response to Hull, suggesting that a few out of-context sentences from an earlier telegram be used as the "backbone" of Hull's so-called report. The sentence to be excerpted referred to official Reich assurances that the violence against Jews would soon end. Later in his March 25 cable, Gordon reported the true situation to Hull: that Jewish expulsions from professional life were imminent, that Nazi denials of anti-Semitic violence were "absurd," and that Jewish German groups issuing public denials of anti-Semitic violence were probably doing so under duress. Still, Gordon suggested that Hull use the coerced Jewish denials along with hollow German reassurances to paint a false picture of amelioration.[36]

But upon receipt of Hull's telegram, Wise and Bernard Deutsch sent off a diplomatic rejection of its unbelievable assurances. "In the name of the American Jewish Congress, we wish to thank you for your prompt report on the situation in Germany, which confirms our fears."[37]

That weekend, the German embassy in Washington telephoned Dr. Wise several times, assuring him that if only the rally were called off, the Jewish situation in Germany would improve. But Wise still would not back down.[38]

Finally, after the American Jewish Committee, the State Department, and the government of Germany had failed to dissuade Wise, the Zionists tried. Stephen Wise was a cornerstone activist in the American Zionist movement. So when the German Zionists whom Goering had ordered to London telephoned Wise as instructed, it was hard for him to deny their request.[39] But the very fact that Zionist officials were asking him to abandon his protest shook Wise deeply.

Public pressures and protests were commonplace to Rabbi Wise. He had lived in controversy for decades. Born in Budapest in 1874, but immediately brought to America, Wise grew up in New York City, where his father, Aaron, served as rabbi of a local synagogue. As a teenager, Stephen committed himself to rabbinical study. At age nineteen, with postgraduate studies in Oxford, he was ordained by Vienna's chief rabbi. Shortly thereafter, Wise accepted his first congregation in New York. In 1897, Wise and other leading Jews established the Federation of American Zionists. The next year, Wise was appointed the American secretary of the world Zionist movement. At the time, Zionism was but a flicker in the imagination of a few determined Jews. It outraged the bulk of world Jewry and was viewed with suspicion by Christians. Defending the movement became a daily chore.[40]

In 1900, Wise became rabbi of a Portland congregation. He was soon involved in turn-of-the-century reform movements, including child labor, women's suffrage, and Negro rights. The governor of Oregon had even appointed him commissioner of Child Labor.[41]

In 1906, Rabbi Wise returned to New York, where scores of thousands of Jewish refugees from Russia, Poland, and Rumania were seeking shelter. He spurned an opportunity to serve at Temple Emanu-El, the fashionable synagogue of the elitist German Jews. Instead he founded the Free Synagogue, operating out of the Hudson Theatre, and later a branch on the Lower East Side. The Free Synagogue established a Social Service Division to aid the deprived and dispossessed—regardless of religion—as they struggled to remain warm, stay fed, and acquire an education. The Jewish masses saw this work as a social crusade. Later Wise joined with Christian counterparts— minister John Haynes Holmes, Jane Addams, and other reformers—to create the National Association for the Advancement of Colored People, which fought for Negro rights and opportunity.[42]

Stephen Wise was an eloquent, feisty, determined, and often self-righteous fighter for the people, a man who found his inner strength and outer support most vitalized when struggling for the underdog against powerful adversaries. In his late twenties, his handsome roughhewn face became familiar on the national political scene. President Woodrow Wilson counted him as a key supporter, and friendships with several Supreme Court justices provided him access to virtually any portal in Washington. Wise's closeness to Woodrow Wilson and his advisers made the rabbi a factor in America's endorsement of Britain's Balfour Declaration. Just after the Great War, Wise was a leading advocate for guaranteed Jewish minority rights, a prime supporter of America's most important labor unions, and a cofounder of the American Civil Liberties Union.[43]

Wise took on the Jewish establishment as well, when in the early 1920s he organized the Jewish masses into the permanent American Jewish Congress.[44]

During the mid-1920s, he supported unions in bitter labor disputes, undeterred by ax-handles and private armies. He fought the Ku Klux Klan throughout the North and the South and was a leader in the protest over the execution of Sacco and Vanzetti. Wise even shook off the wrath of almost every American Jew as press reports distorted his 1925 sermon affirming that Jesus was a Jew whom "Christians deny in fact and Jews deny in name . . . a man not myth, human not God, Jew not Christian."[45]

Wise thrived on controversy and the painful pursuit of his beliefs, no matter how bitter the consequences. He was a man who would sever a lifelong friendship because of a loose comment or cut himself off from his own people rather than retract a statement he believed to be true. And he was accustomed to rallying thousands in bitter, frequently violent battles to achieve a lasting principle.

And yet, as the hour pulled closer for the Madison Square rally, Stephen Wise experienced indecision. He weighed the moral imperative of standing up to Hitler against the risk of provoking the Nazis to unleash an organized pogrom that would leave Jews bloodied across Germany. Would the rally make a difference? Had the protest gone far enough, or was it only starting? Would delay merely provide the Third Reich with the breathing time it needed to organize its destruction of the Jews? Stephen S. Wise, who had stood alone on any issue, fought alone on any battle, could not alone make this decision.

On March 27, Rabbi Wise telephoned the one man in America whose judgment he valued perhaps more than his own—his dearest friend, Supreme Court Justice Louis Brandeis. They spoke briefly and Wise put it to his friend simply. Do it or not? Brandeis answered, "Go ahead and make the protest as good as you can." Wise hung up. His decision was now final.[46]

5. Madison Square

THE RALLY didn't start until after 8:00 P.M., but by 2:30 P.M. on March 27, 1933, people were waiting outside Madison Square Garden. Once the doors were unlocked, a flow of people began that continued for hours. By

5:30, traffic snarled as thousands more jammed the streets around Madison Square. People were backed all the way down the subway stairs. Six hundred policemen formed a blue-coat chain along the crosswalks just to allow pedestrians to pass.[1]

Suddenly, in the midst of the many, came distant sounds of drums and fifes that added distinctly American excitement to the scene. Those people nearest the Garden probably could not see the approaching formation, even as the marching staccato became louder and closer. But then, off on a side street, a drum and bugle corps appeared, all war veterans stepping proudly, with banners denouncing the Third Reich. By plan they were to enter the Garden in a dramatic flourish, but as the streets became thicker the marchers could not move. Up against barriers of mounted policemen, the veterans marched in place, waiting for an opening, their skirls and drumbeats continuing a cadence for the crowd.[2]

Inevitably the streets became chaotic as protesters tried to force through the doors of the Garden. But the aisles and balconies and lobbies of Madison Square Garden were already filled.[3]

Orders went out. The doors were closed with 20,000 inside. But the crowds outside demanded entry and the police started to react. Superior officers rushed in to calm the frenzy. Public loudspeakers were hastily mounted to control an estimated 35,000 anxious citizens crammed into the streets around the Garden. Pleas by police and protest marshals diverted some of the thousands to a second ad hoc rally at nearby Columbus Circle. It wasn't enough. More overflow rallies were frantically set up along the nearby intersections. New York had never seen anything like it.[4] Americans of all persuasions and descents were united against Adolf Hitler, and they wanted their country to do something about it. Decades later they would be accused of apathy and inaction. But on March 27, 1933, the citizens of the United States were anything but apathetic.

Fifty-five thousand were gathered in and around Madison Square Garden. Supportive rallies were at that moment waiting in Chicago, Washington, San Francisco, Houston, and about seventy other American cities. At each supportive rally, thousands huddled around loudspeakers waiting for the Garden event, which would be broadcast live via radio relay to 200 additional cities across the country. At least 1 million Jews were participating nationwide. Perhaps another million Americans of non-Jewish heritage stood with them.[5]

Hundreds of thousands more were waiting in Europe. Congress president Bernard Deutsch had sent out last minute cables to Jewish protest leaders in Latvia, Czechoslovakia, and elsewhere throughout the Continent. Anti-Reich activists across the Atlantic had agreed to hold their protests in abeyance until signaled from New York. When the go-ahead was received, plans were put into effect. Poland was typical. A national day of fasting was authorized by rabbinical bodies. The Warsaw Stock Exchange shut down early. Poland's government even released an order dissolving a large portion of the Polish Hitlerites. Anti-Hitler parades and meetings were granted approval, while police banned counterdemonstrations by Nazi sympathizers.[6]

Inside the Garden itself, the guest speakers were delayed. People were shouting, feet were stamping, chairs were banging. The din was equaled outside, where loudspeakers pleaded for order as the program organizers tried to start. Abruptly in the midst of the tumult, when it seemed the crowd would wait no longer, an eighty-year-old orthodox rabbi, M. S. Margolies, approached the lectern and touched the microphone. The audience came to a sudden silence. The hush spread outside as people strained to hear. Rabbi Margolies chanted a plaintive Hebraic prayer of chilling power, his voice beseeching God in the name of humanity that the persecutions in Germany stop. The chant was heard around the world.[7]

Among the first to speak was Alfred E. Smith, former New York governor and popular Catholic figure. Smith, in his plain-folks style, declared that of all the times he had addressed the public in Madison Square Garden, no rally could give him greater satisfaction because the opportunity to stand up against bigotry was both a duty and a right. He admitted there had been great pressures to keep him from speaking: "I got all kinds of telegrams . . . telling me there wasn't any reason for a meeting, that nothing had taken place [in Germany], that we wanted to avoid the possibility of hysteria at a time like this. Well, all I can say about that is . . . drag it out into the open sunlight and give it the same treatment that we gave the Ku Klux Klan. . . . it don't make any difference to me whether it is a brown shirt or a night shirt." The crowd cheered its approval repeatedly as Smith used down-home lingo, puns, and sarcasm to ridicule der Führer and his Storm Troopers. But before Smith finished, he became stern and in sober tones warned the German nation not to descend into a barbaric war against the Jews.[8]

Bishop John J. Dunn of the Catholic Archdiocese of New York, because of State Department and American Jewish Committee assurances, had reneged on his promise to appear. But other clergymen, including Bishop Francis T. McConnell, refused to back down. Bishop McConnell warned, "People say, 'Why not let Germany run things to suit herself?' My friends, that is just the quickest way to plunge the world into war again. If there is no protest at all against so completely out-of-date a thing as the anti-Semitic movement . . . [then] after a while . . . the situation becomes intolerable and then we resort to force." He added that anti-Nazi rallies and protest actions must continue, even if persecutions in Germany temporarily ceased, until the Nazis were out of power.[9]

The applause and cheers for Bishop McConnell's words were followed by a procession of politicians and clergymen, each likewise committing his supporters to the struggle against Hitlerism. And then the crowd heard from the most experienced economic battle group in America—organized labor.

William Green, president of the American Federation of Labor, pledged the active involvement of 3 million American unionists. "I come tonight in the name of Labor," Green declared, "protesting in its sacred name against the atrocities . . . perpetrated upon the Jewish population of Germany. I transmit to the . . . German trade unions, the masses of the people, the hosts of labor in Germany, and to the Jewish people an expression of sympathy. . . . We pledge to them our moral and economic support . . . [to] do all that lies within our power" to end "the campaign of persecution against the Jewish people in Germany." [10]

Labor's involvement could make any boycott almost totally effective, especially if longshoremen refused to off-load German merchandise at the docks. So Green's words were powerful threats. "We will not remain passive and unconcerned when the relatives, families, and brethren of the Jewish members of our great organization are being persecuted and oppressed," Green promised. [11]

Other eminent figures continued to enthrall the rally, including crusading minister John Haynes Holmes, New York Senator Robert Wagner, *Der Tog* editor Samuel Margoshes, Joseph Tenenbaum of the American Jewish Congress, and Chaim Greenberg of the Labor Zionists. Many more wishing to address the meeting could not, and sent telegrams instead: the Speaker of the House, the governor of Illinois, a senator from California, the governor of Iowa, the Senate majority leader, the governor of Oregon, scores of civic, social, commercial, labor, fraternal, and religious organizations. All condemned the Third Reich in explicit language and expressed solidarity with the movement to overturn Hitler. [12]

The protest rally received such vocal support that the thousands ignored the nonappearance of the American Jewish Committee and B'nai B'rith. Nor did they notice the absence of any message from the one man the nation expected to sympathize—President Roosevelt.

Then, with the audience primed and anxious, Rabbi Stephen S. Wise stepped forward to the most thunderous ovation he had ever received. After many attempts, the crowd finally quieted, and Dr. Wise began. He surprised many by discarding some of the dramatic techniques he often employed. At first he spoke in conciliatory tones, in the hopes of communicating with the people in Germany, "Not out of the bitterness of anger, but out of the . . . spirit of compassion do we speak tonight. . . . We are not against Germany. . . . We are the friends of and believers in Germany—Germany at its highest, Germany at its truest, the German nation at its noblest." [13]

The other speakers had threatened and ridiculed the Nazis. Wise was showing the route away from conflict: cessation of anti-Semitism. He made it clear that even that demand was not an attempt to interfere with Germany's domestic affairs, but simply an insistence upon fundamental human rights or, as he called them, "axioms of civilizations." His manner was calm, steady. [14]

But then he began to build. "To those leaders of Germany who declare that the present situation in Germany is a local German question, we call attention to the words of Abraham Lincoln. Defenders of slavery urged and excused slavery on the ground that it was *local*. Lincoln's answer was slavery is local but freedom is *national*!" The crowd burst into excited approval. Wise kept building, as he demanded "the immediate cessation of anti-Semitic activities and propaganda in Germany, including an end to the racial discrimination against and economic exclusion of Jews from the life of Germany. . . . the human rights of Jews must be safeguarded. . . . Whatever be the threat of reprisal, none of these [demands] can be withdrawn or altered or moderated."[15]

Turning to Jewish leaders in Germany and their advocates in America, Wise disqualified their pleas for an end to the protest as "panic and terror" from those who had failed to fight Nazism before the NSDAP came to power. He vowed the anti-Hitler protest would escalate, even if pseudoameliorations appeared: "Even if life and human rights are to be safeguarded, there must not be a substitution of the status of helotry [serfdom] for violence. Such substitution will not satisfy us"—the throng interrupted with cheers of encouragement—"nor satisfy the aroused conscience of humankind." The crowd offered their own punctuation as Wise declared, "Every form of economic discrimination is a form of violence. Every racial exclusion is violence. To say that there will be no pogroms is not enough. A dry and bloodless economic pogrom remains violence and force."[16] Above the cheering he warned the Third Reich, "And if things are to be worse because of our protest, if there are to be new penalties and new reprisals in Germany . . . then humbly and sorrowfully we bow our heads in the presence of the tragic fate that threatens." But, "Hear the word of a great English statesman: 'Providence would deal good or ill fortune to nations according as they dealt well or ill by the Jews.' This is not a warning, but a prophecy!"[17]

Rabbi Stephen Wise paused to speak the final words of his oration. The crowd hushed. "To this mighty protest Germany cannot fail to give heed and to answer." Then he pointed dramatically to the members of the audience and in a firm voice said, "I ask you by rising to signify to us and to all the world that you agree with us in our stand to bring about justice . . . from Germany to the Jew."[18]

In a thunderous motion, 20,000 Americans rose as one to their feet. The immense noise of the act and the rising voices created a sound that must have seemed like a massive sleeping animal suddenly awakening. That moment of solidarity was shared by the 20,000 in Madison Square Garden, the 35,000 more standing outside the Garden, a million others in supportive rallies in other cities, and millions more in their homes hearing the protest live on radio throughout America and in thirteen nations.[19] The world was warned. Germany was on notice.

Rabbi Wise stood down, ready to accept whatever was Germany's response to his plea, challenge, and warning. Without question, the struggle against Hitler was now in the open.

6. April First

NO DIRECT WORD about a boycott against Germany was actually mentioned at Madison Square Garden. Neither was the budding Jewish War Veterans' boycott or the Polish boycott encouraged at the rally, even though it was an opportunity to expand those movements vastly. The decision was Stephen Wise's. To those who disagreed, Wise would reply, "We have the means and the will to boycott when we want. But now is not right. Let's wait just a little longer."[1]

What Wise was waiting for—strong diplomatic action—was a mirage. President Roosevelt wasn't concerned. And the State Department, B'nai B'rith, and the American Jewish Committee were not going on the offensive. They were simply stalling, hoping the anger on both sides of the Atlantic would dissipate. It wouldn't.

One reason was that the Madison Square denunciations were heard throughout Germany: Der Führer and the NSDAP were termed criminals and barbarians; Germany was accused of rampant tortures and atrocities. As the Nazis saw it, Jewish propaganda was again disabling Germany before she could achieve success, as in World War I.

Although the boycott was not declared then and there as Goering and Hitler had feared, it was threatened indirectly by people with official government titles and authority, by Catholic bishops, and by labor leaders who could start a boycott at the snap of a finger. In the Nazi view, the boycott was already under way. The Congress rally seemed to be the master switch activating a new world movement.

Mass meetings throughout Poland—coordinated to the Congress' rally— had voted to expand the Vilna boycott to all of Poland. The three most important Warsaw Jewish commercial organizations—the Central Association of Merchants, the Central Association of Small Tradesmen, and the Central Association of Jewish Artisans—passed binding resolutions to "use the most radical means of defense by boycotting German imports."[2]

In London, almost all Jewish shops in the Whitechapel district were displaying placards denying entry to German salesmen and affirming the

anti-Nazi boycott. Teenagers patrolled the streets distributing handbills asking shoppers to boycott German goods. And a newsreel showing der Führer
was ceremoniously rejected by a London moviehouse.[3]

In the United States, the withholding of the actual word *boycott* did not
dampen the spontaneous grass-roots boycott led by the 15,000-man Jewish
War Veterans. Within days of the JWV's boycott announcement, the group
established a permanent office to raise funds, and even more importantly to
connect American merchants with eager alternative suppliers in Czechoslovakia, Rumania, England, France, and of course the United States itself.
Thousands of boycott letters were mailed by the JWV to businessmen
throughout the East Coast. Pickets were thrown around East Coast stores
carrying German goods. And a steady publicity program was being well
received by the U.S. media. For example, when two Hoboken, New Jersey,
companies, Pioneer Paper and City Chemical, rescinded orders for hundreds
of thousands of dollars of machinery and pledged to buy no more German
products, the cancellations were accompanied by press conferences and
newspaper articles. Such announcements produced a chain reaction, and
within days of the JWV's boycott declaration the Veterans showed the press
well over $2 million in lost German orders.[4]

Here was the real threat to the Nazis: lost sales. Once lost, many were lost
forever. And when enough buyers actually turned to other sources of supply,
entire markets could be lost as well. Spoken or unspoken, a mushrooming,
even if uncoordinated, anti-German boycott movement was spreading
throughout Europe and America. It was only moments from becoming a
worldwide economic weapon if only the Congress and the other leading
Jewish organizations would give their official support.

Above all of the Nazi dogma, revitalization of the German economy was
the single indispensable feature of Hitler's program. Without a strong economy, the Reich could not rearm and could never begin its conquest of Europe. The Nazis were justifiably convinced that if the National Socialist
revolution brought more unemployment and economic chaos, the German
masses would turn away from the sixty-day Reich. To the Nazis, it seemed
that only the Jews and their boycott were now standing between Germany
and greatness. No wonder Goering had said that Stephen Wise was one of
Hitler's "most dangerous enemies."[5]

Hitler was in his Berchtesgaden retreat Sunday, March 26, 1933, when
he learned that efforts to abort the Congress rally were unsuccessful. He
summoned Goebbels from Berlin for an emergency conference. The two men
held a long discussion of how the boycott and atrocity campaign could be
arrested. Goebbels had been working on the problem. He had just finished a
denial of the atrocities for *The London Sunday Express*, but admitted that
such articles were "inadequate."[6]

Hitler and Goebbels concluded that a preemptive anti-Jewish boycott was the only answer. Longtime anti-Jewish boycott vanguard Julius Streicher would coordinate the action. The party faithful had long awaited this development. Goebbels excitedly hurried back to his Berlin office to polish a statement declaring that Germany's organized anti-Jewish campaign would now begin.[7]

The morning of the March 27 Madison Square Garden rally, Goebbels released a statement warning that "drastic legal proceedings" lay ahead for the German Jews if the New York- and London-centered anti-Reich campaign continued. Goebbels then wired a short party bulletin to Hitler for approval. In his diary that day, Goebbels admitted, "We work through [newspaper] interviews as much as possible; but only a really extensive movement can now help us out of our calamity." By the end of the afternoon, Hitler had approved Goebbels' party bulletin. The Propaganda Minister released it over German radio even before Rabbi Wise's protest broadcast was complete. The bulletin proclaimed that a national boycott against Germany's Jews was to be organized.[8]

The next morning, March 28, German and Nazi party newspapers carried an expanded declaration. The national anti-Jewish boycott was to commence April 1, in order to halt the accelerating Jewish-sponsored anti-German boycott movement and atrocity campaign. The foreign press was told that Hitler was moving to stymie "the anti-German atrocity propaganda which interested Jews have started in England and the United States." Der Führer held Germany's Jews responsible for the foreign agitation, and these "defensive measures" were only the beginning. Officially mandated economic ousters of Jews would commence as well.[9]

The decision was technically made by Hitler in his capacity as chief of the Nazi party, not in his capacity as chancellor of the Reich. For appearances, therefore, the boycott was officially unofficial, to be organized and executed by the party and not the government. To emphasize that the action was in response to the failure of Washington and London to halt the protests in their countries, the announcement specified: The German government would not interfere with the party's boycott "so long as foreign governments do not take steps against atrocity propaganda in their countries."[10]

The NSDAP's preemptive boycott would not begin officially until April 1, but the announcement itself set off a rash of boycotting and expulsions. German medical and juridical societies immediately expelled their Jewish members. In Darmstadt, Mannheim, and numerous other German cities, local SS contingents surrounded Jewish stores, smashed windows, and lobbed stench bombs. Frequently the police themselves demanded the stores close.[11]

The Jewish community in Germany reacted with terror. Previous outbursts had been sporadic, unorganized acts of intimidation and violence against individual families and businesses. But this boycott would be a systematic economic pogrom that would plague every Jewish business and household. No one would be spared. What professional could survive if he could not practice? What store could survive if it could not sell?

At first, Jews and non-Jews, whether in Germany or outside, could not believe that such an official national outrage could occur. No one seriously distinguished between Hitler's party capacity and his role as chief of state. This, then, was the beginning of the fulfillment of *Mein Kampf*, Hitler's explicit forecast of Jewish persecution in Germany, the document all believed—hoped—would never be put into force. The world was shocked. Hitler was going to keep his promises.

Within hours of the Tuesday-morning proclamation, Nazi party headquarters in Munich had formulated precise plans. Under boycott regulations, "no German shall any longer buy from a Jew." The boycott would commence at 10:00 A.M., April 1, a Saturday morning, and continue until the anti-German boycott protest movement in New York and London "ended." [12]

On March 28, the boycott promised to be a long ruinous confrontation for the Jews. In Munich, a hastily formed Central Committee for Defense Against Jewish Atrocity and Boycott Propaganda issued strict guidelines. All local party units were to be involved in both boycotting Germany's Jews and maintaining Nazi discipline. There was to be no violence, no basis for further atrocity stories. But an anti-Jewish boycott, violent or disciplined, would be disastrous for Germany's fragile economy, and virtually everyone in Germany with realistic business sense knew it. Non-Nazi members of the cabinet—a majority—demanded that Hitler cancel the anti-Jewish boycott. He refused. [13]

The next morning, March 30, newspapers in Germany and abroad confirmed that the anti-Jewish boycott proclamation was not just another vague Nazi threat, but a real and organized action. Terrified German Jews now redoubled their panicky campaign to disavow foreign protests and newspaper reports. They pleaded with their New York brethren to cancel any further protest activities, and especially any talk about boycotting German goods. Noted Hamburg banker Eric Warburg cabled his cousin Frederick in New York: "TODAY'S BOYCOTT THREATS AGAINST JEWISH FIRMS IN GERMANY WILL BE CARRIED OUT IF ATROCITIES NEWS AND UNFRIENDLY PROPAGANDA IN FOREIGN PRESS MASS MEETINGS ETC. DOES NOT STOP IMMEDIATELY." [14] Frederick Warburg upon receipt immediately telephoned Cyrus Adler, president of the American Jewish Committee, who composed a paragraph disavowing atrocity stories and any boycott. The statement was forwarded to Committee secretary Morris Waldman for approval. [15]

Waldman quickly approved the statement: "The American Jewish Committee declares that to its knowledge most of the so-called atrocity stories which were reported from Germany to have appeared in the American press did not so appear. No threats of boycott in America have been made by any responsible Jewish bodies. They were irresponsible sporadic outbursts. It is impossible to tell what would happen, however, if the threatened boycott against all Jews in Germany is carried out on April 1st."[16]

In a desperate attempt to mollify the Nazis, the Committee portrayed the Jewish War Veterans and boycott-leaning officials of the Congress as "irresponsible." This deepened the disunity between the Committee and popular Jewish organizations and forced the Committee into an even more isolated antiprotest corner. But the men of the Committee were agonizing over how best to ameliorate the plight of their friends and relatives in Germany. Their legendary judgment and foresight was now narrowed to simply avoiding the calamity of the coming weekend.

To back up the Committee's official statement, Frederick Warburg cabled Eric the following response: "WILL DO AND HAVE DONE MY BEST BUT RECENT GOVERNMENT BOYCOTT ANNOUNCEMENT VIEWED HERE AS CONFIRMATION PREVIOUS REPORTS OF DISCRIMINATION STOP RESENTMENT SO WIDESPREAD NO INDIVIDUAL EFFORTS TO STEM IT LIKELY AVAIL UNLESS GOVERNMENT CHANGES ATTITUDE STOP WILL CONTINUE TO DISCOURAGE MASS MEETINGS AND UNFOUNDED ATROCITY STORIES STOP NO RESPONSIBLE GROUPS HERE URGING BOYCOTT GERMAN GOODS MERELY EXCITED INDIVIDUALS."[17]

The Committee's statements and cables painted the best picture possible for the German authorities. The Nazis, however, convinced that all Jews were part of an international conspiracy, could not understand why the Committee could not control the Jewish organizations of New York and, for that matter, the world. So the Committee's reassurances were ignored. Julius Streicher in his paper *Der Sturmer* described the Jewish threat: "They agitate for a boycott of German goods. The Jew thus wants to increase the misery of unemployment in Germany and ruin the German export trade. German men and women! The instigators of this mad crime, this base atrocity and boycott agitation are the Jews of Germany. They have called those of their race abroad to fight against the German people."[18]

The reaction around the world was immediate. Those who had been reluctant to escalate anti-German protests into declared anti-German boycotts now felt compelled to take the step. During the next two days at neighborhood schools, civic auditoriums, synagogues, and churches, ordinary citizens of every religion and heritage assembled to promise or actually threaten boycott resolutions. Three thousand protesters representing over 100,000 orthodox Jews in Brooklyn vowed a comprehensive boycott. Six thousand in Baltimore, drawn from interfaith circles, gathered to protest at the Lyric Theatre. In Chicago, numerous organizations jammed the mailboxes and telephone lines of the German consulate with anti-Hitler declarations. The Chicago campaign was intensified following a mass protest rally at the great Auditorium Theatre that spilled over into adjacent streets.[19]

In Salonika, Greece, the Jewish community organized a boycott of German trade, especially Germany's locally successful film business. In London, boycott activities escalated with a growing number of previously hesitant trade unionists adding their support. In Paris, in Warsaw, in Cairo, in Dublin, in Antwerp, more protesters were becoming active boycotters.[20]

By midday Thursday, March 29, German business and non-Nazi government officials were alarmed about the consequences should the boycott expand. The disjointed worldwide anti-German boycott was causing millions of reichmarks of lost business. German steamship lines, machinery firms, banks, chambers of commerce, chemical concerns, toy manufacturers, fur companies, every form of exporter—all appealed to the Nazis to halt the anti-Jewish boycott.[21]

There was no time to develop long-range statistics. Forecasting the full damage was impossible because additional thousands were joining the movement each day. Some joined to protect the Jews, some to fight Fascism, some to fight Hitler's anti-union policies, some to fight the party's anti-church activities. And some were joining merely to cut in on lucrative markets Germany had traditionally dominated, such as gloves, toys, cameras, and shipping. But the net result was that jobs and capital would shift from Germany to the economies of other nations—this as the world struggled to lift itself out of the Depression.

A worldwide purchasing embargo now loomed as Germany's major national economic question. And all of it was inextricably bound up with Hitler's treatment of the Jews and the coming April First boycott action.

Hitler's plane arrived from Munich shortly before noon on March 29, 1933. From Berlin's Tempelhof Field he was shuttled under heavy guard to Wilhelmstrasse for a cabinet meeting. Fresh from April First planning at NSDAP headquarters, Hitler was determined to resist the mounting pressure to cancel the *aktion*. The anti-Jewish boycott would continue until the anti-Nazi campaign around the world "abated" or until the Nazis dismantled the alleged Jewish "economic grip on the Reich" and instituted occupational quotas for Jews. Unemployed rank-and-file Brownshirts were already jockeying over anticipated job vacancies.[22]

But Hitler's notions about anti-Jewish boycott benefits were rejected by the non-Nazi cabinet majority, which was convinced the April First action would bring economic disaster. The non-Nazis believed that millions of non-Jewish Germans would suffer as well. Every closed Jewish department store would produce dozens of unemployed clerks—almost all non-Jewish. Every Jewish factory forced out of business would produce hundreds of unemployed laborers—almost all non-Jewish. It was folly to think that inexperienced and largely uneducated Brownshirts could step in and run efficient moneymaking companies. Even if they could, an "Aryanized" company would surely lose most of its foreign business as a result of anti-Nazi boycotting.

The stock market had been plummeting since the original announcement. Siemens electrical manufacturers, down seven points. I. G. Farben chemical trust, down seven points. Harpener Bergbau mining works, down six points. Most other stocks closed three to nine points off. Bonds closed their lowest in years. The initial excuse—end-of-month fluctuations—was no longer believable.[23]

The non-Nazis, led by Foreign Minister Konstantin von Neurath, decided to oppose Hitler's anti-Semitic campaign at the March 29 cabinet meeting. Von Neurath's broad understanding of foreign trade compelled him to defy Hitler—not to save the Jews, but to save Germany. However, when aides handed out the agenda, the boycott issue was not listed. Unwilling to delay any longer, cabinet opponents raised the matter on their own, demanding Hitler rescind the boycott orders.[24]

Hitler refused and reminded the cabinet that the boycott was a defensive action to fight "atrocity propaganda abroad." Hitler insisted that if the NSDAP had not organized a disciplined anti-Jewish boycott, a spontaneous violent one would have risen from the populace. Under party control, violence would be averted. He argued that only when Jews in Germany felt the full effects of the campaign against Germany would foreign Jewish agitators desist. Hitler rebutted the notion that the Nazi action would provoke an international counterboycott, saying that as far as he was concerned, the anti-German boycott was already well organized and under way. To dramatize his point, der Führer described several telegrams from London reporting automobiles cruising the streets displaying large boycott posters. He added that in the United States, anti-Nazi mass meetings and New York radio broadcasts were continuing to harm the Reich.[25]

Goering told the cabinet that he was doing his part to counter Jewish atrocity articles abroad. Describing the feuding between the Zionists and other Jewish groups during the March 25 conference in his office, Goering stated that Zionists had agreed to use their influence to stop the newspaper accounts; this proved it was Jews who controlled the anti-German agitation.[26] Goering's point: The anti-Jewish boycott was merely a defense against a great enemy threatening the Reich. It could not be canceled.

The March 29 cabinet meeting ended without compromise, but with Hitler determined to avoid violence. Hitler had not admitted that he was incapable of canceling the boycott. Goebbels, who forcefully lobbied for the original idea, and Goering, who wielded the "rough and ready" Storm Troopers, were both insisting that Jewish economic expulsions commence at once. The opening of vacancies for unemployed Brownshirts could not wait.[27]

Regardless of the Nazi rationales, von Neurath saw the anti-Jewish boycott as the beginning of a diplomatic and economic war Germany was too weak to win. Immediately after the March 29 cabinet meeting, von Neurath conferred with Finance Minister Schwerin von Krosygk, Vice-Chancellor Franz von Papen, and even Hitler's own confidant, Hjalmar Schacht. The three agreed that only President Hindenburg could stop April First. Their aides would provide Hindenburg with reports proving that if Germany boycotted her Jews, the world would launch a retaliatory boycott that would devastate the entire nation.[28]

That night, Goebbels completed a fourteen-point boycott program that stressed the avoidance of ostentatious violence. There was to be no visible breach of any law. But other instructions overturned any concept of law. For example, Jewish store owners were forbidden to discharge their non-Jewish employees and required to pay two months' advance wages in anticipation of closing. All this was to avoid the criticism that the boycott would increase Aryan unemployment. The NSDAP was now issuing binding directives not only to its party members but to Jews as well.[29]

The next morning, March 30, Goebbels' fourteen points were published in newspapers throughout Germany. The separation between party and state was blurring as boycott directives became publicly accepted. The blur became a total merger later in the day when Prussian Justice Minister Hans Kerrl, a Nazi, officially ordered the dismissal by "persuasion" of all Jewish judges. Kerrl's undersecretary issued a formal declaration: "The boycott received the stamp of legality when it was proclaimed by the National Socialist Party as the expression of the supreme right of the people." The statement qualified, however, that the boycott "must proceed within the limits prescribed by the National Socialist Party."[30] The Justice Ministry statement made abundantly apparent that NSDAP edict was now in fact supralegal.

By Thursday, March 30, no one believed that April First was simply a private party matter. Clearly, this was nothing less than the first official step down the road of Jewish economic annihilation. The British and U.S. governments could no longer stay aloof.

Rabbi Stephen Wise, Bernard Deutsch, and Congress legal experts arrived at Undersecretary of State Phillips' office that Thursday. The department had already learned that the "nonviolent" Nazi boycott was indeed likely to include outbursts of physical violence and mass economic expulsions. Earlier in the day, the outgoing German ambassador had paid a courtesy call on Phillips, ostensibly to introduce his interim replacement. Phillips insisted on arguing against the Nazi boycott, but it was fruitless speaking with the outgoing German ambassador, himself out of favor with the current regime. Now, as Wise entered Phillips' office, the situation was acknowledged critical and getting worse. Shortly thereafter, a cable from chargé d'affaires Gordon in Berlin was brought in describing a violent mood growing among the unpredictable Storm Trooper units throughout Germany. Renegade Brownshirts on a rampage in Gleiwitz had slaughtered four Jews during the night, and Berlin was trying to suppress the report. Other Storm Troopers, loyal to Goering, not Hitler, were planning "a veritable reign of terror" for April First.[31]

Gordon's cable went on: A moderate-minded industrialist, who enjoyed excellent relations with both the United States embassy and Hitler, was recommending that Gordon pay a private visit to der Führer. According to the industrialist, Hitler would be more receptive to a U.S. diplomat than any other foreign liaison. Gordon agreed to bypass the protocol of consulting the foreign minister first, if the State Department in Washington arranged the meeting with Hitler through the German embassy in Washington. Gordon ended his cable with the warning that "almost any development . . . is possible within the near future." Speed was essential.[32]

Phillips had spent much of the day on the telephone relaying news, formulating positions, and doing everything he could to defuse the coming catastrophe.[33] Despite all his efforts, the Nazi boycott was still scheduled to commence Saturday and continue indefinitely as the backdrop for medieval-style rioting, lynching, and plunder throughout Germany. Since the pretext for this rampage was a "defensive" reaction to the Jewish-led, anti-German campaign, Phillips wondered if subduing anti-Reich agitation in the United States could influence the Nazis. But Rabbi Wise and the Congress could not renounce their anti-Hitler protest, nor could they publicly oppose the rapidly expanding independent anti-German boycotts.[34]

These days and nights were a personal hell for Wise as he contemplated what he called his "awful responsibility." Nonetheless, the choice in his mind was clear. "Virtual silence—and silence is aquiescence . . . or supporting this tremendous protest. No matter what the Hitlerites do now, it will be nothing more than . . . [what] would have been covertly performed, protest or no protest."[35]

When Rabbi Wise and his delegation took leave of Undersecretary of State Phillips on March 30, the rabbi insisted that neither he nor the Congress nor the Jews nor the world could back down. If Saturday was to be Day One, so be it.

But Wise did agree that no comments about their meetings would be released to the press. He was determined to keep the pressure on, but was also willing to allow the diplomats a few days. The American Jewish Committee was quietly but forcefully lobbying the administration to demand that the German government halt organized anti-Semitism in Germany.[36] If the FDR government was going to act, it would be now.

Shortly after Wise left Phillips' office on March 30, the undersecretary discussed the crisis with Secretary of State Cordell Hull. At 7:00 P.M. Washington time, Hull wired a response to Gordon's earlier cable requesting permission to meet with and reassure Hitler personally. Instead Hull instructed Gordon to call formally on Foreign Minister von Neurath. "You should make it clear that it is not the purpose of this government to interfere in . . . the domestic concern[s] of Germany," Hull's cable directed, detailing the diplomatic language to be used. "The situation which is now developing, however certainly without the intention of the German government, has assumed an international aspect." Hull's message added, "I am informed that a retaliatory boycott is even now under serious consideration in certain American cities. More important, however, the German Government should appreciate that the human element involved in the situation is such that the friendship of the people of the two countries might not remain unaffected."[37]

Hull had chosen cautious words to convey as strong a statement as the circumstances and his basic philosophy would allow. He was against posing obstacles to foreign trade and meddling in the domestic affairs of another country. But the circumstances demanded this official involvement. Hull ended his cable to Gordon: "You may express to the Minister of Foreign Affairs my deep concern and ask him whether . . . there is anything which the two governments might do either jointly or separately to alleviate the situation."[38] Hull's cable arrived in Gordon's office in the middle of Berlin's night. No action could be taken until Friday morning—the day before the boycott.

While the United States government was trying to avert the April First boycott, the British were also active that Thursday, March 30. The British government earnestly wanted to avoid any involvement unless British citizens were concerned. They felt they were all too often pinpointed as the "guardian angel" of the Jews because of their Palestine mandate. Viscount Hailsham, Secretary of State for War, said as much in Parliament that day· "I assure you . . . [no] British subjects of Jewish descent have been ill-treated in Germany, and the government does not think it has any right to make representations in Germany regarding German citizens."[39]

Nevertheless, in a meeting that March 30 with German Ambassador Leopold von Hoesch, Foreign Secretary John Simon strongly hinted that Britain's official disinterest might not last much longer, especially since the British public and Parliament members—Jewish and non-Jewish—were strongly against Nazi anti-Semitism. Ambassador von Hoesch answered that he had already met with leaders of British Jewry to argue against continued anti-Nazi protest measures, especially a British boycott of German goods. He tried to explain the anti-Jewish boycott as a reaction to economic threats against the Reich, especially American threats. But, added von Hoesch, even if calmer minds prevailed and the anti-Jewish boycott was canceled, Jewish expulsions in Germany were imminent. Simon answered that he could only hope that the anti-Jewish excesses would not push Great Britain and Germany into a public confrontation neither government wanted.[40]

The British government's publicly neutral attitude outraged Lord Reading, a prominent Jewish member of the House of Lords, and president of the Anglo-German Association. That morning, Lord Reading made a strong appeal before Parliament declaring that he could no longer remain silent and that popular sentiment favored an official British protest about the impending anti-Semitic boycott. The House echoed with cheers of encouragement. Later, the Archbishop of Canterbury, among others, endorsed the appeal.[41]

Even as Lord Reading denounced the Nazi regime, senior German Foreign Ministry official Hans Dieckhoff convened an emergency interministerial conference to discuss the accelerating protest and boycott movements around the world. Attending were representatives of the ministries of Economics, Interior, Propaganda, and Transport. Dieckhoff told his colleagues that the latest consular dispatches showed no "organized boycott movement," but rather an uncoalesced gamut of actions by individuals and small groups. More alarming to Dieckhoff, however, was the fact that many of these boycott agitators were non-Jewish, "particularly Anglo-Saxon competitors" who were enthusiastically backing a popular ban on German goods to achieve a lasting competitive edge.[42]

The German officials admitted that nothing could be done to stem the anti-Reich boycott movement except to propagandize against "the horror stories" and avoid anti-Semitic incidents that would "feed the boycott." They agreed that April First was precisely the sort of action that would escalate the popular refusal of German exports. Unless it was canceled, German trade would suffer "far-reaching and serious consequences."[43]

But the men conceded that there was no way of stopping the Nazi boycott against the Jews unless somehow all anti-German agitation abroad ceased at once, and unless German fears of Jewish-led economic punishment dissipated. This they knew was becoming impossible. Party leaders were keeping the rank and file in an emotional state. That day's issue of *Volkischer Beobachter* continued to warn of Jewish economic moves to wreck Germany's new regime. Page one's banner headline claimed that the Jewish boycott against Germany was actually organized by the Communist party. Elsewhere in the paper, commercial leaders denied anti-Semitic actions and pleaded for an end to Jewish-led economic reprisals. Nazi press articles describing real or exaggerated anti-German protests instigated by Jews solidified the resolve of the rank and file to execute the April First *aktion*, and intensified daily Jew-baiting and random violence. In turn, each such incident only convinced more foreigners to refuse German goods. Goebbels' own newspaper bristled that March 30 because it saw "no visible effect" on anti-Nazi agitation. "On the contrary," *Der Angriff* complained, "Germany's countermeasures are being answered with a renewed demand for a boycott of German goods."[44]

Dieckhoff adjourned the March 30 conference on a desolate note, anticipating an economic calamity unless the April First campaign was canceled. But each man left hoping something could be done to change Hitler's mind and forestall the crisis.

A few hours later, Hitler agreed to meet with Reich Savings Commissioner Friedrich Saemisch and Hjalmar Horace Greeley Schacht, Reichsbank president. Hitler trusted few of his associates. But one he did trust was the economic wizard Schacht.

Born in a northern German province of a naturalized American father, Schacht, despite his American roots, was seen by Hitler as a good Aryan and a devoted Nazi. He had served Germany during the pre-Hitler era in several key banking positions, including Reichsbank president. But in 1930 he resigned from the Reichsbank to protest government approval of the Young Plan for finalizing war reparations. Overnight Schacht became a controversial exponent of political economics highly attractive to the rising Adolf Hitler. In a 1931 meeting, the two became enamored with one another. Schacht pledged himself to boost Hitler to the chancellorship by introducing him to the money powers of Germany and by successfully managing the NSDAP's destitute finances. He signed "Heil" to his earliest letters to Hitler. It was Schacht who had coaxed millions of reichmarks in desperately needed campaign support from leading industrialists just before the Reichstag fire. It was Schacht who now pledged to his Führer to reestablish Germany's financial integrity and build a war economy designed for territorial and racial aggression.[45] Schacht was a polished gentleman with a fine German education, who in later decades would fool many into thinking he was just caught up in the Hitler regime, not a real Nazi. Yet in truth, Hjalmar Schacht was the indispensable, enthusiastic player without whom the Reich could not have commenced its genocidal conquests.

Now Schacht, along with Savings Commissioner Saemisch, would argue that the April First boycott threatened all economic recovery. Schacht warned Hitler that the economic damage would be severe, perhaps lasting. If the anti-Jewish boycott and a counter anti-German boycott continued for just thirty days, said Schacht, at least 1 million non-Jewish Germans would be forced out of work by the economic disruption. Moreover, the drop in exports, the disappearance of dependable daily Jewish bank deposits, and the ensuing downward spiral would place a wholly intolerable burden on the nation's finances, especially foreign exchange.[46] Foreign currency for raw materials was the key to rearming the German war machine. So whatever short-term satisfaction would be derived from economic war against Germany's Jews would quickly frustrate overall Nazi ambitions.

It was hard to resist the economic advice of Schacht, but Hitler would not yield. Nor could he. There was now a question of whether greater spontaneous violence might be unleashed if the bloodthirsty Storm Troopers were deprived of the chance to strike German Jewry and muscle their way into the Jewish economic niche.[47]

The only hope now seemed to lay in the presidential palace. President Hindenburg summoned Hitler to an urgent conference. Whether feigned for public consumption or real, Hitler was known to greatly respect the aging war-horse Hindenburg. For sixty minutes, Hindenburg pleaded and demanded that Hitler call off the April First action. Hindenburg's arguments were supported by Schacht, von Papen, and von Neurath, but Hitler held fast. But the anti-German boycotts abroad were accelerating unabated. Der

Führer still held the German Jews responsible for an international economic plot against the Reich. In Hitler's view, the anti-Jewish campaign was still self-defense. Hindenburg refused to accept Hitler's obstinacy. The fate of Germany rode with the ultimate decision. Nonetheless, despite what German diplomats would later call a near "presidential crisis," this meeting also ended in a stalemate.[48]

Friday morning, March 31, Foreign Minister von Neurath and the other seven non-Nazi members of the German cabinet were confronted with a frightening situation. Within twenty-four hours, the Nazis would unleash a total national boycott that within months would force Germany's Jews into pauperism. The action would be accompanied by mob violence that would perpetuate the image of a barbaric Germany. A Leipzig newspaper had already warned Jews against defiance or provocative self-defense. "Should a shot be fired at our beloved leader, all Jews in Germany would immediately be put against the wall, and bloodshed would result which, in its ghastliness, will exceed anything the world has ever seen."[49]

Economic vacancies would be created, but they would be filled by unqualified rank and file Nazis. For example, in Berlin alone, about 75 percent of the attorneys and nearly as many of the doctors were Jewish.[50] Who would take their place? Most importantly, the worldwide retaliation for Germany's anti-Jewish boycott was clearly to be a massive counter-boycott pursued by millions of people who would otherwise limit their protests to petitions and marches. Governments themselves might even be dragged into trade sanctions by popular demand for higher tariffs on German goods and even outright bans. Such initiatives were already under way in the U.S., Poland, and France.

Intervention by the Allied powers for Versailles Treaty violations was even a possibility. Polish anti-Nazi boycott groups were urging military action at that moment to preclude Hitler's threat to occupy the Versailles-guaranteed corridor to the Danzig area. And British groups were talking about a League of Nations petition to enforce the minority guarantees Germany had agreed to.[51]

Waiting for von Neurath the morning of March 31 was an urgent message from U.S. chargé Gordon. A host of other embassies were lodging messages of concern or protest. Fearful German industrialists and bankers were hoping von Neurath and other cabinet moderates could avert the economic consequences the Nazi action would trigger.

The entire cabinet and numerous senior officials were on hand for the fateful March 31 emergency session. Of the eleven cabinet members, only Chancellor Hitler, Interior Minister Frick, and Minister Without Portfolio Goering were Nazis and in favor of the anti-Jewish boycott despite the risks. The remaining eight, led by von Neurath and von Papen, were vehemently opposed. The debates ensued, with tempers rising and accusations flying.

The Justice Ministry warned that the boycott was patently illegal and that the courts might enjoin the entire affair. Finance Minister Schwerin von Krosygk complained that the closure of Jewish enterprises would produce a ruinous loss in sales tax. Hitler answered that the tax revenues would be made up from other sources, Christian sources. Minister of Transport Paul von Eltz-Rubenach told of German ships, such as the *Bremen* and *Europa*, sailing nearly empty because of Jewish-led retaliation. Von Neurath warned of massive diplomatic and economic reprisals, many of which were already under way. Schacht and von Papen supported the ministries, but were unable to convince the Chancellor of the disaster that would follow. Hitler simply continued assuring that the *boykottaktion* would be conducted under the strictest discipline and without violence.[52]

No one believed the assurances. None of the spontaneous boycotts and professional expulsions already sweeping Germany could be characterized as "disciplined." In one case, no more than a letter from a German-American claiming that the founder of the Woolworth's department store chain was a Jew, prompted SA troops to surround six of the stores in Germany and prohibit customers from entering. Even as the cabinet was convening on March 31, Munich Nazis unilaterally declared that their boycott would begin at once. Brownshirts armed with carbines took up positions outside the city's Jewish stores.[53]

Still, Hitler refused to stop the action, now claiming that it had gone too far to be canceled —whether or not the foreign agitation was suspended. Von Neurath exploded and demanded that Hitler as head of the Nazi party call off the boycott. If not, von Neurath would resign. Hitler would not change the plans, and with that von Neurath formally resigned.[54]

At that moment it appeared that the brittle coalition running Germany would collapse. Von Neurath was Germany's last respectable link to the outside world. Von Papen and Hindenburg's personal representative both pleaded with the foreign minister to rescind his resignation.[55]

Von Neurath was despondent and physically weakened over the crisis. He saw his Germany approaching another abyss. He had always felt it his duty to elevate his nation while abiding by a personal moral code. He could no longer be part of a government that would countenance April First. He refused to withdraw his resignation. It was known around Berlin that if von Neurath left, in all likelihood Hindenburg would resign as well. He was the president's favorite and for Hindenburg, perhaps the only redeeming factor in the entire Hitler cabinet.[56]

Without Hindenburg, what? Would the generals take over? Would Hitler and the Nazis be deposed or thrown into civil war? No one could predict. Therefore, it was unacceptable that von Neurath leave the government. Some compromise was necessary. True to form, Hitler agreed not to a compromise, but an ultimatum. He would cancel the Nazi party's boycott if von

Neurath could supply explicit public assurances by Jewish leaders and the governments of the United States, France, and England that they would not participate in any anti-Reich boycott.[57]

The German foreign minister accepted the compromise *cum* ultimatum. He took back his resignation and promised to provide the official foreign assurances Hitler demanded. What was the deadline for producing the statements?

Hitler specified midnight, less than twelve hours away.[58]

The rush began. Von Neurath hurriedly explained the crisis to his senior staff, who set about to secure the impossible. Senior official Hans Dieckhoff was to meet shortly with U.S. chargé Gordon to receive Hull's carefully worded protest of the night before. When they did meet, Gordon dutifully relayed Hull's message threatening a rupture in German-American relations. As instructed, Gordon stressed Hull's desire to do anything diplomatic that might ease the crisis. Dieckhoff immediately answered that an official U.S. statement, published in the American press, repudiating the atrocity reports and denouncing any anti-Nazi boycott could stop April First—if issued in time to meet Hitler's deadline.[59]

Gordon quickly telephoned Undersecretary Phillips in Washington and passed on Dieckhoff's request. The chargé recommended that Hull formulate such a statement. He emphasized that all speed was necessary, that the chances of calling off the Nazi campaign were diminishing with each minute, and that "an eleventh hour breakdown" would be tragic.[60]

Even as chargé Gordon was speaking to Washington, German officials were telephoning their embassies in London, Washington, and Paris, urging similar declarations from Jewish leaders as well as the governments of England and France.[61] The diplomatic telephone and telegraph lines in Washington, London, Paris, and Berlin stayed busy for tense hours. Additional emergency German cabinet meetings assessing the progress were convened throughout the day. But most Reich officials were doubtful. Hitler was demanding the very sort of domestic control that the Western democracies were not empowered to engage in.

As the French, British, and American governments struggled to compose public statements that would not outrage their citizenry and yet satisfy Hitler, popular Jewish leaders were escalating their calls for economic confrontation. In Paris, the newly formed International League Against Anti-Semitism was consolidating French protest groups and announced a unified anti-German boycott to commence at 10:00 A.M., the moment Germany's boycott against Jews started. Merchants throughout France had pledged their cooperation, and efforts were under way during those very hours to force French ministries to join the effort.[62]

In London, the antiboycott placards in shops became more numerous.

And trade unionists began to target crucial industries, especially big foreign-currency earners, such as the German fur industry. One estimate projected Germany's total 1933 loss from this lucrative industry alone at $100 million.[63]

Eleven of the world's leading musicians began drafting a cable to Hitler announcing a boycott of Germany's lucrative cultural enterprises. Led by Arturo Toscanini and Fritz Reiner, the musicians threatened a business that would hurt not only Germany's pocketbook but, perhaps more importantly, her pride. Toscanini, who demanded his name be placed at the top of the protest list, targeted the upcoming Wagner Festival as the first casualty. German tourism, a big foreign-currency earner, was already suffering drastically, because of sympathy with the Jews and the public fear of traveling in a nation besieged by street hooligans. Cancellations had emptied German ocean liners and hotels. Even the great German spas were bemoaning the loss of an elite clientele who were switching summer reservations en masse to rival spas in Czechoslovakia and France. And leaders of the German fur industry, centered in Leipzig, were already nervously discussing an appeal to convince foreigners to halt the cutoff of purchases.[64]

By the close of business, March 31, 1933, German stocks had again tumbled badly. Die Trust fell 10 percent in value. Siemens had dropped 12 percent in value the day before.[65]

Now frenzied, the anti-Jewish boycott machine in Germany continued to make ready. Boycott coordinator Julius Streicher's posters were hurriedly pasted all over Berlin. The posters again cried out for Germans to refrain from buying or associating with Jewish business people because the Jews "excite the world against Germany. . . . They agitate for a boycott of German goods. The Jew thus wants to increase the misery of unemployment in Germany and ruin the German export trade." New orders circulated calling for all Aryan employees of Jewish firms in Berlin to walk off their jobs at precisely 3:00 P.M. on April First and picket their own establishments in protest of the international anti-German boycott.[66]

By the end of the afternoon, the Nazi leadership began to look forward to the next day with increasing desperation and fear. Germany might begin to disintegrate, perhaps even by fire, if Jewish political agitation provoked international military intervention. In the privacy of his diary, Goebbels felt compelled to write, "Many are down-hearted and apprehensive. They believe that the boycott might lead to a war. We can gain nothing, however, but universal esteem by defending ourselves."[67]

As the sun set, the prospects were increasingly dangerous. Someone had to stop the anti-Jewish boycott. So Benito Mussolini stepped in.

Mussolini was the man Hitler mimicked from the beginning even though Mussolini's Facism was not fundamentally racist or anti-Semitic. Italian Jews were, in fact, influential in Mussolini's philosophical development. Five Jews were among the founders of the original Fighting Fasci in March 1919. Three other Jewish activists were commemorated in Fascist history as "martyrs." Mussolini certainly believed in many of the commonly held Jewish conspiracy theories, but he considered the Jewish presence in Italy an asset, assuming all the stereotypical traits in Jews would accrue to the state. As such, several Jews were among his closest advisers.[68]

Hitler deliberately overlooked Mussolini's relationship with Italian Jewry when he patterned National Socialism after Italian Fascism. Hitler's aborted rebellion of 1923, the Beer Hall Putsch, was in fact a bad imitation of Mussolini's successful 1922 takeover by threatening Rome with a nonexistent Revolutionary Legion. And in 1926, Hitler required his followers to give the Roman salute, the trademark of Nazism that was again just an emulation of Mussolini.[69]

Yet Mussolini had repeatedly ridiculed Hitler's anti-Semitic and racist orientation. On March 30, Mussolini had ordered Vittorio Cerruti, the Italian ambassador in Berlin, to register a strong complaint with the Foreign Ministry about the coming April First boycott.[70] Now, with precious few hours remaining, Mussolini instructed Cerruti to try again, this time by going directly to der Führer. Hitler granted an immediate interview to Cerruti, who beseeched him in the name of Mussolini to call off the April First *aktion* and halt Nazi anti-Semitism forever. To make certain der Führer understood Il Duce's feelings precisely, Cerruti read a long telegram from the Italian dictator. Hitler was devastated that Il Duce could take so pro-Jewish a stance. He flew into a rage, screaming, "I have the most absolute respect for the personality and the political action of Mussolini. Only in one thing I cannot admit him to be right and that is with regard to the Jewish question in Germany, for he cannot know anything about it." Hitler continued that he alone was the world's greatest authority on the Jewish question in Germany, because he alone had examined the issue for "long years from every angle, like no one else." And, shouted Hitler, he could predict "with absolute certainty" that in five or six hundred years the name of Adolf Hitler would be honored in all lands "as the man who once and for all exterminated the Jewish pest from the world."[71]

While the diplomats struggled to appease Hitler late on March 31, important Jewish protest leaders were likewise struggling with the emotional question. After much agonizing, two Anglo-Jewish leaders finally agreed to accede to the urgent pleading of the Zionist delegation dispatched to Great Britain several days before. The first was Lord Reading, who one day earlier had lashed out in Parliament at German atrocities. The second was Lord Herbert Samuel, former British high commissioner of Palestine and a great friend of the Zionist movement. Together, they would release a declaration that read: "While sharing . . . the deep feeling aroused in this country at the announcement of the discriminatory action intended to be taken in Germany against Jewish professional men, tradesmen, and others, we deprecate exaggerated reports of occurrences there or any attempts to boycott German goods. Such attempts hitherto made have been unauthorized and spasmodic, and their cessation would in our view conduce to the alleviation of the situation in Germany." British Foreign Secretary John Simon agreed at the same time to hand the German ambassador in London a letter endorsing the Jewish declaration.[72]

Popular protest leaders in America, led by Stephen Wise, however, were unwilling to accede to Germany's threats. Wise's silence, originally intended to allow the State Department to negotiate unhampered, now became a strong refusal to appease Hitler. Even hostile messages from fellow Jews in Germany would not force him to acquiesce. One cable in particular sent that day struck a nerve. Sent by the editors of a prominent Jewish newspaper in Hamburg, it declared: "GERMAN JEWS ACCUSE YOU AND ASSOCIATES TO BE TOOLS OF OUTSIDE POLITICAL INFLUENCES STOP YOUR SENSELESS OVERRATING OF OWN INTERNATIONAL IMPORTANCE AND LACK OF JUDGEMENT DAMAGE LARGELY THOSE YOU PRETEND TO WANT TO PROTECT . . . BETTER SHUT OFF YOUR OWN LIMELIGHT AND USELESS MEETINGS AS SUREST MEANS AGAINST ANTI-SEMITISM . . . THIS IS YOUR MOST IMPORTANT DUTY TO REPAIR YOUR CRIMES AGAINST US." Wise was certain such cables were written under great duress and obviously for NSDAP consumption.[73]

Although popular Jewish leaders refused to appease, the American Jewish Committee was willing. Committee president Cyrus Adler received an impassioned plea the night before from his friend Oscar Wasserman, a prominent banker, informing: "THERE IS NO DOUBT THAT THREATENED BOYCOTT AGAINST ALL JEWS WILL BE CARRIED THROUGH WITH FULL SEVERITY IF SOMEWHERE PROTEST MEETINGS WILL BE HELD OR BOYCOTT AGAINST GERMAN GOODS WOULD BE RECOMMENDED BY JEWS OR WITH JEWISH ASSISTANCE STOP AS GERMAN JEWS ARE FACED WITH UTMOST POVERTY AND DISTRESS IF JEWS IN FOREIGN COUNTRIES CONTINUE TO INTERFERE I REQUEST YOUR HELP SO FAR AS YOU CAN."[74]

On March 31, as the Third Reich was eagerly awaiting a public assurance that American Jews would not fight back with economic weapons or even verbal protests, Adler issued just such a statement, emphasizing his position of authority: "The American Jewish Committee, of which I am president, has taken no part in protest meetings. No responsible body in America has suggested boycott. We have been and are doing all in our power to allay agitation."[75]

In between the British capitulation and the Committee's announcement that day, Horace Rumbold, the British ambassador in Berlin, visited von Neurath to discuss the anti-Jewish boycott. Von Neurath briefed Ambassador Rumbold about Hitler's twelve-hour ultimatum and suggested there was some hope because Jewish and governmental statements from Britain had already been assured. Events were speeding so fast, however, that Rumbold was unaware of his own country's activities in previous hours. Rumbold was, in fact, raising doubts about those British assurances when von Neurath was summoned to the phone. German sources in Washington were calling with the news that American Jewry had issued the announcement Hitler demanded.[76]

It now appeared that von Neurath's impossible task might be completed. The latest updates from his people working in France and with the American State Department indicated that similar statements would be forthcoming. But aside from the American Jewish declaration, which was already public, the other declarations were wholly contingent upon canceling the April First boycott.

It was now up to the chancellor. Despite the encouraging reports, Hitler still refused to cancel the next day's boycott.[77]

Von Neurath could scarcely believe Hitler's refusal. Germany's diplomatic honor had been put on the line. Foreign assurances were solicited under the express warranty that if produced, the anti-Jewish boycott would be canceled. Those assurances were either in hand or forthcoming. Von Neurath was so physically shaken he could hardly function. Von Papen was so furious he tried to convince President Hindenburg to declare martial law. At the same time, urgent appeals were lodged by German shipping, manufacturing, and financial concerns to stop the anti-Jewish boycott at all costs.[78]

Even as last-minute appeals were being made to Hindenburg, the phone rang in chargé Gordon's Berlin office. Undersecretary of State Phillips was calling from Washington with the public statement von Neurath needed. Phillips dictated the declaration: "The situation in Germany is being followed in this country with deep concern. Unfortunate incidents have indeed occurred, and the whole world joins in regretting them. But without minimizing or condoning what has taken place, I have reason to believe that many of the accounts of acts of terror and atrocities which have reached this country have been exaggerated, and I fear that the continued dissemination of exaggerated reports may prejudice the friendly feelings between the peoples of the two countries."[79]

Phillips continued dictating the statement: "I have been told that protest measures . . . in certain American cities . . . would result in a partial boycott of German goods. . . . Not only would such measures adversely affect our economic relations with Germany, but what is far more important, it is by showing a spirit of moderation ourselves that we are likely to induce a spirit of moderation elsewhere."[80]

Hull had caved in, nullifying America's earlier warning of far-reaching repercussions should the anti-Jewish campaign take place. He was prepared to release the new statement to American newspapers Saturday morning. But Phillips qualified the retreat carefully, insisting that Gordon "make it clear [to von Neurath] that he cannot issue such a statement unless you receive definite assurance that the boycott will be called off. You will readily understand that the Secretary would be placed in a highly embarrassing position if, after issuing this statement, the boycott should commence. We shall therefore await a further message from you to the effect that the boycott will be called off. . . . How soon can you get a reply back to us?"[81]

Gordon answered, "The Foreign Minister told me where to get him at dinner. I could be there in five or ten minutes. I can call you back in fifteen or twenty minutes hence." Gordon added that von Neurath had assured him that the British foreign secretary would send a similar statement, but the final details had "not yet been settled." Gordon knew that minutes counted. "I will call him [von Neurath] at dinner at once and will call you back in thirty minutes. I will put the call in now while I am going around to see him." Gordon hung up and immediately phoned the German foreign minister.[82]

At about that time, Hindenburg had undoubtedly contacted Adolf Hitler one last time. Using whatever prestige and influence he could still wield, the president insisted Hitler cancel the April First campaign. All the old arguments were exchanged. Perhaps some new ones. And then for some reason, or perhaps for some combination of reasons, der Führer unexpectedly agreed. The boycott must indeed be stopped.

For whatever reason, Hitler finally agreed the Reich would at this early stage suffer far more than it would gain, and was not yet strong enough to risk the battle. He agreed the tactic of boycotts would be abandoned. Instead, he would proceed against German Jewish economic viability by regulations, legally. Step by step. But Saturday morning's action was now too far gone to be aborted. To do so, admitted Hitler, would probably result in bloodshed at the hands of uncontrollable SA troops outraged by the disappointment.[83]

Therefore, a reluctant compromise was struck that would enable Hitler to satisfy Brownshirt demands for an attack against the Jews, yet limit the economic retaliation by world Jewry. The chancellor would declare "a pause" in the boycott late the first day, then a brief moratorium. If, by Wednesday April 5, foreign agitation had receded sufficiently, the boycott would be dissolved altogether. However, the drive to expel Jews from professions and destroy their place in German society would begin at once.[84]

Hitler then called Goebbels, insisting that SA members loyal to Goebbels and Goering be marshaled and told that the boycott had been curtailed. Goebbels reluctantly prepared a radio announcement suspending the anti-Jewish boycott at 7:00 P.M., April First until the following Wednesday morning—to observe the drastic reduction of foreign agitation and anti-Reich boycott movements. During the Saturday active boycott hours, no violence could be perpetrated. No Jewish store could even be entered, and no Jew could be manhandled. Jewish banks would be exempted by edict to minimize economic disruption.[85]

It was now nearly 11:00 P.M. in Berlin. The world still believed that eleven hours hence, the Nazis would stage their violent pogrom throughout Germany. Chargé Gordon reached von Neurath. He read him Hull's statement disavowing the anti-German boycott, but the German foreign minister, in great distress, admitted it was now too late. Von Neurath said Hitler felt too many SA units were awaiting the moment and could not be disappointed. The only consolation von Neurath could relate was the decision to suspend the campaign at 7:00 P.M., Saturday. Gordon sadly agreed to pass the news to Washington.[86]

Within five minutes Gordon was listening to the radio for Goebbels' announcement limiting the boycott to a single day. But Goebbels' remarks were at once both reassuring and ominous. He made clear that "the boycott will be carried out with iron discipline and no one will be bodily in jeopardy. . . . Every act of physical violence will be punished severely. . . . Provocateurs who . . . incite violence shall be handed over to the police."[87] Then Goebbels, who commanded the personal loyalty of many Storm Trooper factions, added his own threatening postscripts. Instead of downplaying the likelihood of a resumption that next Wednesday, he declared that if atrocity reports and the international anti-Reich boycott movement did not totally subside by Wednesday, the anti-Jewish campaign would be "resumed with unprecedented force and vehemence."[88]

Goebbels left the studio and drove to a hall on the west side of Berlin, where he addressed an already agitated crowd of Brownshirts. In the hypnotic, demagogic Nazi style, Goebbels worked the crowd into a violent frenzy. To cheers, Goebbels shouted, "Tomorrow not a German man or woman shall enter a Jewish store. Jewish trade throughout Germany must remain paralyzed. We shall then call a three-day pause in order to give the world a chance to recant its anti-German agitation. If it has not been abandoned . . . the boycott will be resumed Wednesday until German Jewry has been annihilated!"[89]

Goebbels then admitted to the crowd that the party had not planned on its avowed confrontation with the Jews until Hitler had consolidated more power. "We did not plan to open this question immediately. We had more important things to do." Then, accusing the Jews of "taking bread from German workers" by creating the international anti-Hitler boycott, Goebbels bellowed a stern warning: "We have not hurt one Jewish hair, but if New York and London boycott German goods, we will take off our gloves." The throng exploded with chants of "Hang them! Hang them!"[90]

At midnight in Berlin, chargé Gordon telephoned Undersecretary Phillips in Washington. Gordon was forlorn that some minuscule delay on the State Department's part had been a factor. "As I told you this afternoon," Gordon said, "it was an eleventh-hour breakdown." Gordon added that Sir John Simon's letter disavowing protest and boycott "did not materialize." Under the circumstances, Hull's appeasement statement would be retracted and withheld from public view.[91]

In New York, Stephen Wise finally fell asleep well after midnight that Friday, hoping that history would prove that his steadfast activism against Hitler had not precipitated the events to follow. Those events were in fact long planned by Nazi leaders. The American Jewish Congress protests and the growing Jewish-led anti-Reich boycott merely forced the Nazis to execute their plans much sooner than expected. One reassuring letter from a Berlin confidant reached Wise shortly after April First. It explained: "Over here they have made the Jews and everyone else think that this boycott was only a retaliatory measure because of the action of the Jews in England and America and that nothing would have occurred otherwise. Lies—all lies. It was prepared months ago. I know! . . . Could any country in 48 hours have a complete list of every Jewish shop in Germany . . . including the seamstresses, little shoemakers, tiny shops in basements that sell vegetables, and all this [even] in the smallest hamlets and towns. . . . This was organized to the nth degree." Stephen Wise also hoped that history would confirm that his steadfastness did more than bring the true Nazi intentions out into the open. Wise hoped to prove he actually prevented a bloody medieval outrage.[92]

When Jewish merchants in Berlin arrived at their stores the morning of April First, they found cadres of placard-carrying, arm-waving Brownshirts shooing customers away. All Jewish stores were identified by a yellow spot against a black background, reminiscent of the yellow stars Jews were forced to wear in the Middle Ages. In Hamburg, Munich, Frankfurt, and in every city and most towns throughout Germany, the pickets cried, "Buy German. Don't buy from Jewish stores!" Stink bombs were rolled into Jewish department stores. Judges were hauled off their benches by defendants. Doctors' patients were admonished at the door.[93]

Many stores had been closed days earlier by regional boycotts under way since the first announcement. Despite the pleadings of "Aryan" insurance companies, exuberant SA units did shatter windows and wreck property. Some German citizens actively opposed to the boycott deliberately shopped at Jewish stores, buying the first object they laid their hands on. These people were filmed by Nazi cameramen for exhibition at local theaters; some of them were set upon and stamped on the forehead with the word *Traitor*.[94]

In the most fashionable sections of Berlin, Brownshirts armed with blackjacks and other weapons staged a daylong terror siege that included invading Jewish-owned stores, vandalizing the merchandise, extorting money, and then brutally beating the proprietors.[95] One Jewish attorney was murdered by a mob in Kiel after being dragged from a jail where he was being held after he resisted boycotters.[96]

Throughout Germany, cruel acts of intimidation and destruction formally inaugurated the new era. But much of the outside world was misled about the degree of violence because Goebbels' Government Press Office ordered newspapers to publish only photographs "which are within the limits of the legal boycott." Hence, all photographs showed disciplined SA troops impassively standing outside Jewish stores functioning as no more than informational pickets. On March 31, Streicher's boycott office circulated a statement that a "Communist group" was planning widespread window-smashing and looting; hence, vandalism against Jews was in advance declared to be a Communist, not a Nazi, transgression. Strict censorship and German hysteria over even reporting an incident that would be termed "atrocity propaganda" created a quiescent facade that fooled many Western journalists and diplomats and the rest of the world for decades. They would believe the April First anti-Jewish boycott was essentially nonviolent.[97]

But Stephen Wise was not deceived. He was convinced that even if the more visible acts of physical violence might now be avoided, the quieter acts of violence—occupational ousters, deprivations of civil liberties, cultural obliteration—would continue, until German Jewry was finished. Wise was determined that the rights of Jews not be sacrificed and vowed to fight bitterly until the Hitler regime was toppled by right-thinking Germans who would realize that Hitler's campaign was national suicide.[98]

On April First, *Volkischer Beobachter* printed a photograph of the enemy of Adolf Hitler. It was a picture of Stephen S. Wise standing beside two Congress supporters. Late the night before, Goebbels wrote privately that the struggle against international Jewry "will be a fight to the finish."[99]

April First was therefore Day One. The Nazis had launched their war against the Jews, mobilizing all of Germany. The Jews would launch their war against the Nazis, mobilizing all the world. Anti-Hitler boycotts, protest marches, and meetings were now in store. Germany was to be isolated politically, economically, even culturally until she cast off her Nazi leadership. Germany was to be taught another bitter lesson.

PART II

·

The Zionist Moment

7. The Zionist Solution

THE WORLD awoke to German Jewish refugees. They appeared immediately following April First. But it wasn't the boycott alone. Jews were
being purged from every commercial and professional field. Thousands became victims of random street violence. Tens of thousands more were jailed
on specious charges. Worse, the Third Reich was drafting legislation to
legitimize the illegitimate course of Jewish destruction, even as workers
rushed to construct a mysterious political concentration camp at a pastoral
village named Dachau.

There was no time for elaborate arrangements. Getting out was important, out to anywhere. An extra hour standing still might mean death for any
German Jew prominent in creative, political, or commercial endeavors. By
ship, by train, on bicycle and foot, they rushed to the borders, clutching a few
parcels of luggage or small bundles of precious items: sometimes just a brown
paper bag, cash, some food, pictures of loved ones; often a book, frequently a
diary.

At first they were counted by the dozens, then by the thousands. On April
First, every train entering Denmark was crowded with German Jewish refugees. That same day, hundreds more entered the Netherlands. Dutch border
towns provided temporary shelter and opened their public kitchens to the
fleeing families.[1]

In Paris, hundreds of German Jewish refugees strained charitable organizations to the limit. It was the same in Czechoslovakia and Poland, which
counted at least 3,000 fleeing Jews, and Switzerland, where at least 6,000
had entered, and Belgium, where thousands of Jews fled over the hills to
freedom, many chased by the rifle fire of Reich border guards—and all this in
just the first three or four days following the Nazi anti-Jewish boycott. Non-
bordering European states such as Spain and Portugal, and even England,
also felt the drama of escape as each new ship yielded more desperate German
Jewish citizens.[2]

Within two .weeks of April First, more than 10,000 German Jews had
escaped and were now in need of food, clothing, organization, jobs—a basis
for existence.[3] No Nazi claim of "domestic affairs" could any longer stand.
The crisis was indeed international. Germany's persecution of its Jews was
openly at the doorstep of the world. Newspaper and radio reports from
Germany were now bettered by new evidence: men, women, and children,
homeless, hungry, and clutching the remnants of their lives in small bags.

As in previous Jewish emergencies, the world Jewish community reacted with political agitation against the oppressive force. But this fight would be different. It would not be waged so much by those with access to high office as by ordinary men and women whose great weapon lay jingling in their coin purses. The front lines would be in dimestores and cinemas, in the camera shops and in the haberdasheries, where every person wielded a mighty power: the simple power to reject. The boycott was the long gun whose shell could reach from London or Detroit to Hamburg or Munich. Therefore, local Jewish committees and national associations would not suffice. People would need to be unified in a far-flung, all-encompassing economic war against the Third Reich. An international Jewish body would be needed. And in 1933 there existed only one that maintained a worldwide organization and enjoyed the popular following and political access the anti-Nazi boycott movement demanded.

That body was the Zionist Organization.

Yet in the eyes of Zionists, the outrages of Hitler were nothing unexpected. Zionist ideology predicted periodic Jewish oppression in even the most enlightened lands of the Diaspora, that is, the communities of Jewish dispersion. Such waves of anti-Semitism had been a regular character of Jewish life in Europe since *emancipation* in the mid-nineteenth century, when Jews were allowed to emerge from the ghettos and participate on a less unequal footing with other Europeans. In the twentieth century, Jewish blood was easily spilled, not only by the czar until his overthrow, but also along the Polish-Russian border, where from 1919 to 1921 about 100,000 Jewish civilians were massacred by the Soviet and Ukranian armies during the Polish-Russian War; and in Rumania, where during the mid-twenties nationwide anti-Jewish rioting openly sponsored by the minister of the interior destroyed synagogues and killed innocent civilians.[4]

The rise of Hitler was therefore seen by Zionists simply as the latest anti-Semitic episode. But this time things were different. In a macabre sense, things were ideal. The German Jews were not impoverished Russian peasants or lower-class Polish merchants with few valuables. These German Jews were solidly middle class. They possessed land, homes, furnishings, shares of stock. They were lawyers, doctors, engineers, scientists, artists, civil servants. They owned not storefronts, but department store chains. They owned not pawnshops, but major commercial banks. These men and women who had no place in the German Reich would find an indispensable place in the Jewish nation. From their dispossession would come repossession. Behold: Israel was waiting within the borders of the Third Reich.

Here then was a turning point for Zionism. The task facing the Zionist movement was to maneuver to the forefront of the international Jewish response and interpose Zionism and Palestine as the central solution to the German Jewish problem.

Just what was Zionism, and why did it hold such a confusing position in

Jewish life at the time? Zionism is one of the most misunderstood movements in modern history, both by its adherents and by its critics. Its political patch-work of parties, factions, philosophical feuds, rivalries, improbable alliances, and tenuous coalitions perpetuates the confusion and defies efforts to define the movement in simple, clear-cut terms. But a rudimentary explanation of Zionism is essential to understanding why the movement saw the rise of Hitler as its decisive moment.

In the 1890s, after the pogroms in "uncivilized" Russia, and the Dreyfus prosecution in "civilized" France, Theodor Herzl emerged as the leader of an international group of Jewish thinkers who saw a return to the Holy Land as the solution to Jewish persecution in Europe. Herzl in 1895 had written a pamphlet entitled "The Jewish State—An Attempt at a Modern Solution to the Jewish Question. "The Jewish State," originally written in German under the title "Der Judenstaat," was an extraordinary work. Mixing equal portions of genius and nonsense, human compassion and ruthless prag-matism, a keen sense of history and an impressive utopian notion of the future, "Der Judenstaat" became the bible of the Zionist movement.[5]

In his treatise, Herzl readily admits there is a Jewish problem "wherever Jews live in perceptible numbers." Herzl declares that the Jews themselves "introduced" anti-Semitism by their very presence: "Where it does not exist, it is carried by Jews in the course of their migrations. We naturally move to those places where we are not persecuted, and there our presence produces persecution. This is the case in every country." Thus, Herzl declares that Jewish persecution is not an aberrant facet of bigoted society, but a natural reaction to the appearance of a foreign group—the Jews.[6]

Herzl identifies "modern anti-Semitism" as distinct from religious intol-erance or bigotry; instead, anti-Semitism is a political and economic move-ment itself created by the emancipation of Jews from the ghettos and their strained acceptance into Christian society. Herzl's words: "In the principal countries where anti-Semitism prevails, it does so as a result of the emancipa-tion of the Jews." Herzl asserts that assimilation of Jews into the mainstream of nations was a historical error that naturally produced Christian backlash.[7]

It is the natural Christian backlash, in Herzl's view, not the Jewish re-ligion, that makes the Jewish people a true and distinct nation. That nation, he declares, must procure itself a territory, establish sovereignty, and transfer its people. Herzl specifies Palestine as the ideal home for the Jewish nation if acquired under formal international guarantees. Herzl denigrates gradual colonizing as mere "infiltration" sure once again to stimulate anti-Semitism. International supervision was prerequisite to any population transfer.[8]

Transfer itself was to take place over several decades following acquisition of the land. First would come the "desperate," fleeing oppression and pogroms. Retrained for labor in the Jewish homeland, they would cultivate the soil and build the physical infrastructure of the state. Second would come "the poor," who would create vast labor pools and commercial demand. Then would come "the prosperous" to capitalize on the Jewish State's trade. And finally "the wealthy" would arrive, to join the now well-established Jewish State.[9]

Throughout Herzl states his anticipation that the multitudes of comfortable Jews throughout the world who are not victims of persecution will vigorously oppose Zionism. "Old prisoners do not willingly leave their cells," he writes. Although Herzl specifies that emigration to the Jewish State would be totally voluntary, he threatens that those who do not join would be left behind, cut off from the Jewish people, and ultimately assimilated by the Christian nations. "Hence, if all or any of the French Jews protest against this scheme on account of their own 'assimilation,' my answer is simple: The whole thing does not concern them at all. They are Jewish Frenchmen, well and good! That is a private affair for the Jews alone."[10]

While stressing the element of choice—"He who will not come with us may remain behind"—Herzl assures that once the choice is made, the methods of achieving Zionist objectives will be accomplished without "any voting on it," even if it requires fighting the aspirations of so-called assimilated Jews. Herzl's words: "Perhaps we shall have to fight first of all against many an evil-disposed, narrow-hearted, short-sighted member of our own race." In an even more forceful passage, he declares, "Whoever can, will, and must perish, let him perish. But the distinctive nationality of the Jews neither can, will, nor must be destroyed. . . . Whole branches of Judaism may wither and fall, but the trunk remains."[11]

Herzl's concepts were very much reflective of his times. During the late 1800s, many European groups developed fervent nationalistic movements. These were generally drawn along ethnic lines that saw linguistic, geographic, religious, and/or historic roots as a basis for sovereignty that superseded the ecclesiastic and/or dynastic state. As nationalistic movements drew their ethnic lines, Jews found themselves systematically excluded, or included only conditionally at the tenuous pleasure of the majority. Herzl's thinking made perfect sense in a Europe that persecuted Jews even when they abandoned their religious practices or converted to Christianity. Herzl was correct. Anti-Semitism, not religion, created the Jewish nation.

Herzl's pamphlet, *"Der Judenstaat,"* included a detailed blueprint for building the Jewish State. Two instruments were necessary: first, a "Society of the Jews," to negotiate and manage the affairs of the emerging Jewish nation; second, "The Jewish Company," a strictly commercial entity to liquidate the financial position of Jews in Europe and transfer their wealth to Palestine. According to plan, the Jewish Company would take charge of the assets of each emigrating Jew and provide a compensating value in land, machinery, and homes in the new Jewish State. The Jewish Company would manage the European Jewish businesses and/or Jewish financial matters until they could be sold off to "honest anti-Semites" who would step into the Jews' former economic positions. Herzl promises Christian governments that this Jewish Company would sell off Jewish holdings at a substantial discount. He further entices Christian governments to cooperate in the Zionist program, with a promise of great prosperity to their Christian citizens once Jews totally withdraw from Europe. Until self-sufficient, the new Jewish State would also represent a loyal and lucrative market for the exports of cooperating Christian countries.[12]

The organized withdrawal of all Jews from Europe carried an obvious appeal, even an unintended justification, for anti-Semites. As such, Zionism was as much a threat to comfortable middle-class Jews as anti-Semitism itself. Established Jewish communities insisted they were entitled to be treated like ordinary citizens of any country in which they lived. Herzl's answer to the expected resentment of the Jewish majority was simply to wait. "Great exertions will hardly be necessary to spur on the movement." "[Anti-Semites] . . . need only do what they did before, and then they will create a [Jewish] desire to emigrate where it did not previously exist."[13]

"Der Judenstaat" was an instant success, propelling Herzl to the forefront of the tiny Zionist movement. In 1897, a year after "Der Judenstaat" was published, the First Zionist Congress was convened in Basel, where the Basle Programme was adopted. It called for the legal, international, supervised acquisition of a Jewish State and the orderly, peaceful, and voluntary emigration of all Jews in the world to its boundaries. At the same time, the Zionist Organization was established to function as "the Society of Jews" to lobby for the Jewish homeland and represent all Jews who accepted Zionism. Membership was granted to any Jew who paid the biblical shekel, a token fee equaling about twenty-five cents. Two years later, in 1899, Herzl's "Jewish Company" was founded as the Jewish Colonial Trust Company, a banking entity incorporated in England. In 1901, the Jewish National Fund was established to purchase and cultivate land in Palestine in preparation for the Jewish State. It was prohibited from ever selling any land, once acquired, and would ultimately become the corporate owner of all land in the Jewish homeland.[14]

Deep philosophical divisions gripped the Zionist Organization from the outset. Soon a circle of dissident factions and opposing parties began fighting for leadership of the movement. The chief conflict was between "practical" and "political" Zionists. The "practicals" wanted to settle the Jewish homeland "step by step," gradually colonizing to create the ultimate political reality. The "politicals" eschewed what Herzl had already labeled as "infiltration" and insisted upon a full political arrangement prior to organized settlement.[15]

That full political arrangement was promised in 1917 when England issued its Balfour Declaration committing Turkish Palestine to a Jewish Homeland should the Allies win the War. When the dream seemed likely to become a reality, anti-Zionist Jewish forces, including the world's influential Jewish leaders, fought the prospect bitterly. But in the postwar era, with the Allies devoted to ethnic self-determination for Arabs, Europeans, and even faraway colonial subjects in Africa and Asia, Jewish nationalism was an eminently legitimate even if still controversial aspiration. The League of Nations and the victorious Allies concurred that the Jews should return to their original homeland after an exile of almost 2,000 years.

Although the Balfour Declaration's essence had been incorporated into the Versailles Peace Treaty of 1919, the actual League of Nations Mandate to Britain to oversee the Jewish national home was not finalized until April 1920 at an Allied conference in San Remo, Italy.

Herzl's dream had been realized within barely two decades. The Jewish State was virtually a fact. There were ifs and buts. The declarations did not use the words "Jewish State," but instead used the words "national home for the Jewish people." Moreover, intense last-minute lobbying changed the phrasing to "*a* national home," not "*the* national home." As such, the existing Arab populations were to be a protected group within Palestine's borders. And, of course, the rights of Jews in other countries would not be prejudiced.[16] But limitations aside, the Jews had finally reached the road back to their Promised Land. The obligatory Talmudic incantation "Next year in Jerusalem" now possessed an exciting and real meaning.

During the years before the League of Nations Mandate, the Zionist movement was in nervous limbo, unsure when the creation of the Jewish State would commence, and what form it would take. A long list of Zionist Organization parties, factions, and splinter groups developed. Each was self-righteously convinced that its approach to the Zionist ideal was the best, each claimed to speak for the Zionist movement and the Jewish people, each clamored for its version of Zionism to be recognized by the international community. They disagreed on whether the Balfour Declaration and the League Mandate constituted the long-awaited international sponsorship Herzl had required, with step-by-step colonizing now to be the future focus. Or were the British merely supplanting the Turks as an authority that would continue to refuse Jewish sovereignty? Should Jewish Palestine be a territory associated with Britain, an independent nation, an autonomous canton of a larger British colony, or the Jewish partner of a binational entity in Palestine?[17]

During 1920, amid daily massacres on the Polish border and political uncertainty, eminent Zionist leader Max Nordau espoused a stark new concept some called *catastrophic Zionism*. Nordau, a radical philosopher with a doomsday outlook, had been Herzl's closest ally in Zionism's founding years. In Herzl's dying moments in 1904, his followers insisted Nordau succeed him as head of the Zionist movement. But Nordau refused, preferring to remain outside the upper echelon. At the Tenth Zionist Congress in 1911,

Nordau predicted that if a Jewish Palestine were not granted soon, millions of Jews in Europe would be annihilated by the emerging political forces.[18]

As the slaughter of Jews on the Polish-Russian border and the question of Jewish sovereignty in Palestine were tediously debated, Nordau proposed the immediate transfer of 600,000 pogrom-afflicted Jews to Palestine within a few months—without any real preparation. The assets of these 600,000 Jews would of course come with them. Nordau reportedly predicted that a third of those Jews would starve to death, a third would find Palestine unacceptable and reimmigrate. The remaining third would create a majority or near-majority in Palestine, and the Jewish State would quickly and finally be achieved.[19]

It had been twenty-five years since Herzl first declared "Whoever can, will, and must perish, let him perish. . . . Whole branches of Judaism may wither and fall, but the trunk remains." Max Nordau, Herzl's reluctant heir, was now proposing to extend philosophical writings and dogmatic utterances into reality. The result of his plan, if carried out, would be the accepted sacrifice of hundreds of thousands of Jews, the dispossession and redispersion of hundreds of thousands more, but the survival of enough people with enough resources to achieve the all-important salvation of future generations. Nordau argued that it was better for hundreds of thousands of Jews to perish in the struggle to achieve Jewish redemption in the land of Israel than wait for the cossack's sword to fall.[20]

The Zionist leadership rejected Nordau's plan as frightening and impractical. Although placed on the shelf, Nordau's catastrophic Zionism firmly moved many in the Zionist leadership to believe that the coming decisive moment would somehow arise out of a similar, perhaps even more threatening, tragedy.

One who reluctantly spurned Max Nordau's concept in 1920 was Vladimir Jabotinsky, a fiery maximalist who advocated extreme approaches to Jewish nationalism and Jewish self-defense. However, in an equally controversial move, Jabotinsky ironically sealed a pact with the Ukrainian nationalists responsible for the massacres leading to Nordau's plan. Jabotinsky's agreement established a Jewish militia at the rear of the Ukrainian forces to protect Jewish civilians, many of whom were Zionists. Although violently criticized in 1921 at the Twelfth Zionist Congress, Jabotinsky silenced his foes by dramatically declaring from the rostrum, "In working for Palestine, I would even ally myself with the devil." The curses turned to cheers as the audience endorsed Jabotinsky's rationale with a standing ovation. That ovation was the turning point for many who now came to believe not only that the decisive moment for Zionism would be some coming catastrophe, but also that the solution would require Zionist negotiations with the hand responsible.[21]

January 30, 1933. Adolf Hitler came to power.

During the first days after the Hitler boycott against Germany's Jews, the Zionist movement's hierarchy in Europe and America was busy trying to plot a course of action. Their objective was not to mobilize Jewish and non-Jewish resources for the preservation of Jewish rights in Germany. Rather, they sought a means of turning the miseries of German Jewry into a new impetus for a Jewish homeland in Palestine.

Zionist leadership had, in fact, refused to oppose the Nazi expulsion ideology from the outset. Within twenty-four hours of Hitler's appointment, German Zionists finalized a recently discussed program called Youth Aliya.[22] *Aliya* is the Hebrew term for emigration to Israel; its literal translation is *ascent*. On the premise that there was no longer any future for Jews in Germany, Youth Aliya organized youngsters to find a future in the Jewish homeland. Loving parents, mostly non-Zionists, hoped that one day after Hitler had passed, their children might return to Germany spared the scars of Nazism. The project began none too soon. Within a few months, Jewish children were either banished, segregated, or subjected to quotas throughout the Reich's eduational system. And the Nazi theory of race, which humiliated every Jewish child, quickly became mandatory teaching in all classes.[23] Youth Aliya served a noble purpose in allowing young German Jews to grow up in dignity as part of a historic new future. But it was also a sign to the Nazis that Jews themselves were willing to organize their own expulsion.

The Zionist acceptance of Jewish expulsion was not limited to the Germans. Zionist leaders worldwide saw Hitler's persecution as the fateful beginning. Even a defender of Jewish rights as eminent as Supreme Court Justice Louis Brandeis quietly conceded the right of Jewish existence in Germany. Within a fortnight of der Führer's January 30 appointment, Justice Brandeis shocked Stephen Wise by candidly declaring, "The Jews must leave Germany. There is no other way." An astonished Rabbi Wise asked, "How can five-hundred eighty-five thousand people be taken out of Germany?" Brandeis interrupted, "I would have the Jews out of Germany. They have been treated with deepest disrespect. I urge that Germany shall be free of Jews. Let Germany share the fate of Spain. No Jew must live in Germany."[24]

Nazi leadership, of course, gleefully noted the Zionist acceptance of Jewish expulsion—even if it was clear that the concurrence was perverse, since the Nazis sought Jewish cultural destruction and the Zionists sought a Jewish renaissance. But concurrence or not, the Nazis regarded the Zionists as their enemy personified, and from the outset carried out a terror campaign against them in Germany.

German Zionist officials felt certain their phones were tapped, their mail read, and their office subject to covert entry. Morale was shattered. So precarious was the Zionist position that the ZVfD's headquarters at 10 Meinekestrasse suspended all open correspondence with Zionist bureaus in London and even Palestine. Information was instead passed through secret channels at border towns near Czechoslovakia. In one such report in early March, Czechoslovakian Zionist official Dr. Franz Kahn passed the following briefing to Zionist offices throughout the world: "No Jew can possibly establish relations with the government; all previous contacts are now of no value whatever. The ZVfD expects to be completely closed down. . . . All available cash funds have been either pulled out or sent to Palestine."[25]

But Zionism's threatened status in Germany changed instantly following the March 25 meeting in Goering's office with Jewish leaders. It was after Kurt Blumenfeld's utterance that only the Zionists possessed the international organization capable of stopping the anti-Nazi movement that the Nazi view changed. From that moment on, the Third Reich realized it could exploit the Zionist movement against the Jews. At the same time, Zionists became convinced they could exploit the Nazi movement for the benefit of future generations of the Jewish people.

As soon as Blumenfeld and his colleague Martin Rosenbluth returned home from Goering's office that day, they summoned their associates to discuss Goering's orders. It became clear that the Zionists were suddenly heading the mission to London. This was an opportunity for the Zionist cause to rise to the forefront of the crisis. It was agreed Blumenfeld could not be spared from Berlin for even a few days. Rosenbluth would go. To avoid the appearance that only the Zionist Federation of Germany was talking to British Jewry, other Jewish personalities would have to accompany Rosenbluth. The officials selected Richard Lichtheim, a former member of the Zionist Executive Committee who was currently a leader in Vladimir Jabotinsky's dissident Revisionist Union.[26]

As an afterthought, Rosenbluth and company decided that a member of the non-Zionist Central Verein should also join the mission. This way, Rosenbluth reasoned, if the mission failed, Zionists as a group would not be blamed. Still, it was important to locate a Central Verein member who was not anti-Zionist. The men selected Dr. Ludwig Tietz, son of Alfred Tietz, the German department store magnate and philanthropist. Tietz quickly agreed.[27]

By Monday morning March 27, Rosenbluth, Lichtheim, and Tietz arrived in Britain. They were met at the train station and immediately driven to the Zionist Organization headquarters at 77 Great Russell Street, just near the British Museum. About forty Jewish leaders, Zionist and non-Zionist, had assembled in the board room awaiting their report. The three explained Goering's demands to stop the anti-Nazi protests in England and America. As ordered, they placed a transatlantic phone call to Stephen Wise in a futile effort to cancel his Madison Square Garden rally. That done, the Zionist delegation forecast to their audience that the end of Jewish life in Germany was an inescapable reality. Only Palestine was left as a solution. But most of the assembled Jewish leaders represented the Board of Deputies of British

Jews, a long-established, traditionally anti- or non-Zionist group. These men, and even some of the Zionist officials, seemed to disbelieve the German delegation's prediction.[28]

After the briefing session, Rosenbluth, Lichtheim, and Tietz reported to German Ambassador Leopold von Hoesch as Goering had instructed. Von Hoesch, a non-Nazi holdover from the Weimar Republic, had no taste for National Socialism. Nonetheless, for Germany's sake, and perhaps his own, he asked the Jewish delegation to convince Lord Reading not to resign his presidency in the Anglo-German Association as a protest against Reich anti-Semitism. Von Hoesch also asked that more atrocity denials be sent to anti-Hitler circles in London and New York. Contrary to Berlin's expectations, sympathetic embassy officials allowed the three Zionist leaders a reasonable freedom to move about. So several secret meetings were quickly scheduled.[29]

Lichtheim and Tietz also secured an interview with Lord Reading and implored him to delay his resignation from the Anglo-German Association. Reading became suspicious. In desperation, Lichtheim and Tietz described in detail the Nazi reign of brutality, and how this small achievement might somehow satisfy Goering and in some way delay violence. Reading agreed to delay his formal resignation two weeks, but insisted on venting his outrage about persecution in Germany a few hours later in Parliament.[30]

Late at night on March 29, Rosenbluth, Lichtheim, and Tietz were seated in the lobby of the Russell Hotel, located a short walk from the Zionist Organization. Unsure of their success, uncertain of future events, the tired emissaries somberly awaited their early departure back to Germany the next morning. But in a corner of the lobby, a world news ticker, scarcely noticed before, became a sudden hub of activity. The Nazis had officially announced their boycott of Jewish businesses and professionals commencing April 1 to last until commercial Jewish life was utterly obliterated. In the delegates' minds, this development changed everything. They immediately contacted Zionist leader Chaim Weizmann.[31]

The next day, still relying on the liberty granted by the German embassy, Rosenbluth went from meeting to meeting debating solutions to the German Jewish problem. The tone of many of the conversations changed. The April First boycott represented a turning point in the foreign perception of the crisis. Jewish leaders and British officials who had previously doubted the severity of German Jewry's plight could now see a doomsday rising. Weizmann began talking with wealthy British Jews, including Anthony Rothschild, Lord Reading, Lord Sieff of the Marks and Spencer department stores, and Pinchas Rutenberg.[32] After these initial conversations, Weizmann suddenly departed for Palestine. Ostensibly he left to survey the prospects for emigration in the developing Jewish homeland. But his secret plans involved clandestine meetings with Arab, British, and Zionist leaders to discuss a solution on a vast scale.

While Weizmann and the wealthy Jews of London were conceiving plans to help German Jews within a Zionist context, the German Jews themselves became increasingly desperate. When it was learned Hitler might be dissuaded by formal declarations against any anti-German boycott, Berlin Zionists sent an urgent telegram to the Zionist Organization in London asking for such a proclamation. The cable reached Rosenbluth, Lichtheim, and Tietz about midnight on March 30.[33]

The German Zionist delegation in London panicked. Rosenbluth and Lichtheim dispatched cables to Stephen Wise and the Jewish Agency in Jerusalem, instructing them to notify Adolf Hitler formally that no anti-German boycott would be organized. Rosenbluth and Lichtheim discussed the cables with no one, but signed them in the name of the Executive Committee of the Zionist Organization, thus making the instructions direct orders.[34]

Within a few hours, the Executive Committee discovered the desperate deception and immediately instructed the Jewish Agency in Jerusalem to disregard the cable and delay any message to Hitler. But it was too late. The Jewish Agency had already complied.[35]

"OFFICIAL PALESTINIAN JEWRY HAS NOT PROCLAIMED BOYCOTT GERMAN GOODS STOP ARE SURE BOYCOTT SO FAR SPONTANEOUS ACTION BY INDIVIDUALS AND MAY BE STOPPED IF GERMAN AUTHORITIES WILL NOT CONTINUE ACTIONS AGAINST JEWS." The cable was sent directly to Hitler's office. The Jewish Agency acknowledged the blind execution of the order from London with a telegram reading, "CABLE DISPATCHED TO BERLIN AS REQUESTED DESPITE MISGIVINGS SUPPRESSED BY YOUR SIGNATURE."[36]

Although the ruse had been quickly uncovered, two leading Zionist newspapers in Jerusalem, *Doar ha-Yom* and *Haaretz*, reported the communication, but with no mention of the background.[37] Thus, rank-and-file Zionists in Palestine were put on notice that their leadership opposed any involvement in the fight against Hitler.

Up to the moment the Jewish Agency dispatched its cable to Hitler, Palestinian Jewry had closely followed the dictates of the Zionist Organization in London. However, after the April First action this power flow would be suddenly reversed. Palestine would now make the decisions, especially when it came to the German Jews and Adolf Hitler.

To understand the sudden power shift, one needs to understand exactly what the Jewish Agency for Palestine was. Most observers had long believed that the Jewish Agency for Palestine was an independent entity established in 1922 by the international community after the Allies decreed that Britain work with "an appropriate Jewish agency" to build the Jewish national home. As such, most believed the Jewish Agency was a quasi-governmental unit, with its own appointed bureaucracy exercising its own limited authority over emigration and development in Jewish Palestine, and officially answer-

able to the League of Nations.[38] However, in 1922 the Allies designated the
Zionist Organization in London as the "appropriate" agency. The Zionist
Organization then merely created the Jewish Agency for Palestine to function as the officially recognized administrative body. In reality, the Jewish
Agency simply acted as an alter ego of the Zionist Organization, coordinating
most of its important policy decisions in advance with London.[39] Thus, the
Jewish Agency became the governmentally recognized half of what Herzl
had earlier named "the Society of Jews"—the bargaining agent of the Jewish
people. And in the spring of 1933, the Jewish Agency began to do just that.

8. The Currency Exemption

BARGAINING in earnest with the Hitler regime began on March 16,
1933, a political light-year before the April First Nazi boycott that
would radically change Jewish life in Germany. Four men gathered in
Jerusalem to discuss the German Jewish situation. They were Arthur
Hantke, Avraham Landsberg, Felix Rosenbluth, and David Werner Senator,
all prominent German Zionist émigrés to Palestine. Felix Rosenbluth (who
later changed his name to Pinchas Rosen) was a former president of the
Zionist Federation of Germany; he would later become Israel's first minister
of justice. Felix's brother, Martin, led the late-March Zionist delegation to
London. David Werner Senator was an immigration expert and a member of
the Agency's Executive Committee.[1]

The men talked of the potential for Palestine in the German crisis. Although by March 16 no overt anti-Jewish government action had occurred,
thousands of Jewish professionals, especially in the provinces, had already
been ousted from their positions. They knew that Jews who had never
considered emigrating to Palestine were now inquiring en masse at British
consulates throughout Germany. But uniformly, the German Jews discovered the same problem: Existing Reich currency restrictions forbade taking assets out of the country unless it was "in the national interest."[2]

The four German Zionists also knew that middle-class Jews would not
leave Germany without their property. Yet middle-class Jewish professionals
were ideal prospects for emigration to Palestine because they possessed the
equivalent of £1,000, satisfying British entry requirements. The question
was how to allow them to take that much of their money out of Germany.

It was Felix Rosenbluth who first suggested negotiating with the German government. Perhaps the government would allow a special concession allowing Jews to take the requisite equivalent of £1,000 if they emigrated to Palestine?[3]

The others reacted with astonishment—not at the thought of negotiating with the Nazis, but because Rosenbluth thought it feasible to approach them. Rosenbluth was asked what the Zionists could possibly offer the Nazis to induce them to allow Jews a legal exception to the currency restrictions and help Palestine in the process. Rosenbluth answered: the emigration of a few thousand Jews.[4]

The others were still skeptical. Hitler had vowed never to negotiate with the Jews of Germany, even though Goering had already met twice with Central Verein leaders in an effort to contain Jewish protest in New York. The four men wondered if the British ambassador in Berlin could make contacts and relay the information to the Zionist Organization in London. So they decided to sound out their associates in the international Zionist movement.[5]

A few days later, Senator wrote to the Zionist Organization Executive Committee in London: "We all received the plan with skepticism, even if this should be proposed in an honourable way. But at least it might be important to request an opinion from the ZVfD. . . . In these times you have to consider all the possibilities."[6]

Currency restrictions in Germany were indeed the barrier to an orderly transfer of the wealth and the citizens of Germany's Jewish middle class. Enacted in August 1931 by the Brüning government at the height of a fiscal crisis, the currency restrictions prohibited anyone—Jew or Christian, German or foreigner—from taking currency out of Germany without permission. The restriction was aimed not at Jews, but at speculators and hoarders.[7] But it now loomed as the unbreachable obstacle to Jews emigrating to Palestine—especially since British entry regulations limited all categories of Jews except those in possession of £1,000 [about $5,000]. The restriction ironically suited the German Zionists in Jerusalem because it was precisely those Jews with enough money to qualify whom they wanted. As one German Zionist warned the Jewish Agency, "There is a danger that German Jews with money will go to other countries and those lacking means will come here. We must work on this matter."[8]

Breaching the currency barrier required negotiation. But in late March 1933, what Jew was in a position to negotiate with the Third Reich? Certainly not the traditional German Jewish organizations. As loyal Germans, they would never promote Jewish emigration, precisely because it dovetailed with Nazi intentions. Certainly not the Berlin Zionists, whose organization had already been identified as "the enemy" by the Nazi party.

A go-between would be needed. He would need to be sympathetic to

Zionism, but not directly associated with the Zionist Movement. He would need important connections in the holdover German government, especially in the financial sphere. And he would need to operate in secret. Not even the Zionist Organization in London or the Jewish Agency in Jerusalem could know of his activities. Only the German Zionist Federation hierarchy in Berlin would be aware of his work. The man selected for this mission was a businessman, Mr. Sam Cohen.

Few were undecided about Mr. Sam Cohen. In the minds of some of those he worked with or affected, Sam Cohen was an evil rogue, interested in no more than his own greed at the expense of his people; he was a traitor, a collaborator, a wealthy manipulator, a liar and a fraud, a schemer, a sower and seeker of influence, a man whose fortune bore the bloodstains of Jewish liberty and Jewish aspirations. To others who were closer, Sam Cohen was a munificent man of the Jewish cultural movement, a man who worked tirelessly, often selflessly, to help the Jewish people fight starvation, cultural dissolution, and national dispossession; a deeply religious man, a committed Zionist, a rescuer; a man whose contributions were often unseen but rarely unfelt; a little-known man whose immense importance to Israel deserved a special honored place in the saga of the Jewish people and their redemption.

Each side used him for what it needed: devil or deliverer. Yet few ever understood that Sam Cohen was in fact a little bit of both.

Sam Cohen was born in 1890 in the Polish industrial boom town of Lodz. At age seventeen, he left Lodz to study finance and economics at the University of Marburg in Germany. At Marburg, Cohen developed many vital contacts. After the Great War broke out, he went to Berlin, where he began trading in real estate. War fortunes were won and lost quickly. Sam Cohen's was won. After the war, still in his twenties, Cohen became a partner in a small Berlin bank, Louis Berndt and Successors. He also gained control of a small coal-mining operation in Upper Silesia, Poland.[9]

Cohen's reputation for philanthropy was established during the war. In late 1915, a Jewish relief committee and Warsaw municipal authorities appealed to the occupying German Imperial authorities for permission to distribute food to starving Jews. The kaiser's formal declaration of consent identified "the gentleman Sam Cohen" as one of two authorized purchasing agents and stipulated that "this undertaking has an altruistic character and is not aimed *at any profit*." The words "at any profit" were underlined in the original.[10]

In the 1920s, Sam Cohen was courted for economic aid by a variety of Zionist and Palestinian groups. In late 1923, the Palestine Land Development Company, one of several Zionist Organization land-acquisition corporations, enlisted Cohen's investment of £40,000 to purchase strategic tracts connecting Haifa and the Valley of Jezreel. The development-company director praised Sam Cohen in a letter as "the first to further one of the most important land purchases in the history of Jewish Palestine's development."[11]

In addition to Jewish national redemption, Sam Cohen was committed to Jewish cultural redemption. In 1927, Nahum Goldmann announced that his long-planned *Encyclopaedia Judaica* would be published, the first comprehensive Jewish reference in Hebrew and German. Several donations totaling £210,000 hinged on a major endowment of £50,000 from "a German banker." The unnamed banker was in fact Sam Cohen.[12]

But anonymity characterized many of Sam Cohen's philanthropic and business dealings. Often people at the top didn't even see him, negotiating instead with his attorneys and emissaries. He traveled widely making deals and hearing pleas for donations over dinner. One day in Berlin, the next day in Prague, three days later in Tel Aviv, a week later in Vienna, the next day in Warsaw, two days later in London. He maintained apartments and hotel rooms in all those places, but few knew where he really lived: an opulent castle in Luxembourg.[13]

Now, as Adolf Hitler was preparing to crush Germany's Jews, as the Zionist movement sought to pick up the pieces, Mr. Sam Cohen, his connections, his style, would become the pivotal factor.

Sam Cohen wasted little time. He arrived in Frankfurt in late March.[14] Separate meetings were arranged with two senior government officials held over from the German Imperial and Weimar days. The first was with Hans Hartenstein, director of the Reich Foreign Currency Control Office. It was within his power to allocate foreign currency for uses in the "national interest." The second meeting was with Hans Schmidt-Roelke, director of the Foreign Ministry's Eastern desk, which had purview over the Middle East. Sam Cohen asked both officials for a special currency exemption for Jews agreeing to emigrate to Palestine.[15] The Zionist movement would see to it that German exports were dramatically increased, thus earning additional foreign currency. However, part of that additional foreign currency would have to be set aside for Jewish emigrants, each receiving £1,000 to enter Palestine.[16]

The appeal of a currency exemption was clear, and quickly approved in principle by Hartenstein in consultation with Schmidt-Roelke.[17] During the chaotic first weeks of Hitler's regime, the authority over Jewish affairs was uncertain—indeed that authority would be constantly debated during the life of the Third Reich. In March 1933, senior bureaucrats such as Hartenstein and Schmidt-Roelke could on their own make decisions of great consequence to German Jewry.

Hartenstein's motives were not altruistic. Middle-class Jews would liquidate their existence in Germany. This meant forfeiting all their assets, except for about 15,000 reichmarks (RM), equivalent to the £1,000 needed to enter Palestine. RM 15,000 represented but a fraction of a middle-class Jewish family's accumulated wealth. The rest would be either forfeited to taxes or frozen in blocked accounts. German banks would be enriched by the influx of blocked marks. Jews would quit Germany in an orderly fashion, leaving the overwhelming majority of their wealth behind, as well as economic vacancies that would be taken over by Aryans. Simultaneously, the Zionist movement promoting German exports would not only increase desperately needed foreign exchange and domestic jobs, but would pierce a stake through the heart of the Jewish-led anti-Nazi boycott. At a time when Adolf Hitler was striving to expel Jews, increase Aryan employment, and reconstitute the treasury, the currency exemption would be justified. The Zionists would be awarded a currency privilege allowed no Aryan.

While Hartenstein, along with Schmidt-Roelke, granted basic approval to Cohen's plan, they suggested Cohen work out the operational details with Heinrich Wolff, German consul in Palestine. Wolff was the German official who functioned as the Reich's eyes, ears, and voice in the territory considered to be the center of the international Jewish movement.[18]

Cohen left at once for Palestine.[19]

During these final days of March 1933, Georg Landauer, director of the German Zionist Federation in Berlin and one of the few men who knew of Sam Cohen's mission, lost contact with Cohen. In the hysterical days just before the April First anti-Jewish boycott, Sam Cohen was forced to return to Palestine without reporting to Landauer. However, a letter had already been mailed by Landauer to Cohen's Tel Aviv hotel: "We have received news from interested parties in Frankfurt, with whom you have entered into negotiations. . . . Under present circumstances, we cannot tell the full story publicly, since this would give rise to misunderstanding. . . . Current laws concerning exchanges of capital with foreign countries make the whole thing very difficult. Nevertheless, some progress is already being made. But we will act on any suggestions and will make use of any persons who might be available in this work."[20] Landauer's letter was dated March 31, 1932. The year 1932 was either accidentally miswritten or deliberately misdated. The ZVfD's pattern during those weeks was to sign reports with code names or omit dates on letters, often insisting correspondence be destroyed after reading to protect the author's identity.[21]

By the end of March, Sam Cohen had briefed Landauer's German Zionist associates in Jerusalem, handing the matter over to them for action. They in turn tried to verify Cohen's report through the Zionist Organization via the British ambassador in Berlin. So they took Chaim Arlosoroff into their confidence. Arlosoroff was a member of the Jewish Agency Executive Committee and one of Zionism's most respected personalities. On March 30, 1933, he cabled his friend Professor Selig Brodetsky at the Zionist Organization Executive in London. Arlosoroff's question: Had Germany created a special currency exemption for Jews enigrating to Palestine?[22]

On April 4, during a Jewish Agency meeting, Arlosoroff vaguely suggested it might be necessary to negotiate with the Hitler government about emigration. He made no mention of Sam Cohen's mission. But Arlosoroff was able to obtain tentative permission to visit Berlin and finalize operational details of Cohen's still secret arrangement. After the session, the Jewish Agency sent cable 613 to the Zionist Organization in London: "DESIRABLE NEGOTIATE GERMAN GOVERNMENT EMIGRATION FACILITIES . . . MEMBER EXECUTIVE FORTHWITH PROCEED BERLIN LONDON." [23]

That same day, Professor Brodetsky convinced A.C.C. Parkinson of the Colonial Office to use the British embassy in Berlin as a go-between to determine whether normal restrictions on currency were still in effect. [24] The British inquiry needed to explore several Reich bureaucracies. In addition to the currency-removal restrictions, another regulation rationed foreign currency only to transactions critical to the Reich's economy. For example, British pounds to purchase raw materials qualified for an allocation. [25]

Yet every German citizen had a right to emigrate, a right Hitler's ascent had not abridged. During economic and political upheavals, Germans of all ethnic backgrounds had exercised this right. The Reich Emigration Advisory Office determined how much foreign currency—generally a few hundred dollars—was needed to gain entry to the foreign country. [26]

When on April 5 the British embassy questioned the various Reich offices, it unexpectedly learned that Jews emigrating to Palestine could remove £1,000 to satisfy the British entry prerequisite. British Ambassador Horace Rumbold conveyed the news to London at once. A few days later, on April 8, Parkinson cautiously wrote Brodetsky: "The usual restrictions on the export of foreign currency are still in force, but . . . Jews wishing to take up residence in Palestine who have given proof of possessing £1,000 are granted permission to export this sum by the German authorities." [27]

The British received the information so routinely they probably presumed the currency permission merely represented some gap in the restrictions the Nazis had not yet abolished. [28] London was totally unaware that the currency permission was not a loophole but the result of Sam Cohen's secret contacts with the Third Reich.

When Brodetsky learned on April 8, via the Colonial Office, that the special exemption existed, he realized that somehow the German Zionists had succeeded with the German government. But the times were too volatile to admit openly that Zionists were negotiating with Hitler for the exit of Jews. So in a carefully worded April 13 letter of thanks to Parkinson, Professor Brodetsky tried to cast the exemption as a concession won not by the ZVfD, but by the British. Brodetsky's letter solicitously declared, "We are very glad indeed to see that it has been made possible, through the good offices of His Majesty's Ambassador, for Jews wishing to leave Germany, to settle in Palestine . . . [with] the qualifying minimum £1,000. I should like to thank you most sincerely for your help in the matter, and I hope some means may be found of conveying to [Ambassador] Sir Horace Rumbold our warm appreciation of his assistance in obtaining this most valuable concession." Brodetsky ended by asking permission to publicize the Palestine exemption as a British accomplishment.[29] The British government immediately recognized the maneuver and began planning a defensive response.[30]

At the same time, Brodetsky forwarded copies of Parkinson's confirmation to Georg Landauer of the ZVfD in Berlin, and Chaim Arlosoroff at the Jewish Agency in Jerusalem. When Arlosoroff received the information, he assumed that the exemption would be controlled by official Zionist bodies. He would negotiate the details secretly in Berlin.[31]

But Landauer was worried. He wanted the exemption to cover more than merely the £1,000 entrance fee. After all, Jewish assets in Germany were considerable. An exemption of no more than £1,000 would represent not the planned migration of Jewish wealth, but the orchestrated salvation of a pittance. Parkinson's vague confirmation increased Landauer's uncertainty. So Landauer wrote Brodetsky a follow-up letter: "It would be very good if that note [Parkinson's confirmation] could be interpreted to mean that [Britain's] Berlin ambassador did not merely pass on general information, but that his message was based on a specific ruling by the [German] government. Can you clarify this?" Landauer added, "It is certainly not our goal to merely secure the £1,000 per person, but to obtain formal permission to take along capital sufficient for establishing a new livelihood in Palestine."[32]

Landauer had in mind at least a *second* £1,000 for each immigrant to invest in Palestine. This second £1,000 would be controlled by official Zionist entities on behalf of the immigrant. The immigrant would own it, but the Zionist movement would have the power to use it. As the German Zionists conceived the idea, this massive influx of liquidated Jewish capital would not only bring the first wave of monied Jewish citizens to Palestine; it would deliver the investment capital needed to establish the Jewish State.[33]

9. Redemption or Relief

THE CHALLENGE now was implementation. Even before Professor Brodetsky had received confirmation of the currency exemption, leading Zionist personalities in London began planning a so-called liquidation company. The form this company would take and who would control it would determine the destiny of the Jewish State. Since Zionism's inception, Jewish Palestine had been built an acre and an edifice at a time by donations and dollarless idealists. Herzl had declared that the transplanting of the middle class and their wealth would be the true beginning of the Zionist culmination. So, like the Zionist movement itself, creating the liquidation company became a political struggle.

The first closed-door discussions about creating a liquidation company were organized by Palestine industrialist Pinchas Rutenberg, founder of the Palestine Electric Company. His idea was a company, initially capitalized by wealthy British Jews, to liquidate all Jewish assets in Germany and move the proceeds—along with the people—to Palestine.[1] The idea was once again straight from Herzl's pages.

On the night of April 7, Rutenberg met with Nahum Sokolow and Berl Locker of the Zionist Executive Committee, at Sokolow's London home. In outlining the liquidation company, Rutenberg explained that Lord Reading had agreed to serve as chairman and that the Rothschilds had offered their bank to sell the shares. Rutenberg stipulated that the Jewish Agency would have to manage the company.[2]

However, as discussion about a liquidation company began, a cross-current developed. The world Jewish community began donating large sums of relief money, despite the economic hard times of the Depression. How the money should be spent, and the political solutions to the refugees' status, suddenly threatened the Zionist solution.

Should German Jewish refugees be absorbed into the surrounding countries until the time was right to return to Germany? If Hitler remained in power, at least the refugees would be living in familiar communities: in France, Belgium, and the other haven states.

Or should the German Jews be assisted in Germany proper, thus reducing the factors precipitating their flight? People could be retrained. New employment found. Interim loans arranged. After transition to a new social niche, perhaps a Jewish presence would be accepted by the National Socialist regime, especially once the first waves of anti-Semitic violence ended. German Jews could then retain their German citizenship. Many Jewish organizations favored this approach, including the Joint Distribution Committee, the major international Jewish relief organization. On April 2, the *Joint*—as it was known—opened a giant fund-raising drive in New York to help Jews maintain their existence in Germany. The same day, interfaith meetings were held throughout Canada protesting the Hitler regime and dedicating Canadian relief efforts to helping German Jews survive the times as legitimate citizens of the Reich.[3]

Or should some larger-scale solution be found? Mass resettlement had been a frequent remedy for Jewish crises. After the Russian and Rumanian pogroms at the turn of the century, hundreds of thousands of East European Jews were resettled in America by relief groups, especially the Hebrew Sheltering and Immigrant Aid Society or HIAS. After the Great War, Jews were resettled en masse in various parts of Central and Eastern Europe, and even in special agrarian "colonies" in the Ukraine and Crimea, principally through the efforts of the Joint. Now HIAS was suggesting another mass resettlement, this time in South America. HIAS had quickly convinced several Latin American governments to open their doors to German Jewish refugees, and was readying a worldwide effort to facilitate the mass resettlement.[4]

All of the non-Zionist schemes for relieving the plight of German Jews required vast amounts of donations, which Jews and non-Jews alike were willing to give. But the Zionist movement saw these relief efforts as threats because the solutions excluded Palestine.[5] More important, the donations would divert funds from the Zionist movement. In other words, here was a Jewish crisis, and not only would the answer lie in lands other than Palestine, but the Zionist movement would suffer economic ruin in the process.

Depression agonies had already halted most international Zionist contributions. Many regular fund-raising drives were suspended indefinitely awaiting some improvement in the world economy.[6] Jewish Agency treasurer Eliezer Kaplan summarized the situation: "In 1933, contributions to the Palestine Foundation Fund [the funding arm of the Jewish Agency] have reached an all-time low of £160,000 [about $800,000]. . . . Its [recent] deficit was over £500,000 [$2.5 billion]. Settlement projects of the Jewish Agency Executive were discontinued in 1928. The sole task of the Executive Committee in recent years has been: how to maintain the status quo and prevent bankruptcy."[7] If the Jewish Agency's financial picture did not improve, the question was not *if* the Zionist Organization would go bankrupt, but *when*.

Moreover, Jewish Palestine was desperately undermanned. At a time when impoverished Jews from Poland and Rumania sought entry into Palestine, strict British immigration quotas created seemingly insurmountable barriers. Jewish Palestine's well-known boom economy teetered precariously on the edge of an ever-extending cliff. If the right supply of manpower were not available to pick the oranges, construct the worker housing, and make Palestine's precious few factories function, the whole economy could topple over the brink. For example, during the 1932–33 manpower shortage, all schools were suspended and Jewish students from all over Palestine were trucked to the groves to help with the harvest.[8]

The reminder was constant: Only one category of immigrant was free from quotas—the so-called capitalist in possession of £1,000. So the German Jewish refugees were suddenly spotlighted as the answer to an array of Palestinian problems. But the currency exemption and liquidation company would be futile if Jews were to be saved in a non-Zionist, non-Palestinian context.

On April 4, 1933, Berl Locker of the Zionist Executive in London wrote to Chaim Weizmann, in care of the Jewish Agency in Jerusalem. Weizmann had already left for Palestine to organize for the expected transfer. Having been forced out of the Zionist Organization presidency two years before, Weizmann held no official position. But his prestige among Jews and in governmental circles was indisputable, and indispensable to the Zionist drive for dominance in the fund-raising and relief effort. Aware of Weizmann's sensitive political position, Locker appealed to Weizmann on both pragmatic and historic grounds to help arrange some token act that would help the Zionists take over the relief movement. "In this tragic moment," wrote Locker, "there is much more need for leadership, which is now totally lacking. If we could just succeed in transferring a couple of thousand Jews to Palestine, an appeal for financial help would resonate among all Jewry."[9]

Two days later, Dr. David Werner Senator, one of the four German Zionists in Jerusalem who initiated the Reich currency negotiations, wrote Bernard Kahn, a Jewish relief organizer in Paris. Senator's letter declared, "I believe this catastrophe can only be compared with the expulsion of the Jews from Spain. . . . A large social and constructive aid operation [is needed]." *Constructive* in Zionist parlance meant activities building up Palestine. "If a leader can head this aid operation—and many of us are considering Weizmann—then such an emergency can bring millions of pounds. The Americans and English Jews of German origin are still rich enough today to mobilize for their own flesh and blood enormous sums of money, and they will do it, if we know how to get hold of them the right way." Senator added, "A lot will depend on the drafting of plans, if we know the people; and on negotiations with Jewish organizations in Europe and Palestine."[10]

Senator then revealed to Kahn that a thousand immigration certificates had been issued to the Palestine Office in Germany. Immigration certificates were a controversial matter. The British Colonial Office, which administered the mandate over Palestine, governed the trickle of Jewish emigration to Palestine. Noncapitalists—those not possessing £1,000—were subject to a complicated "Labor Schedule," based on the "absorptive capacity" of the economy. Twice yearly the British government and the Jewish Agency would negotiate how many new entrants Palestine's economy could absorb. Once the figure was finalized—it often fluctuated between 500 and 1,500 per half year—it was wholly up to the Jewish Agency to distribute individual "immigration certificates." How many certificates were allowed for Czech Jewry, Polish Jewry, or any other Jewish community was based on Jewish needs in those countries, how the proposed emigrants would contribute to the social and economic reconstruction of the Jewish homeland and, of course, on the jagged course of Zionist and Jewish Agency politics. Most certificates had traditionally been allotted to impoverished Polish Jews eager to settle in the homeland. Few had been either requested by or granted to German Jews.[11] But Senator saw these first 1,000 as only "the beginning," adding, "it now depends if we can make something out of this accomplishment, because these 1,000 families that come could transform into 1,000 returnees if the appropriate thing is not done for them."[12] To do the "appropriate thing," the Zionists would somehow have to divert relief donations from stabilizing German Jewry in Europe, and use those funds to construct Jewish Palestine.

All the questions of a Zionist versus non-Zionist solution, the relief-fund threat, and Zionist policy during the crisis were debated at an April 9 Jewish Agency Executive Committee session in Jerusalem. Attending were representatives of other Zionist bodies, including the Organization of German Immigrants, which virtually functioned as the ZVfD's alter ego in Palestine. As the meeting opened, only the German Zionists and two of the Jewish Agency's six Executive members—Senator and Arlosoroff—knew of the special currency exemption. And Arlosoroff was unaware that Sam Cohen was the negotiator. However, the others were preoccupied with another question: how Zionists could control the relief donations.

Emanuel Neumann, a prominent American Zionist leader, declared, "In America, two million dollars for the aid fund was collected, and there is not one Zionist among all the 'trustees.' This is a very unhealthy situation."[13]

Some of the participants insisted on organizing an emergency collection under the auspices of the Palestine Foundation Fund. This would guarantee a large share of the money for building Palestine. Others reasoned that such a drive would be confusing, and Zionism's bad reputation for politicized financial mismanagement would repel wealthy Jewish contributors. So to avoid openly involving the Palestine Foundation Fund, yet retain financial control, the participants after much debate suggested the formation of a wholly new refugee fund. The new fund would be organized around Zionist "trustees" who would channel the dollars to both refugees and Palestinian "constructive" projects as they saw fit.[14]

As they argued, Dr. David Werner Senator impatiently reminded them that as each hour passed, more money was being collected under non-Zionist auspices. "Speed is demanded," he said. "Because of our many speeches we lose time and we don't get to the action."[15]

Finally, the men agreed that the special fund would bear a name that did not identify it with Palestine or Zionism. Just after the decision was adopted, Neumann added a condition, that the fund-raising committees in each nation agree *in advance* to "earmark" a suitable percentage for Palestine. Neumann made clear that without such a prearrangement, the Zionists would not participate in the relief effort. One man spoke up, asking if this wouldn't advertise Palestine's involvement and "through this, maybe not enough money will be given." Another in the group explained that only the administrators and trustees, not the donors, would know that some of the money was going to the Jewish homeland. Therefore, "the wealthy will not determine in advance that their contributions will go to Palestine."[16]

All that remained was to secure Weizmann's titular leadership of the fund. Enjoying the respect of both Zionist and non-Zionist Jews, he was obviously the best man for the job and could probably be convinced. But some Executive members were concerned that Weizmann's involvement would threaten Nahum Sokolow, the man who had replaced Weizmann as Zionist Organization president. For much of the session, the men quibbled about how visible Weizmann could and could not be in the new drive. Finally, they agreed that Weizmann *as part of* a committee could dramatically inaugurate the fund-raising drive at an international relief conference in London in early May. By forcing Weizmann to operate with "a committee," the men reasoned, his personality would not dominate the operation.[17]

The gentlemen of the Jewish Agency did not speak very compassionately that day for the plight of German Jews. Their rhetoric was political and practical. They had seen the likes of Hitler before. At the outset of the April 9 meeting, the German Zionists had reported on the situation in Germany: 60,000 arrested; at least four detention camps in operation; constant disappearances; 9,000 doctors out of work. Jews in the big cities might be able to survive, but the Jews must emigrate from the small rural towns. One German representative forecast the problem this way: "Shortly, hundreds of people without means . . . will be arriving. Many will not be suited to the work available here. It is necessary, therefore, to prepare: [refugee] camps, training centers, organization in the settlements."[18] Another German Zionist summarized their intent: "This time, Palestine must be first."[19]

Up to this point in the meeting, Chaim Arlosoroff had said little. Arlosoroff saw the unending dissension of the Jewish Agency as a barrier to decisive action. Instead, he saw himself as the man ordained for the pivotal task ahead: negotiating the resettlement of Jewish citizens and their money from Germany to Palestine. He would do it all by himself if necessary.

Ukrainian-born and German-educated, Dr. Arlosoroff, as head of the political department of the Jewish Agency, functioned as the foreign-minister-in-waiting of the Jewish nation. Although only thirty-four years old in a movement dominated by elder pioneers, Arlosoroff stood out as one of the troika leading the Jewish Agency. His visionary Zionism never thought small. His words were selected carefully, and frequently remembered by those who heard them.[20]

Arlosoroff proffered a hint of his thoughts when he interrupted the bickering gentlemen to state, "The German crisis is a difficult experience for Zionism, and its results will be most important to the future of the movement. The young Jew must ask himself: What is the difference between the

Jewish reaction to this oppression now—in a period of Jewish nationalism—and the reaction before? . . . Since the start of Zionism, this is the first instance when Jews who are considered free have been placed in a situation like this. Also Palestine is put in a special situation for the first time. If Zionism will not do what is required of it, then there will be grave results."[21]

Arlosoroff then alluded to currency regulations as the major obstruction to a political solution to the German situation. But he speculated that the regulations might be overcome by converting assets into merchandise and bringing the merchandise out of Germany. To handle the problem, Arlosoroff said, personal contact with the German Zionists in Berlin would be necessary.[22]

A representative of the German Zionists attending the Jewish Agency meeting, Dr. Zmora, spoke up at this point, saying, "We should not now talk about the specifics of the plan, because we still have to work them out." As Dr. Zmora spoke, Arlosoroff and the German Zionists were aware of the special currency‐exemption and how far discussions had gone. However, most of the others thought Arlosoroff was speaking of some nebulous future plan to be negotiated. To keep the exemption secret, Dr. Zmora proposed that the group dispense with discussing details and simply authorize Arlosoroff and Senator to travel to Berlin to contact the local Zionist leaders in a fact-finding mission.[23]

Arlosoroff and Senator voted in favor. But Neumann couldn't understand why they felt it was so essential to visit Germany. Referring to Rosenbluth and Lichtheim's mission, Neumann said, "Two people from there [Berlin] already went to London, so what is there still to clarify?"[24]

Arlosoroff answered that he would travel to London anyway for a relief conference in early May. So, on the way, he would just stop in Germany to discuss emigration and development plans for Palestine "in a basic and comprehensive way with the Zionist leaders." Arlosoroff suggested that the contact should be by a non-German, and sending several envoys was too expensive. Jewish Agency officers had other pressing duties. Therefore, he alone should do the job. He ended casually, "I thought of going next week."[25]

Neumann objected, "I'm not certain whether it is necessary. . . . Maybe it is still too early." Neumann was suspicious of Arlosoroff's well-known maverick style, and proposed "London be advised on this . . . see what their opinion will be." Careful not to seem too eager, Arlosoroff backed off, saying, "I see that the reaction of the board is not favorable, and I am prepared to forgo my travels."[26]

The meeting ended indecisively with regard to both Arlosoroff's trip and Weizmann heading a Zionist refugee fund. Instead, the gentlemen did as they often did when decisions were necessary—they deferred to the nine-man London Executive Committee. That would take precious time, time that didn't exist in Arlosoroff's view. So Arlosoroff was convinced that a *fait accompli* was the only option.

And secrecy would still be crucial. Arlosoroff had learned a bitter lesson about sharing information with the Executive just the month before. In March, confidential land purchase discussions between the emir of Transjordan and Arlosoroff, and even some of Arlosoroff's privately expressed disparaging comments about the emir, had been leaked to Jewish and Arab newspapers in Palestine and Europe. The leaks obviously came from within the Jewish Agency Executive itself. The disclosures were so damaging to Zionist and Arab conciliation efforts that on March 23, Arlosoroff told the Executive Committee that it could no longer be trusted and might just as well resign. Arlosoroff's comments prompted the other Executive members to recite their own lists of shocking leaks, with each member accusing the others of being responsible.[27]

Arlosoroff also knew that American Zionist representative Emanuel Neumann reported every development to Zionist leaders in New York.[28] Any merchandise-oriented arrangement with the Third Reich would instantly come to the attention of Stephen Wise and the American Jewish Congress. The repercussions would probably destroy negotiations with Germany and obstruct the Zionist refugee fund as well.

If there was to be a transfer of the Jewish nation to the Jewish State, Arlosoroff would have to arrange it alone, and in secret.

10. Arlosoroff's Secret Contacts

QUICKLY the Jewish Agency Executive recognized that Arlosoroff was acting on his own, creating initiatives and making decisions in the name of the Zionist movement. For example, the day before, on April 8, Arlosoroff held an unexpected and historic luncheon at Jerusalem's posh King David Hotel for Weizmann and the leading Arab sheikhs of Palestine. The luncheon was officially arranged on behalf of the Jewish Agency, but the members of the Executive weren't consulted until the night before. Most of the Jewish Agency Executive did attend, but grudgingly.[1]

Arlosoroff's luncheon was the first public meeting between Zionist and Arab leaders. No one understood how Arlosoroff managed to secure Arab attendance. Several of the Arabs owned strategic lands in the Huleh Valley (in Upper Galilee) and Transjordan (the area east of the Jordan River). Behind closed doors, Weizmann and Arlosoroff talked with the sheikhs about glorious things to come, glorious for Arabs and Jews alike, including the arrival of many Jewish newcomers and plenty of commercial development.[2]

Weizmann described the historic meeting as the beginning of a tunnel being dug from both sides with the parties destined soon to meet. The Arab sheikhs announced to reporters after the luncheon that they now realized that the hope of developing their regions lay in cooperating with the Jews, to whom they were now extending a warm welcome.[3]

Stunned by the sudden rapport, Jewish Agency leaders wondered where Arlosoroff's one-man movement would go next. They might have been able to guess, had they known of secret contacts on binational matters between Arlosoroff and Arthur Wauchope, Britain's high commissioner for Palestine. Binationalism was an on-off movement among Zionists and within the British government. Binationalists debated many different formulas for joint or coequal Arab-Jewish national rule in Palestine. But all of them called for some sort of political arrangement whereby Jews and Arabs could achieve their separate but equal national aspirations. Some of Zionism's most influential leaders advocated binationalism in one form or another. Among them were Arthur Ruppin, David Ben-Gurion, Judah Magnes, and Chaim Weizmann, who would in later years support Palestine's partition into separate Arab and Jewish states. Importantly, German Zionism as a movement subscribed to binationalism, and despite frequent disagreements, considered itself Weizmann disciples.[4]

Arlosoroff had vacillated over the years on binationalism, basically because as soon as Arab leaders agreed to any element of cooperation, anti-Jewish Arab agitation would discredit the Arab leaders as traitors representing no one but themselves. But now, in the context of the hoped-for German Zionist and Weizmann-led renaissance, Arlosoroff was convinced there could be no solution to the Jewish problem in Europe without a solution to the Jewish problem in Palestine.[5] Ideas, of course, were easy to come by. It was money—the lack of it—that made the difference between ideas and results. The German currency exemption, however, and other monetary aspects of the Hitler crisis, could finance binational ideas into binational realities.

Arlosoroff, sworn to secrecy by High Commissioner Wauchope, had been since mid-March 1933 negotiating with the Mandate government toward some sort of binational solution. In the initial project, Britain would spend hundreds of thousands of dollars to resettle tenant Arabs displaced by Jewish land purchases. Arlosoroff was secretly advising the high commissioner on how best to spend the money, whether technical education should precede the construction of workman's quarters, and other details.[6] Such a liaison was unthinkable to his Jewish Agency colleagues, but Arlosoroff was convinced these days might actually constitute the live-or-die episode for Zionism. In mid-April Arlosoroff had received two important letters, one from Berl Locker of the Zionist Executive in London, the second from Martin Rosenbluth, the ZVfD liaison to London. Locker's letter stressed the urgency of

Zionists quickly dominating the international relief and fund-raising effort, and of solving the German Jewish problem through Palestine: "Brodetsky and myself feel this is the last moment for us to make our voice heard, if we do not want to be the fifth wheel on the wagon." Locker added, "We still think it possible today to procure large sums . . . in connection with the situation in Germany. . . . We must act, to make our voice heard, and to prevent the new 'Help Fund.'" Locker emphasized, "The main point is: . . . We must at least tell the public that we place the question of Palestine at the center of the matter."[7]

Rosenbluth's letter reinforced the inspiration that these were sudden and historic moments in Jewish history, moments that would terminate Jewish life in Europe and deliver the Jewish homeland to the Jewish nation. However, Rosenbluth also warned of a solution that would exclude Zionism and Palestine. "I fear that we shall be forced to fight [an idea] in the next few days which is basically against a special role for the Jewish Agency and Palestine." Rosenbluth maintained that if the non-Zionist solutions could be debunked or supplanted, the relief effort could be not only politically lucrative but commercially profitable to Jewish companies. "Here [in London] the belief is widespread that the slogan 'German Jews to Palestine' will be very attractive from the financial viewpoint. . . . They think, moreover, that it is no disaster if certain groups make attempts at obtaining big financial means for colonization of German Jews in Palestine on a more merchant-like basis."[8]

Verification of the Zionist assumption that Jewish life was officially over in Germany came swiftly. On April 7, Hitler promulgated the first formal anti-Semitic decree, summarily dismissing virtually all Jewish government employees. Other decrees were readied to outlaw almost all non-Aryan attorneys, judges, jurors, or Jewish dentists and doctors working with social health plans. Simultaneously, the Nazis themselves elevated Palestine to new importance by abruptly halting the flow of refugees. National Socialism of course wanted Jews out of Germany. But in the first days of April, as thousands fled, the Reich realized that the refugees were a liability they could not afford. Nazi leaders such as Goebbels were certain that Jewish refugees in France, Great Britain, and other haven countries would naturally become the core of the anti-German crusade. Nazi economic planners such as Schacht were convinced that the outflow of Jewish businesspeople would cripple the nation's commerce, especially in foreign trading. And the Reich assumed that fleeing Jews would smuggle out whatever wealth they could, thus further debilitating the German economy.[9]

Germany's crackdown on escape was at first sporadic. On April 3, Reich border guards fired at Jews as they frantically scrambled over the hillsides into Belgium and Holland. That same day, border police had stopped a trainload of Jews just before it entered Czechoslovakia. That night, Reich authorities announced that no Jew could leave Germany without a police exit visa. And in Breslau the police actually confiscated all Jewish passports. Later, guards were posted every fifty yards along some border points to prevent Jewish flight.[10]

Hitler's unexpected problem now was how to get rid of his country's Jews in an orderly fashion that would not pose a threat. The answer was methodical emigration with a gradual usurpation of Jewish status by Aryan replacements. One locale that could absorb thousands of German Jewish citizens, yet isolate them politically, was the stretch of desert and swamp at the far end of the Mediterranean Sea called Palestine. To the Nazis this territory was a convenient dumping ground, in a sense a remote, self-run concentration camp. To the Zionists, this territory was the Promised Land destined to be a Jewish State.

Arlosoroff saw the forces of good and evil, pain and prophecy racing toward one central point in time. Following the divisive April 9 Executive session, Arlosoroff remained convinced that the Agency's factionalism could not be overcome in time to seize the historic moment. Arlosoroff concluded that he alone would orchestrate the final negotiations for the liquidation of Jewish existence in Germany and its transfer to Eretz Yisrael.

On April 13, 1933, Arlosoroff met with a worried Rutenberg. To succeed, his liquidation company would need thousands of middle-class Jews to purchase small blocks of noncontrolling stock. Rutenberg feared that the rival plan for a Zionist refugee fund would ruin everything. People would not buy shares in a liquidation company that wasn't expected to return dividends for ten years *and* donate additional money to a relief fund as well. One or the other, probably both, would be unsuccessful. Rutenberg said he would rather see his liquidation company delayed or canceled than launched on a path of failure.[11]

The next day, April 14, Arlosoroff and Weizmann met at an experimental agricultural station near Tel Aviv with High Commissioner Wauchope and Sir Phillip Cunliffe-Lister, the British colonial secretary, who had just arrived from London. Cunliffe-Lister was the cabinet officer with direct purview over England's colonies and the Palestine Mandate. Together, Wauchope and Cunliffe-Lister possessed the power to change radically the course of Jewish nationalism in Palestine. Cunliffe-Lister had already talked to Rutenberg in London about transplanting German Jews to Palestine via a liquidation company. Essentially, the colonial secretary approved.[12]

But the many thousands, perhaps hundreds of thousands, of German Jews could not possibly dwell in the tiny enclaves that comprised Jewish Palestine. In 1933, only about 4 percent of Palestine's 10,000 square miles was in Jewish possession. Most of this land was concentrated in enclaves around Jaffa-Tel Aviv, the northern Mediterranean coast, Haifa and the Galilee. Large tracts were reserved for cultivation. About 20 percent of Palestine was Arab-owned. The Mandate government owned the remaining

70 percent, and half of that was uninhabitable desert. So more room would clearly be needed.[13]

As the two Zionists and two British officials spoke, their attention turned to the swampy Huleh Valley in northeast Galilee. All previous Zionist efforts to purchase this land had been stymied by either government obstruction or radical Arab pressure on the Arab landowners. But Cunliffe-Lister and Wauchope could guide this swampland from Arab ownership to Jewish control. And by meeting's end, they appeared so inclined.[14]

Most of Arlosoroff's meetings with Rutenberg and with the British were still either secret or arranged by Arlosoroff working alone. And although they were conducted more or less under the color of the Jewish Agency, most Agency officers learned of the episodes only after the fact. No wonder that a few hours after the secret April 14 rendezvous with Weizmann, Wauchope, and Cunliffe-Lister, Arlosoroff's maverick actions were finally confronted. Arlosoroff was briefing the Executive Committee about his meeting the night before, in which Rutenberg threatened to abandon his liquidation company because it could not succeed alongside the fund-raising campaign. Arlosoroff explained that London would have to decide which operation should be executed, the fund or the company. Ludwig Pinner, one of the German Zionists attending the session, objected to the continuing delays. "The initiative in this matter came from us," Pinner said. "We intended to begin work immediately . . . but as organized Zionists we turned to the Jewish Agency Executive. Then a 'battle for authority' began."[15]

Emanuel Neumann then spoke up angrily. "I cannot express an opinion on these issues, since activities are being undertaken without my knowledge. This is a scandal which I cannot simply ignore. I hear everywhere, even in the street, of important matters which are unknown to me. Meetings are called without us. I will not participate in any discussion until all members of the Executive are provided with full information on every matter." Neumann then ticked off the sources of his irritation. "Among the things which I heard outside were: discussions with the colonial secretary, the Huleh, discussions with Rutenberg, and so on. It will perhaps turn out that there are other matters which are not known to us."[16]

The exchange closed with Neumann insisting that London be consulted for authority to undertake any special action—this, a direct attempt to control Arlosoroff.[17] But Arlosoroff would not be stopped.

The next day, April 15, Arlosoroff contacted Rutenberg and Weizmann to help decide the next step. Rutenberg conceded that the donations fund took priority over the liquidation company because each lost day meant lost revenues. Moreover, non-Zionist fund-raising was an even greater threat to Zionism.[18]

On April 16, the Jewish Agency gathered again. Arlosoroff admitted that he had taken the initiative once more by formally inviting Weizmann to head up the fund-raising operation. Arlosoroff defended his action, declaring, "We are neglecting a historical opportunity and betraying our mission. . . . I warn the Executive. A delay for internal reasons will backfire on us." The Executive members realized that Arlosoroff now was personally shaping the highest level of Zionist politics.[19]

Neumann was furious: "We did not decide to ask Dr. Weizmann to head the appeal. We decided to send a telegram to London to inform our colleagues there of our views and ask their opinion. If someone has approached Weizmann on this matter, it was done prematurely and without authorization. . . . One cannot behave in this manner. . . . There is Rutenberg, and there is Weizmann. They negotiate. Negotiations are undertaken with them. We have no place in this as an Executive. . . . They arrange matters and come to us afterwards . . . to vote and decide. Is this an Executive or a fiction?"

Continuing in anger, Neumann declared, "Here we learn that an agreement has already been completed between Weizmann and Rutenberg. In that case—what are we doing here! I do not even know exactly what Rutenberg's plan or what Weizmann's intentions are. . . . Things have gone too far. . . . I therefore inform you that: A, I am resigning from the [special German crisis] committee; B, I retract my vote on our earlier decision concerning the [fund-raising] operation to be headed by Weizmann, as I did not then know of Rutenberg's proposal; C, I agreed then to Dr. Arlosoroff traveling to Germany and London—at the moment I see no point in this, and I accordingly retract my agreement."[20]

The others attending, including Arlosoroff, tried to reason with Neumann, stressing that all the bickering was trivial compared to the crisis in Germany, and the crisis Zionism would suffer unless it quickly interposed itself in the solution. Dr. Senator tried to convince Neumann to continue working on the German problem. Neumann answered, "I cannot retract my resignation." Senator then announced, "In that case, I also resign."[21]

The meeting abruptly ended, with Zionism's response to Hitler still undecided. After Arlosoroff left the room, Neumann instructed the secretary to cable London in code all that had transpired.[22] Energies would now be spent not on relieving Jewish agony in Germany, but in finding some way to prove who was boss in the Zionist movement.

Yet Arlosoroff's momentum was not stalled. Two days later, April 18, Arlosoroff organized a day trip to the Huleh for Weizmann, Cunliffe-Lister, and Wauchope. Stopping at a point near Tiberias and the Sea of Galilee, the men talked and came to a meeting of the minds. Cunliffe-Lister stated that Britain was in principle in favor of Jews taking over the Huleh. He would even recommend to the British cabinet that Transjordan lands be used for Jewish emigration as well—subject to three stipulations: First, if Jews moved to Transjordan, an extra military unit would be needed for the area, and its £30,000 annual expense would have to be borne by the Jews. Second, the Zionist press must refrain from any mention of extending the Jewish National Home into Transjordan. Third, the Jewish Agency would be superceded by a specially chartered company to carry out the settlement.[23]

During the conference, Colonial Secretary Cunliffe-Lister did most of the talking, while High Commissioner Wauchope tried not to commit himself. However, at one point Wauchope asked Weizmann directly when the transfer would begin. Weizmann replied, "It must either happen in the next year or two, or would have to be put off for ten years."[24]

Rutenberg's liquidation company now became all the more pivotal, as did Arlosoroff's personal negotiation with the Third Reich as the official representative of the Zionist movement. The Jews of Germany would have to be steered to Palestine. But without genuine authority, Arlosoroff was certain the Nazis would not cooperate. And even then, he was unsure just how far the Reich would go.[25] So when Arlosoroff discovered Neumann's telegram 620, sent in code to the London Executive in an attempt to discredit Arlosoroff's authority and block his visit to Berlin, Arlosoroff dispatched his own cable:

"SPECIAL 622: OUR TELEGRAM 620 DISPATCHED . . . WITHOUT MY/ SENATOR CONSENT OR KNOWLEDGE STOP . . . INFORMAL CONVERSATION PURPOSE COORDINATE RUTENBERG SCHEME NOT ILLEGAL BUT VERY HELPFUL . . . DELAY ACTION OWING TO INTERNAL CONTROVERSY . . . ENDANGERING PALESTINE PARAMOUNT POSITION IN EMERGENCY ACTION AND RESULTING MORAL LOSS ZIONISTS."[26]

Arlosoroff's main goal now was to wrap up Jewish Agency business quickly and leave for Berlin. In yet another Executive session, held on April 19, Arlosoroff declared that approval for this trip had already been granted and that "Mr. Neumann's retraction of his vote does not change the situation as far as I am concerned. I am therefore prepared to travel." Neumann, still suspicious, suggested that the matter at least be tabled until the next session. Arlosoroff replied, "I do not agree to a delay." Finally, Senator, who knew why Arlosoroff needed to visit Berlin, broke in and said, "There is already a decision, and if there will be a demand [from London] to change it . . . then we will discuss it." Arlosoroff added decisively, "I shall prepare to travel."[27]

On April 22, Cunliffe-Lister held a secret meeting with two of the most important Arab personalities in Palestine. One was the emir, who owned much of the Huleh lands; the other was the Mufti of Jerusalem, the virulently anti-Jewish leader who by intimidation, bribery, and family influence kept the fires of violence and confrontation in Palestine stoked. After Arlosoroff learned of the meeting, his outlook toward an immediate binational arrangement dimmed. Apparently, the mufti had maintained his usual rejectionism. This convinced Arlosoroff that the path to binational coexistence would be a spiral that first settled Jews on land surrounding their existing enclaves and only later expanded to the Huleh. In the meantime, despite difficulties, settlement in the Transjordan would be necessary for the coming waves of German Jews.[28]

On April 23, just a few days before Arlosoroff was to leave for Berlin, one last Jewish Agency session was convened. In the background, the pauperization of the German Jews was clearly accelerating. Disenfranchisement not obligated by government decree was implemented by popular fanaticism.[29] What's more, Jewish Agency leaders were convinced that if Hitler succeeded, the crisis in Germany would be reenacted in Austria, internationalized Danzig, and perhaps even Rumania.[30] They were intensely aware that their response now would be noted by anti-Semitic regimes elsewhere in Europe.

At the April 23 Agency meeting, Rutenberg was called in to explain personally his liquidation company, now provisionally named the Palestine Development Corporation. As Rutenberg explained his concept, it became clear that his liquidation company would in fact absorb most of the Zionist institutions, including the Jewish Agency, the Jewish National Fund, and the Palestine Foundation Fund. Arlosoroff hoped that the company's shares would be split fifty-fifty between Zionist institutions and private investors, but the precise percentages couldn't be guaranteed.[31]

The concept was so mammoth that some Executive members could not comprehend exactly how it would work. Others were uncertain where the Zionist movement would find the money to purchase 50 percent of the company's shares. The questions and debate continued until Arlosoroff angrily chastised: "Some fifty days have been lost since March tenth, and each day is worth one hundred thousand pounds [in Jewish donations going to other sources]. We have already lost half the company's capital. We cannot continue to talk."[32]

But the gentlemen then disagreed over whether Rutenberg's company should be purely commercial, syphoning German Jewish wealth to Palestine via business ventures, or whether the company should actually oversee resettlement. Senator was against the company engaging in any relief activities. Rutenberg was shocked. "If I had wanted to found a commercial company," Rutenberg complained, "there would have been no need for me to come here. The operation is intended to be *both* commercial and ethical."[33]

However, after an acrimonious debate, the Executive unanimously endorsed Rutenberg's company as a "purely commercial" venture engaging not in the transfer of people, but in the transfer of money. This new approach to solving the German Jewish question stressed not political negotiations with the Reich for relief, but commercial negotiations with the Reich for business.[34]

There was no time to lose. Arlosoroff asked German Consul Heinrich Wolff for a letter of introduction to the German government so he could initiate discussions of emigration and property transfer. Wolff was happy to comply, preparing a letter to the Berlin Foreign Ministry that glowingly described Arlosoroff as an important Zionist official who had been instrumental in good relations between the Jewish Agency and Germany.[35]

Introduction in hand, Arlosoroff made ready to leave Palestine. However, just before he left, the members of the Jewish Agency Executive Committee insisted on a last-minute confrontation. On April 25, they demanded once and for all to know exactly why Arlosoroff was going to Germany. Arlosoroff at first denied that his trip was really very special. But when Neumann absolutely insisted the trip be canceled and that the authorizing vote be rescinded, Arlosoroff finally blurted out, "I don't wish to be a football . . . to be condemned for my bad behavior." In a moment more he admitted his true mission.[36]

German assets must be liquidated and transferred to Palestine. A structured institution—say, an emigration bank—would be necessary. Arlosoroff would organize it, probably through future negotiations with the German government. Arlosoroff claimed that the negotiations were not actually possible at this tense moment. Instead he might just lay the groundwork with the German Zionists in Berlin for government negotiations to come.[37]

Senator, the man who started the currency exemption negotiations six weeks earlier, saw his plan disintegrating. Arlosoroff's authority was now clearly in dispute. Senator declared he would also travel to Germany. This Arlosoroff opposed, believing that as a German, Senator's negotiations would be doomed. Ukrainian-born Arlosoroff insisted that he would go, Senator would not, and that was that.[38]

What now for Senator and his German Zionist colleagues, so eager to convert their currency exemption into a viable program? How could they lift this opportunity out of the miasma of Zionist factionalism and save the transfer? They doubted that the man they had taken into their confidence, Chaim Arlosoroff, visionary and dynamic as he was, was capable of accomplishing the feat. What Zionist official could, given the Jewish Agency's political strife?

Mr. Sam Cohen was still in Palestine and paid a visit to Consul Heinrich Wolff that same day, April 25.[39] Sam Cohen had a plan.

Cohen was connected to a company named Hanotaiah Ltd., which in Hebrew meant "the planters." Hanotaiah (Ha-noh-tay-ah) essentially existed as a profit-making subsidiary of a settlement organization called the Young Farmers Association. Hanotaiah's main business was buying and selling land, especially for orange orchards, and providing equipment needed for citrus cultivation.[40]

Cohen explained his idea. The consul approved and provided Cohen with what amounted to a rival letter of introduction, describing Hanotaiah as an important land-investment firm—citing several million dollars in business over the past four years. Partially explaining what Hanotaiah had to offer,

Wolff wrote, "Up to now, Hanotaiah has bought pumps, pipes, and so forth in Czechoslovakia, since they are cheaper than in Germany." Wolff knew that pipes were one of Germany's most important exports. The letter explained that Yugoslav and Italian firms were soliciting Hanotaiah's pipe orders as well. But Hanotaiah would purchase all future pipes and other agricultural equipment from Germany if the merchandise could be paid for with the frozen assets of German Jews.[41]

It was very complicated. But, wrote Wolff, all would be explained by Hanotaiah's representative, who would travel to Germany to negotiate the deal.[42]

Arlosoroff left Palestine for Berlin on April 26, 1933. Mr. Sam Cohen left for Berlin shortly thereafter.[43]

11. Stifling the Boycott

ZIONIST LEADERS, during April 1933, sought to cooperate with the Nazi Reich to arrange the orderly exit of Jewish people and wealth from Germany. But during the very same weeks, Jewish groups throughout the world were struggling to resist and topple the Reich to keep Jews in Germany as citizens. Boycott and protest were everywhere.

April 1: *Paris*, the International League Against Anti-Semitism made good on its threat to declare a boycott, effective 10:00 A.M. until the downfall of Adolf Hitler or the resumption of full rights for German Jews. *Istanbul*, Jews distributed circulars urging a boycott of all German products.[1]

April 2: *Toronto*, a mass protest meeting cosponsored by Jewish and Christian clergy adopted the boycott. *Paris*, Cardinal Verdier publicly assured the chief rabbi of Paris that Catholics would actively support the anti-Hitler movement.[2]

April 3: *Salonika*, 70,000 Greek Jews gathered in a mass protest against Hitler. *Panama*, fifteen leading Jewish firms announced the cancellation of all orders of German merchandise.[3]

April 4: *Bombay*, Jewish protest meetings condemned the Hitler regime.[4]

April 5: *New York*, 15,000 leftists protested both Nazism and those Jewish and governmental leader's going slowly in the fight against Hitler.[5]

In Poland, the national boycott against Germany was enforced by mob violence. On April 6, Reich Ambassador Hans Moltke officially demanded an end to the violent boycott and its semiofficial encouragement. The Polish Undersecretary of State angrily told Moltke to his face that the Polish government did not desire to interfere with the boycott. Anti-German boycott violence was so extensive in Upper Silesia that the German Foreign Ministry declared "the situation altogether unbearable" and threatened to complain to the League of Nations.[6]

In England, on April 9, the fear of Polish-style boycott violence prompted police in London and Manchester to insist all storeowners, under pain of prosecution, remove "Boycott German Goods" window posters. The next afternoon, boycott suppression was excitedly debated in Parliament. Home Secretary Sir John Gilmour denied that the police were acting on express government orders. Just to make sure, Winston Churchill called for an official end to the suppression, to which the home secretary answered, "Certainly."[7] Meanwhile, Britain's Labour-dominated boycott movement continued to expand. By April 15, *The Daily Herald*, quoting industry sources, estimated the fur boycott alone would cost Germany $100 million annually.[8]

Similar scares faced the Reich from all over Europe.

April 13: *Bucharest*, German trade was already suffering from a semiofficial boycott because the Rumanian National Bank refused to allocate foreign currency for German imports (in retaliation for Reich barriers to Rumanian goods). Now Rumanian Jews formally joined the popular purchasing embargo, thus eliminating many barter deals as well. In Ploesti, Jewish merchants refused three carloads of German porcelain despite frantic price reductions by the shippers. Other German industries in Rumania were similarly afflicted.[9]

April 17: *Antwerp*, the fur boycott was extended to Belgium following a binding resolution by Jewish fur traders.[10]

April 19: *Belgrade*, the anti-German boycott in Yugoslavia was so damaging that local Nazi surrogates began an intense but futile counterboycott to pressure Jews to abandon the fight.[11]

The spirit of the anti-Nazi boycott was fueled not only by persistent organizers, but by encouraging press reports. For example, the sudden termination of Germany's April First action was explained by the world press as Hitler's retreat from economic retaliation.[12] This convinced many that the best defense was a better offense.

Encouragement continued. Berlin newspapers began to report Germany's foreign trade for the first quarter in a dangerous decline.[13] On April 9, Hjalmar Schacht, Hitler's newly appointed head of the Reichsbank, surprised a conference of international bankers in Basel by reducing Germany's foreign debt with a $70-million dollar check. Although the payment severely drained reserves, Schacht hoped to inject some believability into Germany's credit. But the financial press reported the "show of strength" as a mere desperate maneuver.[14] Financial writers pessimistically pointed to the extraordinary

German economic dislocation directly caused by Hitler's anti-Jewish policy. The press emphasized that the economic problems included both external backlash and massive internal disruption resulting from the sudden subtraction of the Jewish middle class from the commercial mainstream.[15]

On April 10, Germany announced that Jewish veterans would be exempted from sweeping anti-Jewish occupational expulsions—at Hindenburg's request, in the name of fairness. *The New York Times* attributed the "softening" not to sentimentality, but to the world protest and resulting economic chaos within the Reich. A week later, the *Times* carried another story repeating the theme, adding that a quiet but cohesive lobby within German economic circles opposed continued anti-Semitic activity.[16]

In a radical move on April 22 that would have been impossible in later years, a group of German industrial associations unanimously rejected official government reports citing a recent 9 percent *gain* in manufactured exports, especially machinery, textiles, and steel. In their daring announcement, the industrialists admitted they had actually suffered a heavy *decline*.[17]

Pessimistic newspaper and radio reports were vital to keeping the anti-Nazi boycott movement alive, because every boycott thrives on the appearance of success. It matters little whether a business decline is actually due to a boycott or to seasonal fluctuations, strikes, material shortages, or the phases of the moon. People want to see evidence of damage. When they do, the devoted redouble their devotion and the uncommitted see real value in the protest and jump on the bandwagon. In April 1933, such evidence was abundant for those opposed to Adolf Hitler.

On April 26, British Embassy Commercial Counsellor F. Thelwell in Berlin ended a twenty-two-page economic forecast with the words "If as time goes on the effects of bad foreign trade make themselves felt in industrial employment in Germany and money is not forthcoming for schemes of work and settlement, the pressure of economic distress may yet prove strong enough to break the political stranglehold which Hitler has put upon the country."[18] Germany could not afford a boycott.

What's more, the American Jewish Committee in New York, the State Department in Washington, the Foreign Office in London, and the Jewish Agency in Jerusalem were all becoming aware that protest and boycott were the only effective restraints on Nazi policy.

For example, on April 5, Berl Locker of the Zionist Organization Executive Committee in London readily acknowledged the power of the protest in a letter to a colleague: "It is clear that these [British protest] actions, added to the general anti-Nazi attitude of the press . . . have surely caused the [April First] anti-Jewish boycott to be limited to a single day." Despite this awareness, Locker admitted in the same letter, "My friends and I have attempted to energetically counter the so-called *Greuelpropaganda* [atrocity stories]. . . . We also made efforts to counteract the proclamation of an [anti-

Nazi] boycott [in Britain] and we were successful, at least with the official organizations. Of course, we cannot directly influence the individual merchant. . . ."[19] In the first week of April, Locker also advised the Jewish Agency in Jerusalem that for tactical reasons, Zionists in all countries should avoid participating in the struggle against Hitler. Locker feared that open criticism of Hitler would precipitate crackdowns on German Zionism and jeopardize contacts with the regime.[20]

Both the American State Department and the British Foreign Office were equally aware that pressure and only pressure was restraining the Reich. British and American legations around the world reported the distress the anti-Nazi protest and boycott movement was causing the German government. But while aware of press reports attributing the so-called softening of Hitler's campaign to sudden economic distress, the British and American diplomatic communities continued to preach noninterference, political reassurance to the Reich, and economic cooperation as the wisest method of reducing anti-Semitism in Germany.

In the case of Zionism, the State Department, and the Foreign Office, their hands-off policy was in pursuit of ideals. Zionists, of course, were seeking détente with an enemy to achieve Jewish nationalism. American and British diplomats were seeking an illusory peace by an ineffective strategy later to be labeled *appeasement*. But the American Jewish Committee's antagonism to anti-Nazi activity defied even their own definition of Jewish defense.

In early April, Committee president Cyrus Adler received an anguished letter from a friend writing from Paris. The man was ruined, living from moment to moment as a refugee. Adler's frightened friend sought to debunk the Committee's belief that German atrocities were in the least bit exaggerated. Over several neatly typed pages, the refugee listed typical disappearances, beatings, and murders: Herr Kindermann disappeared for several days until his frantic family received a letter from a Nazi commander to pick up his body. Herr Krell disappeared until one of the Nazi torture houses called with the news that he had thrown himself out a fourth-floor window. Herr Naumann, seized by Brownshirts, dragged through the streets, beaten over his entire body, and then forced to suffer as pepper was sprinkled on his wounds, died shortly thereafter of a skull fracture and blood poisoning from the pepper.[21]

Adler's friend beseeched the Committee to "not take the slightest notice of assurances . . . whether they come from Jewish or non-Jewish sources, from within Germany or from without. The real truth is only known to those Jews who are condemned to live in Germany under the present government, and they dare not breathe a word about what is going on, because they would pay for such information with their lives."[22]

In a final insistent paragraph, the refugee begged Adler, "You free Jews in free countries, demand restoration to German Jews of their civic, social and economic rights. The only practical way to attain this end is to boycott all German goods except where they come, without a doubt, from a Jewish manufacturer or producer."[23] But Adler would not change his position.

Unshakable evidence about Nazi horrors arrived on April 6, when Adler and B'nai B'rith president Alfred Cohen received a cable completely invalidating the denials of German atrocities that German Jewish leaders had issued and the Committee had earlier published. But instead of making the information public to expose the truth, Adler and Cohen wired the news verbatim to Secretary of State Cordell Hull: "APPEAL OF GERMAN JEWISH ORGANIZATIONS TO AMERICAN JEWS TO CEASE PROTESTS DEFINITELY MADE UNDER INTIMIDATION STOP GOERING INVITED FOR SECOND TIME JEWISH LEADERS STOP . . . HE WAS EXTREMELY ABRUPT DEMANDED IMMEDIATE INTERVENTION THAT JEWS ABROAD DISCONTINUE HORROR LEGEND/BOYCOTT CAMPAIGN OTHERWISE GERMAN JEWS WOULD BEAR CONSEQUENCES STOP . . . JEWISH LEADERS OBLIGED OUTLINE PLAN TO GOERING TAKE UP CONTACT WITH JEWISH LEADERS ALL COUNTRIES FOR DENYING HORRORS/DISCRIMINATION/BOYCOTT."[24]

Adler and Cohen assured Hull that the facts would be temporarily "withheld from publication." Hull acknowledged in kind within hours: "I HAVE RECEIVED YOUR TELEGRAM . . . SHALL BE GLAD TO FIX A TIME FOR FURTHER DISCUSSION OF THE SITUATION."[25]

Adler and the Committee continued to deprecate publicly Jewish efforts to boycott Germany or even organize protest. Committee people would always point to the instructions of German Jewish leaders to stop all protests and boycotts and not believe the exaggerated stories of Nazi brutality. Yet Adler and his colleagues knew those German Jewish admonitions to be false, spoken under the truncheon, and, in fact, no more than tools of Nazi propaganda.

At first, the Committee was partly successful in muzzling Jewish protest. For example, on April 2, while many were still trying to determine the truth about German atrocities, the Joint Distribution Committee held a relief conference. The Joint traditionally avoided political controversy to protect its internationally recognized status as a neutral relief agency, analogous to the Red Cross. Officiating at this April 2 meeting were Committee leaders Cyrus Adler and Joseph Proskauer. Quickly, the Joint's position at the conference was seen not as neutral, but committed *against* anti-Hitler activism. The rostrum speakers openly repudiated efforts by Jewish organizations to boycott German imports. Finally, Rabbi Jacob Sunderling from Hamburg rose to recite the truth about Nazi tortures in Germany. Proskauer and another gentleman cut short the rabbi's remarks, arguing that such speeches had no place in a relief conference. The crowd objected loudly. One person shouted, "We don't want to hide anything. Let him go on!" Rabbi Sunderling tried to make himself heard, his eyes welling with tears as his words were being ruled out of order. Finally, since Rabbi Sunderling would not be muffled and the audience demanded he be heard, the chairman summarily adjourned the meeting. But the audience would not leave, so Proskauer stepped to the platform to emphasize the point: The meeting was over. Rabbi Sunderling would not be heard.[26]

On April 6, Adler wrote to a leader of the Jewish War Veterans accusing the JWV of having "furnished a pretext for the German [anti-Jewish] boycott." A copy of Adler's letter reached J. George Fredman, commander in chief of the JWV and head of its boycott committee. Fredman bluntly answered Adler: Our action "needs no apology. . . . Our organization was the only one which started right, kept straight and is still right on the situation. . . . Jewry should be united in this movement—it is the only weapon which will bring the German people to their senses." Adler, in an April 19 reply, lectured back, "I wish to reiterate and even strengthen the statements I made heretofore. The American Jewish Committee, in objecting to boycotts, demonstrations, parades, etc. was acting in accordance with the wishes of leading Jews in Germany as directly conveyed to them over the long distance phone from Paris where they were entirely free to talk. . . . I cannot use language sufficiently strong to indicate my hope that you will discontinue the form of agitation which you started."[27]

Soon the Committee's reluctance was no longer seen by the great masses of American Jews as wisdom and behind-the-scenes tactics. Instead, the Committee—together with B'nai B'rith—was viewed merely as meek and silent; or worse, a saboteur of the anti-Nazi movement. So although the Committee and B'nai B'rith retained some element of "establishment" recognition and access, the American people opposed to Hitler—Jewish or not—rejected them.

The rejection soon became public. In conjunction with an early-May protest action, an editorial in the leading Yiddish daily, Der Tog, bitterly attacked the Committee and B'nai B'rith for their "policy of fear and silence." In a stunning rebuke, the editorial asked, "What do Messrs. Adler and Cohen propose? . . . Silence and nothing else! . . . [Our] people are determined to fight for their very life. . . . The voice of the masses will be heard."[28]

Their voices were indeed heard, not only in America, but in Nazi Germany.

12. Fear of Preventive War

BECAUSE German foreign policy included supervising exports, the Reich Foreign Ministry became the clearinghouse for all the disheartening boycott news regularly transmitted by German consulates and trade missions throughout the world. These reports invariably came across Foreign Minister von Neurath's desk and were distributed to Schacht, Hindenburg, and Hitler as von Neurath thought necessary.[1] During April 1933, Berlin's most important in-boxes were brimming with frightening boycott and protest news from around the world. Some boycotters were clever enough to increase the Reich's anxiety by sending their boycott announcements directly to the Foreign Ministry in Berlin.

Those business leaders who found Hitler's financial policy suicidal also sent their bad news to the Foreign Ministry. Munster's Chamber of Commerce reported canceled orders from Holland and France. Offenbach's Chamber of Commerce reported boycotts of their goods in Belgium, Egypt, Denmark, and Finland. There could be no mistake, according to the Offenbach report. Many retail establishments, such as those in Copenhagen, prominently displayed signs reading "No German Bids Accepted."[2]

Matters worsened. Quickly, the leaders of Germany realized that the anti-Hitler boycott was threatening to kill the Third Reich in its infancy, either through utter bankruptcy or by promoting an imminent invasion of Germany by its neighbors. When the Nazis consolidated power in early March, Polish officials openly reinforced troop strength along the Polish Corridor. This was in response to der Führer's bellicose threats to seize the Versailles-created territorial bridge.[3] In late March, the anti-Nazi boycott helped push Poland from a heightened defensive posture to a near-hysterical readiness to invade Germany.

On April 7, von Neurath, Schacht, and other key officials briefed Hitler about the Reich's perilous condition in the wake of the accelerating anti-Nazi backlash. Emphasizing that various neighbors were actively contemplating a preventive war with Germany while she was still weak, von Neurath told Hitler, "The gravity of the dangers threatening us should not be underestimated." Foremost among the potential invaders was Poland, determined to preempt any territorial compromise. Other neighbors to the east—Rumania, Yugoslavia, Hungary, Czechoslovakia—would have to be kept on friendly terms, principally through trade, to preclude any anti-German alliance with Poland. The West was also threatening. Von Neurath reminded Hitler that when German Chancellor Brüning told a newspaper in early 1932 that Germany would consider stopping all reparations, France mobilized for possible invasion. The foreign minister warned that France might resume her threatening posture if the Reich persisted in its policies.[4]

Von Neurath did not have to remind Hitler what happened when Germany defaulted on reparations payments in 1923. France did invade. The political chaos resulted in cyclonic inflation.

The foreign minister was plain about the Reich's absolute military vulnerability. He assumed that France was the strongest military power in the world. Germany could not challenge her in the least, and lagged five years behind the might of even her lesser enemy, Poland. Moreover, Europe vigorously opposed Germany's efforts to rearm. And Hitler's cabinet knew that the Jewish protest and boycott movement was in the forefront of political agitation to keep Germany a weaponless nation. So von Neurath was forced to list Germany's main defensive assets not as guns and bombs but as international goodwill and her value as a trading partner.[5] Von Neurath's military statement to Hitler concluded, "We shall first have to concentrate our political activity on economic questions, in order to avoid in all circumstances warlike complications with which we cannot cope at the present time."[6]

Then Schacht told Hitler the dismal economic truth. Things were far worse than in 1930. Then, foreign exchange reserves totaled RM 3.3 billion, which Schacht considered dangerously low. Current reserves had dwindled to merely RM 450 million. Therefore, the end of foreign exchange and, hence, viable international commerce was now in sight. Every last sum of foreign currency was being gathered, even from German banks overseas. Within months—perhaps sooner—"foreign exchange would no longer be available." Some way must be found to prepare the nations trading with Germany for the abrupt cessation of payments, said Schacht, stressing his hope that hostile reactions—like those feared from the French—could be avoided.[7]

But Schacht had an idea, perhaps the only idea capable of saving trade relations. Massive blocked accounts that is, frozen bank accounts—would create a giant pool of blocked reichmarks, called *Sperrmarks*, which Germany could use to pay obligations. Debtors would have no choice but to accept the reichmarks, and they would be usable almost exclusively in Germany.[8] The true owners of such blocked accounts—foreigners and emigrants—presumably could not all use their sperrmarks at once, especially since they could not be removed from the country. Thus, the Reichsbank could trade them freely.

Schacht's idea was to elevate this shell game to a pseudolegitimate financial technique to save the German economy. During the April 7 conference, Schacht predicted that so many new blocked accounts could be generated that there would be money left over for "the new needs of the Reich." Hitler ended the April 7 conference by insisting that Schacht's plan get under way at once.[9]

But the situation deteriorated rapidly. On April 12, German Ambassador Moltke in Warsaw reported that the anti-Nazi boycott was inciting the Polish people and their leaders to military edginess. "Everywhere the slogan is: destruction of everything in Poland which is still German, and boycott of everything which comes from Germany," wrote a distressed Moltke. "Everywhere straw men labeled Hitler are being burned." He added that the Polish government's open support for the "boycott against German goods as legitimate and useful" was incontestable. Moreover, reported Moltke, the Polish foreign minister had warned him that any retaliation against Polish Jews or any others of Polish extraction living in Germany would be met with dangerous Polish countermeasures, the "consequences [of which] were unforeseeable." [10]

On April 22, German Ambassador to Italy Ulrich von Hassell reported worse news from Rome. In a one-sentence telegram, Hassell relayed highly reliable information from circles close to Czech President Thomas Masaryk that Prague was planning to support "Polish intentions of preventive military action at the German eastern border." No longer confined to preemptively occupying demilitarized zones in the Polish Corridor, Poland's military threat now included an actual invasion of Germany proper. And as feared, Czechoslovakia was primed to join her. Von Neurath passed Hassell's telegram directly to President von Hindenburg. [11]

The next day, April 23, Ambassador Moltke responded to an urgent inquiry from Berlin seeking his confidential assessment of the chances of a Polish invasion. Moltke answered with the known arguments circulating in Poland. Persuasively in favor was the growing feeling that Germany under Hitler would one day attack Poland. Since war was inevitable, Polish leaders were convinced they should conquer the East Prussian region of Germany at once while Germany was still weak and unarmed. The arguments against such a preemptive invasion were Poland's exaggerated fears of nonexistent German weapon stockpiling, the financial cost, and Poland's doubts about her own military capability. In balancing the pros and cons, Moltke concluded that the chances of an invasion were even. [12]

In an attached memo, Moltke listed proof that Poland was readying should the decision to invade be affirmed. Poland's war industry had increased production 100 percent since Hitler took office, placing large orders for airplane engines, munitions, field kitchens, and the other staples of war. Polish representatives were even then in France purchasing heavy artillery and antiaircraft guns. Reserve officers had been called up. And troops due to be discharged had been kept on for additional months of duty. In an ominous show of force, the government had ordered the rapid deployment of 30,000 soldiers and artillery at Vilna just the day before. [13]

On April 25, at 12:45 P.M., German Ambassador Walter Koch in Czechoslovakia dispatched an urgent telegram to Berlin: "THERE IS NO DOUBT THAT A PREVENTIVE WAR IS BEING CAREFULLY CONSIDERED AT THE PRAGUE CASTLE WHERE THE THREADS OF ALL INTERNATIONAL PLOTS AGAINST GERMANY COME TOGETHER. . . . RECENTLY [PRESIDENT] MAS-

ARYK SPOKE OF WAR AS A MATTER OF COURSE. I AM CONVINCED THAT POLAND'S INFLUENCE HERE IS CONSTANTLY PRESSING FOR A PREVENTIVE WAR, AND THAT THE CZECHS HAVE THE INTENTION TO INTERVENE ACTIVELY." [14]

Koch's telegram was received in the Foreign Ministry at 4:00 P.M. Two hours and forty-five minutes later, Hitler and the entire cabinet assembled to consider the prospect of an imminent invasion.[15] As they saw it, Poland would act to protect her borders. Czechoslovakia would take advantage of the situation and at the same time strike at German anti-Semitism. France might move to counter border tensions and preclude any plan to discontinue reparations.

Von Neurath pleaded, "The situation is so tense that provocations from our side must under all circumstances be avoided."[16]

The Jewish question and the anti-Nazi boycott were a common aggravating factor in Germany's intensifying economic and military problems. Polish Jews had successfully inflamed Poland from defensive concern to war hysteria through their violent anti-German boycott and protest movement. German officials were in fact astonished that the historically anti-Semitic Polish people would allow Jewish persecution in Germany to become the pretext for a war. But it was happening. The anti-Nazi movement in Czechoslovakia was encouraging Masaryk's government to join the opportunity. Masaryk believed anti-Semitism to be an evil unacceptable to Christianity. The international boycott was frustrating every Reich effort to earn the foreign exchange needed to keep France at bay. Events were fitting into the Nazi conception of war: a cataclysmic conflict caused by Jews through economic and propaganda means. But Germany simply was not ready.

The Third Reich had raging problems. Perhaps cunning diplomacy and the self-interest of the world could dampen many of those problems. But at every turn the anti-Nazi protest and boycott movement threw fresh fuel on the fires. There was no longer any doubt. The boycott would have to be stopped.

13. Message to Schacht

FOLLOWING the lesson of April First, Nazi leaders sought to avoid noisy anti-Semitic outbursts that would provoke more headlines and retaliation. Instead, they planned the methodical destruction of Jewish existence in

Germany—not through riots, no longer through declared boycotts, but through exclusionary regulations and private purges. Julius Streicher sadly admitted when the anti-Jewish boycott was rescinded, "I have a feeling that the boycott battle will not be further taken up. . . . This will prove a disappointment to millions of Germans. . . . It was not easy to yield, but Adolf Hitler can only proceed one step at a time." [1]

Yet as in any radical movement, NSDAP activists were constantly trying to outdo each other. In this vein, a hysterical drive for Nazi purity was announced April 12: So-called un-German books would be burned in giant bonfires across Germany on May 10. [2]

In response, Stephen Wise and the Congress on April 19 called an emergency meeting of 1,000 Jewish delegates representing 600 New York-area Jewish organizations. As usual, the delegates shouted for the Congress to finally proclaim the boycott. Jewish groups could then begin organizing. But once more Wise refused the call. [3]

Wise felt that the formal boycott was so valuable a weapon it should be held back just a little longer while the spontaneous, unorganized movement hinted at the damage to come. And he wanted to announce the formal boycott as part of a worldwide Jewish retaliation declared by an international Jewish body convened in a dramatic flourish for that very purpose. Specifically, Wise envisioned a World Jewish Conference in Geneva during September 1933. And deep inside, he probably harbored doubts stemming from Zionist pressures to hold back on the boycott. [4]

So Wise answered the shouters: "The time has not yet come for an official boycott—we still have other weapons." When delegates insisted on stronger action, Wise pleaded with them: "We are not going to disclose our campaign so that Hitler . . . will know our next move. I will not be your leader if I cannot be trusted." [5] Instead of launching the official boycott, the delegates unanimously agreed to a monumental parade to take place the night of the Nazi book burnings. [6]

Newspapers on April 27 carried the announcement that the 600 New York-area Jewish organizations would ask their 2 million members to march through Manhattan in a display perhaps equal to the Victory parade of 1919. [7] The performance would have to be impressive, if only for one spectator who would be in America at the time: Hjalmar Schacht.

Schacht was coming to the United States in early May to confer with American officials. The Reich hoped somehow to maintain good economic relations with the United States. Exports and foreign currency—these were the precious remedies to massive German unemployment, a weak, unarmed German military, and a continuum of material shortages. Schacht's mission was therefore all-important.

The May 10 parade in many ways was a repeat of the Madison Square Garden effort. The American Jewish Committee and B'nai B'rith opposed every detail. However, this time their disapproval was not waged privately, but in the media in a desperate attempt to dissuade millions of Jews throughout the country who wanted to organize against Hitler. Of the many public attacks the Committee launched against the May 10 plans, the first major condemnation said it as well as any: "We nevertheless consider such forms of agitation as boycotts, parades and mass meetings and other similar demonstrations as futile. They serve only as an ineffectual channel for the release of emotion. They furnish the persecutors with a pretext to justify the wrongs they perpetrate and . . . distract those who desire to help with constructive efforts."[8]

At the height of the parade preparation, in a rebuke to the Committee, the April 29 *New York Times* editorialized in favor of protest—Jewish and non-Jewish—as the only means of making Nazi leaders take note. "The thing that must drive home most surely to the mind and conscience of Germany's rulers is the outcry of the non-Jewish world. . . . The Nazi rulers do know . . . that the heads of Christian churches everywhere have been foremost in the protest."[9] The editorial reinforced Wise's strategy of making Jews the vanguard of a larger, interfaith movement. Shortly after the editorial, non-Jewish participation in the march accelerated. By May 4, in addition to 250,000 Jews, 50,000 mostly non-Jewish AFL unionists promised to march.[10]

That day, May 4, the luxury liner *Deutschland* was tugged into the docks of Manhattan. Wealthy German industrialists and prominent German politicians were aboard. But once the lines were tied, the reporters who assembled on the deck were not seeking out magnates or mayors. They were looking for Reichsbank president Hjalmar Schacht, the man the German media called "the Wizard." When they found him, at breakfast in the dining room, the question was immediately put: Is the Reich planning a propaganda campaign to counter reports of German atrocities?[11]

"What atrocities?" Schacht demanded defensively. "I have not seen any." "Why don't your papers enlighten you?" he barked. "Why don't your papers tell the truth? Why do your papers spread warlike feelings?" The Wizard then pulled out a *New York Times* clipping from the day before about a planned Nazi demonstration in honor of a German shot by the French during their 1923 occupation. Another article in the same *Times* edition mentioned tensions on the Franco-German border. With Schacht's voice rising in ferocity, he declared, "When you print stories like this you are stirring up warlike feeling. That kind of stuff makes for war!" Unable to control himself further, Schacht crumpled the *Times* clipping and ceremoniously threw it on the deck.[12]

On May 6, at noon, Schacht visited Secretary of State Cordell Hull's Washington office. They spoke briefly with Hull expressing confidence that Germany and the United States would enjoy a new economic partnership. At 1:00 P.M., Hull and Schacht drove up to the White House. Standing in front was FDR. Photographs of smiling men were snapped. They walked into the vestibule as a military band played the German national anthem and martial divertimenti. Lunch was served promptly. With Schacht seated next to the president, the two talked for some time about economic problems affecting both countries.[13] At one point, Roosevelt stood up and proposed a toast to President Hindenburg. Schacht returned the gesture by proposing his own toast to Roosevelt and conveying the best regards of Adolf Hitler. A half hour remained for some private talk, away from the crowd and the White House photographer. Schacht sat on the sofa next to Roosevelt. FDR immediately made it plain that Hitler's policy toward Jews had been costly to Germany's economic and political recovery. The American people, said the president, were quite unsympathetic to Germany, not even liking the newsreel scenes of Nazis marching in uniform. FDR called American outrage a hurdle to be cleared if economic success was to be achieved for Germany.[14]

Reminding Schacht that Secretary of State Hull was a believer in free trade, Roosevelt alluded to an extraordinary increase of mutual trade. Schacht asked how? FDR answered that the details would be worked out later, but it would allow Germany to repay its massive debts to other countries.[15]

That night, just before midnight, Schacht cabled the Foreign Ministry in Berlin detailing all that Roosevelt had said.[16]

When Schacht went to bed, late on May 6, there were scintillas of encouragement in the air. But the next day, the news was again bad. Larger boycott groups were organizing. And I. G. Farbenindustrie, one of Germany's colossal conglomerates, publicly admitted an extraordinary export slump due to anti-Nazi trade reprisals. Sales of some Farben commodities had fallen by as much as half. Farben, a leading foreign-currency earner, was one of the few sources Schacht had been relying upon to buy time.[17]

As a crowning touch that May 7, the American Jewish Congress cabled Schacht a courteously humiliating summons: "RESPECTFULLY INVITE YOU TO JOIN REVIEWING STAND OF HUGE DEMONSTRATION TO BE HELD IN NEW YORK ON MAY 10 . . . TO DEMONSTRATE EXTENT OF SOLIDARITY OF AMERICAN CITIZENS OF ALL FAITHS IN RESPECT TO POLICY OF YOUR GOVERNMENT IN REDUCING ITS JEWISH POPULATION TO SECOND-CLASS CITIZENSHIP."[18]

Later, Schacht reportedly confided to a friend, "Is there nothing in America to talk about but the Jewish question? That's all I hear: Jews, Jews, Jews and the Jewish question!"[19]

The next day, the Munich Chamber of Commerce released a report verifying that drastic adverse trade developments were indeed due to the worldwide anti-German boycott. The report concluded with a plea for the German government to counteract.[20]

That same day, May 8, Schacht met in FDR's office with the president, Secretary Hull, and German Ambassador Hans Luther. There was perhaps one way Schacht could stunt the anti-Nazi boycott movement. The gamble would have to be taken before the May 10 protest matured into a formal declaraton of economic war against the Reich. The gamble involved American creditors holding either German municipal bonds or general German commercial debts. Schacht had warned before that Germany would be unable to pay its debts if a boycott deprived it of the normal trade required to amass foreign exchange. At this rate, Germany would indeed run out of foreign currency within weeks. There was now nothing to lose.

So Schacht surprised FDR, Hull, and Luther by announcing that Germany would soon stop paying interest on American loans, and then stop paying all external debts generally. Ambassador Luther nervously resettled himself in his chair, waiting for FDR's response. Hull became visibly agitated. Schacht himself mentally prepared for Roosevelt's outburst. But Schacht was amazed when FDR just slapped his thigh in a jovial display and laughingly roared, "Serves the Wall Street bankers right!"[21] The president of the United States did not comprehend

But Hull understood completely. Five billion dollars in debts would be defaulted on, $2 billion of which was held by Americans. And he understood the timing. Coming just before the World Economic Conference in London, and arising out of a conversation with the president, the German move would certainly seem like some bizarre fiscal connivance to prop up the Hitler regime at the expense of America and her allies. Now Hull was outraged. The countless brutalities against Jews and the escalating campaign of legalized Jewish dispossession in Germany did not ruffle the secretary of state. But tinkering with Hull's emerging economic order was a capital offense that excited him to a fighting stance.[22]

Hull summoned Schacht to his office the next day. The secretary had been able to explain the ramifications to Roosevelt and secure the president's condemnation. When Schacht arrived, Hull deliberately began searching through papers on his desk, pretending Schacht was not standing in the doorway. Only after several minutes did Hull finally acknowledge Schacht's presence with the words "I am to give you this from the president." He handed Schacht an envelope. Wary of what was happening, Schacht asked if he should read the contents at once. Hull said yes. Schacht carefully pulled the short note from the envelope and read it silently. It was in fact a message from Hull, reading, "The President has directed me to say to you in regard to . . . the decision of the German Government to stop [payments] . . . on obligations externally sold or externally payable, that he is profoundly shocked." Schacht replaced the note in its envelope, said nothing, but sat down at Hull's desk.[23]

Schacht was barely seated when Hull exploded. "I was never so deeply surprised as I was yesterday afternoon by your announcement. My government is exercising every ounce of its power to bring [our] . . . nation out of the depths of awful panic conditions, back in the direction of normal prosperity. Just as real progress is being made, you come over here and, after sitting in confidential conferences with our officials . . . suddenly let it be given out from our doorstep that Germany suspended these payments. . . . It is greatly calculated to check and undermine American efforts to restore domestic business conditions."[24]

Schacht apologized, claiming he had not foreseen the implications of his statement. Not true. Schacht was trying to coerce America and the world away from the boycott movement and into continued economic support of the Hitler regime. Emerging as it did from a White House conversation, it indeed appeared as though the president understood and agreed to Germany's reneging on its debts so long as a boycott was making it impossible for her to pay. Hull refused to accept Schacht's excuses, and scowled, "Any person ought to realize the serious possibilities of such steps."[25] But scowls were unimportant. The Wizard had begun to work his magic.

In the days before the May 10 march, Stephen Wise continued to walk a tightrope between Jewish powers. On the one side was the great mass of American Jewry, eager to declare an official boycott. On the other side was the tiny faction of mostly German-American Jews represented by the Committee and allies in B'nai B'rith. In a May 9 letter to Albert Einstein, Rabbi Wise complained, "In America, I am sorry to say, there is *no* unity of opinion and action. Things are made infinitely more difficult for us by American Jews of German descent who believe they owe it to their German past to disbelieve the stories of Hitlerish barbarism and brutality. . . . The result is that, what with the [coming] London Economic Conference and the lack of pressure on the part of the rich German [American] Jews, the Administration has found it simpler not to act."[26]

Hjalmar Schacht, surrounded by America's anti-Hitler tumult, understood that on May 10, hundreds of thousands of American citizens would assemble to denounce the Reich. Schacht knew that the newspapers would continue to print anti-Nazi news, one article giving rise to another, fueling the boycott.

Indeed, some columns addressed Schacht directly. One *New York Times* article just before the May 10 parade capsulized the intended drama. Headlined "HEAD OF REICHSBANK, HERE FOR WHITE HOUSE TALKS, FACES OPPORTUNITY TO GAUGE CRITICISM OF NAZIS," the article wished Schacht "all good luck" in his efforts to rehabilitate Germany's battered economy. However, the article predicted, all his efforts would hinge on ending the Reich's anti-Semitic campaign, which carried with it constant economic retaliation by the rest of the world. Noting that "it is said that his word is law in all that pertains to finance and economics in Berlin, it is fortunate that it is upon the ears of Dr. Schacht himself that will fall" the voices of anti-Nazi protest. The article warned Schacht to listen and face the facts: The anti-Nazi boycott was killing the German economy.[27]

And now Samuel Untermyer, one of America's most prestigious and forceful Jewish leaders, was filling Stephen Wise's leadership vacuum. In a speech that made headlines just before the May 10 parade, Untermyer urged all Americans to ban all German products and services. Untermyer called the simple act of boycotting the "obvious remedy."[28] The masses were now demanding unity against Hitler.

At noon on May 10, Jewish commerce in New York stopped as promised. Employees, customers, and owners alike took their leave to return home and prepare for the afternoon's event. This spectacle would dwarf even the March 27 rally. Indeed, the parade swelled to 100,000 strong.[29]

They marched under Jewish banners, Zionist flags, anti-Nazi placards, and military pennants. They wore dapper business suits, dirty smocks and work shirts, army uniforms, rabbinical robes, white collars, and habits.[30] Shoulder to shoulder they marched in the face of Nazi threats to retaliate, in defiance of the forces of fear among their own people. In this moment they were united.

Chanting anti-Nazi slogans and vowing to resist Hitler, the crowds, fifteen deep on either side of the street, urged the protesters to escalate the fight. If there was any question of leadership, it was settled now. Roars of applause and volcanic cheers greeted a hat-waving Stephen Wise at every corner. For hours, Wise, 100,000 behind him, marched south toward Battery Park. Along the way, cheering people in windows showered the parade with ticker tape and confetti. At Seventeenth Street, thousands of assembled labor unionists, their ranks extending to the East River, flowed into the mainstream. At City Hall, Mayor O'Brien and other dignitaries stood on the steps of a reviewing stand. It took more than four hours for the protesters to pass.[31]

Despite the late hour, the throng gathered at Battery Park. There, the speakers condemned Hitler and his Reich. The cries for resistance were silenced only when the rally was officially closed by the playing of "The Star Spangled Banner" and the anthem of Jewish resistance, "Hatikva." Similar rallies were held in other cities, including Chicago, where 50,000 braved the rain. Those too old, too young, or too weak to walk joined the caravan of 500 cars and trucks that brought up the rear.[32]

The American people had a message. They were speaking in unison. And the most important man listening could not help but hear their warning.

From Washington, Schacht contacted an old friend, David Sarnoff, the president of RCA, and accepted an invitation to a May 12 private dinner party at Sarnoff's home. The Wizard knew that about a dozen Jewish leaders had also been invited—including Stephen Wise. Both the Reich and influential American Jews had been seeking a private parley to see if some ceasefire could be arranged.[33] The dinner seemed to be a perfect opportunity.

But when Justice Brandeis learned that the much-debated dinner was actually to take place, he counseled Stephen Wise against the meeting. Brandeis was privy to rumors in official circles that Hitler might soon back down due to international economic pressure. Any symbolic gesture to Schacht now would be the wrong signal. Wise agreed with Brandeis, but decided to attend the Sarnoff dinner if only to counterbalance the voice of American Jewish Committee leaders who had been invited.[34]

As expected, the dinner was a complete failure. After the meal, Schacht warned the Jewish representatives that outside interference "would only make matters worse." No one cared to comment, and Schacht took his leave.[35]

The next day, May 13, Schacht received an urgent call from James MacDonald of the Foreign Policy Association. Having just conferred with Roosevelt, MacDonald insisted on meeting with Schacht. Schacht was scheduled to leave aboard an ocean liner later that night, but he rearranged his remaining hours for the urgent meeting. That afternoon the two men met. MacDonald's message: Time was running out for Germany. According to MacDonald, the mood in France was suddenly turning uglier. There was talk about "partitioning Germany and making up for what was left undone in Versailles."[36]

He pleaded with Schacht to convince Hitler to do something—exactly what, MacDonald did not know—but *something* to avoid the possible dismemberment of Germany. Schacht thanked MacDonald for the concern, but warned that such a dismemberment would not be accomplished as easily under Hitler as it was following Germany's war defeat. The Wizard tried to feign a facade of strength and courage, but as he boarded the vessel for the return trip to Europe, he had indeed concluded that the Jewish question was destroying Germany's interests in America. Only after intervening days of transatlantic solitude did Schacht compose an urgent cable to Chancellor Hitler informing him of the unsuccessful dinner with Jewish leaders and MacDonald's dire warning that France and others were entertaining the notion of dismantling Germany forever.[37]

14. Mr. Sam Cohen's Deal

GERMANY'S destitute foreign-currency situation, aggravated so severely by the Jewish-led boycott, had a swift impact on the Zionist currency exemption. The exemption had been approved to defuse the boycott, increase

German exports, and generate more foreign currency for the Reich. But the anti-Hitler boycott was as virulent as ever and expanding daily. Palestine itself, which stood to gain a windfall from the exemption, was as active in the boycott as any nation. Ironically, despite Nazi hatred for Jews, Jewish Palestine was vital to the German economic strategy.

At the turn of the century, when the Zionist movement was headquartered in Germany and its official language was German, Herzl and his circle looked to Kaiser Wilhelm as the logical sponsor of the Jewish State in Palestine. Herzl promised Imperial Germany a perpetual commercial and military outpost, as well as a colony of German culture in the Holy Land. From Jewish Palestine, the German Empire could anchor a highly desired sphere of influence in an undeveloped Mideast ripe with commodities and cheap labor, and equally in need of German merchandise. Jewish Palestine would be to Germany what India and Hong Kong were to England. In return, Kaiser Wilhelm was to persuade his ally, the Turkish sultan, to make Jewish Palestine a German protectorate. Although Herzl and the kaiser met twice in 1898 to consummate the arrangement, the kaiser ultimately withdrew his support.[1]

Although colonial status had not been arranged, Zionists continued to look to Germany for commercial, cultural, and political support. During the Great War, Britain enunciated the Balfour Declaration and similar pledges to various Arab potentates, intending to create local rebellions in the Turkish Mideast. Only the German government's intervention saved the Jewish population in Palestine from annihilation at the hands of the Turks, who suspected Zionists and Jews in general of favoring the Allied cause against Turkey.[2] (The same Turkish regime systematically slaughtered 1.5 million Armenians during the same years for many of the same political reasons.[3])

After Palestine was mandated to the British, Zionists switched allegiance to the United Kingdom. But extensive ties to Germany remained. In fact, during the postwar years, German leaders fashionably showed their support for Jewish nationalism through Germany's Pro Palestine Committee. A leading plank of this support pointed to Palestine's reliable place in German commercial and diplomatic recovery. This view prevailed right up to the Hitler ascendancy.[4]

Yet Palestine's importance to Germany was more vital after Hitler than before. In the decade since the Jewish Agency had been established, Jewish Palestine had flourished, even amid a worldwide Depression. While this tiny corner of the Mideast by 1933 accounted for only 0.1 percent of Germany's overall exports, it was a disproportionately important customer for certain vital Reich industries such as fertilizer, farm equipment, and irrigation pipes.[5] Far beyond its own consumption, however, Palestine was now the crucial gateway to expanding German exports throughout the emerging Mideast market: Egypt, Iraq, Lebanon, Syria, North Africa. This market was deemed essential by the Reich if certain strategic raw materials Hitler craved for war were to be acquired via bilateral trade agreements.

But the *Yishuv*—that is, the Jewish population of Palestine—was not following the direction of the Zionist Organization leadership. Despite official Zionist calls to abstain from anti-Nazi activities so as not to jeopardize Zionism's commercial and political ties with Germany, the rank and file said no. As early as February 1933, Jewish newspapers in Palestine began urging a boycott, and merchants in great numbers complied. On March 27, the Revisionist newspaper *Doar HaYom* expressed the popular sentiment in a defiant editorial: "Listen Hitler," the Jews of Palestine will not display "criminal apathy." World Jewry, the paper predicted, would rise up "as one man" to boycott Germany. Palestine would set the example: "No German machines, no German textiles, no German films, no German medicines, no German books and newspapers will be bought."[6]

Official Zionist rejection of the anti-Nazi movement, which became public just before the April First action in Germany, changed the nature of the boycott in Palestine. It quickly became a grass-roots trend spreading *in spite of* Zionist leadership. Hence, it was no different from the boycott in America and many other countries. People wanted to boycott and fight. Leaders refused. Thus, in the days after April First, many Palestinian newspaper editorials—heavily influenced by Zionist institutions—became stunningly silent about the German situation. No longer was boycott advocated. Tel Aviv's Chamber of Commerce tried to keep its merchants in line by resolving against any boycott, insisting that world trade was too valuable to the continuing Palestine boom.[7]

Since mainstream Zionist officials refused to confront Hitler and insisted on continuing mutual trade, it was only logical that the Revisionists would assume the vanguard of protest. Revisionists—the followers of Vladimir Jabotinsky—rejected the Zionist Organization, advocated paramilitary Jewish self-defense, and pursued a maximalist territorial claim in Palestine. Their ranks were composed largely of East European Jews, especially Polish Jews. What Revisionists did around the world was often a direct reflection of Jewish activism in Poland. Naturally, Revisionists in Palestine agitated for an emotional, often violent, boycott of anything German.

In fact, in late March 1933, as the Zionist leadership's stance toward Hitler crowned a constellation of other Revisionist political grievances, Jabotinsky advocated an open break with the Zionist Organization. Since 1925, his Revisionist Union had enjoyed special dissenter status within the Zionist Organization. But now Jabotinsky was determined to lead his Revisionist Union toward an actual takeover at the coming Eighteenth Zionist Congress in Prague, scheduled for August 1933. However, when the Revisionist hierarchy gathered in Kattowice, Poland, in the last week of March, they could not agree on tactics; nor could they bring themselves, in the face of the Hitler threat, to abandon the Zionist Organization. Jabotinsky knew that the rank and file was with him. So, in an action that stunned the movement, Jabotinsky dissolved the entire Revisionist leadership structure, declaring he would lead by personal fiat.[8] In his fight to evict the existing Zionist leadership, the anti-Nazi boycott would be the single most visible arena of confrontation.

Doar HaYom, the Revisionist newspaper in Palestine, and Betar, the paramilitary Revisionist youth corps, were relentless. Tactics included public humiliation of businessmen trafficking in German goods, mass recruitment of boycott pledges from merchants, picket lines, disruptive demonstrations, and incessant editorials condemning those who traded with Hitler. Many thousands of dollars' worth of German orders were canceled in Tel Aviv and Jerusalem in the first days of April alone.[9]

Berlin clearly understood that much of Palestinian Jewry was in the forefront of the anti-Nazi boycott. By mid-April, Consul Heinrich Wolff was dismally reporting that the boycott was seriously damaging all German economic interests in the area. Many German businessmen in Palestine desperately sought to issue oaths repudiating Hitler's crusade; such oaths were useless. By May 1933, Consul Wolff informed Berlin that the boycott movement had made the crucial transition from a merchant-based protest to a consumer protest. The results: Agfa film sales, very poor. Of 626 physicians in Palestine, 452 were Jewish and no longer prescribing German medicines; German pharmaceutical houses were in ruin. No more German films were being screened; Ufa film distributors were devastated. Buying loyalties were abruptly transferred to Belgium, Holland, France, and Sweden, even when those products were more costly.[10]

The Zionist rank and file in Palestine were waging economic war against Hitler—with or without their leaders' permission.

An anti-Hitler Yishuv violently hostile to German merchandise was the accurate Nazi perception in Berlin when Chaim Arlosoroff arrived in early May—and when Mr. Sam Cohen arrived shortly thereafter. Acting separately, both men discovered that the precious Zionist currency exemption had been abrogated by the Germans. When the first German Jews approached Reich authorities seeking their special allotment of foreign currency—about RM 15,000 worth of British sterling—they were sent on bureaucratic runarounds, or told they could obtain only RM 10,000, a third shy of the equivalent needed to enter Palestine. Many who took what they could were nonetheless turned back at the border by Reich guards.[11]

Foreign exchange was essentially exhausted, and the Reich was about to suspend most of its external obligations. Currency Control director Hans Hartenstein had only granted the exemption on the promise of extra foreign currency flowing into Germany as a result of boosted German exports. Since the Jews had failed to keep their side of the bargain, the exemption was stricken.

Arlosoroff must have certainly been discouraged. After spending weeks to secure the cloak of authority for his visit to Germany, the deal was dead. Just as he feared, too much time had been wasted.

Actually, the deal was never really very alive. Georg Landauer, director of the ZVfD, knew as early as mid-April that the growth of the Jewish-led anti-Hitler movement had prompted the Reich to renege on the exemption. In an undated letter, sent sometime between April 14 and April 17, Landauer cautiously complained to Professor Brodetsky of the Zionist Organization in London that German Jews were receiving only two-thirds of the £1,000 needed to enter Palestine. If emigrants could not obtain "the minimum in accordance with Palestine immigration law," the currency exemption would not be workable, wrote Landauer. He asked Brodetsky to confirm again via the British whether the exemption was still formally in place.[12]

The British now found themselves being dragged in as the medium of negotiation—a role they did not want. And Brodetsky's overly thankful letter of April 13, 1933, to A.C.C. Parkinson, falsely identified the British as having won the exemption. Two days after receiving Brodetsky's letter, which also asked to publicize the exemption as a British deal, Parkinson telephoned the Foreign Office and explained the situation. A Foreign Office functionary commented, "Professor Brodetsky needs careful watching, as he is only too anxious to maneuver His Majesty's Government into acting or appearing to act as the protectors of the Jews in general in foreign countries and not merely of those Jews who possess British or Palestinian nationality." Parkinson drafted a response explictly denying that the British were involved in the currency concession. He added that since Nazis were paranoid about foreign interference, "from the point of view of the Jews in Germany, it would seem wiser not to suggest that a concession had been made as the result of representations from abroad."[13]

But just after Brodetsky received Parkinson's denial, Landauer's new request came in. So Parkinson was asked to verify again whether the currency exemption was formally in place. In view of the crisis, Parkinson reluctantly agreed to once more ask the British embassy in Berlin to make inquiries.[14] But at this stage, inquiries were useless. The one common ground between Germans and Jews—emigration to Palestine—had become off-limits because the boycott of German goods had dried up the essential lubricant of any deal: money.

Only money could reopen the dialogue between Zionists and Nazis. Here Arlosoroff, the planner, could only fail. But Mr. Sam Cohen, the doer, could possibly succeed. While Arlosoroff slowly struggled to conceive a legally valid plan, Sam Cohen quickly presented the Reich with a marks and pfennigs proposal Germany would find irresistible.

Cohen started by retaining attorney Siegfried Moses. Moses was experienced in government as the postwar food controller of Danzig. He was active in Jewish communal affairs as director of the Jewish Workers Aid Society in Berlin until 1923. And he was attuned to business as the former manager of the prominent Schocken department store in Zwickau. Moses had one other important credential. He was president of the German Zionist Federation.[15]

So while Chaim Arlosoroff was in Berlin on behalf of the Jewish Agency, Sam Cohen would be able to pose as the official emissary of Zionism. And who in the Third Reich would doubt him when Siegfried Moses, president of the ZVfD, stood at Cohen's side? This kind of window dressing was exactly why Cohen hired Moses.[16]

The ZVfD leadership—Landauer and Moses—"allowed" Cohen to usurp the negotiations, believing that the official international Zionist bodies were politically inert. German Zionism needed a pragmatic, resourceful person who could quickly, without consulting anyone, consummate a deal with the Reich; someone who could speak the language of the Reich—a language now dominated by the nouns of commerce. The Reich, unaware of the charade, would believe they were dealing with the official Zionist movement. But they would in fact be negotiating bilateral trade and emigration with a single man.

In early May 1933, that man, Sam Cohen, returned to the two senior bureaucrats who had originally granted him the currency exemption in late March: Foreign Currency Control director Hans Hartenstein, and Hans Schmidt-Roelke of the Foreign Ministry's Eastern desk. In his new meetings, Cohen told them about Hanotaiah Ltd., which bought land from Arabs and sold it to Jewish settlement groups for orchard development. Cohen explained his company's impressive activities, which included vast imports of pipes, fertilizers, and other agricultural items—all traditionally purchased from Czechoslovakia, with eager sources in Yugoslavia and Italy bidding for the business.[17]

Then there were the key issues of liquidation and emigration. Any emigrant, Aryan or Jewish, was subject to several currency regulations. Once a German emigrant liquidated his assets—stocks, bonds, property—those reichmarks were frozen as sperrmarks in a blocked bank account. The émigré would then automatically forfeit 25 percent of the account to the Reich Flight Tax, the standard government claim on the assets of any German emigrant. This left 75 percent of the emigrant's assets intact. Of this 75 percent sum, the Emigrant Advisory Office would recommend how much could be removed and/or converted into foreign currency to satisfy a receiver nation's entry requirements. This allowance was generally 200 to 500 reichmarks—under $200. The remainder of his holdings were left behind, still frozen in a German bank as sperrmarks.[18]

But there were ways to transfer the value of these sperrmarks out of Germany. It was a bit convoluted, but very much in practice by emigrants and foreign businesses. Essentially, the owner of the blocked marks would swap his sperrmarks for someone else's foreign currency in another country. The swap was always at a loss to the owner of the sperrmarks. Potential swappers or buyers were usually foreign businesses in Germany wanting cheap reichmarks. International manufacturing companies, oil firms, and banks were typical foreign buyers. But whoever bought sperrmarks could pay for them only outside Germany, usually with foreign currency reposing in a bank in Amsterdam, London, or Paris. German banks regularly sold sperrmarks by this method. No merchandise transactions were necessary because the prospect of a cheap reichmark was inducement enough.[19]

In practice, then, if a German citizen decided to emigrate, he would sell off all his assets, realizing, say, RM 100,000, equal to $33,000. That entire RM 100,000 would be deposited in a blocked account, and automatically suffer a 25 percent Flight Tax. Of the RM 75,000 that remained, the emigrant would be allowed to take with him only a few hundred reichmarks, which would be converted to francs, dollars, or whatever currency was needed to satisfy immigrant entry requirements. The emigrant would then own just under RM 75,000 in a blocked German account he could no longer spend. Before departing Germany, he would go to a bank and offer to sell his sperrmarks to the highest bidder. A foreign buyer would be found, offering perhaps RM 60,000 for the 75,000 sperrmarks, paying with the equivalent in foreign currency from a foreign bank account. If agreed, the two would simply swap bank accounts. Thus, the foreign buyer would purchase RM 75,000 marks for the foreign equivalent of RM 60,000. And the emigrant would have successfully transferred his money out of Germany, albeit at a loss of about 20 percent after discounts to the buyer and bank commissions. After delays of perhaps months, the transaction would be complete.

Aware of sperrmark transfer techniques, Sam Cohen started dealing. First, find a way to generate enough foreign currency for the German Jewish emigrant to enter Palestine; this amount was £1,000. Then, transfer additional amounts of the emigrant's money to help develop Jewish Palestine, which would be the only allowable destination for the transferred cash.

Under Sam Cohen's plan, the money would never really leave Germany. Instead, Hanotaiah Ltd. would shift its purchases of farm equipment from Czech to German exporters. These German exporters would be paid with reichmarks from the blocked emigrant accounts. When the equipment was sold for pounds sterling in Palestine or elsewhere in the Mideast, Hanotaiah would find some way to compensate the emigrant for the sperrmarks used to pay for the equipment. This compensation would not necessarily be cash. It might be *value*—giving the emigrant some orchard land, some agricultural equipment, or a farmhouse. Naturally, Hanotaiah Ltd. alone would determine the "value" of the land or equipment and how much of it equaled the £1,000 needed to enter Palestine.[20]

In summary, Sam Cohen's complicated transfer procedure called for the

German Jews' assets to be frozen in special blocked accounts of which the emigrant could convert RM 15,000 into £1,000 to gain entry to Palestine. But instead of actually receiving the RM 15,000 or £1,000, the emigrant would receive land or equipment that Hanotaiah Ltd. said was "worth" RM 15,000 or £1,000. This would technically satisfy British immigration requirements. The prospect of Hanotaiah inflating the true value of land, equipment, or farm buildings to artificially equal the RM 15,000 was obvious. Herzl had in fact predicted that Jewish wealth could be transferred by assigning an inflated value to land that had been acquired without cost or quite cheaply. Compared to Germany's standard of living, Jewish Palestine's boom was still a primitive economy where labor could be found for a few pounds daily, where simple domiciles could be erected for well under £100.[21] Cohen's scheme promised massive windfalls for Hanotaiah and good business for Germany, as the emigrants' assets were divided between Zionism and the Third Reich—in the Reich's favor.

Cohen's idea seemed credible to the Germans. By linking the purchase of German goods to the settling of German Jews in Palestinian orchards and the circuitous capitalization of the Jewish national home, the anti-Nazi boycott could now be broken. The Zionist movement would be obliged not only to refrain from and oppose any boycott, they would be obliged to aggressively sponsor German exports. Moreover, the systematic egress of German Jews would create vast pools of blocked marks that Germany could use to pay debts. Sam Cohen's deal was more than business; it was brilliance. Every German pipe sold, every German chemical purchased, every pound of foreign currency earned contributed toward another dunam and another citizen for Eretz Yisrael. At the same time, every economic or diplomatic knife slash at Hitler merely lacerated the hopes for a Zionist solution. The deal carried abundant political and economic incentive for the Reich.

And the deal was good for Zionism. Once the emigrant arrived in Palestine, possibly penniless, he was essentially obliged to work the land to stay alive. Hence, middle-class German Jews would be steered to Jewish agriculture in the Promised Land.

This cashless transfer did resemble a twentieth-century update of indentured servitude, but the Zionists, needing money to purchase land and men to work it, were committed to social engineering and occupational retraining. Philosophically, they were devoted to converting the Jews from merchants and bankers in Europe into farmers and laborers in Eretz Yisrael.

This goal was also acceptable under Nazi theory, which sought German Jewry's expulsion to their own land in Palestine and their conversion to occupations detached from international commerce. In effect, the Zionist ideal and Sam Cohen's offer were exactly what the Nazis had in mind.

Hitler and von Neurath were waiting at the Wilhelmstrasse government complex the morning of May 11, 1933. In walked Britain's Ambassador Sir Horace Rumbold. Rumbold tried to defuse the urgent atmosphere by explaining his request for an audience as a formality with each new chancellor. Hitler brushed aside this explanation, declaring that statesmen outside Germany could not understand what was happening inside the Third Reich. The Poland situation was a bad problem, said Hitler, a problem created by the Versailles Peace Conference. Hitler wanted the Polish Corridor moved east so Germany could absorb the territory now occupied by the Corridor. Otherwise, tension between Poland and Germany would remain.[22]

Hitler abruptly turned to Germany's massive unemployment. He vowed he would not allow the Aryan work force to become deteriorated and demoralized. Labor conscription—drafting an essentially unpaid work force to engage in great public works—was the only solution. Suddenly, switching topics again, Hitler identified Marxism as the party's great target. Marxism would be destroyed. Der Führer did not directly refer to Marxism as a Jewish movement, but there was no doubt in Rumbold's mind whom he meant.[23]

Rumbold kept trying to get a word in during Hitler's ramblings. Finally, the ambassador was able to speak, and he brought up the treatment of Jews under National Socialism. No sooner had Rumbold uttered the words than Hitler became excited, working up to a trancelike state. Der Führer stood up as though addressing thousands in a stadium. "I will never agree," he shouted with sweeping oratorical gestures, "to the existence of two kinds of law for German nationals. There is an immense amount of unemployment in Germany, and I have . . . to turn away youths of pure German stock from the high schools. There are not enough posts for purebred Germans, and the Jews must suffer with the rest!"[24]

Hitler warned the world in the presence of his imaginary throng, "If the Jews engineer a boycott of German goods from abroad, I will take care that this hits the Jews in Germany!"[25] It was as though the moment were filled with cries of mass adulation, as though the swelling fury of the crowd itself were fueling Hitler's verbal violence, as though he could see the scores of thousands with their white palms exposed in a rhythmic Nazi salute, producing ear-splitting roars of *"Seig Heil, Seig Heil."*[26]

But the room was empty. Except for Hitler, von Neurath, and Rumbold. When suddenly the imaginary crowd seemed to dematerialize before Hitler's eyes, and not before, a frightened Rumbold tried to calm the chancellor by claiming that the anti-German boycott placards had probably already been removed from the store windows of London's East End. Rumbold wanted to mention that foreign boycott or not, German Jews were German nationals as much as anyone else, and entitled to the full protection of law. But he was afraid to rekindle Hitler's maniacal flame.[27]

In a somewhat milder manner, Hitler then unexpectedly brought up Palestine. He zeroed in on Jewish immigration policy, telling Rumbold that he understood that Jews wishing to settle there could not gain entry unless in possession of £1,000. Hitler thought this was a good idea. If Germany had required such a financial test for the East European Jews who had settled in Germany since the Great War, there would now be no Jewish question facing the Reich. But without such a requirement, Hitler declared, lower-class, impoverished Eastern Jews had brought in every form of disease and caused rampant demoralization.[28]

Hitler, now totally calmed down, told Rumbold that Germany knew how valuable a good relationship with England was. Rumbold answered cautiously—and Hitler did not seem provoked—that no country, especially a great country, could live in today's world "in isolation surrounded by a Chinese wall." Hitler agreed. Rumbold cautiously continued, explaining that the economic, trade, and even internal policy of one country necessarily caused reactions in other nations. Still no flare-up. Rumbold, still cautious, acknowledged that the treatment of German Jews might be described as "internal affairs" by Germany. But the reactions to that policy—no matter how Germany described them—were clear. In England, Germany was forfeiting the sympathy gained during recent years.[29]

As Rumbold took his leave, Adolf Hitler seemed more reasonable. Rumbold couldn't help thinking that although he was speaking to a fanatic beyond the reach of reason, the meeting had ended on pleasant terms.[30] Rumbold did not know it, but the spontaneous comments of this interview would echo for seven years as Hitler's policy toward Palestine.

On May 11, other Reich leaders were equally worried about the international economic backlash. Economics Minister Alfred Hugenberg, one of the non-Nazi cabinet members still in power, issued a "Decree for the Protection of the Retail Trade," exempting Jewish retailers and certain others from recent sweeping anti-Semitic regulations. Hence, any international boycott of German merchandise would also affect Jewish businessmen. And, in desperation, many German export corporations were actually dismissing their Christian employees stationed abroad and replacing them with Jews.[31] The hope was that somehow world Jewry might then lessen its campaign.

But boycott organizations only continued to gain strength and support. The newly founded American League for the Defense of Jewish Rights and the Jewish War Veterans had finally begun large-scale organizing. And boycott groups in Poland, France, and England were making plans to create a common international front.[32]

By mid-April, the effects were dramatic. England had already supplanted Germany as the single largest exporter to Denmark and Norway, two of Germany's leading customers. Reich sales to Finland were drastically down. Many U.S. stores found merchandise labeled "Made in Germany" virtually unsalable. American retailers urgently sought alternative suppliers in Japan,

Czechoslovakia, and England, especially for glassware, toys, china, and sausage. Competitor countries happily rushed in to reap the boycott's benefits.[33]

Total Reich exports were down 10 percent in April. That initial decline was limited because of many unexpired contracts. Reich economic sources were convinced the May figures would be calamitous. With roughly half the German workforce employed by just 2 percent of the companies in Germany, the successful boycotting of even a limited number of cartel industries would be disastrous. Food prices in Berlin were already reflecting the concern, bread and other items escalating 4 percent weekly.[34]

Meanwhile, Germany's border crisis grew hour by hour. Poland's proinvasion military hawks found widespread support among a population inflamed by Jewish boycott committees. Czechoslovakia's known pro-Zionist stance and her readiness to join a preemptive strike only intensified German nervousness about her eastern border.[35] By May 11, the invasion threat had doubled, because France was consumed by what Reich officials called "war fever," fueled by boycott committees and the press.[36]

Events were culminating. The destruction of Hitler's tenuous regime—from without or within—loomed as the crisis of the hour in Berlin. German officials and corporate leaders had been dispatched to the cities of Europe and America to try to blunt the attack. Their efforts were unsuccessful. Government clarifications, token protective decrees and threats of unrestrained retaliation against German Jews were also unsuccessful.

Hitler had sworn never to compromise with the enemy. But with bankruptcy and invasion at the door, the discussions with Sam Cohen intensified. Hjalmar Schacht was in America at the time. So the contact point was the Foreign Currency Control Office headed by Hans Hartenstein.

The struggling Reich believed that developing Palestine as a springboard for crucial trade with the Middle East was a desirable thing, as was the organized emigration of Germany's Jews. But desirable as those things were, all of them might somehow be achieved without Sam Cohen and the Zionists—or at least they could be achieved on Germany's own timetable. However, if the boycott continued much longer, there might be no future for National Socialism. The main question was whether the Zionists could really intervene, not only in the boycott, but also in the anti-Nazi protest movement that was flaming a war fever among Germany's neighbors.

Perhaps so. Even though the Nazis and the Zionists were enemies, the two now needed each other.

On May 12, Sam Cohen was already in the Polish industrial town of Lodz, where he was born and raised, and where he had commercial and political connections among mainstream Zionists, Revisionists, and other Jewish circles.[37] While Cohen was in Poland, the German Zionist Federation found itself in a complicated position. Landauer and his colleagues had originally conceived the transfer concept in mid-March. That was when they called upon the services of Cohen to negotiate the original currency exemption. The exemption procedures were to be worked out secretly as a *fait accompli* by Chaim Arlosoroff on behalf of an ad hoc Zionist combine led by German Zionists. But in April it had become painfully clear to Landauer and his ally in Jerusalem, David Werner Senator, that Arlosoroff, working officially, could not engineer the mammoth task entrusted to him—the organized transfer of an entire society. So they turned once more to Sam Cohen to travel to Berlin and negotiate, as though he were the representative of the international Zionist movement. In fact he was representing no more than Landauer's ad hoc faction. The authentic envoy, Arlosoroff, was also in Berlin, believing he would arrange the transfer. He was unaware, however, that the German Zionists had decided to consummate the agreement via Cohen.

The convoluted intrigue played Cohen and Arlosoroff against each other, depending upon the changing perception of which man could deliver the fastest results. But by mid-May, Landauer was losing his tenuous control over the situation. Because Landauer felt Sam Cohen's deal would turn German emigrants into modern-day indentured servants, he tried to manipulate Cohen out of the negotiations and bring Arlosoroff back in.[38] However, without Cohen, Landauer was uncertain exactly how to reestablish communication with the Reich. One idea advanced to Arlosoroff suggested that he contact his old schoolmate Magda Friedlander, whose stepfather was Jewish. Magda and Arlosoroff had been friends during their youth. Magda could now be immensely valuable. She was after all the wife of Paul Joseph Goebbels. But Arlosoroff refused. He had heard that his onetime friend was now among the most rabid Nazi fraus in Germany. Once she had even thrown white mice from a balcony to disrupt a pacifist film.[39]

Landauer and Arlosoroff found themselves in a political doldrum. Unable even to approach the government, they confined their activities to studious deliberations on the fine points of any future plan. Would it conform to international law? Could other countries, even the League of Nations, guarantee or oversee the operation? These theoretical details were put into memos and discussed between them. But their ideas never reached the German government.[40]

Even as Landauer and Arlosoroff hypothesized, the boycott was undeniably reaching into Germany in ever more destructive ways. On May 12, for example, the prestigious Leipzig annual fur auction was held. Ninety percent of the world's fur industry was in Jewish hands, and French, Dutch, British, and American furriers boycotted the event totally. Reich sources admitted that the entire auction was a failure as $3 million worth of furs were withdrawn for lack of buyers.[41]

A decision had to be made, and only Hitler could make it. An accommodation—a deal—with the Jews would be necessary. Their weapons of economic retaliation and political agitation were devastating Germany. If those weapons could be neutralized long enough for Germany to recover economically, to rearm its military, then all glories would be within reach of the Aryan people.

A deal made perfect sense, for all the known reasons. Unemployment, foreign currency, raw materials, economic recovery, political rehabilitation, military rearmament. Those were the logical reasons. Yet Hitler had always defiantly resisted logical reasons, and he undoubtedly could have continued resisting them until the Reich broke apart. Adolf Hitler was not a servant of logic. He was, after all, the man who in 1945 fought until the last minute in his concrete cloister and even then chose to destroy his own life and scorch Germany with it rather than capitulate. So what then compelled der Führer to acquiesce to the logical dictates of the crisis? It could well have been his own madness.

In his conversation on May 11 with Sir Horace Rumbold, the British had the outlandish nerve to lecture him, Adolf Hitler, on the correct treatment of the Jews—even though, in Hitler's mind, the British themselves, like the rest of the world, indeed recognized the Jews were parasites. Had the British not erected financial barriers to keep the foul, impoverished Eastern Jews out of Palestine? On May 11, Hitler pointed out to Ambassador Rumbold that had Germany erected such financial barriers, the Eastern Jews would never have migrated into the Reich. But Rumbold did not see the validity of Hitler's claim. In Hitler's mind, they were all hypocrites.[42] Very well, he would see how well England liked the very Jews they were pretending to be concerned about.

Adolf Hitler would arrange for those very "disease-carrying" and "demoralizing" Eastern Jews to flow out of Germany and into British Palestine. He would give them the financial wherewithal to overcome British financial barriers, or for that matter the financial barriers of the United States or any other country. Der Führer revealed this attitude just a few days later to Bernard Ridder, publisher of a New York-based German-American newspaper, *Staats-Zeitung*. In the interview, Hitler confessed he would "gladly pay their [the Jews'] freight to the U.S. and make them a present of a bank account in addition if America would only harbor them."[43] For years, Hitler would continue to harp on this theme: The British didn't want the Jews, otherwise why would they establish a £1,000 Palestinian entry requirement that Jews obviously could not meet? And yet Britain and the other nations maintaining financial requisites for immigrants were constantly assailing him. They could conveniently do so behind their £1,000 protective shields.[44]

Hitler would play a racial trick on the British. He would give them the Jews they sought so self-righteously to protect.

And so, as compelling as the logic, was the madness. Quite probably it was that very fleeting moment of madness that made it easier for Hitler to do the logical thing for the illogical reason.

On May 13, 1933, the German Zionists were still perfecting theories, still wondering how to approach the government. Arlosoroff was studying a short, six-point memorandum from Landauer, suggesting the Zionists "offer the German government a large influx of foreign currency to create a basis for negotiations about assisting in emigration." The emigration would be linked to massive land acquisition based on transferred German Jewish assets. But suddenly Siegfried Moses, ZVfD president, still listed as Sam Cohen's solicitor, was contacted by the Foreign Currency Control office. The message was brief: Sam Cohen's deal is accepted.[45]

What Sam Cohen deal? Dissatisfied with his cashless version of transfer, Landauer had cut Cohen out of the negotiations. How was it that the Economics Ministry was now signaling the acceptance of a deal with Sam Cohen?

Siegfried Moses, to avoid prejudicing whatever was happening, simply telegraphed the information to Cohen in Poland, in care of the firm Ben Mazur Brothers, 46 Poludniowa Street in Lodz: "MINISTRY INFORMED TODAY BASIC CONSENT REACHED."[46]

On May 19, the Reich economics minister directed a formal declaration to Sam Cohen of Hanotaiah Ltd., outlining the deal. Jewish emigrants would contact Hanotaiah and purchase real estate and agricultural equipment as Hanotaiah saw fit. Bearing the sales contract, the emigrant would then contact both the Emigrant Advisory Office and the Foreign Currency Control Office. The emigrant would then be allowed to exchange his blocked marks for Hanotaiah's land and equipment. No cash was involved unless the Emigrant Advisory Office specifically recommended it, and even then only "the absolute minimum necessary to establish a new existence" in Palestine. A case-by-case review would ensure the least possible release of foreign currency. In return, Hanotaiah would use the emigrant's sperrmarks for the "purchase of all kinds of [German] raw materials, pipes, iron constructions, agricultural machines, fertilizers, pumps, fertilizing machines, and chemicals." For the time being, up to 1 million reichmarks of purchases would be allowed. The Economics Ministry declaration cited "the previously held negotiations between Mr. Cohen and Ministry assistants" and Cohen's assurance "that the same goods until now were bought in Czechoslovakia, and now, because of the [new] regulation improving the position of the German Palestine emigrant, they are to be purchased in Germany."[47]

The German Zionists had constructed a maze of political intrigues. They had shifted their loyalties from Arlosoroff to Cohen to Arlosoroff. Unaware of the intrigues, Arlosoroff persisted in formulating a visionary *fait accompli*. But Cohen hadn't gone away. He had continued his ruse, negotiating on behalf of the Zionist movement—even though he represented nothing more than an orchard company.

Meanwhile, the German government felt certain it had triggered the breakup of the boycott because the Zionist movement would now be in the German export business. German Jewish wealth and emigrants would be transferred in a flow wholly dependent upon the purchase of German merchandise and commodities. The Jews of the world would now have to choose between fighting Hitler and building Palestine, preserving the old or securing the new.

Sam Cohen's deal was, in fact, only the preliminary agreement. When discovered by the international Zionist hierarchy, it would be considered inadequate, delivering too little money and too narrow a variety of merchandise to Jewish Palestine. If the Jewish State was to be built, it needed more than Hanotaiah's transactions, more than the sale of a few dunams of orchards. It needed the building blocks of a new society—everything from taxis to bridges. And it needed more than the mere transferred value of a million reichmarks; it needed a sizable portion—in cash—of the billions that constituted German Jewish wealth. The result of a broadened transfer would be more than the expansion of Hanotaiah's few settlements, it would be the expansion of *all* settlements, and the towns and villages, into an economically, geographically, and politically cohesive state—Israel. A massive, historically irreversible agreement was sought—a final solution to the persecution of Jews.

The plan was not a rescue or a relief project. If it was, the Zionists would have labored for an agreement for Jews fleeing Germany without regard to *where* they sought refuge. Instead, Jews would be allowed to bring assets out of Germany to rebuild their lives, but only if they liquidated their European existence and rebuilt those lives in Palestine.

The correct word, then, for Mr. Sam Cohen's deal, and the arrangements to follow, was not *rescue*. It was not *relief*. It was in fact *transfer*—the point between the philosophical spheres where Zionist and Nazi circles touched.

15. Judgment on the Sand

EVEN BEFORE Sam Cohen's deal was verbally accepted by the Reich Economics Ministry on May 13, 1933, it became impossible to confine knowledge of the secret negotiations to a select few. German Zionist circles in Germany and Jerusalem were aware of developments, as were key Zionist leaders in London, including Weizmann, Rutenberg, and Professor Brodetsky. And in late April, the Jewish Agency Executive Committee finally learned of the project. Who knew how much, and at what point during the first hush-hush weeks of negotiations, created a chaotic scenario.

For instance, Sam Cohen was still in Poland when Siegfried Moses received word on May 13 of the Reich Economics Ministry's acceptance.[1] So the German Zionists were unaware of the height or breadth of the deal, although they probably suspected it might include Hanotaiah.

After Sam Cohen first secured the currency exemption in late March 1933, he quickly convinced the Reich to link an emigrant's currency grant to the purchase or attempt to purchase orchard acreage from Hanotaiah. Cohen did this without the ZVfD's permission.[2] The Emigrant Advisory Office had agreed to the linkage because they were guarding against citizens removing currency from Germany for merely a temporary stay abroad. A good-faith attempt to purchase acreage from Hanotaiah was a reasonable indicator of an emigrant's sincere intent to relocate permanently.[3]

Reich recognition made Hanotaiah the "preferred" Palestine land broker and transfer authority for German Jews. But Hanotaiah was unacceptable to the ZVfD because its transaction terms left little choice of relocation or cash for German Jews. ZVfD director Georg Landauer was originally able to thwart the Reich's Hanotaiah requirement by encouraging individual emigrants to protest the condition or substitute another Palestinian land broker in place of Hanotaiah. Landauer had thought this effectively cut Hanotaiah out.[4]

But Landauer soon learned that Hanotaiah was back in the arrangement. Cohen briefed Landauer on the new arrangement sometime between May 14 and May 17. From Cohen's description, Landauer suspected that Hanotaiah was no longer just the "preferred" land broker but the chartered company entrusted with the future of German Jewish emigrants. Cohen was bluntly told his monopoly was out of the question. He tried to reassure the German Zionists that Hanotaiah actually held no monopoly, but the ZVfD leadership was not convinced. They insisted Cohen issue a formal disavowal of any monopoly to the Reich. Cohen answered that he had already made that point perfectly clear during negotiations.[5]

The Economics Ministry's official May 19 confirmation of Sam Cohen's deal was delivered to Siegfried Moses, who was still listed as Cohen's solicitor. Landauer studied the document but found no indication of a Hanotaiah monopoly. He concluded that Cohen's deal was in fact a limited arrangement between the German government and a private Palestinian company that would not obstruct the official Zionist bodies from negotiating the larger transfer Arlosoroff was still formulating.[6]

The same day, May 19, Arlosoroff finalized his transfer ideas. The grandiose project was outlined in a personal memo marked TOP SECRET. The centerpiece of the plan was a "Liquidation Bank." Rutenberg had originally talked of a liquidation *company*, but ownership of the company had become a political issue, and Arlosoroff was now convinced the solution was a publicly supervised transfer, not a privately controlled migration. Arlosoroff's Liquidation Bank would be internationally recognized, probably under the aegis of the League of Nations. Relying on Weizmann's good relations with both the British government and Mussolini, Arlosoroff proposed that the bank's funding be secured by joint British-Italian sponsorship with international Jewish contributions. Merchandise would of course be the nexus between Germany and the Zionists.[7]

In fact, Arlosoroff's May 19 transfer plan was essentially the same as Sam Cohen's deal, with two basic improvements. First, German exports would not be limited to agricultural wares. Any German product or commodity would be included. Arlosoroff's memo listed items as varied as automobiles, building materials, dyes, and pharmaceuticals.[8] His thought was not just the expansion of orchards, but the creation of a thriving urban and rural society.

Second, Arlosoroff's transfer would not be cashless. Emigrants would receive their £1,000 entrance money in hand, and then transfer an *additional* sum that would be used in trust by Zionist institutions to develop the country. This additional money was essential. Thousands of Jews could not be suddenly transferred to primitive Palestine without the roads, schools, hospitals, ports, and other fundamentals of a twentieth-century nation. Many of these had to be constructed virtually from scratch. Arlosoroff's Liquidation Bank would take over the blocked assets of German Jews, use them to pay for German exports, sell them in Palestine, and give proceeds of the first £1,000 to the immigrant, minus a small percent for administration.[9] Transferred cash beyond the first £1,000 would be invested in infrastructure. In this way, Palestine would receive the maximum merchandise and investment capital. The Jewish immigrant would receive the maximum cash.

In addition, Arlosoroff's May 19 memo listed Germany's inducements: a gateway to the Middle East market, increased employment, and the foreign-currency opportunities of unhindered exports. Moreover, the Zionist transfer would be seen as the minimum of "fair play" toward German Jewry that Western leaders had publicly called for in recent days. Thus, Hitler could both remove the Jews and be recognized as assisting in their national aspirations.[10] Arlosoroff's memo demanded all Jewish "sentimentality" about negotiating with the Nazis be rejected. Emotionalism, he argued, would not gain Jews their homeland.[11]

But Arlosoroff appended one important stipulation to his memo. German Jewish transfer must be wholly voluntary. This was a mandamus from Herzl. The Jewish State awaited only those who would ascend to it: Emigration was *aliya*, the Hebrew word for ascent. No Jew would be forced to liquidate his German existence.[12] Arlosoroff's plan combined the best elements of international law, bribery, and freedom of choice. All his hypothesizing had created a workable transfer, guaranteed by law and motivated by self-interest.

When Arlosoroff completed his top-secret memo on May 19, he was unaware that the Reich had already agreed to Sam Cohen's deal. When apprised of the unexpected development, probably that same day, Arlosoroff did not agree with Landauer's assumption that Cohen's pact was a limited deal. Arlosoroff believed it was *the* deal. But they were all still guessing. Cohen himself could not be located in Berlin to explain, because on May 19 Cohen had suddenly surfaced in London.[13]

Arlosoroff had to move quickly lest a man and his orchard company supplant the entire international Zionist movement and seize control of the fate of the Jewish nation.

His first task was to circulate word that the official proposal of Zionism was in the hands of Chaim Arlosoroff, head of the Political Department of the Jewish Agency—not Sam Cohen, orchard broker. More important, transfer must provide emigrants with as much of their cash as possible and Palestine with as many building materials as possible. On May 20, in a wide-ranging interview with Robert Weltsch, editor of the ZVfD's *Juedische Rundschau*, Arlosoroff detailed all the proposals of his plan, which only twenty-four hours earlier had been marked TOP SECRET.[14]

The interview was printed in the *Rundschau's* May 24 edition. In it, Arlosoroff pinpointed the problem for Jews. They no longer needed refuges, asylums, or other temporary solutions to their persecution. Jews needed an endpoint in their quest for self-determination. Palestine was this endpoint. There Jews would find the glory of self-imposed struggle. After the struggle they would find agrarian opportunities if they chose, industrial opportunities if they chose—whatever they chose, for the choosing would now be free from anti-Jewish decrees or concessions from on high. Through liquidation, Jews would achieve independence—for the first time in 2,000 years.[15]

"This leads me to a central question . . . the liquidation of capital and holdings belonging to German Jewish emigrants," Arlosoroff explained in the article. "There appears to be no way out for people whose fortune exceeds the amount of foreign currency normally permitted . . . under present laws. . . . It makes no sense to ignore it or to think that it can be solved without an agreement with the German government. . . . The only way out is to . . . provide a benefit to both parties."[16]

Nazi censors ordered the newspaper seized. The Reich Press Office routinely suppressed troublesome editions and sometimes closed publications down altogether. In this case, the first for *Juedische Rundschau*, the edition was merely confiscated.[17] No reason was given, but that same day, to clarify matters, the Reich Foreign Ministry transmitted a written guideline to the British embassy, ostensibly in response to their earlier inquiries regarding the original currency exemption.[18] The Reich specified: "The emigrant must first of all give convincing evidence of his serious intention to transfer his domicile abroad *permanently* [Reich emphasis], and must produce a certificate from the Emigrant Advisory Office that his proposals are economically realizable and that the capital which he wishes to take with him is of suitable amount for beginning a new existence abroad." [19] The reference—without naming it—was to Sam Cohen's cashless or near cashless orchard settlement scheme. An accompanying message warned that publicity be strictly avoided. Whatever cash German Jews were allowed would severely burden monetary reserves, and if too many emigrants applied, the intensified fiscal strain would force a curtailment of the entire arrangement. [20]

The Nazis had effectively muffled Arlosoroff. So Arlosoroff left the country to promote the position that a Jewish exodus from Germany should guarantee as many emigrant assets as possible. Arlosoroff went to Prague, where on May 25 he urged an audience to act unemotionally for the benefit of Germany's Jews and indeed the entire Jewish people. The most pressing issue, he told them, was the immediate transfer of German Jewish youth. "We do not want them to become psychic cripples." Second in line, Arlosoroff said, should be laborers from ages seventeen to twenty-two, who would build and cultivate for a dramatic national expansion. Then would come the settlers, rural and urban. These new settlers, the commercial and agrarian lifeblood of the nation-to-be, should not be exploited by competitive and unviable programs—a reference to Sam Cohen's deal. Instead, Jews should pool their resources in a single *officially sanctioned* program. That program would have to include German merchandise. Undoubtedly, many in the crowd were boycott advocates, but he urged them to be realistic and understand that Jewish assets must be made liquid and transferable. And this would require an understanding with the German government that would hinge on exports. This theme was repeated in a public address in Warsaw on May 27 and in newspaper interviews published in Europe and Palestine that week. [21]

Arlosoroff tried to circulate his notions as the true position of the Zionist movement. But with a secret deal already ratified by the German government, Sam Cohen was far ahead of him. And Cohen was now in England, making arrangements with the rest of the Zionist hierarchy. Enough speeches had been made. Arlosoroff hurried to London.

In London, Mr. Sam Cohen had been very busy. On May 19, shortly after his arrival, Cohen telephoned Martin Rosenbluth, the German Zionist dispatched to London by Goering to stop the anti-Hitler movement. Rosenbluth was now stationed in London as the Zionist Organization's liaison with the ZVfD. Cohen briefed Rosenbluth on the deal and asked for an immediate meeting to discuss its implementation, but warned that Landauer and company were extremely dissatisfied with the arrangement. However, after hearing Cohen's preliminary explanations, Rosenbluth was convinced that Landauer must be sorely mistaken. Cohen's deal seemed fine, especially in light of the Jewish Agency quarrels and sniping, which prevented any decisive action in April. So just after he hung up, Rosenbluth dashed off a short note to Landauer reminding him that German Zionists had received reports of the squabbling in Jerusalem and London, and perhaps Cohen's deal was not so bad.[22]

During the next several days, Cohen explained the lucrative potential of his deal to the Zionist Executive Committee in London. Seeking to broaden the benefits, the Zionist Executive urged him to submit his private agreement to "national control." That would mean sharing the agreement with the official land-settlement firms such as Yakhin, owned by the Mapai-controlled Histadrut workers organization. Cohen agreed. The Executive then asked him to return at once to Palestine to personally handle negotiations between Hanotaiah, Yakhin, and other companies. They promised the Jewish Agency's full support and gave him a letter of authority dated May 30, 1933: "The Executive Committee has taken note of your agreement with the German Ministry of Economics and would be gratified if you were successful in bringing about an agreement for joint implementation of the plan between Hanotaiah, Yakhin, and other appropriate societies. We are pleased that you agree with the idea of national supervision for this project."[23] By relying on Cohen, the Zionist Organization preserved its own deniability. If tumult arose over any deal with Hitler, they could just blame a private citizen acting alone.

Frustrated and travel-weary, Arlosoroff arrived in London on June 1, almost two weeks after Sam Cohen. The challenge facing Arlosoroff was to unravel the complicated arrangements Cohen had woven. At stake was a nearsighted business deal that would squander Zionism's one great chance, probably its last great chance, to bring the Jewish people en masse to Palestine.

Upon arrival, Arlosoroff went to Zionist headquarters at Great Russell Street for a conference with Nahum Sokolow, president of the Zionist Organization, Berl Locker of the Zionist Executive, David Werner Senator of the Jewish Agency Executive, and Martin Rosenbluth and Leo Herrmann of the ZVfD. Arlosoroff made his appeal. He began with an analysis of Zionism's precarious status in Germany and claimed the future was in the hands of young German Jewish leaders. The older leaders, such as Landauer, would be emigrating to Palestine in the near future. Arlosoroff called their abandonment of the work in Germany "deplorable," adding that they would be hard to replace.[24]

As to transfer, there was only one solution, argued Arlosoroff: an internationally guaranteed Liquidation Bank. Without it, Jewish assets in Germany would soon dwindle to nothing. Only personal savings and reserves were buffering the present misery. With those depleted, the narrow Jewish employment possiblities remaining in Germany would utterly pauperize the community. Moreover, German currency was so weak that the absence of international guarantees could collapse any system limited to reichmarks.[25]

Arlosoroff was sure that when German Jews discovered they could not remove large amounts of their money through Sam Cohen's deal, they would postpone emigrating to Palestine until they were destitute. In that case, their indispensable capital contribution would be squandered. Or they would resort to widespread smuggling. The Nazis would invariably catch many of the smugglers, and the Jews would suffer even worse. Without larger cash permits, the overwhelmingly non-Zionist German Jewish population would simply reject Palestine as a realistic option.[26]

The Executive Committee and the German Zionists heard Arlosoroff's compelling explanations. It was now a choice between Sam Cohen's deal or Chaim Arlosoroff's transfer. A long discussion ensued. Arlosoroff answered the questions persuasively. By meeting's end the decision was made: in favor of Arlosoroff.[27]

Arlosoroff was instructed to proceed to Jerusalem and establish an official institution to supervise the Liquidation Bank. Rosenbluth and Senator would coordinate the program in Berlin. Arlosoroff would control the entire operation.[28] There was no time to enjoy the triumph. With his instructions and authority clearly laid out in writing, Arlosoroff left the conference for a meeting across town with Colonial Secretary Cunliffe-Lister.

At 5:00 P.M. in an office at the stately House of Commons, Professor Brodetsky and Arlosoroff met Cunliffe-Lister and A.C.C. Parkinson. Speaking in a clear, forceful manner, Arlosoroff impressed upon Cunliffe-Lister that Jews were finished in Germany. Their only way out was his transfer plan: children first—this captured Cunliffe-Lister's sympathy the most; laborers second—Cunliffe-Lister understood the need for this advance group and was receptive to bending the immigration-certificate system to the emergency.[29]

Arlosoroff then began to explain how the transfer would work. The Liquidation Bank would gather in Jewish assets and use them to export German goods to Palestine. Cunliffe-Lister's facial expression changed. His reaction to a flood of German wares displacing British wares on the Palestinian market was as Professor Brodetsky feared. Cunliffe-Lister interrupted, "Where do we come in? You will be increasing German exports at our [British] expense."[30] Throughout all the secret meetings with Weizmann, Arlosoroff, and Arab leaders in Palestine during April, Cunliffe-Lister had been willing to cooperate on a glorious new plan for the area, a plan of binational self-determination that would solve a host of Arab and Jewish problems and produce a modern Jewish State in the process. There would be commerce, technology, and prosperity for all. Great Britain would reap the financial benefits, selling basic materials and consumer goods to a developing

Palestine. The notion of Germany replacing Britain as Palestine's greatest commercial partner had not even occurred to Cunliffe-Lister.

Arlosoroff tried to minimize Cunliffe-Lister's bad reaction. Perhaps the League of Nations, in overseeing the Liquidation Bank, could structure things so as not to harm British commercial interests. Cunliffe-Lister stopped the discussion cold and snapped, "Do what you like, but don't tell us!"[31]

Arlosoroff realized that opposition to trading with Germany would be everywhere. But he was convinced that economic inducements were the only way to prompt Germany to cooperate in the transfer. Next, it was necessary to contact Sam Cohen.

Exactly how the Zionist Executive explained the withdrawal of support for Cohen is unrecorded. Cohen had already set things in motion under the Zionist Organization's preliminary May 30 authority. Meetings had been scheduled in Palestine between Hanotaiah, Yakhin, and other companies. But ultimately, Cohen was forced to step back and allow Arlosoroff to assume control of the transfer. The difficult negotiations must have stretched over several days, because not until June 4 was a cable dispatched to Hanotaiah Ltd. in Palestine: "JOINT IMPLEMENTATION OF SAM COHEN PROJECT REQUIRED UNDER NATIONAL CONTROL. DISCUSSION BY ALL PARTICIPANTS NECESSARY. DELAY MEETING FOR ARRIVAL COHEN ON 12TH [JUNE], ARLOSOROFF 15TH." The cable was signed "ARLOSOROFF/COHEN."[32]

Arlosoroff intended to use the Hanotaiah agreement as a springboard for formal negotiations with the Reich that would produce a transfer controlled by the Jewish Agency. However, Arlosoroff quickly learned that the German government, believing Cohen and Hanotaiah represented the Zionist movement, had indeed granted Hanotaiah complete responsibility for Jewish emigration to Palestine.

On May 19, the day the Reich confirmed Cohen's deal in writing, the British Passport Control Officer in Berlin received new instructions governing the issuance of capitalist certificates for Palestine. Previously requiring evidence of £1,000 in hand, he was now told "not to insist on the production by the applicants of a currency export permit." Instead, the passport officer was "to accept as evidence" proof of capital in "reputable banks in Holland, Switzerland, etc." And he was to "take into consideration as capital the value of machinery, stock, immovable property, etc."[33] What's more, whenever Jews applied for their currency permits at Reich offices, they were handed a notice referring them to "the firm Hanotaiah Ltd. (the solicitor Siegfried Moses), on the basis of an agreement which has been concluded, sells settlement sites, etc., against payment of the purchase price into a blocked account."[34] The cashless or near-cashless transfer was formally in place. And Hanotaiah was totally in charge.

Quickly the word reached the ZVfD in Berlin from prospective emigrants all over the country. Hanotaiah did indeed hold a monopoly, despite the assurances of Sam Cohen. Emigrants found they could leave Germany—but only if they left behind most of their holdings to be divided between Hanotaiah and the Reich. By June 9, Landauer was forced to concede in a letter to a colleague in Breslau that he had been deceived by Cohen. Landauer promised to intervene at once to strike down the Hanotaiah exclusive.[35] He knew that non-Zionist, middle-class German Jews would simply not leave everything behind for a new life in Palestine. If they were to be convinced to start a new life in the Jewish national home, they must be allowed to take some of their old life with them.

Palestine was ready to explode. Internal Zionist politics had produced a dangerous undercurrent to the German emergency. Revisionist forces led by Jabotinsky were challenging the entire leadership of the Zionist Organization—which was becoming increasingly Mapai-dominated. Jabotinsky planned a dramatic appeal for floor votes at the upcoming Eighteenth Zionist Congress to oust the existing leadership and install himself and his circle.[36] At stake was the very philosophy of Zionism.

In simplified terms, Mapai, or Labor Zionism, saw Palestine as a home for a Jewish elite that would toil in the noble vocations of manual work and farming. Their orientation was communal, socialist. They wanted collective farms and villages. Moreover, Labor Zionism desired the many, but not the multitudes. Mapai's Israel would not be for every Jew—at least not in the beginning. At first Israel would be for the approved cadre of pioneers. And Mapai wanted gradual "constructive programs" to build the Jewish Homeland—dunam by dunam.[37]

Revisionist Zionism rejected Jewish exclusivity. They wanted a nation of ordinary Jews in a mixed urban-rural society. The system would be free enterprise not socialism. And Revisionism believed that Palestine could not be acquired a nibble and a shipload at a time. Only by rapidly transferring the largest number of Jews in the shortest amount of time would the Jews constitute a sudden majority in Palestine that could declare the State. With specific unpleasantries about starvation and exposure deleted, Revisionism was very much an updated version of Max Nordau's catastrophic Zionism.[38]

All the conflicts of Mapai-dominated Zionism and Revisionism became life-or-death issues with the rise of Hitler. How many Jews to bring to Palestine, how quickly, from which socioeconomic-national category, and by what means were all fighting questions. Whether to work with the Hitler regime, or combat it through an economic boycott, only heightened the confrontation.

The battle techniques of Revisionism and Mapai also differed. Mapai was expert at political warfare—not so much *by* the rules as *for* the rules. Preoccupied with legalisms, they favored sudden organizational and government meetings that would yield repressive regulation. For example, in December

1931, a Mapai-engineered Zionist Organization decree urged all registered Zionists to avoid membership in Jabotinsky's Revisionist Union.[39]

Revisionists, on the other hand, were heavily Fascist and profoundly influenced by Mussolini. Neither Vladimir Jabotinsky nor Benito Mussolini approved of Hitler's twisted version of Fascism. Nonetheless, Jabotinsky's legions were wrapped in many of the same fabrics. The paramilitary Betar youth corps trained in military camps and wore the same characteristic brown-colored shirts found in Germany. Revisionists claimed their brown was the color of the earth. But a German brown shirt and a Jewish brown shirt were practically indistinguishable when laid side by side. On one occasion, in mid-April 1933, a Betar parade through Tel Aviv was attacked by Labor Zionists who claimed the brown outfits were so reminiscent of Nazi uniforms (even though nothing resembling a swastika was displayed) that the march itself was a provocation to violence.[40] True to Fascist ideology, the fist and the shout were the preferred methods of achieving Revisionist goals. Labor Zionists, especially David Ben-Gurion, were fond of calling Jabotinsky the Jewish Hitler.[41]

During the spring of 1933, every Zionist decision was calculated for its impact on the coming elections for control of the Eighteenth Zionist Congress. As the sniping intensified, Revisionist sympathizers were increasingly shut out of the Mapai-controlled Histadrut labor exchanges. Palestinian Revisionists found they could not earn a living. Revisionists in turn became professional strikebreakers, available for Palestinian employers suffering from Histadrut labor actions. This was especially true in the vast orchard business, where a strategic strike could forfeit a harvest and cripple an entire settlement.[42]

While Revisionists were trying to topple the Mapai labor monopoly in Palestine, Labor Zionist leaders were touring hundreds of East European towns and villages, hoping to convert traditional Revisionist voters. Typical was the May 5, 1933, visit of Ben-Gurion to Riga, Latvia. No sooner had Ben-Gurion stepped from the railway station than a band of Betarim pelted him with rotten eggs. Mapai supporters rushed to Ben-Gurion's aid. Police were called to disperse the fight.[43]

Politics was in fact a vital factor when the Zionist Executive in London persuaded Cohen to merge his Hanotaiah deal with Yakhin, the Mapai-controlled land firm. Whoever controlled the German Jewish money and immigrants, directed votes and financial resources that could be wielded in the war for control of Zionism.

Advocating the anti-Hitler boycott became part of Revisionism's campaign for popular support. On April 28, despite official Zionist calls to abstain from anti-Hitler agitation, Jabotinsky delivered a forceful condemnation of Nazi relations with Palestine. It was the first speech by a foreign Jew ever broadcast by Poland's state-controlled radio. Speaking alternately in

French and Polish, Jabotinsky called for a rigid worldwide boycott of German goods, to be led by Palestine.[44]

By May 10, boycott agitation in Palestine was so severe that the Executive Committee of the Vaad Leumi (Zionist national council in Palestine) threw into open debate its official ban on anti-Nazi boycott activities. On May 16, German Consul Heinrich Wolff—unaware that Sam Cohen's deal had already been approved—warned Berlin of the Vaad Leumi action, and urged acceptance of the Hanotaiah arrangement as a quick countermeasure. Wolff's cable cited anti-German violence, including a recent arson at the Jerusalem consulate, as proof that the Reich should move fast.[45]

On May 17, Consul Wolff, still unaware of the deal, again openly implored his government to approve the Hanotaiah arrangement. Wolff explained that when Jews in Palestine read about 300 American Jewish organizations actively engaged in boycott and the failure of the Leipzig fur auction, they cannot resist joining the movement. Only by linking the export of German goods to Jewish agricultural settlement, argued Wolff, would Palestinian Jews learn that boycotting Germany would hurt their own interests.[46]

On May 18, Mapai stepped up its antiboycott campaign. Pointing to the arson at the German consulate, they claimed boycott and terrorism were part of the same Revisionist platform. In a saccharin editorial on Kol Israel radio, Labor proclaimed, "Screaming slogans calling for a boycott . . . are a crime. . . . We are all anxious about our brethren in Germany, but we have no quarrel with the representatives of the German government in Palestine."[47]

Ironically, the intrigues and alliances crossed all logic and labels. Revisionism urgently sought the mass influx of Jews from rural and urban classes. Yet it was the Mapai leader Arlosoroff who was working to transfer hundreds of thousands of German Jews to Palestine. Transferring with them would be the money and merchandise needed to establish the very mixed society Revisionism wanted but which Mapai was philosophically opposed to. Obstructing this transfer was the boycott, most staunchly advocated by the Revisionists.

But to the Zionist movement, the realities were not as important as the perceptions. Secrecy and distrust kept the movement polarized and paralyzed at the very moment when world Jewry needed it most.

Zionist attitudes toward Germany were not the only flashpoint in Palestine. Of equal ferocity was the controversial binational question. Many Zionists were motivated by a sense of fair play, but far more were convinced that Jews would for the foreseeable future constitute a minority in Palestine unable to thrive without the cooperation of their Arab neighbors.

Almost all binational talking was done by Zionists as they put forth endless plans of ethnic parity—as opposed to numerical equality—in a national government, or in side-by-side federated national states, or in some compromise thereof. Zionists perceived limited successes when Arabs would even listen in silence to such proposals—and even then Arabs listened in secret, fearing reprisals by Arab extremists.[48]

Every Arab extremist had a counterpart on the Jewish side who was emotionally antagonistic to the binational idea. These Zionist rejections were overwhelmingly Revisionist, but often came from Mapai and the religious or Mizrachi camp as well.[49]

In the spring of 1933 Chaim Arlosoroff sought to bridge the gulf between the two peoples. Virtually acting alone, he was pulling together the sudden realities of the day to create a binational moment that would probably never again present itself. Now, for the first time, perhaps the last time, there would be money to make things work: money to compensate Arabs for displacement, money to upgrade Arab villages, money to purchase Arab dunes and swampland at exorbitant rates and one day reclaim them for Jewish use. All this money was in the homes and bank accounts and storerooms of German Jewry—soon to become deposits in the Liquidation Bank. With the potential strength of billions of reichmarks behind him, Arlosoroff, working with Weizmann and the German Zionists, was orchestrating the most promising scenario yet for binational cooperation in Palestine.

As early as a week after Hitler came to power, Arlosoroff, as the Zionist foreign-minister-in-waiting, had been fervently seeking out who among the Arab leaders would be receptive to a parley. Victor Jacobson, prewar Zionist envoy to Turkey, still enjoyed extensive Arab contacts. Jacobson was selected by Arlosoroff in mid-February to travel to Egypt and Syria, not to "engage in negotiations, [but] . . . to put out feelers wherever he thinks advisable, . . . supply information to Arab and Moslem leaders, and find out whether we could do anything with the help of these leaders to reach an understanding with the Arabs of Palestine."[50]

Feelers turned to fruition on April 8 when Arlosoroff was able to convene the much-publicized luncheon at the King David Hotel in Jerusalem with Weizmann and key Arab dignitaries. Informal communiqués after the gathering spoke in glowing terms of binational cooperation. The antagonistic reaction from both sides was swift.

Arab radicals condemned the Arab moderates who had attended the luncheon and issued the declaration of a cooperative future. Most of the hostility was aimed at Emir Abdullah of Transjordan, who controlled much of the land in Transjordan and who was at the forefront of the conciliation. The Palestinian Arab newspaper *Falastin* reported that efforts were under way in Syria to block the rapprochement, and that in the towns of Transjordan an anti-Abdullah protest movement was fast developing. Another publication, *Al Jamia Al Arabia*, editorialized that memoranda, special reports, and stormy meetings were no longer sufficient to counter the Zionist arrivals, and that in the light of the King David Hotel luncheon, some other way must be devised to remove the menace.[51] This kind of language was less a veiled threat than a promise. Assassination was the known punishment for moderation.

Jewish radicals were equally irate. Mizrachi—the major religious Zionist party—publicly demanded Arlosoroff's resignation on the grounds he had no authority to convene the extraordinary luncheon.[52] The ranks of Revisionism went further and demanded Arlosoroff be relieved of his life. One Revisionist leader in Lodz, Poland, declared at a news conference that if a Jewish court-martial existed, Arlosoroff would be condemned to death; he reportedly added that his own hand would not tremble if asked to carry out the sentence. Another Revisionist leader, this one in Warsaw, allegedly stated that any Jewish youth who fired a shot at Arlosoroff would become a saint.[53]

Undaunted, Arlosoroff continued his binational efforts, enlisting the active support of the British. The first fruits of these secret initiatives came quickly. By the end of April, Palestine's high commissioner had announced the resettlement of one hundred Arab families evicted when their absentee Arab landowners sold land to Zionists. The high commissioner stressed that Jewish agricultural methods were to be employed. The unnamed architect of the resettlement plans was Chaim Arlosoroff, who had been secretly working on the program for some time.[54]

Simultaneously, a model Arab community was being sponsored by the Jewish residents of Netanya, the Jewish colony just north of Tel Aviv established in part by Hanotaiah and Revisionist leaders. Netanya residents included a number of American Zionists, many of whom were devout binationalists. Several of these residents, Hebrew University Chancellor Judah Magnes among them, convinced Hanotaiah to rehabilitate the nearby run-down Arab village of Umm Khaled. Under the plan, Hanotaiah would provide each household with ten dunams (2½ acres) of land, a house, an area for animals, and additional dunams for vegetable growing and citriculture. In a confidential May 1 report, United States Consul in Jerusalem Alexander Sloan explained that Hanotaiah had agreed to assist "provided it is given complete title to a certain section of sand dunes facing the sea on which it now holds a 99-year lease." Sloan explained that "Hanotaiah Ltd. is interested politically in the betterment of Arab-Jewish relations."[55] Naturally, the better Arab-Jewish relations were, the less difficult it would be to conclude land sales.

The binational initiatives of spring 1933 found not only Jewish takers but Arab takers as well. Suddenly, for the first time in Palestine's turbulent history, moderate Arabs were standing up. With the security of German Jewish money forecast by Arlosoroff, many Arabs were finally willing to say *yes* to coexistence. For example, shortly after the King David Hotel luncheon, the Transjordan Opposition scheduled a major anti-Zionist conference for May 18. But the conference was postponed when pro-Zionist Arabs violently disrupted the meeting.[56]

On May 24, dozens of Arab sheikhs and property owners, representing twenty-three villages and a large town in Transjordan, visited the white, mazelike structure housing the Jewish Agency in Jerusalem. The assembled leaders collectively invited Zionists to purchase Arab land in Transjordan for the mass setttlement of Jews.[57]

That same day, Jewish Agency chairman Emanuel Neumann met with W. J. Johnson, treasurer of the Palestine government. Neumann was always lobbying for the British to allocate as much of Palestine's tax money and other fiscal resources to Jewish projects as to Arab projects. That day, as Johnson explained some of the government's big development plans—housing for British troops and the accretion of a huge monetary reserve—Neumann asked how then would the resettlement of displaced Arabs be financed? Johnson replied that the money wouldn't be provided from the government's normal revenues.[58]

Where will the money come from? asked Neumann. Johnson at first tried to evade the question. But Neumann pressed until Johnson, stipulating the strictest confidence, admitted that the specifics of a £2-million Palestine development loan had been secretly approved by Sir Cunliffe-Lister when he visited Palestine in April. The fine points, just completed, were being rushed to London in the next airmail pouch for Cunliffe-Lister's signature. Such a development loan had been debated for two years without agreement. Therefore, Neumann was amazed as Johnson itemized the details: first, a water supply system for Jerusalem and Haifa, possibly with a drainage grid. Neumann interrupted and said such a massive endeavor would cost at least £350,000 for Jerusalem alone. Johnson corrected him: £480,000. Second, an oil port at Haifa costing anywhere from £150,000 to £200,000. Third, port improvements at Jaffa, no figure mentioned.[59]

Johnson then described some of the Arab settlement programs. To start, a program of general assistance, say, £50,000, to help Arab villagers in the hill country; Neumann guessed this money was designed to *buy* political support for the new situation. Additional money would resettle Arabs displaced by absentee landlord property sales to Zionists. Neumann guessed resettlement would cost a few hundred thousand pounds. Johnson said no, it would be "much more than that."[60]

Central to the plan was an "Agricultural Bank" capitalized with £100,000 from the new fund and an additional £500,000 from the Prudential Insurance Company or its executives, perhaps Barclays Bank, and Anglo-Zionist investors. To avoid any sectarian character, Englishmen would manage the Agricultural Bank; a three-man bank advisory committee would include a Jew, an Arab, and the Palestine director of agriculture. Once in place, the Agricultural Bank would permit both Jew and Arab to purchase and settle land throughout the Palestine plains.[61]

Johnson mentioned other projects: irrigation plants, hydrographic surveys, Arab municipal improvements, water for remote Arab villages. All this money would be borrowed by the Mandate government from the great new fund. The interest rate would be no more than 3½ to 5 percent because the British Treasury would guarantee repayment. Neumann remarked, "Very cheap money indeed." Johnson answered that the Treasury was willing to guarantee repayment, thus assuring the low interest rate, because Palestine would generate huge purchases of British exports.[62]

Johnson and Cunliffe-Lister were unaware of it at the time, but Britain's special inducement—massively increased exports to Palestine—was to be eliminated in favor of a bitter concession to Nazi Germany. A week later, on June 1, during the meeting with Arlosoroff, Cunliffe-Lister finally discovered this and realized that all the binational plans, many of which were already under way, were now of primary benefit only to Jews and Germans. Britain would lose—and not just trade. For Germany's winnings would include breaking the boycott and gaining the economic recovery she needed to rearm.

Chaim Arlosoroff was one of the most provocative thinkers of his day in that he tried not to overwhelm, but to transform. In an era of extremes, his efforts to combine the hostile forces around him were almost too theoretical to succeed. Rumors of a deal with Hitler only accelerated the controversies swirling around him. By early June 1933, Arlosoroff was in fact a threat to so many groups that people measured themselves by how vehemently they opposed him.

His Jewish friends began to fear and hate him. Arlosoroff was a top Mapai leader, but Labor-aligned moderates could hardly contain their fury that the prodigy of the Zionist movement was abandoning all Zionist discipline. Unilaterally he was formulating and executing policy—binational breakthroughs with the Arabs and controversial trade-offs with the Nazis. Arlosoroff was by himself engineering the fate of societies and nations, not in theoretical, discreet ways leaving plenty of doors open for retreat, but by one stunning *fait accompli* after another. Arlosoroff was dangerous to Mapai and to the others of moderate mainstream Zionism. He was giving away the Promised Land to the Arabs, and in so doing giving away the Eighteenth Zionist Congress elections to the Revisionists. Arlosoroff would have to be stopped.

His enemies among the Jews were convinced there was no greater nemesis. Arlosoroff was a special foe of Revisionism. It was Arlosoroff who in late 1931 conceived the decree against membership in Jabotinsky's Revisionist Union. The calls for his assassination were so commonplace during early 1933 that it was rumored Revisionist circles were merely debating whether to kill him before or after the Eighteenth Zionist Congress. According to one such rumor, Vladimir Jabotinsky himself was said to have quashed a far-gone Palestinian conspiracy by cabling the ringleaders a one-word instruction: "NO."[63] More than rumor was an odious Revisionist pamphlet published by Abba Achimier, the editor of the Revisionist newspaper *Hazit Haam*. Achimier's pamphlet, entitled "Manifesto of the Sicarii," explained a new secret society based on an ancient sect of Jewish assassins from the Masada era. The Sicarii carried short Roman daggers and assassinated Jewish leaders found guilty of consorting with the Roman enemy.[64] Arlosoroff was consorting with all of Revisionism's greatest enemies: the British, who occupied the land; the Arabs, who refused to make room for Jewish destiny; and the Germans, who were dedicated to annihilating the Jews. Arlosoroff would have to be stopped.

His enemies among the Arabs saw him as the one Zionist willing to push past the historic barriers. Arlosoroff was too willing to use the new powers and wealth arising out of the German crisis to create a new binational community that would make the battle cries of Arab rejection obsolete. To Arab extremists, Arlosoroff was the most dangerous Zionist in Palestine. Not because he sought to conquer. But because he sought to combine. Arlosoroff would have to be stopped.

His enemies in Britain were created unexpectedly. Suddenly the British government realized that Chaim Arlosoroff carried the key to economic turmoil or triumph in Palestine for either Britain or Germany. The transfer as London had originally envisioned it would be a boon for the British economy that would blossom into an extended economic sphere of influence over the entire Mideast. That prize was now going to Germany. Arlosoroff's dreams would play right into Hitler's plans. Arlosoroff would have to be stopped.

And his newest enemy was the one enemy people knew the least about. His name was Mr. Sam Cohen. Cohen had masterminded an international economic and political coup. If successful, he alone would control millions of dollars, thousands of people, and large tracts of land. One man working alone could, if allowed, deliver the Jewish nation to the Jewish homeland. Cohen could be this private messiah. But now Arlosoroff was obliterating it all. Cohen was being robbed of both his promise and his profit. Arlosoroff would have to be stopped.

The question was: Who would stop him, and how?

The passions of Palestine, its dreams and disappointments, all focused on a single man. When Arlosoroff departed London in the first week of June, he was returning to a land whose potentials he loved. Too few in Palestine would accept the clarity of his ideas. But Arlosoroff had visions from the beginning.

When he was only twenty-two years old, in 1922, Arlosoroff first visited Palestine and encountered the reality of a land inhabited by one people of the present while cherished by another people of the past. The young Zionist wrote, "Let us not overlook the following fact: there is in the country a massive [Arab] nation . . . and it makes no difference if we call it a national movement or not. . . . We have only one way: the road of peace; only one national policy: a policy of mutual understanding. . . . Peace and agreement cannot grow overnight. The road to it is long and requires much work." 65

For years Arlosoroff had sought peace by the forces of reason. All efforts failed. In June 1932, one year after becoming the political secretary of the Jewish Agency, Arlosoroff wrote a disconsolate letter to Weizmann, predicting that soon only two options would remain: "narrowing down the geographical area [in Palestine] in which Zionism will materialize." That failing, a man of peace such as Arlosoroff in desperation advocated a brief coup, hoping that this position of power could result in coexistence.66

But such transient suggestions as armed revolt were outmoded because the German crisis would at last allow him to create realities with money where reason had failed.

As Arlosoroff traveled across Europe, rumors were everywhere. He was sealing a pact with Hitler, and forging a new binational political party with pro-Zionist Arabs, and was even ready to publish an Arab-Zionist newspaper. Shortly after Arlosoroff left Poland in early June, the Polish Revisionist newspaper Die Welt accused Arlosoroff of trying to make peace with Hitler and warned; "Get off the Jewish stage, Dr. Arlosoroff!" On June 9, the Palestinian Revisionist newspaper Hazit Haam declared, "At a time when the people of Israel in Palestine and abroad are in a defensive war of honor against Germany . . . an official of the Jewish Agency suggests not only a cancellation of the boycott but also a promise of a market for German imports. . . . This should be viewed as putting a knife in the back of the Jewish people while attempting to stretch out the hand of friendship to the Hitler government." 67

The animosity of the Jewish masses, the desperation of German Jewry, and the momentus failure or success that might emerge within the coming days could not help but cast the thirty-four-year-old Arlosoroff into a deep depression. As he journeyed home to Palestine, Arlosoroff's gloom was only worsened by a sequence of missed trains, lost wallets, and strange delays. Everything had gone wrong, and Arlosoroff felt the omens were not good.68

Arlosoroff had hoped to meet his wife Sima in Egypt and enjoy the train ride back to Tel Aviv together. But the mishaps forced him to board a ship in Naples that didn't arrive in Egypt until June 13. The superstitious Arlosoroff asked Sima to instead meet him at 6:00 A.M. on the fourteenth at a Palestine train station along the way.69

Arlosoroff and Sima arrived in Tel Aviv at 9:00 A.M. on June 14 and went straight to their Tel Aviv apartment at 82 Yarkon. There Arlosoroff hugged his children for the first time in over a month. Later that day, he visited his mother. And he conferred with various Zionist officials. Throughout the day, his dejection remained clearly visible to those he met.70

That night, Arlosoroff tried to find solace playing with his infant son Shaul. One of Shaul's favorite games was to remove his father's ring from his finger and replace it. But this day, when Shaul removed the ring, he replaced it on his mother's finger. Arlosoroff cried out, "Not yet." [71]

On June 15, Arlosoroff, still tired from his travels, continued meeting on the transfer question. It is rumored that among those he spoke with was Sam Cohen.

The next day, June 16, Arlosoroff lunched with High Commissioner Arthur Wauchope. After lunch, they visited a village that Arlosoroff said would become a major center for transferred German Jewish youngsters. At the end of the afternoon, Arlosoroff went back to Tel Aviv, arriving at 5:15 P.M., in time for *shabbat*, the Jewish Sabbath. [72]

At about sunset, Sima and Arlosoroff tried to soothe their nerves with a quiet dinner at the Kaetedan boardinghouse on the beach north of Tel Aviv. It was a favored establishment of Mapai leaders. [73] After dinner, Arlosoroff wanted to walk along the deserted seashore around the Kaetedan, but Sima was afraid. Just that day, the Revisionist newspaper *Hazit Haam* had issued what many considered a public death threat. The article attacked what it called an alliance between Hitler and the Mapai party engineered by Arlosoroff. "There will be no forgiveness for those who have for greed sold out the honor of their people to madmen and anti-Semites. . . . The Jewish people have always known how to size up the betrayers of the nation and their followers, and it will know today how to react to this crime." [74]

Arlosoroff had lived with threats for some time. When informed in early 1933 that he was at the top of a fanatic Revisionist group's hit list, Arlosoroff at first refused protection, saying, "No Jew would kill *me*." Not long after, however, Sima heard footsteps outside their door late at night. Situated as they were in a Jewish neighborhood, they concluded the prowlers were Jewish. So Arlosoroff finally agreed to post a guard outside his home. The threat from the Arab side became equally real, forcing Arlosoroff to carry a pistol while traveling through Arab areas. But before leaving for Germany, Arlosoroff had deposited his pistol with a friend, and had not yet reclaimed it. So on the night of June 16, Arlosoroff was unarmed. [75]

The moon was not out that night. As Sima and Arlosoroff began walking, little could be seen except the red running lights of freighters in the Mediterranean to the west and the sparkling crescent of lights formed by Tel Aviv and Jaffa to the south. Before long they had strolled so far north there was nothing but solitude, sand dunes, and the foamy fizzles of the sea. But then Sima noticed two men following, a short one and a tall one who seemed to waddle as he walked. [76]

Soon the two men quickened their pace and passed Sima and Arlosoroff. Sima was frightened, but Arlosoroff reassured her. "Don't worry, they're

Jews." The two men were now ahead, but they then stopped. The taller one began to urinate into the sand as the Arlosoroffs came closer.[77] Finally, the Arlosoroffs saw the lights of a distant Jewish housing development. They left the seashore and meandered through the new neighborhood, discussing the construction that everywhere rose from the sand. An hour later, they returned to the beach, arms entwined, and began walking south, staying close to the waterline. After a while the two men again appeared, walking slowly so the Arlosoroffs could not help but pass. When they did, the two men sped up and in turn passed the couple. This passing and falling back occurred several times as the Arlosoroffs continued walking south.[78]

When the Arlosoroffs neared a Moslem cemetery on the outskirts of Tel Aviv, Sima noticed a donkey carcass lying on the shore. And then, just ahead at the cemetery, the two men stopped entirely, turned, and positioned themselves on either side of the Arlosoroffs' path. As the Arlosoroffs passed between the men, the taller one shined a flashlight in Chaim's face and said, "*kamah hashaa*"—an erroneous construction of the Hebrew phrase for "What time is it?"[79]

Just then the other man pulled out a Browning automatic and a bullet flashed into Arlosoroff's chest. He dropped to all fours, his life spilling onto the sand. The two assailants fled into the dunes as Sima screamed in horror, "Help, help! Jews shot him!" The bleeding Arlosoroff immediately corrected her, saying, "No, Sima, no."[80]

At first Sima struggled to help Arlosoroff crawl. Finally she helped him stand. Sima supporting him on her shoulders, they walked toward some people summoned by the shot. As bystanders took Arlosoroff's bleeding body, Sima ran back to the Kaetedan to call police and an ambulance. As she raced into the lobby, she cried, "They've shot Chaim" and begged for help. Meanwhile, people on the beach carried Arlosoroff to the roadway and began looking for someone to take him to a hospital. But this was shabbat, 10:30 P.M. No automobile traffic. In desperation, a bystander sounded the horn of a parked car. The car's owner came out and at once agreed to drive Arlosoroff to the hospital.[81]

Arlosoroff was lying on the gravel of the roadway, still bleeding, his jacket under his head as passersby kept asking who had done the shooting. Arlosoroff answered, "I will tell everything, but let me rest." Finally the automobile was brought around and Arlosoroff was helped in and rushed to Hadassah Hospital. Along the way, Arlosoroff remained coherent, but still refused to answer any questions.[82]

At the hospital, the doctors were ill prepared and indecisive. This being shabbat, there was no surgeon on duty. Arlosoroff reached the emergency room at eleven-thirty—about an hour after being shot. The first surgeon arrived before midnight but would not operate until joined by three other specialists still en route. While waiting, the staff tried to make a weakened

Arlosoroff comfortable. By this time, word had spread throughout Tel Aviv. The loved-hated son of Zionism had been shot. Political friends and associates began gathering around his bed. They and the police asked him question after question. But Arlosoroff was too faded to respond cogently.[83]

They were all helpless. Nothing could be done. Arlosoroff had just a few powerless moments remaining. No one expected him to speak. But with the last air in his lungs he turned toward the mayor of Tel Aviv, Meir Dizengoff, looked up, and whispered in soft tones, "Look what they have done to me."[84]

And then he died.

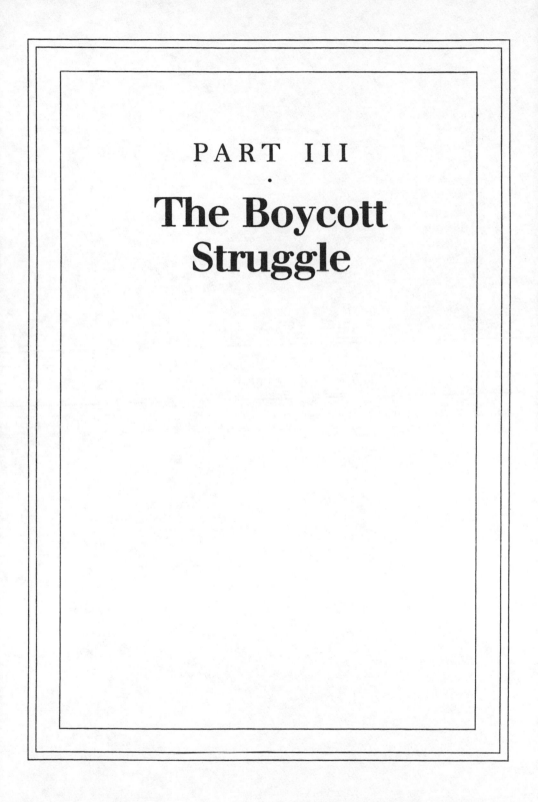

PART III
·
The Boycott
Struggle

16. Sam Cohen Resumes Control

LESS IMPORTANT than the death of Arlosoroff became the question: Who killed him? In London, members of the House of Commons immediately demanded an inquiry. In Warsaw, all Jewish newspapers featured black borders of mourning on their front pages. Memorial services were held in Vienna, Paris, and many other cities. Rewards for the capture of Arlosoroff's assailants were posted throughout Palestine. His funeral was attended by the largest assemblage in Palestine's history, between 70,000 and 100,000 persons. Arab and Jewish leaders alike and the entire consular corps paid their homage to the man generally assumed to be the brightest ascendant of the Zionist movement.[1]

Quickly the Revisionists emerged as the logical, and to a larger extent, the most suitable culprits. Police squads raided the apartments of leading Revisionist figures, including Abba Achimeir, the editor of *Hazit Haam*, who had so vocally editorialized for Arlosoroff's murder as recently as the day of the crime.[2] There they found a Betar activist named Abraham Stavsky, who had arrived from Poland just a few months earlier but was now eager to return. Sima Arlosoroff identified Stavsky as the man who held the flashlight, and Polish Revisionist Avi Rosenblatt as the one who fired the pistol. Some weeks later, Abba Achimeir himself was accused of masterminding the plot.[3]

Whether or not Stavsky, Rosenblatt, and Achimeir were the actual murderers will never be known. Sima Arlosoroff was under tremendous pressure from Mapai leaders to maintain her damaging testimony despite doubts.[4] In the months that followed, the murder investigation was besieged by bought-and-paid-for Arab confessions, false witnesses, manufactured evidence, bizarre theories, dramatic revelations, and unanswerable questions. Within a year, Rosenblatt, the alleged triggerman, and Achimeir, the accused ringleader, were both acquitted due to conflicting evidence. Stavsky, however, was found guilty and condemned to death. A long appeal finally released him on an evidence technicality.[5]

Eyewitnesses, real and induced, former police officials, and even private detectives continued announcing dramatic denials and reversals for years after the trial. Mapai leaders, satisfied that Revisionism was implicated—whether or not juridically guilty—would refuse to discuss the case even decades later. Revisionists and their sympathizers, determined to cast off a "blood libel," produced numerous theories to clear their names. Usually the theories blamed Arabs, sometimes they blamed British agents, and one far-fetched story even blamed Goebbels, who supposedly wanted to obliterate the last shreds of his wife Magda's Jewish associations, including her former friend Chaim Arlosoroff. Five decades after the conflict, recriminations still fly among Zionist leaders when the question of Arlosoroff's murder is raised.[6]

But if the aftermath was bitter, the moment of conflict itself was torment. Jabotinsky's biographer remembered it this way: "For those who did not live during that agonizing summer of 1933, it is difficult, almost impossible, to imagine the dreadful atmosphere of violent animosity that permeated Jewish life all over the world, particularly in Palestine and Poland."[7] Mapai exploited the tragedy to its maximum. A broad anti-Revisionist movement sprang up uniting a range of Zionist ideologies behind Mapai. These groups collectively advocated the banishment of all Revisionists from Zionism. One policy statement declared, "No intercourse whatever with Revisionism! Let our motto be: Expel the Revisionist gangs from Jewish life!" Jabotinsky was often held personally responsible. Pamphlets called him a "bloodthirsty beast."[8] David Ben-Gurion, who would become Israel's first prime minister, admitted he was "less interested in whether Stavsky is the murderer than in Jabotinsky." Ben-Gurion declared that Jabotinsky bore total responsibility because he was Revisionism's "commander, leader, and mentor."[9]

Emulating the very violence they were decrying, Mapai forces called for "avenging our Arlosoroff" with a bloody reprisal against Jabotinsky. Polish newspapers in early July 1933 printed rumors that Jabotinsky, fearing an attack, had canceled his forthcoming lecture tour. Jabotinsky refused to cancel the tour, but was persuaded to accept a bodyguard.[10]

At each tour stop, he was heckled and harassed. At Brest-Litovsk, home town of accused assassin Stavsky, the throng became vicious. Young Polish Revisionist leader Menachem Begin remembers the event as traumatic: "An inflamed crowd tried to stone him [Jabotinsky] and we surrounded him, creating a human wall to absorb the stones."[11] In the town of Pinsk, Begin remembers the emotional chill as he heard his idol Jabotinsky plead, "The inciters tell you that I educated young Jews to murder one of their own people, while I have devoted my whole life to saving Jews, . . . to defending them from pogrom and assault." Begin controlled his emotions that day as he sat behind Jabotinsky, prepared to jump out in case a rock was thrown. But he recalls that another Jabotinsky aide trembled and wept.[12] The Revisionist movement was crumbling. The staunchest advocates of Jewish defense had become outcasts among their own people.

Hostilities continued as Mapai forces hammered away at Revisionism, labeling it a Fascist misfit of Zionism, and harassing Jews who supported Jabotinsky. Jabotinsky himself was portrayed as the Jewish Hitler, commanding forces analogous—somehow even linked—to Nazi Storm Troopers. And yet in truth, it was not the stalwarts of Jewish militancy, the Revisionists, who had constructed avenues of commercial and political détente with the Third Reich. It was the forces of Mapai.

And as Revisionism fell to one knee in the summer of '33, the anti-Nazi boycott fell with it. For to adhere to the boycott was to carry out Revisionist dogma. To reject the boycott was to reject Vladimir Jabotinsky.

The campaign to reject the Revisionist-tainted boycott in Palestine reached a formal level even before Arlosoroff was assassinated. In fact, while Sam Cohen and Arlosoroff were still in London, at the beginning of June, the Mapai-dominated institutions of Palestine were already scurrying to implement Cohen's merchandise deal—whether funneled through Hanotaiah Ltd. or supervised by national Jewish authorities. For example, on June 6, an ad hoc coalition assembled at the Tel Aviv Chamber of Commerce. There were representatives from the Jewish Agency, the Vaad Leumi, the Jaffa-Tel Aviv Chamber of Commerce, the Histadrut, the Citrus Center, the Association of Farmers, the Manufacturers Association, and the Organization of German Immigrants, which was the Palestinian counterpart of the ZVfD. These groups formed something called "The Conference of Representatives of Institutions in Connection with the Question of Clarifying Trade Relations with Germany"—*The Conference of Institutions* for short.[13] Their purpose was to explore the many ways Sam Cohen's deal could benefit Palestine commercially.

The Conference of Institutions was afraid to assume an openly anti-boycott stance. So on June 6, they carefully adopted a nonstance. They didn't endorse the anti-Nazi boycott. Nor would they oppose it. Effectively this was of course a vote to accept German goods.[14]

A week later, Sam Cohen returned to Palestine from London. The previous few weeks had been filled with sudden triumphs and reversals for Sam Cohen. In mid-May, he was able to feign legitimacy to the German government and walk away with a cashless transfer that would bring badly needed agricultural materials to his sand dunes soon to be orange groves. Despite the resistance of the ZVfD, Cohen was able to sail to London and on May 30 gain the written endorsement of the Zionist Organization to include Mapai-owned grove companies. However, after Arlosoroff had been given superseding authority, Sam Cohen refused to relinquish control.

On June 15, Cohen went to see German Consul Heinrich Wolff in Jerusalem and presented the obsolete May 30 letter from the Zionist Organization endorsing Hanotaiah's cashless transfer. Cohen then asked Wolff to help him expand his limited agreement from 1 million to 3 million reichmarks.[15] To convince Berlin that he was the one man capable of breaking the boycott against Germany, Cohen offered an ace.

Among the most vehement anti-Nazi newspapers in Palestine was *Doar HaYom*, the official Revisionist publication. *Doar HaYom* had been a pioneer in the economic war against Germany. When the boycott itself became an issue within Zionism, *Doar HaYom* steadfastly supported boycott agitation, often publishing encouraging columns by Vladimir Jabotinsky.[16] Somehow Mr. Sam Cohen acquired a financial interest in *Doar HaYom*. He was then able to replace the pro-boycott editor with a freelance writer named Moshe Smilansky.[17] Smilansky was already the editor of *Bustani*, official journal of the citrus growers. *Bustani* under Smilansky was a well-established proponent of better German-Palestinian trade relations; Germany was after all Palestine's second-largest customer for Palestine's number-one export: citrus.[18] During his June 15 meeting with Consul Wolff, Cohen explained that *Doar HaYom*, which had been so vocal a boycott advocate, would suddenly become silent on the issue.[19]

Consul Wolff agreed to give Cohen full backing both to expand his agreement and to overcome any ZVfD opposition in Berlin. That same day, Wolff sent the Reich Foreign Ministry a long memorandum, "Increase of German Exports Against Payment into Sperrkonto [Blocked Accounts] to Palestine for the Purpose of Breaking the Boycott." Wolff's report asked his superiors "to urgently prevail upon the Reich Economics Ministry" to implement their deal with Hanotaiah quickly. Wrote Consul Wolff, "Only through the admittance of exports, as is proposed by Hanotaiah, will it be possible to effectively counteract the anti-German boycott here."[20]

Wolff then explained why it was imperative for Germany to break the boycott in Palestine first. "The anti-German boycott is making progress not only in Palestine but in the entire world." But now, argued Wolff, the world Jewish community was looking to Palestine for leadership, instead of the other way around. This political inversion had taken place since April. He added, "[Since] Palestine is now . . . calling the tune . . . then everything that . . . counteracts the boycott in this country [Palestine] would have beneficial effects for us elsewhere, e.g., the United States."[21]

Wolff's intelligence about the shift in world Jewish affairs was accurate. This view was especially acceptable to Berlin because it fit the Hitler conception of an international Jewish conspiracy headquartered in Jerusalem. Building on this foundation, Wolff's June 15 letter encouraged Berlin to increase the incentive to Zionism by expanding Hanotaiah's license in quality and quantity. Wolff estimated that a RM 1 million ceiling would allow only thirty or forty German Jews to emigrate to Palestine. "In the eyes of the Jews," wrote Wolff, "this is but a drop in the bucket." Wolff's suggestion: increase the ceiling. "Every day would constitute a gain. . . . Do it as quickly as possible."[22]

Consul Wolff's second idea was the germ of the key financial potential of the entire agreement. The idea called for German Jews "who do not yet wish to emigrate but who would later on wish to settle in Palestine or neighboring areas to pay for exports into the Hanotaiah Sperrkonto [blocked account]."[23] This was Sam Cohen's answer to Arlosoroff's Liquidation Bank. Cohen's new arrangement would permit masses of German Jews—declared emigrants or not—to deposit their assets for safekeeping. Call it an escape hatch, an insurance policy, or an investment. Thousands of German Jews would surely take advantage of the opportunity. This would create a massive frozen cash pool for Hanotaiah's use.

The resulting extra millions in German merchandise would be too much for Hanotaiah to distribute in Palestine alone, so the firm would establish a re-export system throughout the region. Wolff pointed out that this "could constitute a possibility of breaking the boycott in Egypt and Cyprus" as well, and cut in on French competition in those markets.[24]

To countercheck any efforts by Georg Landauer and his circle to discredit Cohen, Wolff sprinkled his memo with assurances of Cohen's authenticity as the syndic of Zionism. "Mr. Sam Cohen showed me a letter . . . from the Zionist Central Organization [sic] in London, which shows that the Central Organization is effectively working on eliminating obstacles which could arise from Jewish circles against Hanotaiah's plans, insofar as those circles are pushing for an increasingly organized boycott movement." Wolff then referred to the joint telegram sent some days before by Arlosoroff and Cohen to Hanotaiah, instructing that no action be taken until they both arrived in Palestine, at which time Hanotaiah's private deal would be submitted to "national supervision." Wolff referred only to the "national supervision" fragment of the telegram, implying that this proved that Hanotaiah's position was official. Hanotaiah's official status, wrote Wolff, "would take the wind out of the sails of those radical circles which are pressing for continued boycott."[25]

Citing Cohen's dedication to eradicating the boycott, Wolff advised Berlin, "Sam Cohen feels that it is urgently necessary to use the local press . . . to defeat the boycott," adding that Cohen now controlled *Doar HaYom*. Wolff explained, "Today a contract is to be signed which will provide Mr. Smilansky with decisive influence on the newspaper [*Doar HaYom*]. Smilansky . . . is prepared to exert all his influence against the boycott movement. I believe this . . . will significantly enhance an anti-boycott mood."[26]

Lest his unabashed support for Cohen and the upbuilding of Palestine arouse suspicions in Berlin, Consul Wolff was careful to qualify: "I need not emphasize . . . that I am not making these statements in the interest of the Jews, but only because I see in this plan a significant means of employment, considering Germany's precarious economic conditions. The Jews would benefit from the implementation of these plans; but in my opinion, our own advantage would be considerable and the best deals are always those which benefit both parties."[27]

Consul Wolff's motives were in truth an amalgam of sympathy with Zionism, loyalty to Germany, and efforts to ensure his own survival. He was no Nazi, and no anti-Semite. He did not seek the expulsion of Germany's Jews. But as Weimar Germany's liaison with the Jewish national home, he embraced the basic tenets of Zionism, doing what he could to further a cause sanctioned by the League of Nations. On the other hand, situated in the capital of the mythological Jewish conspiracy, with a Jewish wife, Consul Wolff was in a precarious position. He tried to straddle the fence and stay alive doing it. For this reason, his paragraphs were constantly weighted to the point of literary clumsiness with the words "to break the boycott." Whatever words he chose, they were almost always shown to Zionist personalities in advance, including Sam Cohen. In fact, his June 15 memorandum ended with a postscript implying that Cohen was virtually looking over his shoulder. Wolff appends, "P.S. Sam Cohen just informs me that the Jewish National Fund, headed in Palestine by Ussischkin, and Baron Rothschild's representative are in full agreement with Sam Cohen's proposed activity, which gives added significance to his work, insofar as it constitutes an anti-boycott measure."[28]

Wolff's postscript name-dropping Ussischkin and Rothschild was just another undisguised reminder to the Reich that Cohen was the only man who could overcome the boycott and at the same time solve the problem of a Jewish presence in Germany. And undoubtedly Wolff himself believed that Sam Cohen was the authorized agent of the Zionist movement. After all, during this June 15 meeting, Cohen had displayed obsolete letters of authority that out of context could easily be misconstrued. Ironically, Cohen's ruse was due to be spoiled as soon as Chaim Arlosoroff could present his superseding authority to Wolff. In fact, by June 9, the Zionist Executive in London had already sent the Jewish Agency in Jerusalem a cable specifying Arlosoroff's total authority in the transfer question.[29] But for some reason Cohen felt confident enough to set in motion, on June 15, this new request for an expanded Hanotaiah license.

The next day, June 16, before Arlosoroff could schedule a meeting with Consul Wolff, Arlosoroff was assassinated. So, as far as Consul Wolff knew, Cohen was still the legitimate representative of the Zionist movement, and the Hanotaiah deal was the sanctioned medium of transfer. As such, there was little standing between Sam Cohen and his plan for near-cashless indentured servitude for German Jews as a means of building the Jewish national home.

But such a transfer was a calamity Georg Landauer in Berlin could not allow. If Sam Cohen had arranged a deal for Hanotaiah, that was one thing. But Hanotaiah was not the authorized trustee of the Jewish people. Landauer was determined to make that clear to the German government.[30]

Building on the rapport established by Cohen with the Economics Ministry, Landauer felt confident enough to make his own approach. On June 20, 1933, Landauer had a letter delivered to the Economics Ministry proposing for the first time a formal conference with the ZVfD to develop an official plan to export merchandise to Palestine against the blocked accounts of Jewish emigrants. Landauer implied that various "interested parties"—meaning Hanotaiah—had already applied for this "basic idea." But Landauer warned that any such transaction would depend upon the involvement of the Anglo-

Palestine Bank, the only Palestine bank Zionists trusted. The point was not explictly written, but Landauer was trying to say that blocked accounts should be entrusted to a *bank*, not to a private real estate company. Landauer's note added that the director of the Anglo-Palestine Bank, Mr. E. S. Hoofien, had just arrived in Berlin from Tel Aviv, and asked if they could all get together for a discussion.[31]

That same day, June 20, the Reich Foreign Ministry received via diplomatic pouch Consul Wolff's June 15 letter suggesting a broadened version of Sam Cohen's deal.[32] Landauer's June 20 letter to the Economics Ministry was sufficiently vague that the government had no reason to suspect that the two letters were not part of the same negotiating effort. In fact, they were diametrically opposed.

While Landauer was cautiously making his first formal entreaty to the Third Reich, Sam Cohen was moving rapidly in Palestine to garner the backing he needed to claim legitimacy. During the last week of June the Organization of German Immigrants convened a meeting in Tel Aviv chaired by Arthur Ruppin. Ruppin had been influential in the Zionist movement for years. Also attending were representatives of Hanotaiah, Yakhin (Mapai's land company), and Sam Cohen. Cohen spoke first, reporting on transfer prospects and developments to date. There is no record of what method he used to convince the group to circumvent Georg Landauer and the German Zionist Federation in Berlin. But unaware that Cohen's deal was an inequitable cashless arrangement, the conferees agreed there was now no need to interfere with Cohen's progress. They voted to create a commercial coalition between Yakhin and Hanotaiah Ltd.[33] This was the very coalition originally envisioned by the Zionist Executive in London before Arlosoroff arrived to demand that Cohen's deal be executed through official institutions.

One of the German Zionists, Felix Rosenbluth, drafted a compact binding Hanotaiah and Yakhin to immediately negotiate joint implementation of Sam Cohen's deal.[34] As one of the German Zionists who originated the transfer concept in mid-March 1933, Rosenbluth was a fitting choice to draft this agreement. Later, he would change his name to Pinchas Rosen, and as Israel's first minister of justice, become the architect of Israel's judicial system.

Instructions went out to the representatives of both Hanotaiah and Yakhin, already in Berlin, to begin hammering out the details of sharing Hanotaiah's privilege. Representing Yakhin would be Lev Shkolnick, who as Levi Eshkol would become Israel's third prime minister. Representing Hanotaiah would be its director and part-owner, Moshe Mechnes.[35]

Sam Cohen had now won the renewed endorsement of the German Zionists in Palestine and the agreement of Mapai. He was authorized to proceed to Berlin as soon as possible to negotiate an even larger emigrant asset allowance from the German government. The men backing him, however, were still unaware that Sam Cohen's project was cashless.[36]

On June 25, Ludwig Pinner, a leading German Zionist in Palestine,

wrote a somewhat accusatory letter to Landauer in Berlin, dismissing Landauer's criticism of Cohen's Hanotaiah plan as the words of a "rival." Pinner
could not understand how Landauer could be so antagonistic to Sam Cohen's
plan when the ZVfD itself, represented by Siegfried Moses, was Cohen's
obvious sponsor.[37]

Landauer responded to Pinner at once with a bitter, albeit somewhat
suspect, denial. "I once again repeat," wrote Landauer, "that the agreement
between Hanotaiah and the Reich Economics Ministry was not made on the
suggestion nor with the help of the ZVfD. . . . Siegfried Moses [ZVfD
president, who originally worked as Cohen's attorney] dealt with the matter
only as a solicitor hired by a firm. . . . The matter reached us . . . as a *fait
accompli*."[38] Landauer was trying to disclaim knowledge of the deal and
dismiss Moses' brief involvement as unrelated to Moses' post in the ZVfD. In
truth, the ZVfD, Landauer, and Moses had originally sponsored Cohen, but
Cohen continued negotiating.

Trying to explain how Sam Cohen's plan endangered emigrating German
Jewry, Landauer added, "What Mr. Sam Cohen says about his activities here
for the good of the revocation of regulations for emigrants is pure nonsense.
. . . The text of the agreement with the Ministry is not known to us. . . .
[But] for some days doubt has arisen about whether the cash sum will be at
the free disposal of the clients. . . . I would warn people before they enter into
a contract with Hanotaiah, because the emigrants would then find an existence only as settlers of Hanotaiah."[39]

Landauer's protestations from Berlin were too late. Cohen was using his
freedom of movement and speech in Palestine to influence key Zionist
personalities and organizations to make him the de facto envoy of the Zionist
movement. In addition to the Organization of German Emigrants and important elements of Mapai, Cohen recruited the Jewish National Fund to his
side. As official landholder of Zionist property in Palestine, the JNF was
among the most powerful Zionist institutions. Its leader, Menahem
Ussischkin, had already threatened the Jewish Agency in April 1933 that he
opposed many of the plans for German Jewish capital transfer, and might be
forced to sponsor his own rival plan. Now at the end of June, in exchange for
Ussischkin's support, Cohen promised to arrange the transfer of blocked
JNF monies in Germany.[40]

Large sums were indeed accruing in JNF's German bank accounts from
domestic relief donations. If Sam Cohen used his connections to transfer this
money, substantial funds would be available for wholesale land purchase in
Palestine. So on June 25, 1933—the day Pinner wrote his letter to Landauer
supportive of Sam Cohen—Ussischkin wrote two letters of his own. The first
went to Sam Cohen at his London address: "Let me once again request that
you use your influence at the Ministry in Berlin [so] . . . funds presently
being collected for the Jewish National Fund, and monies already held in

escrow, be transmitted here without delay. Per our conversation, you have understood that these funds are now urgently required here for land purchases to be used for new settlements. A steady stream of German Jews is presently immigrating into Palestine and the first thing they ask for, with good reason, is to have a piece of land on which to settle and make a living."[41] Ussischkin dispatched a similar letter to the JNF office in Berlin, with special tributes to Cohen added into the text. To obviate any doubts, Ussischkin specified, "We have given Sam Cohen carte blanche in this matter."[42]

By June 25, 1933, Cohen had accumulated enough written testaments of legitimacy to overcome any challenge from Landauer and the ZVfD. More important, he had Consul Wolff. And so, on June 24, even before all the supportive conferences and letters had become facts, Sam Cohen again visited Wolff and asked for assistance in fulfilling his promise to Ussischkin and in stifling any attempts to discredit Hanotaiah's efforts. Wolff dutifully obliged by sending an urgent letter to the Foreign Ministry in Berlin "as a follow-up to my report of June 15 on Sam Cohen's activities to break the boycott." This letter, however, mixed careful qualifications with the consul's usual unmitigated support for Cohen. Wolff was walking a tightrope between Zionist voices and Nazi ears. He was by now aware that although Cohen had assembled an arsenal of prestigious endorsements, his legitimacy was still very much in question. So Wolff formulated his sentences cautiously: "Today, Mr. Sam Cohen told me the following, which I have no reason to doubt since from reports I have about him I conclude that he is most reliable."[43]

Wolff continued, "In order to secure the necessary broad approval among Jewish circles . . . Mr. Sam Cohen several days ago held a meeting attended by the main local industrial representatives, workers, planters, and the Jewish National Fund, among others. On that occasion Mr. Sam Cohen obtained the concurrence of the . . . organizations for his plan [to bring German exports to Palestine]. The industrialists are especially interested in importing German machinery, which could amount to . . . some £300,000 [roughly RM 4 million]."[44]

Consul Wolff's June 24 letter added that this extraordinary development would be enhanced if Jewish National Fund money could be transferred, despite existing currency prohibitions. Acknowledging that circumventing the currency regulations was highly unusual, Wolff still made "a plea that if possible Mr. Sam Cohen be supported in this matter. In all these questions, my point of view is that the danger of the boycott, which in my opinion threatens not only in Palestine but in the whole world, can only be counteracted when the Jews come to the conclusion that the German government—speaking only from an economic point of view—is prepared to make a generous accommodation."[45]

Wolff asked Berlin "if a decision could be speeded up" on his June 15 request to expand Hanotaiah's deal from RM 1 million to several million.

Wolff then mentioned an additional incentive: substantial payment in actual foreign currency. Apparently, Sam Cohen envisioned generating so much foreign currency by widespread sales of German merchandise in Palestine and neighboring countries that he could afford to pay about 60 percent of the purchase price in actual foreign currency, the remainder coming out of blocked emigrant accounts.[46]

Consul Wolff claimed in his June 24 letter that Cohen was now off in Europe to wage his antiboycott campaign. Since there was little time to spare, Consul Wolff asked that the Reich's decision be sent not only to the Jersualem consulate but also "to Mr. Sam Cohen in care of the [German] consulate in Geneva, where he will look for messages to him, as he and I have agreed."[47] It was almost as though Sam Cohen had become part of the German diplomatic and trade apparatus, selling German goods, arranging for the emigration of German Jews, supplying foreign currency, stimulating German employment and breaking anti-Nazi boycotts. This, of course, was the desired appearance. But no matter how much Sam Cohen's pro-Reich activities were deliberately overaccentuated to evoke Nazi cooperation, there existed one salient, inescapable common ground: The national aspirations of both Nazis and Zionists hinged on the successful removal of Jews from Germany to Palestine.

And yet there was one major problem. German Jews simply didn't want to leave.

17. Jews, Zionists, Germans, Nazis

THE UNWILLINGNESS of German Jews to be forced from their country loomed as formidable an obstacle to transfer as any presented by German government policies or Zionist organizational strife. In fact, even if German Jews did consider a temporary hiatus from their beloved Fatherland, they envisioned other European countries as havens. The last place on their minds was Palestine. Historically, Zionism had always been a German Jewish taboo. Yet in 1933 the leaders of this shunned splinter were suddenly elevated to the status of spokesmen and agents of German Jewry—a people they did not represent. A broken-line triangle between German Jews, Zionism, and Nazism was the key to Zionism's sudden ascent as Jewish custodian for the Third Reich.

Nazi mythology accused Jews of being an alien factor in German society.

But in truth, Jews had lived in Germany since the fourth century A.D. As elsewhere in Europe during the Middle Ages, what German Jews could do and say, even their physical dress and appearance, was oppressively regulated. Confiscation of property and expulsion were frequent. Worse, anti-Jewish mobs often organized hangings and immolations at the stake. Even when left alone, German Jews could exist only in segregated ghettos subject to a long list of prohibitions.

The pressure to escape Germany's medieval persecution created a very special kind of Jew, one who subordinated his Jewish identity to the larger Christian society around him. Assimilation became a desirable antidote, especially among intellectuals during the Age of Enlightenment. When Napoleon conquered parts of Germany in the early nineteenth century, he granted Jews emancipation. But after Napoleon was defeated, the harsh German *status quo ante* was restored. The taste of freedom, however, led affluent and intellectual Jewish classes to assimilate en masse. Philosophically, assimilationists no longer considered themselves Jews living in Germany. Instead, they saw themselves as Germans who, by accident of birth, were Jewish.

Many even succumbed to the German pressure to convert to Christianity. German Jewry lost to apostasy many of their commercial, political, and intellectual leaders. A far greater number were convinced that Jewish ethnic identity should be denied, but nonetheless saw quintessential value in the tenets of Moses. These German Jews developed Reform Judaism. But even many of Reform Judaism's pioneers ultimately converted to Christianity.[1]

Between 1869 and 1871, Germany granted Jews emancipation from civic, commercial, and political restrictions, although certain prohibitions against high governmental, academic, and military office remained in force. Emancipation allowed acknowledged Jews to assimilate comfortably into German society. Germany's Jewry seized the chance to become equals. They changed their surnames, adopted greater religious laxity through Reform Judaism, and frequently married non-Jews, raising the children as Christians. Outright conversion became common.

In fact, of approximately 550,000 Jews in Germany who were emancipated in 1871, roughly 60,000 were by 1930 either apostates, children raised without Jewish identity by a mixed marriage, or Jews who had drifted totally away. Even those consciously remaining within organized Jewish "communities" neglected their remnant Jewish identity. The Jews of twentieth-century Germany, like their Christian neighbors, embraced national identity far more than religious identity. In the minds of German Jews, they were "101 percent" German, first and foremost.[2]

When political Zionism emerged shortly after emancipation, its principal leaders were Germanic, spoke German, and looked to Germany as the sponsor of a hoped-for Jewish home. Imperial Germany viewed Jewish notions of self-removal as a curiosity that appealed to basic anti-Semitic precepts. But German Jewry vehemently rejected Zionism as an enemy from within. Assimilated cosmopolitan Jews feared any assertion that they did not belong to Germany, any implication that Jewish loyalties were not to the Fatherland. The religious sector reacted with equal condemnation. Clinging to their communal existence, and unwilling to return to the Promised Land until beckoned by the Messiah, religious German Jews saw Zionism as sacrilege.[3]

So in 1897, when Herzl selected Munich as the site of the First Zionist Congress, Jewish leaders throughout Germany publicly protested until the convention was relocated to Basel. Anti-Zionism was one of the few Jewish topics Reform, Orthodox, cosmopolitan, and ghetto Jews could agree on.[4]

In the years after Basel, the movement earnestly tried to find acceptance among Germany's Jews. From 1905 to 1911, Zionism's world headquarters was seated in Cologne. But the overwhelming majority continued to revile it. In *The History of German Zionism*, German Zionist chronicler Richard Lichtheim recalls that "nowhere was the opposition of Jews to the new movement so widespread, principled, and fierce as in Germany." In March 1913, fed up with Zionist efforts to organize the withdrawal of Jews, the Central Verein, representing over half of German Jewry, expelled any member who advocated loyalty to any land other than the German Fatherland.[5]

When World War I broke out, it was an opportunity German Jews had awaited to prove they were patriotic, fully integrated Germans. About 100,000 Jews fought, 80,000 in the trenches. Some 12,000 were killed. And yet the persistence of Zionism still brought German Jewish patriotism into question. After Britain's 1917 Balfour Declaration promised a Jewish national home in Palestine, German Jews frantically avoided any identification with Zionist activities that might be interpreted as a link with Germany's enemy Britain.[6]

Before 1933, fewer than 1 percent of the *Yishuv*, or Jewish community in Palestine, had immigrated from Germany. In 1912, only 8,400 out of roughly 550,000 German Jews elected to pay the token shekel of Zionist membership. In 1927, German Zionist affiliation had grown to about 20,000. But that figure included many so-called *non-Zionists*, who endorsed Jewish philanthropic settlements in Palestine but wholly rejected the concept of Jewish nationalism. Many of these non-Zionists became financially involved simply to create an economic dependence that would allow them to control the more militant wings of the movement.[7]

Because the world headquarters of the Zionist Organization remained in Berlin during World War I, German Zionists were able to rise to an influential niche in the movement. Their connections with the kaiser's government were used to influence Turkey, to cancel violent Ottoman measures against the *Yishuv* after negotiations for the Balfour Declaration commenced in early

1917.[8] Even though the international seat of the movement shifted to London when the Jewish National Home was established, German Zionists retained an important place in Zionism. Their influence within the movement was still intact when Hitler came to power in 1933.

Zionism could have been expected to appeal to Nazis because the prospect of sending Jews back to Palestine appealed to the intellectual ancestor of Nazism, Martin Luther, leader of the Protestant Reformation.

In the early 1520s, the rebel monk Luther looked to the Jews as a potential following free from what he termed "papal paganism." So protective of Jews was Martin Luther that church superiors branded him *semi-Judaeus* or half-Jew. But in the late 1520s, Luther began showing irritation with German Jewry's refusal to abandon Judaism.[9]

In the early 1540s, Luther underwent a startling philosophical transformation, from archdefender to archassailant. In 1543, Luther published a vitriolic anti-Semitic pamphlet entitled "On The Jews and Their Lies" that virtually specified, down to the phrasing, the height and breadth of Nazi-style political anti-Semitism.

Luther's words: "They have been bloodthirsty bloodhounds and murderers of all Christendom for more than fourteen hundred years in their intentions. . . . Thus they have been accused of poisoning water and wells, of kidnapping children, of piercing them through with an awl, of hacking them in pieces, and in that way secretly cooling their wrath with the blood of Christians." There was no doubt in Luther's writings. He employed endless repetition to avoid any mistake. And in this pamphlet his point was clear: "The sun has never shone on a more bloodthirsty and vengeful people."[10]

Luther insisted that the Jews had enslaved Germans. Luther's words: "In fact, they hold us Christians captive in our own country. They let us work in the sweat of our brow to earn money and property while they sit behind the stove, idle away the time, fart and roast pears. They stuff themselves, guzzle and live in luxury and ease from our hard-earned goods. . . . Thus they are our masters and we are their servants."[11]

Luther suggested a solution to the Jewish problem in Germany: force them to return to Jerusalem. Luther's words: "[The Jews] should as we said, be expelled from the country and be told to return to their land and their possessions in Jerusalem, where they may . . . murder, steal, rob, practice usury, mock and indulge in all those infamous abominations which they practice among us, and leave us our government, our country, our life and our property . . . undefiled and uncontaminated."[12]

He vehemently rejected the notion that ghettoized Jews were held captive in medieval Germany. Luther's words: "We surely did not bring them from Jerusalem . . . No one is holding them here now. The country and the roads are open for them to proceed to their land whenever they wish. If they did so, we would be glad to present gifts to them on the occasion; it would be good riddance. . . . They must be driven from our country. Let them think of their fatherland [Jerusalem]. . . . This is . . . the best course of action, which will safeguard the interest of both parties."[13]

Luther knew Germany's Jews would be "loath to quit the country, they will boldly deny everything and will also offer the government money enough for permission to remain here." And so he explained a seven-point program for wiping out German Jewry. Luther's words: "I shall give you my sincere advice: First, to set fire to their synagogues or schools and to bury and cover with dirt whatever will not burn, so that no man will ever again see a stone or cinder of them. . . . Second, I advise that their houses also be razed and destroyed. . . . Instead they might be lodged under a roof or in a barn. . . . This will bring home to them . . . that they are living in exile and captivity, as they incessantly wail and lament about us.[14]

"Third, I advise that all their prayer books . . . be taken from them. Fourth, I advise that their rabbis be forbidden to teach henceforth on pain of loss of life and limb. . . . Fifth, I advise that safe-conduct on the highways be abolished completely for the Jews. . . . Sixth, I advise . . . that all cash and treasure of silver and gold be taken from them. . . . Seventh, I recommend putting a flail, an ax, a hoe, a spade, a distaff, or a spindle into the hands of young, strong Jews and Jewesses and letting them earn their bread in the sweat of their brow."[15]

Luther's program called for the abolition of Jewish rights, the seizure of their assets, the destruction of their homes and synagogues, concentration in misery, and forced labor. However, Luther suggested that his final step, forced labor, would be so impossible for the lazy, untrustworthy Jews that it would by itself lead to negotiation over their assets, and then expulsion: "Then let us . . . compute with them how much their usury has extorted from us, divide this amicably, but then eject them forever from the country."[16]

Luther asserted that any Christian who showed mercy toward a Jew would himself burn in the fires of Hell. His treatise's parting instruction were as follows: "Act like a good physician who, when gangrene has set in, proceeds without mercy to cut, saw and burn flesh, veins, bone, and marrow. . . . Burn down their synagogues, forbid all that I enumerated earlier, force them to work, and deal harshly with them. . . . Therefore it would be wrong to be merciful. . . . We must drive them out like mad dogs. . . . I have done my duty. Now let everyone see to his. I am exonerated."[17]

Luther's advice about Jewish persecutions and expulsions was espoused in 1543, after the principles of the Lutheran movement had already been formalized in the Augsburg Confession of 1530.[18] Consequently, the Luther Solution was at first not widely taught in the church schools that Luther had so profound an influence over. But it was kept alive in the seventeenth and eighteenth centuries by renegade churchmen. The Luther Solution was revived as a national issue in the second half of the nineteenth century. The German Jews had been emancipated in 1871, thus becoming visible in all sectors of German life. Visibility had always been a fear of the Jews. The fear was vindicated this time as well.

Adolf Stoecker, the Court and Cathedral Preacher of Berlin, led the reaction in 1874. He used his church position to organize an anti-Semitic political party that included many clerics dedicated to expunging the Jewish presence from German society. Stoecker was in fact dubbed "the Second Luther." His relentless Judophobic preaching included the now familiar slogan "The Jews are Germany's misfortune." The words were taken from Luther's original treatise.[19]

Stoecker and other anti-Semitic German nationalists were the impetus behind the Union of German Students, an anti-Jewish society organized in 1881. The Union, represented at every major university, included a large number of theological students who became the carriers of church-disseminated anti-Semitic dogma at the turn of the twentieth century.[20]

Two rabid German national anti-Semites who gained prominence during the Stoecker heyday were Houston Steward Chamberlain and Theodor Fritsch. Fritsch, in the late 1880s, helped form anti-Semitic political parties that would later evolve into the NSDAP. The Nazis referred to him as their spiritual leader. Chamberlain became Hitler's personal inspiration.[21]

In 1917, a Germany gripped by war lavishly marked the four-hundredth anniversary of Luther's Reformation. It was the perfect moment for a Luther revival. As Germans struggled to defend the Fatherland, Luther's ideology of territorial and ethnic destiny gave them conviction and encouragement.[22]

A few years later, a defeated Germany was again looking to Luther, this time for strength and solace. During the 1920s, the church literally became an extension of German nationalism. The purity of German blood, the sanctity of German religion, and the destiny of the German people were all woven into a virtual theomania. Integral to this movement was the compulsion to exclude Jews for all the reasons Martin Luther had enumerated four centuries earlier.[23]

Anti-Semitic German nationalists outside the church resurrected the Luther Solution. They called themselves Nazis. In their campaigns to recruit support, Brownshirts spoke the familiar phrasing of Germany's religious patriarch. From the street corners they constantly reminded that Martin Luther was beckoning Germany to expel the Jews.[24]

In spring 1933, Hitler reflected the weight of Luther's words upon his own thought. During a newspaper interview, Hitler asked who was "prepared to harbor . . . those who have poisoned the wells of Germany, of the whole Christian world. Gladly we would give each and every one of them a railroad pass and a thousand mark note for pocket money to be rid of them."[25]

From Luther's treatise "On the Jews and Their Lies": "They have been

. . . murderers of all Christendom for more than fourteen hundred years . . . poisoning water and wells. . . . The country and the roads are open to them to proceed to their land whenever they wish. If they did so, we would be glad to present gifts to them on the occasion; it would be good riddance."[26]

Julius Streicher's newspaper *Der Sturmer* bannered the Luther slogan in every issue: *"Die Juden sind unser Ungluck!"*—The Jews Are Our Misfortune![27] And one of Streicher's anti-Jewish picture books was titled after the Martin Luther adage "Trust no fox in the field and no Jew under his oath."[28] In Germany, preaching Jew hatred was as good as preaching the gospel.

When Streicher was captured by the Allies in 1945, they confiscated his personal copy of "On the Jews and Their Lies." At the Nuremburg War Crimes Trials, Streicher, a philosophical descendant of a centuries-long tradition, explained his actions with these words: "Martin Luther would very probably sit in my place in the defendant's dock today if this book had been taken into consideration. . . . In the book "[On] The Jews and Their Lies" Dr. Martin Luther writes that . . . one should burn down their synagogues and destroy them."[29]

Martin Luther gave rise to nothing less than a jagged and saltatory lineage of Jew-hating German nationalists that culminated in the men and women of the Nazi movement.

The Nazis had always glossed over Zionist aspirations for statehood. Hitler believed that Jewish laziness, decadence, and impurity made Jewish nationhood an impossibility. In Hitler's words, spoken in the first days of Nazi organization: "The establishment of a [Zionist] state is nothing but a comedy."[30]

Instead, the Nazis seized upon the one aspect of Zionism they approved of: the condemnation of a Jewish presence in Germany and the desire to remove Jews to Palestine. On April 6, 1920, in Munich, Hitler explained the Nazi willingness to embrace Zionism with these words: "To reach our goal, we must use every means at our disposal, even if we have to make a pact with the devil himself." Ironically, Vladimir Jabotinsky had spoken essentially the same words several months before, when he declared to the Twelfth Zionist Congress: "In working for Palestine, I would even ally myself with the devil."[31]

A few months after his April 1920 promulgation, Hitler made the point again, at a Munich beer hall. While he was preaching his doctrine of Jewish expulsion, someone from the crowd hollered something about human rights. Hitler answered sharply, "Let him [the Jew] look for his human rights where he belongs: in his own state of Palestine."[32]

Hitler's foremost theoretician on Judaism and Zionism, Alfred Rosenberg, adopted Hitler's willingness to exploit Zionism. Writing in 1920 in the Nazi newspaper *Die Spur*, Rosenberg demanded that Germans lay aside all feelings of antipathy: "Zionism must be actively supported so as to enable us annually to transport a specific number of Jews to Palestine, or, in any case, across our borders."[33]

With the appointment of Adolf Hitler, the moment was ripe for a hateful alliance; Nazis and Zionists working in concert for a Jewish exodus. In the first months of 1933, German Zionists knew they faced either total demise or ultimate vindication.[34] So, in a bold move, the ZVfD launched a two-sided campaign: first, to convince the Nazis to recognize Zionism as the custodian of Germany's Jews; second, to convince Germany's Jews to admit that yes, German Jewry belonged in Palestine.

On January 31, 1933, within twenty-four hours of Hitler's appointment, the ZVfD newspaper, *Juedische Rundschau*, asserted that the defense of Jewish rights could be waged only by Zionists, not mainstream Jewry. After the May 10 Nazi book burnings, *Juedische Rundschau* mourned the loss as did all Jews, but could not resist publicly labeling many of the Jewish authors "renegades" who had betrayed their roots.[35] The anti-assimilationist barrage continued weekly with Zionist aspersions sounding painfully similar to the Nazi line discrediting the German citizenship of Jews.

It became that much harder for German Jews to defend against Nazi accusations of illegitimate citizenship when a loud and visible group of their own continually published identical indictments. It was as mainstream German Jewry feared, and as Nazi philosopher Alfred Rosenberg made clear in his anti-Semitic teachings: "If an organization inside the state declares that the interests of the German Reich do not concern it, it renounces all its civil rights."[36] Zionism had become a tool for anti-Semites.

The Hitler hierarchy was at first unwilling to work with Zionism, lest the rank and file misunderstand the association. In fact, by March 1933 the ZVfD was clearly marked for extinction.[37] But all that changed when Stephen Wise rattled the boycott and protest saber at Germany. The critical minute for Zionism had come during the March 25 meeting with Goering. The Zionists stepped forward and offered to try to dissuade Wise from holding his Madison Square Garden rally. In that instant, the Zionist relationship to National Socialist goals underwent a rapid transformation, from theoretical to practical.

Sensing the change, *Juedische Rundschau* called in an April 7 column for Zionists and Nazis to be "honest partners."[38] Instrumental in developing this partnership was ZVfD activist Kurt Tuchler, whose many acquaintances in the NSDAP included an Austrian-born engineer named Baron Leopold von Mildenstein, an SS officer dealing with Jewish affairs. Tuchler wanted to convince von Mildenstein's circle that the NSDAP should openly promote Jewish nationalism. If von Mildenstein could write a pro-Palestine article in Goebbels' widely read newspaper, *Der Angriff*, it might sway many in the party and the government. Von Mildenstein was receptive, but insisted that he could write a believable piece only if he actually toured Palestine. So Tuchler invited von Mildenstein to Palestine. In late April 1933, both men and their wives boarded an ocean liner for Palestine. The Nazi party and the ZVfD each had granted permission for the joint trip. Von Mildenstein approved of what he saw in the kibbutzim and in Tel Aviv. He even learned a few Hebrew words. Many photographs were taken, numerous mementos were dragged back to Germany. An elaborate illustrated series was published about eighteen months later in *Der Angriff* under the title "A Nazi Goes to Palestine." Goebbels' newspaper was so proud of the series that a commemorative coin was struck in honor of the voyage. On one side was a swastika. On the other side a Star of David.[39]

Von Mildenstein rapidly became the party expert on Zionism. He was said to have read Herzl's *"Der Judenstaat"* and insisted his subordinates do likewise. One of these subordinates was a man named Adolf Eichmann. Von Mildenstein, and later Eichmann, developed the Jewish Section of the Reich Security Main Office, which in the late 1930s coordinated Jewish emigration policies. In the early 1940s, Eichmann's domain would change from emigration and Zionism to deportation and genocide, as he orchestrated the shuttling of millions of Jews to the gas chambers of Europe.[40]

The Nazi recognition of Zionism that began in April of 1933 was apparent because the Zionists enjoyed a visibly protected political status in Germany. Immediately after the Reichstag fire of February 27, the Nazis crushed virtually all political opposition. Through emergency decrees, most non-Nazi political organizations and suspect newspapers were dissolved. In fact, about 600 newspapers were officially banned during 1933. Others were unofficially silenced by street methods. The exceptions included *Juedische Rundschau*, the ZVfD's weekly, and several other Jewish publications. German Zionism's weekly was hawked on street corners and displayed at newsstands. When Chaim Arlosoroff visited Zionist headquarters in London on June 1, he emphasized, "The *Rundschau* is of crucial importance today for the Zionists. Every day it gets fifty to sixty new subscribers." By the end of 1933, *Juedische Rundschau*'s circulation had in fact jumped to more than 38,000— four to five times its 1932 circulation.[41] Although many influential Aryan publications were forced to restrict their page size to conserve newsprint, *Juedische Rundschau* was not affected until mandatory newsprint rationing in 1937.[42]

And while stringent censorship of all German publications was enforced from the outset, *Juedische Rundschau* was allowed comparative press freedoms. Although two issues of *Juedische Rundschau* were suppressed when they published Chaim Arlosoroff's outline for a capital transfer, such seizures were rare. Other than the ban on anti-Nazi boycott references, printing atrocity stories, and criticizing the Reich, *Juedische Rundschau* was essentially exempt from the so-called *Gleichschaltung* or "uniformity" demanded by the Nazi party of all facets of German society. *Juedische Rundschau* was free to preach Zionism as a wholly separate political philosophy—indeed, the only separate political philosophy sanctioned by the Third Reich.[43]

In 1933, Hebrew became an encouraged course in all Jewish schools. By 1935, uniforms for Zionist youth corps were permitted—the only non-Nazi uniform allowed in Germany. When the Nuremburg Laws in late 1935 stripped German Jewry of their citizenship, it became illegal for Jews to raise the German flag; the same law, however, stipulated that German Jewry could raise the Star of David-emblazoned Zionist flag.[44]

The ZVfD's quick success in lobbying the Zionist option to the Reich advanced the priority of their second imperative: convincing German Jewry to relinquish ten centuries of German national existence. But the bulk of German Jewry wanted another solution to their predicament.

They wanted to stay, even as second-class citizens—even reviled and persecuted. The hot springs and baths, the outdoor *Konzerten* of Bach and Mozart, the readings of Goethe, Oriental carpets on the floor, exotic fruits from Africa, a noble tradition they had fought for, died for, profited by. These people were integrated. They were Germans. They wanted to stay, even as helots.

Zionism said no. While mainstream Jewish organizations were frantically assembling theories and position papers suggesting a tapered-down but still German national existence, the Zionists were doing the opposite. On June 21, 1933, a long ZVfD memorandum was sent directly to Hitler outlining those Zionist tenets that were consistent with National Socialist ideology. For example: "Zionism believes that a rebirth . . . such as that in German tradition resulting from a combination of Christian and national values, must also come about within the Jewish community. Racial background, religion, a common fate and tribal consciousness must be of decisive importance in developing a lifestyle for Jews too. . . . Zionism's objective is to organize Jewish emigration to Palestine in such a way that it improves the Jewish situation in Germany. . . . Jewish settlement is based on agriculture. All productive work, be it of an agricultural, craftsmanship, or industrial nature, is performed by Jewish workers who are inspired by a new, idealistic work ethic."[45]

The German Zionist memo to Hitler contained the obligatory appeals to Nazi prejudices about Jewish laziness and calculated comparisons between the two movements. This was the only way to converse with the Nazi regime. Nazis were philosophically trained to dismiss as standard Jewish trickery any logical, civil, and legal arguments by Jews laden with words of justice and compassion. On the other hand, Nazis weren't fooled by the obvious Zionist use of Aryan rhetoric. Rather, they viewed the Zionists not as partners, but as agents who would act not out of interest for the Reich but for their own Jewish national aspirations. And while the Zionists indeed spoke in the Aryan context, they recognized fully that they were speaking to an enemy of the Jews, an enemy who understood that Zionist approaches were not for the sake of the German state, but for the sake of the Jewish state. This mutual understanding was even set down in writing in the Zionists' June 21 memo to Hitler: "For its objectives, Zionism feels able to enlist the cooperation of a basically anti-Jewish government, because dealing with the Jewish problem does not involve sentimentality." The memo added that it was precisely that absence of Zionist sentimentality about the anti-Semitic regimes it worked with that committed the worldwide Zionist movement against the anti-Nazi boycott.[46]

Perhaps no more dramatic example of German Zionism versus German Jewry exists than a *Juedische Rundschau* article entitled "Wear It with Pride, the Yellow Spot!," written by editor Robert Weltsch. This article appeared April 4, 1933, as one of the first German Jewish comments following the shock of the aborted April First anti-Jewish boycott action. Decades after the fact, Weltsch's article is held up as an act of courage comforting the Jewish community in a moment of anguish while the nation around them was reviving the medieval concept of Jews wearing an identifying yellow spot on their clothing.

In fact, Weltsch's article was a barbed chastisement of German Jewish assimilation in Germany at the very moment when Jews were struggling to preserve their legal status as citizens. Weltsch's words:

April 1, 1933 will remain an important date in the annals of the German Jew and the entire Jewish people. The events of that day have not only a political and economic, but also moral side. . . . Our concern is the moral aspect. . . . On April 1, the German Jews received a lesson which goes much deeper than even its embittered and today triumphant opponents can guess. . . . Our concern is how does Jewry react to all this.

April 1, 1933 can be a day of Jewish awakening and Jewish rebirth. If the Jews want it to be. If the Jews are mature enough and possess sufficient inner greatness. . . . We must recommend that during these days the publication which stood at the cradle of Zionism, Theodor Herzl's *Judenstaat*, be distributed among Jews and non-Jews in hundreds of thousands of copies.

We Jews who have been brought up in the spirit of Theodor Herzl are not accusing today—we only seek to understand. And to ask ourselves where our own guilt lies, how we have sinned. . . . Jewry bears a heavy burden of guilt because not only did it not heed Theodor Herzl's call, it even partially ridiculed it. . . . It is not true that the Jews are traitors to the German nation. If they have committed treason, it was directed against themselves, against Jewry.

Because every Jew did not proudly bear his Jewishness, because he wanted nothing to do with the Jewish question, he shares the guilt for all Jewry's humiliation. Despite all the bitterness we feel reading the National Socialist calls for [an anti-Jewish] boycott . . . we can still be grateful . . . for one thing. The [boycott] guidelines state in paragraph 3: . . . "this concerns businesses which belong to members of the Jewish race. Religion is irrelevant. Businessmen who have been baptized Catholics or Protestants or dissidents of the Jewish race are, for the purposes of this decree, Jews."

This is a reminder for all traitors to Jewry. He who sneaks away from the community [by assimilating] in order to improve his own situation should not be rewarded for his treason. This attitude toward renegades contains the beginning of a clarification. . . . To be a renegade is shameful; but so long as the world put a premium on it, it appeared to be advantageous. Now it is an advantage no longer. A Jew is being identified as such. He is given the yellow spot.

The fact that the boycott leadership decreed that boycotted businesses be identified with "a yellow spot on a black background" is a tremendous symbol. This measure is meant to be a stigma, a show of contempt. We accept it, and we want to make it a badge of honor. . . . Among other symbols and inscriptions, many store windows were painted with a big Star of David. Jews, pick it up . . . and carry it with pride!

. . . If National Socialism recognizes this state of affairs, it would no doubt wish as its Jewish partner a Jewry which values its honor.[47]

Only a few of the dramatic catchphrases from Weltsch's article have been remembered, hence the myth that his words were an act of comfort. But for the 97 percent of German Jewry who rejected Zionism and accepted German assimilation,[48] Weltsch's denigrations and dramatic calls for a bold abandonment of ten centuries of German existence were painful and foreboding. His words signaled the beginning of what Diaspora Jews had always feared about Zionism—the day it would be used as the legal and moral pretext for forcing Jews out of European society.

The broken-line triangle between German Jews, Zionism, and Nazism, now filled in by tears, blood, and hate, explains how a fringe minority of German Jews—numbering just a small percent of the community—assumed emergency custody of 550,000 men, women, and children. Based on that custodial privilege, the Zionist movement in Palestine, Germany, Great Britain, and America continued to debate how best to claim the Jewish nation waiting within the borders of the Third Reich.

18. Jews Lead the World to Boycott

MOST JEWS in America and Europe committed to political and economic battle with the Reich were also avid Zionists. But many of them possessed a Diaspora Zionist orientation; that is, they valued the right to live in the nations of the world as coequal to, not mutually exclusive with, the *right of return*.

To most Diaspora Jews, the tug of Palestine and the right of assimilated citizenship elsewhere represented a *choice* rather than a *conflict*. With the ascent of Hitler, these Jews would not tolerate one right to be subordinated to the other. While their political agitation often included demands to open the gates of Palestine to German Jews, care was taken not to abandon the struggle to defeat Nazi persecution of those Jews who wanted to stay. In fact, as Hitler became a progressively deadlier menace, most Jews felt the work for Palestine should be prioritized *second*. First and foremost was the battle to save German Jews in the context of their right to live freely in Europe.

That meant boycott and protest. It was emotionally impossible for Jewish circles to do otherwise. The daily reports of outrageous atrocities and persecution cried out for a punitive reaction.

Examples: In mid-May 1933, *The Manchester Guardian* and *The London Jewish Chronicle* reported that a Berlin Jew picked up by Storm Troopers was not seen again until his body was discovered two weeks later amid sewage outside the city. The victim had been "horribly mutilated, his face had been smashed in and his lips had been cut open."[1]

On June 9, *The Jewish Chronicle* reported how a squad of four Brownshirts broke into a Berlin dressmaker's apartment at 2:30 A.M. The Nazis decided to "squeeze the Jewish blood" out of the eighteen-year-old son. "In front of the parents they . . . started beating him with whips. One sat on his head, another on his feet, and the other two beat him for ten minutes. All the time, the parents were ordered to keep their eyes wide open and watch the scene. . . . [Then] they decided . . . to cut out a swastika on his forehead so that he should remember 'the good times of Nazi rule.' But, not with a knife was the . . . work done, but with their revolvers. Each of the four Nazis kept hitting the boy on the head, so as to form the wound into a swastika. The boy's face was a mass of raw flesh, and so was most of his body." The Brownshirts left the house with a warning not to " 'tell stories about Nazis.' "[2]

In late June, *The Jewish Chronicle* reported the invasion of a Jewish clothes merchant's home in the fashionable section of Berlin. SA hooligans "broke down the doors of Herr Friedenberg's flat and attacked him savagely, beating him for an hour on end with their rubber truncheons, chairs, or anything that came to hand. His groans and cries could be heard out in the street."[3]

German Jews knew that it was better to endure silently. To complain was to be marked as a purveyor of *Greuelpropaganda*, which would only bring more hooligan punishment upon a victim's family and business—not to mention actual prosecution, which generally meant shipment to the Dachau concentration camp. Family and friends frequently did not even know the grisly details. The local NSDAP unit would often order the body to be either cremated or buried before the family was notified. And the Jewish Burial Society was under explicit instructions to not reveal information about the physical condition of any corpses.[4]

Nonetheless, a fraction of the sadistic tales did leak out, mainly via the scores of refugees who streamed out daily. Relief sources estimated that 90 percent of the Jews reaching Poland by June 1933 had suffered physical violence. About 25 percent of the refugees, including women and young girls, still bore the wounds of torture.[5] And travelers—businessmen, diplomats, and academics—regularly brought back stories of uncontrolled street violence.[6]

Of course, the Third Reich tried to deny that *any* anti-Jewish violence was occurring in Germany. In an interview in mid-June 1933, Hitler tried to assure a *Colliers Weekly* correspondent: "Perfect calm reigns in Germany. Not a street has been destroyed. Not a house. . . . If only all Americans could come over here! They would look about and ask themselves where is this revolution, where is this terror, where is all this destruction and chaos I've heard about?"[7]

Such calming statements were not convincing in the face of repeated public promises by prominent Nazis to kill every Jew in Germany. Just a few weeks before Hitler's statement to *Colliers Weekly*, Nazi boycott leader Julius Streicher told a meeting in Nuremberg that if Germany went to war, every Jew in Germany would be killed. At the same time, Nazi leaders in Danzig issued a secret memorandum, a copy of which was obtained and published by *The London Daily Herald*. The memo claimed, "Final punishment of the enemies of the German nation, in the first rank of whom are the Jews, will be ordered by Hitler at the right moment. . . . That which tomorrow may be a holy duty must today be left undone."[8] At the same time, a prominent German physician published in a German medical journal his solution to the Jewish problem: sterilization.[9]

Even the American Jewish Committee, which had tried to pretend the atrocities did not exist, was compelled by mid-June 1937 to admit that anti-Jewish violence in Germany was rampant. In a booklet entitled "The Jews in Nazi Germany," which they released to the media, the Committee detailed count after count of Nazi brutality. *The New York Times* endorsed the Committee booklet as a believable bill of particulars of the Reich's anti-Jewish campaign and advised the public to reject all German denials.[10]

The question before the world now was whether the Hitler regime could be smitten down quickly—certainly before it pauperized German Jewry, but more important, before it could carry out the recurring Nazi promise of destruction to 550,000 Jewish men, women and children. Protest and boycott were the only weapons at the disposal of those who opposed the Reich.

So the protests and boycotts continued. City after city hosted Madison Square-style rallies throughout the month of May. Melbourne, Philadelphia, Buenos Aires, Warsaw, Marseilles. The protest movement in England was especially contagious. Raucous mass demonstrations started in Manchester and swept through Newcastle, Leeds, Birmingham, and Glasgow. The protests culminated in an overflow rally May 16 at London's Queen Hall.[11]

During May, the boycott movement continued to spread, especially where there were Jews to fire the issue. *Cairo*: The League Against German Anti-Semitism demanded that all Egyptian Jews lead a national boycott of German goods and services. *Gibraltar*: One thousand Jewish merchants vowed to boycott all German merchandise. *Paris*: Filmgoers cheered a band of Jewish youths who disrupted a German film; more disruptions were promised for any future German screenings.[12] *London*: The extensive boycott against German ocean liners was in large part due to Jewish passengers switching to British and Italian vessels; prior to the boycott, half of all Anglo-Jewish ocean travelers sailed on German ships.[13]

Buenos Aires: German commercial interests in Argentina were powerless to stop the accelerating boycott organized by Argentinian Jews; the Argentine boycott not only involved German ships and products, but called for depositors to transfer accounts from German to Argentine banks. *Paris*: The League Against Anti-Semitism began proliferating the boycott throughout the provinces by opening boycott offices in Lyons, Nice, and Marseilles.[14] *Amsterdam*: Two boycott groups printed thousands of "boycott stamps" to be used on envelopes and parcels. The stamps featured a swastika transmuted into a four-headed snake behind prison bars over Dutch, French, and English inscriptions urging boycott. They quickly became an international boycott tool. In late May, sample stamps were delivered to New York for the American movement by a Dutch physician. But the Jewish War Veterans were already mailing an American version at the rate of 10 million per week.[15]

A sudden growth in the boycott was also spurred when national trade unions became active in the movement. British trades were sympathetic from the beginning in March 1933. But by late May, guided by Jewish industrialist Lord Melchett, the powerful Trades Union Congress (a union federation) declared the anti-Nazi boycott a mandatory pursuit for its members. The T.U.C. instructed member unions, Labour party supporters, and Cooperative Societies to bring the benefits of boycott to British manufacturers.[16]

At about the same time, the Dutch Federation of Trade Unions and the Social Democratic Labour party in Holland adopted a stance identical to British labor. Britain's ambassador at The Hague reported that the boycotters acknowledged the "harmful effect such a boycott would have on Dutch agricultural exports to Germany . . . but decline to be deterred by such considerations."[17]

If anyone in Berlin dreamed that the mid-May deal with Sam Cohen would act as an automatic boycott circuit breaker, they quickly realized they were mistaken. During late May, German consulates throughout the world continued to report attacks on Reich commercial interests. On May 24,

Hitler was handed a report on the entire foreign-trade question. Protectionist trade policies coupled with the growing international boycott were listed as the two principal reasons for Germany's dwindling exports. The report explained that the boycott itself was a joint reaction by Jewish groups and labor unions. The prospects: bleak.[18]

By June, data from the previous months was starting to pile up in Reich offices like delayed battle casualty reports. The news was always worse than expected. Germany's vital trade surplus for the first four months of 1933 was down more than 50 percent from the 1932 figure, dropping from RM 70.2 million to RM 35.4 million.[19] Throughout North Africa, ordered and shipped German goods were being refused, resulting in staggering losses. Egyptian refusals alone amounted to about $500,000 weekly.[20]

Specific German industries were hit hard. Reeling from the failure of the Leipzig fur auction, in June the fur industry was authorized to proclaim: "Jews in the fur trade are welcome in Leipzig."[21] But Jews in foreign countries who controlled almost all wholesale fur transactions were keeping their promise to destroy Germany's fur business. Jews were also heavily represented in the international textile market. Britain's most outspoken boycott leader, Lord Melchett, headed one of England's textile conglomerates. So when Germany's already suffering textile industry suddenly lost another RM 1 million in sales, the Reich readily conceded that the boycott was responsible.[22]

Perhaps the most devastating and visible loss struck the German diamond industry. Previously Germany had employed 5,000 diamond workers, even as thousands of Dutch polishers went jobless. In the last days of May, Holland's mostly Jewish diamond traders collectively refused to send any more gems to Germany for polishing or cutting. In less than a week, 4,000 unemployed Dutch diamond workers were hired in Antwerp and Amsterdam to handle the diverted business. Germany's lucrative diamond industry was dismantled overnight.[23]

The Jews were striking back. Not in the shoulder, where the enemy was armored, but in the region of the wallet, where the enemy was tender and exposed.

By early June 1933, the specter of collapse was hovering over the Third Reich. On June 6, Hjalmar Schacht sent a grim letter to the Führer reporting that as of May 31, only RM 280 million in gold and foreign-exchange reserves remained in the Reichsbank. There was now "the great danger that the foreign exchange available will no longer be adequate for the orderly payment of the millions needed daily in German foreign trade transactions. This danger is all the greater, since the constant reduction of available foreign exchange reserves causes foreign trade to shrink more and more." Schacht then confirmed what foreign newspapers had already published, that Germany's positive trade balance—that is, her vital surplus of exports over imports—for the first quarter of 1933 was *less than half* the 1932 figure: down from RM 94 million to RM 44 million. Schacht warned that a drastic decline in trade was now "dangerously imminent."[24]

"We should not wait for such a situation to occur if we do not want to jeopardize payments for imports, especially of raw materials and semi-finished goods, the processing of which forms the basis for the *employment of a highly qualified German labor force*."[25] The words, underlined by Schacht, carried an ominous message. Germany's exports were mainly finished goods, which relied upon the imported components. It was one thing for Germany to default on its past debts, bonds, and intergovernmental obligations. But if Germany could not continue the day-to-day purchasing needed to keep its people working, they would suddenly stop working.

Schacht demanded an immediate prohibition on paying foreign-exchange obligations incurred before the bank crisis of July 1931, except those required by the Standstill Agreement, which froze most of Germany's debts as part of a restructured repayment plan. This measure would barely allow Germany to continue day-to-day business.[26] France's ambassador in Berlin, André Francois-Poncet, visited Reich Foreign Minister von Neurath the next night, June 7, to protest that French creditors would be severely affected. Von Neurath defended the move as a natural consequence of the export decline.[27] It was Germany's old argument against the boycott. How could she honor her international debts when her ability to pay was dependent upon exports that were being refused throughout the world?

American complainers were more outspoken. Chief among them was John Foster Dulles, an attorney representing American banks. Ironically, Schacht had always believed that the threat to default on American holders of German bonds, due to a lack of foreign exchange resulting from the boycott, would be a major incentive for Americans to reject the anti-Hitler campaign. But Dulles' written protest promised even more retaliation: "I believe that if Germany inaugurates such a system, your outgo of *devisen* [foreign currency] will continue to be very substantial and your income of devisen will be very sharply reduced due to increased obstacles and prejudices against the use of German goods and services." The last clause bore the familiar ring of anti-Nazi boycott phraseology. Dulles' message added, "There is already a considerable element which is discriminating against the use of German goods and services. This may prove to be merely a passing phase, or it may crystallize into a well-defined national attitude. In my opinion it will crystallize if . . . [Germany] alienates that important element of our population which is represented by the holders of German bonds."[28]

Punctuating his threat with the statement "Defaulted bonds do not evaporate," Dulles listed retaliatory measures beyond a boycott, including a court-ordered seizure of German private and public assets in the United States. An attached memo actually itemized some of the assets that could be liquidated: the vessels and revenues of three German shipping lines; the property and funds of the German-Atlantic Cable Company; the AEG and Gesfurel electric companies; and the United Steel Works; plus the deposits of at least two major German banks in the United States. Together the targeted assets represented $155 million. But Dulles promised that the seizures would extend even to unrelated German firms abroad that owed money to the targeted German debtors.[29] In other words, Dulles was threatening a systematic repossesssion, confiscation, and liquidation of Germany's international commerce.

Currency and debt manipulations bought time, but precious little of it. Nazi leaders were frantic and divided on how best to fight the boycott. Increased threats were offered. In a June 10 *Volkischer Beobachter* editorial reprinted in America, Hitler's philosopher Alfred Rosenberg warned, "The fate of the Jews . . . might become worse if world Jewry does not give up its isolation plan against German business."[30] But boycotters ignored such threats, believing that Nazi persecution was proceeding as swiftly as possible—boycott or not.

In one test case, the Reich used its precious remaining influence with a foreign power to outlaw a boycott movement. This happened in Latvia, one of the strongest boycott centers in the Baltic region. In late May, the German embassy sought court restraint for Jewish student groups urging a boycott of German films. Then in early June, shortly after the All-Latvian Jewish Conference and various Socialist groups voted to officially sponsor a boycott, the Reich hit back with a German boycott of Latvian butter. Germany promised that butter was only the beginning. In truth, the Reich could not afford to disrupt more bilateral trade than that; butter was selected only because such a ban was already needed to protect the domestic German butter market. But for Latvia, the warning was sufficient. Within a week, von Neurath had concluded an agreement in London with the Latvian foreign minister to ban all further anti-Nazi boycott activities in Latvia. However, while the agreement did reduce open anti-Nazi organizing, Latvian boycott groups in fact remained in the forefront of international boycott actions.[31]

But the Latvian case was isolated. The anti-Hitler movements in other countries were only becoming more organized and more comprehensive. One of the most threatening precedents was being set in England by an elderly gentleman named Capt. Walter Joseph Webber. Captain Webber, who earned the nickname "the Gallant Captain," established a system of "boycott certificates" for British stores. Just as the NSDAP in Germany had circulated window certificates for Aryan businesses free of Jewish commercial dealings, so Captain Webber's organization in England would begin distributing window certificates for stores in strict compliance with the anti-Nazi boycott. Those stores not displaying certificates would be blacklisted and, if necessary, boycotted themselves. If Webber's vigilant inspectors found any breach, the certificate would be removed.[32]

At first, Captain Webber set June 15, 1933, as the deadline for compliance. But when a multitude of shops asked for extra time either to return or to sell off at discount their remaining German inventory, the deadline was extended to July 1. When the certificates were finally released, 5,000 were affixed to store windows in England the first day alone. Many went to non-Jewish concerns. Adherence was strictly enforced in Jewish neighborhoods. For example, late one Friday night, Mr. Isaac Angel's London toy store was found with German stock. An angry mob of about a thousand protesters surrounded the store and became so menacing that mounted police were dispatched. The incident ended only when the frail Captain was summoned and escorted through the crowd to confer with Mr. Angel. The protesters finally dispersed when assured the German toys would be sent back, whereupon a certificate of compliance would be issued.[33]

Despite the economic and psychological impact of local and national boycotts, what the Nazis feared most was a coordinated global operation. For instance, when a haberdasher in London considered refusing to sell German gloves, where was he to find alternate sources of gloves? When an optical house in Newark considered switching its long-established German source of ground lenses, where were the new lenses to come from? Locating new distributors, hammering out new commercial relationships was not an overnight process. Even when the outrages of Nazism provoked merchants to discontinue stocking German goods, this could be done only for a few months before their own businesses would begin to suffer for lack of merchandise. Sympathetic businesspeople and consumers were only too happy to cut off German goods permanently if someone would only locate alternates of identical quality and price.

Germany's competitors in France, Canada, England, Czechoslovakia, America, and Holland were glad to fill the void. But how were the cutlery manufacturers in Sheffield, England, to discover the neighborhood cutlery stores in Pittsburgh and Krakow? How were the quaint chinaware shops of Oslo and Buenos Aires to locate the china factories of Rumania?

By 1933, commerce had become so international a complex that only a global organization could fundamentally shift commercial traffic over and around the well-entrenched German export system. And the boycott organizers understood this from the beginning.

These organizers knew that boycotts become successful not by asking people to stop buying and selling what they have traditionally bought and sold, but by asking people to *switch* their buying and selling loyalties. New loyalties, once rooted, would become equally difficult to dislodge. Without high-quality, price-competitive alternative sources of supply, the anti-Hitler boycott would be no more than an emotional, briefly punitive commercial reprisal. But with an international clearinghouse to reroute the rivers of commerce, Germany would be left deserted and destitute—not for just a few months, as she weathered the attack, but in a systematic fashion that would remain in force until Germany collapsed from within.

The major boycotters of America, Holland, England, France, and Poland, looking forward to the moment of international consolidation, almost universally adopted the same slogan: "Germany will crack this winter!"

19. Germany Will Crack This Winter

TIME was what the Reich needed. When the Reich could no longer pay its obligations, Germany would be bankrupt. That moment had been technically postponed for years by rationing foreign exchange to only the most important transactions. But with Reichsbank reserves hit so hard by both the boycott and the Depression, there would soon be nothing left to ration.

In fact, in early June 1933, the German government was forced to permit the American Jewish Congress and other groups to send a multimillion-dollar Jewish relief fund to Berlin. The decision was of such importance that final approval could be granted only by Hitler himself. It was a difficult approval, because accepting relief funds was an admission that German Jews were being economically destroyed—something the Reich continued to deny. But the dollars were too badly needed to prop up the foreign-exchange scarcity. Moreover, when recalcitrant NSDAP activists tried to seize the funds from Berlin banks, claiming that the Congress money belonged to a hostile organization, the government quickly intervened and cash distribution to Jews resumed. The threat that future relief dollars would not be sent to Germany was too perilous a possibility to allow any interference.[1]

But relief funds were mere drops of water to the cash-thirsty Reich. In plain English, they were already broke. Only Schacht's clever acts of desperation were postponing a mass shutdown of German industry.

For example, shortly after Sam Cohen's deal was concluded, the Reich Economics Ministry realized the potential of using blocked marks and merchandise to pay desperate creditors. A similar arrangement was set up with a new American syndicate managed by the Harriman Company Harriman would purchase German merchandise for about 150 American individuals and companies owning blocked accounts in Germany. It worked this way: American importers would pay only 75 percent of their merchandise invoices in actual U.S. currency. But these dollars would never reach the German manufacturer; they would go into the Reichsbank reserve. The Reichsbank would then pay the German exporter in blocked marks. The remaining 25 percent of the invoices would be paid to a U.S. escrow account in dollars. To consummate the transaction, the U.S. creditor would take over the dollar escrow account in America and the German manufacturer would take over the creditor's blocked account in Germany. The Economics Ministry expected to promote about RM 25 million in exports by this technique.[2] The U.S. creditors were so desperate they were willing to traffic in German exports to slowly regain part of their assets frozen in Germany. In the process, Germany earned foreign currency and kept industry working a little longer.

Another trick for time was the proliferation of bilateral bartering. With little or no cash to pay for raw materials and semifinished goods needed for industry, Germany could resort to the barter system, a straight exchange of goods or commodities. For instance, Germany could swap its coal for another country's cotton, or German pharmaceuticals for another country's metal ore. In this way, a bankrupt Germany could keep manufacturing components flowing to German industry, and the population would remain working.

But such tricks were dependent upon one essential factor: the inherent value of German goods. Once German merchandise did become essentially valueless, Germany could gain yet a little more time with domestic tricks, charades, and outright thefts. For instance, the Reich could offer subsidies to stave off an industry's disintegration. By early June, such subsidies were frequent. For example, on June 6, Goebbels granted a RM 10 million subvention to the German film industry.[3] But crippled by cinema boycotts, the German film industry would take many months, perhaps years to rebuild.[4] How long could such subsidies continue?

Or the Reich could broaden its artificial protection of domestic industries. Such protection already existed for numerous commodities such as eggs and wheat. But whenever the government banned competitive supplies from neighboring countries, those countries always retaliated with similar restrictions on German products. So one German economic sector would flourish for a moment, while several others paid the price. For example, trade with Rumania was almost nonexistent by June 1933 because Germany's protectionist ban on many Rumanian farm products provoked a reciprocal ban on most German wares.[5] How long could the Reich protect selected economic sectors at the expense of others?

Or the Reich could expand its rigid wage and price controls. But that creates shortages, black markets, and even bankruptcies. In fact, such bankruptcies were regularly occurring. Defunct companies were simply absorbed into ever larger cartels to keep the employees working. But how long could unprofitable businesses continue federating before they created one prodigious industrial failure? How many such failures could the Reich prop·up with subsidies? And how many shortages could the Reich endure before work was forced to a halt for lack of materials?

Or the Reich could fool the millions of unemployed Germans into believing they were actually gainfully employed. With over 5 million still jobless, employment schemes were an obsession of the Third Reich. For example, in May, Hitler announced "compulsory volunteerism" as a substitute for actual employment. Most of these schemes simply relocated the worker. Heavily reliant on Nazi jingos and fatally underfinanced, the substitute work programs were aptly summed up in a mid-May report by British commercial attaché F. Thelwell: "Schemes for [re]settlement and for the provision of work . . . are being dealt with together, and . . . such a state of confusion exists and such obviously fantastic plans are being discussed, that it is quite impossible to form any rational or coherent picture of what will ultimately be done."[6] How long could such schemes continue to fail before the populace saw them as placebos?

Or the Reich could continue squeezing its own citizens and companies. This it was already doing to the Jews, with the overwhelming approval of the anti-Semitic population of Germany. Jewish assets in Germany probably exceeded RM 10 billion.[7] But the Nazi business usurpers were so inept that Aryanized businesses frequently failed, creating even more unemployment. Moreover, by spring 1933, the company takeovers began extending into the non-Jewish sector as any suspect business was subject to confiscation by party kommissars (locally appointed party controllers). The situation became so precarious that Nazi leaders such as Hugenberg, Goebbels, and even Hitler were incessantly chastising NSDAP kommissars to *stop* their takeovers. On May 20, for example, Goebbels warned kommissars, "We will not permit the country's business to be destroyed by dilettantes."[8] How long could productive businesses be neutralized before the collective loss created an insurmountable crisis?

The Nazis knew the answer to all these questions. If exports fell too low, Germany as a nation would again be faced with starvation. It had happened just fourteen years earlier; it was still fresh in many minds. In the winter of 1919, a besieged Germany was blockaded into submission, starved into defeat. To the Nazis, the anti-German boycott of 1933 was in many ways a reminiscent tactic. There were no enemy ships in the seaways, no hostile divisions at the bridgeheads. But as effective as any blockading frigate or infantryman was this boycott that blocked German goods from being sold, blocked foreign exchange from being earned, and blocked the means of survival from entering Germany.

How many months could Germany survive once the boycott became global, once commerce was rerouted around Germany? The boycotters adopted a slogan: "Germany will crack this winter." In Berlin many believed those words. On June 14, Britain's Ambassador Sir Horace Rumbold reported to British Foreign Secretary John Simon on an hourlong conversation with former German Chancellor Heinrich Brüning. The meeting was held in great anxiety because Brüning was convinced his phones and mail were monitored. Rumbold conveyed Brüning's belief "that economic conditions might deteriorate to such an extent in the autumn or winter as to produce a very serious situation in this country." Rumbold added his own validation: "I have heard from a direct source that the Chancellor [Hitler] himself is very apprehensive of the economic conditions which are likely to obtain towards the end of the year."[9]

Two weeks later, on June 30, Rumbold sent Simon another report, this one describing the unparalleled political and economic chaos dwelling in Nazi Germany. Rumbold's report closed with a flat assertion: "The Chancellor is concentrating his attention on the problem of reducing unemployment in the realization that his stay in office depends to a great extent on the economic situation next winter."[10]

Germany's economic viability had indeed become a phantasm of lies, tricks, and facades. And then came the very thing the Reich was dreading: boycott consolidation. Since the spring, both the Jewish War Veterans in New York and the Polish boycott committees in Warsaw had talked of joining forces. On June 3, Lord Melchett and the British Trade Unions Congress took the initiative and issued formal invitations to the independent boycott committees of the world to assemble in London on June 25 to establish an international boycott council.[11]

Melchett titled the boycott convention the World Jewish Economic Conference. The name was a wordplay on the intergovernmental meeting then under way in London, the World Economic Conference, convened to stimulate trade, especially with Germany. As it turned out, Germany's hopes for increased trade evaporated. So threatening were the World Economic Conference delegates that Schacht's plan of default had to be suspended for fear of provoking extraordinary retaliation, such as the liquidation of German property abroad as promised by John Foster Dulles. A Reich cabinet meeting called on June 23, shortly after the World Economic Conference, reported: "Pessimistic as were the expectations with which the [German] delegation went to London, they were outdistanced by far. Germany found among all states an attitude that hardly could be worse."[12] Melchett's Conference planned to finish the job.

The Jewish War Veterans and the American League for the Defense of Jewish Rights—America's two vanguard boycott groups—accepted Lord Melchett's invitation at once through ALDJR president Samuel Untermyer, one of American Jewry's most respected champions. He was renowned as the man who broke the "money trusts," as the former law partner of Committee leader Louis Marshall, as a major figure in the victory over Henry Ford, and as a regular crusader against civil rights injustice. His leadership was all the more meaningful to the boycott movement since he was a popular rival of Stephen Wise, who had yet to declare a boycott. However, in accepting Melchett's invitation, Untermyer asked if the conference could be postponed two weeks, giving Untermyer and his associates time to wrap up affairs in America. Melchett quickly agreed and a new date was set: July 15.[13]

Preparations began in earnest. Boycott groups from Holland, France, Poland, England, America, Latvia, and from thirty other nations would attend. Successful boycott ideas would be exchanged. Inefficient methods would be analyzed and improved. Separate committees would focus on techniques for organizing trade unions, manufacturers, and consumers. Most important, all the groups would bring long lists of manufacturers and sellers seeking alternatives to German goods.[14] These lists would be put together, making the international boycott group a commercial clearinghouse first and foremost. In the meantime, those anxious to replace German goods continued their haphazard struggle to find one another via advertisements in a boycott publication, *The Jewish Economic Forum*, published by Lord Melchett.

Egyptian importers of silk stockings want supplies "similar to the Chemnitz products." British ornament distributers invite carved wood from any non-German sources. Poland's leading importer of cleaned graphite seeks non-German alternative supply. British cap manufacturers need cap fasteners produced anywhere but Germany. Hungarian, Yugoslavian, Swiss, and Czech firms want gloves, hats, glues, and foodstuffs to replace German products. The French State Railways offers special discount freight rates for shippers seeking to avoid German trucks and rail lines.[15]

Such inefficient methods would be short-lived. At the July 15 World Jewish Economic Conference all the emotionalism, anger, and resentment of the boycotters would be transduced into pure business. The mercantile expertise of centuries would be but a rehearsal for the biggest and most important commercial brokerage network in Jewish history. If the deals were right, German Jewry could be saved.

Once the global boycott became a reality, the slogan "Germany will crack this winter" could well become a prophecy.

Mr. Sam Cohen, on June 24, 1933, concluded a fruitful meeting with German Consul Wolff in Jerusalem. A number of boycott-breaking ideas were discussed, and Consul Wolff was eager to notify Berlin. In a memo marked "URGENT," sent that day to the Reich Foreign Ministry, Wolff reported, "Mr. Sam Cohen . . . had informed me today that he will most likely . . . attend a Jewish congress in London, planned for the middle of July, which is to make decisions concerning the Jewish boycott against Germany . . . throughout the most important countries of the world." Wolff predicted "that the boycott resolution will be passed" since Jews everywhere believe "the boycott is the only weapon which can do appreciable damage [to Germany]." [16]

It went on: "If Mr. Sam Cohen is now going to attend what I might call the 'boycott congress,' he is doing so . . . in his capacity with Zionism here and with the Jewish Agency; [and] to put the brakes on the congress by working behind the scenes. . . . He will try . . . to sell his anti-boycott plans to influential attendees of the London congress. This includes if possible, Stephen Wise and attorney [Samuel] Untermyer, both of whom are arriving from America to attend the congress." [17]

Consul Wolff added that Cohen's tireless anti-boycott efforts were being continuously subverted by Jewish and Zionist groups who maintained that Hanotaiah's 1-million reichmark permission was too small a concession to trade for the politically volatile act of abandoning boycott. Playing right into the Nazi mentality, Wolff labeled the RM 1 million license as "insignificant in view of the magnitude of [Jewish] economic problems and the wealth in Jewish hands. . . . The only successful measure to counteract increasing Jewish hate and hostility for Germany would be a more generous accommodation on the part of the German government. It is of course understood that such an accommodation would be in the economic rather than in the political area." [18]

Consul Wolff's letter was another lobbying effort to expand Sam Cohen's deal to several million and broaden it to cover future as well as present Jewish emigrants. In the Nazi party's view, "future" emigrants included every Jew in Germany. In allying with Consul Wolff, Cohen found his most effective advocate. Even as Wolff was mailing his June 24 letter, the Economics Ministry in Berlin was notified of the Foreign Ministry's full endorsement of the consul's recommendations. [19] Consul Wolff was after all Germany's man in Jerusalem. Berlin relied upon him. So did Sam Cohen.

Consul Wolff would not fail him. In yet another fortifying effort, sent three days later, Wolff sent a personal note to his colleague Kurt Prufer, who supervised the Foreign Ministry's Eastern Department. "I have become more and more convinced that Mr. Sam Cohen's way is the only one which will enable us to overcome the Jewish anti-German boycott movement," Wolff wrote. "Mr. Sam Cohen has been successful in not only provoking the interest of all appropriate local authorities and individuals for his plans, but also in obtaining the most extensive authority for implementation under [Jewish] national supervision. . . . This is the only way . . . something can be done about the wave of boycotts." To drill home the perception of Cohen's validity, Consul Wolff added assurances that there would be no subsequent opposition to Cohen or Hanotaiah, "not from the orchard growers, or the big Zionist funds, or worker groups or from any other party." [20]

For the moment, such assurances were essentially correct. Leading Zionist institutions, desperate for fast action in the face of the growing boycott, had indeed endorsed Cohen. On July 2, the ad hoc Conference of Institutions convened a meeting attended by representatives of the Histadrut labor conglomerate, the Manufacturers Association, the Organization of German Immigrants, and other official entities. These men indeed represented official Jewish Palestine, and they reiterated their belief that breaking the boycott was the only way to save the Jewish wealth of Germany. But the men also verbalized their fear of a popular backlash. By now, the Third Reich's hot-and-cold pogrom was so heinous, and the public cries for boycott so vehement, that few could envision public acceptance of any economic liaison with Germany. The Chamber of Commerce representative reminded the gathering that in a previous session on June 6, they had voted to take no stand for or against the boycott, functionally defeating any boycott plan. The June 6 resolution had been withheld from public view following the Arlosoroff murder. But the representatives now felt they could no longer delay if German immigrants were to successfully transfer their assets to Palestine. The representatives voted to encourage a merchandise arrangement with the Reich.[21]

The next day Consul Wolff resumed his campaign. On July 3, he dispatched a letter marked "VERY URGENT" to the Reich Foreign Ministry relating the various tactics boycotters would try and credited Cohen with providing inside information. "Mr. Sam Cohen, . . . who because of his intimate knowledge of local conditions, called some other matters to my attention, . . . for example . . . the British and French, to exploit the difficulties experienced by German export efforts in Palestine, . . . intend to establish a clearinghouse which with the help of local Jewish firms would list present German suppliers and then be in a position to offer British and French substitute merchandise at lower prices. Mr. Sam Cohen informs me that Jewish [Zionist] circles to date do not favor such an enterprise, and I believe him, because Sam Cohen and his friends are strong Zionists who want to facilitate the immigration of German Jews to Palestine by way of Hanotaiah's imports. . . . [But] they must demonstrate that by organizing this German Palestine trade they can make a special contribution to Palestine [outweighing the value of the boycott]."[22]

Wolff's July 3 letter warned Berlin how advanced the Palestine boycott was. "What is happening in Tel Aviv . . . is that young men are inspecting every store, demanding to see company orders and invoices to determine the origin of merchandise."[23] The consul urged approval of his earlier request to expand Hanotaiah's transfer permission in both cash limit and in the type of merchandise allowed.

When Wolff first requested the expansion in late June, he enticed the Reich with assurances that Cohen's deal was broadly supported through "national supervision," and with promises that Cohen would separately import £500,000 worth of machinery, paying mostly with foreign currency. But Wolff now advised the Reich that Cohen's role as a boycott breaker was so crucial that Berlin should circumvent "national supervision" and grant Hanotaiah an outright monopoly on *all* German imports to Palestine.[24] Cohen had originally agreed to "share" his commercial ventures with publicly responsible companies such as Yakhin to avoid profiteering and engender public control. But now Cohen would share the profits and the decisions with no one.

In his July 3 letter, Consul Wolff also indicated that Cohen was no longer willing to pay any foreign currency for the special orders of machinery. The consul acknowledged that Berlin would not like this retreat, but stressed that if Germany expected to break the boycott, it should cooperate with Cohen. Wolff suggested all outstanding questions be resolved at a meeting with Cohen in Berlin on July 13.[25] Then expansion of the original deal, separate arrangements for machinery imports, and exact foreign-currency requirements could be settled.

"Immediately afterwards," Wolff wrote, "he plans to go to the [July 15] 'boycott congress' in London."[26] The implication was clear. Mr. Sam Cohen's work at Melchett's July 15 boycott conference would hinge on the deals he could arrange in Berlin on July 13.

The protest situation in England was almost a mirror image of America. The general British population was shocked and angered by Germany's anti-Jewish regime. Christian and Jewish lay and religious leaders favored strong punitive measures. His Majesty's Government preferred to remain silent, but frequently acceded to the wishes of the people and Parliament to lodge formal objections with the Reich. Yet in England, as in America, the biggest obstacle to a united protest and boycott movement was the coterie of leaders standing at the helm of the Jewish community.[27]

As in New York, London's Jewish community was divided into an East European class congregated in the East End, and the more gentried West European, heavily Germanic families of the West End. These two groups often looked upon each other with reproach. The East Enders—working people and struggling merchants—were accustomed to noisy protests to secure their rights. West Enders preferred dignified methods of coping with injustice toward Jews.[28]

The British counterpart of the American Jewish Committee was a small group of self-appointed gentlemen called the Anglo-Jewish Association. The seeming counterpart of the American Jewish Congress was an elected representative body called the Board of Deputies of British Jews. However, the Deputies pursued defense missions in their own sedate manner. And unlike the Congress, the Deputies were known for being either anti-Zionist or non-Zionist. So, while they were indeed elected, they often did not represent popular Anglo-Jewish desires.[29] Therefore, in their custodial approach to Jewish affairs, the Deputies found a greater kinship with the conservatives of the Committee than with the rabblerousers of the Congress.

In the protest and boycott vacuum created by the Anglo-Jewish Association and the Deputies, there arose many grass-roots Jewish and interfaith groups determined to boycott. Such ad hoc entities as the World Alliance to Combat Anti-Semitism, Captain Webber's Organization, and Lord Melchett's Anglo-Jewish Trades Council generated a militancy directly threatening Anglo-Jewry's established leadership.

The disunity came to a climax during July 1933, when Lord Melchett's circle was determined to stage massive protest and boycott actions in London. Among the most important was the July 15 World Economic Jewish Conference. The custodial mentality of Anglo-Jewry's leaders caused them to issue statements claiming the planned World Jewish Economic Conference—and its constituent groups from thirty-five nations—was an "unauthorized" gathering of Jews to be ignored.[30] At first, conference organizers refused to be intimidated. They enjoyed mass support, buoyed each time they vowed publicly to hold the boycott conference with or without the sanction of traditional Anglo-Jewish leaders. But as the barrage of discrediting statements by established Anglo-Jewish leaders mounted, it became clear to Lord Melchett that British Jewry was not ready to wage economic battle with Hitler. By July 7, he was forced to announce a postponement of the conference until autumn. The official explanation cited a need for several national boycott committees to coordinate further.[31]

But Lord Melchett correctly understood that Jews alone could not execute a successful boycott. They were dependent upon winning Christian cooperation. That would be impossible as long as official Jewish organizations denounced the boycott and the boycott conference as illegitimate. It was therefore time for a showdown.

In a surprise move on July 12, Lord Melchett's representatives attended a meeting of the Joint Foreign Committee, the foreign policy arm of the Board of Deputies and the Anglo-Jewish Association. All policies on the German crisis were technically formulated through this bilateral deliberative body and reflected the decisions of the Deputies and the Anglo-Jewish Association.[32] The JFC's approbation was therefore imperative.

During the meeting, Lord Melchett's advocates presented an eight-point memorandum requesting the JFC step aside and acknowledge that reaction to the Hitler crisis was solely within the purview of a special ad hoc committee to include Lord Melchett and other boycott notables.[33] If they did not wish to join the boycott, at least they could be silent while others took up battle.

Abdicating authority on the greatest emergency facing twentieth-century Jewry would not be an easy act for the Joint Foreign Committee. Zionist stalwarts attending the session lobbied against Melchett's superseding committee because it promised boycott as an official policy, thus derailing hopes for a transfer to Palestine. Many of the regular Jewish leaders fought the abdication for all the known reasons of fear and caution and because it was an admission that their leadership was bankrupt.

But enough JFC members either buckled under Lord Melchett's pressure, chose to be relieved of the responsibility, or secretly backed the popular movement. After a bitter debate, a majority ratified Melchett's memorandum—six in favor, three against.[34] Thus, an ad hoc committee now superceded the established Anglo-Jewish authorities on all questions regarding Nazi Germany. The boycotters could approach the Christian community and British government as the designated and legitimate voice of Jewry, thus ending months of public disunity.

Neville Laski, president of the Deputies, and Leonard Montefiore, president of the Anglo-Jewish Association, saw Lord Melchett's coup as virtual insurrection. Indeed, the London-based *Jewish Chronicle* described the Joint Foreign Committee unheaval as a "Palace Revolution." And the New York-based *Jewish Daily Bulletin* described the confrontation as "the possible overthrow of the present leaders of British Jewry."[35] The boycotters accepted these descriptions and lost no time in wielding their new power. They quickly called for the Deputies to ratify Melchett's takeover of the JFC and adopt a formal boycott resolution at the Deputies' next meeting, July 16.[36]

Neville Laski immediately swore in a press interview that if the Deputies passed Melchett's boycott resolution, he would resign at once.[37] But conference organizers disregarded Laski's threat. If on July 16 the Deputies ratified the JFC takeover and a boycott resoluton, it would segue perfectly into London's mass protest and boycott march planned for July 20. These formal and popular mandates would then set the dramatic and authoritative foundation for a World Jewish Economic Conference that fall to rally the world in a coordinated boycott.

At the end of the day on July 12, the Reich realized that its future might indeed soon be decided by Jews—unless somehow Lord Melchett's deeds could be undone. In this climate, German officials prepared for the next day's meeting in Berlin with Mr. Sam Cohen.

20. July 13 at Wilhelmstrasse

WILHELMSTRASSE was the name of a street, and the name of a block of German government buildings. In both senses, Wilhelmstrasse designated the seat of German government. Although built during the reign of

Frederick the Great in the mid-eighteenth century, Wilhelmstrasse's exterior lacked any hint of grandeur. Its monotonous two-story length was interrupted by nothing more distinctive than a simple entrance flanked by two wrought-iron light fixtures, topped by a tiny balcony.[1]

The Wilhelmstrasse interior had been updated to suit the new Germany. Swastika emblems and flags had been hurriedly added to all the empty spaces. Anyone entering the building could not help but sense the lack of continuity between this Reich and the two before.

It was to the depths of this complex of government offices that Mr. Sam Cohen reported on July 13, 1933, ready to discuss the final details of assuming personal custody of the fiscal and physical future of German Jewry. If all went as expected, his RM 1 million license, granted in mid-May, would be expanded to a perhaps limitless concession sufficient to transfer the assets of thousands of German Jews—those few who wished to emigrate to Palestine, and those of the majority who frankly could not afford to rule out the option. Those German Jews who did elect to move to Palestine would find their existence essentially limited to working the citrus groves of Hanotaiah's acreage. Those depositors who would not leave Germany or who chose another destination would find their assets already transferred and invested in their name in Palestine.

Sitting atop this mammoth transaction would be Mr. Sam Cohen. For his contribution to the Zionist cause he would of course collect a suitable commission in the form of Hanotaiah's profits. Undoubtedly, these profits could then be reinvested in other worthy Zionist projects. Hence, he could derive immense personal satisfaction from his venture. But beyond simple profits, it must have been clear that as transfer agent of the German Jewish community, Cohen would become the all-powerful middleman of the Jewish nation-in-waiting. For him this was a climactic moment.

It had been a tortuous, intrigue-filled journey to this hour. He had shuttled between Jerusalem and London, Berlin and Warsaw, and many points along the way. He had outmaneuvered his critics, outdistanced his sponsors, and outlived his competition. He had been quick, clever, and undaunted as he perfected the art of selective omission, distorted appearances, and a promise for everyone. By these powers he had assumed the unquestioned role of broker for the Zionist movement and the Jewish people. He walked into the conference room, prepared to quibble about percentages of foreign currency and procedures of liquidation, but emerge one way or another with everything he wanted.

And there, sitting in the conference room, waiting for the meeting to commence was Georg Landauer, director of the Zionist Federation of Germany. With him was David Werner Senator of the Jewish Agency Executive.[2] Those first moments were undoubtedly tense as Sam Cohen greeted the men whose authority he had cleverly usurped and misrepresented. Landauer could have easily denounced Cohen then and there as a fraud who had engineered a massive international conspiracy to corrupt Reich currency regulations. But would Landauer be believed? By the same token, Cohen, the man the German government had come to trust as their anti-boycott champion, could have denounced Landauer and Senator as rebellious elements within the Zionist movement who refused to go along with the sanctioned policy of cooperation with Germany. But would Cohen be believed?

On the other hand, why should either side become accusatory and forfeit a crucial meeting with Reich officials to arrange the all-important transfer? The resulting fiasco could eradicate any chance of negotiating on any formal and congenial basis as "partners" in good faith. So Cohen and Landauer remained cool with no sign of hostility or rivalry. They would both negotiate as Zionists for the best transfer arrangement Germany would grant them.

When Currency Control director Hans Hartenstein and his assistants, as well as Foreign Ministry experts and a Reichsbank director[3] joined the Zionists, they were totally unaware that Cohen and Landauer were not part of the same team. Almost a month before, on June 20, Landauer had made his first formal entreaty to Hartenstein by delivering a memo asking to broaden the transfer concession beyond that originally granted to Hanotaiah in mid-May. That same day, Hartenstein received a copy of Consul Wolff's request to expand Cohen's agreement. There was no reason to believe that these two requests were not the same. When Landauer somehow learned of Cohen's July 13 meeting to discuss the wider permission, Landauer contacted Hartenstein and asked to be included. Hartenstein of course agreed.[4] Proceeding under this mistaken impression, Hartenstein and his colleagues commenced the July 13 meeting as though both Cohen and Landauer were partners. Neither Cohen nor Landauer disturbed the illusion.

The most pressing issue for Hartenstein was foreign currency. Consul Wolff's letter on behalf of Cohen had offered more than half the merchandise price in actual foreign currency. This startled Landauer. The more foreign currency the Reich received, the less the emigrants received. To deliver foreign currency would not be a transfer as much as a discount purchasing plan. The Germans turned to Cohen and asked about Consul Wolff's original foreign-currency promise.[5] The Foreign Ministry aides almost certainly carried copies of Consul Wolff's letters. The Reichsbank director would be anxious to report an influx of needed foreign exchange to Hjalmar Schacht. And Hartenstein could only justify setting aside the £1,000 Palestine entry money in actual sterling if some larger sum of foreign currency flowed into Germany. But with no extra foreign exchange coming in, how could the cash-desperate Reich participate in this transfer scheme at all?

The Reich negotiators were told that initially the transfer must confine itself to blocked marks, with no foreign currency involved. The Zionists undoubtedly offered a rationale they would later use to deny breaking the boycott, namely that the absence of foreign currency deprived the Reich of the basic benefit of a true merchandise sale—foreign exchange. Without foreign exchange, the transaction was precisely the noble endeavor the Zionists claimed it was—a transfer.[6]

The Reich negotiators provisionally accepted the arguments of the Zionists and agreed to extend a low limit of transfer without foreign currency—a few million, the precise figure would be worked out later. However, after this first stage, some percentage of foreign currency would be required, just as Wolff had promised several weeks earlier.[7]

The rest of the meeting concentrated on transfer procedures. Landauer's concept called for two clearinghouses. Landauer explained that the first would be headquartered in or affiliated with a major German bank to convey the reliability needed if German Jews in great numbers were to participate. Emigrants would deposit their money in numbered blocked accounts. A corresponding clearinghouse would be established in Palestine, comprised of leading merchandise importers. This second clearinghouse would actually import the German wares and then instruct the German clearinghouse to remit merchandise payments from the blocked accounts. At that point, the German exporter was satisfied.[8]

When the Palestinian importer sold the merchandise for sterling, that money would be deposited in a corresponding numbered Palestinian bank account. Upon arrival in Palestine, the emigrant would take over the Palestinian account, thereby transferring part of his assets in cash.[9] He was then able to start a new life.

Landauer stressed that the second clearinghouse in Palestine must also be in a reputable financial institution and suggested the Anglo-Palestine Bank. He intended to cut Sam Cohen out of his caretaker role by reducing Hanotaiah to just one of the many importers, none of whom would be entrusted with actual disbursements of money. That job, asserted Landauer, was unalterably the province of a bank, not a real estate company.[10]

Landauer added that the certainty and speed of the emigrant receiving his money once in Palestine would be the key to convincing Germans to emigrate.[11] None would want to move penniless to a new land. They would prefer to hang on indefinitely in Germany waiting for conditions to improve.

Landauer's insistence on quick payment and bank supervision must have certainly hit Sam Cohen as a threat to his entire plan. Cohen had never intended to turn much cash over to the emigrants. He had intended to reimburse them mainly with a parcel of land, cheap farm structures, or perhaps some agricultural equipment, all at a value he himself would set.[12] In this way, Hanotaiah and Cohen would reap the windfall profits that would justify battling the Jewish world by breaking the boycott. Moreover, Hanotaiah expected to control all the transactions through its own bank accounts, reimbursing emigrants' transfers at its own rate.

But Landauer understood that German Jews would never accept destitution in Palestine over destitution in Germany. The transfer plan had to be attractive. Families could not arrive in Palestine only to be shocked by the loss of their transferred assets and the virtual necessity of settling on the sandy acreage designated by Hanotaiah. The word would quickly filter back: Go anywhere but Palestine. The transfer would be a short-lived get-rich-quick scheme for Cohen. But the dream of bringing the Jewish people of Germany to Palestine would be dissolved.

Cohen's reaction to Landauer's presentation is unknown. He probably knew enough to say little and go into action later. But however he reacted, there was no hint to the Germans that Hanotaiah and the ZVfD were not in perfect coordination. The illusion was sustained. As the meeting ended, Hartenstein asked Landauer to crystallize all transfer questions into a brief memo.[13] At the same time, Reich bureaus would consider the foreign-currency disappointment.

Although the Reich's decisions were not finalized at that moment, it seemed clear that Germany would agree to a multimillion-reichmark arrangement encompassing a gamut of merchandise, and they would forgo foreign-currency benefits for the time being. Hitler's Reich had too much to gain from the transfer under almost any format. First, the Reich and the Zionists knew that the transfer and the boycott could not coexist. Merchandise could not be used as the medium of transfer if it could not be sold somewhere. The Zionists would be forced to sabotage the boycott if they expected to sell German merchandise.

Second, export orders meant jobs in Germany. This was as important as breaking the boycott. Hitler was desperately striving to rehabilitate Germany's work force. With exports already drastically reduced, the merchandise could be *dumped*, let alone transferred at market value, and the government would be satisfied, because German men and women would continue working.

Third, once commenced, the transfer benefits would escalate. Foreign currency would quickly become a demandable part of the bargain. Furthermore, the purchase of German machinery, cars, and equipment carried the promise of German spare parts and service technicians to keep them in good working order for years to come.

Fourth, Hitler's Reich craved a Germany without Jews. On a political agenda dedicated to economic recovery, the elimination of the Jews was nonetheless paramount. Transfer was Germany's hope for a Jewish exodus. The need to promote emigration became ever more compelling in mid-July as German Jewish refugees actually began returning to Germany. With capital punishment facing the dispenser of so-called atrocity stories, with Germany doing all it could to inhibit foreign journalists from reporting all but the most concretely verifiable incidents, many German Jews had wrongly presumed that the period of anti-Semitic violence in Nazi Germany had passed. The Reich interned most of these first returnees in a concentration camp. But when the repatriation began to reach into the hundreds, Germany feared she might actually regain many of the 30,000 Jews already frightened away.[14]

Transfer was crucial to the Third Reich. Both sides knew it.

The Wilhelmstrasse meeting took place just before the July 16 Board of Deputies vote on the boycott and on the Joint Foreign Committee takeover. The Reich made clear what it expected the Zionist herarchy to do. The German Zionists made clear what they expected in return. Nazi Germany was ready to deliver. The next move was up to the Zionist hierarchy.

21. The World Jewish Economic Conference

THE WORLD JEWISH ECONOMIC CONFERENCE was still waiting for a new date, but once scheduled, its success seemed assured. It would rally the Jews of the world in a new sense of self-defense. They would replace their leaders with men who accepted the credo so aptly described in the premiere issue of Lord Melchett's boycott journal, *The Jewish Economic Forum*: "In these days, when international wars are fought with economic weapons, and peace treaties and alliances take the form of trade agreements, a conscious awareness of the economic role of Jewry in the affairs of the world is not only desirable but necessary for the preservation and future development of our people. From this day forth we shall confront our enemies not with weak appeals to their dormant humanity, but with the irresistible argument that it does not pay to persecute us."[1] Late on July 13, the rallying slogan "Germany will crack this winter" appeared to be a promise the Jews would keep.

But things started to change the next morning. On July 14, Joint Foreign Committee co-chairman Neville Laski called an emergency meeting to rescind Lord Melchett's takeover resolution of July 12. Melchett himself did not attend the sudden session.[2] After little discussion, the abdication of July 12 was unanimously rescinded. Melchett's original eight-point takeover memorandum was then redebated clause by clause, with a shorter seven-point proposal resulting. The new proposal covered much of the same ground but in more ambiguous language. More important, the revised proposal changed Melchett's status. Instead of Melchett leading a panel that would *supersede* the Joint Foreign Committee, the JFC voted to remain active, but *include* Lord Melchett and other representatives of popular organizations previously beyond the JFC's horizon. While the vital clause advocating boycott was toned down, the boycott suggestion itself was not deleted.[3] In short, the JFC retained control of foreign policy for the Jewish community, but agreed to become more responsive to popular demands.

Lord Melchett went along with the replacement proposal for the sake of unity. He was convinced there was too much "squabbling over mere words." Whether the boycott bore an "official" imprint was not as important to him as that the boycott became *organized*. If working through established channels instead of around them was the best way to create a unified anti-Nazi front, so be it.[4]

But the new question was: Would Melchett sway establishment Anglo-Jewish leaders to boycott, or would they convince Melchett to join the ranks of quiet diplomacy and foresake his movement?

The Board of Deputies, co-parent body of the Joint Foreign Committee, was prepared to induct Lord Melchett. But a sudden "technical arrangement" delayed board ratification.[5] The technical problem was not explained, but the JFC probably could not formally induct Lord Melchett for one embarrassing reason. He was not Jewish.

In fact, Lord Melchett was of assimilated German Jewish stock that in the late nineteenth century relinquished its Jewish identity. His father married a Christian woman, and Melchett himself was raised Anglican. On July 15, 1933, he was still a prominent member of the Anglican Church. Despite his Anglican affiliation and a Christian mother, which under Jewish law established that he was indeed not Jewish, Lord Melchett maintained a considerable Jewish identity. Somewhere deep inside he knew he was a Jew. This Jewish identity could not find expression in ritual because he was an Anglican. Instead, Melchett became a leading funder and organizer of Zionist projects, including Palestine's embryonic industrial works. When Hitler rose to power, Melchett's inner summons propelled him to the forefront of the boycott movement.[6] A good Zionist and a good boycotter he was. But neither of those distinctions earned him a place on the Board of Deputies or the Joint Foreign Committee. The JFC had restructured itself twice in two days to accommodate Melchett. But one precept could not be overridden. He had to be Jewish.

So on June 15, Lord Melchett converted. It was planned as a secret ceremony, but it quickly produced headlines from New York to Jerusalem, as all the picturesque details were chattily published below banners such as "WELCOME BACK" or "LORD MELCHETT COMES HOME."[7] This done, he was now ready to assume his place spiritually as well as physically in the economic war against Germany.

Melchett now came under increasing pressure from those who opposed the boycott conference. The traditional leaders of British Jewry, such as Neville Laski, rejected any formal boycott in fear of Reich retaliation against German Jewry. But Anglo-Jewish leaders also harbored a special fear that transcended the Hitler emergency. For decades, the Jewish people had fought the fallacies of economic internationalism contained in the Protocols of the Elders of Zion. And here was the very proof Jew-haters would use to verify their claims.[8] After all, was not the boycott conference's avowed goal to smother Germany's industries, choke off its foreign exchange, and topple its government?

The Zionist hierarchy in London continued its active resistance to the conference because boycott and transfer were mutually exclusive. Ironically, in expressing themselves, the Zionist hierarchy in London could speak with three voices. First, they were the voice of Zionism. Despite popular Zionist demands for protest and boycott, the hierarchy was denouncing any anti-Nazi agitation as a barrier to a Reich accommodation for Palestine. Second, the Zionist hierarchy functioned in England as the voice of Germany's Jews. German Zionist Martin Rosenbluth had set up the official German Jewish liaison office in London.[9] Third, Zionists often spoke for popular Anglo-Jewry. The men at the helm of the Zionist Organization frequently held key leadership positions in Diaspora Jewish groups. Most of these groups were actively Zionist, so it was only natural that Zionist notables should lead them.

The triple Zionist voice in London was becoming increasingly assertive. For instance, Zionist Organization president Nahum Sokolow was also the president of the Federation of Polish Jews in Britain. The Federation reflected the boycott fervor of their landsmen in Poland, America, and Palestine. Yet at a mid-July rally held at the height of London's anti-Nazi agitation, Sokolow, in his capacity as Federation president, advised an anti-Nazi Polish-Jewish rally to forgo boycott plans.[10] And Chaim Weizmann and other key Zionist figures repeatedly advised the Deputies to persist in their non-boycott policy.[11]

The Zionist hierarchy and establishment Anglo-Jewish leaders knew they would have to abort Melchett's conference decisively—and quickly. By mid-July, American boycotters Samuel Untermyer and George Fredman were already in London conferring with European boycott advocates. All were anxious for Melchett to reschedule the conference.[12] However, Zionist and traditional Anglo-Jewish leaders suddenly learned that they would be joined in opposing the conference by one of the boycotters' own, one whose counsel would be heeded. No one could accuse this opponent of not being in the forefront of the anti-Nazi movement. He had just arrived in London from America, and he was as determined as anyone that the World Jewish Economic Conference never take place. His name was Rabbi Stephen Wise.

Wise was dedicated to a worldwide boycott of Germany and equally committed to supplanting the old Jewish leadership that advised silence in the face of Hitlerism, but Wise was against the conference. His reasons were political, strategic, and personal.

Politically, Melchett's convention was openly intended as a counter-convention to the World Economic Conference then meeting in London. As such, the boycott convention would undercut President Roosevelt's initiative to revive the world's depressed economies. If the London intergovernmental meeting failed alongside a World Jewish Economic Conference that claimed success, Jews would surely be blamed. Wise believed that major Jewish American involvement in the counterconvention would only alienate FDR, whose sympathies Wise was still trying to arouse.[13]

Strategically, the Melchett conference had divided Anglo-Jewish leaders from the masses. Like Melchett, Wise saw the advantage of working within the established leadership system and creating a united front. A publicly discredited boycott convention in London would hurt the boycott's quest for legitimacy and broad acceptance. Moreover, Wise was hoping to maneuver such establishment leaders as Neville Laski and Leonard Montefiore into a coalition with American and East European Jews that would create the World Jewish Congress.[14]

Personally, and perhaps most important, while Melchett was the spiritual sponsor of the conference, it was clear that Wise's old rival Samuel Unter-myer was the popular hero of the boycott movement. Conference organizers openly agreed that their conference represented a *coup d'état* among the Jewish people. They announced that the anti-Nazi boycott would be the springboard for a worldwide Jewish organization that would supplant all major established groups.[15] If the World Jewish Economic Conference did convene, Untermyer would be catapulted to a dominant position in both the anti-Nazi movement and world Jewish leadership. Wise was convinced this leadership belonged to him and to his long-sought and soon-to-be World Jewish Congress.[16] Two world Jewish organizations could not exist side by side. It would be Wise or Untermyer to lead the Jewish people to battle against Adolf Hitler. And so, as is often the case, the struggle to achieve justice was subordinated to the struggle to claim the credit.

Therefore, Wise urged Lord Melchett to turn away from an ad hoc boycott and instead join him in creating the World Jewish Congress. Once constituted by such organizations as the American Jewish Congress, the Board of Deputies, and France's Alliance Israelite Universelle, the new World Congress—imbued with Wise's fighting spirit—would be a powerful defense force. This new Congress would dramatically proclaim the coordinated global boycott.[17]

Suspicion and confusion had spread among the world's boycott circles from the moment in early July when Lord Melchett announced the postponement. Although calculated to strengthen the offense against Hitler, the postponement in fact delivered a damaging blow to boycott momentum.

Many boycott organizers had already journeyed to London to participate. Their time, effort, and money was now wasted. By the second week of July, with no new conference date set, Polish boycotters warned Lord Melchett that with numerous boycott committees ready to assemble, they might insist on going ahead without him in either Paris or Amsterdam.[18]

The fear of a sell-out by their own leaders was intensified following the publication of two news items. The first was an early-July story in the *Frankfurter Zeitung* alleging that Anglo-Zionist leader Sir Herbert Samuel, former high commissioner for Palestine, had promised Germany's ambassador in London that any formal British boycott action would be stymied by public denunciations from Neville Laski and Leonard Montefiore. Normally, such German press notices were viewed skeptically.[19]

But then the Jewish Telegraphic Agency distributed the story unchallenged on its international wires. In an accompanying report, the JTA announced that its London bureau had verified the *Frankfurter Zeitung* claim: "It is definitely learned here that an agreement was reached during the latter part of March between certain Jewish leaders and the German Ambassador." The JTA juxtaposed this confirmation to a reminder that Laski had promised to resign should a formal boycott resolution be adopted by Melchett's group.[20]

The JTA's confirmation was given the widest credence in Jewish newspapers throughout Europe and America.[21] Since it came at the same time as vague media reports about reversals of the Joint Foreign Committee takeover, boycott organizers concluded that Lord Melchett was caving in to establishment pressure to kill the World Jewish Economic Conference slowly, via a series of postponements. The London *Jewish Chronicle*, acknowledging the demoralizing effect of the *Frankfurter Zeitung* story, staunchly denied that Melchett had capitulated, and even castigated the JTA's London bureau "confirmation" as a false item that really originated in the JTA's Paris office.[22]

Clearly, each day that passed without a firm boycott announcement only heightened the suspicion and rebelliousness of the boycott community. Then Neville Laski used his authority as president of the Board of Deputies to postpone until July 23 both the boycott vote and ratification of the JFC's new composition.[23] No reason was given. Lord Melchett's people, sensing further disaffection in the boycott movement, issued statements that the conference would definitely take place in early October.[24] But delays could no longer be tolerated by the boycott community. The Deputies' boycott-vote postponement, July 16, was the final signal.

On July 18, Samuel Untermyer and a team of boycott associates announced that the World Jewish Economic Conference would be convened within forty-eight hours—not in London under the auspices of Lord Melchett, but in Amsterdam under Untermyer's guidance. The announcement was met with immediate support by all boycott groups.[25]

An article in *The New York Times* correctly identified Untermyer's move as a battle between Eastern European and Western European Jews for the leadership of the Jewish people. "Among the Western Jews," explained the article, "it was the German branch . . . to which leadership was willingly granted. . . . The present situation is that Poland, with her 4.5 million Jews—the largest colony of them in Europe—threatens to assume by sheer weight of numbers the direction of the racial protective battle."[26]

Many Polish Jews were Revisionist Zionists. Hence, Untermyer's move also portended a victory for Revisionism within the Zionist movement over the question of whether to fight the Nazis. The last paragraph of the *Times* article delineated the stakes: "The only question now is which part of the race shall assume the new leadership. That will be decided in Amsterdam and London."[27]

Although Lord Melchett was convinced that Stephen Wise's World Jewish Congress would yield a more effective boycott, Melchett was unwilling to relinquish the momentum of his own ad hoc movement. So when Untermyer announced the Amsterdam Conference, Melchett publicly promised either to attend or to send his own representatives as the British delegation.[28]

Untermyer's sudden, well-publicized leadership leap boosted him to the vanguard of the anti-Nazi movement. For the moment he had even eclipsed Wise as the single most revered champion of Jewish rights. Even the leaders of the American Jewish Congress, Wise's personal power base, began to doubt whether Wise was still the man to follow.[29]

Dr. Wise tried to reassure his own loyal supporters in a late-July letter to the Congress Executive. He denied responsibility for the Melchett conference delays, but insisted that only the World Jewish Congress could or should lead the boycott struggle: "Personally, I have a suspicion that . . . the American Jewish Committee inspired the plan . . . to head off the Melchett-Untermyer Conference." Wise added, "It is almost impossible in writing to tell you the story of . . . my own meetings in London with the gentlemen in respect to the Congress. . . . [Zionist leader] Dr. Goldmann and I labored with them time and again. I mean especially four men: Laski, Major Nathan [a Melchett boycott ally], Montefiore, and Lord Melchett." Wise insisted that his goal was united action toward a World Jewish Congress that would represent all Jewish people.[30]

He indicated that the supraorganization's planning commission would assemble in Prague during late August, just before the Eighteenth Zionist Congress. Wise assured that "a world boycott decision might well be reached in Prague." Even though many members of the World Jewish Congress would come from the solidly anti-boycott camp, Wise reasoned that established Jewish leaders would be outvoted and forced to submit to popular demand. He had taken pains to explain to conservative Anglo-Jewish leaders that a de facto popular international boycott already existed: "In Poland, it is incredibly good; in Czechoslovakia, fantastically good; in France, good; in England, fair; in America, very good." [31]

Ultimately, Wise expected to win Jewish unity against Hitler. But in his late-July letter to New York he drilled home his determination that he would have to be the man to lead such an international movement. It could not be Untermyer, even though Untermyer's worldwide following was already in place. "[I] adhere to my judgment," Wise wrote, "that a world boycott cannot be publicly proclaimed by any *one* group in world Jewry. This is our grievance against Untermyer and his two fellow musketeers." [32]

Rabbi Wise accused Untermyer of actually wrecking the boycott: "Without conferring with anyone, they took this great step [the Amsterdam Conference] in such a way as to do a minimum of hurt to German commerce and a maximum of damage to the Jewish people." [33]

But Congress leaders in New York were wondering whether Wise's World Jewish Congress would really be effective, especially with its inclusion of so many establishment anti-boycott leaders. In a rebellious action taken even before Wise wrote his late-July letter of defense and explanation, the American Jewish Congress suspended the subsidy for Nahum Goldmann, Wise's chief organizer in Europe. One hour after receiving a cable informing of the suspension, Wise objected in a letter he hurriedly mailed without even correcting spelling errors. "I cannot understand this," he protested. "This is only another way of saying there shall not be a World Jewish Congress. . . . That decision should not and cannot be made while I am in Europe. . . . It would be just as impossible to run the American Government without Washington, as the World Jewish Congress without the services of Goldmann. . . . Very earnestly, I protest against such a decision which should only have come after conference with me." [34]

Stephen Wise was methodically erecting an international boycott apparatus in his own way. He did not want to be rushed. But many others would not wait.

Provided with only forty-eight hours' notice, not all of the thirty-five national boycott committees could attend the suddenly convened World Jewish Economic Conference in Amsterdam. Only sixteen national committees actually sent delegates. They came from Lithuania, Belgium, France, Finland, Czechoslovakia, Egypt, Poland, Latvia, and other countries. Britain's delegation represented Lord Melchett as promised. Ten more national committees, unable to attend due to the conference's off-on nature and the suddenly switched site, sent telegrams of solidarity. To avoid any appearance of rivalry, Untermyer labeled the two-day gathering as *preliminary* to the actual conference Lord Melchett was still planning to host in London in October. [35]

From the moment on July 20 that Untermyer called the several dozen delegates to order in the hall of Amsterdam's Carleton Hotel, the conference was a procession of militancy. Each representative declared what damage his countrymen had wrought on German trade, what steps had been and could be taken to integrate non-Jewish anti-Nazi movements.[36] The Dutch delegates were among the most active, boasting a 40 percent decline in Reich exports to Holland.

Fiery speeches and a feisty determination to crack German economic staying power created an impressive spectacle that finally put the world on notice that some element of the Jews was united in the war against the Third Reich. One of the most stirring testaments to the conference was recorded by *The New York Times*, which saw the convention as so important to Germany's survival that they flew their veteran Berlin correspondent, Frederick T. Birchall, to London to cover the event. When the conference moved to Amsterdam, Birchall followed.[37] His front-page coverage began:

AMSTERDAM, July 20—In this city upon free Dutch soil where, almost four hundred years ago, Jews driven from Spain and Portugal found a safe refuge, establishing a colony which in the next generation produced the great philosopher Spinoza, some thirty representatives of world Jewry met today to deal with Germany's modern revival of Jewish persecution. They elected Samuel Untermyer of New York president and adopted this resolution:

"Whereas . . . unanimous outcry, protests and demonstrations of Jews and non-Jews throughout the civilized world against the incredibly inhuman policy toward the Jews of Germany have been unavailing . . . Whereas the Hitler government has repeatedly expressed its determination . . . to annihilate them economically, to deprive them of their citizenship . . . and eventually exterminate them . . . now, therefore, be it Resolved, That boycotting of German goods, products, and shipping . . . is the only effective weapon for world Jewry and humanity by way of defense and protection of Jewish rights, property and dignity in Germany. . . . We earnestly urge all the men and women of the civilized world, irrespective of race or creed, to support and join in this movement against brutal fanaticism and bigotry and to help lead it to a victorious conclusion and until the last traces of barbarous persecutions have been eliminated."[38]

The declaration of war officially proclaimed, the soldiers of Israel broke up into three businesslike commissions. The French, the Polish, and the Czechs composed policy resolutions. The Dutch, the Egyptians, and the Americans handled organizational questions. The British, the Belgians, and the Lithuanians tackled financing problems.[39] Commercial rerouting was of course the real power of the conference, and this was made clear in the newspaper coverage. One of Birchall's reports, for example, explained, "The matter of supplying equally satisfying substitutes for German exports at no greater cost . . . is regarded as the real key to making the boycott efficient. . . . The meeting will organize methods of obtaining and supplying this information in the minutest detail."[40]

The World Jewish Economic Conference was the spectacle Germany had hoped somehow to delay. In vain, the Nazis wondered if perhaps individual conferees might be intimidated. If any of them were German Jewish refugees, their families back home could be targeted. The German consul-general in Amsterdam inquired of the Carleton Hotel manager if any of those attending were German? The manager checked with Samuel Untermyer. Untermyer gave the manager a message for the consul, which Birchall of the *Times* discreetly reported this way: "Mr. Untermyer suggested that the Nazi Consul might be invited to go to a warmer climate."[41]

Working with great speed, the conferees unanimously established the new world organization they had promised. Named the World Jewish Economic Federation, it would be headquartered in London, with Lord Melchett as its honorary chairman and Untermyer as its president.[42] International media coverage and a broad multinational character seemed to imbue Untermyer's new Federation with the legitimacy it desperately needed to be taken seriously. But this legitimacy was intolerable to Stephen Wise, who saw his rival Untermyer on the verge of global success. Wise began a subversion campaign.

Working through conservative Dutch leaders analogous to the American Jewish Committee, Wise issued salvo after salvo accusing Untermyer's people of representing no one and misleading world opinion. The principal mouthpiece for these attacks was David Cohen, a leader of the Dutch Jewish Committee. While the conference was in session, Cohen declared publicly that Untermyer had no right to convene his group, and that organized Dutch Jewry had not been consulted and in fact deplored the entire convention.[43] Cohen then issued an "American" statement authorized by Wise in London condemning Untermyer's gathering and incongruously declaring that the great majority of American Jews were not in favor of any boycott whatsoever against Germany.[44] Such pronouncements by Stephen Wise, the acknowledged leader of America's protest movement, did the expected damage to discredit Untermyer's new Federation.

Untermyer shot back with a widely circulated press statement castigating Wise's "apparent determination to discredit every movement he cannot lead." He publicly challenged Wise "to tell Jewry frankly whether or not he personally favors a boycott," since no one had yet been able to solve the mystery.[45] There was no answer because Wise was proffering different postures at different times, trying to walk a fine line between the protest movement and the establishment leaders he needed to bring his World Jewish Congress into reality.[46]

22. Reversals and Reprieves

EVEN AS the Amsterdam conference was struggling for acceptance, anti-Nazi reaction in London continued its schizophrenic course. The Jewish masses were demanding that all Britain boycott German goods. Jewish leaders were counseling against vocal protest or organized boycott.

The dichotomy became most visible on July 20, 1933, the day of a giant protest and boycott parade. West End Jewish leaders had bitterly opposed the demonstration; all Jews were asked to not participate, and non-Jews were cautioned to ignore any that did march.[1]

Despite the denunciations, the July 20 parade was universally proclaimed the largest demonstration ever undertaken by British Jews, bearing all the drama of the May 10 rally in Manhattan. London newspapers reported closed shops throughout Jewish districts, a cross-section of participants, and a sea of banners: MAKE GERMAN GOODS UNTOUCHABLE . . . BE LOYAL TO THE BOYCOTT AND AVOID GERMAN GOODS. Braving searing summer heat, the estimated 50,000 formed an orderly column, at times two and a half miles long, and urged the thousands of spectators to join the movement.[2]

The intent was to create an unmistakable wall of unity. But the newspapers could not avoid mentioning that West End Jews "took no part in the demonstration except to stare at the thousands of their co-religionists straggling past." Irrepressible notices of condemnation were issued by the Board of Deputies and the Anglo-Jewish Association even as the protestors marched, giving a bewildering approach-avoidance character to Jewish defense.[3]

Nonetheless, on the day of the London march, British labor provided a pivotal display of solidarity. The National Joint Council, comprised of the Trades Union Congress, the Labour party, and the Parliamentary Labour party, circulated a binding boycott manifesto to its members. Citing a long list of prohibited German merchandise, the directive asked workers to announce to "shopkeepers and others when purchasing goods or services that they will not buy from the country whose government has so outraged the conscience of the world." The manifesto closed with this assurance: "Against an awakened and sensitive public opinion no tyranny can stand."[4]

British labor's logic was sound, but it became difficult to mobilize Britain when protest and boycott were incongruously disowned by Jewish leaders themselves. Christian perceptions could not penetrate the complex Jewish fears of becoming highly visible or triggering dormant British anti-Semitism. They saw only unfathomable inaction.

On July 19, traditional Anglo-Jewish leaders reached a turning point. For decades, the stalwarts of the Board of Deputies and the Anglo-Jewish Association had remained steadfastly anti- and non-Zionist. But since the German Zionist mission to Britain at the behest of Goering in March, Anglo-Jewish leaders slowly came to see Zionism as the answer to German Jewry's dilemma. The Zionist solution gained momentum after the July 13 meeting at Wilhelmstrasse, when Werner Senator went to London to join high-ranking Zionist officials to lobby for transfer.[5]

On July 19 at 5:00 P.M., the Joint Foreign Committee held its decisive session. Neville Laski devoted much of the meeting to a clause-by-clause review and modification of the seven-point compromise memorandum of July 14. Laski then explained that the list of new members would be much shorter than originally suggested. It would include Melchett and his boycott colleague Maj. J. L. Nathan, but no others from the boycott community. And while the original list did name leading Anglo-Zionists, the final list would upgrade Zionist representation to include the movement's most influential voices. Chaim Weizmann was one of those discussed. Ultimately, the list of twelve additional names to be inducted included Zionist Organization president Nahum Sokolow, former Palestine attorney general Norman Bentwich, Palestine academic Philip Hartog, Zionist investor Sir Robert Waley-Cohen, and the non-Zionist president of the Jewish Agency (oversight) Council Osmond d'Avigdor-Goldsmid.[6]

Laski then read a classified briefing based on an interview with Gen. Jan Christian Smuts, deputy prime minister of South Africa. Smuts, formerly of the British Imperial War Cabinet, was, together with Chaim Weizmann, mainly responsible for the Balfour Declaration. Although not Jewish, Smuts was one of Zionism's most important supporters. On condition that the press not be informed, Laski revealed that Smuts was "optimistic as to the future of the Jews in Germany." *Optimistic* was a word thus far unheard in the lexicon of the Hitler crisis. Laski mentioned some important developments in Germany, adding Smuts' personal advice: "Take the long view of the situation," do not allow "discretion to be overridden by sentiment," and remain strongly opposed to an organized boycott. The JFC members were impressed by the briefing and decided that Smuts' news could be read in secret at the next Board of Deputies meeting—just before the boycott vote.[7]

Laski finally read a letter from Nahum Goldmann inviting the JFC to attend Stephen Wise's World Jewish Congress gathering in Geneva in early September.[8] This was Wise's coordinated global boycott. Laski and the JFC decided to defer acceptance of Goldmann's invitation, thus increasing the ambiguities about Anglo-Jewish cosponsorship of an international boycott Jewish conference.[9]

It was all very confusing. On July 12, Lord Melchett's eight-point take-over memorandum called for an international conference to convene in October. Presumably, this was to be the rescheduled World Jewish Economic Conference. Heightened pressure then focused on Lord Melchett to abandon any conference with ad hoc boycott leaders and instead work within the system. On July 14, Neville Laski engineered a rescission of Melchett's July 12 coup, and Melchett's eight-point memorandum was replaced by a new seven-point proposal, which still mentioned an October conference. But presumably, the reference was now to Wise's World Jewish Congress. Wise even wrote back to New York, "It represents a great triumph for the democratic and nationalistic Jewish ideals. For the first time, these London gentlemen have been forced to . . . sit down and publicly confer with representatives of the Jewry of the world—something they have never done before." [10]

Then Samuel Untermyer's Amsterdam conference founded the World Jewish Economic Federation, whose inaugural convention would still be held in London in October under Lord Melchett. Now, on July 19, a new world gathering in London was being discussed for October, this one sponsored by Zionist and Anglo-Jewish leaders to focus on "relief" and fundraising to the exclusion of boycott. [11]

So many rival suggestions for a world Jewish gathering were vying for recognition by July 19 that nobody was sure which idea was under discussion at any given time. Laski's move to defer a decision to accept Goldmann's invitation to Wise's World Jewish Congress only prolonged the confusion. The longer such confusion existed, the less likely anyone *except* the Deputies could properly organize a conference—which is why Untermyer suddenly called his Amsterdam conference. Similarly, Stephen Wise decided he could no longer wait for the Deputies to co-convene the World Jewish Congress. So Wise and other Congress advocates scheduled something called the Second World Jewish Conference for early September in Geneva, which would finally construct a worldwide anti-Hitler boycott—with or without the Anglo-Jewish establishment.

Melchett was trying to walk a line between his own grass-roots support and the establishment Joint Foreign Committee of which he was now a member. So after the boycotters in Amsterdam proclaimed him chairman of the World Jewish Economic Federation, Melchett felt compelled to issue press statements denying his involvement and counseling against any "officially proclaimed" boycott. Yet at the same time, his own boycott journal, *The Jewish Economic Forum*, assured boycotters that the long-awaited anti-Nazi "conference" would indeed convene in October in London. To pacify conservative Jewish leaders, however, it would be called a *general* conference, not an *economic* conference. But Melchett promised that the preliminary work in Amsterdam would be a major focus. The *Forum* stressed that whether the boycott was proclaimed or unproclaimed, official or unofficial, was not as important as ensuring that the boycott was indeed *organized*. [12]

However, Melchett's equivocation soon gave way to indecision. Perhaps the boycott was not a good idea. Melchett was an ardent Zionist. Like the

The April First anti-Jewish boycott
(Courtesy of the National Archives)

Jewish War Veterans picketing a store selling German goods. (Courtesy of Jewish
War Veterans of the U.S.A.)

Colonel Morris Mendelsohn (Courtesy of
the Jewish War Veterans of the U.S.A.)

Thousands turned out for the Jewish War Veterans' March 23, 1933, anti-Nazi
parade, inaugurating the boycott against Hitler. (Courtesy of the Jewish War
Veterans of the U.S.A.)

Rabbi M.S. Margolies steps to the microphone to chant a prayer for God's intervention during the March 27, 1933, Madison Square Garden protest rally. The chant was broadcast around the world. (Courtesy of the National Archives)

Stephen Wise addressing a protest rally at Battery Park, May 10, 1933. (Courtesy of the American Jewish Congress)

Bishop Francis T. McConnell (*left*) and Stephen Wise (*right*) lead interfaith protest at Madison Square Garden rally. (Courtesy of the National Archives)

The May 10, 1933, protest sent a clear message to the Third Reich. (Courtesy of the American Jewish Congress)

Georg Landauer, director of the German Zionist Federation, worked for an emigration agreement between the Third Reich and the Zionist Organization. (Courtesy of the Leo Baeck Institute, New York)

Siegfried Moses, president of the German Zionist Federation, helped Sam Cohen gain entry to negotiate a private agreement with the Reich. (Courtesy of the Leo Baeck Institute, New York)

Historic King David Hotel luncheon held with Chaim Weizmann, Chaim Arlosoroff (*front row, fourth and fifth from left*), and Arab leaders, April 8, 1933. (Courtesy of the Central Zionist Archives)

TELEGR.
GRANDSTEINER - PRAHA

PRAHA

**GRAND HOTEL
STEINER
PRAHA**
Telefon 64872, 60778, 60661

1. *Vor allen Dingen ist es nötig einen falschen Eindruck wegzunehmen, der vielleicht hier und dort besteht, als ich oder die Bank ohne Mandat, in ... falsch ... Eifer, in ... hinein ... wäre, aus dem Sie, die besser Verstehenden, sich und uns nun mit Mühe befreien müssen.*

E.S. Hoofien's nervously scribbled notes from the Hotel Steiner lobby while waiting to be questioned about the Transfer Agreement before the Political Committee at the 18th Zionist Congress.

Uss. definitely wants you to get out of it, — don't be mistaken about it.— he only gives you a proper motive for doing it

Note passed to Hoofien during questioning before the Political Committee at the 18th Zionist Congress.

Arthur Ruppin (*middle*) and Georg Landauer (*right*) attend a meeting of a Palestine School for recently transferred German Jewish children, circa 1935. (Courtesy of the Leo Baeck Institute, New York)

Mr. Sam Cohen (Courtesy of Esther Aharony, private collection)

Chaim Arlosoroff (Courtesy of the Central Zionist Archives)

others in the JFC, he had heard Laski foreshadow a great development for German Jews. Was it better to continue the struggle to topple the Hitler government—a prospect that seemed more difficult as each day passed, a prospect that carried the certainty of bloody reprisals, but a prospect that made the Jews the sole force willing to organize the war against Nazism internationally? Or was it the heartbreaking duty of Jewish leaders to renounce the fight in advance, struggling instead to save who could be saved, convert the anguish of Nazi Germany into the future of Jewish Palestine, and thus solve such tragedies forever more? Melchett was unsure. Others in Anglo-Jewish leadership were unsure. The decision would be made on July 23, at the Deputies' final meeting of the season, when the JFC's pro-Zionist shift and the boycott would both come up for debate and a vote.

The Board of Deputies was a representative Jewish body. But a core of longtime elected members, including Neville Laski, were able to control the votes in part because of chronic roll-call absenteeism.[13] However, for the July 23 final session, 185 Deputies packed the auditorium. Many would support the Laski line. But many were determined to vote the boycott through.

After dispensing with questions of kosher slaughter, honorary mentions of academic achievements, and congratulations on the seventieth birthday of one of the Deputies, the topic finally turned to Germany.[14] Laski began by assuring the Deputies that the many delays were misleading. During previous days, JFC members had been busy working with Jewish organizations throughout the world to alleviate the plight of German Jewry, including initiating "constructive" assistance. "Constructive" in Jewish relief parlance meant the rebuilding of Palestine. Laski acknowledged that for the first time he would attend the Zionist Congress and that this should be interpreted as a major change in the Deputies' longtime antagonism for Jewish nationalism.[15]

Laski then alluded to enormous efforts under way to liquidate German Jewish assets. He declared emotionally that he yielded to no man in his sincerity or the sincerity of his colleagues. Laski readily acknowledged that others at the gathering, especially those who supported boycott, did not see "eye to eye" with him, but he would not challenge their sincerity either. The audience applauded.[16]

But the Deputies had still heard no persuasive reason to abandon the boycott. Deputy Joseph Wimborne objected that too much of the Jewish public had been "in the dark" about negotiations with Germany. Whatever it was that Jewish leadership was doing, it was not helping Germany's Jews. Mr. Wimborne demanded "more information" and "brass tacks." Laski answered that certain matters were still secret and could not be divulged in public. Deputy Percy Cohen spoke up, agreeing that the Jews had been fighting on "too narrow a front" and that it was time to broaden the offensive.[17] Boycott was the obvious alternative.

Deputy Michael Levy then urged Laski and his colleagues to heed the warning of British Jews who had just three days earlier staged a spectacle of protest through London. The people, declared Mr. Levy, "want to be led." But unless the board took that lead, "the masses would lead themselves."[18]

Laski saw the mood. So he invoked his privilege as president and declared that the boycott debate would now go into secret session to explain certain developments that could not be uttered in public. There could be no outside observers, no reporters, no minutes. All the Deputies participating would be sworn to secrecy as well. Laski promised that after his statements, the Deputies would understand the secrecy.[19]

Presented with such drama, the Deputies reluctantly agreed. With all outsiders barred, the stenographer's pen capped, and the doors closed, Laski read from the document given to him by General Smuts. In this moment of decision, with the Deputies torn between the instinct to fight and the inclination to allow their leaders to engage in quiet diplomacy, Smuts' secret document would have to make the final, compelling case against boycott.[20]

After reading the document, Laski delivered an impassioned hourlong speech explaining why it was now absolutely necessary to forgo the boycott against Germany. When he concluded, Laski felt certain he had swayed the Deputies, even those adamantly pro-boycott. Again using his authority as president, he limited other speakers to five minutes each, saying that it was "a poor case that could not be stated in that time." Only one or two pro-boycott Deputies were permitted to speak.[21]

Many had come to demand that their leaders organize a boycott fight against all odds for persecuted German Jewry. They saw this as their duty to God and man. But they had heard the hard facts of Jewry's endangered position. And although their organizations officially rejected Zionism, as individuals they believed in the destiny of Jewish people to finally find redemption and peace on the soil of their forefathers. Torn between the anger in their veins and the vision in their hearts, one by one they cast their votes to battle or to build.

The vote: 27 to boycott, 110 against. Two hours after it had begun, the secret session was adjourned.[22] No boycott.

In July 1933, influential Anglo-Jewish leaders committed themselves to the Zionist solution of the German Jewish crisis. In so doing, they would help bring to sudden fruition the dream of Jewish nationhood. Unlike previous Jewish emergencies, this time Palestine would come first. When the next persecution descended upon a Jewish people, Israel would be there to receive them.

That noble goal was also desired by Jews advocating combat with the Reich. But they believed the better answer was boycott. For them, Wise's Second World Jewish Conference would indeed be the last chance to organize. And Wise wanted it that way. He was counting on his ability to achieve a dramatic eleventh-hour breakthrough, producing the unified economic death blow needed to end Hitlerism.

But plans were even then afoot to undermine Wise's culminating efforts. Just after the Deputies' final July 23 vote, Nahum Goldmann, the main Congress organizer, arrived back in Geneva and promptly wrote a short letter about a fund-raising question to his friend Mr. Sam Cohen, who had by then reached London. At the end of the letter was this addendum: "Stephen Wise is presently in Paris and will arrive here [Geneva] Thursday evening."[23]

The events of July 1933 represented more than a series of reversals in the evolution of the Jewish response to Hitler. They represented a reprieve for the Third Reich, a letup in the anti-German offensive. This reprieve could not have come at a more decisive moment.

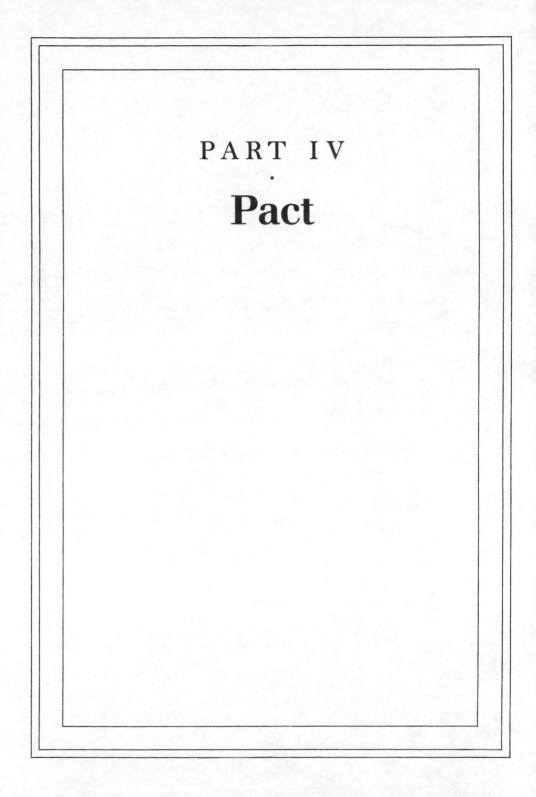

PART IV
·
Pact

23. Druck von Unten

THE THIRD REICH'S campaign of social, economic, and political terrorism against Jews was endless. During June 1933, the chain of anti-Jewish government decrees was itself overshadowed by numberless unofficial acts of repression. For example, Jews were no longer allowed to advertise in the phone book or rent stalls in the Frankfurt markets, and were terminated en masse from hundreds of German companies. Even companies owned by Jewish principals could no longer withstand the popular demand to fire all Jewish employees.[1]

The paper pogrom against Jewish economic participation was the dull edge of the knife. The sharp edge was a continual stream of anti-Jewish boycott actions, many of them violent. For example, in late June, scores of Jewish merchants in Essen and Muenster were picked up and delivered to concentration camps. In Frankfurt, thousands of frenzied Storm Troopers paraded through the streets chanting "Kill the Jews" and demanding that Jewish shops be closed.[2]

These acts of terror were widely publicized throughout the world. In fact, in mid-June *The London Sunday Referee* actually published a Berlin street map locating a dozen Nazi torture houses.[3] The daily outrages in Germany only heightened the moral justification for anti-Reich action. So in spite of the Zionist hierarchy, the Deputies, and the American Jewish Committee, the grass-roots anti-Nazi boycott continued to widen. In simple terms, men and women all over the world of all religious and political beliefs were repulsed by the very thought of conducting business as usual with Nazi Germany.

The crippling effects of international retaliation were only magnified by domestic business disruption caused by the disintegration of the Jewish economic sector, and the pillaging of non-Jewish German companies by NSDAP cells. The battering from without and the deterioration from within weakened Germany during late June to a state of near collapse, and the hairline cracks were beginning to show.

The greatest pressure came from those without jobs. Chain-reaction unemployment triggered revolutionary chaos as the jobless began redefining their loyalties. Nazi splinter groups became rampant. Many such groups consolidated their popularity with time-buying employment tricks. For example, local Nazi groups began forcing factory owners to rehire men let go because business was down. Companies refusing to do so were subject to a thorough financial review. Those with any cash reserves were obligated to rehire the men until those reserves were totally depleted. In Upper Silesia, managers of closed coal mines were arrested; the mines were then reopened by a Nazi kommissar determined to keep them operating until the very last moment. Elsewhere throughout Germany, bankrupt Jewish storeowners were threatened with a charge of "economic sabotage" unless they reopened. Once again, the intent was to keep the employees working beyond the moment of economic infeasibility and right up to the instant of economic exhaustion.[4]

Such employment tricks did buy the Third Reich a little more time. But in many ways the time was not bought in the name of Adolf Hitler as much as in the name of dissident Nazi splinter groups unhappy about rampaging unemployment. To survive, these dissident groups needed to guarantee their adherents—for just a little while longer—what every political machine needs to guarantee its followers: jobs.

To head off political insurrection, Hitler set in motion a series of party absorptions that digested allied right-wing parties, such as the Center party and the Nationalist party. But the real threat was not vestigial parties, it was Nazi splinter groups, which in their fanatic frustration were about to stage a second coup, this one more violent than the first.[5] Goebbels, a chief fomenter of this second wave, did not fail to egg on his supporters. In a speech in Hamburg on June 24, he declared, "The revolution is not yet finished. Worse events are still in store."[6]

In June 1933, Hitler named businessman Kurt Schmitt to be Economics Minister. In Schmitt's view, saving Germany's economy stipulated a return to normalcy, a drastic reduction in anti-Jewish provocations, and an end to interference by kommissars. Hitler approved of Schmitt's approach, but when Schmitt tried to impose his restrictions, Nazi fanatics refused. On June 30, the four highest-ranking NSDAP subordinates in the Economics Ministry began rallying Nazi commercial organizations to oppose Schmitt's appointment. They favored Dr. Otto Wagener, Reich Kommissar for Business and Industry, a longtime party economic leader, chief of the kommissars, and a man of immense power due to his control over thousands of private-sector jobs.[7]

No time was wasted in suppressing the rebellion. Dr. Wagener and his assistants were promptly sent to a concentration camp. The charges were summed up as attempting to "rob the Führer of his freedom of decision."[8] This set off a wave of anarchy, with mid-level Nazi leaders jailing businessmen and taking over companies.[9]

Later that day, June 30, British Ambassador Rumbold reported the chaos in a letter to Foreign Secretary Simon. "Can he [Hitler] control them? . . . Nobody can foresee the actions of leaders like Frick, Goering, Ley, and Wagener, who seem to possess authority to incarcerate anyone at a moment's notice. . . . It is doubtful whether the Nazi leaders in the provinces even trouble to refer to Berlin for authority to make arrests.[10]

The madness continued for days, with contravening Nazi authorities ordering private businessmen to make large donations, abrogate contracts, suspend debts, rehire workers and postpone layoffs. Those who did not seem to cooperate fully were arrested and tried by party bureaus.[11] In many instances, fear and fear alone kept companies operating.

On July 2, Hitler gathered all major SA and SS leaders at Bad Reichenhall and admitted what the diplomats had been saying for weeks—the success of the Third Reich depended wholly on a solution to the unemployment crisis. And he was aware that the swelling ranks of unemployed Brownshirts were creating the impetus for a second revolution. He promised to crush ruthlessly any such action because any second wave would only bring chaos.[12] That chaos would probably result in civil war.

Hitler's July 2 rebuke did not work. The hairline cracks were becoming distinct as the unemployment panic escalated the batteries against German business. A Bavarian director was told to consider himself lucky for being ordered to contribute as little as RM 30,000 to the local Nazi unit. The Berlin Municipality was forced to hire unemployed men to work in imaginary public works programs. The Municipality announced that its normal creditors would therefore not be paid.[13]

A prominent Saxon Nazi employed as a salesman was unafraid to inform the British embassy's commercial section that his local faction had decided to forbid all foreign goods and rule Saxony's commerce as they saw fit. When the embassy staffer reminded the man of Hitler's speeches forbidding interference with private enterprise, the salesman answered that the Nazi leaders of Saxony "had lost patience" with the government and would do as they pleased.[14]

The anarchy was most visible in a massive resurgence of anti-Jewish boycotts. Such boycotts had been forbidden shortly after the aborted April First attempt. Reich leaders knew that of all the foreign provocations, boycotting Jews was the most likely to provoke like retaliation. Yet provincial Nazi units, in open defiance of instructions from Berlin, ordered local newspapers to publish boycott notices. In many districts, party members were ordered to denounce for arrest any Aryan seen entering a Jewish store.[15]

Anti-Jewish boycotts of course increased general unemployment. Although it appeared as though Jewish commerce was being diverted to Aryan businessmen, thereby increasing Aryan employment, the exact opposite was true. Jewish firms ruined by boycott were invariably forced to fire their German employees and default on their debts.

The spiraling effect on employment of these Jewish defaults was made clear to Hitler personally during these first days of July. His new economics minister, Kurt Schmitt, appealed for an emergency meeting to discuss the imminent bankruptcy of Germany's second-largest department store chain, the Jewish-owned Hermann Tietz stores. The massive Tietz chain operated over one hundred stores throughout western Germany, employing 14,000 people directly and providing employment to thousands more who worked for Tietz suppliers. Furthermore, there were several other Jewish department stores that, like Tietz, had been boycotted into near bankruptcy. Schmitt explained to Hitler that if these chains went bankrupt—Tietz in particular—the entire German economy would suffer a major overnight increase in unemployment. The employees of Tietz and many of its suppliers would lose their jobs, and hundreds of creditors would be ruined. Schmitt told Hitler the only solution was to reach somehow into dwindling government reserves and provide Tietz with a special subsidy. Hitler was outraged. The very thought of diverting precious government funds to subsidize a Jewish enterprise was blasphemy. At that point, Schmitt showed Hitler a stack of financial analyses of what would happen if Tietz went out of business. For example, the financial condition of food-processing plants, whose products were well represented in Tietz's stores, would be dangerously weakened. The excited debate lasted two hours. But in the end, money was found to bail out the Tietz operation. It was a stunning lesson in economics for Adolf Hitler.[16]

Der Führer took immediate steps. On July 5, Hitler addressed an open letter to the leading Nazi officials of Brunswick to stop mass arrests and trials of businessmen and industrialists. Hitler stressed that business must be allowed to function normally. The next day, Hitler's minister of labor issued a similar warning to the so-called Nazi Cell Organization, which included numerous bottom-echelon clerical workers. Later on July 6, Hitler chastised key party leaders in Berlin for National Socialist experiments that were destroying the remnants of German industry. "History will not judge us," he warned, "according to whether we have removed and imprisoned the largest number of economists but . . . whether we have succeeded in providing work."[17]

But once more Hitler's warnings went unheeded. The cancerous decay of German business was spreading. In a report to Washington, American chargé Gordon, described how explosive the unemployment issue was: "The tremendous pace at which the new revolutionary wave . . . [is] sweeping over Germany . . . shows that what is known here as the 'Druck von Unten'—that is to say, the *pressure from below* on the part of the rank and file of the Nazi Party who feel that . . . they have in no wise obtained the material benefits which . . . they feel are due them . . . is still a very acute reality." Gordon added that Germany was on the very brink of the so-called "second revolution," and Hitler had decided to stop it.[18]

And so on July 11, Hitler announced that "the revolution was over." Interior Minister Frick circulated a grave warning to all high-ranking government and police authorities, stipulating in plain German: "The Chancellor has made it clear beyond doubt that the German revolution is closed. . . .

The foremost task of the government is now to lay intellectual and economic foundations. . . . But this task will be seriously endangered by further talk of a continuance of the revolution, or of a second revolution. He who talks thus must realize that . . . he is rebelling against der Führer himself and will be treated accordingly. Such utterances . . . are particularly calculated to expose the German economic system. . . . the marked fall of unemployment, must in no circumstances be disappointed." [19]

The warning was again ignored. Transparent references to a "marked fall in unemployment" fooled no one. When 5 to 6 million wage earners in a country of approximately 15 million households have been out of work for two or three years, they know it. Only food on the table can change such people's minds. The talk of a second revolution was indeed a frantic attempt by these 5 to 6 million jobless Germans to transfer their political loyalties to anyone who could finally accomplish that one heroic deed: put some food on the table.

Along with Frick's warning, an announcement was issued to all newspapers by Rudolf Hess, Hitler's personal deputy, ordering all boycotts against Jewish-owned department stores to stop, explaining: When the Third Reich "finds its most important task to provide work and bread for as many unemployed Germans as possible, National Socialists cannot . . . deprive hundreds of thousands of employees . . . of their jobs in department stores and enterprises which depend on them. I therefore strictly forbid all members of the NSDAP to take any actions against department stores or similar enterprises." [20]

In the frenzy to survive, it was not only the poor and unemployed who demanded change, but also the rich and powerful. If Hitler was going to rehabilitate the German work force and rearm, continued support from the magnates of German industry was vital. And Germany's leading industrialists enjoyed vast alliances with the underarmed, understaffed, but nonetheless fully organized German military, the Reichswehr. [21] The Reichswehr was still an uncertain factor in German politics. At the end of the second week of July, the wealthy needed immediate reassurance.

On July 13, 1933, a panel of German industrial leaders and financiers met with Minister of Economics Schmitt to hear the government's plan to seize business back from the Nazi factions. Schmitt outlined a seven-point policy, and it was just what they wanted to hear. Businessmen were to be given full police protection against Nazi interference. Government price controls would be dropped. An advisory council, comprised of Carl Bosch, Gustav Krupp, Fritz Thyssen, Karl Siemens, and thirteen other German executives, would be granted a special voice in future economic decisions. Cartels and markets were to be stabilized. The department stores were to be fully protected from "irresponsible elements." Various so-called fighting organizations of middle-class Nazis were to be dissolved. [22]

In particular, Schmitt was alarmed about the sudden rise of massive middle-class economic associations. The Estate for Handicraft and Trade was the most threatening. This Estate originated in May 1933 as a paper-shuffling party bureaucracy committed to the Nazi doctrine of native crafts and small enterprise. In recent days, however, the Estate had grown to an enormous membership and had taken a defiant position against big business. More important, the Estate had asserted itself as the *sole* competent authority in economic organizing and was even obligating employers to join its ranks. The Estate represented more than just a threat against big business. It represented an alternative power base with the potential to intevene and redistribute jobs. And so Schmitt assured that the Estate would be dissolved at once to avoid the danger that a "whole series of non-authorized persons would engage in experiments and seek to build up a sphere of influence so as to realize all kinds of plans." [23]

Schmitt reassured the gathered executives that the new seven-point program would commit the Hitler regime to economic recovery through *traditional* business methods. The industrialists heartily approved. Gustav Krupp said a word of thanks on behalf of the "German economy" [24] for the last attempt to rescue capitalism in the Third Reich.

While Schmitt was reassuring German industrialists on July 13, Hitler was espousing the new economic philosophy to a party leadership conference in Berlin. He tried to explain that in politics a single swift and decisive blow was required, but "in the economic sphere other laws of development must determine our action. Here we must move forward step by step without suddenly destroying what already exists and thereby imperiling the basis of our own existence." Hitler stressed that he was preoccupied with his prime economic task: restoring the German worker's job and consumer power. [25]

Though Nazi leaders agreed that the paramount issue was jobs, there was now considerable disagreement over the best way to preserve and restore them. Schmitt and Hitler in their new alliance with the German magnates had their ideas. But the Estate, which pursued a more common man's commerce, had its ideas. If any entity could play a role in a second revolution, it was this new Estate. [26]

So the next day, July 14, the Reich issued a new emergency measure stating unequivocally that the Nazi party was the only legitimate party in Germany. Political activities were limited to privileged members of the party. No new parties of any kind could be initiated. This was a telling emergency measure since the Nazis had been the only real political party since April, and even the remnants of their right-wing affiliates had been wholly absorbed in late June. Whatever Estate leaders were planning, under whatever name, Hitler would not allow it. United States Ambassador Dodd, explaining the new law to Washington, commented, "There can be little doubt now that this law was directed not so much against the defunct political parties as against attempts to split the Nazi Party from within." [27]

A few days after the July 14 proclamation, Hermann Goering was vacationing on the Island of Sylt in the North Sea when his entire Prussian cabinet suddenly assembled on the island for an urgent conference. The next day, Goering cut short his vacation and flew back to Berlin. At the airport he said little except that he would move "with an iron hand" against the enemies of the state.[28]

Goering then convened an emergency conference of all the Prussian prosecutors, police chiefs, presiding judges, Gestapo heads, and senior SA and SS commanders. Wholesale arrests of entire dissident Storm Trooper units were already under way, but Goering wanted arrests stepped up. Prosecutors were ordered to clear their dockets of all but dissident cases to provide the swiftest possible punishment.[29]

On July 15 the final figures for Germany's balance of trade were made public. For June, the surplus dropped 68 percent compared to the month before; for the entire first half of 1933 it was down 51 percent. That six-month loss would have been greater except that the anti-Hitler boycott had not really commenced until late March. Overall export volume had also dropped, almost 9 percent from May to June. France's purchases alone decreased by 25 percent, finished goods suffering the greatest losses.[30]

The German Chamber of Commerce issued a brave report admitting that the export decreases were caused by the "growing shutting out of German goods from many countries." The word *boycott* could not be used. And *Deutsche Bergwerks Zeitung*, the newspaper of the powerful Ruhr industrialists, editorialized that the latest figures now made the acquisition of foreign exchange and the increase of exports the Reich's greatest priority.[31] All this occurred about the time Samuel Untermyer proclaimed that his World Jewish Economic Conference would suddenly convene in Amsterdam.

Outrages against Jewish citizens, especially the anti-Jewish boycott, increased the legitimacy of Untermyer's demand for a worldwide economic war against Germany. So the suppression of "atrocity propaganda" was revived as a Reich imperative. It now became clear to Goering that the only real way to diminish atrocity tales was to outlaw the atrocities themselves. The new adamancy about suppressing anti-Jewish acts and forbidding business interference was certain to provoke mass disobedience. The ranks would insist on taking drastic measures to redistribute Germany's remaining economy, and of course deprive Jews of whatever remaining resources they enjoyed.

United States Ambassador Dodd warned of the coming clashes in a July 17 letter: "Hitler realizes that any further attempts at Nazification of business and industry might throw the German economy completely out of joint and thus imperil the existence of his regime." Dodd predicted, "Many of Hitler's followers will resent this sudden change of policy as a betrayal of the Party's program." To illustrate the likelihood that dissident Nazi groups might set up their own kommissar-dominated mini-governments, Dodd quoted a recent warning by Interior Minister Frick: "Any form of auxiliary government is incompatible with the authority of the totalitarian State." Dodd ended his letter by focusing on the "danger that the numerous extremists in the Nazi Party may get out of hand once they realize they have been deceived."[32]

On July 23, Goering called a press conference and announced extraordinary measures to combat any insurrection among the ranks. First, a political prosecutor's office was established to work with the Gestapo. Second, all violations of law that interfered with German reconstruction and offenses against the Storm Troopers, Stahlhelm, or the police would be punished ruthlessly "no matter by whom they are committed." The families of persons convicted of such offenses would be disqualified from any unemployment or relief benefits. Third, a sentence of fifteen years to life imprisonment and possibly death by decapitation would be imposed on "any person who kills, plots, or instigates to kill a policeman, a member of the Storm Troopers or Stahlhelm; or who brings into Germany foreign periodicals or pamphlets with political content, which may be regarded as treasonable in the sense of existing decrees . . . proscribing certain organizations . . . [or] the formation of new parties."[33]

Although the law seemed designed to protect Nazi party units, the real object was to prevent members of the party from turning on each other in a bid for control. Any encouragement of such action, especially if violence were involved, would be deemed by Goering an act of "atrocity propaganda." And any Brownshirt advocating violent anti-Jewish behavior would simply be accused of infiltrating SA ranks to foment atrocity propaganda. Any provocative leaflets or unauthorized newspapers preaching disobedience or loyalty to new factions would be deemed "foreign" and once again "atrocity propaganda." Goering stressed that dissemination of atrocity propaganda was punishable by death.[34]

Despite the sternest of government warnings, anti-Jewish boycotts continued unabated and in the most public fashion. Newspapers throughout Germany published locally ordered boycott ordinances in open defiance of der Führer's orders. For example, the *Dortmund Generalanzeiger* circulated a boycott ordinance on behalf of the local party unit. The *Chemnitzer Neuesten Nachrichten* publicized a boycott sponsored by the Chemnitz Chamber of Commerce. And at the height of Goering's demands that public violence against Jews be abolished, Julius Streicher's followers arrested 300 Jewish shopkeepers in Nuremberg and marched them through the streets in a humiliation rite. The embarrassed Bavarian authorities quickly released the Jewish internees and warned the local press not to mention the incident further.[35]

By late July, a clash of fanatics seemed unavoidable. To the lower-downs, the Reich's economic failures seemed a symptom of laxity and loss of faith. One local NSDAP unit even refused to rescind its boycott when directly admonished by Berlin. Their answer: "We don't need to check with Berlin. On this matter the platform of the Nazi Party is clear. That is good enough for us."[36]

It is unknown how far the "second revolution" had advanced by July 25. There is no way to know whether the threat was greatest from the forces of former economics minister Hugenberg, Nazi theoretician Julius Streicher, imprisoned chief kommissar Otto Wagener, the growing throngs of the Estate for Handicrafts and Trade, or any of a dozen other coalitions and political factions. But on July 25, action was taken.

Precisely at noon, 1 million policemen, Storm Troopers, and SS officers whose loyalty to Hitler could be assured, brought Germany to a standstill. Everything was searched. Trains, cars, waiting rooms, railway stations. The countrywide operation lasted about an hour. The results were never revealed, since the action was executed under Goering's decree promising death to atrocity mongers.[37]

But even the mobilization of a million men could not restrain the *druck von unten,* the pressure from below.

No one knew the precise answer: whether the total breakdown would come in a week, a month, or in two months—or whether it would come at all. That was the question that kept people guessing. But the clear connection between Germany's jobless and national unrest was widely known. All the desperate Nazi speeches and economic alarms of July 1933 were openly reported in the newspapers of London, New York, Paris, Amsterdam, and Washington.

Yet in the face of those headlines and seductive encouragements to strangle the Reich economically, key Jewish leaders were doing all they could during July to block the anti-Nazi boycott. Clearly, the Third Reich was prone, in chaos over unemployment, frantic for time to save its economy, and unable to withstand further erosion of its export trade. But imponderables plagued the international Jewish community: Could the boycott work fast enough? If it did succeed, would German Jewry not be left in ashes beneath the rubble of the Reich?

Those who rejected boycott in favor of the Zionist solution questioned whether Jews could ever truly win such a war, and if they did, would the battles only continue from generation to generation? They believed that the only way to win such wars was to avoid them. If constructing Palestine could achieve the Zionist ideal of Jewish independence, then the victory would not be transient; it would be everlasting. This was the torment of the times for Jewish leadership: to fight fire with fire, or to fight fire with foresight.

24. Landauer vs. Cohen

I N THE MINDS of Zionists, Jewish life in Germany could not be saved, only transferred. Even if Hitler and the German economy were crushed, Jewish wealth in Germany would be crushed with it. The wealth had to be saved. Through the speedy liquidation and transfer of that wealth, the Jewish Homeland could be built, thus creating the refuge needed for a mass transfer of the people. Zionism had declared from the moment of Herzl that anti-Semitic regimes were not to be opposed. They were to be cooperated with in the transfer of Jews and their assets.

As Landauer saw it, vast amounts of money—from immigrants as well as so-called potential immigrants—would be at the disposal of Zionist institutions. Thus, a virtually endless bank account could finance Palestine's development: roads, water supply, housing, and the unique Zionist enterprise of coaxing the desert into bloom.

The great threat to this reach for utopia was Landauer's erstwhile partner, Mr. Sam Cohen. During the July 13 meeting, Landauer had stressed that an agreement could be realized only under the supervision of a special Zionist clearinghouse controlled by the Anglo-Palestine Bank, the bank most Jews and Zionists trusted. This stipulation would deprive Hanotaiah of its monopoly on the futures and fortunes of German Jewry.

The Anglo-Palestine Bank could of course be relied upon to implement the decisions of the Zionist Organization. Established in 1902, the oldest and most respected bank in Palestine was owned by the Anglo-Palestine Company. The Anglo-Palestine Company was in turn a wholly owned subsidiary of the Jewish Colonial Trust Company. All controlling shares of the Jewish Colonial Trust Company were owned and managed by the Zionist Organization in London.[1]

Although the bank was still a small financial institution, this transfer project held the potential to make the Anglo-Palestine Bank one of the world's strongest. Years later, Anglo-Palestine would indeed become one of the top one hundred banks in the world. And it would change its name to Bank Leumi—the most important bank in Israel.[2]

To ensure that Sam Cohen would not again intercept the transfer, Landauer decided the ZVfD would maintain constant communication with both the Economics and Foreign ministries. So on July 14, the day after the Wilhelmstrasse meeting, Landauer sent a letter to Currency Control director Hans Hartenstein, with a copy to Hans Schmidt-Roelke at the Foreign Ministry. Landauer's letter was a simple confirmation that, as requested during the July 13 meeting, a memo crystallizing transfer procedures would be delivered shortly. Until then, wrote Landauer, "I find it important to re-emphasize in advance what I said during that session: It is of the utmost importance that the clearinghouse proposed for Palestine be a public organi-zation which enjoys the full confidence of the Jewish public. . . . Only the Anglo-Palestine Company is available for this purpose."[3]

In a not so subtle move to preclude another Sam Cohen trick, Landauer explained to Hartenstein why he was reiterating his position even before further negotiations. "I want to avoid the possibility of losing this resource through any individual negotiations which might take place prior to the implementation of the overall agreement."[4]

With German unemployment soaring, and with transfer as the only ready means of breaking the boycott, Landauer was feeling eminently more con-fident than just weeks ago when he was afraid to even contact the govern-ment. That surge of confidence was apparent in the July 14 letter as Land-auer made it clear the Zionists would not agree to just any deal. They wanted the deal that was right for Palestine. And so Landauer's short letter closed with what must have appeared like a warning, or even a threat. "I wish to emphasize this in writing beforehand because I consider it important to inform you that the [Zionist] authorities which will be dealing with emigra-tion to Palestine will hardly be able to agree to any other method." Schmidt-Roelke was a little astonished when he read that language and he penciled two exclamation marks next to it in the margin.[5]

Landauer also moved against Cohen at the very center of Cohen's power, Hanotaiah Ltd. Lev Shkolnick, manager of Yakhin, was to negotiate in Berlin the final details of joint implementation with Sam Cohen and Hano-taiah co-owner Moses Mechnes. By June 30, Mechnes had arrived but nothing concrete could be done without Cohen, who was still en route from Tel Aviv to Trieste, and from there to Geneva and then London before finally reaching Berlin to finalize specifics. Employing an old technique of Mr. Sam Cohen himself, Landauer used the opportunity of Cohen's absence to meet with Mechnes and other Hanotaiah personnel to extract a promise that they relinquish any transfer monopoly.[6]

At the same time, Yakhin's desire for a joint venture with Hanotaiah quickly dissipated. Telegrams sent by Hanotaiah to Yakhin were answered in vague terms. Yakhin managers realized they no longer needed their com-petitor Hanotaiah. By mid-July, the publicly controlled Yakhin, which gave the private company Hanotaiah its air of public sanction, had disassociated itself from Sam Cohen[7] and was ready to support Landauer.

Landauer spent almost a week polishing his two-and-a-half-page transfer memorandum, which was typed on the stationery of the *Palastina Amt* or the Palestine Office. The Palastina Amt was the actual Zionist emigration office and thereby colored Landauer's memorandum as *the* official emigration and transfer proposal. On July 19, it was delivered to Hartenstein at the Foreign Currency Control Office. A copy went to Schmidt-Roelke at the Foreign Ministry with a cover letter that again made the point: "I emphasize that our offices in Palestine are particularly anxious to see money and transactions handled by agencies which enjoy the trust and confidence of the public."[8]

Landauer also sent a letter that day, July 19, to E. S. Hoofien, general manager of the Anglo-Palestine Bank, who was then in London. Landauer's letter asked Hoofien to establish a bank-supervised trust company in Palestine ready to commence on a moment's notice. He made it clear that speed was essential because there was always the threat of Sam Cohen.[9]

To further neutralize Cohen, Landauer urged Hoofien to have the Anglo-Palestine Bank people in Jerusalem "keep in close contact with the German Consul." Just as Wolff had been the avenue to Cohen's recognition at Wilhelmstrasse, so would Landauer's project receive official endorsement—if only Wolff would transmit his approval.[10]

Even before Hoofien received Landauer's July 19 memo, the London Zionists were busy preparing for a massively enlarged transfer plan. Werner Senator, who had attended the July 13 Wilhelmstrasse meeting, was preparing a major report to the Zionist Executive in London that outlined the new proposals formulated by Landauer. At the same time, Professor Brodestsky asked his contact A.C.C. Parkinson once more to request the assistance of the British Foreign Office. Senator would be returning to Germany to finalize details of the transfer. To drape Senator in the cloak of legitimacy, Professor Brodetsky wanted the British embassy to allow Senator to use their offices.[11] Foreign Office officials objected that the whole request was "another of Professor Brodetsky's attempts to get us identified with Zionism abroad." But the Colonial Office ultimately struck a compromise whereby Senator would be allowed to call at the embassy but would not be allowed the use of embassy facilities such as telegraph or telephone.[12]

Landauer had indeed gone to extraordinary lengths to reclaim the authority to conclude the agreement with Germany. He had convinced Hanotaiah to withdraw from its monopoly. Yakhin had retreated from joint participation with Hanotaiah. E. S. Hoofien and the Anglo-Palestine Bank would quickly establish a bank-supervised trust company in Palestine. Anglo-Palestine Bank people in Jerusalem would convince Consul Wolff to switch his endorsement from Cohen to Landauer. Landauer was staying in very close touch with Hartenstein, with copies of everything going to Schmidt-Roelke. And Senator, of the Jewish Agency, would be joining Landauer soon as the official representative of the Jewish government in Palestine, complete with British embassy trappings.

At stake was literally the future of the Jewish national home. If the huge transfer expansion the Reich planned was put into force through Sam Cohen, Jewish emigrants would quickly discover an essentially cashless existence in

Palestine. By the time they discovered the unattractiveness of Cohen's transfer, their money would nonetheless become blocked marks in Hanotaiah's special bank account. Only Cohen would have use of the money. When bad experiences became widely known, German Jewry would seek refuge anywhere but the Jewish national home.

But if Landauer's project were put into force through the Anglo-Palestine Bank, German Jewish émigrés would be free to pursue whatever existence they chose in Palestine. They would have the £1,000 entry money in hand, and shortly after they arrived, as German goods were sold, they would receive even more of their money, perhaps a second £1,000. In a nation like Palestine, where wages amounted to no more than a few pounds daily, a £2,000 head start would guarantee a comfortable life. The transferred Jews would in turn become consumers, purchasing familiar German goods coming in as part of the transfer. This in turn would support the transfer of even more German Jews.

Shortly after Landauer's transfer memorandum to the Economics Ministry was delivered, Hartenstein invited Landauer to a conference to discuss details of the transfer. It was finally going as Landauer wanted. He was in control. To make sure all aspects of the negotiations remained fully in hand, he asked his friend Herman Ellern, of the Ellern Bank of Karlsruhe, to visit Schmidt-Roelke beforehand and support Landauer's initiative.[13]

At Wilhelmstrasse on July 20, Hartenstein was most cordial as the meeting began. But as the conversation progressed, Landauer probably wondered if they weren't talking about two wholly different concepts. Landauer's memorandum outlined the *future* expansion of the transfer. Yet Hartenstein explained the transfer had already been expanded two days before. With whom?

With Mr. Sam Cohen, explained Hartenstein. Cohen had assured the ministry that the ZVfD would organize a special Hanotaiah office in its Berlin headquarters to serve as the German clearinghouse. Hanotaiah's main office in Tel Aviv would function as the Palestinian merchandise clearinghouse. Hanotaiah would process all Palestinian transactions through its bank accounts in Palestine, which would be opened in both the Anglo-Palestine Bank and the German-controlled Temple Bank.[14] Was it not exactly as Landauer had insisted: two clearinghouses, one in Germany, one in Palestine—with the money channeled through the Anglo-Palestine Bank?

Hartenstein then showed Landauer a letter on the stationery of Economics Minister Kurt Schmitt, signed by Schmitt's deputy, Dr. Reichart. Dated July 18, 1933, the letter to Hanotaiah confirmed, "On the basis of the renewed negotiations between Mr. Sam Cohen and my experts, I am willing to support the emigration of German Jews to Palestine by allowing the following facilities for an extended transfer of their assets." The second paragraph authorized voluntary deposits into Hanotaiah's blocked accounts for both actual emigrants and for any other Jew considering emigration or "willing to participate in the development of Palestine."[15] That covered every Jew living in Germany.

Reflecting the uproar about unemployment and the dramatic decrease in exports of finished goods due to the anti-Nazi boycott, the Schmitt-Reichart authorization specified that "finished goods" would be exported to Palestine to achieve the transfer. The order acknowledged that deposits made by German Jews would be handled through "an office at the German Zionist Federation, Berlin, Meineckestrasse 10." Yet Landauer, director of the ZVfD, hadn't even been consulted.[16]

The letter also stipulated that German Jews, upon arriving in Palestine, would receive cash from the merchandise sales.[17] Landauer had emphasized how important cash would be in enabling Jews to rebuild their lives and making mass emigration viable. But Landauer was certain that Cohen would keep most of the sale cash, repaying emigrants with whatever parcels of sandy acreage Cohen felt sufficient.

The July 18 order listed Hanotaiah's initial expanded permission as RM 3 million—$15 million—and superseded Cohen's original RM 1 million deal. Unlimited additional permissions were allowed, but the letter demanded an unspecified minority percentage of foreign currency for transfers beyond the first RM 3 million. Dr. Reichart was explicit: "I wish to point out what my experts have repeatedly and decidedly emphasized to Mr. Cohen, that after the 3 million reichmarks have been used up . . . foreign exchange must be received in payment" for at least part of the purchase price.[18]

The final words of the permission letter indicated that emigration to Palestine was absolutely linked to German exports to Palestine. If Germany was to continue providing precious foreign exchange to emigrants to meet the British entry requirement, she could do so only as part of an overall export program. The first RM 3 million then was an inducement. Thereafter, the Third Reich wanted real money.[19]

Landauer was now forced to crack the illusion of partnership and told Hartenstein, "I cannot acknowledge that Mr. Sam Cohen or Hanotaiah are authorized by responsible national institutions." As for Cohen's clearinghouse office at the ZVfD, Landauer declared that it simply did not exist. He added, "I doubt very much if Mr. Sam Cohen or Hanotaiah have the possibility to satisfy [reimburse] the emigrants if they do not sell the goods in an appropriate manner." And such sales would essentially be impossible, Landauer said, since in truth Hanotaiah was an orange grove company, not a retailer or a distributor. "Therefore," Landauer declared, "I cannot assume the responsibility of advising emigrants to undertake their financial transactions with Hanotaiah."[20]

Hartenstein, undoubtedly shocked, answered, "Mr. Sam Cohen has been accredited by the German Consul General in Jerusalem. . . . He is a leading person and has all the authorizations of national institutions." Therefore,

Hartenstein said, he would allow Hanotaiah's expanded permission to stand. Hartenstein tried, however, to reassure Landauer with a promise to watch Hanotaiah's work and make sure Cohen's company lived up to all expectations.[21]

Landauer would not yield. He told Hartenstein that he could not trust any program implemented by Hanotaiah. As the head of the ZVfD, which controlled the Palastina Amt, he was therefore going to counsel all emigrants that anyone transferring via Hanotaiah was doing so at great financial risk. At the same time, he was going to instruct the Zionist authorities immediately to establish a competitive trust company supervised by the Anglo-Palestine Bank as outlined in the transfer memo of July 19.[22] This was a tense moment. Landauer was speaking to a high German government official. He was declaring that he would create an economic organization to frustrate an important export program. Landauer's adamancy came at a time when high-ranking Nazi officials were being sent to concentration camps for proposing alternative economic plans. It was a time when Economics Minister Kurt Schmitt had received Hitler's authority to crush anyone who did not fully cooperate with economic directives.

But the exodus of Jews to Palestine, the employment that would result from the exports, the foreign currency that would be earned, and most significantly the anti-boycott effect of finalizing the transfer were all too vital to let lapse. So Hartenstein backed down and agreed to stay Hanotaiah's expanded permission briefly, pending a verification from the Foreign Ministry, through Consul Wolff, of Cohen's authority. If Hanotaiah was discredited, Hartenstein would vest the transfer authority with the ZVfD and allow Hanotaiah to participate as a mere importer. However, if Cohen was vindicated and the much-touted Anglo-Palestine Bank trust company did not quickly come into existence, then Hanotaiah would be granted full transfer authority—and Landauer could tell the emigrants anything he chose.[23] With that compromise, Landauer left the Economics Ministry and went right to work.

A coordinated plan of action was called for. It began that same day, July 20, with Hermann Ellern, who had access to Schmidt-Roelke at the Foreign Ministry. While traveling back to Karlsruhe, Ellern had made contact with Landauer, probably during a train stop at Frankfurt. After learning of the unexpected Sam Cohen development, Ellern telegraphed Schmidt-Roelke: "WILL SEND YOU COMMENTS RE TRANSFER PLAN TODAY STOP WOULD APPRECIATE YOUR CONSIDERATION OF SAME IN IMPLEMENTATION DIRECTIVES"[24]

The next morning, Landauer sent an urgent correspondence to Anglo-Palestine Bank director Hoofien in London. He explained the sudden crisis, how apparently between the July 13 Wilhelmstrasse conference and Landauer's follow-up July 20 meeting with Hartenstein, Cohen had made additional unauthorized representations to the Economics Ministry that once again placed the entire transfer in his hands. In writing his letter, Landauer tried to control his anger. "It is clear that the Reich Economics Ministry and the Foreign Ministry should not have done this thing without asking us. Mr. Sam Cohen's behavior is for me entirely unclear. He has operated with the most impossible remarks. For instance, he said that he will get an office with us, and he is our authorized agent." [25]

Cohen's coup could be reversed, but "only if all parties in Palestine establish an office within the week to take over the merchandise and if the APB immediately takes the initiative." Landauer urged Hoofien to "treat this matter urgently" and his letter ended with the simplest distillation of the crisis: What happened in the next few days would "decide in the long run the fate of German-Jewish emigrants' money." [26]

Once Hermann Ellern arrived in Karlsruhe, he sent Schmidt-Roelke his personal transfer suggestions. These closely followed Landauer's ideas. This was to show Schmidt-Roelke the widespread acceptance of Landauer's viewpoint. Ellern added his comments: "This plan is intended to facilitate for Jewish emigrants the transfer of a majority of their assets to Palestine and reopen a large market for German products. This proposal [however] may have been overtaken by events, namely the agreement . . . with Hanotaiah." [27]

Ellern's demarche continued, "I am in close contact with the ZVfD in this matter and feel a personal obligation to inform you of some misgivings, since I want to take a position as early as possible with respect to matters which might be harmful to all parties concerned. . . . Last night I was told at the offices of the ZVfD that, contrary to statements made by Mr. Sam Cohen, there is no question of opening a Hanotaiah office. . . . Also, I have spoken with a representative of Yakhin who stated that Mr. Cohen is not speaking for that company." [28]

To retain his own credibility, Ellern disparaged Cohen carefully: "I don't know Mr. Cohen personally and have no reason to doubt his veracity, but I have gained the impression that a transaction of this magnitude, if it were to be conducted solely by Hanotaiah, would not be greeted with universal trust and confidence. This also conforms to various opinions which I have heard about Hanotaiah in Palestine." [29]

Realizing his assertions went against everything Schmidt-Roelke had been told, Ellern explained, "Mr. Cohen is a very clever businessman and his sweeping powers of attorney and letters of recommendation may be based on the fact that the situation in Germany is not well known there [in Palestine] and that every idea is welcomed which could conceivably lead to a transfer of capital . . . by emigrants, thus facilitating the establishment of a new existence for these emigrants in Palestine, as well as to again make the Palestine market accessible to Germany." [30] This last comment was a clear reminder that the boycott in Palestine could be stilled only by the Zionist authorities there.

Expanding on the issue of official Zionist approval, Ellern asserted that Yakhin and Palestinian workers "who are a key element, will have no part of it if Hanotaiah is put in sole charge." Ellern added the manufacturers, importers, and Jewish consumers of Palestine to the list of "will nots." Summing up, Ellern wrote that such widespread opposition "would of course damage the main objective: the stimulation of German exports. All these dangers would be obviated if the leadership role in this matter were to be entrusted to the Anglo-Palestine Bank rather than Hanotaiah. . . . Under no circumstances should the name Hanotaiah be used in the designation of the account." In conclusion, he urged Schmidt-Roelke to accept Landauer's transfer memorandum.[31]

Ellern's letter would reach Schmidt-Roelke by Monday, July 24. At the same time, Schmidt-Roelke would receive a letter from Hartenstein following the revelations of the Landauer meeting.

Dated July 22, Hartenstein's letter explained how Landauer had urged the Hanotaiah transfer decree be set aside in favor of a bank-supervised transfer. "He [Landauer] indicated . . . that in view of news he had received from Palestine during the last few days, he had serious doubts whether Mr. Sam Cohen and Hanotaiah could be considered legitimate. . . . Hanotaiah, he said, is just one of several plantation companies, which would now have an undesirable monopoly. He [Landauer] doubted that Mr. Cohen would be successful in selling, without loss, the merchandise valued at RM 3 million which Hanotaiah plans to buy. Under these circumstances, he [Landauer] and his friends could hardly assume the responsibility of recommending to Jewish emigrants to make deposits . . . to the account of Hanotaiah because they have reason to fear that the equivalent funds would not . . . be paid back to depositors."[32]

Here was the point. Either the emigrants received their money in Palestine and could reconstruct their lives there—or they did not. Clearly, the Jews would not give up Germany to live a life of poverty in Palestine.

Hartenstein's July 22 letter continued, "I do not have sufficient information about conditions in Palestine and about the attitude of the various organizations to be able to react to Dr. Landauer's misgivings. Nor am I in a position to examine Mr. Cohen's legitimacy, and have in this respect fully relied on your point of view, which is based on the reports of the Consulate General in Jerusalem, some of which I have seen." Prudence dictated, wrote Hartenstein, that he stay Hanotaiah's permission and "request the Consulate General in Jerusalem to provide a statement whether the proposed procedure . . . guarantees for the emigrants the receipt of their money immediately upon arriving in Palestine, or whether the agreement with Hanotaiah should be put on a broader basis by including the appropriate national Jewish organizations." He urged Schmidt-Roelke to speak with Landauer directly and take the other steps necessary to determine once and for all who represented Zionism: its official institutions, or an enterprising gentleman named Mr. Sam Cohen.[33]

Monday morning, July 24, Schmidt-Roelke read letters from Hartenstein, Ellern, and others suggesting that Sam Cohen was a fraud, that he was incapable of selling the merchandise except at a great loss, and that German emigrants would never receive much if any of their transferred assets. A message was dispatched to Consul Wolff: "After negotiations with Cohen, Hanotaiah has obtained authority to transfer a total of RM 3 million via exports to Palestine. After conclusion of negotiations, Zionist Federation and the Jewish Agency expressed doubt as to Cohen's authority to negotiate for Palestine authorities. They declare Hanotaiah monopoly to be undesirable and doubt that RM 3 million worth of goods can be transferred without loss. . . . Doubts expressed also on whether emigrants would receive their money immediately and without loss. Local Jewish organizations therefore had misgivings about authorizing payments to Hanotaiah. Request info on whether misgivings are justified, especially whether it is true that Hanotaiah does not have support of appropriate authorities in Palestine, which is the exact opposite of what Cohen indicates."[34]

Schmidt-Roelke and Hartenstein would have summoned Cohen himself to clarify the questions. But Cohen was not in Germany. He had gone back to London to coordinate with the Zionist Organization and do what he could to quash the chances for a unified world boycott.

25. Race for Credibility

E.S. HOOFIEN in London did everything possible to assist Landauer in supplanting Sam Cohen. On July 26, he sent a cable to Heinrich Margulies, Tel Aviv manager of the Anglo-Palestine Bank, instructing Margulies to convince the German consul to rescind his endorsement of Sam Cohen.[1] Even as Hoofien was cabling Margulies in Jerusalem, however, Consul Wolff was traveling to Tel Aviv to speak with Hanotaiah and others about Sam Cohen's authority, whether Hanotaiah could indeed distribute RM 3 million worth of German goods, and whether Cohen's transfer plan was cashless. The Hanotaiah people answered Wolff as honestly as possible. First, Hanotaiah had no plans to distribute merchandise. Second, they had no plans to reimburse the emigrants with much cash once they arrived in Palestine. Major deductions would be made for construction materials, land, and other charges.[2] When the transaction was complete, the emigrant would possess little more than the land, some equipment, a farmhouse, and probably some sheds. These answers—which substantiated the criticisms against Cohen— were going to be hard to handle in the consul's report to Schmidt-Roelke.

Hoofien's July 26 cable to Margulies reached Margulies the next morning. Margulies immediately telephoned Consul Wolff, who agreed to discuss the situation. Margulies left Tel Aviv for the consulate at once.[3]

During the ninety-minute meeting, Wolff said that in March, Berlin expected to lose the boycott battle in Palestine. Sam Cohen changed all that by presenting his anti-boycott plan. Wolff added that Cohen was the first to suggest transfer ideas. After Hanotaiah received its first permission in mid-May, competitors came to the consulate to complain. Wolff said he answered them all the same way: "Why did you come so late? Somebody has outrun you."[4]

Now that Hanotaiah possessed the monopoly, warned Wolff, Palestinian competitors must not interfere. The consul called the crosscurrents against Cohen a dangerous game. Margulies answered that he represented the Anglo-Palestine Bank, not any group for or against Hanotaiah or Sam Cohen. The bank's position was that it did not understand how it had been suddenly dragged into the arrangement since it had no relationship with Cohen or Hanotaiah, and had never authorized Cohen to speak on its behalf.[5]

Wolff assured that Cohen had not spoken in the bank's name, but that Cohen did have a letter from the Zionist Organization stating his transfer deal would be under "national supervision." Also Ussischkin, head of the Jewish National Fund, had endowed Cohen with official authority to transfer JNF monies from Berlin to Palestine. So, asked Wolff, was this sudden declaration about the illegitimacy of Sam Cohen a mere "sting" against Cohen, or was the intent to disrupt the transfer itself?[6]

Margulies denied any negative intentions regarding Cohen or the transfer. He wanted to state only that Cohen had no connection with the bank, and the bank was therefore free to choose whether to join the transfer project or not. At this Consul Wolff asked why might the Anglo-Palestine Bank not participate? Margulies answered that the bank did not want to associate its good name in so vital an enterprise when the partner was a little private company, "which after all is not exactly the Deutsche Bank." Here Margulies sensed that Wolff was trying either to persuade him or at least to discover the real fiscal reasons behind Anglo-Palestine's hesitation. So Margulies allowed himself to be nudged in that direction.[7]

Wolff did as expected, explaining that he had concluded early on that the original RM 1 million permission granted to Cohen was too small: "I said to myself that in comparison to the big sums which are being mobilized for the Jews, one million marks is cat shit, and therefore I urged the sum to be increased." But with the new 3-million-mark ceiling, and unlimited renewals, what was the bank's objection?[8]

Margulies shot the demerits off in quick succession. A: Hanotaiah's financial capability was limited. B: Hanotaiah could not even guarantee proper land purchases. C. A transfer limited to plantation investments was unacceptable, especially since recent immigrants were learning such investments were risky. D. Hanotaiah could never generate enough plantation sales even to approach the RM 3 million figure.[9] Hence, whatever immigrants would be receiving in exchange for their blocked marks would be vastly inflated.[10]

Then Margulies talked plain politics. Whoever was going to traffic in great quantities of German goods, said Margulies, was exposing himself to the worst kind of public criticism before the whole world. The outcry would be too much for any one private company. If the arrangement were under the aegis of official Zionist bodies, that outcry might be muffled. But even still, the protests might be so strong that official entities might also retreat from the project.[11]

Margulies then carefully shifted to a gentle threat that in view of the obstacles, only Anglo-Palestine could make the transfer work. In so many words, he declared that if the bank did withdraw, leaving only the German Temple Bank and Hanotaiah, the project would indeed be doomed. Wolff's facial expression changed as he comprehended Margulies' ultimatum. The consul became a bit threatening himself and said, "Then the prospects would be very pessimistic. . . . The Jews would not get out of Germany."[12]

This was a moment not for diplomats but for hard bargainers. Margulies put up a good front. He nonchalantly agreed yes, "prospects really are pessimistic." With that, Margulies said it was now up to the bank's board of directors to approve or disapprove Cohen's project, and in Margulies' personal opinion, the decision would be no. He would of course stay in touch with the consulate.[13]

Margulies hurried back to his office to type a full report to Hoofien. "I am now quite positive," Margulies wrote, ". . . that the Consul General . . . has skillfully profited from circumstances, using Sam Cohen as a 'scab' to create a *fait accompli*, that is, before the Zionist institutions could decide whether they would tolerate any breach of the boycott." Wolff wanted to show Berlin how fast he could conquer the boycott in Palestine. Now that all sorts of problems had developed with the consul's choices, suggested Margulies, Wolff "does not want to let his men fall and thereby exchange them for the more bothersome and much less sure partnership of the [same] institutions" he sought to avoid in the first place.[14]

"We have made a great mistake in not getting in touch with the Consul earlier," Margulies told Hoofien. But, added Margulies, "I believe I can change the Consul's stand considerably. . . . *He is urgently interested*, and in Berlin they understand that such a key situation . . . is worth far more than three million marks. If we do not want to let the whole thing fall or to fight it, and if we want instead to really attain a really 'reasonable' arrangement and to participate, then two things are necessary: you [Hoofien] must begin to act on this matter in Berlin; and I must negotiate here. The negotiations here are very important . . . because if we show the Consul our readiness to cooperate, he would probably abandon his exclusive pro-Hanotaiah position." [15] Margulies raced to make the airmail bag to London and then cabled a distilled version of his letter to Hoofien just in case. [16] That done, Margulies called for an immediate conference with the Conference of Institutions which had authorized Cohen a month before.

Even as Margulies was typing his letter to Hoofien, Consul Wolff was preparing his report to Berlin. This was going to be complicated. He would have to tell the painful truth, but in such a way as to not make himself look either foolish, incompetent, or worse—in league with Mr. Sam Cohen.

Wolff's July 27 report turned out to be a confusing review calculated to protect all his prior endorsements of Cohen, while carefully qualifying them to correspond to the newly known facts. The report began: "I have no reason for changing . . . what I have said in previous reports." Wolff then admitted that Hanotaiah was indeed not the only settlement firm in Palestine, but added that Cohen was the first to suggest a plan and that the plan had been endorsed in writing by the Jewish Agency and other Zionist institutions. It was not until after Cohen secured his "monopoly-like agreement" that "Hanotaiah's competitors . . . realized that they too should conclude an agreement." [17]

The consul then reaffirmed the need to stand by the Hanotaiah monopoly because "it places Sam Cohen in a position of exerting a calming influence upon boycott tendencies. . . . For instance in London, from where yesterday he sent me a telegram 'My work is progressing satisfactorily in London also.' " [18]

It was easy to paint Hanotaiah's critics as jealous competitors. But explaining away Cohen's intentions on reimbursements and his inability to distribute merchandise would be harder. Wolff's tactic was simply to leave some questions unanswered and confuse the issues with contradictory statements. For example, he readily conceded that emigrants would not receive their money immediately, but then asked why that was even relevant since the whole idea was to convert German Jewish deposits into agricultural wares. He similarly admitted that Hanotaiah was incapable of distributing general merchandise, but then asserted that Hanotaiah never was interested in such merchandise. Wolff then simply reaffirmed unswerving support for the Hanotaiah agreement, "even if it results in a monopoly."

Perhaps Consul Wolff thought he could pretend that the question of cash reimbursements was not really a valid issue. Perhaps he thought that his open acknowledgment of Hanotaiah's inability to deal in general merchandise would imply that Cohen might organize the merchandise distribution on his own outside Hanotaiah proper. The fact that Wolff followed his candid admissions with a staunch reinforcement of the Hanotaiah agreement strongly suggested to Berlin that the problems were no real obstacle to a successful transfer.

As for the Anglo-Palestine Bank, Wolff wrote that he sensed Hoofien was orchestrating the bank's withdrawal, which would obviously "make the transaction for the Jews more difficult." The consul related his warning to Margulies that withdrawal would only result in a total "cancellation of this and similar projects." [19] In other words, Wolff was advising transfer through Hanotaiah, or no transfer at all. Wolff added that if Jewish groups propagandize against Hanotaiah, "We should stifle this by clearly letting the Jewish Agency know that by sabotaging the Hanotaiah project, it will not smooth the way for other agreements." [20] Wolff's report summed up with a warning he expected the Foreign Ministry to pass on to Hartenstein: "By sabotaging the Hanotaiah plan the Jews would only cut off their noses to spite their faces by making further agreements impossible." [21]

Consul General Heinrich Wolff was the Third Reich's man in Palestine. He had been handling this question from the outset. He was the closest man to the Zionist political scene. Consul Wolff had openly admitted there were problems with the project, but insisted these problems should not be allowed to impede the agreement. There was no other authority on Palestinian affairs the Foreign Ministry could turn to. Howsoever problematic his advice seemed to be, Consul Wolff was to be relied on. Schmidt-Roelke could make no other decision.

Mr. Sam Cohen and Hanotaiah Ltd. would remain in full control of the transfer.

Late in the afternoon, July 27, 1933, as Consul Wolff was reinforcing Cohen's credibility, Heinrich Margulies was continuing his campaign to debunk Cohen once and for all. Margulies went to the Conference of Institutions. Although Landauer, the Anglo-Palestine Bank, and Yakhin had renounced Cohen, the Conference's authority was still intact. Since the Conference included all the key commercial associations plus the Organization of German Immigrants, their endorsement was still a mighty one. Its members were interested primarily in trade with Germany. And Hanotaiah and Cohen had promised to bring plenty of it under the most advantageous financial conditions. In fact, since the merchandise was actually being paid for in Germany from blocked emigrant accounts, all sorts of lenient payment forms could be arranged. However, Margulies was able to convince the businessmen that whatever commercial benefits and windfalls they hoped to realize from the transfer would be wholly endangered if the project were controlled by Hanotaiah, a private concern that was truly in competition with all the business entities present.[22]

A member of the Organization of German Immigrants, Mr. Ney, conceded that his group had been rethinking the Hanotaiah plan. A special Organization subcommittee had adopted an alternative plan, which Ney read aloud. It involved founding a tiny corporation of ambiguous purpose that, like Hanotaiah, would transfer assets by merchandise. Ney at first claimed the emigrants would be reimbursed. Not with money, though, but with some sort of nonmarketable investments in new companies. The conferees quickly saw this as just another version of Hanotaiah's plan, but instead of giving emigrants inflated property, they would be given shares in perhaps worthless companies. The undisguised pilferage was so transparent to the businessmen gathered and to Ney himself that Ney actually became embarrassed over the scheme. Ney withdrew the proposals, which Margulies termed "grotesque," just minutes after they were introduced.[23]

Ney's scandalous proposal was strong proof that only a proper trust company, supervised and controlled by the Anglo-Palestine Bank, would deliver the benefits of transfer without abusing the interests of the German Jews. Neither Mr. Sam Cohen, Hanotaiah Ltd., or any other private entity could be trusted—only the Anglo-Palestine Bank.

Just after Margulies left the conference session, he cabled Hooflen in London: "RESOLUTION CONFERENCE . . . BANK SHALL UNDER ALL CIRCUMSTANCES ACCEPT ACTING AS AGENT WITH OR WITHOUT HANOTAIAH TEMPLE BANK STOP SECONDLY ASK YOU INTERVENE BERLIN VIEW CONTINUATION ALL TRANSACTIONS WITH BANK STOP THIRDLY ASKED ME CONTINUE CONCENTRATING WITH CONSUL GENERAL STOP PLEASE INSTRUCT ME INFORM CONSUL . . . ONLY CONFERENCE PLUS BANK SHALL BE AUTHORIZED NEGOTIATE."[24]

Hooflen's response was immediate. "INFORM CONFERENCE BANK PREPARED TO ACT STOP YOU MAY INFORM CONSUL ACCORDING YOUR CABLE."[25]

On July 28, Margulies also tried to bring the Jewish Agency to the anti-Cohen team. On July 17, the Conference of Institutions had cautiously approached the Jewish Agency with a copy of the Conference's resolutions on trade with Germany. The object then was to secure the Agency's sanction. But the Jewish Agency had refused at the time, undoubtedly reacting to the Conference's usurping its authority. Now Margulies was asking the Agency—in the name of the bank that was itself owned by the Zionist Organization—to specifically authorize the Conference of Institutions as the sole legitimate negotiator of the transfer. Margulies also wanted the Agency to notify Consul Wolff that Sam Cohen was indeed not acting on its behalf. For compelling evidence, Margulies presented copies of Landauer's original

July 19 transfer memorandum, and various letters and cables illustrating that the problem almost entirely revolved around Sam Cohen. The Jewish Agency promised a quick answer.[26]

That same day, July 28, Margulies received in the mail a copy of Landauer's July 21 letter to Hoofien describing the shock he received at Hartenstein's office when he learned of Sam Cohen's new deal. The letter quoted the Hartenstein-Landauer dialogue almost verbatim. It was now clearer than ever to Margulies that the day would be won or lost on the word of Consul Wolff. Margulies sent another note to Hoofien, acknowledging receipt of the Landauer letter and indicating he could now see "that the matter is coming to a head." He told Hoofien he would go back to Consul Wolff to "emphasize more strongly the removal of Sam Cohen-Hanotaiah than I did yesterday, when I was forced to restrain myself." Margulies explained that his tactic would focus on Wolff's false or at least misunderstood endorsements of Cohen—endorsements "he was now obligated to correct, either of his own volition or in reply to a request for confirmation which the Reich Foreign Ministry would send him."[27]

Margulies, at that moment, was unaware that Wolff had already replied to the Foreign Ministry's request for confirmation, retreating not an inch in his support for Cohen. Nonetheless, Margulies dispatched to Wolff a copy of Landauer's July 19 memorandum, with a short cover note identifying it as the "official" memorandum of the ZVfD.[28]

Then, in a longer letter to Wolff written that day, Margulies suggested that Wolff's exaggerated endorsements of Cohen were about to be unpleasantly exposed. Margulies explained how he had just received a report about the actual conversation between Hartenstein and Landauer, including Hartenstein's request that the Foreign Ministry obtain a "confirmation from the German Consul . . . about the authorization of Mr. Sam Cohen."[29]

Margulies was letting Wolff know that he was aware that Berlin was doubting Wolff's original words. Margulies' July 28 letter went right to that issue: "On the basis of our talk yesterday, I was pleased to notice that Mr. Sam Cohen had not declared to you at all that he was the representative . . . of our bank, or any other central national institution. It seems to me, then, that the gentlemen at the Reich Economics Ministry have misunderstood your recommendation of Mr. Sam Cohen, and after the explanations which I have received from you, and vice versa, I suppose that you yourself will initiate the correction of this misunderstanding."[30]

Margulies' July 28 letter repeatedly reminded that without the Anglo-Palestine Bank, no goods would be sold, the project would not be trusted by the people, and the entire transfer "would have such minimal chances of succeeding" that German emigrants would have to be advised not to work through Hanotaiah.[31]

Margulies hoped to be sufficiently threatening to compel Consul Wolff to rescind his recommendation of Sam Cohen lest he endanger Germany's interest and his own credibility. But the suggestion of embarrassment to Consul Wolff, and the promise of a foreign policy and trade fiasco for Germany were all conveyed with cordial language and roundabout phrasing. No threats are taken so seriously as those spoken with a smile. Margulies was smiling in every sentence.

He ended his polite missive: "And you, my very esteemed Consul General . . . understand that in this case the unexpectabilities can play a very great role. And these unexpectabilities lay not so much in the hands of those who deposit their money in Germany, but are in the hands of those who must sell the merchandise here." Margulies then put Wolff on notice that the Conference of Institutions would soon present a plan for a unified transfer scheme. After presentment they expected the consul to renounce the Hanotaiah plan and endorse the new group.[32]

On July 28, while Margulies was keeping up the pressure on Consul Wolff in Jerusalem, E. S. Hoofien of the Anglo-Palestine Bank in London was planning his strategy for intervening in Berlin. Hoofien was studying the problem when he received a visit from two men: Moshe Mechnes and Mr. Sam Cohen. The Hanotaiah co-owners wanted to discuss details of their transfer, which was to be funneled through an account at the Anglo-Palestine Bank. Hoofien asked them to sit down, and the conversation went right to the conflict.[33]

Wasting no words, Hoofien told them he harbored the greatest apprehensions about Hanotaiah's recent arrangement with the Reich Economics Ministry.[34]

It would have to be reversed. If Hanotaiah would not reverse it of their own accord, the Palestinian community and the Anglo-Palestine Bank would reverse it for them. The logic was simple. If Landauer's ZVfD specifically recommended against the Hanotaiah method of transfer, German Jews would never participate. German Jews wanted a safe and reliable transfer. The least hint of instability would scare them off. Of course, many Jews would prefer the financial risk of transfer via Hanotiah to the physical risk of remaining in Germany. But even these assets would not be usable by Hanotaiah. In order to extract the value of blocked assets, Hanotaiah and/or Sam Cohen would have to sell the merchandise in Palestine. This would never happen. With the Anglo-Palestine Bank, Yakhin, and the Conference of Institutions abstaining from the whole operation, Cohen's transfer would become untouchable. The goods would be boycotted either because they were of German origin or because they represented an outlawed commercial treaty. The Germans would drop the unworkable project and surely rule out any future dealings with Hanotaiah or Sam Cohen, and for that matter with Zionists altogether.

Hoofien, in essence, told Hanotaiah on July 28 that they were the proud possessors of a worthless, exclusive deal, but that there could be a compromise. He conceded that Hanotaiah had every right to conduct its plantation business, but no right to acquire a monopoly. Furthermore, Hanotaiah should not sell merchandise, nor should it be the controlling factor in the transfer with reimbursement to emigrants at its own discretion. Hoofien's compromise was this: First, the Anglo-Palestine Bank would establish a transfer account for Hanotaiah Ltd., but it would be an ordinary account, with the bank assuming no responsibility and stating so openly. Second, the funds processed through the account could pay only for land and agricultural wares—no general merchandise. Third, Hanotaiah would get no monopoly; the bank would grant identical privileges to competitive plantation companies. Fourth, Hanotaiah must "stick to its role as a plantation company." [35]

Cohen was hearing an ultimatum and it was coming from a bank that embodied the authority of the Zionist Organization. This was a moment of hard choices. All of nothing, or part of something.

Cohen chose something. Mechnes approved. They then handed Hoofien the July 18 transfer decree and asked him to propose any amendments he felt proper. They would return to Berlin and ask the Economics Ministry to ratify the changes. [36]

Mr. Sam Cohen had finally agreed to withdraw. There was no need for recriminations, no need for explanations about all the previous reversals and intrigues. That was all past. Call it bad communications. What was important now was Cohen's pledge to withdraw—spoken before his partner Mechnes and the head of the Anglo-Palestine Bank with no further possibilities for misunderstandings.

All that remained was for Consul Wolff to switch his recommendation to the new trust company of the Anglo-Palestine Bank and the Conference of Institutions. Margulies was doing everything possible with the consul himself. Hoofien would work on Schmidt-Roelke.

An interagency correspondence was dictated by Hoofien from Anglo-Palestine Bank's London office to Landauer at the ZVfD. This rendered the impression that the two entities regularly coordinated on projects and communicated informally. While the note was addressed to the ZVfD, it was wholly intended for the eyes of Schmidt-Roelke. [37]

Hoofien's correspondence stated, "During the last few days I have heard from you as well as from Mr. Sam Cohen that . . . the Reich Economics Ministry will approve certain procedures for transfer of Jewish capital to Palestine . . . in such a manner that our bank is to open an account with the Reichsbank into which funds for the credit of Hanotaiah are to be deposited. I have thereupon immediately expressed my surprise to you over . . . a linkage between our bank and Hanotaiah without our bank having been consulted." [38]

The note admitted that Hoofien had asked his mangers in Palestine to check on Sam Cohen's activities, authorizations, and any accreditation he enjoyed with the German consul. "Today, I received a reply," Hoofien declared, "which stated—similarly to the very information I received from Mr. Cohen—that we had in no way authorized this, that furthermore, the official Jewish authorities had never authorized Mr. Cohen's actions, and that Mr. Cohen had never informed the Consulate General of either. However, the Consulate General has informed our office that it is firmly in favor of a monopoly for Hanotaiah."[39]

Rejecting Consul Wolff's warnings, the correspondence first cited Wolff's words: "As the Consul General puts it, if we opt out, the matter will proceed without us, with only Hanotaiah and the Temple Bank participating." Hoofien then did just that—he opted out. He explained, "Hanotaiah is a plantation company and nothing else. Nor is it the only one. . . . To appoint Hanotaiah as a central point for Palestinian imports from Germany . . . would be . . . giving it an impossible task. If we were to state that funds are deposited in our account with the Reichsbank and we were therefore participants in the transfer operation, we assume a moral obligation to the German public which we are not prepared to undertake. Will you therefore be good enough to inform the Reich Economics Ministry that we regret to be unable to participate in the arrangement described in the letter of July 18."[40]

After opting out, Hoofien pointed out, "The possibility appears to remain open that the operation be implemented without our participation, as the Consul General in Jerusalem has indicated . . . but I doubt very much that it would amount to very much if the German and the Palestinian public finds out that we had seen fit to decline."[41]

As he did with Mechnes and Cohen, Hoofien gave the Reich a respectable way out. He related the entire conversation with Cohen and Mechnes that day, including his offer of working with Hanotaiah so long as they limited their involvement to plantation activities, garnered no monopoly and subordinated to the bank's trust company. Hoofien asserted that both Cohen and Mechnes "told me they are prepared to comply with our wishes in every respect" and willing to ask the Reich to adopt whatever amendments Hoofien felt correct.[42]

What would be correct? "I am prepared to establish in Palestine an agency for handling exports from Germany and to come to an appropriate agreement with the Reich Economics Ministry, if you [Landauer] tell me that the Economics Ministry desires this. I would be prepared to travel to Berlin for that purpose." Hoofien added that just as he was dictating the correspondence, he received another cable from the Conference of Institutions. The Jewish Agency had joined forces with the Conference, thus unifying Zionist support for the Anglo-Palestine Bank's efforts.[43]

Hoofien explained that the Conference "speaks with authority. It is composed of representatives of all leading Jewish authorities . . . [and it] informs me it will ask the Consulate . . . to consider the Conference along with our bank as the sole representatives of Jewish authorities in Palestine."[44] Hoofien's point: The Anglo-Palestine Bank, the pivotal financial institution, and the Conference of Institutions representing all the important commercial and political entities, all wanted the Hanotaiah agreement changed. Even Mr. Sam Cohen and Hanotaiah now wanted the agreement changed.

Only one man now stood in the way of doing the correct thing. That man was Consul General Heinrich Wolff. Hoofien put the burden on the consul, stating that once the Jewish delegation presented its bona fide authority, "it will of course be up to the Consulate General whether it will comply with this request." He added that if Consul Wolff truly understood the powers represented by the Conference of Institutions, "he will hardly fail to do so."[45]

Hoofien's correspondence to Landauer intended for Schmidt-Roelke was received at the ZVfD's Berlin office on July 31, 1933. Landauer promptly delivered it to Schmidt-Roelke's office with a note attached: "Herewith a copy of a letter addressed to me from London by the Director of the Anglo-Palestine Bank, Mr. S. Hoofien. . . . While this letter is written in the style of an interagency correspondence, it contains some important information which I do not wish to fail to bring to your attention." Landauer promised to telephone later.[46]

Schmidt-Roelke was confronted that day, July 31, with a thicket of reports, memoranda, and cables about whether Sam Cohen was the man the Third Reich thought he was. But Consul Wolff, the Reich's man on the scene, had investigated all the charges. Wolff reported simple business jealousy as the basis for the sudden criticisms. He recommended in the strongest terms that the Reich honor the Hanotaiah agreement and ignore the criticism. Whatever shortcomings were implicit in the plan would in time be overcome.

But now the head of the Anglo-Palestine Bank himself had written that Wolff had misstated the facts about Cohen. If Cohen himself agreed that the consul had misunderstood Cohen's authority, that would surely settle the matter. Without Cohen's clarification, there was virtually no way to decipher who was correct.

Clearly, the only solution was to bring Cohen and Landauer together with other interested parties to discuss the issue face to face. Schmidt-Roelke instructed one of his key subordinates, Dr. Eberl, to contact Cohen in London, apprise him of the conflicting information and Hoofien's statement that Cohen had voluntarily withdrawn from the transfer.[47] Dr. Eberl's July 31 communication to Cohen, including the full text of the July 28 Hoofien letter, arrived in London the next day.

Late on August 1, Sam Cohen wrote back to clarify all questions. "My Esteemed Dr. Eberl: I am addressing this letter to you because you have conducted all negotiations with me and are fully familiar with the subject matter. I have for more than 3½ months spent my entire energies, my capabilities, my intentions, and my influence preparing the groundwork for my project in Palestine. I have worked with equal intensity on the implementation of this project in Prague, Amsterdam, and London. All the influence and connections that I was able to muster and which were accessible to me have made it possible for me to bring this project to fruition despite great obstacles.[48]

"Without the Hanotaiah group in Palestine," he continued, "including the farmers, the cooperative societies, industrialists, and merchants, it would never have been possible to find interest for the project. All appropriate authorities in Palestine and London have approved of my project. This purely personal success is begrudged me by dirty competitors and their henchmen. The competition has used every means at its command to destroy the project. Anything they could not accomplish by countervailing arguments and objective proof they tried to do by slander."[49]

If there was any doubt in the Foreign Ministry's mind about Cohen withdrawing from the transfer, or admitting Hanotaiah's inability to execute the merchandise sales, or his willingness to subordinate to the Anglo-Palestine Bank, the next sentences settled the question. Cohen's words: "No objective arguments are possible against my project and against Hanotaiah; it is the only company in the country which can, with my help and collaboration, implement this contract. No bank is necessary for its implementation. Hanotaiah has sufficient capital to do so. . . . Success is absolutely guaranteed."[50]

Cohen added: "Mr. Hoofien has told me in so many words that he had no intention whatever to destroy this agreement and that he had no objection to it whatsoever. The only reason for his writing that letter [of July 28] to Dr. Landauer was the latter's statement that he could obtain a better agreement. Mr. Hoofien told me that he would assume no responsibility for a possible cancellation of this agreement and that he would charge Dr. Landauer with that responsibility."[51] These were potentially deadly words against Georg Landauer, a German Jew, a man who had stood before the Reich and promised to frustrate—in fact, defy—economic decrees designed to stimulate employment, break the boycott, and achieve Nazi goals.

At that moment nothing was easier in Nazi Germany than denouncing a Jew for economic sabotage. Such a denunciation—justified or not—usually resulted in immediate detention in Dachau without trial. Many such detainees were never heard from again. It was Landauer's good fortune that Schmidt-Roelke was an old-school statesman from the Weimar days. Had Cohen's words been read by an NSDAP kommissar, they would not have been glossed over.

Cohen reminded the Reich of his transfer's central usefulness to them—the sabotage of the anti-Nazi boycott that was threatening to crack Germany that winter. Cohen's words: "Personally, I wish to emphasize that without the Hanotaiah group and without my intensive efforts and work, it would be impossible to sell any significant amount of merchandise in Palestine during the next six months. I have made my services in their entirety available to you and to the Reich Economics Ministry for the next six months."[52]

Cohen could have hardly been more explicit. Hanotaiah's transfer bore no time limits, no financial ceilings, and indeed was structured to accommodate emigrants for years to come. But both sides knew there would not be years of fruitful transactions if the Reich could not survive the coming winter—"the next six months." As usual, Mr. Sam Cohen selected his words carefully, and emphasized them only with good reason.

Defenses, denials, and derogations recorded, Cohen, however, declined Eberl's invitation to meet with Landauer.[53] It is unclear whether Sam Cohen was actually afraid to return to Germany. He had continually assured the Foreign Ministry he would be available to come to Berlin from London during this period if questions arose. Now at this pressing moment, however, he refused to sit down with Landauer, and claimed to be preoccupied, presumably with transfer and anti-boycott business. "If it were not for the fact that I am presently engaged in negotiations in London in that matter which cannot be postponed," Cohen wrote Dr. Eberl, "I would have come to Berlin for further personal discussions."[54]

Cohen amplified slightly on these pressing London meetings. He claimed they involved Pinchas Rutenberg, who after "long and difficult negotiations" was won over "for my project. . . . He is the single most influential industrialist and could become one of the largest consumers [of German machinery]. Tomorrow I am to negotiate with Tel Aviv's deputy mayor and hope to enlist him in my plans also."[55] Cohen's correspondence rarely lacked the power of important names and pending breakthroughs. This correspondence was no different.

There is no way to know why Cohen refused to meet with Landauer, but Cohen did write that Moshe Mechnes would be in Berlin and could be called upon for any further meetings.[56] Hence, the decisive confrontation Schmidt-Roelke had hoped for would not materialize. Nonetheless, one more final negotiating session in Hartenstein's office would be needed to resolve somehow the question of who should take possession of the transfer and on what terms. A date was set: August 7, 1933.

26. The Transfer Agreement

THE AFTERNOON of August 7, 1933, the Zionist delegation arrived at 76 Wilhelmstrasse and announced their appointment to a lobby guard who was expecting them. He escorted the group to the Economics Ministry's conference room. They entered one by one: Georg Landauer, director of the German Zionist Federation; E. S. Hoofien, director of the Anglo-Palestine Bank; Arthur Ruppin, Zionist Organization emigration specialist; and Moshe Mechnes, co-owner of Hanotaiah Ltd. Hans Hartenstein, director of the Foreign Currency Control Office, courteously greeted the Jewish leaders and did his utmost to make them feel welcome.[1]

Undoubtedly, it wasn't until then that Mr. Sam Cohen was shown into the room. His mustache neatly trimmed, his necktie arranged in a perfect knot, Cohen was looking elegant as always, bearing up well under the circumstances. In his August 1 letter to Dr. Eberl, Cohen had promised not to attend this confrontation, but that was probably before he learned of Consul Wolff's July 27 report of absolute support. Wolff's report had not been rescinded by the Foreign Ministry, so as the meeting began Mr. Sam Cohen still held the power of the transfer.[2]

The Reich and the Zionist delegation talked for some time. Money. Emigration. Boycott. Regulations. Timing. Public opinion. Boycott. Foreign exchange. Exports. Boycott.[3]

Hoofien and Landauer tried their best to persuade Hartenstein that there would be no successful transfer if it was controlled by Sam Cohen and Hanotaiah.[4] Senator believed that without a viable transfer, the Reich would find no relief from the anti-Nazi boycott.[5] But Cohen's position was that his vast personal connections could accomplish what the official Zionist bodies and even the Anglo-Palestine Bank could not—break the boycott.[6] After all, they were subject to public pressure. As a private businessman, Cohen was not. Mechnes, who had promised to abide by Hoofien's London compromise, only wanted Hanotaiah to be properly included in whatever arrangement was finally approved.[7]

However, Hartenstein was unable to decide in favor of Hoofien and Landauer. He could not overrule the Foreign Ministry and was obliged to create a transfer authority with whichever Zionist group was accredited by Consul Heinrich Wolff. In the Reich's view, perhaps Wolff and Cohen were right: Perhaps public entities could not successfully wage war against the boycott; only carefully placed saboteurs such as Cohen could stop the movement. As far as Berlin knew, Cohen had been instrumental in disrupting decisive boycott activities in London, Amsterdam, and elsewhere. Therefore, even though he was probably convinced it was a mistake, Hartenstein was obligated to maintain the existing RM 3 million agreement in favor of Sam Cohen. Landauer and Hoofien refused to accept this and urged Cohen to relent. But Cohen would not.[8]

As the deadlock continued in Berlin, a corresponding scenario was taking place in Jerusalem. Margulies and a delegation from the Conference of Institutions were meeting with Consul Wolff, urging him to amend his endorsement at once in view of the decisive and final conference under way at that very moment in Berlin.[9] Wolff was unwilling. To reverse himself now would make him look incompetent if not altogether untrustworthy.

The Palestinian delegation continued to plead and pressure. They insisted that Hoofien was the only authorized negotiator, and that the Anglo-Palestine Bank's trust company could be the only transfer entity. The delegation even offered to guarantee Hanotaiah a prominent position within the trust company, if the consul would only broaden his endorsement.[10] Time was running out, but Wolff would not budge.

Thousands of miles away, the meeting in Hartenstein's office dragged on in deadlock. Cohen and Hoofien agreed that a monopoly was necessary for a successful transfer, but each man insisted his side be entrusted with that monopoly.[11] With no progress visible, Hartenstein was undoubtedly preparing to call the meeting to a close.

Meanwhile, in Jerusalem, Consul Wolff bickered stubbornly with the Zionist delegation until they finally said something that changed his mind. There is no record of what sudden convincing argument Margulies and the conference delegates raised. But Wolff was vulnerable within the new Nazi context. He had a Jewish wife and close ties with Jewish organizations in Palestine. He even had secret business dealings with Sam Cohen, including some land the consul had acquired through Hanotaiah.[12]

At exactly 1:30 P.M., Jerusalem time, Consul Wolff sent a telegram to the Foreign Ministry: "FOR REICH ECONOMICS MINISTRY FOR THIS AFTERNOON'S MEETING. IN VIEW OF GROWING OPPOSITION TO SAM COHEN AGREEMENT IN PRESENT FORM . . . A COMMITTEE FORMED SOME TIME AGO TO DEAL WITH TRADE WITH GERMANY AND CONSISTING OF PLANTERS, INDUSTRIAL WORKERS, IMPORTERS AND CONSUMERS, HAS TAKEN UP THE TRANSFER MATTER UNDER LEADERSHIP OF ANGLO-PALESTINE BANK. IT BELIEVES THAT IN VIEW OF ITS BROAD REPRESENTATION IT CAN ABSOLUTELY GUARANTEE THE IMPLEMENTATION OF THE TRANFER PLAN. A DELEGATION VISITED ME TODAY, STATING THAT HOOFIEN HAS BEEN GIVEN UNLIMITED AND SOLE AUTHORITY FOR . . . THE TRANSFER PLAN. AN OVERALL UMBRELLA ORGANIZATION IS BEING FORMED. THE COMMITTEE WOULD WELCOME THE INCLUSION OF HANOTAIAH. MY IMPRESSION IS THAT IN VIEW OF THESE DEVELOPMENTS THE TRANSFER PLAN HAS CHANCES FOR SUCCEEDING ONLY ON THAT BROAD BASIS AND AM RECOMMENDING TO SAM COHEN THAT HE JOIN."[13]

At precisely ten minutes after two in the afternoon in Berlin, a messenger from Deutsche Reichspost walked into the Wilhelmstrasse offices of the Reich Foreign Ministry and handed them Consul Wolff's telegram. It was routed to the Palestine desk within the Eastern Department.[14] In another part of the Wilhelmstrasse complex, the Hartenstein conference was nearing a frustrating end. Hartenstein might then have told Hoofien and Landauer that the Economics Ministry reluctantly had no alternative but to stand by the Hanotaiah agreement. But at about that time, the officer on the Palestine desk saw that Consul Wolff's telegram was actually intended for Hartenstein's meeting. He immediately telephoned the message over to Hartenstein's office.[15]

Hoofien, Landauer, Cohen, and the others had not yet left the conference room when the news was brought in. A moment of silence passed as the telegram's contents were noted. It is unknown whether Hartenstein then read the words aloud, or whether he simply handed the handwritten note to Cohen. Whichever it was, Mr. Sam Cohen got the message.[16] He had finally run out of endorsements. Wolff's new recommendation was clear. Cohen was gracious in defeat. He agreed to relinquish his transfer to a trust company to be established by the Anglo-Palestine Bank. Hanotaiah would step back and function as just one of several participating plantation companies.[17] It was over.

Three days later, on August 10, Hartenstein issued a revised decree authorizing Hoofien to create two transfer clearinghouses, one under the supervision of the ZVfD in Berlin, one under the supervision of Anglo-Palestine's trust company in Palestine. The Berlin corporation was named Palastina-Treuhandstelle zur Beratung deutscher Juden GmbH—the Palestine Trust Society for Advice to German Jews, Inc. As was the Reich vogue, an approporate acronym was immediately invented: Paltreu. Corresponding to Paltreu was Haavara Trust and Transfer Office Ltd. in Tel Aviv. Often called Haavara Ltd. for short, this corporation was organized under the Palestinian commercial code and operated by business managers. Its stock was wholly owned by the Anglo-Palestine Bank.[18] *Haavara*, the Hebrew word for transfer, quickly became a synonym for *transfer*.

Paltreu and Haavara would each manage two separate accounts or *Kontos*. Konto I was for existing emigrants. They would deposit their marks into Paltreu's German-based blocked account. German exports would then be sold in Palestine, the proceeds being deposited in Haavara's balancing account. Hartenstein's decree specified that the equivalent of the blocked marks "will be paid out [by Haavara] in cash in Palestine pounds upon request." The transfer would indeed give the emigrants the cash they needed to restart their lives.[19]

Konto II was reserved for so-called potential emigrants or those wanting to invest in Palestine as a Jewish national home. German Jews could voluntarily deposit their marks into this second konto, but they could not be transferred until all the actual emigrant depositors of the first konto had been reimbursed. As such, these potential millions upon millions of frozen reichmarks represented a long-term money pool the Zionists could utilize for capital investments and development projects. Those who stayed behind would continually finance the expanding Jewish home for those who agreed to leave.[20]

Several additional letters of confirmation and procedural refinement were exchanged between Hoofien and Hartenstein in the days immediately after that August 7 meeting. Those several letters were bureaucratically attached to official Reich decree 54/33. Together they became what was to be known as the Transfer Agreement.[21]

After beseeching the supporters and allies of the Jews for decades, the Zionists realized that the moment of transfer would come not from friends but from foes, as Herzl had predicted.

Forty years of struggle to create a Jewish State had come to a sudden and spectacular turning point. For forty years there had never been enough money, never enough land, never enough men. So long as those essential factors were lacking, the Jewish State was *also* never to be. But in an office at Wilhelmstrasse on August 7, 1933, this all changed. A few men working with telegrams, letters of introduction, images, the power of prejudice and pretense, a few men who saw an opportunity for salvation within the abyss of Nazi injustice, those few men had simply arranged it.

Henceforth when Jews would be threatened, as Jews always were, as Jews always would be, they would have a nation of their own to come home to. A nation no Jew could enter as a refugee or a stranger, a nation all Jews would enter as full citizens.

The price of this new nation would be the abandonment of the war against Nazi Germany. Whole branches of Judaism would wither, but the trunk would survive—Herzl's words. This one time, this crucial and un-parelleled time, the emergency would be used to secure a future, not ransom a past. From this crisis of humiliation, agony, and expulsion would come sanctuary, nationhood, and a new Jew, with a new home to call his own. These few men were willing to make those decisions. Was it madness? Or was it genius?

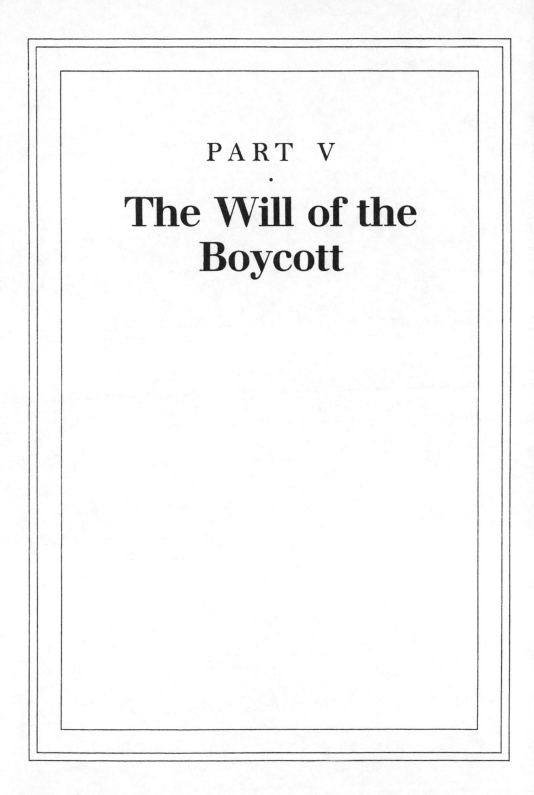

PART V

·

The Will of the Boycott

27. Now or Never

IT WAS one thing for the Zionists to subvert the anti-Nazi boycott. Zionism needed to transfer out the capital of German Jews, and merchandise was the only available medium. But soon Zionist leaders understood that the success of the future Jewish Palestinian economy would be inextricably bound up with the survival of the Nazi economy. So the Zionist leadership was compelled to go further. The German economy would have to be safeguarded, stabilized, and if necessary reinforced. Hence, the Nazi party and the Zionist Organization shared a common stake in the recovery of Germany. If the Hitler economy fell, both sides would be ruined.

David Werner Senator made the Zionist stake in the Reich's economy clear to the Zionist Organization. On July 24, in London, even before the Transfer Agreement was consummated, Senator presented a long, complicated, and confidential memo to the Zionist Executive. His memo outlined just how big the transfer would become. It would be more than just a trust company—it would become an actual Liquidation Bank, although Senator's memo advised "this name should of course be avoided." Such a large enterprise, Senator suggested, would have to be supervised by a combine of European and American shareholders.[1]

Most importantly, this massive Liquidation Bank would issue development bonds that "would be quoted on the international stock markets— London, New York, Cairo . . . and Jerusalem, if a stock exchange later materializes there."[2] Ultimately, an institution for transfer trading was created in Palestine. It later became the Tel Aviv Stock Exchange.[3]

The development bonds of this Liquidation Bank would provide capital for the Jewish State's infrastructure, just as Arlosoroff and Herzl had envisioned. Because these bonds would be backed up by blocked accounts, Senator raised an unforeseen issue—the need to stabilize the German mark. Boycotts and bad economics had made the reichmark an endangered currency. The less valuable reichmarks were, the more marks it would take to equal a pound or a dollar, and hence the greater the exchange loss endured by the transferring emigrant. Therefore, to avoid emigrants receiving progressively less, the German government would have to provide a guarantee to keep transfer marks flowing at levels sufficient always to pay interest and principle on the development bonds—no matter how badly the mark devalued.[4]

These were complicated concepts of high finance that Senator was presenting. They were hard to comprehend and might be harder still to implement. But in paragraph 16 of his memo he estimated just how much money was at stake. The bonds sold against the blocked deposits of German Jews could amount to $150 million in just two years. These bonds might require a mere 7 percent interest, with repayment of principle waived during the first five years. Thereafter, the principle would be paid in equal installments over two decades.[5]

The Zionists were suddenly taking charge of a massive store of frozen cash. They could use that cash to create a bank. That bank could raise capital to build the State of Israel through development bonds that would be repaid out of the Palestinian commerce created by the development. Even then, payment would occur under the most advantageous rates. The bonds would be backed up by German Jewish sperrmarks to be stabilized by some hoped-for Reich guarantee of the marks needed for bond repayments, even if the mark devalued due to the deteriorating Nazi economy. Otherwise, the value of a pool of reichmarks, say RM 1 million, could dwindle to virtually nothing.

Senator's July 24 memo admitted that "it would be possible to obtain such a transfer guarantee . . . only against certain concessions on the Jewish side. . . . We might offer . . . certain export facilities for German goods. Such facilities are already being sought with some anxiety by the German government in view of the recent rapid decline in German exports." Here Senator was probably talking about extending exports to the entire Near East, perhaps beyond. Senator also suggested that the Liquidation Bank should actually make development loans to Germany "and thus make possible an increased employment program on the part of the German government."[6]

Senator's memo acknowledged that the Zionists knew just how desperate the Germans were. Senator's words: "From preliminary negotiations . . . with the Economics Ministry, we know that special importance is attached to any measure . . . to counteract the present tendency of German exports to decline. The German government knows very well from experience during the War, that a decline in exports means not only the loss of orders for a year or two, but that [trade] obstacles . . . increase progressively, and that reconquering markets once lost is possible only with great difficulty and expense, and even then only partially." Acknowledging that the boycott had already battered German exports to the breaking point, Senator declared that Zionists could at least "help Germany . . . avoid the almost certain rupture of commercial relations."[7]

Reflecting a keen awareness of Hitler's unemployment problem, Senator added, "We know that one of the principal aims of the German government is to provide work for the unemployed." Senator explained that the residual Jewish community in Germany would have little chance to earn a living unless overall employment improved. As such, "We shall have to . . . offer the German government some help with their program for providing employment." For example, the Liquidation Bank, in addition to providing employment loans, would itself purchase shares in major German enterprises, such as the railroads.[8]

Senator's long transfer memorandum wasn't the only report the Zionist Organization Executive considered in late July. At about the same time, a second memo came through Leo Motzkin, head of the Committee of Jewish Delegations in Geneva.[9] It spoke not of high finance and long-term loans but of high crimes and long-term damage to the Jewish people of Germany. The report began, "For close on six weeks . . . I have been in contact with Jews in all stations of life. Professors, doctors, solicitors, manufacturers and businessmen, young and old, from towns as far apart as Danzig and Aachen. . . . They one and all affirmed that they were living in a veritable Hell. . . . The actual number of cruelties and of violence perpetrated against Jews . . . will never be known. Those reports which have penetrated abroad, are only a small fraction of what has actually occurred."[9]

After listing a series of atrocities, and confirming the utter bleakness of a Jewish future in Germany, Motzkin's report divided German Jewry into five categories. First, the "genuine Zionists," who were quickly leaving Germany without thinking of who would stay behind to organize the exodus. Second, the non-Zionist now hoping to find safety in the Zionist movement. Third, the anti-Zionists willing to go to Palestine if no other place was available, but this group's emigration would be contingent upon taking "German culture, German customs, German manners, and the German language with them."[10]

The fourth category was comprised of establishment Jewry, who "attribute the entire disaster which has befallen German Jewry to the Eastern Jews, who are all Zionists. They do not want to go to Palestine. . . . [They believe] the Jews in Germany should be satisfied with being considered an inferior species of humanity. The fifth category are the . . . German Nationalist Jews. They are not 100 percent but 101 percent German."[11]

The point: Except for the small percent who were genuine or newly converted Zionists, almost all of Germany's established Jews still reviled the Jewish national home and the Zionist philosophy. They were desperate but seemed to prefer a German death to a Palestinian life. However, the report emphasized the "undeniable fact that young German Jewry, even from the fifth category, are turning to Jewish nationalism. What we have not been successful with during 30 years, Hitler has accomplished for us overnight."[12]

The report's conclusion: "The majority of the older generation of German Jewry cannot be moved, they are too deeply rooted in the soil of the country. A large portion does not want to leave. But the Youth are anxious to start a new life as Jews and every effort should be made to rescue them from . . . utter destruction." However, the report added that while emigration would save the young, only an intensified international boycott would help the older generation survive in a hostile Reich.[13]

"The boycott of German goods in various countries is having a very material influence on German trade and the effects are undeniably being felt," the report asserted. [And it is] the only weapon which might . . . [influence] the present order to restrain the violence of the rank and file." The report recommended that the "boycott be increased and extended. Concentrated action against a few more industries will intensify the already serious economic situation in Germany and will force the present order to change its tactics." [14]

The report presented through Motzkin may have seemed like a reasonable compromise. Transfer the true believers to Palestine. At the same time, continue boycotting to force Germany to curtail persecution of those remaining. Unfortunately, the Third Reich was willing to release any number of Jews for Palestine as a means of expulsion, but it was unwilling to let them remove any of their assets unless the Zionists intervened against the boycott. Unless assets preceded emigrants, there would be no real nation to emigrate to. Motzkin's boycott report was rejected. Senator's report for stabilizing the German economy was accepted. It was simply a matter of priorities.

What began as a purely noble task in the minds of a few German Zionists quickly diluted into a grand bazaar of business opportunities. The notion of tranfer was itself steeped in business transactions with Germany. When complete, Palestine would possess the commercial-industrial framework needed to supply a population's needs, provide jobs, and qualify the Jewish State as a member among nations in world commerce. This was sensible. A true nation was more than a haven, more than a commune. It was a land whose citizens could live, work, and prosper in peace. Therefore, the transfer of industrial machinery to build factories was intrinsic to state building as surely as the transfer of hospital beds and irrigation works.

Israel's commerce was to be as diverse as any nation's. In fact, this was a special feature of Zionist self-determination. Whereas Jewish economic opportunities had historically been confined, the opportunities in Israel would be unlimited—including the opportunity to earn one's bread by sweat and labor in fields and factories.

But in the summer of 1933, as the transfer apparatus developed, the lines between welfare and windfall blurred. What was state building, and what was pure commercialistic opportunism? Indeed, this conflict represented the critical flaw in the actions of Mr. Sam Cohen. For his flaws, Cohen was replaced with a fleet of brokers and enterprises that did enjoy the Zionist Organization's seal of approval, but were nonetheless just as commercialistic. So it soon became impossible to distinguish between the unhappy burden of doing business with the Third Reich to facilitate emigration, and the gleeful rush of entrepreneurs frantic to cash in on the captive capital of Germany's Jews.

For example, in the summer of 1933 a new publishing company was formed in London, headed by leading Palestinian publisher Shoshana Persitz. Its board included such notables as financier Robert Waley-Cohen, Hebrew University chancellor Judah Magnes, Palestinian industrialist Pinchas Rutenberg, and JNF director Menahem Ussischkin. The venture would be called the Palestine Publishing Company. Its feasibility hinged on the purchase of £80,000 ($400,000) worth of printing presses and other lithographic equipment from Germany, only half of which was to be paid in actual pounds. The remainder would be paid out of blocked marks. To complete the transfer, Palestine Publishing would deposit minority shares instead of money in the balancing account. Thus, a new industry was created for Palestine that would have been financially impossible except for the transfer.[15]

In early August, several of the original transfer conceptualizers in Jerusalem, including Felix Rosenbluth and Arthur Landsberg, formed Exim, a company to import German steel via the transfer apparatus. The first transaction called for RM 500,000 in German steel, only 40 percent of which would be paid in foreign currency. The remainder would be paid in blocked transfer marks. There was no particular public character to their enterprise, no charitable by-product of Exim sales. Although steel was vital for housing and factories, Exim was in fact just a company selling German steel products via transfer.[16]

In August another group of investors decided to establish a brewery in Palestine. The German government agreed to transfer brewery equipment valued at RM 750,000 (about $250,000), 90 percent of it paid by sperrmarks. The balance would be foreign currency supplied in part by the American Economic Committee for Palestine in New York.[17]

The Palestine Publishing Company, Exim, and the new brewery represented just a fraction of the Palestinian-German business ventures that came into play during July and August as the bonanza that lay within the transfer became known in business circles. Were these business deals little more than taking advantage of the crisis facing German Jewry? Or were they legitimate efforts to build the Jewish home by developing the Palestinian economy? All enterprise in Palestine of course expanded the Jewish national economy by providing jobs, services, products, and capital. But then again, in 1933, all nations and their citizens were struggling to recover from the Depression. Those who placed the boycott against Germany before lucrative business deals were sacrificing in the fight against Hitler. Palestinian entrepreneurs simply concluded that they could not afford to be part of that fight. A nation was being built. For now, there could be no wars. Only alliances.

An alliance with Germany based on trade quickly shifted the Zionist emphasis from the people caught in crisis to the money caught in crisis. By late July, transfer activists spoke increasingly of "saving the wealth" and "rescuing the capital" from Nazi Germany. The impact on the German Jews themselves seemed to be a subordinated issue. It was this very accusation that led to the rejection of Mr. Sam Cohen. And it was to avoid private-sector exploitation that the Zionist Executive had convinced Cohen to bring his mid-May deal under "national supervision." This meant sharing the transfer with the rival company Yakhin, operated by the Histadrut, the official labor conglomerate essentially controlled by Mapai. Yakhin and Hanotaiah had eventually signed a binder of cooperation, but Yakhin ultimately joined the Conference of Institutions.

However, at a July 31 Histadrut Executive session called to review the transfer, Histadrut leaders acknowledged that from the outset their main interest was forming a special investment combine to usurp the project from Hanotaiah. Then the Histadrut leaders unveiled a plan for a sort of mandatory loan that German emigrants would extend to a Yakhin subsidiary called Nir, which would purchase German goods for sale in Palestine using blocked funds. But instead of depositing all the proceeds in the Palestine balancing account, thus completing the transfer, Nir would essentially convert two-thirds of the transaction into a mandatory fifteen-year loan, using the money for large land purchases and housing construction.[18]

One of the leaders attending the July 31 meeting objected, "Frankly, this imposed loan has a bad smell. The Jew in Germany might claim he is being forced to loan money, while the Jew in the States is not." Such hesitation was brushed aside, however, as Histadrut leaders agreed that "constructive" tasks were of the highest priority. And unless a public body such as the Histradrut seized control, "it will turn to a gang of speculators."[19]

The attitude of Histradrut officials was typical of Mapai leadership and their allies, who saw the wealth of German Jews as the most precious hostage held by the Third Reich. As part of this thinking, Georg Landauer and the ZVfD fought for German regulations that would prevent German Jews from saving their wealth by any means other than investing it in Palestine. On August 17, ten days after the Transfer Agreement was sealed at Wilhelmstrasse, Landauer sent a letter to Hans Hartenstein. Landauer's words: "We looked for methods to make sure that sums which flow to Palestine in the framework of the presently granted three million mark concession are indeed invested there. We are also looking for solutions to prevent people using this concession in a roundabout way to establish a sure means of livelihood in other countries."[20]

Landauer recommended that ZVfD certification of emigrants be contingent upon purchasing land in Palestine, extending a loan to Nir, or participating in any approved Palestinian investment. Landauer's words: "Therefore I would like to suggest that the Emigrant Advisory Office . . . receive instructions whereby emigrant applications based on contracts with Palestinian colonization companies receive priority status." Landauer reminded Hartenstein that the legal basis for such an arrangement was essentially already on the books by virtue of currency regulations that obligated the Emigrant Advisory Office to verify exactly how much cash an individual needed in order to relocate.[21]

Landauer's August 17 letter closed with a preemptive defense against the obvious criticism: "Of course we don't want to prevent the emigration of Jews into other countries. We only want to secure the application of the three million mark concession in the sense that it was granted."[22] But Landauer and his associates knew that without money, a refugee was escaping to a life of soup kitchens and near starvation, a life that almost always precluded an entire family fleeing together for simple lack of cash. Moreover, refugees were barred access to the United States and other countries unless they possessed enough money to prove they would not be public charges.

Yet without the special certification Landauer requested, the transfer might have proven a false boon. Many German Jews were desperate to leave Germany for a short time, hoping the Hitler terror might subside. German Jews were quite willing to transfer their money briefly to Palestine and then retransfer it to a desirable destination such as Holland or France. However, the awesome impact of the ZVfD certification process was that, with few exceptions, a German Jew could not save himself with any of his assets unless he did so through Palestine.

Penniless refugees were already straining the charitable resources of Europe. It had been a Zionist strategy from April 1933 to divert relief donations for constructive work in Palestine. Chaim Weizmann had delivered a number of speeches to Jewish groups in this vein, urging them to look only to Palestine and relinquish any serious effort to maintain refugees in Europe. One such speech on May 29 in Paris was printed verbatim in Jewish and Palestinian newspapers for weeks thereafter. At a time when Nazi racial scientists were accusing Jews of being or transmitting an infectious racial disease, Weizmann's choice of words was ironic: "And here I must speak frankly of a very painful and delicate subject: these refugees are themselves the germ-carriers of a new outbreak of anti-Semitism."[23]

The effect of Weizmann's Herzlian rhetoric was to make Jews in neighboring haven countries wonder if they were not importing German anti-Semitism by caring for the refugees. Weizmann's true point was made elsewhere in the speech: "It is true that thanks to generous hospitality . . . some tens of thousands will find refuge in France, in Czechoslovakia, in Switzerland, or in Holland; but . . . we must entertain no illusions. . . . The world is already full—and the countries abutting on Germany will soon become saturated. . . . What is going to happen to those 200,000 [German Jews] who may find themselves on the pavement tomorrow or the day after tomorrow? They are condemned to a fate which is neither life nor death." The answer was not a haven in Europe, said Weizmann. The answer was a home in Palestine.[24]

Weizmann urged Jews to fight for national rights, not civil rights. Energies were to be devoted away from combat with the Reich, and toward the creation of Israel. Otherwise, the same drama would merely act itself out in country after country due to the irrepressible character of anti-Semitism. This time, the crisis would have to create not a temporary haven but a permanent home. Weizmann's blunt and idealistic words marked the Zionist leadership as being unwilling to protect Jewish rights in Europe at the very moment when Jews most needed protection.

Focusing on Palestine as the only legitimate destination for large-scale emigration, the Zionist Organization rejected opportunities to resettle German Jews in havens or homes other than Eretz Yisrael. For example, in mid-July Australia announced a willingness to accept thousands of German Jewish families for settlement in the northern region around Darwin.[25] Longtime Jewish colonization organizations had successfully settled a thousand Jewish families in the Crimea and another thousand in the Ukraine during the first half of 1933,[26] and a proposal for an actual Jewish homeland in Manchuria had come from Japan. For years, thousands of Russian Jews and British Jews had been living in Shanghai and other Asian cities. Most had arrived after the Russian Revolution; others represented British commercial interests. Japanese leaders controlling Manchuria well remembered the help of Jewish financier Jacob Schiff in defeating the Russians during the Russo-Japanese War of 1904–1905. So they responded favorably to ideas advanced by Shanghai Zionists to convert part of Manchuria into a Jewish homeland.[27]

But the Australian, Russian, and Manchurian settlement opportunities were rejected by the Zionist Organization. Resettlement meant further dispersion and little more than another scenario for persecution, as Jews would again become guests of a host nation. A return to their own land in Palestine constituted the only end to centuries of catastrophic nomadism.

The Zionist stance made it clear: Palestine or nothing. Now or never.

28. The Larger Threat

As the Zionists prepared for a Palestine now-or-never operation, Hitlerism spread dramatically to almost every country where people of German heritage lived. Exploiting whatever local bias seemed most suitable, hyphenated Germans created Nazi-style parties determined to infect their host countries with Aryan ideology. By summer 1933, the Nazi menace was rapidly becoming global in nature.

AUSTRIA. *Vienna, July 22*: The Austrian press and cabinet are divided on whether to introduce Jewish quotas into the professions and college. *Innsbruch, August 2*: Anti-Semitic attacks in the provinces increase as Austrian Nazis manhandle Jews and paint the word *Jude* on Jewish homes. *Vienna, August 14*: Jewish merchants discover a silent anti-Jewish boycott is in force, spurred on by the Austrian Nazi party.[1]

MEXICO. *Mexico City, July 24*: An organization of Nazi ideologues known as Confía, backed by right-wing industrialists, asks the government to declare Jewish businessmen foreigners and raise their taxes 500 percent. *Guadalajara, August 18*: Local authorities will investigate all Jewish businessmen for commercial code violations.[2]

CZECHOSLOVAKIA. *Prague, May 31*: Nazi students at the University of Prague disrupt plans to appoint a Jewish professor, and urge the ouster of all Jewish teachers.[3]

HOLLAND. *Amsterdam, August 20*: A Dutch Nazi party creates numerous anti-Semitic incidents. The Dutch government prepares regulations forbidding brown shirts and Nazi insignia.[4]

UNITED STATES. *Chicago, July 29*: German-American social groups organized into Nazi cells demand the swastika flag fly over the German-American exhibit at the Century of Progress. Fair officials refuse. *Springfield, New Jersey, August 9*: Seven thousand members of a German choral society holding an outdoor songfest are unexpectedly "bombed" by a low-flying plane dropping leaflets urging them to turn to Hitlerism.[5]

RUMANIA. *Czernowitz, June 21*: The Nazi-style Iron Guard succeeds in convincing military officials to ban a local newspaper critical of anti-Semitic activities. *Bucharest, August 15*: Denying an Iron Guard claim that a student quota for Jews has been instituted, education officials admit the shortage of space has necessitated limiting the number of students, but say religion is not a factor.[6]

CANADA. *Hamilton, July 11*: The Swastika Club erects eight-foot signs on the beaches declaring "No Jews Allowed on Shore Within 800 Feet Either Way of this Sign." *Toronto, August 16*: The 400 Swastika Club members disrupt a Jewish softball game by unfurling Nazi flags and chanting "Heil Hitler." The melee escalates into a citywide riot involving 8,000 people. Police patrol Jewish neighborhoods until 4:00 A.M. to prevent attacks by roving gangs. Afterward the police ban the display of the swastika in any form.[7]

HUNGARY. *Debreczen, August 27*: Hungarian Nazis affix anti-Jewish posters. Local Storm Troopers guard against the signs, but police finally move in, arrest the Nazis, and remove the placards.[8]

ENGLAND. *London, July 20*: British Fascists wearing black shirts and swastikas hold a counterdemonstration as British Jews protest Hitlerism. Special police units guard against Fascist threats of violence. *London, July 30*: Several leading papers, including *The Daily Mail*, print articles praising Hitlerism. A swastika appears prominently at the top of *The Daily Mail*'s column, and its publisher Lord Rothermere personally endorses the Nazi movement.[9]

BRAZIL. *Rio de Janerio, August 2*: Brazilian Nazis, known as the Integralite party, commence a campaign to "cleanse" the nation of Jews, who "came to Brazil to rob the poor Brazilians." Integralite advocates a "Fascist Fatherland."[10]

PALESTINE.. *Jerusalem, April 1*: The Arab leadership adopts Hitlerism as the long-awaited anti-Jewish weapon. The Mufti of Jerusalem, leader of Palestine's Arab community, notifies the Reich that "Mohammedans inside and outside of Palestine welcome the new German regime and hope for an expansion of fascist and anti-democratic regimes in other countries." He adds that Mohammedans everywhere will assist any Nazi campaign designed to "damage Jewish prosperity." *Haifa, June 1*: German Christians stage a march complete with swastika-bedecked Brownshirt uniforms.[11]

POLAND. *Bendzin, August 15*: Polish Brownshirts end an anti-Semitic rally after police orders to disperse, but then rampage through the streets molesting Jewish citizens. Police reinforcements finally curtail the disturbance. *Czestochowa, August 21*: Following random street attacks against Jews, Polish Fascists receive prison sentences, their publication is suspended, and their headquarters is closed.[12]

IRAQ. *Baghdad, August 20*: Nazi sympathizers accelerate a wave of persecution against the ancient Babylonian Jewish community. In one disturbance, Arabs waving black Fascist flags with anti-Jewish inscriptions march through a Jewish district. Policemen look on passively as Jews are beaten.[13]

SWEDEN. *Stockholm, June 10*: Government authorities discover Reich plans to spend $10 million to propagandize for a massive Germanic state occupying all of north central Europe. Led by Swedish Nazis of German ancestry, a first step will establish a Nazi newspaper and publishing house. *Malmö, August 21*: Although townsfolk throughout Skane Province resist Nazi ideology, Swedish Nazis successfully recruit among Lund University students.[14]

In late June and early July, a number of Nazi organs, especially in Rumania and Austria, called for an international Aryan convention to arrange the forced emigration of all Jews from all countries to a "Jewish National State." One convention call noted that Palestine could not hold the millions of Jews in the world. Therefore, a larger receptacle, equally remote, would be designated. Madagascar was suggested. By late June, Nazi parties in twenty-two countries agreed to participate in the movement.[15]

Those Jewish leaders who hoped Hitlerism might somehow just go away, or that somehow Hitler could be reasoned with, were finally convinced by the summer of 1933 that there would be no compromise. At the height of Germany's unemployment panic, on July 2, Hitler reassured a nationwide gathering of SA leaders that while the tactics might become more restrained, there was no thought of altering the ultimate goal of National Socialism: the speedy annihilation of Jewish existence.[16]

By summer, Hitler's words and deeds forced Jewish leaders to begin viewing German Jews as utterly doomed. For example, by late July, Stephen Wise sent a report home from Europe advising the Congress, "I have a mass of cumulative evidence which proves that the Jewish situation in Germany is hopeless." A few days later, Dr. Joseph Tenenbaum, a leading Congress boycott proponent, told Congress officials that it was no use delaying the boycott proclamation in the hope German Jewry might be saved. "This hope," said Tenenbaum, ". . . now seems to have gone forever."[17]

If Nazism survived, Germany's Jews would all perish. If Nazism was overturned amid economic upheaval, German Jews would suffer bloody reprisals. But the question was now larger than the 600,000 Jews in Germany. In the minds of Jewish leaders, the future of millions of Jews throughout all Europe was at stake.[18] Whatever was done now would set the example for other governments coping with the rise of Nazism.

When Zionist leaders of the Mapai camp looked at this global threat to Jewish survival, it only reinforced their determination to force the crisis to yield a Jewish State. Could Jews be successfully resettled in Eastern Europe, in Latin America, in Western Europe, even in the United States? Traditional anti-Semitism and the new Nazism thrived in all lands. Some of those Nazi and anti-Semitic movements would flourish, others would recede. But the threat would always remain—whatever color shirt, under whatever color flag. A Jew outside his homeland was a Jew waiting for the next pogrom.

Some of the most effective fighters are those who use their adversaries' own weight and power against them. This was the Mapai Zionist defense. Out of the attempts to destroy would emerge the final impetus to attain victory for the Jewish cause: a State.

But the overwhelming majority of Jews and Zionists had not given up on Jewish existence in the Diaspora. They were not willing to pay the price of Mapai's defense strategy. They could not stand still and suffer Hitler's blows in the hope that those blows could be converted to victory strokes. These Jews could not stand by and witness the disintegration of Jewish communities in Europe. They had seen all reasonable efforts to stymie the Hitler plan fail. Moral persuasion, diplomatic pressure, economic warning shots— all of it had failed. Defense-minded Jews saw only one solution: boycott, rigorous and comprehensive, until Germany cracked wide open. Germany would have to be crushed, not merely punished.

Here was the tearing dilemma: Should Jews transplant to their own nation in Israel, abandoning existence in a world that in Jewish terms could be judged only by the *degrees* of Jewish hatred found from one place to another, from one era to the next? Or should Jews stand their ground and defend their right to exist anywhere in the world? It was a choice. Plain and simple. A choice.

29. Near the Cracking Point

THOSE who chose to fight Hitler had every reason to be encouraged during the summer of 1933. German industry was crumbling in an increasingly publicized chain reaction of crises.

Shipping and transatlantic passenger travel had been a strategic foreign-currency earner for the Reich. But anti-Nazi boycotting had virtually bankrupted the entire industry. In late July, at the Hamburg-American Line's annual stockholder meeting, chairman Dr. Max von Schinkel and all board directors announced their resignations with this statement: "The disaffection in the world toward Germany and the boycott movement are making themselves strongly felt. This has severely hurt the Hamburg-American's business and is continuing to hurt . . . German shipping generally."[1] *The Philadelphia Record*, in commenting on the shipping bankruptcies, editorialized: "In a civilized world, the Nazis cannot hound 600,000 fellow Germans out of existence because they happen to be Jews without arousing international indignation. Resentment makes itself felt—and rightly—in a widespread refusal to buy goods or travel on the ships of a great nation lapsed into ugly barbarism."[2]

At about the same time, the Solingen Chamber of Commerce, in the heart of Germany's ironmaking region, was predicting the same fate for the iron industry, given the "tremendous decrease of export possibilities." Heavy machinery exports alone were only half their profitable 1930 level.[3] The medical industry, was also reeling. Berlin, once renowned as the medical capital of Europe, was suffering a 50 percent decline in its lucrative foreign patient market. German educational institutions received an even more damaging blow. Foreign endowments, vital to Germany's academic funding, diminished by over 95 percent.[4]

The declining German export surplus—down 68 percent from May to June—continued dropping during July and early August. The export surplus over imports was the traditional measuring stick of overindustrialized Germany's ability to pay for the raw materials needed to keep its factories running and pay its monthly debt service of RM 50 million. But by summer,

Germany's trade balance was so decayed that the export surplus was becoming outmoded as a true indicator of the Reich's decline. So little foreign currency had been earned that Germany could not purchase many vital raw materials. And German industry had reduced normal imports of raw materials because chain-reaction shortages had halted or slowed certain manufacturing processes. The trade-balance ratio was further moderated by canceling nonessential imports. For instance, the rubber used in sport shoes was simply eliminated. So the *total export* figure—without regard to surplus ratios—was by summer becoming the more valid measure. Overall exports to its European neighbors had dipped at least 23 percent in the first half of 1933, compared to the previous year, according to the Reich's own figures. Total exports were reported down to RM 385 million.[5] The true losses were probably far greater, since statistical falsification was official Nazi policy. But even these admissions were ominous to a nation absolutely dependent on abundant exports.

Added to boycott damage was the worsening domestic economic dislocation caused by Jewish pauperization. In those businesses where Jews were well entrenched, the result was calamity. Germany's vast wine industry was a perfect example. Prohibiting Jews from growing grapes or manufacturing and selling wine threatened to wipe out large sectors of the German wine industry. Non-Jewish vintners, including many active Nazis, pleaded with the government to stay the exclusion. One Palatinate Nazi publication, *Landauer Anzeiger*, openly admitted that without the Jews, the region's wine business would be utterly wrecked, adding that if "the Jews' share in the wine trade heretofore amounted to 80 percent, one comes to the conclusion that even under the most favorable conditions, wine growers will only sell half the amount of wine this fall that they . . . must sell. In view of the growers' great indebtedness, there rises the danger of a ruinous price catastrophe."[6]

A companion move to exclude all Jews from the Palatinate tobacco industry could not be implemented because there was simply no one to replace them.[7]

An analogous situation occurred in the metallurgical field. In mid-July, Nazi kommissars demanded the ouster of the six Jewish members of the industry's trade organization. The six were the most knowledgeable experts in the field. Almost as soon as the Aryan substitutes were installed, however, the organization realized no one else could do the job. So the six ousted Jews were immediately rehired as "consultants."[8]

Equally damaging to the German economy was the wholesale departure of foreign business. Prior to 1933, hundreds of European and American companies maintained sizable operations in Germany. But by summer 1933, Germany was witnessing mass corporate flight. Each foreign firm that withdrew from German soil left a wake of unemployed Germans and lost opportunities for other, interacting German businesses. The German government often tried to suppress news of such departures, but the banks knew the truth: defaulted loans, diminished deposits, and a virtual cessation of normal lending.

Desperate directors of Germany's prestigious Dresden Bank hoped to call upon the international banking fraternity for help. In a dramatic written appeal sent in mid-July to a major French bank, the Société Générale, Dresden Bank frantically declared, "The atrocity propaganda . . . harmful to German trade . . . is based on lies and distortions of fact. Complete tranquility reigns in Germany, and any non-Party person on the spot can convince himself that no one is hindered in the lawful pursuit of his private and professional affairs. We would be glad if, in the interests of international trade relations, you would spread the truth and do your utmost to bring about a speedy end of the boycott of German goods."[9]

The highly unusual plea provoked an equally unusual response from Société Générale, which had for decades enjoyed cordial professional relations with Dresden Bank. Société Générale's response, which ultimately reached the world's newspapers, answered that "on opening our mail we find an amazing circular from your esteemed bank. We beg to draw your attention to the fact that a French business would never presume to send propaganda material in business correspondence. We are thus compelled to assume that the tactlessness of your letter arises from an inborn lack of taste. As for the systematic persecution of Jews by your government, we know what to believe. We know . . . doctors have been driven from hospitals, lawyers struck off, and shops closed down. . . . Every nation is a master in its own home, and so it is not our business to interfere. . . . Nevertheless, we are free to turn our business sympathies to our friends and not to a nation which aims at destroying individual liberty. We assure you, gentlemen, that we will continue to esteem your bank, but we cannot extend our sympathy to Germany in general, for we cannot hide our belief that the National Socialist Party will extend its lust for power to other countries at the first opportunity. You ask us to pass on this circular. Rest assured we will do so, and our answer with it. Yours truly, Société Générale, Paris."[10]

The continuing deterioration of the Nazi economy in the summer of 1933 triggered yet another sequence of time-buying tricks. The first was a series of special multimillion-reichmark industrial subsidies. But the regime was running out of reichmarks. The government turned to the Reichsbank, but it, too, lacked sufficient resources to help. So the Reichsbank itself applied for a loan.

Sometime around the end of July, German go-betweens approached London brokers for an embarrassingly small loan of RM 40 million, or slightly more than £3 million. Once known, the request caused a round of derisive laughter in the London financial community. The *Investor's Review* broke the news with a mocking tidbit in its August 5 issue: "We have seen a letter written by a financial broker in Berlin . . . [that] throws a lurid light on the dreadful condition to which Hitlerism has reduced Germany. . . . The writer states that he has been asked by the German Reichsbank itself to negotiate for it a loan . . . of 40 to 50 million marks! That the Reichsbank, formerly perhaps the greatest financial institution on the Continent, should have come begging to London for . . . a paltry sum is . . . alarming. . . . So it is not surprising to hear that authoritative opinion is that Hitlerism will come to a sanguinary end before the New Year." [11]

With London a forfeit market, Germany turned to New York to help finance one of the department store subsidies, this one for Kaufhaus des Westens. An even smaller sum was requested, this time just RM 14.5 million, or about $5 million. Chase National said no. Germany then approached the lesser financial markets of Europe. One after another, each said no. Many refused even to consider the loan. The Hitler regime finally turned inward and demanded that the Dresden Bank extend the RM 14.5 million. Dresden had already suffered department store defaults and was extremely reluctant to advance further funds. But the Reichsbank insisted, backing up the arrangement with an amorphous "guarantee." [12]

In reporting on the RM 14.5 million loan fiasco, American Consul General in Berlin George Messersmith confirmed that the loan begging was done at the behest of Hjalmar Schacht. The dismal failures, reported Messersmith, made it crystal clear to Schacht that "foreign banks irrespective of nationality are for the present avoiding to increase in any way their commitments in Germany." The Wizard had publicly admitted as much to the Berlin correspondent of a Dutch financial newspaper, *Algemeen Handelsblad*. Answering a question about the economic consequences of the Reich's anti-Semitic campaign, Schacht declared, "Germany does not reckon in any way further upon international financial assistance." [13]

In a second interview shortly thereafter, published by the German paper *Deutsche Allgemeine Zeitung* using an Amsterdam dateline, Schacht warned if the world would not buy German products, then Germany would simply not pay her debts, or do so with such financial instruments such as scrip, a form of I.O.U. Schacht declared that in the face of declining foreign trade, Germany's creditors could take such paper guarantees or get nothing. [14] Even Schacht could no longer deny that Nazi Germany had become diplomatically and economically isolated. The economic recovery the Nazis so fervently sought was becoming more and more a mirage.

More time-buying tricks would be needed. To keep shipping industry employees working just a little longer, stringent rules enacted in mid-August required German businesses to ship their goods via German vessels. Companion regulations prohibited currency payments to foreign shipping companies, thus forcing almost all travelers passing through Germany to sail on

German vessels. But the ill-conceived assistance actually robbed German lines of an important profit center—bookings and transshipping on foreign vessels.[15]

An equally self-destructive rescue was imposed upon the textile industry, where unemployment in some places reached 50 percent. Recovery had been blocked at every turn by the boycott. So the Nazis slightly changed the design and color of regulation uniforms. Idled looms switched on and mill payrolls increased as textile companies scurried to produce materials for the new uniforms. But an impoverished public could not produce enough demand, and much of the new goods was dumped at great loss on foreign markets. Thus, sales revenues slumped in the face of increased production.[16]

Another trick was the outright bribery of foreign officials and cash incentives to special-interest groups purchasing German goods. For example, in August, I. G. Farben, one of Germany's largest employers, negotiated with the Rumanian government to lift their quasi-official ban on German merchandise, which was protectionist in origin but regularly flamed by anti-Nazi boycott groups. Via the German legation in Bucharest, with the full endorsement of the Foreign Ministry, Farben offered Rumania a complex but irresistible bargain.

First, Farben would purchase RM 17 million worth of Rumanian grain, about half of which would actually be imported into Germany to compete with German produce. The remaining RM 9 million would be sold by Farben to other countries. Second, Farben would broker 100,000 tons of Rumanian wheat to the world market, and even pay a 10 percent price support, in effect subsidizing Rumanian wheat farmers.[17]

Third, of the foreign currency received by Germany in selling Rumanian products, the equivalent of RM 2.5 million would be handed to the Rumanian National Bank. What's more, roughly 25 percent of the sales within Germany would be converted into foreign currency and also handed to the Rumanian National Bank. Fourth, much of the worldwide grain shipments would be shipped aboard Rumanian vessels, in direct competition with German lines. All this was in exchange for Bucharest's granting permits for RM 13.6 million worth of I. G. Farben products to be sold in Rumania.[18]

Despite the lopsided arrangement, Farben was forced to grease the deal further with a bribe of RM 250,000 to high Rumanian government officials for "party purposes." An additional RM 125,000 went to the National Socialists of Rumania, presumably to guarantee their consumer support for Farben's products. To quiet public opposition to trading with Germany, Farben earmarked a RM 125,000 slush fund "for exerting influence on the press and on [key] persons."[19]

But after all the bribes had been paid and the commercial favors and foreign-currency concessions granted, I. G. Farben could continue employing its assembly-line workers just a little longer. And Germany would retain about RM 10 million in badly needed foreign currency. Beyond the short-term benefits, the complex arrangement dramatized a bitter reality: The anti-Nazi boycott had made it easier and more profitable for Germany to sell another nation's products on the world market than to sell her own.

There seemed no way for the Nazi leadership to counteract the boycott successfully other than hope that the transfer would prompt world Jewry to call off its economic war. But despite actions by the Zionist leadership to scuttle the boycott, popular Jewish momentum would not subside. In early August, a frustrated Adolf Hitler held a meeting at Obersalzberg with two Americans influential within New York's National City Bank organization. One was Henry Mann, a vice-president representing the bank's German operations. The second was Col. Sosthenes Behn, who was both a bank director and the chairman of International Telephone and Telegraph (ITT). The two Americans reviewed for Hitler the U.S. mood against Germany. Behn then questioned just how safe foreign investments were in Nazi Germany. Hitler reassured Behn that foreign capital such as General Motors' was safe if used according to regulations. Hitler remonstrated that the sordid picture of a violent Germany hostile to foreign business was just another figment of atrocity propaganda. That led to talk about the anti-Nazi boycott. And here Hitler became visibly excited. "These senseless measures are not only harmful to Germany," ranted an enraged Führer, "but, by weakening German purchasing power on world markets, to other nations as well." Hitler vehemently insisted that the boycott would "eventually collapse all by itself." Therefore, said Hitler, it would be best to say and do as little as possible.[20]

In early August, Goebbels was showing equal distress about the boycott. Speaking to a festival at Stuttgart, Goebbels admitted he looked forward to the day when the Reich "will have burst the iron boycott with which the world has encircled us."[21] Shortly thereafter, Goebbels felt unable to abide by der Führer's advice to pretend the boycott didn't exist. Addressing the annual NSDAP Congress at Nuremberg, Goebbels confessed, "We still feel ourselves handcuffed and threatened by this cleverly thought-out plot. . . . This boycott is causing us much concern, for it hangs over us like a cloud."[22]

The regime tried to delude the grumbling population with manipulated unemployment statistics. For example, the number of jobless was artificially decreased by subtracting Jews, Marxists, and pacifists. Additionally, German males aged sixteen to twenty-five were removed en masse from their jobs to make way for older family men. The young Aryans were then steered to voluntary labor camps, where they could keep some unemployment payments and yet be removed from the jobless rolls. Those who refused voluntary labor were deprived of their unemployment benefits and taken off the rolls anyway.[23]

Women were also being fired in great numbers, under the Nazi notion that good Aryan women should make way for men in the job market. Many of these women were relocated as domestics, receiving little more than room and board. Others were instructed to have children and keep house. In either case, essentially jobless women were excluded from the unemployment figures. Thousands of male German family heads were likewise excised from the jobless ranks, either by engaging them in meaningless public-works programs, where they earned virtual pittances, or by resettlement onto farms.[24]

More tangible illusions were created by coercing employers to overstaff. By mid-August, Ruhr mining firms were employing 30,000 more than market demand justified. Some of this was accomplished through a shorter work week, which robbed those who did have a job of the full wage they normally received. And no one was allowed a second job. Such "black labor" was strictly *verboten*.[25]

Indeed, the jingoism of the Nazi economy had by August 1933 become a mere symbol of disappointment to millions of Germans. The July unemployment panic had receded somewhat after dissident Storm Troopers were rounded up. However, the laissez-faire business climate espoused in the July Schmitt-Hitler covenant, and the prohibition against violent anti-Semitic activity, were by August cast aside as unenforceable rhetoric.

Time was running out for Germany. Winter was approaching. Construction, farming, public works, and voluntary labor camps were all wholly dependent upon outdoor activity and good weather. With no part-time or off-season work available, it would be a winter of desperation and dissatisfaction.[26]

Goebbels could plead "the handcuffs" of the Jewish-led anti-Nazi boycott, but such excuses only encouraged dissident factions to assert their own authority as they had during the July unemployment panic. Realizing that the regime would stand or fall with the popular mood that winter, the Reich leadership anxiously made preparations. The Ministry of Finance and party groups established "voluntary" appeals for the unemployed whereby contributions were automatically deducted from a wage earner's pay.[27]

A second campaign urged farmers, especially those in East Prussia, to store unthreshed crops in their barns. Then, instead of farm employment ending with the harvest, it would continue through the winter months as the harvest hands threshed the grain. But by mid-August, the campaign had proved unsuccessful, as cash-hungry farmers sold their crops early. In droves, harvest help was already returning to the city awaiting the next bit of relief from the Third Reich.[28]

A brilliant solution to the entire unemployment scene was finally conceived by Chancellor Hitler himself. His idea: Compel 200,000 working women to marry and quit their jobs, thus making room for 200,000 men to support families. The 200,000 newly married women would have babies and set up new households requiring furniture, appliances, and other household products, which would create the demand for another 200,000 men who could then marry a second group of 200,000 women who would once again create households demanding products for a third 200,000. This process would continue until all eligible women were retired from the work force and firmly planted in households making babies, thus creating ever-increasing consumer demand.[29]

In the fervor of the times, mass marriages were certainly possible. But a marriage without money could not generate instant demand for furniture and appliances. The 200,000-marriages plan was typical of the Nazi approach to economic recovery, and among diplomats the proposal became a laughable example.[30]

"Bread and wurst for all" was the Nazi slogan sung in Berlin. But in the provinces far from Berlin, where Nazi factions ruled, the people wanted results. In the lead story of the August 21 *New York Times*, correspondent Frederick Birchall, upon returning to Berlin from covering the Amsterdam boycott conference, speculated on the question: "The prospect for the winter therefore is far from promising. But how far the economic crisis can affect the Nazis' hold upon Germany is extremely doubtful. 'Bread and wurst for all' was their promise. But if they cannot fulfill it, who is to put them out? And with whom can they be replaced?"[31]

A few days later, a follow-up article appeared in the *Times*, datelined Berlin but without a byline. After explaining the duplicity of the most recent unemployment statistics, the article warned, "Both the statistical and the propagandistic efforts of the National Socialist regime are tokens of its realization that it stands or falls with its solution of the unemployment problem. The entire country is watching these efforts with both hope and skepticism. The labor situation during the coming winter is expected to determine the fate of Hitlerism itself. Indicative of the mood of a large section of the population is this doggerel which your correspondent has heard repeatedly during my travels throughout Germany:

> If Hitler doesn't give us bread,
> We'll see to it he'll soon be dead."[32]

On August 24, 1933, *Chicago Daily News* correspondent John Gunther reported from Vienna: "Dr. Hjalmar Schacht . . . narrowly escaped assassination by disaffected Storm Troopers, it is said today in the Prague newspaper *Sozial Demokraten*, copies of which were received here. According to reports, 'Dr. Schacht noted some days ago that he was being followed by mysterious individuals and appealed to the secret police [Gestapo] for protection.' Yesterday, three Storm Troopers were arrested and five others fled, it is said, when Dr. Schacht was followed by police officers to trap the alleged assailants. A search . . . revealed a plan of assassination. Dr. Schacht was thought to be too conservative in his policies and hotheads wanted to make the Nazi revolution more socialistic." Gunther added that the report was unconfirmed.[33]

The anti-Nazi movement watched the signs of Germany's crumbling economic and political house and drew encouragement. The boycotters believed that to save Europe from Nazism, the example would have to be set in Germany. The price of war against the Jews would have to be commercial isolation and economic ruin. And so the boycotters took their slogan seriously: Germany was to crack that winter.

30. Untermyer Takes Command

THE FUTURE of the anti-Nazi boycott and its hoped-for winter victory was ultimately dependent upon one factor and one factor alone: *organization*. Because the major Jewish bodies had spurned boycott, the movement resided in the basements, front parlors, and spare rooms of such devoted leaders as Samuel Untermyer, Captain Joseph Webber, and thousands of nameless workers around the world. Ad hoc boycott organizations, while enjoying massive popular support, also lacked money. Untermyer personally donated most of the money involved in his activities.[1] The funds supporting the Captain Webber Organization undoubtedly came out of Captain Webber's own pocket. Working with such meager resources, boycott leaders tried to fight both Adolph Hitler and established Jewish organizations whose comparatively superior assets were devoted either to sabotaging the boycott or to remaining harmfully neutral.

The crisis of organization had become clear when Untermyer convened his Amsterdam conference. After the headlines had run and battle strategies were plotted, the resulting World Jewish Economic Federation was an organization without an infrastructure. They hoped Lord Melchett could maneuver British Jewish organizations into joining the Federation, but that hope was shattered by Anglo-Jewish leaders, the Zionist hierarchy, and Stephen Wise, each for their own reason.

Shortly after Amsterdam, Lord Melchett quietly disassociated himself from the Federation. Melchett's uncle, Sir Robert Mond, took his place, but Sir Robert's involvement was more symbolic than functional. By early August, Melchett had dropped out of the boycott movement altogether. The longtime Zionist had decided that the best way to beat Hitlerism was to use it to establish the Jewish State. The value of Melchett's shift from the boycott solution to the Zionist solution was readily apparent. By early August, Zionist groups in London were talking publicly about nominating Melchett for president of the Zionist Organization at the coming eighteenth Zionist Congress. *The London Jewish Chronicle* even editorialized in favor of his election.[2] By August 1933, Lord Melchett had completely turned the other way.

Untermyer's World Jewish Economic Federation at this point had no address, no telephone number, no field offices, no real structure, but Untermyer did enjoy one powerful resource: the people. In just a few months he had displaced Stephen Wise from the vanguard of Jewish defense. To millions of Jews and non-Jews alike, Untermyer was the hero of the hour, standing alone against Hitler where all other Jewish leaders had feared to tread. Untermyer intended to use his popular support to pressure the boycott-leaning, but still boycott-reluctant American Jewish Congress to abandon Wise and immediately join the movement. This would avoid the delay of waiting for Wise's Second World Jewish Conference, to be held in September.[3]

As Untermyer wrestled with the boycott's organizational problem, he also realized just how crucial American participation was. At the Amsterdam conference, Untermyer learned that although devoid of formal organization, the boycott was working well in Europe and the Mediterranean region. Holland, Czechoslovakia, and Poland, for example, were nations with well-entrenched, highly effective boycotts. Egypt was enforcing a virtually hermetic trade blockade.[4]

Untermyer understood the reasons for initial boycott successes in Europe and the Mediterranean even in the absence of a true organization. First, the countries were all smaller, less populous, and less enthnically diverse than the United States. A smaller group of leaders could rally a greater portion of the national population. Second, the lines of commerce in Europe were not as diversified as in America. Choking off a number of strategic commercial channels in many European countries was enough to smother German exports. Third, the boycotts enjoyed the official support of labor organizations, East European Jewish religious bodies, and, to a certain extent, the national governments themselves. So greater resources were available, thus injecting the understaffed movements with an unexpected stamina.[5]

On the other hand, the boycott in America was lagging behind badly. German imports to the United States for the first six months of 1933 had dropped at least 22 percent below the 1932 level.[6] But imports would have to quickly dip to 50, to 70 percent of their 1932 level, as they had in European markets, if Germany was to crack. Untermyer knew that to achieve that effectiveness, he would need what he didn't have: a well-financed organization capable of covering the vast territory of the United States.[7]

On July 31, Samuel Untermyer sailed from Plymouth, England, in triumph. During a press conference just before the ship departed for New York, Untermyer asserted that his Amsterdam conference was a total success, especially given the short notice. He insisted that the boycott, with just a little more intensification, would win. "The spontaneous outpourings by non-Jews as well as Jews," Untermyer proclaimed, "confirms the view that it [the boycott] may be regarded as a worldwide uprising of civilization . . . regardless of race and creed, against the most incredible crime of many centuries."[8] In a week, Untermyer would arrive in New York, the new Jewish champion. He would then call the Jewish population of America to his side. He hoped the Congress leadership would follow.

August 3, 1933, 8:15 P.M., in a conference room at the New Yorker Hotel, American Jewish Congress president Bernard Deutsch convened a special meeting of the Administrative Committee. Under Congress bylaws, the Administrative Committee decided policy; the Executive Committee implemented the decisions. As soon as the Administrative session was called to order, Deutsch explained the crisis: First, Samuel Untermyer was sailing back to New York. Second, the Amsterdam conference had "received wide publicity here." Third, upon his return, Untermyer would "be met with a great deal of acclaim by welcoming committees." Deutsch was forced to concede that Untermyer had singlehandedly overshadowed the Congress. He had proclaimed the global boycott while the Congress had not made a decision. The Congress' reluctance to join the boycott movement was now a "storm raised on all sides by various branches of the Congress demanding a determined stand."[9]

Deutsch explained that the Congress was still awaiting the signal from Dr. Wise, at that time in Europe. Wise had been cabled for his "latest views" and for instructions, since the boycott decision was due to be announced at the August 6 Executive Committee meeting. This decision had already been delayed innumerable times. Then Deutsch related Wise's answer: Joining the boycott now "would be undesirable and dangerous. . . . It is now absolutely necessary to postpone any decision" until the Second World Jewish Conference preparatory meeting in Prague, August 18.[10]

The world was demanding action. Wise was counseling delay. What was to be the August 6 Executive announcement, boycott or no boycott?[11]

The members argued back and forth. The reluctant ones weren't exactly sure why they opposed the boycott: Maybe it wouldn't work. . . . Maybe it would offend a fragile joint consultative agreement recently worked out with the American Jewish Committee and B'nai B'rith—this to make some feeble effort at unity. . . . Maybe Wise would look bad if the boycott were declared in his absence and against his specific advice. . . . Maybe a Jewish-led boycott would alienate the Christian community—and the old fear, boycott might provoke German reprisals against the Jews.[12]

Dr. Joseph Tenenbaum, a staunch boycott proponent from the start, chastised his fellow leaders: "If the American Jewish Congress does or does not decide to declare the boycott, the conditions of the Jews in Germany could not be made more serious. . . . Now is the time for action, because in the last six weeks, an unparalleled rabid anti-Semitism has broken out. . . . Hitler has declared that 'there is going to be no mitigation of the Jewish question.' . . . The boycott is being carried on without the Congress . . . because the Congress did not have the courage or the conviction to come out . . . with a stand." [13]

Tenenbaum predicted that the American Federation of Labor would follow the example of England's Trades Union Congress and openly declare for the boycott. He pointed out that in Europe, especially France and Poland, the boycott was extremely effective, and America's contribution could make the difference. The moment was late, Tenenbaum admitted, but if the Congress did not proclaim its support for the boycott at the August 6 Executive session, it would be *too* late. Citing the demands by Congress leaders all over the country, Tenenbaum formally proposed instructing the Executive Committee to proclaim the boycott at their August 6 meeting and to "concentrate all efforts" to make it work. [14]

Mr. Leo Wolfson followed Tenenbaum's emotional plea by suggesting the August 6 meeting be postponed until Stephen Wise returned from Europe. Mr. Isidore Teitelbaum went further and recommended that the whole boycott notion be abandoned as a bad idea; he preferred to fight Germany "diplomatically and by appealing to the sense of justice and American fairplay to help the Jews in Germany." [15]

Wolfson's and Teitelbaum's suggestions sparked immediate rebuttals by boycott advocates. Mr. Morris Margulies declared, "We have all the information on this problem that we can ever have. . . . We should not wait for Dr. Wise for further action." He emphasized that Samuel Untermyer and only Samuel Untermyer had brought about an effective boycott, and the Congress should immediately back his boycott group. Mr. Herman Speier chimed in that the Congress could not "declare" a boycott if it wanted to, because the boycott was already under way. The best the come-lately Congress could hope to do was "endorse" the existing movement. But this was urgent, if only to help Untermyer. [16]

As the conflict focused on Stephen Wise's leadership failure, Mr. Zelig Tygel urged his colleagues to decide for the boycott and simply cable the news to Wise in Europe. [17] Dr. Samuel Margoshes, an early boycott proponent, reminded them that Samuel Untermyer was sailing back to America with the power of Amsterdam behind him. Everyone knew that Untermyer would build a "great and important boycott movement throughout the U.S. . . . We should join forces with him now, setting up an organization which includes the American Jewish Congress." Margoshes deplored Wise's strategy of delay: "The time to act is *now* . . . not a delay for two or three months." [18]

It was near midnight. The Congress men were weary of debate. Votes were called for Wolfson's motion to postpone the August 6 meeting. Just before the votes were cast, Tenenbaum reiterated his plea against delay. [19]

Twenty-two of the twenty-five assembled men cast votes. Ten to endorse the boycott on August 6. Twelve for postponement. The new date for a decision would be August 20, 1933.[20]

Late in the morning on August 6, 1933, the French liner *Paris* sailed past the Statue of Liberty. Samuel Untermyer was aboard, triumphantly returning to America as the foremost adversary of Adolf Hitler. Awaiting him was a Jewish community eager to follow and a non-Jewish community ready to join. As the *Paris* neared the city, it was met by chartered boats bedecked with huge placards proclaiming Untermyer "Our Leader" and congratulating him for a great achievement in Amsterdam. A band aboard one boat struck up welcome music as it followed the *Paris* into dock. As soon as the gangplank was lowered onto Pier 15, two dozen representatives of Jewish and civic organizations along with a gaggle of reporters scampered up to Untermyer's cabin for a hearty round of congratulations and an impromptu press conference.[21]

Untermyer told of the great gains made against Nazi economic survival, but declared America must now catch up to other countries. "It is not a fight of Jews, but of humanity," Untermyer said. "We are embattled for every liberty-loving citizen of whatever race or creed."[22]

Waiting on the pier itself when Untermyer descended the gangplank were 5,000 cheering supporters: Jewish War Veterans and American Legionnaires in full uniform, members of the Zionist Organization of America, Hadassah, and numerous other Jewish and non-Jewish groups. They had been waiting for hours. As the fiesty seventy-five-year-old crusader was helped through the crowd, he stopped to address a shipside reception committee. As he finally reached the street, 10,000 more supporters were waiting for him to pass.[23] The cheers for Untermyer were cheers for the boycott. The American Jews who had lagged so long behind their compatriots in other countries were now grateful that someone would lead.

Untermyer was ushered to a waiting car. From West Fifteenth Street, he was whisked by police motorcycle escort uptown to the American Broadcasting Company, where a national radio hookup was waiting.[24] From WABC studios, Untermyer sought to rally the nation and force the existing Jewish organizations, especially the Congress, to join the boycott fight. His words were addressed to both Jews and non-Jews: "My Friends: What a joy and relief and sense of security to be once more on American soil! The nightmares . . . through which I have passed in those two weeks in Europe, listening to the heartbreaking tales of refugee victims . . . beggar description. I deeply appreciate your enthusiastic greeting on my arrival today, which I quite understand is addressed not to me personally but to the holy war in the cause of humanity in which we are embarked."[25]

He quickly turned to the boycott's biggest obstacle—Jewish leaders. First, the American Jewish Committee: "A mere handful in number, but powerful in influence, of our own thoughtless but doubtless well-intentioned Jews seem obsessed and frightened at the bare mention of the word *boycott*. It signifies and conjures up to them images of force and illegality, such as have on occasions in the past characterized struggles between labor unions and their employers. As these timid souls are capitalists and employers, the word and all that it implies is hateful to their ears.[26]

"These gentlemen do not know what they are talking or thinking about. Instead of surrendering to their vague fears and half-baked ideas, our first duty is to educate them . . . [that] the boycott is our only really effective weapon. . . . What then have these amiable gentlemen accomplished or expect to accomplish . . . by their 'feather-duster' methods. You cannot put out a fire . . . by just looking on until the mad flames, fanned by the wind of hate, have destroyed everything. What we are proposing and have already gone far toward doing, is to prosecute a purely defensive economic boycott that will undermine the Hitler regime . . . by destroying their export trade on which their very existence depends."[27]

Untermyer then turned to the Congress and Stephen Wise: "I purposely refrain from including the American Jewish Congress in this appeal because I am satisfied that ninety-five percent of their members are already with us and that they are being misrepresented by two or three men now abroad. . . . I ask that prior to the [World Jewish Conference preparatory] meeting to be held this month in Prague . . . they instruct these false leaders in no uncertain terms as to the stand they must take . . . or resign their offices. One of them, generally recognized as the kingpin of mischief-makers, is junketing around the Continent engaged in his favorite pastime of spreading discord, asserting at one time and place that he favors and supports the boycott, and at another that he is opposed or indifferent to it, all dependent on the audience he is addressing."[28]

With the nation listening, Untermyer explained how the whole world had already made "surprising and gratifying progress" in the economic war against Nazism. It was the United States and England that were the most "inadequately organized." He admitted, "With us in America, the delay has been in part due to lack of funds and the vast territory to be covered, but it is hoped that this condition will soon be corrected. The object lesson we are determined to teach is so priceless to all humanity that we dare not fail.[29]

"Each of you, Jew and gentile alike, who has not already enlisted in the sacred war should do so now. . . . It is not sufficient that you buy no goods made in Germany. You must refuse to deal with any merchant or shopkeeper who sells any German-made goods or who patronizes German ships. . . . To our shame . . . there are a few Jews among us, but fortunately only a few, so wanting in dignity and self-respect that they . . . travel on German ships where they are despised. . . . Their names should be heralded far and wide. They are traitors to their race.[30]

"In conclusion . . . with your support and that of our millions of non-

Jewish friends, we will drive the last nail in the coffin of bigotry and fanaticism that has dared raise its ugly head to disgrace twentieth-century civilization."[31] In his sermon from the studio, Samuel Untermyer rightly expected the Jews of America to cast off their old leadership and join his defiant crusade.

The next morning, August 7, Untermyer received a phone call from an indignant Bernard Deutsch, president of the American Jewish Congress. Deutsch explicitly condemned the radio speech as a vicious attack against Wise. Exactly how Untermyer answered is unknown, but the spunky boycott leader must have certainly prevailed. That afternoon, a special four-man Congress delegation conferred with Untermyer about joining his movement.[32]

Untermyer varied little from his broadcast. He welcomed their cooperation. A Congress fund-raising campaign must be launched in concert with the American League for the Defense of Jewish Rights, which was the American alter ego of the World Jewish Economic Federation. These funds were desperately needed to spread the boycott to the American interior, where it was strong but far from complete. Untermyer was unyielding that Wise be instructed without further delay to announce the Congress in favor of the boycott.[33]

Immediately after the Congress delegation left Untermyer, they cabled Wise in Europe urging him, in view of enormous public pressure, finally to declare himself in favor. The cablegram also made clear that the Congress intended to join forces with Untermyer's group. The decision would be ratified on August 17 and announced to the public in an Executive Committee session on August 20.[34]

That morning, August 7, Congress leaders and Samuel Untermyer in New York had every reason to believe a successful boycott alliance was soon to be consummated that would bring down the German economy. They had no way of knowing that even as they were solidifying their plans, a group of Zionist leaders and Mr. Sam Cohen were meeting in Berlin with the German government to seal the Transfer Agreement, thus creating not an economic boycott but an economic bond between Germany and Palestine.

Stephen Wise was not pleased when he received the Congress' August 7 cablegram. He had worked political miracles to achieve his moment in Geneva, but the Amsterdam gathering had obviated the need for any World Jewish Congress meeting to plan or declare a global boycott. Untermyer had already done it.

And now, while Wise was still in Europe, his power base in America was on the brink of merging with Untermyer's essentially nonexistent organization. This was a threat to everything. In Wise's view, Untermyer's Federation would not only dilute anti-Nazi boycott resources, it would create the world-wide entity Wise himself was hoping to establish.

The Congress' cable heralded nothing less than the triumph of Samuel Untermyer and the dethroning of Stephen Wise. Wise wired back: UNANIMOUS DECISION GENEVA CONFERENCE SEPTEMBER FIFTH ESSENTIAL . . . DECISION ALMOST CERTAIN FAVOR PUBLIC BOYCOTT BUT MUST [BE] SOLEMNLY . . . PROCLAIMED INTERNATIONAL JEWISH AUSPICES GENEVA STOP SUGGEST YOUR RESOLUTION [AUGUST] 17 AUTHORIZE YOUR REPRESENTATIVES GENEVA PROPOSE BOYCOTT RESOLUTION . . . UNTERMYER AMSTERDAM FIASCO EVERYWHERE DISCREDITED MELCHETT DECLINED CHAIRMANSHIP URGE POSTPONE DECISION CONCERNING COOPERATION TILL GENEVA.[35]

His message: a boycott resolution now would undermine the Second World Jewish Conference. Joining forces with Untermyer, who represented no one and was not worthy to lead the boycott, would also undermine the Conference. In other words, continue doing nothing.

Wise saw no value in helping Untermyer in the struggle against Hitler. The show would have to go on in Geneva. And as far as Wise was concerned, it would have to be a one-man show.

Stephen Wise was now careful to retain the support of the American Jewish Congress. On August 14, a few days after receiving the demand to declare for the boycott, Rabbi Wise did just that. In a speech to the Prague Jewish Community, Wise stated publicly, "Decent, self-respecting Jews cannot deal with Germany in any way, buy or sell or maintain . . . commerce with Germany or travel on German boats." And he promised that a preparatory commission meeting the next day would make vital decisions to be implemented at the Second World Jewish Conference in Geneva on September 5.[36]

When word reached New York of Rabbi Wise's boycott declaration, reporters contacted Untermyer for comment. With restraint aimed at a strategic union with Wise's forces, Untermyer issued a one-sentence statement: "I am pleased to learn that at last Rabbi Wise has definitely come out in favor of the boycott."[37]

The next day, August 15, the World Jewish Congress' preparatory commission met in Prague. Wise told the commission that the Second World Jewish Conference would almost certainly make the global boycott official.[38] Whereas Untermyer's World Jewish Economic Federation envisioned grandiose plans for rerouting commerce around Germany, it lacked the branch offices, the postage, the telegraph accounts, the mimeographs, the phones, the sheer manpower possessed by the member organizations of the emerging World Jewish Congress. Only Wise's boycott machinery could wield the global network needed to cripple the Third Reich.

Responding to enormous public pressure, American Jewish Congress officers felt compelled to ignore Stephen Wise's request not to pass a boycott resolution. At the Congress' August 17 Administrative meeting, many members felt unable to remain publicly silent any longer. After a long, discordant debate, Dr. Samuel Margoshes proffered a compromise resolution authorizing Stephen Wise to vote at Geneva in favor of boycott. But it also directed the Congress' Executive Committee to announce on August 20 that it was finally ready "to cooperate with all Jewish agencies now engaged in . . . the boycott movement, [so] . . . a consolidated boycott organization may . . . enlist the support of the Jewish as well as the non-Jewish population of America."[39] A majority voted for Margoshes' resolution.[40]

After consideration, Untermyer agreed to the compromise, subordinating to Wise's World Jewish Congress. Untermyer's movement, imbued with fight but devoid of organization, would now have to wait until early September, when the Geneva Conference would declare a worldwide boycott. It would be Wise's way. Yet Untermyer, even though surpassed, had succeeded. He had forced the American Jewish Congress to commit to a boycott without further delay. Of course, each day was precious if a winter triumph was to be won, but Untermyer knew he could not create his own national and worldwide infrastructure during the few weeks he would wait to join his movement to the Stephen Wise-built organization.

There would now be no turning back. In a little more than forty-eight hours, the American Jewish Congress, the world's largest Jewish confederation, representing hundreds of thousands of American Jews, speaking for 25 percent of all the Jews in the world, comprising hundreds of Jewish men's clubs, sisterhoods, neighborhood groups, labor associations, and synagogue congregations, would finally join the economic war against Adolf Hitler.

Almost none of the reporters who showed up Sunday morning, August 20, knew why the Congress Executive had called an emergency session. Dr. Joseph Tenenbaum, chairman of the Executive Committee, had announced the meeting in a press release the night before, but carefully avoided any reference to boycott.[41] Nevertheless, the conference room at the New Yorker Hotel was crowded with reporters and Congress leaders.

Bernard Deutsch began almost routinely, calling for an emergency program to assist German Jews. But then Deutsch shocked the audience by declaring that the last element of the program would be full implementation of the anti-Nazi boycott in America.[42]

Congress officials explained that they had waited this long clinging to hopes that President Roosevelt would publicly condemn Nazism, as the leaders of other nations had. Deutsch and Wise had used every private channel to induce Roosevelt to speak out, but the president would do nothing to help. He would not even lift artificially tightened procedures that were each day denying visas to desperate German Jews applying at the U.S. consulates in Germany. These visa refusals were occurring even as other nations had opened their arms to thousands of refugees. The result was a miserable and overcrowded refugee situation in Europe that the United States refused to help alleviate.[43]

"The American public may rightfully ask," said a frustrated Deutsch, "why the United States government continues to maintain diplomatic silence in relation to a country whose treatment of its nationals betrays every humane instinct, and where Americans are repeatedly assaulted, arrested, and forcibly detained; where American firms are ordered to dismiss their Jewish employees; . . . and whose government has the temerity to send paid political propagandists into the United States to spread racial hatred and bigotry."[44]

It was incomprehensible, Deutsch said, that the United States had long ago severed commercial relations with Russia and had still not granted the Soviet Union diplomatic recognition—this to protest Russia's abuse of her citizens and her refusal to abide by international accords. Yet economic and political relations continued to thrive with Germany. *Why*, demanded Deutsch forcefully, were *communist* agitators being deported from the United States when "every steamer arriving from Germany brings new propagandists, Nazi cells."[45]

When Dr. Tenenbaum took over the podium, he continued the theme. "We do not know," said Tenenbaum, "who bears the responsibility for persuading the president . . . to yield his native impulse of magnanimity and sense of justice. . . . While the people, the leaders of thought and science in this country, and the leaders of the Senate and the House of Representatives have allied themselves in protest against the atrocities and inhumanities . . . the administration has singly failed in its duty."[46]

Tenenbaum, who had researched the legality of international boycott action, defended the anti-Nazi campaign as an obligation of civilization inherent in the League of Nations charter. "Every people," Tenenbaum declared, "has a right, nay a duty, to refuse to support the economic structure of a country which threatens its life and property—there can be no greater moral justification for taking such an extreme step."[47]

Reciting statistics testifying to the bleakness of Germany's trade, and explaining how Germany's overindustrialized society was dependent upon commercial prosperity, Tenenbaum predicted, "If Nazi Germany can be encompassed by a cordon of economic quarantine, . . . a well-organized boycott, there is no doubt that the so-called 'second revolution' which Hitler dreads will soon come to pass."[48]

Turning to the losses American investors would suffer if Germany's commerce and bond-repaying ability collapsed entirely, Tenenbaum stated, "There are times when material benefits fade into insignificance in comparison with the moral obligations incumbent upon humanity. If Germany is permitted to continue on the steep road leading to utter disintegration of all that civilization stands for, [toward] war and moral pestilence, [then] the sacrifices which humanity will be forced to offer . . . to rid itself of this gigantic menace will exceed everything imaginable in . . . material goods."[49]

Tenenbaum then introduced the Congress' boycott consultant, Dr. Max Winkler, economics professor at City College of New York. Winkler explained how Nazified statistics hid the true economic hardship in Germany and how German industrial dependency made the boycott the one anti-Hitler weapon that could triumph.[50]

There were more noble statements about the need to fight Hitler, the value of the boycott, the justification, and the devastating effects the boycott would inflict. As the speeches continued, however, many listening began to understand that this was rhetoric. The local leaders at the meeting knew that the time for talk and expectations had passed. Americans needed concrete organization, a *plan*. A speaker was making a theoretical point when the group suddenly became unruly. A man in the audience yelled out, "Get on with really doing something about the situation!" Another cried, "Instead of leading the masses . . . Mr. Deutsch and Dr. Wise obstructed the boycott movement and did not fulfill their duty to the Jewish people!" A rabbi shouted, "We must throw a *cherem* [an excommunication or curse] upon Jews who handle or import German goods!" Others bitterly protested that so much time had been wasted.[51]

Then Joseph Schlossberg, secretary-treasurer of the Amalgamated Tailors' Union, stood up and advised against *any* boycott, anti-Nazi or otherwise. Schlossberg charged that boycotts were mere propagandistic devices designed to "pour gas on the fires of the working world." They were bad for labor.[52]

That statement led to chaos as delegates angrily denounced Schlossberg's comments. Dr. Tenenbaum could barely gavel the group back to order. One prominent labor lawyer rose and declared that Schlossberg stood alone, that all the labor unions—Jewish and non-Jewish—were "in favor of the boycott of Hitler and his gang."[53]

Amid the tumult a rabbi stood to speak. His name was Rabbi Jacob Sunderling. Months before, he had risen to speak of the indescribable horrors confronting Jews in Germany at an emergency conference chaired by members of the American Jewish Committee. Then he had been silenced. But since that dramatic moment in early April, Rabbi Sundering had become a leading figure in anti-Nazi circles.

No longer a man to be swept aside at a public meeting, Rabbi Sunderling spoke and the crowd listened: "I rise, as a German Jew. I rise as a man whose kith and kin at present are suffering from all these things you have heard and we know. And if I deplore one thing, I deplore that even a discussion is taking place as to the necessity of the boycott. I am in favor one thousand percent of a boycott—in spite of the fact that I know my own people will suffer."[54]

He then explained in his humble way, and in the simplest words possible, what every Jew in the world needed to grasp if European Jewry was to survive: "Ladies and gentlemen, don't you understand. We still believe that . . . a diplomatic manner at certain places in Europe or here will finally bring results. [It] will not. For one reason—we are left alone. We have to fight our own battle. We have to die our own death. If we are not going to help, nobody is going to help. They will register facts. They will deplore things. But they will not *do* things unless the Jew takes the step that he is going to do things.[55]

"Where do you belong? With whom do you want to be reckoned? Are your ours—or are you our enemy!" He made it clear that there could be no middle ground for any reason. "And if you are *not* with us, you are against us. *That is the boycott!*"[56]

Many in the audience wept openly. Others tried to hide their tears. Action was needed. A plan, or at least a leader. That was clear to everyone at the conference. They called out for Samuel Untermyer. So in a unanimous resolution, the Executive Committee voted to summon the boycott crusader from his home to give whatever guidance he could.[57]

When Untermyer's elderly figure appeared at the door, the entire meeting—pro-boycott and against—rose to their feet in spontaneous cheering. Untermyer could offer the crowd no more specifics than Tenenbaum or Max Winkler because they were all awaiting the organizational structure to be formed at Geneva under Stephen Wise. Nonetheless, Untermyer gave them hope. His words were brief: "I want to thank you for having invited me. And I congratulate you upon . . . the resolution for boycott. It was what I had been hoping and wishing for, and I know that so many of your people were in favor of it. . . . You may remember the effect of the Jewish boycott on Henry Ford. . . . Well, what we did there on a small scale, we can accomplish on a large scale. . . . [Germany] cannot stand the economic strain that is being put on her. . . . [but] this is not a subject for oratory. This is a subject for work. Good, hard, practical work." The leader of the world boycott exhorted them, "I hope you will go forth from here and every one of you do his share. If you do, Germany will crack this winter!"[58]

Every person in the room was aware of the calendar. Precious few days remained to push the Third Reich into upheaval. In this moment of potential triumph, it was essential that all Jews unite throughout the world. At least for a few months, until victory over Hitler had been achieved. They were also aware that the next day, August 21, the most organized Jewish entity in the world was to gather in Prague. On August 21, the Zionist movement—all its factions and wings, it parties and coalitions—would convene the Eighteenth Zionist Congress.

Untermyer told the audience he had just cabled Zionist leaders at Prague urging them to join the boycott movement. And it was well known that the Revisionist Zionists were intent on making Prague a battleground to dethrone Mapai and lead Zionism to total war with Germany. If in the presence of their own collective consciences as Jews and Zionists, the Eighteenth Zionist Congress would follow the Revisionist and rank-and-file demand to devote the Zionist movement to the boycott, the Hitler regime *would* crack.

All eyes now turned to Prague.

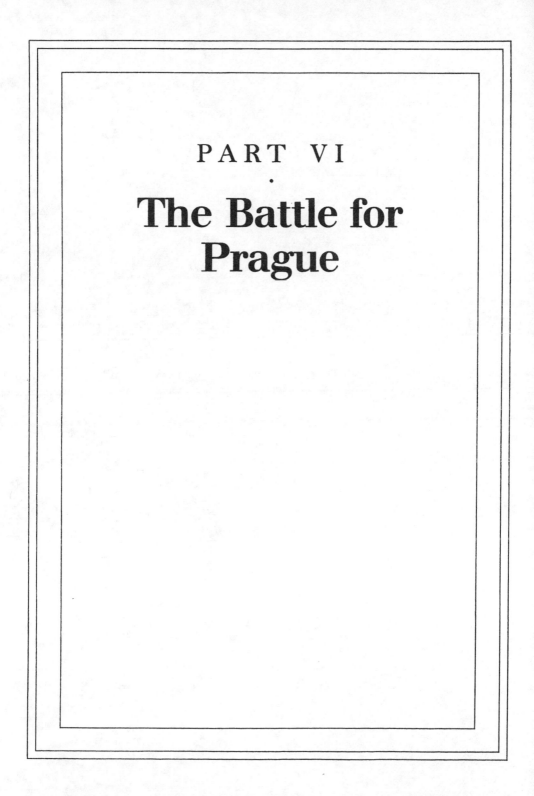

PART VI

·

The Battle for
Prague

31. Pre-Congress Maneuvers

I N ZIONISM'S great moment of challenge, the movement was a confusing and contradictory patchwork. The Zionist Organization was a government without a land. Under its authority existed territorial federations from every country, religious and philosophical unions, political parties, factions, and splinter groups. Each was embroiled in ideological and personality struggles pitting faction against faction, creating bizarre, often transient alliances. Frequently there were separate alliances for separate issues. One faction might join its philosophical nemesis on a religious issue, and then oppose that same temporary ally on an immigration question. As such, Zionism resembled any democracy, which is after all little more than a civilized method of constant disagreement.

It would be an oversimplification to characterize the clash between Mapai and Revisionism solely as a dispute over the Hitler crisis. Broad issues divided these two camps: labor policy, immigration attitudes, economic philosophy, religious identity, and sovereignty questions. But as the Eighteenth Zionist Congress approached, the constellation of conflicts between Mapai and Revisionism focused most spectacularly on the Zionist response to Nazism.

The Mapai-Revisionist clash was hardly the only rift in Zionist politics. For example, the movement was divided over whether Chaim Weizmann should resume the presidency of the Zionist Organization. In July 1933, Weizmann had actually journeyed to the American Zionist convention in Chicago in part hoping to commit U.S. delegates to support him for reelection at Prague. Stormy Chicago convention scenes cut the American Zionist community into equal halves, with Stephen Wise leading the half staunchly opposed to Weizmann's return.[1]

Adding to the rift was a Weizmann precondition for resuming the presidency: the total expulsion of all Revisionists from the Zionist movement. Therefore, a vote for Weizmann was a vote to expel Jabotinsky and his supporters. That drove Stephen Wise of the General Zionist party even further into the Revisionist corner, because a vote for the Revisionists was not only a vote for the boycott, it was a vote against Chaim Weizmann.

Another major conflict pitted the religious Mizrachi Zionists against the Zionist Organization itself. This struggle, essentially revolving around questions of religious predominance in Jewish Palestine, was as important as the Weizmann issue because Mizrachi held a decisive swing vote. So at Prague, Mizrachi support for the Revisionists would be, in large part, an effort to force religious planks on the more secular mainstream Zionists.

Despite assumed alliances, the question of whether Revisionists or Mapai would prevail was indeed unanswerable. Mapai tried to ensure their success by continually comparing Revisionism to Nazism, and by spotlighting the Arlosoroff assassination as proof that Revisionists were terrorists who had no place in the Zionist movement.[2]

Just before the worldwide elections for delegates to the Zionist Congress, the Revisionists themselves succumbed to a party squabble and actually split into separate majority and minority parties. The majority followed Vladimir Jabotinsky personally. The minority, led by Meir Grossman, called themselves alternately Grossman Revisionists or Democratic Revisionists. The split was essentially internecine; the two factions still acted in concert on vital issues. But this temporal split allowed Mapai-influenced Zionist election boards to disqualify the majority Jabotinsky candidate lists in many locales, based on technicalities.[3]

In mid-July, Congress election bureaus opened in virtually every country on every continent—from traditional Zionist strongholds such as Poland and Canada to scant Zionist communities in Uruguay and New Zealand. Depending upon the Zionist rules in any given country, voters could cast their votes for any party strong enough to qualify for the local ballot. The parties in turn sent delegates to the Congress based on electoral strength. Any Jew paying the token biblical shekel (about twenty-five cents) could vote.

It took days to count the votes—more than half a million worldwide. Charges and countercharges of terrorism at the polls and vote fraud led to numerous post-election disallowances and recounts. But when it was all over, Mapai had garnered 44 percent of the delegates, up from its approximate third achieved in the previous election two years before. The two Revisionist parties attracted about 20 percent of the vote, down from the approximate one-fourth captured two years earlier.[4]

The defeat dashed Jabotinsky's dream of leading a worldwide voter revolt against the Zionist establishment. Whereas Revisionism with alliances had previously held a tenuous half-control over the movement, the Revisionists were now the third most powerful. Moreover, with Mapai able to wield an alliance of the second-ranked General Zionists and the tiny Radical Zionists, Revisionism became an isolated minority within the movement.[5] The power of Mapai's accusations and the Arlosoroff murder backlash was overshadowing the Revisionist stance on Hitler. The only way Jabotinsky could now save his movement, and force Zionism to join the anti-Nazi campaign, was through a floor fight at the Eighteenth Zionist Congress itself. Jabotinsky was convinced that with the world watching, he could rouse the hearts and consciences of delegates, regardless of party.

Mapai was equally determined that its 44 percent control be used to expel the entire Revisionist community—about one-fifth of the Zionist movement—and then to transform the whole Zionist Organization into a mere extension of Mapai itself. To achieve this, Mapai would have to block any public debate of the Hitler threat that could sway the other delegates into a sudden emotional coalition with the Revisionists.[6]

A strong minority of Zionists were motivated by religion, but the others were motivated by a history of anti-Semitism. The overwhelming majority were common people: cobblers, teachers, doctors, journalists, clerks. They had held the hands of tortured refugees, and had read smuggled letters from those still within the Reich. Like all other Jews, Zionists were enraged. The strongest boycott movements were in heavily Zionist communities in Palestine, Poland, Egypt, and France. This anti-Hitler devotion cut across all party lines—Mapai, Revisionist, Mizrachi, General Zionist, Radical Zionist.

But the cobblers and shopkeepers of the Zionist movement followed leaders. In many instances, these leaders, particularly the Revisionists and the religious Mizrachi, had concluded that Zionism was obligated to join with Jews throughout the world and combat Nazism. But the leaders of Mapai and their allied factions had concluded that Zionism's only *realistic* response was to work with the German regime and save Jewish wealth for the future of the Jewish nation, so Palestine could quickly become strong enough to commence the true in-gathering. These Mapai leaders were implementing a painful decision in the face of monumental popular resistance. Mapai was in fact leading a war of salvation. They would do what was necessary with the same vigor and ruthlessness as anyone fighting a war of bullets, bombs, and boycotts. This ruthlessness would include silencing the opposition.

At Prague it became obvious that silencing the widespread opposition would be a major challenge. The dominant Zionist community in America—New York—had sent a definitive demand that the Prague Congress publicly endorse and join Samuel Untermyer's boycott movement.[7] Similar sentiments were pouring in from local Zionist bodies around the world. In many ways, the Zionist Organization was facing the identical crisis the American Jewish Congress was facing. In both cases, rank-and-file membership and local leaders demanded boycott; in both cases key influential leaders stymied and frustrated the decision.

From the beginning, the Third Reich had seen the Eighteenth Zionist Congress as the dramatic moment when the international Jewish conspiracy, all according to established Nazi myth, would consolidate and finalize the economic demise of Germany. A prime Reich motivation in cooperating with the German Zionists and the Zionist hierarchy was to divide the movement, bribe it into submission, and rob it of this moment of consolidation. The Amsterdam Conference had been explained away by Zionists and establishment Jewish leaders as an unauthorized and meaningless meeting of dissidents without power. Stephen Wise's upcoming Geneva conference was being dismissed in the same vein. Zionist leaders assured the Reich that the

Prague Congress was the pivotal Jewish meeting, the only conference with the power to declare and implement Jewish policy—and that policy would reject boycott in favor of transfer cooperation.

But the Nazi mind had always visualized Zionist congresses as the birthplace of Jewish conspiracies. Consul Wolff had appealed to this fear in early July when he promised Berlin that Mr. Sam Cohen and associates were doing all possible to cancel the Congress "because they expect the speeches and resolutions . . . will cause increased hostility and anti-German boycott."[8] And indeed, since spring, the German Zionists had been pressuring the Zionist Executive in London to cancel or postpone the event. Their final attempt, a collective petition written from Strassburg on August 4, warned: "It is absolutely clear to us, that today no Zionist Congress will convene without raising a sharp protest against the German government. The German government in turn . . . will be forced to react to this protest by prohibiting the Zionist organizations . . . and organized *aliyah* . . . and by making it impossible to free Jewish capital from Germany; it should also not be ignored that this reaction could mean considerable danger for body and life of a large part of the German Zionists. . . . We demand that you . . . postpone the Congress. . . . We beg of you that this last warning, which comes from responsible people of the movement in Germany, be taken into serious consideration."[9]

Much as the Zionist Executive in London sympathized with the plight of German Zionists and accepted their rationales, the Executive could not stop the Congress. Any attempt to do so would demonstrate a clear capitulation to Hitler's threats. If the Executive did not convene the Congress, someone else would, no doubt the Revisionists, who would then have the working proof that the Zionist Organization was no longer serving the interests of Jews. London insisted the Congress be held.[10]

Unable to postpone the Prague Congress through pressure on German Zionists, the Nazis gambled that the Transfer Agreement, sealed on August 7, would force the Zionist movement to silence the rank and file. Hans Hartenstein expressed as much in an August 10 letter to Schmidt-Roelke, explaining the Transfer Agreement: "It seems to me that this way really affords the best guarantee of the strongest possible effect on Jewish boycott measures."[11]

However, Nazi hopes of an innocuous Eighteenth Zionist Congress soon dissolved. The very day the Transfer Agreement was sealed, August 7, Samuel Untermyer returned to America to rally Jews, non-Jews, and loyal Zionists to boycott. On August 11, German chargé d'affaires in Washington Rudolf Leitner brought Cordell Hull a *New York Times* transcript of Untermyer's national "call to boycott" broadcast, and protested in the sternest terms. Hull was himself a strong advocate, perhaps the architect, of FDR's noninterference policy. But by now even Hull had been caught up in the national outrage and answered Leitner with a rather unrestrained castigation of Nazism. He recited a litany of German atrocities, asking what Leitner realistically expected anyone to do. "The best remedy," Hull said, "will be for the German people or the German government or both to stop whatever may be their activities against the Jews. [Only] This will enable us to make suitable appeals to discontinue the boycott." [12]

Convinced the Prague Congress would not be canceled, the Reich began a sequence of highly visible warning shots to convince it to abstain from the anti-German crusade. Pressure on the German Zionists escalated. Leaders were suddenly arrested, meetings were inexplicably broken up, and ZVfD records were arbitrarily confiscated. On August 16, in a public appeal, the ZVfD's newspaper *Juedische Rundschau* declared, "It is not the duty of the Congress to declare war, but in a Zionist spirit, through practical measures to bring about spiritual encouragement and relief in the situation. . . . This is why German Zionists urged that the present Congress should not be held. . . . Since, however, the Congress was not postponed, it is the duty of the . . . [Zionist] Executive to establish a spirit of creative responsibility . . . to enable mass Jewish emigration from Germany to Palestine." [13]

Of course, no one even tried to organize Zionist elections in Germany. When it became obvious that the Congress might declare war against Hitler, German Zionists decided against sending an appointive delegation. Even German Zionists wholly unconnected with the Congress were beseeched to leave Prague prior to the opening session to avoid any mistake. Although newspaper accounts around the world repeatedly emphasized the German Zionist nonpresence, in truth, Martin Rosenbluth would secretly attend as the ZVfD observer and do his best to curtail boycott activities. [14]

The ZVfD's highly visible disassociation from Prague did not matter to the Nazis. On August 17, Hitler's personal newspaper, *Volkischer Beobachter*, published its lead article on the Eighteenth Zionist Congress, written by Alfred Rosenberg, Hitler's philosopher and the NSDAP's chief foreign policy official. Insisting that the boycott was coordinated by "Zionists," Rosenberg promised retribution against all those "guilty of conspiracies and against all their accomplices"—a clear reference to German Zionists. The fact that Lord Melchett had assumed a renewed leadership position in the Zionist movement and was expected to play a major role at Prague was proof to Rosenberg that "the London castle of the Zionist leader, Melchett, is actually the center of world Jewry for the anti-German boycott." In an unmistakable warning, Rosenberg wrote, "Germany will watch Congress developments closely in the conviction that while the real intentions will not be disclosed in the public speeches, secret resolutions will be adopted along the lines laid down by *The Protocols of the Elders of Zion*. . . . Actual decisions will result from secret discussions between gentlemen from New York, Amsterdam, Paris, and London." [15]

Germania, the Catholic newspaper controlled by Deputy Chancellor Franz von Papen, similarly warned, "We shall have to follow the dealings of this Congress closely, for international Jewry, as we have often experienced in the past, will not itself openly join battle, but will make other forces work for it." [16]

New York Times correspondent Hugh Jedell summed up German apprehension in a report filed from Berlin on August 18: "The Zionist Congress . . . is probably of more lively interest to the new Germany than was the World Economic Conference." Jedell explained that the Prague convention held the power to stimulate the anti-Nazi boycott. [17] What would be decided by the Zionists in Prague would probably have more impact upon Germany's economic recovery than all the trade accords the Reich could negotiate. And Germans knew it.

In response to the accusatory columns of Alfred Rosenberg and other Nazi spokesmen, *Juedische Rundschau* published an uncommonly defiant editorial denying that the Prague conference would join the boycott but explaining why those same conferences would almost certainly denounce the Nazi ethic. "Surely not even the Nazis expect us to agree that the Jews are an inferior race," *Juedische Rundschau* declared. The Nazis promptly suspended *Juedische Rundschau* for six months. [18] This was yet another warning shot. The Zionist privilege in Germany could be rescinded with the scrawl of a pen.

The constitution of the Zionist Organization called for its General Council to convene just before each Congress. This council, commonly called the Actions Committee, was comprised of several dozen officials, proportionately drawn from the various parties. The Actions Committee's duty was to decide all policy, including the management of the Congress itself.

If the Revisionists were allowed their minority rights on the Actions Committee, they would demand that the Congress debate the German crisis and vote on the boycott. And they would block Mapai's supremacy on other issues. Mapai could count on the support of substantial elements of the General Zionist and Radical Zionist parties. But other groups, particularly the religious Mizrachi, could be expected to align with the Revisionists to stymie Mapai intentions. So Mapai knew it was imperative to exclude the Revisionists from their rightful place on the Actions Committee. [19]

The Actions Committee's first session was scheduled for late on August 15. That same day, while en route to Prague, Vladimir Jabotinsky received notice that he would not be granted a visa to enter Czechoslovakia. The alleged reason: Jabotinsky did not request his visa through the Eighteenth Zionist Congress Bureau, which automatically issued them. Instead, in a deliberate act of disassociation, Jabotinsky applied through normal consular channels. It was refused, allegedly as an oversight. In truth, the Czech Home

Office feared Jabotinsky's presence might lead to violence.[20] Consequently, Jabotinsky could neither assume his place on the Actions Committee nor lead his supporters through the political obstacle course Mapai was planning.

Jabotinsky's supporters quickly demanded their seats on the Actions Committee nonetheless and began pressuring the Czech Foreign Ministry to grant the visa.[21] Mapai countered by trying to cancel the Actions Committee altogether through their coalition majority. At the last minute, Leo Motzkin, chairman of the Actions Committee, was forced to announce a postponement of the opening meeting. The General Zionists, however, broke with Mapai on the issue, reasoning that Mapai's hegemony could eventually extend to other parties as well.[22] The General Zionists, controlling almost 25 percent of the delegates, could have teamed up with the Revisionists and Mizrachi to overwhelm Mapai's unilateral move. So Mapai backed down.

On August 17, at 4:30 P.M., the Actions Committee finally met. Chaim Weizmann, a General Zionist, boycotted the session and requested his name be removed from the Congress speaker list altogether because the Revisionists had been allowed to participate.[23] After two hours of preliminaries, Revisionist Joseph Schechtman demanded that the Congress concentrate on the German Jewish crisis, emphasizing that "the Congress must not remain silent on the boycott."[24]

Nahum Goldmann, Radical Zionist and Geneva conference organizer, agreed that the German Jewish crisis would have to be raised, probably in a special session, but that the boycott itself should not be mentioned.[25] Goldmann, like Wise, wanted the worldwide declaration to be pronounced at Geneva and nowhere else.

Dr. Arthur Ruppin, one of the principal transfer negotiators, insisted that "at this Congress we cannot confine ourselves to reproaching the German government for its sins against the German Jews. Our criticism must be coupled with a constructive scheme [for developing Palestine]. The relation between the two must be well balanced. We must not forget that the execution of any constructive plan presupposes goodwill on the part of the German government. . . . If we fail to find the right solution, the German government will solve the Jewish problem in its own one-sided way."[26]

The Actions Committee finally decided to discuss the issue of German Jewry at a special session. But any specific plans or resolutions would be made by a special "German Commission," which would make a decision *for* the Congress.[27] The Revisionists accepted this because under the rules, if they disagreed with the commission majority, they could submit a minority report and insist upon a floor vote to see which was acceptable. This was the best method of ensuring that Revisionist boycott demands would finally confront the delegates.

The decisions to discuss the German question openly and appoint a commission were preliminary victories for the effort to mobilize the Zionist movement against Nazi Germany. But Mapai leaders at the August 17 Actions Committee session felt the most urgent question was not Hitler; it was Jabotinsky. They wanted to quash all discussion and action against the Nazis and instead devote all energies to combating Revisionism. This in mind, Mapai leader David Ben-Gurion recited a list of Jewish Palestinian "acts of terror" and demanded a second special commission on the assassination of Arlosoroff—even before the murder trial in Jerusalem concluded. Stephen Wise, representing the American Zionists on the Actions Committee, needed Revisionists to enforce the boycott within the Zionist movement; and, of course, so long as the Revisionists remained in the Zionist power structure, Weizmann would not accept the presidency. So Wise counseled against any such investigative commission. Recriminations, said Wise, had no business at a Congress with such important matters to decide.[28] Nazism was the crisis, not Revisionism.

Then Berl Katznelson, one of Ben-Gurion's closest associates, asked to be recognized for an urgent motion. "I regret not taking part in the discussion about the situation of German Jews," said Katznelson. "I felt, however, that I could not participate in a discussion about German Jewry before delivering the message which my friends from Palestine have entrusted to me." Katznelson then read a prepared statement: "The murder of Arolosoroff has revealed to us the terrible abyss that confronts the Zionist Organization. Thorough investigation has confirmed our fears. . . . Within one of the parties which belong to the Zionist Organization, within the Revisionist party, there exist terrorist groups. I emphasize: *groups*, not *a* group.[29]

"The very existence of such groups is a heavy blow to the Zionist movement, to its moral character, and to its political driving power. The existence of this impurity in our midst is a national disgrace, a betrayal of the culture of our generations. . . . It is the foremost duty of the Zionist movement . . . to extirpate this evil from our midst before it begins to destroy our hopes."[30]

Hours of vicious and accusatory debate ensued, but the decision to appoint an anti-Revisionist commission was postponed.[31] The Revisionists had survived, and their anti-Hitler program still had a chance in a floor fight.

But Mapai might yet prevent that floor fight if only somehow the Revisionists could be excluded from the Congress *presidium*. The presidium was the ruling coalition panel created by the Actions Committee. Seated at the front of the Congress hall, it was empowered to decide parliamentary points, recognize speakers, and rule on agenda questions. Normally, the presidium was constituted according to relative party strength.

So a renewed smear campaign against Revisionism was waged by Mapai leaders in the anterooms and newspapers of Prague. The hope was to sway delegates to support Mapai's demand that the Revisionists be excluded from the presidium. Ben-Gurion told reporters that Revisionism was nothing more than "Hitlerite pseudo-Zionism" and that Labor's struggle against it was "a fight for life and death in the strongest sense of the word."[32]

The public denigrations were picked up by wire services and printed in the newspapers of the world. The Jew-vs.-Jew antagonism disheartened Jews and sympathetic non-Jews alike. Many around the world had looked to the Zionist Congress as a major event in the war against the Third Reich, only to now witness a spectacle of recriminations.[33] Zionist priorities became self-evident. And only Germany took pleasure in the display, since the war against Revisionism was for all intents and purposes a surrogate war against the anti-Nazi boycott.

To balance the public perceptions of the Congress as a convention of squabbles devoid of concrete action, Mapai decided to present openly its proposals to help German Jewry. Mapai's plan was a synthesis of noble long-range hopes and immediate short-term realities attainable through the still secret Transfer Agreement. It called for the salvation of approximately 250,000 German Jews over the next ten years. This figure represented about half the Jews still in Germany. The presumption was that half of German Jewry had already lost all means of economic survival with no hope of regaining a livelihood.

The plan worked this way: Approximately a thousand Jewish families could be settled in Palestine at once. The rest of the quarter million would quickly emigrate to other countries, especially the United States, which for years had enjoyed a virtually unused German immigration quota. As more land was purchased and developed in Palestine, a percentage of the Jews who had emigrated to other countries would emigrate again, this time to their final destination, Eretz Yisrael. This long-term, two-stage emigration to Palestine would take place over the next decade and ultimately account for between 60,000 and 100,000 of the quarter million emigrants envisioned. The remainder—60 to 75 percent—would assimilate into the first-stage receiver nations.[34]

Mapai's plan, formulated by Dr. Arthur Ruppin with the Transfer Agreement in mind, was a sudden open admission that Palestine simply could not solve the entire German Jewish crisis. The most it could do was absorb a thousand families at once, and unspecified thousands more over a period of years. Of course, the unmentioned aspect of the Mapai program was that Ruppin's plan would actively help only those German Jews willing to commit themselves to Palestine as a *final destination*.[35]

While dressed up with huge numbers, Mapai's plan was seen by many as little more than an amorphous rescue notion. It added almost nothing to the thousand emergency immigration certificates granted by the British government that spring. And the Mapai plan was not particularly fulfilling in a Zionist sense because the protracted two-stage immigration scheme could be expected to fail as European-cultured German Jews simply restarted their lives in first-stage countries and forgot about any commitment to Palestine five or ten years later. However, Ruppin knew that all German Jewish emigrant deposits in the proposed Liquidation Bank were to be reimbursed only at the moment of ultimate arrival in Palestine. If out of a quarter million German Jews, only 1,000 families arrived in Palestine immediately to collect reimbursements, and no more than 50,000 to 100,000 came to collect over the span of a decade, the transfer would carry immeasurable added significance to Palestinian development. Ruppin's plan meant that few transferred assets would be repaid, and what was repaid would be stretched over many years.

The Revisionists immediately rejected Mapai's concept as too little for too few over too long a period of time. Revisionists instead called for all-out political and economic isolation of the Hitler regime until either it rescinded its anti-Semitic terror—which was unlikely—or Jews were allowed to depart for Palestine with all of their belongings and possessions so they could properly rebuild their lives.[36] The Revisionist plan was militant and defensive, yet Palestine-oriented. In fact, it was simply the common man's plan spoken of throughout the world by Zionist and non-Zionist, Jew and non-Jew: combatting Hitlerism with all political and economic weapons while at the same time bringing the persecuted Jews to Palestine.

On Friday, August 18, when the Actions Committee met to reconsider the presidium question, the rival parties were again deadlocked, primarily because Mizrachi continued to support the Revisionists' right to participate in the movement. But before the Friday session was over, Mapai forces had succeeded in creating the special Commission on Palestinian Terrorism. The new commission was designed to indict the Revisionist party wholesale for Arlosoroff's murder and sentence the party's hundred thousand worldwide members to an ultimatum: renunciation of Revisionism or permanent expulsion from the Zionist movement.[37] Dusk brought the sabbath and prevented further debate on the presidium.

But during the Sunday session, August 20, the presidium question was again fiercely contested. The Revisionist role had by then become underscored. Late that day the Actions Committee learned of the American Jewish Congress decision to formally join Untermyer's boycott movement. A cable sent by Untermyer to Louis Lipsky, American leader of the General Zionist party, specifically called upon officials to read a "boycott manifesto" to the Prague delegates and urge a resolution joining the economic war.[38]

The "boycott manifesto" received by Lipsky was specifically phrased to appeal to the General Zionist delegates because they had the potential of teaming up with the Revisionists, the Mizrachi, and the Radical Zionists to defeat Mapai's staunch anti-boycott policy. The manifesto contained profuse praise for General Zionist chief Chaim Weizmann as "the greatest statesmanly Jewish leader of our generation, and eloquent reminders that "the present Congress is amongst the most important in Palestine's history." Untermyer's manifesto assured that "Germany is being kept uninformed about world opinion. Boycott is the only language they understand. Only an economic collapse will open the eyes of the German people." Most importantly, Unter-myer stressed that boycott and Palestine-oriented rescue were not mutually exclusive: "The boycott logically goes hand in hand with the movement that I heartily support: to settle in Palestine as many Jews as the limited pos-sibilities and the territory of the land can absorb."[39]

Untermyer ended with a reminder: "If world Jewry and the civilized world will in the meanwhile not stop, and [instead] tolerate Germany's medi-eval crusade, then global anti-Semitism will be encouraged, . . . then your only chance of helping your persecuted brothers will be lost.[40] Whether this manifesto, which essentially advocated the Revisionist strategy, would be read aloud to the Congress delegates and its message then voted on was a decision for the presidium.

The Sunday Actions Committee lasted well past midnight. Mapai would not agree to seat any Revisionists. The Revisionists used their minority power to block the formation of any presidium without them. Finally, the deadlocked session simply broke up. The argument-weary Actions Commit-tee members returned to their hotel rooms to catch a few hours of sleep before the Congress officially opened Monday evening—for the first time in its history, without a presidium.[41] As the leaders of the Zionist movement fell asleep, just before dawn Monday, no one could predict what would happen.

32. The Eighteenth Zionist Congress Opens

SEVEN HILLS inhabited by Gothic cathedrals, Romanesque monuments, and regal halls have made Prague "the city of a hundred spires." A network of bridges spanning the Vltana River link the city's left and right banks. On the left, the medieval Hradcany Castle, towering above a vast complex of gardens, parks, and gray-brown churches. On the right, the congested "old city," with its narrow streets, clock towers, and art galleries.

Jews had always represented a major cultural and economic segment of Bohemia. Prague's Althneuschul, the oldest existing synagogue in Europe, was completed in 1270. The synagogue's narrow interior, graced by rib-vaulted ceilings and high windows, boasted a large, ornate banner of friend-ship bestowed in 1648 by the German monarch Frederick III. A Jewish Town Hall was erected in Prague's Jewish district during the sixteenth century; a large clock featuring Hebrew numerals was added in 1754. Split between Czech and German identities, the Prague Jewish community was known for its illustrious rabbis, scholars, and artists.[1]

By 1930, Prague, with its Jewish population of 40,000, was respected as a bastion of Jewish rights and Zionist activism. Czechoslovakia's first president, a Catholic named Thomas Masaryk, felt it his Christian duty to help obliterate anti-Semitism. He enjoyed close contacts within the American Zionist movement, including Justice Louis Brandeis and Stephen Wise. Under Masaryk, Czechoslovakia had opened its arms to fleeing German Jews.[2]

The Congress was not the only Zionist event in Prague during late August. The Jewish athletic contest, the Maccabi Games, headed by Lord Melchett, was to be held in Prague, as was the Women's International Zionist Organization convention, the General Zionist party convention, and the Jewish Agency General Council assembly. The streets of Prague were bedecked with pennants and flags emblazoned with the Star of David. Blue and white bunting was everywhere. Large signs along major thoroughfares welcomed over 10,000 Zionist visitors in six languages—with Prague's traditional German conspicuously absent.[3] As the sun came up on "the city of a hundred spires" on August 21, 1933, it was the most logical, hospitable place in Europe for a decisive international Zionist uprising against the Third Reich.

All afternoon, spectators and participants filed into Prague's massive Lucerno Concert Hall. Undercover police guarded against threatened Nazi disruption. As spectators entered the great hall, they saw a huge portrait of Theodor Herzl hanging above the stage, framed by Czechoslovakian and Zionist flags. Beneath Herzl's portrait, just next to the speaker's podium, an empty chair draped in black signified the loss of Chaim Arlosoroff. By 8:00 P.M., about 5,000 people had entered, with more thousands outside unable to squeeze in. All seats, and even aisle standing space, were occupied.[4]

The atmosphere was tense; the expected clash between Mapai and Revisionism was the topic of conversation throughout the audience. Shortly after 8:00 P.M., Actions Committee chairman Leo Motzkin appeared. To a round of applause, Motzkin led members of the Actions Committee, all in tuxedos, to their seats on stage. Then David Ben-Gurion, now representing the greatest power in the Zionist movement, led his Mapai delegation to their chairs. As they walked, they enjoyed a long ovation from Labor's vast supporters in the hall.[5]

Other VIPs were about to walk onstage when suddenly a cheering was heard from outside the hall. The audience turned around to see. It was Jabotinsky. His supporters had successfully pressured the Foreign Ministry, and his visa was finally issued. Jabotinsky took his seat, buoyed by the hearty cheers of Revisionist supporters throughout the hall.[6]

When the tumult subsided, the inaugural ceremony continued. The audience rose as Zionist Organization president Nahum Sokolow led a diplomatic corps, which included Masaryk's personal representative, the Polish ambassador in Prague, a British embassy official on behalf of Britain's Mandate, and Greek and Spanish diplomats representing the League of Nations. The Zionist Organization, having been accorded quasi-governmental status by the League of Nations, was not just an association of activists; it was the officially recognized Jewish-government-in-waiting. In fact, virtually the entire future Jewish government was at that moment waiting in Lucerno Hall. Applause continued until the diplomatic corps had all taken their seats onstage.[7]

Sokolow then gaveled three times, bringing an immediate hush to the hall. He declared the Eighteenth Zionist Congress officially called to order. This brought a resounding cheer from the delegates. Sokolow then nodded to the choral director, who led a choir of refugees, formerly of the Berlin Opera House, in a short program of Hebew songs followed by Handel's Hallelujah Chorus. Each diplomat then offered a brief greeting, followed by a special statement of solidarity from Neville Laski of the Board of Deputies. His remarks provoked a long ovation.[8] If the traditionally anti-Zionist forces Laski represented were dropping their opposition, it was indeed a new era for Zionism.

Preliminary ceremony out of the way, Dr. Sokolow returned to the podium for his keynote address. To avoid German, the traditional Congress language, Dr. Sokolow alternated between English, French, Hebrew, and occasionally Yiddish. When he mentioned Chaim Arlosoroff, the entire assemblage spontaneously rose in a short tribute of silence.[9] However, the real power of his message was a crystallization of the historic choice facing the world.

"We come together on this occasion in a time of tribulation and suffering," Dr. Sokolow began. "Emancipation has been shaken at its foundations, . . . thrown into confusion as by an earthquake. We are suddenly faced with the *ruins* of Jewish emancipation in one of the greatest countries in Europe."[10]

His voice shaking in emphasis, Dr. Sokolow continued: "The falsehood of assimilation and mimicry endeavored to make our people believe that anti-Semitism was a passing episode which would be quickly overcome, a bogey to frighten children. . . . It is a bitter irony that the assimilationist movement should have been strongest in Germany." He suddenly stopped and exclaimed in English, "Germany of Goethe, Schiller, and Lessing, where are you now!"[11]

Speaking more to the Jews of the world than to the Zionists in the hall, the elderly Sokolow then asked a dramatic question: "Jewish people! How long can we go on like this? Time presses, the ground gives way beneath our feet. Whatever it is not too late to save must now be saved. . . . Zionism must in these days become the concern of the entire Jewish people and of the human race. . . . The maintenance of the status quo has become impossible. . . . How do you picture safeguarding the future existence of the Jewish people, which is now at the mercy of the ax? And to the civilized world, I ask, shall this nation ever and forever be in vagabondage, shall our people ever and forever shift about, . . . yearning to find rest, and never find it? Is this not a situation which mocks the most elementary conceptions of humanity and civilization?"[12]

"What then is to be done?" he demanded. "If it is impossible to restore the refugees to their country, or to receive them into another country, then the country of their ancestors must be given to them. Nothing is more straightforward or more just. That is the problem which faces the international political world." Emotionally answering his own question, Sokolow exclaimed, "The idea of Zionism as the solution of the Jewish question must now again rise before the world like a new daylight!"[13]

He conceded that a grand scale of action was now needed. "Two ways are open for the solution of this problem, one easy and one difficult. The easier way is to get excited, to protest and argue. The more arduous way is that of increasing tenfold the work of the Palestine Foundation Fund and the Jewish National Fund." He then stood down from the podium to a thunderous standing ovation.[14]

Mapai leader Berl Katznelson closed the inaugural session with a stirring eulogy of Arlosoroff, calling him the "young and gifted leader upon whom the entire Zionist movement laid its hopes. . . . The entire Congress must mourn him. . . . The bullet which wounded Arlosoroff also wounded the heart of the entire movement."[15]

The delegates had been moved by Nahum Sokolow, crying out for a solution of the German tragedy and its implications for Palestine. But Mapai wanted the delegates to know they had an equally pressing crisis to consider—the implications of Arlosoroff's murder for the Zionist movement. As the ceremonial opening of the Congress ended, the delegates still did not know which of those two issues would predominate. That question would be answered during the next days at the working sessions, when Mapai and Revisionist forces would vie for which crisis was the most important.

33. The First Leak

THE POMP and passion of the Eighteenth Zionist Congress' opening session belied its internecine undercurrents. On August 21, prior to Dr.

Sokolow's opening gavel, the Mapai and Revisionist camps had each gathered to review tactics.

The Revisionist strategy counterposed a nine-point plan for Palestine addressing a range of Zionist issues.[1] But Vladimir Jabotinsky himself understood that political triumph in the days ahead was impossible. So at the Revisionist strategy conference, Jabotinsky told his followers to look beyond the Prague convention. He fully expected Mapai to successfully isolate Revisionism. But, he predicted, after two years of Mapai-dominated leadership, the Zionist movement would be utterly frustrated. "The Congress of 1933," he declared, "is paving the way for a Revisionist victory [at the next Congress] in 1935." For this reason, Jabotinsky commanded his followers to refrain from any emotional outbursts during the proceedings—unless the Laborites tried to convert the Congress into a kangaroo court for indicting and expelling the Revisionists for Arlosoroff's assassination.[2]

While the Revisionists expected little immediate success for their Zionist goals, they did demand immediate action on the Hitler crisis. In a moving speech, Jabotinsky insisted that all energies be expended to force the Congress to join the boycott movement. Nothing less than a "merciless fight" would be acceptable, cried Jabotinsky. "The present Congress is duty bound to put the Jewish problem in Germany before the entire world. . . . We are conducting a war with murderers. . . . [We must] destroy, destroy, destroy them—not only with the boycott, but politically, supporting all existing forces against them to isolate Germany from the civilized world."[3]

That same afternoon, as Jabotinsky was exhorting his followers to postpone their political grievances in favor of the war against Nazism, Labor leader David Ben-Gurion, speaking to the Mapai strategy conference, demanded that his supporters do the opposite. The most important task of the moment, Ben-Gurion declared, was to cleanse the movement of Revisionism and extend Mapai's political borders to cover the entire Zionist Organization. The Labor party, controlling 44 percent of the delegates, *was* the movement, Ben-Gurion said. This new reality, Mapai leaders explained, required a new constitution to enable the Zionist Executive to expel "undisciplined" groups and/or deprive them of their rightful share of immigration certificates. Ben-Gurion proposed giving Revisionists the Inquisitional choice of pledging allegiance to the new Mapai-dominated organization or leaving the movement altogether.[4]

After their strategy conferences, Revisionists and Mapai attended the inaugural Congress session. But the peril dramatized by the words of Dr. Sokolow did not mitigate their factional conflict. No sooner had the ceremony concluded then the Actions Committee huddled for another emergency session to form a presidium. Committee members bickered all night, with the Revisionists refusing to allow a debate on the Arlosoroff assassination, insisting instead on debating the German crisis. This only redoubled

Mapai's unwillingness to allow the Revisionists a place on the presidium, which would ultimately decide such questions. The Actions Committee's all-night meeting again ended without a decision. The deadlock meant that the Congress would have to function without a ruling coalition.[5]

Several hours after the Actions Committee again broke up in frustration, the Tuesday-morning August 22 session of the Congress convened. Working sessions would be held in Prague's City Council chamber. Weizmann again refused to attend because the Revisionists still had not been purged. And when Dr. Sokolow gaveled the Tuesday-morning session to order, the delegates could plainly see that no presidium had been formed. For want of a better solution, Sokolow ran the session.[6]

Without a presidium, agenda questions could not be decided, so the most pressing issues were not discussed. Instead, the session's main feature was a speech by Professor Selig Brodetsky, a General Zionist and the Zionist Organization's liaison man to the British government. Brodetsky pleaded for Palestine's gates to be opened, asserting that hundreds of thousands of Jews could and should be absorbed into Palestine during the coming few years. Thereafter, within a decade, millions of Jews could live and thrive in Israel.[7]

The whole subject of "how many, how fast" was quite controversial among the delegates. Brodetsky's notion of "hundreds of thousands" as opposed to Mapai's "one thousand family plan" put Mapai on notice that their two-stage protracted emigration plan was insufficient. The crowd cheered Brodetsky's words, which resembled the Revisionist point of view. But to avoid any hint of General Zionist sympathy for the Revisionists, Brodetsky added a eulogy for Arlosoroff. And the eulogy led to a reprimand. "This Congress," warned Brodetsky, "must once and for all settle the problem of unity of Zionist efforts. Unity of Zionist efforts does not mean that all Zionists shall think alike, but it can mean and must mean that all Zionists act alike." Here Brodetsky alluded to the coming Mapai move to force Revisionists to renounce Revisionism or suffer banishment from the movement. In a telling defense, Professor Brodetsky declared, "It is not an Inquisition, but discipline for which I ask."[8]

Following Professor Brodetsky's speech, the Actions Committee went into yet another session, this one to discuss the ultimate recommendations of the special Commission on German Jews. As expected, disagreements dominated. By late that Tuesday morning, the special Commission on German Jews joined the other Zionist deliberative bodies and declared a deadlock. The Revisionists would be allowed to present their minority position to the full Congress for a vote.[9] The commission's conflicting recommendations were to be presented at the Congress session that Tuesday afternoon, but with no presidium to rule on agenda questions, the scheduled German debate was postponed.[10]

The Tuesday-afternoon session was confined to more public speechmaking and more closed-door political haggling over the formation of a presidium. Despite pleas by peacemakers and intermediaries, all compromises were rejected. Yet unless the presidium deadlock was broken soon, the question would be forced to the floor.[11]

While virtually all important Congress functions on August 22 had been frozen by factional conflict, the editors of *Vossische Zeitung* in Berlin were reviewing an extraordinary piece of information. Their Eighteenth Zionist Congress coverage featured a wrap-up of developments, but added to the Prague summary was a leaked report that a trust company organized in Berlin had successfully negotiated a transfer of Jewish assets to Palestine. According to the report, the agreement would allow Jews to purchase up to RM 3 million of German machinery and receive credit for the sales in Palestinian accounts. Furthermore, emigrating German Zionists could transfer an additional RM 3 million capital to Palestine in cash.[12]

Vossische Zeitung's transfer item, however, was slightly incorrect. It was unlikely that any authoritative Reich governmental or ZVfD source leaked the news because the item confused machinery purchases and emigration assets as separate matters. It is more likely that the news was leaked by unofficial Nazi sources in Germany or dissident Zionists in Prague. In either case, the delegates would soon have to decide one way or the other: boycott Germany, or purchase Nazi merchandise to facilitate emigration and an assets transfer. The *Vossische Zeitung* article would appear in the next day's editions.

The Wednesday-afternoon August 23 session was as embroiled as any other. No presidium was available to decide agenda questions, especially the burning issue of whether the Arlosoroff assassination or the Hitler menace would be the focal point of debate. In frustration, the religious Mizrachi party introduced a motion for a floor vote to bypass the Actions Committee deadlock, allowing delegates to directly elect a presidium with equal representation for all parties. This motion was blocked by Mapai as being irregular. Mizrachi refused to accept Mapai's veto, forcing a vote on the very question of voting. This maneuver Mapai could not block. The vote on the question to vote would resolve the presidium fiasco once and for all.[13]

As the vote was getting under way in Prague, news of the Transfer Agreement had spread all over Germany, and most major German papers were carrying the item.[14] But those newspapers had not arrived in Prague by the afternoon vote. So the Transfer Agreement was not yet a factor. The vote on the presidium question would be a contest strictly on the issue of Revisionist isolation versus Mapai domination.

All Mapai delegates of course voted to defeat Mizrachi's motion. Mizrachi and Revisionist delegates voted in favor. The General Zionists and Radical Zionist delegates, however, were divided along intraparty lines. A tense Congress waited as the 300 delegate votes were counted one by one. Not until the last moment was the outcome clear: 149 votes for the Mizrachi-Revisionist motion, 151 against. The motion to vote was defeated by two votes.[15]

Immediately thereafter, Mapai forces nominated Leo Motzkin to become Congress president and oversee personally the formation of a presidium. Mizrachi and the Revisionists immediately declared they would not participate. And that afternoon, Motzkin and Mapai leaders formed a presidium mostly of Labor Zionists, with token General Zionist and Radical Zionist representation.[16] The Eighteenth Zionist Congress would henceforth be run by Mapai.

News of the Transfer Agreement had not yet reached the eyes and ears of delegates in Prague. But the ZVfD in Berlin was quite aware that within hours the news would become common knowledge around the world. To help shape the thrust of the revelation, the ZVfD issued its own press release during the afternoon of August 23. The release confirmed that an agreement had indeed been reached between the ZVfD and Economics Minister Kurt Schmitt allowing transfer to Palestine of RM 3 million in Jewish assets via merchandise sales. The ZVfD hoped its announcement would be hailed as an important breakthrough.[17]

At the same time in Prague, Dr. Arthur Ruppin told reporters that he would present the Congress delegates with an explanation of the agreement reached with the Third Reich. He would say little more than that it did in fact provide for the transfer of RM 3 million—about $1 million—through the purchase of German goods via the Anglo-Palestine Bank. Between the German papers arriving in Prague, news of the ZVfD's statement, and Dr. Ruppin's announcement, the entire Congress was by nightfall blazing with speculation about the possibilities and ramifications of a Reich-Zionist transfer agreement.[18]

Although the Transfer Agreement was sealed on August 7, 1933, with verbal commitments, the fine technical points weren't completed until August 22, even as the Congress was in session. By the morning of August 24, the news had reached the newspapers of all Europe, America, and Palestine.[19] Zionist delegates in Prague entered the Thursday, August 24 morning session of the Congress anxious to know more. Each had his own notion of whether the agreement represented a betrayal of the Jewish people or a daring move to save the German Jews and create a national wellspring for Eretz Yisrael.

With a Mapai-controlled presidium now in place, the twice-delayed session on the Hitler crisis could now take place. Three major agenda items were scheduled. First, a report by Sokolow summarizing "the state of the Jewish people" around the world—a traditional address that had been postponed over the question of how vocally to condemn German persecution. The second presentation would explain Ruppin's proposed two-stage immigration scheme and the Transfer Agreement. The day would end with a Congress decision on commission resolutions committing the Zionist movement either to fight Hitler, or work with him. The Revisionists pinned their hopes on this final event; if somehow they could present their minority report and force a debate on the merits, they believed they could sway the consciences of the delegates.

This was also the day the Nazis were listening with keenest attention. Nazi officials had unmistakably warned: The sterility of the Congress' German resolution, the uncompromising suppression of any boycott or protest mandates, and the complete absence of any hostile demonstrations against Germany—these would be the prerequisites for future cooperation.

So in his speech, Sokolow did his best to sound defiant yet avoid affronting the Reich. His references to Germany were oblique: "The tragedy of the Jewish Diaspora has been revealed in Germany in a manner that is without precedent for centuries. . . . Not only German Jewry, but the whole of the Jewish people is attacked when one speaks of the inferiority of the Jewish race, and when Jewish honor is degraded in so extreme a fashion. . . . It is impossible for us to let anti-Semitism display its fury without our energetic, emphatic protest."[20]

However, Sokolow quickly added, "It is not our task to influence or criticize the internal developments of the German people, which have gravely suffered through the war and its consequences. We are not gathered here to criticize any one nation or any one state. It is not part of the program . . . of the Zionist Organization to break its [shepherd's] staff over this or that state organization, this or that economic system. Our duty is to speak the truth."[21]

On the other hand, Sokolow, using the words of Justice Brandeis, cried out to a cheering throng, "The Jews will never forget and never forgive Germany's insult. . . . Jews will respect ancient Spain more than present Germany because it is better to have a complete exodus of Jews than be degraded in this manner." The cheers continued as Sokolow ended with the rousing but empty warning, "There is now no capitulation, no surrender, no yielding words!"[22]

Such oratory walked a tightrope between the expectant Jewish world and the attentive Third Reich. But if the delegates had any delusions, the next speech, the anxiously awaited report of Dr. Ruppin, changed their minds. Dr. Ruppin's first words were these: "My address on the adaptation of German Jews to Palestinian life, and their settlement therein, will lead you down from the high peaks of political debate into the low valleys of economic problems."[23]

A procession of economic statistics followed. Ruppin detailed the numbers of persecuted German Jews out of work, profession by profession, and explained why they held no hope for any other livelihood under the Nazi regime. He then outlined the emigration plan. Two hundred thousand Jews would leave Germany for a variety of nations. Because of water shortages and economic unreadiness, Palestine could accept only 1,000 families now—about 4,000 persons. Only 50,000 to 100,000 more could come over the next decade.[24] "I am afraid I must disappoint all those," said Dr. Ruppin, "who had hoped to say that Palestine would absorb just so many German immigrants in just so much time. . . . The number of German Jews who can be taken into Palestine depends on the capital which they bring with them and on the sums which are contributed to that end by world Jewry. It is very difficult at the present moment to say anything about these factors."[25]

It was all sounding very fiscal for an exodus. And, of course, Dr. Ruppin was not mentioning that German Jewish assets would not be reimbursed unless the German Jews actually reached Palestine's shore. Yet he did make one point eminently clear: "We shall of course help only those Jews who want to go to Palestine. Emigrants choosing some other country are of course perfectly free to do so."[26]

The burning question of the Transfer Agreement was then summed up in barely a sentence or two. He merely explained that the question of German Jewish capital held great promise because an emigration agreement had been reached with the Reich. Who had arranged the agreement? "A few months ago," Dr. Ruppin said, "Mr. Sam Cohen had the wisdom to conduct with great care and diligence negotiations with the appropriate authorities in Germany . . . enabling Jews who wish to emigrate to Palestine to take with them part of their capital in the form of currency and merchandise. You will later on be informed of some of the details in this matter by the German Commission. On the basis of these negotiations, I feel . . . there will be no obstacles to an organized immigration of Jews from Germany along with permission to take a part of their property."[27]

Sam Cohen, attending the Congress as the alternate delegate from Luxembourg, did not hesitate to grant press interviews immediately afterward. Cohen confirmed that it was he who had convinced the Reich Economics Ministry during more than two months of negotiations to transfer German Jewish assets to Palestine.[28]

As the Thursday-morning session closed, things were still rather unclear. The newspaper items about the Transfer Agreement had been short and indistinct. Dr. Ruppin's "presentation" amounted to a fleeting, ambiguous mention, treating the issue as a proud achievement. And the entire arrangement had been successfully placed on the shoulders of none other than Mr. Sam Cohen. If a backlash occurred, Cohen would receive it. For his part, Cohen was willing to risk such a backlash. In exchange for providing the official Zionist institutions with deniability, Cohen was getting his hard-earned glory. Ironically, shortly thereafter, Dr. Ruppin saw to it that most drafts of his speech not already printed deleted any reference to the Transfer Agreement or Mr. Sam Cohen.[29] Dr. Ruppin apparently preferred history to believe he had never even mentioned the subject.

34. Showdown on Nazism

THURSDAY EVENING, August 24, brought the showdown on Nazi Germany. The Congress reconvened just a few hours after Dr. Ruppin's parenthetical transfer disclosure. The agreement's full import had not yet been realized. On first hearing, it sounded like a noble project. German Jewish emigrants would be allowed to take part of their assets to Palestine. Who could argue with such an arrangement? But the maze of provisos and special conditions attached to Haavara were as yet unknown. The magnitude of merchandise traffic, the cooperative economic ventures between the Reich and Palestinian sources, the planned Liquidation Bank, the facts about mandatory loans, the actual mechanism of transfer, and the financial dangers to the German Jews—these were all unknowns.

Besides, there wasn't time to delve into the serpentine issue of transfer. The big issue now facing the delegates was the ultimate resolution on Germany. The German Commission had formulated two majority resolutions, reciting the particular grievances and vested interests of Labor, General Zionists, Radical Zionists, and the Mizrachi. But these contradictory, taped-together resolutions were so devoid of affrontive language toward Germany, so transparently submissive,[1] and so disallowing of the anti-Nazi boycott that the Revisionists flaty rejected them. By blocking the unanimous approval required to adopt a resolution, the Revisionists forced their own boycott-mandating minority resolution to a floor debate and vote.

This was the moment Revisionists had waited for. If famed orator Vladimir Jabotinsky could evoke the passions of the delegates to vote for the minority resolution, that single moment of delegate disobedience would determine the fate of the Jewish war against Hitler. The anti-Nazi boycott was truly desired in the hearts of almost all Zionists; only the marshaling demands of a small group of Mapai-aligned leaders was staying a formal worldwide Zionist commitment to boycott. A Congress resolution would be the justification any Zionist body from Paris to Hong Kong needed to devote its resources to the fight. Of course, leading that worldwide act of Jewish self-defense would be Jabotinsky. This would reestablish the leadership of Revisionism within the movement.

Shortly after the session was gaveled to order, presidium chairman Leo Motzkin told the delegates that the Actions Committee had created a special Commission on German Jews to study the problem and prepare binding resolutions for the Congress.[2] The secretary then read the Mapai-backed majority resolution: "The Eighteenth Zionist Congress . . . considers it to be its duty to give expression . . . to its consternation at the tragic fate of the German Jews, and its indignation at the discrimination and degradation inflicted upon them. After a century of Jewish emancipation, . . . developments in present-day Germany have gone so far that half a million Jews have been deprived of their elementary human rights, [so far] that through the official sanctioning of racial prejudice the dignity and honor of the Jewish people are insulted, and [so far] that a policy and legislation are enacted whose fundamental principles must destroy the bases of existence of the Jewish people." [3]

Words of "consternation" characterized the remainder of the resolution. Soft nouns and verbs together with lofty introductory clauses were present throughout. When the resolution mentioned the "suppression of the rights of the Jews by all the powers of the State, unique in its scope and inconceivable in the twentieth century," it called the persecution a vindication "of the century-old Jewish question as depicted by . . . Theodor Herzl." [4]

The resolution ended with the sentence "In conjunction with our protests . . . the determined will of the Jewish people to rebuild its National Home . . . will represent the strongest proof of our national solidarity with the Jews of Germany." [5]

In other words, Hitler would be fought and the rights of the Jewish people would be preserved by one means and one means only: a Jewish State.

On the other hand, the Revisionists' minority resolution was nothing less than a boycott declaration, even though it cleverly avoided using the actual word *boycott* and even abstained from mentioning Germany by name. If the Revisionists had wanted a mere symbolic protest, they would have injected far more inflammatory language, but they earnestly wanted their resolution to win. They deliberately avoided trigger words that would make the resolution unacceptable to the average delegate, even the delegates of Mapai. Yet the phrasing conveyed the essence of an unmistakable commitment to economic war.

The Revisionist resolution stated: "The Congress welcomes the decision by the Jewish masses in all countries to use their purchasing power and their economic influence . . . as a factor of world trade for the benefit of the products of only those states which constitutionally recognize the principle of full equality for their Jewish citizens. The Congress is resolved to actively and energetically support the Zionist movement in extending and organizing every serious attempt to implement this just protective measure of the Jewish masses." [6]

But the Revisionist argument would never be heard. Motzkin announced that after the resolutions were presented, there would be no debate, this by decision of the Mapai-dominated presidium. Revisionist delegate M. Hoffman, founder of Betar, stood and objected. The Revisionists had a minority resolution, and according to the rules, this had to be openly discussed. Radical Zionist Nahum Goldmann answered against debate, asserting that the Commission on German Jews had already debated these resolutions back and forth for days without any progress. He urged that the Congress show unity by considering only the Mapai-based resolution.[7] For Goldmann, avoiding the Revisionist boycott declaration also preserved the illusory world boycott premiere that Wise's World Jewish Congress coveted.

Loud protest broke out as the Revisionists demanded a proper debate for their minority resolution. Amid the tumult, Jabotinsky was finally allowed to make a brief statement, actually a plea: Nazism was endangering the "securest foundations of the existence of all Jews the world over. . . . It must be regarded and treated as the affair not only of German Jews but of the entire Jewish people. It is therefore the duty of world Jewry to react with all means of just defense . . . against this attempt to destroy the Jewish people."[8] Beyond those few words, no other remarks were allowed.

Motzkin then read the Mapai resolution once more. His elocution was so stilted and so artificially exalted that Jabotinsky openly mocked him by caricaturing the words even as Motzkin spoke. At one point, in an exaggerated inflection, Jabotinsky recited a famous Latin quotation: *"Quousque tandem, Catilina, abutere patientia nostra?"* The quotation referred to Cicero's complaint against a noisome speech in the Senate by Roman archcriminal and conspirator Catiline—"Oh, please, Catiline, tell me how long you will continue to abuse our patience!"[9]

Motzkin ignored Jabotinsky's ridicule, completed his reading, and then ordered the assembly to vote. The Revisionists demonstratively refused to participate. In the uproar, perhaps just to achieve some sort of decision, all the weary non-Revisionist delegates—including Mizrachi—voted for the majority resolution—265 votes. Because the Revisionists refused to vote, no nays were registered.[10]

When the Revisionists then demanded that their minority resolution at least be put to vote, Motzkin and the presidium denied that motion as well.[11] This crushed the last Revisionist hope that perhaps both the innocuous majority resolution and the minority boycott resolution might both be adopted. At this the Congress lapsed into utter pandemonium.

The Revisionists in a group began a disruptive walkout. Threats and insults were shouted as the Mapai and Revisionist forces faced off. Ushers trying to intervene were themselves manhandled by angry Betarim. Jabotinsky and his wife were suddenly surrounded by a band of Mapai ruffians. One jostled Mrs. Jabotinsky, which brought a cadre of Betarim running. The battle was on, with shouts of scorn and praise for Jabotinsky flying as fast as punches and jabs. Only a squadron of police could separate the combatants. Both sides were ousted from the hall, and the doors locked. Jabotinsky was invited to press charges, but declined.[12]

In that hour of supreme opportunity, neither fist nor voice was raised to

Hitler. It was so much easier to fight each other. And so the moment of consolidation slipped past.

The Zionist Organization had failed. But the question remained: Would the Zionist *movement*—the men and women around the world who believed in the righteousness of both the Jewish nation and Jewish defense—would these people accept that failure? There was a time to be a Zionist, and there was a time to be a Jew. Only one issue could make any of them understand the difference. That issue was the recently revealed, but little understood, Transfer Agreement.

35. Interpellation

GERMANY liked what happened in Prague on August 24. Before the end of the day, the six-month suspension of the ZVfD's *Juedische Rundschau* had been lifted without explanation. As if to vindicate itself, the *Rundschau* quickly printed Congress coverage that explained, "Within the Congress it was of course only the small, but very militant Revisionist group which wanted to convert the Zionist Organization into a sort of fighting unit. This group . . . [proposed] a boycott resolution. . . . The Congress defeated this motion by a vast majority whereupon turbulent scenes ensued. . . . The Congress . . . clearly demonstrated that Zionism does not fight with weapons of that sort."[1]

Der Deutsche, the newspaper of the Nazi Labor Front, devoted most of its August 25 front page to a positive reaction to Dr. Ruppin's emigration plan. "The view of the Zionist Congress represents a proposal which is acceptable and interesting," *Der Deutsche* said. "Without doubt, Jews living in Germany have all kinds of opportunities to get along in the world, even outside Palestine. . . . The emigration of a large part of the Jews from Germany would, aside from other things, provide room for German unemployed." *Der Deutsche* added, however, that the question of just how much in Jewish assets could be transferred was still in debate.[2]

German newspapers took care to continue their scintillating leaks about the Transfer Agreement.[3] Many Jews around the world were beginning to understand what this Transfer Agreement was all about. It was more than just an assets transfer. It was an assets transfer *in exchange* for a merchandise market in Palestine.

Holders of German bonds, loans, and investments around the world, had all been implored to forgo the material gain of trafficking in Nazi wares to alleviate losses should the Reich economy collapse. But now the Zionist Organization was willing to betray the boycott in exchange for the same economic stimulus many in the world were being urged to relinquish. In the minds of boycotting Jews, the Transfer Agreement was an unthinkable breach of the boycott—dressed up with emigration, rationalized by the urgent need to develop Palestine, but nonetheless a great breach of the boycott.

Anti-transfer telegrams began arriving in Prague by Friday morning, August 25. *Paris*: "DEEPLY SURPRISED AT NEWS ABOUT RUPPIN'S NEGO-TIATIONS WITH NAZI GOVERNMENT RE EXPORT CAPITAL JEWISH EMI-GRANTS IN THE FORM OF NAZI GOODS STOP . . . AGREEMENT IS INAD-MISSIBLE BECAUSE IT COUNTERACTS THE BOYCOTT MOVEMENT AND IS IMMORAL FOR JEWS STOP. . . WE ASK YOU TO DISAPPROVE THESE NEGO-TIATIONS STOP . . . signed DEFENSE COMMITTEE FOR PERSECUTED GER-MAN JEWS."[4]

Warsaw: "WE HAVE LEARNED ABOUT RUPPIN'S STATEMENT RE AGREE-MENT ALLEGEDLY CONCLUDED WITH GERMAN GOVERNMENT CONCERN-ING EMIGRATION GERMAN JEWS STOP WE REJECT CATEGORICALLY IDEA OF NEGOTIATIONS WITH NAZI GOVERNMENT STOP SHOULD SUCH NEGO-TIATIONS AND AGREEMENT REALLY HAVE TAKEN PLACE THE UNDER-SIGNED ORGANIZATIONS PROTEST IN THE NAME OF MANY MILLIONS OF POLISH JEWS STOP . . . OUR PROTEST ALL THE MORE VIGOROUS SINCE THIS AGREEMENT WAS CONCLUDED ON EVE OF WORLD JEWISH CON-GRESS IN GENEVA signed CENTRAL UNION OF MERCHANTS CENTRAL UNION OF JEWISH CRAFTSMEN CENTRAL UNION OF RETAILERS."[5]

New York: "SOME DAYS AGO I SENT LIPSKY LONG CABLE URGING BOY-COTT RESOLUTION . . . ASKING IT TO BE READ TO CONVENTION ON WHICH I RESPECTFULLY INSIST STOP FEEL CONVENTION SHOULD ALSO VOTE ON BOYCOTT RESOLUTION REGARDLESS signed UNTERMYER."[6]

Telegrams from important members of the Zionist community did not dissuade Mapai forces from enacting their program. The Friday-morning August 25 session began with an announcement by Ben-Gurion that hence-forth *halutzim* must be accorded precedence for labor immigration certifi-cates to Palestine.[7] Halutzim were the young pioneers of the Zionist move-ment. Idealistic youths would enter the program, then move on to training camps known as *hachsharah* to learn the manual and agricultural skills as well as philosophical insights needed to become leaders in Eretz Ysrael. When Jewish Palestine had a place, selected halutzim immigrated, and as-sumed key positions in the labor force and on kibbutzim. By 1933, more than half the Jewish Palestinian work force and about 80 percent of the kib-butzniks were halutzim. The vast majority of this Zionist vanguard were steeped in European socialist thought and were active members of Mapai.[8]

But in Germany, there were fewer than 3,000 halutzim,[9] and many of those were non-Germans residing in the Reich. Clearly the pauperized German Jewish masses—traditionally not involved in Zionist youth training—would have great difficulty being selected for entry to Palestine. However, Mapai wanted the worker immigrant quota filled not so much by German halutzim as by halutzim from Poland, Czechoslovakia, Rumania, and other nations. Dr. Ruppin had in fact hinted that the great Palestinian structure to be yielded by the German crisis would have to serve the needs of Jewish communities throughout Europe, and not just Germany.[10]

Halutzim of course were far better prepared for the rugged living and working conditions in Palestine. Many a middle-class immigrant, similar to the German Jews, had failed in Palestine for lack of the necessary manual or agricultural training. But Ben-Gurion drove home his ideological priorities when he told the Congress that Friday morning why halutzim should be taken first: "If this is a class war, we shall carry it on. But the problem between capital and labor cannot be decided at the Zionist Congress. . . . The Zionist Congress is concerned only with the most rapid building up of Palestine." Nor was Ben-Gurion interested in widening the halutz program to encompass those who were not true believers of the Mapai mold. In fact, he had every intention of keeping undesirable elements out, including the Revisionists.[11] The result would be a Jewish State cast in the image of Mapai.

Ben-Gurion's demand provoked criticism from the other parties, who understood that Mapai's control would now allow it to usurp the entire immigration certificate system. But while the Mizrachi, General Zionists, and Radical Zionists were busy responding to Mapai's immigration position, Revisionist delegates were thinking about the Transfer Agreement. Although they had walked out en masse the night before when their boycott resolution was denied a vote, they had decided to remain for subsequent sessions. The Transfer Agreement, still shrouded in ambiguity, had raised a storm of protest around the world. If the agreement was what the Revisionists suspected, the details had to be aired before the delegates, the world media, and world Jewry.

The presidium could block almost any attempt to debate the transfer issue. But one of the Revisionists believed he could circumvent the presidium by invoking the right of *interpellation*. The parliamentary procedure of interpellation guaranteed delegates the right to introduce a special question for clarification. In the middle of the Friday session, Meir Grossman stood up and announced; "The Democratic Revisionist faction poses the following question. . . . In yesterday's newspapers there was a report that an agreement has been concluded between Zionists and the German government . . . that Palestine will purchase 3 million marks' worth of goods from Germany and that in return the German government will release a like amount of the property of the Jews."[12]

Grossman's unexpected comments captured the attention of the delegates. He went on to protest that the Transfer Agreement would divide the Zionist movement from a world Jewry bent on boycotting Hitler. "We consider this agreement to be an outrage and not compatible with the Jewish people's moral and material interest," declared Grossman. "We are asking the Executive whether this agreement was concluded with the Executive's encouragement or knowledge and whether agencies or offices of the Zionist Organization are participating in these negotiations.[13]

"We consider clearing up this matter to be urgent and important, particularly since yesterday the majority of the Congress refused a general debate about the events in Germany and has thereby made a detailed investigation of these events impossible. We expect the Executive will reply to this inquiry quickly and thereby give the Congress an opportunity for discussion. My faction has raised this subject because it is one more proof of the need for vigilance. We are beset by dangers and certain people are not as reliable as we had thought." At that, Grossman received an outburst of applause from the delegates.[14]

Up to that point, the Zionist leaders involved in the Transfer Agreement had been able to avoid the question of their involvement. Ruppin had identified Mr. Sam Cohen as the negotiator of the deal. If in fact the Transfer Agreement had been negotiated by and was to be implemented under the Zionist Organization or its components, the Congress plenum would have the right to discuss and ratify the question.

Grossman was waiting for his answer. The curious and by now apprehensive delegates of all the parties were waiting. What was the Transfer Agreement and who was responsible for it?

The presidium conferred briefly, and Grossman received his answer: Due to the approaching sunset, the Congress would adjourn for Sabbath. Motzkin gaveled and the session was over.[15]

Before the delegates and reporters dispersed, however, Jabotinsky called an impromptu press conference outside the hall. Over one hundred journalists and scores of delegates gathered around as the fiery orator delivered the full anti-Nazi speech he had been prevented from presenting the day before. He tore into both the Congress' refusal to join the boycott and the Transfer Agreement. "We sympathize with the position of our German brethren. Let them remain loyal to Germany. But Hitlerism is a danger to the sixteen million Jews all over the world, and . . . the German Jews cannot influence us not to fight our enemy. Our enemy must be destroyed!"[16]

Jabotinsky then declared that because the Zionist Organization had refused to establish the international network needed for the boycott, the 100,000 members of the Revisionists, all their offices and resources all over the world would do so. There would be no haggling over leadership with such people as Samuel Untermyer. The Revisionists would cooperate fully with all existing boycott groups. As for the Transfer Agreement, Jabotinsky flatly denounced it as humiliating. He vowed that the Jews in Palestine would never abandon the boycott, never purchase German goods imported via the agreement, and that the agreement and those connected with it were doomed. Jabotinsky called for the Jews of the world to unite, abandon the Zionist Organization, and take up their rightful place in the economic trenches confronting Hitler.[17]

The Saturday-night session, just after Sabbath, was reserved for general debate. Mapai and their allies wanted to suppress any discussion of the Transfer Agreement and instead continue the verbal war against Revisionism. But before the chair could designate the first speaker, Meir Grossman again invoked his privilege of interpellation. "Yesterday we addressed an urgent interpellation to the Executive and asked for a reply," Grossman stated. "In the meantime, the English press had published reports about an agreement between Germany and Zionists—a matter which the English cannot understand [referring to Germany's trade advantage]. We request that the Executive . . . reply today to our urgent inquiry."[18]

Presidium chairman Motzkin answered, "In the bylaws about interpellations, there is nothing that says when an interpellation is *urgent*."[19]

Grossman shot back, "I propose that the Congress determine the urgency of our interpellation and instruct the Executive to provide a reply sometime tomorrow."[20]

At this point Berl Locker spoke up. Locker was the Executive member who had worked with Sam Cohen on his initial deal in May. Locker stated, "The interpellation referred to by Mr. Grossman has no connection with any action or negotiation conducted by the Executive or ordered by it. In view of today being the Sabbath, the Executive has had no opportunity to conduct a meeting. But it will deal with the interpellation at its next session and will inform the Congress whether it will submit its findings in this matter to the Congress or to a committee."[21]

Before Grossman could respond, Motzkin said, "We acknowledge this statement by the Executive. I only wish to say that it is entirely up to the Executive whether it gives or does not give an answer. We will now proceed with the general debate."[22]

Locker had forestalled an unpredictable delegate reaction first by lying about the Executive's involvement, and then by appearing to be reasonable by offering to investigate and then report either to the Congress *or* to a committee. The *or* was carefully added so the Executive could simply make that report to a "committee" and yet live up to the promise uttered before the entire plenum.

To turn the Congress away from the transfer and back to Mapai's preferred enemy, Palestinian Labor leader Zalman Rubaschov—who would later become Israeli president Zalman Shalazar—then launched an acidic attack against the Revisionists, characterizing them as "gangrene" that had to be cut away at the proper time. Jabotinsky, upon hearing Rubaschov's words, demonstratively stood up and walked out of the hall. Rubaschov all the more emphatically urged his fellow Laborites to remove the "pernicious, obnoxious elements in our midst."[23]

Joseph Schechtman, a Jabotinsky associate, rose to voice a Revisionist rebuttal. However, before his first sentences were complete, the entire Mapai delegation stood up and walked out. Even as they were exiting, Schechtman denounced their "milk and water resolution on the German situation" and the Congress' refusal to join the boycott as "capitulation to the forces of Hitlerist Germany."[24]

When the session finally resumed, Revisionists were anxious to demand more details of the Transfer Agreement. But the proceeding was interrupted by what many believed was a staged emergency. Someone dramatically handed Motzkin a telegram: Motzkin reacted with a look of shock. The presidium then passed the telegram around, conspicuously whispered among themselves, and announced that the session would be adjourned at once.[25]

The presidium made no formal announcement, but word quickly spread that the cable had come from Palestine. It claimed that one of the Revisionists on trial for the murder of Arlosoroff had "confessed to the crime." Mapai could now rally the Congress in a moment of passion to expel the entire Revisionist party. The Laborites were ecstatic. The Revisionists reacted to the news with confusion and fear.[26]

Both camps were milling about in the lobby when Jabotinsky reentered from his previous walkout. Supporters nervously explained news of the cable from Palestine. Jabotinsky immediately broke into laughter. He summoned all his followers to a caucus and urged them not to despair. "I guarantee that the telegram is a fake. . . . It is late, and I advise you to get some sleep. And when you wake in the morning, you will find out that the telegram was a fake."[27]

The next day, the Congress delegates quickly learned the "confession cable" was in fact a fake.[28] Still, the false alarm had served to foreclose debate one more day on the truly pressing issue: the Transfer Agreement. But that issue would soon become irresistible. The Nazis were waging a propaganda war, and they had more news to release.

36. The Golden Orange

REICH OFFICIALS reacted nervously to Jabotinsky's break with the Zionist Organization. His August 25 announcement that Revisionism would use its international facilities to coordinate the boycott prompted Nazi leaders to suspect that Jabotinsky was Zionism's other hand, working for the demise of Germany's economy. Alfred Rosenberg, Hitler's personal theorist on Jewish and Zionist affairs, printed a stinging editorial in the August 26 *Volkischer Beobachter*. Rosenberg labeled the watered-down majority resolution on the German situation as "shocking interference in the internal political affairs of Germany." Because the Congress "was not courageous enough to expel the Jabotinsky-led group," Rosenberg concluded that "Jewry is instigating a new campaign against Germany." He warned that the texts of Congress resolutions would be rigorously examined to determine exactly what Zionism's policy would be.[1]

Jabotinsky tried not to disappoint the worried Nazis. His followers openly organized boycott meetings with visiting businessmen in Prague. One idea was to make sure that importers switching to non-German suppliers had no difficulty establishing new credit.[2] The logic was inescapable. If a Jewish-sponsored global finance network could *promote* German exports, a Jewish-sponsored global network could *undermine* German exports.

Jabotinsky also announced that he had sent a cable to Samuel Untermyer: "SHOULD LIKE TO COORDINATE REVISIONIST BOYCOTT ACTIVITY WITH YOUR FEDERATION STOP PLEASE INSTRUCT YOUR PARIS REPRESENTATIVE." Elias Ginsburg, a key Jabotinsky organizer in America, was already one of Untermyer's main boycott activists. To underscore his willingness to support Untermyer, Jabotinsky assured Ginsburg, "I need not add what decisive importance we attach to Mr. Untermyer's personality and to the Federation headed by him. It is our fervent wish to coordinate all our activity with this powerful factor."[3]

Outside Prague, where Jews were beginning to feel a deep sense of betrayal, there was open talk of renouncing the Zionist Organization altogether if the price of allegiance required abandonment of the holy war against Hitler. One of the most outspoken was, of course, Untermyer. During an August 27 Youngstown, Ohio, address to B'nai B'rith lodges from three states—broadcast nationally by CBS radio—Untermyer appealed to the B'nai B'rith rank and file to break with their national leaders and fall in behind the boycott crusade. "Your representatives in the East . . . made a grave mistake in aligning you with the American Jewish Committee in opposing the . . . boycott, which is the only weapon available . . . [against Hitler's] barbarous campaign of extermination. You are thereby unwittingly denying to your stricken brethren in Germany . . . [their] only hope of effective relief."[4]

He explained, "These gentlemen [the Committee] are a self-appointed, self-perpetuating body who represent no constituents other than themselves. Unlike your organization, they have no specific mandate from any section of the Jewish people and therefore are accountable to no one for their self-appointed task." B'nai B'rith members needed to understand how they had been misused, Untermyer said. The Congress had "seen the error of its ways, and has had the courage to break away" and join the boycott movement. Would not B'nai B'rith do the same?[5]

Turning to the Zionist Organization and the Transfer Agreement, Unter-myer's threats were equally unbuffered. "The Zionist Organization had no business to enter upon any such negotiations." And he warned, "If they accede to any such terms, or to any terms other than to offer to take care of the very limited number of German Jews whom they can locate in Palestine or care for . . . [then] they will rightly destroy their organization in this country."[6]

Untermyer, a leading American Zionist and Palestine contributor, knew that the American wing of the Zionist Organization was an indispensable column upon which the entire world movement balanced. American num-bers, American contributions, and American political involvement made American Jewry a powerhouse in Zionism. That power could be shut off—or reconnected to another house, especially the house of Revisionism, which wanted to establish a rival worldwide Zionist organization.

The boycott champion told B'nai B'rith that he well understood the reasoning of many Prague delegates. "[They] had been warned if they voted for a boycott, the absurd abortive negotiations . . . to permit German Jews to be taken out of Germany would be terminated." Untermyer declared that he wished the negotiations *would* be terminated, because "It is playing into the hands of the enemy, and destroying the only opportunity . . . to liberate their victims by bringing about the certain economic downfall of the Hitler regime.".[7]

Summoning Jews and non-Jews everywhere to resist the idea of the Transfer Agreement, Untermyer ended his say with these words: "It is sim-ply inconceivable that we should ever become parties to such an unholy compact."[8]

It was clear to Nazi party leaders that dissident Zionist elements might override the relationship Germany had forged with the Zionist Organization. So, on August 27, more leaks ran in the Berlin press. This time, though, the items were not on the Transfer Agreement per se, but one of the purely commercial undertakings between Palestine and Germany. The subject was oranges.

Germany not only held the power over Jewish Palestine's future growth, Germany held the power over Jewish Palestine's very existence. The bulk of the Jewish Palestinian economy was based on just one factor: citrus exports, accounting for about 80 percent of exports and almost as much of the gross national product. Great Britain was the leading purchaser. The second largest customer was Germany. Third Reich importers accounted for roughly 19 percent of the Palestine crop and in 1933 were expected to increase their buying substantially as crop yields grew. Without an utterly successful or-ange sale for the 1933–34 season, the Palestinian economy would be under-mined overnight.[9]

Palestine did not thrive on a mixed economy. Its so-called factories were generally no more than workshops. Its second most important product was soap, representing just a few percent of its gross national product.[10] More-over, oranges lived by their own clock. They had to be picked, processed, packed, shipped, distributed, and sold on a very tight schedule. Delaying any leg of the journey just a few weeks could devastate the entire crop.

Palestine's 1932 orange crop was 4.3 million cases—roughly a million cases more than the 1931 harvest. In mid-1933 most experts were expecting the coming season to yield more than 6 million crates. Fruit brokers declared Palestine was "drowning in fruit." And yet the world was in a state of depres-sion. Foreign currency in Germany had been curtailed for most nonessential imports. What's more, Spanish oranges were threatening to dangerously undersell Palestinian Jaffas.[11]

Nothing could have been easier for Germany than to disallow Palestinian orange imports. The result would have been sudden, perhaps insurmounta-ble, economic disaster for Palestine. But Germany had several reasons for wanting Palestine's orange trade to flourish. For one, if Palestine was to be the receptacle for Germany's Jews, it would need to be viable. Purchasing Jaffas was therefore as essential to Nazi planning as solving the Jewish question. In fact, to a large extent, purchasing Jaffas *was* solving the Jewish question. What's more, a continuing German purchasing power in Palestine was the greatest motive for the Zionist movement to abstain from the boycott. If Germany could not sell her exports, there would be no money to purchase 15 percent or more of the 1933–34 citrus crop.

Furthermore, in view of the expected hardships, all food questions in Germany had been commandeered by both the Reich Ministry for Food and the Nazi party's department for agrarian trade, known as the Land-handelsbund. Wholly apart from the transfer contacts, negotiations had been under way for some months between the Landhandelsbund, German Zion-ists, and Palestinian citrus brokers.[12] Germany wanted to buy extra oranges, but could not find the foreign currency.

On August 27, the Berliner *Tageblatt* led the German press in leaking the story: A massive agreement was nearing completion. The Landhandelsbund would take about RM 10 million in Palestinian citrus from the coming crop; in return Palestine would take double, perhaps triple that amount in German products. No cash was involved; it was a straight barter. All goods and produce would be shipped on German vessels.[13]

Jews were confused and provoked by the emotionally charged, still hazy Transfer Agreement. But this clearly understandable mutual trade pact be-tween Palestine and Germany ignited the Jewish and even the non-Jewish community to almost universal outrage against the whole question of Zionist dealings with the Hitler regime. Quickly dubbed the "Golden Orange," the revelations suddenly focused the issue clearly in almost everybody's mind. Palestine and Germany were business partners.

At first, the orange deal was not believed. London papers only skeptically picked up the story for their August 27 late-Sunday editions. Scores of angry citizens immediately called Zionist Organization headquarters in London demanding information. When the Zionist Organization denied all knowledge of the orange barter, people turned to the Jewish Telegraphic Agency for details. The JTA, however, could provide little more than what it reprinted from the Berlin papers.[14]

Astonished correspondents from the major newspapers and wire services in London and Palestine also tried in vain to verify the report. No one knew anything. In Prague, Zionist leaders issued only emphatic disclaimers that whatever this supposed orange agreement was or wasn't, it was wholly unrelated to the Transfer Agreement.[15]

Boycotters were trying to make Germany starve that winter. They could not believe that Palestine would stymie this effort so near success with a food barter for a cashless Reich. British boycott champion Captain Webber was quick to issue a statement of disbelief: "The chief purpose of the German Land Trade League [Landhandelsbund] is to throw ridicule upon the Jewish boycott. Last week I heard a rumor that the Land Trade League was endeavoring to launch something of this kind and personally received assurance from the Zionist Organization that there was nothing whatever in it. Any agreement between Germany and Palestine is naturally an agreement between Germany and Jews; therefore the Zionist Organization would be the first to hear about it. I feel sure that tonight's report has no foundation in fact. I consider it an attempt to belittle us, particularly in the eyes of the United States."[16]

Everything was getting confused. The Transfer Agreement . . . the barter deal. Surely they were part of the same arrangement? Or were they? The media, the diplomatic community, the world's Jews, the Zionist movement—they were all understandably mixing apples and oranges in comprehending the two agreements. Answers were demanded. Attention focused on the Monday night August 28 plenary session. Not only was Grossman's interpellation due to be answered, but the delegates were scheduled to debate Arlosoroff murder allegations openly. Delegate emotion was clearly keyed up, and the debate promised to be explosive. Congress organizers could not allow the confrontation.

So the session was simply canceled.[17]

Lacking any credible rebuttals to orange deal reports, hesitant American, European and Palestinian journalists filed dispatches. The articles ran in the Tuesday, August 29, editions.

New York Times: NAZIS REPORT DEAL WITH PALESTINE . . . *"Berlin.* A remarkable announcement by the German Land Trade League [Landhandelsbund] . . . indicates, if correct, that the much-heralded Jewish boy-cott of German goods has certain qualifications. . . . The arrangement, ac-cording to this announcement, provides that Germany will import 8 million to 10 million marks' worth of Jaffa oranges, . . . [and] Palestine . . . will take 20 million marks' worth of German industrial products. The exports to Palestine are to consist principally of agricultural machinery, motors, re-frigerators, textiles . . . and machinery for . . . small manufacturing plants for buttons, leather goods, wicker furniture, and similar household goods. . . . The goods will be shipped on German vessels."[18]

Palestine Post: PALESTINE TRADE WITH NAZIS . . . "*Berlin*. The Handels-bund . . . of the Nazi Party, has stated that the agreement with Palestine whereby . . . oranges were to be imported into Germany in exchange for the import of . . . manufactured articles is the result of negotiations carried on within the last three years with various Palestinian cooperatives. It also states that a German commission will proceed to Palestine to arrange the details."[19]

Jewish Daily Bulletin: BRITISH, PALESTINE GOVERNMENTS, ZIONISTS DENY REPORTS AS NAZIS REVEAL ORANGE DEAL . . . "*London*. Consider-able mystification exists here as to the purported Nazi-Palestine agreement . . . with the general impression that the reports . . . are incorrect, and an attempt to create feeling among the Jews that will lead to a breaking down of the boycott. . . . The Palestine government and the British Colonial Office here deny any knowledge of . . . this astonishing and ambiguous agreement. It is pointed out [by Jewish and Zionist sources] that . . . apart from the moral aspect of the deal on the anti-Nazi boycott, the agreement would represent a bad bargain."[20]

Haaretz: ON THE QUESTION OF THE AGREEMENT FOR AN ORANGE SHIPMENT TO GERMANY . . . "*Berlin*. The Landhandelsbund . . . of the Nazi Party [said] . . . the agreement for a shipment of 18 million marks' worth of oranges . . . has *not* yet definitely been completed. Negotiations are being held at the Reich Ministry for Food."[21]

Sharply worded denunciations from Zionist leaders and rank and file throughout the world poured into the special post office in the Congress hall. One of the most threatening came from Rabbi Abba Hillel Silver of Cleveland, one of American Zionism's towering figures. Repeating the es-sence of his protest, Rabbi Silver told a Jewish Telegraph Agency inter-viewer: "If the reports of those two deals are correct, and I for one find them unthinkable and inconceivable, then every Jew who goes to Palestine be-comes an importer of German goods into Palestine, and this at a time when we deny Jewry . . . of the world the right to trade with Germany."[22]

Unable to conceal his fury, Rabbi Silver declared, "Why, the very idea of Palestinian Jewry negotiating with Hitler about business instead of demand-ing justice for the persecuted Jews of Germany is unthinkable. One might think that the whole affair was a bankruptcy sale and that the Jews of

Palestine were endeavoring to salvage a few bargains for themselves. Palestinian Jewry should be showing the way to unified action and not be willing to victimize the rest of the world for a million crates of oranges."[23]

Understanding full well that the JTA would distribute his remarks throughout the world, Rabbi Silver made the following declaration: "This is a test case. Always Palestine has asked the Jews of the world to sacrifice for Palestine. Now the time has come to ask, will Palestine make a commercial sacrifice for the fifteen million Jews of the world? We say to the Palestinian Jews, *we* won't trade with the enemy and we won't permit the Jews of Palestine to."[24]

Untermyer sent Prague a cablegram demanding that Zionist leaders comprehensively deny the orange agreement. The news was "probably untrue," said Untermyer's cable, and was undoubtedly "spread to injure the boycott that is daily growing more formidable." He then insisted the Eighteenth Zionist Congress disown any pact trafficking in Nazi merchandise, for "world Jewry will tolerate no dealings with Germany and will denounce any body that dares thus to sell our birthright for a mess of potage. We are loyal Palestinians," warned Untermyer, "but the outcome of this struggle is vastly more important than selling oranges."[25] Specifying the consequences, Untermyer threatened that unless the orange agreement was immediately investigated and denied, a convention of American Zionists would be summoned forthwith to repudiate the agreement, order the immediate recall of the entire U.S. delegation from Prague, and formally disassociate American Zionism from the Zionist Organization.[26]

If American Zionist organizers ordered their thirty delegates home, about 10 percent of the Congress would depart. Even American Mapai delegates would be obligated to return if Untermyer could persuade Mapai's American headquarters to pass a binding resolution recalling them. Non-American elements of Mizrachi and Revisionism would be happy to follow, thus subtracting another thirty or forty delegates. And since the American delegates held great power in the General Zionist party and the small Radical Zionist party, perhaps another ten delegates would also be compelled to walk out. Untermyer therefore had the power to trigger the departure of sixty to eighty delegates, or about 25 percent of the entire Congress. But beyond mere numbers, the American delegation played a politically and financially indispensable role in almost every Zionist effort, and this, too, would be lost.

He had done it before. Just one month earlier, Untermyer had created—on a moment's notice—the World Jewish Economic Federation in Amsterdam. And less than ten days before the Eighteenth Zionist Congress, Untermyer had swayed the American Jewish Congress to abandon Stephen Wise's leadership and by resolution compel him to declare for a boycott. The strongmen of the American Zionist movement were all in Prague. Untermyer could operate in America unchallenged, and had indeed already convinced New

York regional Zionist organizations to demand Prague pass a boycott resolution.[27]

Untermyer wasn't to be toyed with, and Congress leaders knew it.[28]

The Tuesday morning August 29 session at Prague could not be postponed. Among the first scheduled to speak was Rabbi Stephen S. Wise, boiling with grievances against Mapai. First, Labor was close to engineering the return of Chaim Weizmann as president of the Zionist Organization; Wise despised Weizmann and was determined to prevent his reascendance. Second, because Mapai feared the boycott Wise would proclaim at Geneva and the competition of his World Jewish Congress, Mapai leaders had suddenly forced the Actions Committee to withdraw its endorsement of the Geneva conference. Third, Mapai leaders had encouraged the Board of Deputies to withdraw their co-sponsorship of the Geneva conference and convene their own counterconference in conjunction with the Zionist Organization, this one to coordinate worldwide relief donations.[29]

Wise was not winning. The best way he could strike back at Mapai was through a dramatic defense of the Revisionists, tying in the unacceptable policies of Weizmann for good measure. Wise began his speech with a stinging rebuke of Weizmann's address in Chicago advocating restricted Jewish settlement. One by one, Wise went on to discredit a range of other controversial Weizmann attitudes. If the delegates supported Weizmann, warned Wise, the movement would never recover.[30]

Continuing the attack, Wise lashed out directly at Mapai's plans for selective immigration for halutzim, who were steeped since childhood in the idealistic workers' society Mapai hoped to achieve. "Utopia!" cried Wise. "This is what Mapai is planning to create in Palestine. You may actually make a utopia out of the land of Israel, but don't delay its resettlement for the sake of this possible utopia." At this the Revisionists applauded loudly, while Mapai people rose to shout denigrations and denials. Wise went on, accusing the Laborites of trying to create a society in Eretz Yisrael where everyone who did not think like them or belong to their political party would be unable to gain entry or find work. Once more, the Revisionists cheered, while Mapai people hollered catcalls.[31]

At one point, Chairman Motzkin had so much difficulty restraining interruptions, he admonished that if Mapai did not behave he would punish them by letting Wise speak past his time limit. This threat tamed the unruly ones briefly; that is, until Wise ended his provocative speech, declaring that the "Congress must create peace among the factions. The majority represented by the Labor party is responsible for continuing the work in Palestine. But they must not say that only those Jews can enter who share their views." The entire Revisionist group then stood and applauded wildly, shouting congratulations. The Mapai group hissed and booed, calling Wise "ignorant" and a "liar," claiming the Revisionists had fed him lies.[32]

Wise's abrasive speech, coming from a leader of American Zionism, was a great blow to Mapai's prestige at the Congress. His comments conspicuously lacked any reference to the Transfer Agreement or the orange deal, probably because as breaches of the boycott he felt these issues should be confined to the Geneva Conference. However, others had not forgotten. Meir Grossman rose again to demand an answer to his interpellation.

"Three days ago," Grossman shouted, "we were told we would have a reply. . . . I believe we have shown fairness in waiting for it this long." Aware that Berl Locker had previously promised an answer to either the Congress plenum *or* a "committee," Grossman tried to head off a closed-door disclosure. "We will not be satisfied with merely a reply to the Political Committee. We want a reply to the Congress. I am asking the chairman whether the Executive will give us a reply."[33]

Locker answered: "The fact that so few plenary sessions have been held is the reason that Grossman's interpellation has not been answered until now. But this is our reply: The Executive has . . . determined that the negotiations referred to in the interpellation had not been ordered by the Executive. We are prepared, however, to furnish additional details to the Political Committee. We will leave it up to the Political Committee whether or not it will communicate this reply to the plenary session."[34]

Chairman Motzkin added: "I wish to remind all concerned that the bylaws state the following about a reply to interpellations: *'Reply can be given orally or in writing; it can also be refused by the Executive with reason therefore.'* "[35]

If Locker thought that he could deny the Executive's responsibility because the Anglo-Palestine Bank controlled the arrangement, Grossman here too, was one step ahead. "Inasmuch as Mr. Locker has declared that the Zionist Organization has nothing to do with the negotiations," Grossman added, "I wish to ask whether or not the Anglo-Palestine Bank is subject to supervision by the Executive?"[36]

The answer was obvious. Virtually everyone in the hall knew that the Zionist Organization owned the Anglo-Palestine Bank through subsidiaries and essentially controlled it through the Executive. Before Locker could respond, however, a Mapai delegate, Israel Mereminski, stood up and intervened. "To begin with, the Executive has stated that it has nothing to do with the agreement," Mereminski said. "In the second part of its statement, the Executive declared that . . . this was a matter for the Political Committee." Defending Locker from the need to answer further, Mereminski rhetorically asked, "Does the Executive mean that it refuses to make a comprehensive statement before the Political Committee—which deals with all political matters affecting the Congress—has had a chance to examine the matter and decide whether . . . the matter is to be submitted to the Congress? If this is the case, I believe it is sufficient reason not to reply to Grossman's inquiry."[37]

Locker interjected, "In my opinion, the Executive is entitled not to reply to an interpellation by stating the reason therefore. . . . The Executive wishes to . . . furnish all details in its possession to the Political Committee. That should put an end to the matter."[38]

Motzkin added a helpful clarification: "Mr. Locker's statement should be understood to mean that the Executive will make its statements to the Political Committee; the Congress will then be entitled to deal with it. It is of course possible, Mr. Grossman, that after you have heard the Executive's statement to the Political Committee, you will withdraw your interpellation."[39] Motzkin's comment held out hope that perhaps if Grossman—an alternate member of the Political Committee—were briefed privately behind closed doors, he would understand the sensitivity of the issue and spare the full Congress a floor report.

But Grossman brushed aside any compromise. And since the Congress was due to hold its final session the next day, he added a new demand: "I propose that the Congress order the Executive to make its statement to the Political Committee *today*, and that the matter be submitted to the [full] Congress this evening or tomorrow morning."[40] This was the key demand. By having the statements made to the Political Committee within a few hours and reported at once to the floor, the delegates could then learn all the details and vote on rescinding the Transfer Agreement before the Congress disbanded.

Motzkin looked out at the faces of the delegates. For days, they had been bombarded by rumors, press leaks, and flying allegations. Rank and file back home were all demanding to know the truth about the Transfer Agreement. A response to Grossman's interpellation had been delayed three times, debate had been clotured, and sessions had been canceled.

It could go no further. Chairman Motzkin turned to Berl Locker and said, "We ask the Executive to furnish its statement to the Political Committee *today*." Cheers burst forth from the Revisionists. Before they became carried away, Motzkin added, "As to the second part [reporting the findings to the full Congress], we will talk about that tomorrow. We will now proceed with the general debate."[41] It is doubtful that in their exuberance the Revisionists were still paying attention. What was important was that finally the delegates would learn what they needed to know about the negotiations with Germany, and what in fact was the Transfer Agreement.

37. The Political Committee

ELIEZER SIEGFRIED HOOFIEN was scribbling notes nervously. The Dutch-born Jew had enjoyed a meteoric rise within the movement since his early days as a financial assistant in the Cologne office of the Zionist Organization. During World War I, as manager of the Anglo-Palestine Bank, he had averted financial disaster by printing temporary banknotes when the Ottoman currency fell. After the war, as director-general of the Bank, E. S. Hoofien was involved in virtually every aspect of Palestine's commercal growth.[1]

When the potentials of German transfer were in danger of being lost, E. S. Hoofien was called in like a financial savior to redeem the opportunity. Indeed, he had almost single-handedly devised the transfer's intricate banking procedures. To the small circle of Zionists who knew of his recent accomplishment at Wilhelmstrasse, he was a true hero.

But now E. S. Hoofien was scribbling notes nervously. The bespectacled man had enjoyed barely a few days rest in a Czech border hotel upon completion of his crosscontinental jaunts.[2] He had worked so hard to achieve something of historic value, something he could be proud of, a redemption and foundation both. Deeply motivated, he saw the work as a Zionist's task, not a banker's task. He knew he had the blessing of the leadership. But now he was being called to defend himself before hostile questioners. Laying responsibility for the Transfer Agreement on the shoulders of Mr. Sam Cohen was not sufficient. Everyone by now knew the Anglo-Palestine Bank was involved. So E. S. Hoofien, it seemed, would have to intercept the blame. This he did not want to do.

The Political Committee was to convene at 5:00 P.M. that day. Hoofien would be the main witness. As fast as possible, he began outlining notes on a short stack of Grand Hotel Steiner stationery, each sheet crested with the hotel's coat of arms. "First of all, it is necessary to remove a false impression which perhaps exists here and there," Hoofien wrote, "as if I or the Bank, without being authorized, only out of a misconceived zeal, have intruded into a political adventure"—he scratched out the word "adventure" and wrote in "undertaking"—". . . have intruded into a political undertaking from which you, those who understand things better, are now obligated to liberate yourselves.[3]

"When the late Arlosoroff learned of Hanotaiah's negotiations, he cabled to that company that they had no right to let this agreement remain a private one, but that it should be put under national control. This telegram does exist and I have seen it."[4]

Hoofien clearly specified that the Executive was in charge, not the Anglo-Palestine Bank or E. S. Hoofien. "Dr. Senator [of the Jewish Agency Executive] was present at Mr. Sam Cohen's talks with the Ministry of Economics. Our [bank's] office in Palestine informed the [London] Executive by letter about this matter as soon as we became involved. It is the ZVfD which demands this agreement and our participation.[5]

"The Conference of Institutions . . . in which all authoritative institutions of the Yishuv [Palestinian Jewry] are represented, also explicitly demanded our intervention. . . ." Hoofien explained why the Transfer Agreement was imperative. The Third Reich was pauperizing all of German Jewry. The only way to stop this was economic intervention wherein Zionism could claim the right to salvage some of the assets via merchandise. "Our rationale is as follows: we, i.e. the Palestinian economy, cannot renounce our claims on Germany. We cannot afford the luxury of rejecting merchandise for which our economy does not incur any debit and which in effect constitutes merely the settlement of a just debt. To reject the merchandise would be tantamount to making a present to Germany [of the Jewish assets]. And that is what the opponents want the Yishuv to do. But the Yishuv has acquired its economic thinking in the school of hard knocks and it will accept the goods."[6]

Continuing his defenses, Hoofien wrote, "The counterargument makes use . . . of the sentimental issue, namely that with today's Germany one cannot enter into understandings or even negotiations. The Yishuv skips this argument because it knows that it cannot cash a debt from a debtor without speaking with him and without settling the matter. Even in the resolutions adopted [by the Congress] about an organized emigration, negotiations and agreements with the German government are needed—you have yourselves skipped this argument.[7]

"The opponents cannot say either, as I have heard during talks and discussions, that the thing should be done, but by no means by an official body. The Yishuv has no understanding of such a cowardly"—Hoofien stopped, crossed out the word "cowardly" and replaced it with "evasion"—". . . has no understanding for such an evasion. If it suits Jewish interest that Palestine cashes its debts from Germany, and if it suits Jewish dignity that negotiations are being led, . . . then it is the right and obligation of the Yishuv's main economic institutions to handle this matter. . . . If it does not suit the Jewish interest and pride, then nobody should do it."[8]

Broaching the question of the worldwide outrage, Hoofien wrote, "If the Jewish masses are upset—which is justified—and oppose seeing clearly the importance of the matter for the Yishuv, then the duty of the people's leaders is to instruct and enlighten the people, . . . not give in cowardly . . . and sacrifice the interests of Palestine's construction to public opinion.[9]

"The second argument . . . is that this agreement breaks the boycott. . . . Notwithstanding the fact that the boycott has *not* been formally declared as part of the Zionist Organization's political program, and without analyzing here the question of whether the boycott is a right or wrong weapon, . . . it must be stressed explicitly once more that the whole argument is wrong and based on erratic reasoning. Boycott makes sense if [transferred assets] are realized by something other than purchased goods. But when the merchandise has no other equivalent, and in fact represents the compensation for our claims, then boycott is pure insanity." [10]

Hoofien continued writing defenses, rationales, and elucidations. His point of view focused totally on the necessity of saving Jewish assets. If the anti-Nazi boycott were successful, he believed, German Jews would be pauperized anyway. Why not convert part of that tragedy into reconstruction in Palestine and thus help avoid future emergencies through the establishment of a Jewish State? To resist this imperative, asserted Hoofien, would create war between Zionists and the Zionist Organization. [11]

"If you want to enter into this absurd conflict with the Yishuv, whereas the whole world—after a quiet future analysis . . .—evaluates how much the Yishuv has been right and how much you have been wrong, so do what you please. Only do not pretend that you have not been warned explicitly and at the proper time. I consider your decision—" There was no time to complete the notes. [12] The Political Committee session was at hand.

Hoofien took his notes into the meeting room. Members of the committee included Meir Grossman, Stephen Wise, Menahem Ussischkin, David Ben-Gurion, and many others. Testifying were E. S. Hoofien, Berl Locker, Dr. Arthur Ruppin, and Mr. Sam Cohen. [13]

Locker began by stating that the Zionist Executive "did not conduct negotiations which led to the conclusion of the Transfer Agreement with Germany. Mr. Sam Cohen, who was in London early in June, showed the Executive a letter . . . from the German Ministry of Economics, which resulted from negotiations conducted by Mr. Cohen on behalf of Hanotaiah. The German government intimated in that letter its readiness to allow Jews emigrating to Palestine to take with them RM 15,000 in cash and RM 10,000 in goods produced in Germany. The agreement provided for a total of RM 1 million, and the German Ministry was prepared to extend the agreement at a later stage. It was then contemplated to form a Liquidation Bank. . . . During those conversations with Mr. Cohen, it was thought that it would be better if his agreement were not confined to Hanotaiah, but embraced other organizations as well. The Executive was in no way in charge of negotiations." [14]

The next witness was E. S. Hoofien. In front of him were his notes detailing full complicity by the Zionist Executive. But Locker has just asserted that the Executive was totally uninvolved, that the whole matter was Sam Cohen's doing. If Hoofien read from those nine pages of stationery, he would utterly discredit Locker, Mapai, and the entire Executive, and probably kill the Transfer Agreement.

So instead of reading from the front of the stationery, Hoofien read from the reverse sides which bore little more than his handwritten chronology of events. "On May 19," Hoofien began, "the German Ministry of Economics addressed a communication to Mr. Sam Cohen, putting forward the proposals to which Mr. Locker has already referred." Opposition then arose to Hanotaiah acquiring a monopoly. In July, he [Hoofien] conferred with Dr. Landauer in Berlin and suggested that the Anglo-Palestine Bank was really "not anxious" to be involved in Cohen's agreement. A Conference of Institutions was then formed in Palestine, recalled Hoofien, reading his chronology almost line by line. They urged that "the Transfer Agreement be taken in hand."[15]

Hoofien recalled the August 7 Wilhelmstrasse meeting and his subsequent efforts to complete all the procedural details. He admitted that the Anglo-Palestine Bank did help create the Berlin trust company that would serve as the Liquidation Bank. But Anglo-Palestine's only function, he argued, would be holding German merchandise sale proceeds until German Jews arrived in Eretz Yisrael to be reimbursed. The motive was to collect in an organized fashion the money belonging to emigrating German Jews. And, he said, the negotiators were guided throughout by the Conference of Institutions.[16] Hoofien had avoided implicating the Zionist Executive by identifying the Conference of Institutions as the source of his authority. Locker's story stood unchallenged.

Then Dr. Ruppin testified. He argued that without some agreement with the Reich, organized emigration would be impossible. Nothing in the agreement violated the boycott because no new currency would come to Germany as a result of the transactions. Dr. Ruppin did not explain that after the first 3 million reichmarks were transferred, all other merchandise transfers would involve at least partial payments in foreign currency. Nor did he discuss the numerous associated commercial enterprises that were being organized partly on transfer assets and partly on foreign currency.[17]

Question: Was it still possible to abolish the Transfer Agreement? Ruppin said it was indeed possible, but such an act would be utterly irreconcilable with the interests of Zionism, Palestine, and German Jewry.[18]

Final testimony was rendered by Mr. Sam Cohen, whose comments were brief. He basically reiterated the assertions of Hoofien and Ruppin, adding that the original currency exemption allowed emigrants bound for Palestine to take the necessary £1000, but the details were "not settled. That concession could easily be withdrawn." By negotiating the Transfer Agreement, the currency exemption was totally stabilized. Proof that it was not advantageous to Germany, said Cohen, was the fact that Reich currency authorities opposed much of the plan because it failed to provide Germany with foreign currency.[19]

Numerous questions were asked by the Political Committee members. Hoofien provided most of the answers. Would the Transfer Agreement allow

Germany to dump goods on the Palestinian market, thus destroying locally manufactured wares? *Not really.* Would the Transfer Agreement increase employment opportunities for German workers? *Obviously yes, but not all that much.* Did German officials act in a hostile, denigrating manner? *No, generally, and besides, the agreement was good from the Jewish point of view.* How many families could really emigrate with part of their assets in the near future? *Probably about 2,000 families. About 650 individuals had already emigrated . . . [and] brought with them £650,000 [more than $3 million].*[20]

At one point Menahem Ussischkin, chief of the Jewish National Fund, started criticizing the Transfer Agreement and the Anglo-Palestine Bank's role in it. As a founding father of the Anglo-Palestine Bank, Ussischkin's comments were taken seriously. Putting aside the moral questions, Ussischkin asked, how could a bank involve itself in anything as controversial as this? A gentleman sitting next to Hoffien scrawled a note to Hoofien: "Uss. definitely wants you to get out of it—don't be mistaken about it. He only gives you a proper motive for doing it." Hoofien nonetheless cited the bank's political obligations. At this, the gentleman next to Hoofien slipped him another note: "You have put the case of the A.P.B. very well *but . . .* a bank runs away from anything political. . . . They don't know what the depositors will do."[21]

Questions continued. There were so many complicated facets to the Transfer Agreement: moral, financial, practical. What would the British say, their trade interests in Palestine having been severely diluted? How should Zionist leaders answer angry Jewish critics? Just how badly would the Transfer Agreement hurt the anti-Nazi boycott? Was it Zionism's destiny to work with anti-Semites as Herzl had commanded? Or was Zionism's larger obligation to fight the persecution of Jews? The rationales and criticisms went back and forth. Was it better to fight Hitler, or concede the battle and convert Nazi persecution into a salvation for the Jewish people? All the known arguments were posed and counterposed, considered and reconsidered.[22]

When the Political Committee meeting was over, most of its members were thoroughly confused. On the surface, it was easy to shout denunciations as though everything was either black or white, but the issues were so monumental, so emotional, and laced with so many imponderables that it became impossible for most members to adopt clear postures of either endorsement or rejection.

Some compared the confrontation with Hitler to the confrontation with the Egyptian pharoah. Then, too, it was a question of freeing a stubborn and reluctant people from captivity, freeing them with their cattle and goats and possessions. Was Moses to refrain from negotiating with the pharoah? If he had, the Jews would have never made an exodus to Israel with possessions needed to establish themselves. Hitler was the new pharoah, pro-Transfer people argued. The German Jews were the descendants of the slaves reluctant to depart. As in pharaoh's day, without negotiation, there would be no freedom, no Israel.

With all their biblical schooling, however, these well-meaning men forgot that Moses would not compromise and that freedom for the children of Israel was secured not by prizes but by plagues.

The moderates who emerged from the August 29 Political Committee session were still undecided about the Transfer Agreement, but the extremes of Zionism—Mapai and Revisionism—had only reinforced their earlier attitudes. Mapai still saw transfer as the beginning of national actuation. Revisionists more than ever saw transfer as a betrayal the Zionist movement was duty bound to rescind. Now that representatives of all parties had heard Political Committee testimony about at least the superficial aspects of the agreement, the Revisionists believed they could appeal to the delegates for a resolution of nullification. As expected, the only way Mapai could block this was by intensifying their allegations that the Revisionists killed Arlosoroff.

Grossman's interpellation called for the Political Committee to make a report at the Tuesday night session or the final session on Wednesday morning, August 30. But the committee needed far more time. Mapai's forces also needed more time to lobby for a resolution indicting the Revisionists for Arlosoroff's murder. Furthermore, routine Congress business had not yet been completed because of all the delays. Congress leaders were forced to extend the convention until September 3.[23]

After the Political Committee adjourned, its members went directly to the main hall for more floor debate. At 9:15 P.M. the general session was called to order by Motzkin. The frustration expressed by the initial speakers reflected just how rankled the delegates were becoming and how impatient they were for a united stand. One eloquent Austrian General Zionist, Oskar Gruenbaum, blamed both the Revisionists and Mapai. "I keep imagining a picture. We are all fighting on ice and the ice breaks and we don't realize that we are drowning. If we continue with a policy like this, then the waves will drown us and you will share the guilt that Jewry loses its last chance—Zionism."[24]

The next speaker was a Polish Mapai delegate who reflected rank-and-file Mapai disillusionment with their own party's response to Hitler. "We are overlooking the big picture for the details. The big national disaster, the German tragedy, this we exploit for money collections and colonization. But this is not enough. The whole Jewish world in Europe is psychologically ready for an emigration. What are we doing to organize this movement? . . . One thousand to two thousand certificates in view of the agony of six hundred thousand Jews is a terrible shame."[25]

Later, Berl Katznelson, one of Mapai's central figures, stepped to the dais. His goal was to marshal delegate frustration against Revisionism and undo the losses suffered earlier when Stephen Wise battered the entire Mapai position from his ostensibly neutral General Zionist corner. So Katznelson's speech fired first at Wise. "Dr. Wise is a prominent personality and his voice . . . is heard all over the world. But when this voice is used . . . to spread false concepts, then this is very dangerous." Attacking Wise for being a labor crusader in America but anti-Labor while in Prague, Katznelson declared, "There are Jews, Zionists, who are very radical. They get excited about liberty, progress, labor rights, and democracy. But all their radicalism and their progressive concepts they confine to the non-Jewish world. When they come to us, they forget the basic concept of organized labor and social rights. In regard to America, Dr. Wise is a very progressive man." Katznelson then turned to the Revisionists and cried, "In America, it would be impossible that Dr. Wise become the speaker of [fascist] black forces.[26]

"Here it is possible. Here people, who in regard to the world in general can be called almost socialist, here they can operate even with . . . the Revisionists. While here, he [Wise] has chosen to associate himself with those who are helping to create an atmosphere similar to Hitler's."[27]

Addressing delegates critical of Mapai's lackluster reaction to the German crisis, Katznelson cried, "It is not our fault that we did not come to the Congress with proposals. Zionism fell into a terrible disaster. Our movement is purely a movement of liberty. Now that it has been stained with blood, we cannot proceed with constructive labors. . . . If you had read . . . [news of the Arlosoroff murder] in the press of Eretz Yisrael . . . which arrived here today, then you would understand this Congress cannot do anything, until it has been freed from this disgrace."[28]

Revisionist hecklers shouted out, "Then why did you convene the Congress?" Katznelson shot back, "*That's* why we convened it. You thought you could play a double game. You act like you don't know anything [about the Arlosoroff murder], but others came and revealed it."[29]

At this point, Grossman, seeking to remind the audience about the Transfer Agreement, yelled in Yiddish, "How does it go with your *business?*" The word business was uttered by Grossman not in Yiddish, but in English with a hostile inflection.[30]

Katznelson, hearing this, attacked Grossman for insisting on interpellations about the Transfer Agreement while refusing to discuss the Arlosoroff issue. "I admire the equanimity of Grossman," Katznelson said sarcastically. "He's got time and he can remain in silence [on Arlosoroff]. But there are things which don't let him rest [such as the Transfer Agreement], and which he demands should be dealt with immediately at the Congress. This he demands, when the matter can be brought forward to the press. But he, the man of the Democratic Revisionists, remains silent when every day things are published [about the Arlosoroff case] which bring only shame . . . to our movement." Hitting hard with the murder accusation, Katznelson cried,

"Only one of us has been slaughtered so far. Nobody can guarantee that tomorrow a second will not fall. . . . Therefore the first *business* of the Congress is to liberate Zionism from this right now!" Like Grossman, Katznelson broke from Yiddish to speak the word "business" in English and with an equally if not more demonstratively hostile tone.[31]

This is how it went. Hour after hour, night after night. The crisis in Germany was omitted from the agenda. The menace of Hitlerism was bypassed. The Nazis must have been smiling.

By Wednesday morning, August 30, Political Committee members had slept a night on the subject of the Transfer Agreement. Some convinced members became uncertain; some uncertain ones became convinced. Hence, there was still no unanimity when the Political Committee convened its second meeting that morning.

The session opened with a background talk by Professor Selig Brodetsky, who had been deeply involved in the transfer negotiations. He explained how the Zionist Organization had taken decisive steps early on in response to the rise of Hitler. Information was obtained through British government channels, and Neville Laski of the Board of Deputies and Leonard Montefiore of the Anglo-Jewish Association were influenced to avoid an "open struggle against the Third Reich." This was done to keep the lines of communication open between the Zionist Organization and Berlin. The Transfer Agreement had obviously created great dissatisfaction throughout the Jewish world, Brodetsky conceded, but he insisted the agreement was needed if German Jewish emigration was to be organized.[32]

Professor Brodetsky's comments, however, gave Stephen Wise no satisfaction. Wise demanded to know how Nazi propagandists could be prevented from seizing upon the Transfer Agreement to discredit the entire anti-Hitler boycott movement. Brodetsky could not provide a sensible answer.[33]

Mindful of Untermyer's ultimatum that the Congress either disown the Transfer Agreement or suffer the recall of the American delegation, Wise laid down an ultimatum of his own. Either the Political Committee clarify how the Transfer Agreement was *not* a gross breach of the boycott, or Wise would issue a statement on behalf of the entire American delegation condemning the agreement. Such a move would almost certainly trigger the recall Untermyer had promised. Transfer advocates heatedly protested, but Wise insisted he would take public action unless the committee did as he demanded.[34]

Recriminations and threats continued throughout the day as the Political Committee struggled to resolve the transfer controversy.[35] No progress was made, but by meeting's end it had become clear that Mapai's grasp on the Congress—when it came to the transfer question—was indeed weakening. There was now the clear possibility that the unpredictable Congress delegates could be swayed against the agreement. To that end, the Revisionists began planning a minority resolution calling upon the full Congress to repudiate the Transfer Agreement and forbid any future pacts with Germany.

True, the Revisionists' earlier minority boycott resolution had been a total failure, but during that fight, they'd had Stephen Wise working *against* them. The Revisionists could now count on a dismayed and angry public and the support of Stephen Wise to give their resolution at least a chance.

The Wednesday August 30 Political Committee adjourned just in time for the members to reach the main hall to attend the last session of open debate. The Revisionists were ready to make transfer the big issue. No Revisionists were scheduled to speak that night, but when Berl Locker came to the dais, the Revisionists were ready.

Locker was trying to improve Mapai's image of being too preoccupied with factional feuding to have responded properly to the Hitler crisis. Therefore, much of his speech was devoted to a compassionate reading of the German Jewish tragedy and Mapai's reaction to it. "I know that immediately, when the first news about events in Germany arrived," Locker said in a dramatic voice, "every Zionist and also every Jew asked himself how is it possible to get out as many Jews as possible from Germany and how can they be brought to Eretz Yisrael." At this, the Revisionists in the audience burst into conspicuous laughter, with several shouting, "Through an agreement!"[36]

Instantly, Locker stopped to answer the hecklers, declaring, "If I am not wrong, and I am sure that I am not, two days before the murder of Arlosoroff, an article appeared against Arlosoroff because of his position on the question of German Jewry, and in the same paper Jabotinsky wrote that it is possible [for the Revisionists] to come to an agreement with Hitler."[37]

"False quotations! False quotations!" shouted Jabotinsky's supporters.

"False quotations?" Locker answered. "It won't help you anything if you call these quotations false. I assure you, such things were written." Believing the interference to be over, Locker proceeded with his address. But the Revisionists continued to heckle, shouting out "certificates," in castigation of Mapai's decision to force an immigration certificate priority for their own halutzim even over the German Jews themselves. Locker continued, "I can only say to the people that call out the word 'certificate,' that you have a comfortable point of view [not being responsible for quota negotiations with the British as Mapai people were]. When we succeed in obtaining a big number of certificates, then you like it. But when the government only gives us a few, then who is guilty—the Zionist Executive, Weizmann and Mapai?" Revisionist hecklers answered the question: "The [socialist] internationale!"[38]

The scorn and skirmishing continued until late that evening. Once again, nothing was accomplished. But just as Mapai had been able to block the Revisionists from rallying the delegates to oppose the Transfer Agreement, so had the Revisionists been successful in preventing a successful purge of their party from the Zionist structure.

Mapai understood that it was losing its war to destroy the Revisionists. Just after the session adjourned, Mapai leaders convened an all-night emergency session of the Actions Committee to plan their strategy for ultimate victory.[39] The big push would come the next day.

38. Hatikva

THROUGHOUT the Congress, a special Commission on Palestinian Terrorism was the scene of venomous attempts by Mapai to link the entire Revisionist party to the assassination of Arlosoroff. The Revisionists, as minority members of the commission, had blocked any unanimous recommendations to the Congress as a whole. But Mapai had finally succeeded in scheduling a special session exclusively devoted to the question of violence. That session was Thursday, August 31. The expected climax had attracted hundreds of additional spectators and journalists who jammed the delegate benches and visitor galleries. Squads of Prague policemen were stationed throughout the hall in anticipation of fighting.[1]

Mapai's majority resolution was virtually an enabling act permitting Mapai to indict and expel Revisionism. The resolution instructed the Actions Committee to convene *after* the Congress adjourned and the delegates left Prague. A special panel would be established to conduct an investigation in Palestine. The Actions Committee was then empowered "in the most effective manner . . . to remove from the Zionist Organization those elements which are responsible [for violence]."[2]

Chairman Motzkin read the resolution to the delegates, adding that there would be no discussion. Jabotinsky jumped to his feet demanding a debate with speeches limited to three minutes. He promised that the Revisionists would be courteous and careful. Motzkin asked if Jabotinsky would agree to the presidium reviewing his statement in advance and censoring any comments they did not approve. "Never," he shouted. "We don't accept censorship!" He pleaded with the delegates not to "tolerate a procedure which makes caricatures" of Zionist democracy. But unable to do better, Jabotinsky finally agreed to read an edited declaration that welcomed an investigation, so long as it also probed the class warfare of Mapai that he said created such crises.[3]

Several futile, angry Revisionist delays followed, but when it was over, 179 over 62 voted to establish the investigative panel. When the Revisionists tried to offer their own minority resolution, it was ruled out of order. Jabotinsky desperately pleaded to come to the dais and make a statement of defense as a Jew speaking to other Jews. He was denied. "Justice is dead!" the Revisionists screamed. "Lie! Lie!" others shouted. "Judicial murder!" they wailed. A fracas ensued. The door to exile had been opened. The Revisionists would exit through it, but only fighting. Chaos continued for fifteen minutes, but that did not change the vote.[4]

During the last week of August, the Reich continued its propaganda war, releasing more leaks about negotiations between Germany and Zionism. The Zionist hierarchy stuck by their defense: The Transfer Agreement was nothing more than a private deal engineered by a private citizen named Sam Cohen and supervised by a private financial institution, the Anglo-Palestine Bank. This story sufficed for a few days as international Jewish furor became diluted by the continuing confusion. Moreover, the more spectacular orange deal disclosures were so impossible to verify that many dismissed it as just another Nazi fabrication designed to divide Jewish solidarity.[5]

But on August 31, the Reich inflamed the entire subject again by leaking to the Berlin press the complete text of the Transfer Agreement—decree 54/33, dated August 28, 1933. In sterile bureaucratic language, the published text clearly explained to the world that the ZVfD was officially involved and that Palestine had been given an exclusive Jewish assets transfer privilege.[6] The ZVfD, under the circumstances, was forced to confirm the Reich decree. So newspapers in Europe and America reported that the Transfer Agreement between official Zionist institutions and the Third Reich was now corroborated.[7] As if deliberately to mix the orange deal and the Transfer Agreement in the public mind, that same August 31 the Fruit Department of the Landhandelsbund announced that the Jaffa orange pact was now sealed following negotiations with two major Palestinian cooperatives under the aegis of George Halperin, an official of the Anglo-Palestine Bank.[8]

All the subdued rage was rekindled. Jews throughout the world unleashed a barrage of protest. The Warsaw Jewish Community sent Prague an immediate condemnation. The Jewish War Veterans in New York wired to Chairman Motzkin notice of JWV resolutions denouncing the Transfer Agreement, the orange deal, and any other negotiations between Zionism and Hitler's Germany.[9] London's *Jewish Chronicle*, reflecting Anglo-Jewry's shock and disbelief, actually reprinted the text of the Transfer Agreement as a joke with the following preface: "And what a decree! The first section is headed 'Transfer of Property to Palestine' . . . and it must be read in full for its rich humour to be appreciated."[10] Unfortunately, it was no joke. Every word released in the Berlin papers and reprinted in the *Jewish Chronicle* corresponded to the actual text of decree 54/33. By September 2, in the shadow of the latest disclosures, even some of the staunchest transfer advocates in Prague were changing their minds.

The only group available to lead any antitransfer crusade, however, was the discredited Revisionists. The Revisionists knew that while they were indeed voted *persona non grata*, they retained immense popular Jewish support on the question of resisting deals with Germany. The Eighteenth Zionist Congress would disband the next night, September 3. Within hours of the final session, many delegates would have to rush to Geneva in time for Stephen Wise's Second World Jewish Conference. However, there was now such widespread hostility to the reported deals with Germany, there was indeed a strong possibility that in the final hour of the final session a Revisionist-led minority resolution rescinding the Transfer Agreement could be voted through. The likelihood of that actually happening would be forecast at the upcoming Political Committee meeting, where final party positions on the transfer would be outlined.

The Political Committee was called to order at eight-thirty that evening, September 2. Transfer opponents were not disappointed. Dr. Israel Waldmann of the Radical Zionists said that his party had concluded the agreement was "dangerous" and had to be rescinded. But the Radicals insisted rescission be handled in a way that would not disgrace the Zionist movement. "In view of all the complications," Waldmann said, "we would be satisfied if [a secret] internal resolution were passed asking the Actions Committee at its next meeting to instruct the Anglo-Palestine Bank to withdraw from the agreement." Meir Grossman countered, "We will insist on an open resolution at the Congress against the agreement, and disavowing . . . negotiations with the German government."[11]

Mapai members of the committee staunchly defended the transfer. They maintained that the boycott, even the German crisis itself, was secondary to the needs of Palestine. Palestine represented a historic obligation. The boycott and the German crisis were transient. Berl Katznelson summed up this way: "We must save Jews of Germany, and their property, and arrange their transfer to Palestine. Therefore, all the discussion and excitement about the Transfer Agreement is misplaced. The anti-Hitler boycott is a means to a goal—not a goal in itself."[12]

Rabbi Cziransky, from Poland, supported Grossman's view: "In addition to thinking of German Jewry, we must also consider Jews in other countries, where Hitlerism may develop. Therefore, the Transfer Agreement and the negotiations with the present German government must be condemned by the Congress in the strongest possible manner. Polish and world Jewry will regard this as a national betrayal!"[13]

Stephen Wise declared that world opinion was absolutely hostile to the agreement and adamantly for the boycott, and this could not be disregarded.

He absolutely rejected Mapai's position that the need to settle Palestine took precedence over every other facet of Jewish life, including the boycott. Wise warned that this was only the beginning: "We have opened the door." The Agreement would be "followed up by all kinds of filth, and advantage will be taken of the *abmachung* [deal]." It would divide the very integrity of the anti-Hitler "Jewish front." Wise insisted the Congress pass a "definite and unequivocal resolution against the Agreement." [14]

Hoofien answered the critics, especially those who blamed Anglo-Palestine. He emphatically denied that the bank or manager George Halperin were even indirectly involved with the orange deal. As for the Transfer Agreement, "It is not true that the bank negotiated with the German government on its own account. The initiative was taken by representatives of German Zionism and various Palestinian interests. The bank did not wish to be involved in a political issue." But ultimately, Hoofien conceded, he was willing to get out, if only someone could get him out without embarassing condemnations. "If the proper organ did decide against the Agreement," Hoofien said, "the bank would certainly withdraw, but it would be inadvisable to refer to the bank in any resolutions put to Congress." [15]

Dr. Ruppin protested, "If the Congress does revoke the agreement, it will be assuming a very heavy responsibility; it will endanger the existence of many German Jews. The Transfer Agreement in no way interferes with the boycott movement, since no new currency will flow into Germany as a result of the agreement. . . . Abolition . . . would also endanger the existence of the Zionist institutions in Germany, as well as facilities for emigration from Germany." Everything would be lost, he tried to explain. [16]

The tide suddenly turned when Ruppin dropped the cover story they had all been maintaining that kept the Zionist Executive out of the picture, and thereby avoided the question of Congress approval. He finally admitted it: "The negotiations were conducted with the knowledge of the Executive. Senator was fully aware of all that had been done." This disclosure now placed the agreement squarely within the authority of the Congress. [17]

Then came Professor Selig Brodetsky's turn. Brodetsky, the transfer liaison in London, was finally prepared to make a difficult statement. He tried to re-create how the best of motives had been in all their hearts as the Zionist movement was torn between the instinct to fight Hitler and the need to negotiate. "Many people [in April 1933] were anxious to involve the Zionist Organization in the boycott movement," he recalled. "But all parties held different opinions as to the advisability of the boycott. If direct negotiations could be entered into with the German government with regard to the position of German Jews, very few people would object." [18]

Brodetsky then explained how the Zionist Executive had been overtaken by events. "When Mr. Cohen visited London in May, the draft agreement was nearly completed, and the question was not whether he *should* or *should not* go on, but whether it should remain an agreement with a private plantation organization, or whether wider interests should be included." He then admitted, "The responsibilitiy of the Executive was therefore somewhat different from that which could be implied from our earlier speeches.[19]

"[We] had to face the dilemma as to whether it was more important to enable more Jews to leave Germany with some of their property for Palestine, or whether on balance the agreement should be revoked in view of its conflict with the boycott movement." And then he said it: "On the whole, it would be best if the bank would withdraw from the agreement."[20]

Meir Grossman, having heard Brodetsky's solemn words, declared the Revisionists would move that the Congress adopt an explicit resolution of nullification. He and Stephen Wise presented the text: "As long as the Jews of Germany have not received their former legal rights again, and as long as the German government does not . . . enable Jews the right of free emigration including taking all their property, the Zionist Congress considers it inadmissible that . . . the Zionist Organization or its subordinate institutions [such as the Anglo-Palestine Bank] sign any agreement of any kind with the present German government."[21] The resolution drafted by Grossman and Wise incorporated the quintessential strategy of Moses: "Let my people go, with all their possessions, and the plagues shall not stop until you do."

But Mapai's top echelon stiffened. Mapai political leader Moshe Shertok (Sharett), who later became Israel's foreign minister, decried the entire conversation. "It has been suggested that negotiations were conducted with the consent of the Executive. This is not true," rebutted Shertok. "The Jerusalem Executive certainly never considered the question, and it was officially informed only on the very eve of the close of the agreement." He deplored even the suggestion of a conflict between the interests of Palestine and the Diaspora. Shertok declared that if the agreement could in fact facilitate the transfer of German Jewish property to Palestine, and enable Jews to settle in Eretz Yisrael, then it could not be interfered with.[22]

A Mapai resolution was set forth: "The Congress refers to the Actions Committee for careful examination the question of the Agreement with the German government for the transfer of Jewish capital to Palestine, with an instruction that nothing shall be done . . . contrary to the attitude of the Congress on the German Jewish question."[23] The "attitude of the Congress" was the majority resolution passed the night of August 24 that declared Zionism and emigration to Palestine as the appropriate reaction to the Hitler regime.

With Stephen Wise and Brodetsky against the transfer, a large sector of the General Zionists were now ready to renounce the agreement. The Radical Zionists were on record as desiring the agreement's abolition if it could be done discreetly. The Revisionist and Mizrachi antagonism toward the agreement was well known. And even such notables as Leo Motzkin had finally decided the agreement was bad. In fact, Motzkin was now determined to attend Wise's boycott conference in Geneva as soon as the Prague Congress ended.[24]

Mapai knew they were becoming isolated on the issue. The Transfer Agreement could indeed be repudiated the next day at the final Congress session. In the absence of a Transfer Agreement, there could only be boycott, and boycott meant the return of Revisionism. It could not be allowed.

Mapai had one more resolution they could wield. It was introduced that Saturday night, September 2, at the 9:00 P.M. general session. The new resolution stated that as part of Zionist discipline, no individual or group within the Zionist Organization would be permitted to conduct foreign policy, contact foreign governments or the League of Nations, or engage in any activities of a political nature that infringed on the prerogatives of the Zionist Executive. This outlawed all forms of anti-Nazi protest, including campaigning against the Transfer Agreement. Under the resolution, all those who broke the discipline provisions would be suspended and tried by a special tribunal. Upon a guilty verdict, the tribunal would be empowered to expel the person or party from the Zionist Organization.[25]

The delegates reacted to Mapai's discipline resolution with a storm of outrage. Members of all other parties filled the hall with loud protests and accusatory declarations. The battle raged for hours as the Revisionists and others tried to prevent a vote. But Mapai held on with their 44 percent and with a few allies in other parties.

At some weary moment during the night, Mapai called for a vote. Some said it was 3:00 A.M. Some said it was after dawn. The delegates had been without sleep, they were hungry, they were worn out. No one could tell how many delegates even knew the vote was being taken. Mapai's discipline resolution was carried. Out of 300 delegates, 152 voted for the resolution, 13 against.[26] Mapai won.

On September 3, 1933, at 4:30 P.M., the final session of the Eighteenth Zionist Congress began for 300 delegates plus alternates, disputed representatives, special participants, and observers. They had train and boat tickets in their pockets, too much bloodshot in their eyes, and precious little patience in their dispositions. Many came from Zionist strongholds in the United States, Poland, and France. But many also came from remote Zionist enclaves in Chile, Yemen, and Hong Kong. In the hall, the delegates spoke twenty or thirty different languages, often all at once. Even the official proceedings were conducted in at least three languages. The delegates had varying levels of sophistication. Some were true believers. Some were skeptics. Some demanded to lead. Some wanted only to follow. But whether dark-skinned or fair, Asian or European, powerful or inconspicuous, they all had one thing in common. Each had one vote.

On this last day, all the untied strings had to be knotted. The Congress was more than a forum for debate about the Hitler crisis. Russian anti-

Semitism, immigration certificates for Yemenites, land prices in Palestine, dialogue with Arab leaders, training facilities for halutzim, agricultural experiments on kibbutzim, loan agreements with London banks, reorganization of the Jewish Agency, relations with non-Zionists, the Palestinian school system, Sabbath enforcement—there were a hundred pressing emergencies. Most delegates concerned themselves with one or two or five or six of the emergencies, and merely voted in blocs on other issues.

On this last day, the many special commissions and committees that had been deliberating for days on each and every pressing issue would finally present their recommendations to the plenum. The custom was for these voluminous resolutions to be read in rapid succession for lightning votes designed to get the overworked, overspent delegates out of the hall and back to wherever was home.

As in other years, the various commission, committee, and subcommittee chairmen read their long, complicated resolutions on everything from budget allocations to religious questions. With record impatience, the delegates ayed and ayed, sending resolution after resolution into the statute books. However, even the debate-battered Zionist delegates in their last hours could not help but withhold their vote and demand discussion when strange and unexpected resolutions began appearing. The first unexpected resolution was a subtle change in the Zionist Organization's constitution that permitted the Actions Committee to convene subsequent congresses at three-year intervals instead of biannually. The assembly argued this radical change long and hard, but in the end Mapai's votes carried the resolution.[27]

The next resolution of importance addressed the question of Dr. Weizmann. For days, Mapai had been trying to convince him to return to the presidency of the Zionist Organization. Weizmann had rebuffed all pleas because Mapai had failed to expel the Revisionists. Finally, Weizmann sent word—without actually visiting the Congress hall—that he would not accept the presidency, but would chair a new London-based entity to be known as the Central Bureau for the Settlement of German Jews. The Bureau would coordinate all relief, emigration, and political issues affecting German Jewry, including Haavara. In Palestine, a sister entity called the German Department would be headed by Dr. Ruppin.[28]

In essence, Weizmann no longer needed the helm of the Zionist Organization to guide the destiny of the Jewish national effort. That destiny now reposed within the borders of the Third Reich, and within the numbered accounts of the Liquidation Bank, Paltreu, and Haavara. Since Weizmann's bureau would operate semi-autonomously in tandem with the Zionist Executive, Weizmann and Mapai could make their own decisions without factional obstruction. In Weizmann's view, the Zionist Organization, with all its parties and points of view and cumbersome committees, was too inefficient for the task at hand. A state was to be built while flames were all around.

The resolution creating the new bureau was passed.[29] Most of the delegates voting had no way of knowing they were creating an elite entity that during the next fifteen years would make virtually all the life-or-death rescue decisions for German Jewry.

As had been proven on the back of the Revisionists, it did not pay to oppose Mapai. But on the resolution regarding the Transfer Agreement, the Revisionists were hoping the delegates would rise up and vote their consciences. The press, the letters and telegrams, the phone calls, the late-night clashes, the quiet, introspective personal moments of regret that most delegates had felt would almost certainly compel them to vote to rescind. On the other hand, Mapai looked upon the Transfer Agreement as the cornerstone of everything to come: the buyer of land, the builder of schools, the sponsor of halutzim, the redeemer of the Jewish future. Weizmann's bureau, the priority for halutzim, the unrivaled domination of Mapai—all of it was contingent on the next vote.

Mapai had already been busy making private assurances to delegates about the meaning of their resolution: Yes, there were major problems with the agreement and its conflict with the boycott. Those who had engineered the agreement had even expressed a willingness to scrap it, but a humiliating floor rejection was not the way. At the very next meeting of the Actions Committee, the entire program would either be brought into harmony with the boycott or be rescinded as the public wanted. These were the impressions held by a great number of delegates, including some of the most influential, such as American delegation co-leader Louis Lipsky, a close associate of Weizmann, who had just been appointed to the Zionist Executive.[30]

Political Committee chairman Michael Ringel read the majority resolution paragraph requiring the "Congress to turn over the question of the interpellation of August 24 to the Actions Committee with the instruction that nothing shall be done . . . contrary to the attitude of the Congress on the German Jewish question."[31]

Then it was Meir Grossman's turn: "I am proposing the following minority resolution: 'As long as the Jews in Germany have not received their former legal rights again, and as long as the German government does not . . . enable Jews the right of free emigration taking all their property, the Zionist Congress considers it inadmissable that the Executive of the Zionist Organization or its subordinate institutions sign any agreement of any kind with the present German government.' "[32]

Grossman turned to his fellow Jews and told them, "In full conscience of the responsibility and in the interest of the German Jews and not less in the interest of all of world Jewry, we have to be fully aware that we are not allowed in any way to weaken the atmosphere of protest in the Jewish world today. We were told that the Executive had no relations whatsoever to this action. But I rather declare that at least three members of the Zionist Executive knew about this 'action.' Therefore we [the movement] have given this 'action' our national signature and seal, and I consider it a breach of *national discipline*."[33]

Grossman had turned Mapai's own weapon against them. The Transfer Agreement, maintained Grossman, was the ultimate breach of discipline. His closing words: "It is impossible to leave this Congress without condemning this 'action.' Neither the Executive nor one of the institutions under its guidance has the right to sign an agreement with a government engaged with us in a daily struggle. Our resolution must liberate the Zionist Organization from the damage which has been done to it by this agreement!"[34]

Berl Katznelson, on behalf of Mapai rose to answer: "After the declaration of Mr. Grossman, I am forced to say the following: In the Political Committee this question was discussed . . . at great length in a number of sessions. . . . It was the express wish of the committee to avoid if possible a Congress debate on the question. In every parliamentary body it is understood that there are sometimes important foreign-policy issues which have to be treated discreetly, and by persons who are thoroughly familiar with the subject."[35]

Katznelson then charged Grossman himself with a flagrant breach of discipline. "We have seen today how many people who sit in confidential bodies leak news which we explicitly decided was confidential," rebuked Katznelson. "They do it if the matter can be exploited for party affairs. . . . The majority of the [Political] Committee clearly understood that it is the main task of Zionism and a Zionist duty to negotiate as Jews and as Zionists and to help the Jews in all countries who are forced to emigrate. They have to be supported to save their life and also their property. Therefore negotiations have to be led, even when it involves negotiations . . . with hostile factors. This is the way Zionism has been understood since the days of Herzl.[36]

"The idea of a Liquidation Bank is also connected with negotiations and very often with very difficult, bitter circumstances. A short time ago, a decision established [Weizmann's] Central Bureau, which today should be engaged in transferring Jews with their property from Germany to Eretz Yisrael," Katznelson said. "On this resolution, which is also connected with certain negotiations, Grossman voted in favor."[37]

Katznelson ended his appeal declaring, "We don't believe that it is possible to draw a financial agreement into a political debate. Any Zionist body must agree that Eretz Yisrael is the primary thing and it is the primary duty to save Jewish lives and Jewish assets from all dangers to which they are exposed."[38]

A choice lay before the weary delegates. The final session had begun at 4:00 P.M. Sunday. It was now close to dawn on Monday. Many were confused about the details of the issue, but many also seemed to sense that it placed Judaism and Zionism at a crossroads. The Transfer Agreement, the liquidation and transfer of German Jewish assets . . . yes—this would create the State.

So they voted yes. Yes to allowing Zionist leaders to make the painful, complicated decisions in the privacy of caucus rooms and conference chambers. In so doing, many fully understood that their decision was indeed yes for the Transfer Agreement, yes for the road to nationhood, and yes for a decisive historic move to intervene in the continuum of Jewish dispossession and persecution.[39]

In full recognition that Israel was to become a reality, seventy-seven delegates suddenly and solemnly asked that the white banner emblazoned with the light blue Star of David, for decades the symbol of the Zionist movement, be officially designated the national flag. They also moved that "Hatikva," for decades the symbolic hymn of the Zionist movement, be officially designated the national anthem. Both motions were adopted.[40] Now they had a flag, a song, a treasury, and a people. Land was the only element they were missing. That, too, would come through the power of the Transfer Agreement.

A few closing speeches were made, and at about 9:00 A.M., after seventeen hours of debate and soul-searching, the Eighteenth Zionist Congress was adjourned. The delegates walked from the hall singing their national anthem, "Hatikva." In Hebrew it means "hope."

PART VII
·
Decision at Geneva

39. The Second World Jewish Conference

THE LAST POLITICAL ACT of the Eighteenth Zionist Congress was the unison singing of *"Hatikva."* But the aftertaste of this Congress left many in the movement embittered and confused about the facts. Some believed the Transfer Agreement would be sent to the Actions Committee and quietly revoked. Many believed that the Transfer Agreement was officially condoned as a distasteful but necessary act to save German Jews and their assets for the Jewish national home—but purely commercial agreements such as the orange deal were explicitly forbidden. Others remained under the impression that the agreement was merely a contract between Sam Cohen, the Anglo-Palestine Bank, and the Third Reich—with absolutely no official Zionist involvement. And there were those who believed that neither the Transfer Agreement nor the orange deal actually existed.[1]

For instance, shortly after the Congress, the London *Jewish Chronicle* commented on the two agreements. On the orange deal, the *Chronicle* reported, "It is now stated definitely that, strictly speaking, no such agreement exists." On the Haavara, the *Chronicle* reported, "It has been brought about mainly by a private commercial concern in Palestine—Hanotaiah. The Jewish Agency has stated, in somewhat cryptic language, that it 'does not participate' in any way in . . . the agreement. . . . Mr. Sam Cohen, who is said to have conducted the negotiations, leaves no doubt as to Zionist cooperation. . . . We leave it to others to square Mr. Cohen's words with the categorical denials . . . recently heard in Prague."[2]

Modern View, St. Louis' Jewish weekly, issued a call to Zionist officials to end the confusion. "A veritable storm of protest from every part of the Jewish world has greeted the report from Berlin [of an orange deal]. . . . [It] may be part of a Nazi scheme to discredit the sincerity of the anti-German boycott, [but] it behooves the Zionist [authorities] to issue a frank denial . . . [and] quickly."[3]

When a reporter asked Stephen Wise how the agreements could have been approved, he replied, "None of us at the Zionist Congress could be certain of the facts. . . . I fought against it in the Political Committee. I was defeated by two groups; one consisting of those who denied in the most categorical manner that there was any such pact, and the second . . . who took the position that . . . to not purchase goods from Germany is no more than assenting to partial expropriation [by the Nazis]."[4]

And Zionist Executive member Louis Lipsky published a front-page statement in *The New Palestine*, official newspaper of the Zionist Organization of America, declaring, "The specific agreement about which there has been so much discussion in the press has been referred to the next meeting of the Actions Committee. I understand the enterprise is to be abandoned by its initiators."[5] When he wrote those words, Lipsky was unaware that the Actions Committee meeting he mentioned was in fact never held. On the day in question, almost no one showed up; the committee lacked the quorum needed to convene.[6]

But continued German leaks, many of which were published unchallenged in Palestinian newspapers, compelled many to believe that the Transfer Agreement *did* in fact exist and in some way involved the Zionist Organization officially. This growing group of angry believers continued to demand that the agreement be revoked and the boycott adhered to. Typical was a comment in *The Jewish Chronicle*: "We cannot overlook the broad and ugly features of the situation. . . . Half a boycott won't save the German Jews!"[7]

On September 5, 1933, delegates from Jewish communities around the world arrived in Geneva. Many had come directly from Prague. Once in Geneva, among fellow boycotters, these delegates underwent a rapid change of attitude. In the pressure-cooker atmosphere of the Eighteenth Zionist Congress, the word "boycott" was essentially *verboten*. Anyone even uttering it was immediately put on the defensive. Now in Geneva, the exact opposite was true. Anyone who dared rationalize trading with the enemy was a traitor, and all boycott traitors were to be exposed.

Stephen Wise had promised the world that he would lead an international boycott organized by the established Jewish organizations of Europe and North America. Furthermore, the American Jewish Congress had promised that the structure conceived in Geneva would be placed at the disposal of Samuel Untermyer. With the Third Reich announcing ever more barbarous anti-Semitic measures in spite of the Transfer Agreement, and precious few days before winter to effect the death blow, the Geneva delegates were determined to do what they could not do in Prague: create a worldwide boycott organization and stop the Transfer Agreement.

The Second World Jewish Conference would be brief. It was agreed in advance that what was needed was not speeches, but organizing. Whereas the delegates who attended the Amsterdam conference all represented homespun boycott groups, the one-hundred delegates from twenty-four countries assembled on September 5 in Geneva's Salle Centrale did indeed represent a substantial sector of establishment Jewry. The list included: the Committee of Jewish Delegations, Paris; the Central Union of Bulgarian Jews, Sofia; the Federation of Polish Jews, Warsaw; the League of Jewish Women, Geneva; the Board of Deputies of Rumanian Jews, Bucharest; the Yugoslavian Association of Synagogues, Belgrade; the American Jewish Congress, New York

City; and Jewish umbrella groups from Copenhagen, Vilna, Geneva, Florence, Warsaw, and Madrid. Attending as Mussolini's personal envoy was Rabbi Angelo Sacerdoti, the chief rabbi of Rome. Even Zionist officials were there, including delegates from the Zionist Federation of Switzerland, Dr. B. Mossinson of the Vaad Leumi, and Leo Motzkin of the Actions Committee.[8] The absence of the British Board of Deputies was especially noted, but Anglo-Jewry was ably represented by the British Federation of Jewish Relief Organizations, the Federation of Synagogues, and the Inter-University Jewish Federation.[9]

At about 8:00 P.M., Rabbi Stephen S. Wise walked onto the stage to a standing ovation and proclaimed the conference officially convened. After telegrams of encouragement from Jewish communities all over the world were read, Wise stepped up to the lectern. This was his moment.[10]

"Ladies and gentlemen. . . . Jews the world over are agreed that the overshadowing problem throughout Jewish life today is bound up with the situation of the German Jews. . . . It is no less true, ladies and gentlemen, that the German Jewish problem is itself overshadowed and dominated by *one question*, which must be answered by the World Jewish Congress. . . . That question is: Shall there be a world boycott of all . . . products manufactured in Germany?"[11]

The crowd erupted in loud applause. Then, without mentioning the Zionist Organization by name, Wise broadened his question to include the negotiated agreements on everybody's mind. "Put even more simply, shall Jews have any relation whatever, industrial or economic, with a nation which has declared war . . . against the Jewish people everywhere?"[12]

He then described the difference between the initial boycott and what he now had in mind. "The Jewish boycott movement from the beginning has been absolutely *spontaneous* . . . not imposed from above. It grew out of the anguish of the Jewish masses, who inevitably reacted to the declaration of war against them by taking in hand the only weapon accessible to the Jewish masses." The question, said Wise, was *organization*.

"I have no apologies to offer for the failure of the American Jewish Congress up to this time to declare a boycott. . . . It is easy enough for the unorganized and the irresponsible to make threats against Germany. . . . Throughout six months we have waited and waited, hoping against hope that it would not become necessary.[13]

"Today, we who are responsible and authorized representatives of millions of Jewish people in many lands, face a grave question. . . . Can we . . . wait any longer?" In his best oratorical style, Wise answered his own question. "We can no longer expect the Jewish people to stand by our side and to place their faith in us unless we declare before this conference that the time has come for an organized, *organized*, ORGANIZED boycott—*tuchtig und grundlich* [total and efficient] against Germany!"[14]

Those assembled were not a valiant band of grass-roots leaders with plenty of energy but no organization. Rather they were the directors of established Jewish organizations with budgets, field offices, printing facilities, and paid staffs. What they could accomplish in a week would take an Untermyer months to achieve. They commanded resources not only in the major cities but in the smaller cities and villages. Waiting to gather these men and women under one roof to pool their combined international resources was worthwhile. These people could make the boycott victorious. They accepted Wise's explanation of delay.

"We of the American Jewish Congress," Wise shouted, "could not, would not, did not seek to organize and proclaim a *world* Jewish boycott. . . . Throughout six months, I have maintained this because I believed that such a boycott could be declared *only* by a body such as meets tonight in Geneva and speaks on behalf of millions of Jews. Whatever decision may be reached by the World Jewish Congress will be supported to the limit by the American Jewish Congress, indeed by all America's Jewry, the largest Jewry on earth, consisting of more than a quarter of the world's Jewish population."[15]

If there were voices of question about Stephen Wise's place in the boycott movement, those voices now seemed stilled. Nothing would stop this assembly from pooling resources to economically strangle Hitler's Germany. The delegates knew they would have to stop the Transfer Agreement as well. And they had every intention of forcing the Zionist Organization to abandon it.

Those who had made it to Geneva, including Wise, were badly in need of sleep. So the conference adjourned after Wise's opening address. But as the delegates filed out of Salle Centrale late that September 5, 1933, they were united in their determination to spend the next two days planning to force Germany to crack that winter.

Under the unwritten code of the boycotters, Jews found handling German goods were to be branded as traitors and blacklisted. So in the first days of September, spontaneous calls went out in various countries to compel the Zionist Organization to stop its deals with Germany.[16] If not? *Cherem.*

For centuries, the cherem had been the curse of untouchability imposed against the Jewish people's greatest enemies and most reprehensible sinners. Once pronounced by a rabbi against a non-Jew or inanimate object, the person or object became untouchable for Jews. Once pronounced against a Jew, the Jew was either excommunicated or shunned or both. Anyone breaching the cherem would himself fall under the cherem. Obedience to this concept varied from community to community. Modern Jews would literally ignore a cherem. Orthodox Jews, however, considered the cherem as inviolable as the Sabbath itself. Moreover, the collective effect of numerous rabbis joining in a cherem decree could sway even a non-Orthodox Jew into obedience. In 1933, when deep religious traditions were ingrained in the large majority of Jewish households, the concept of cherem was powerful for a large part of the world Jewish population, especially in Europe.[17]

On September 6, the Assembly of Hebrew Orthodox Rabbis of the United States and Canada was concluding its annual convention in New York. Two honored speakers addressed the group. The first was William Sweet, representing FDR's National Recovery Administration. Sweet flew in from Washington to urge the rabbis' influence for the NRA, which was advocating a boycott against companies not cooperating with the national recovery effort. The second speaker was Untermyer, who denounced those bargaining with Adolf Hitler to salvage "a few possessions" belonging to German Jews. Untermyer told the rabbis that a cherem was the only answer to such traitors. And it should be cast at once if Germany was to crack that winter.[18]

Once pronounced, the decree would be binding upon hundreds of orthodox congregations under the Assembly's authority. Synagogue members would be ordered not to handle any German merchandise. They would be obligated to extend the cherem of untouchability to those who did. If the Zionist Organization became untouchable, Orthodox Jews, including the Mizrachi, would literally have to separate themselves from the movement.

Cutting religious Jewry off from Zionism was a radical step, but many endorsed it. On the day of the ceremony, the convention even received a radiogram of encouragement from Rabbi A. J. Kook, chief rabbi of Palestine. But Untermyer believed excommunication would isolate too many Jews and instill the boycott with a religious character that non-Jews could not relate to. He therefore urged a cherem confined to German goods alone. This prompted several rabbis to protest disruptively. But the majority deferred to Untermyer, voting for a cherem of untouchability, but not excommunication.[19]

The solemn ritual began when two tall black candles were set on a table several feet apart, then lit. A rabbi wearing the traditional *talis* or prayer shawl, blew three times on the *shofar*, the twisted ram's horn traditionally sounded on the Day of Atonement. Following the shofar blasts, the chief rabbi of Newark, Rabbi B. A. Mendelson, chanted the decree in Hebrew: "In the name of the Assembly of Hebrew Orthodox Rabbis of the United States and Canada and other rabbinical organizations that join us in our beliefs, we take upon ourselves . . . as leaders of Israel, to decree a cherem on everything manufactured in Hitler's Germany. From today on we are to refrain from dealing in all basic materials such as metals, textiles, and other things . . . which come to us from the Nazis. . . . We urge all to not knowingly violate this boycott which we have this day decreed."[20]

Rabbi Mendelson then took his gavel and ritually extinguished the candle flames. As the flames turned to smoke, many in the room were heard to mutter softly, "Like this, for Hitler."[21]

The spirit of the cherem was developing among the conferees in Geneva. The first working session on September 6 revolved around creating a viable worldwide boycott and the ultimate form of the World Jewish Congress. Leading off the deliberations was Nahum Goldmann, one of Zionism's most respected figures. He began with a confession: "What I could not say at Prague, I am stating from this platform as a good Zionist and a member of the Action Committee: Zionism is not in a position to handle the problem of Jewish rights in the Diaspora and can only handle the work of upbuilding Palestine. . . . Palestine is no solution. The solution must come from within Germany in order to avoid shattering Jewish rights in other countries."[22]

Goldmann told the delegates, "There must be two separate Jewish organizations—one for Palestine upbuilding and another to conduct the fight for Jewish rights. The latter should be proclaimed at this conference." He acknowledged that such a world body would be incomplete without the Board of Deputies. "Of all the Western European groups, the most difficult one for us to include is the English one. . . . [But] I am convinced that eventually we will succeed in winning the Board of Deputies . . . None of us underestimates their importance."[23]

The Deputies had in fact been close to joining Wise in sponsoring the Geneva conference. But the Zionist hierarchy in London had persuaded the Deputies to abandon all projects not in harmony with Zionist policy. This Goldmann knew, but was reluctant to verbalize. "I do not wish to go into detail as to why the Board of Deputies has so far remained aloof from taking a positive stand," Goldmann said. But, he added, when the World Jewish Congress became a reality, the Deputies would be unable to resist joining. Therefore, the first task of the conference, urged Goldmann, was to create the organization needed to conduct a "bitter," well-planned war against Nazi Germany.[24]

In the afternoon session, delegates debated whether their organization should be appointive or democratically elected. Dr. Henryk Rosmarin, a Polish General Zionist who had just arrived from Prague, bitterly argued, "A few days ago an agreement was signed between Germany and Palestine which brings shame upon the Jewish people. . . . This was possible [because] there is no . . . democratically elected representation of the Jewish people. [Zionist elections elected parties, not individuals.] If such a [democratically elected] authority were in existence," Rosmarin assured, "no Jew would dare . . . enter into negotiation with the Hitler government."[25]

Stephen Wise later that night spoke of Zionist-Nazi deals during a formal address. He had intended to review the threat to international law posed by the Nazi regime, this for the benefit of the local press, which carried some influence over the Geneva-based League of Nations. The boycott was not really part of the address. But just a few minutes into his speech, Wise suddenly stopped to issue an unexpected public warning to the Zionist Organization: "I do not believe that the boycott has been ruthlessly trampled upon and violated by our fellow Jews or their representatives in Palestine," Wise said. "[But] if it be proved to me that any Jew in or out of Palestine, or any representative of any group of Jews, has been so base as to attempt to do business with Germany for the sake of profit and gain, I attest that life will not be bearable for any such man. . . . We are not rebuilding a Holy Land, out of which the Law and the Prophets came, in order to make a land of profits for some by their dealings with the German government."[26]

As Wise uttered those words, he was really envisioning the orange deal. He was trying to rationalize the Transfer Agreement itself as a regrettable but understandable necessity. He quickly followed his warning with a qualification: "But it is only fair to add, the Reich makes its own laws. Those laws are ruthless. . . . What shall a Jew in Germany do if Germany says to him: You may go out, you may leave this Reich, . . . you can leave this Hell . . . but you can only take part of your money with you. The rest you must leave us for purchase of wares. You can leave on no other condition. I could understand the Jews in Germany [concluding] . . . that if they cannot go to Eretz Yisrael any other way, they may as well go that way.[27]

"It may be that if you and I were in Germany, we too would pay the penalties which a ruthless, lawless Hitler government might exact from us. But I repeat there will be no patience . . . for any Jew on earth if, for the sake of profit, he violates the will of the Jewish people and the dictates of human conscience by doing business with Germany!"[28]

Wise's condemnation, indeed the condemnation of the Jewish world, was provoked by disclosures about the orange deal and the Transfer Agreement. But in fact they were just two of literally dozens of major commercial arrangements being negotiated between Palestine and Germany even as Wise spoke. There were breweries, bakeries, steelworks, cement factories, irrigation systems, printing presses, medical facilities, and a host of other state building enterprises. Wise and the other protesters didn't really understand what was happening, or how fast.

40. A "Central Jewish Committee"

SEPTEMBER 7 was the day of decision for the Second World Jewish Conference. The tone was set by the first speaker at the morning plenary session, E. Mazur of the Federation of Polish Jews. Mazur could barely control his rage as he cried, "The entire agreement agreed to by the Zionist

Exec, is a *schande* [in Yiddish, a shameful disgrace]. And this conference must issue a protest resolution against [both] the agreement and the negotiations. . . . The boycott is the only [defense] means at our disposal. Using it will prove that we still have the power to resist. [Therefore] the boycott must be organized in such a way that Jews will be morally unable to break it." The delegates warmly applauded.[1]

C. Rasner, also of the Federation of Polish Jews, joined his colleague in condemning the agreements with Nazi Germany and urged the delegates to vote specific sanctions against them. "The agreements made by Zionists with Germany are a *schande*," protested Rasner. "If the Zionist Congress did not have the courage to condemn them, that is its own business. We must do it— in the sharpest possible manner."[2]

At this point Nahum Goldmann spoke up. As co-organizer of the World Jewish Congress, and as a major figure in the Zionist movement, Goldmann was a powerful voice at the conference. The day before, he had publicly confessed his failures at Prague, and then called for a world body dedicated to an international boycott, but things now were getting out of hand. Delegates were openly talking about binding resolutions of condemnation that would undoubtedly extend the boycott to the Zionist Organization itself if the transfer were not rescinded.

"I didn't have any intention of participating in this discussion," Goldmann said, "but I'm really forced to. . . . [Don't] interrupt me because I only have ten minutes [under the rules]. . . . Among the Jewish public an [anti-Zionist] campaign has started because of the agreement which was signed between a land settlement company in Palestine, which is a private company, and the German government. . . . Inasmuch as I am among those who had nothing to do with it, but who are one hundred percent in favor of it and are prepared to share the responsibility for it, let me say a few words on the subject—not to make converts . . . but rather to clarify it for you and the Jewish public, which is here represented by the Jewish press. Unfortunately, this wasn't possible at the Zionist Congress.[3]

"First of all," Goldmann explained, "the Zionist Organization has not signed any kind of agreement. It was not even involved in the negotiations. Hanotaiah made this agreement and a Zionist bank participated. The [Reich] foreign-currency management authority decided to permit an exception for Jews who emigrate to Palestine. This does *not* signify a breaking of the boycott. Boycott means throttling of exports from Germany and of the influx of payments into Germany. Here we are dealing with money which is *already in* Germany; thus when these goods are later sold, no additional money flows into Berlin."[4]

Goldmann's rationales were not working. In desperation, he tried to make the conferees understand: "We are told we must make no deals with Germany. This is absurd! A people must be able to negotiate with any state in the world, especially during a state of war. Think of the negotiations concerning prisoners of war in Switzerland between the warring nations. . . . Whát is involved here is that these people who are emigrating from Germany would otherwise become beggars."[5]

But Goldmann's impassioned speech was not lessening their conviction that the Transfer Agreement would have to be stopped. A frustrated Goldmann, co-convener of the conference, flatly declared, "I am telling you that we will not permit this forum to be used for anti-Zionist maneuvers and I am asking you not to insist on resolutions which are directed against the Zionist Organization. The conference is to decide about the boycott question. But what has been done here [with the Transfer Agreement] was absolutely necessary and is not a crime."[6]

The next delegate answered, "Contrary to the opinion of Dr. Goldmann, this conference *is* authorized to deal with the question of agreements with the German government because this subject is organically connected to the question of the boycott." Another delegate added, "Dr. Goldmann has forgotten to talk about the . . . oranges of Palestine. . . . What will happen is this: There will be a store in Palestine which will be proclaiming boycott of German goods, and the store next door will be selling them!"[7]

Dr. B. Mossinson of the Vaad Leumi, Jewish Palestine's national council, then stood to ask the delegates not to blame Palestine. Mossinson proclaimed that he was personally against the agreements, and Palestine as a whole was boycotting German merchandise vigorously. "This agreement was made by individuals," pleaded Mossinson, "and only individuals are guilty of breaking the boycott." Dr. Mordechai Nurock followed with a demand that "every traitor of the boycott must be designated a strikebreaker." Dr. Nurock used the term "strikebreaker" advisedly, since it was the term Mapai ascribed to Revisionists who sought employment outside the Histadrut combine.[8]

Dr. Rosmarin, however, tried to end the discussion with reason and understanding. "The boycott broke out spontaneously," he began. "Jewish public opinion started it earlier than did the politicians. . . . The leadership probably did not have the courage to proclaim the boycott publicly. . . . It is no secret for anybody that at the Zionist Congress there were great differences of opinion, but I have the courage as an organized Zionist to say from this platform that the boycott should have been proclaimed there.[9]

"Yet even if we can understand the misgivings that existed there, there must not be any misgivings here," Dr. Rosmarin said. "If we had proclaimed the boycott three months ago, today there would be no disunity in public opinion. The Palestinian agreement hurts us because it hurts our dignity and it weakens the Jewish people in its fight.[10]

"It is obvious that the discussions . . . have been passionate, but there are situations—moments in the life of people—when *no compromises* are possible. I am in agreement with those who have spoken against the transfer and . . .

want to proclaim the boycott. I am asking you to not waste any more time with discussion. The matter has been decided. Let's concentrate on what we need for the boycott battle. Assistance, implementation, the activities of the various committees, and so on." [11]

Those in the hall instantly applauded Rosmarin's clarity, but Rosmarin's call was not heeded. Goldmann continued trying to persuade his fellow Jews not to break with the Zionist Organization. He also disclaimed the orange deal—which he openly condemned as profit-motivated and inexcusable. But to the end, he defended the Transfer Agreement as a historic Zionist obligation. [12]

After many hours of discussion, much of it outside the formal sessions, the delegates made a decision. At some future date, Jewish elections would be held throughout the world, creating the desired democratic representative body. In the meantime, a so-called Central Jewish Committee would be appointed, probably headquartered in Paris or Geneva, comprised of ten or twelve Jewish leaders. This elite committee would immediately coordinate the boycott efforts of all Jewish organizations represented at the conference. [13] Presumably, this Central Jewish Committee would link up alternate suppliers with anxious buyers in the promised rerouting of world commerce around Germany, extend the consumer boycott from the major cities to provincial areas, and vigilantly oppose any barter or bilateral trade arrangements with the Nazis.

Later that day, after the delegates had struggled over the wording for hours, a boycott resolution was finally formulated. It called for a worldwide Jewish boycott to be coordinated by the Central Jewish Committee, so that "the Jewish people may not abandon legitimate, honorable, and peaceful resistance to the war waged on the Jewish people." No mention was made in the resolution of the Zionist Organization's agreements with Germany, but commercial or other relations between Jews and Nazi Germany were expressly forbidden. [14] At this point, the chief rabbis of Rome and Florence walked out. They had been arguing on Mussolini's behalf against any boycott resolution at all. Having failed, they no longer wanted to be associated with the conference. [15] The other conferees remained, but few if any of them were certain about their decisions.

Formal general debate resumed at nine-thirty that night. The last speaker, at about 11:00 P.M., was Leo Motzkin, who issued a solemn appeal. He asked the boycotters to understand the Zionists who had negotiated the Transfer Agreement, asserting, "Even this step on the part of some Zionists, who in this way attempted to save as much German Jewish capital as possible, can be justified; we must not speak of treason against the Jewish people. You must understand this! [16]

"Personally, I was one of those in Prague who was against this agreement. And my rationale was as follows. Despite the fact that in this manner thousands of Jews are saved and their move to Palestine is thereby made possible, it breaches Jewish solidarity. . . . But at the same time I must ask you to understand that this is really not a manifestation against Jewry."[17]

Technically, the Transfer Agreement had been consigned by the Eighteenth Zionist Congress to the Actions Committee, which Motzkin chaired. His last words to the conference delegates that night were: "I have from the very beginning stated that this is a big mistake. I will attempt to keep this mistake from being made."[18] Motzkin had in fact decided to do all in his power to strike the agreement down at the next Actions Committee meeting, due to convene within weeks.

But Motzkin's appeal seemed ineffective. The conference's boycott resolution was on a collision course with the Zionist movement. If the Central Jewish Committee were established, it would extend its influence into Palestine, thus making sales of German merchandise there impossible. It would block foreign investment in transfer enterprises. It would quickly have an impact on the Anglo-Palestine Bank. A secondary boycott would ultimately extend to the Zionist Organization itself. And, of course, the resolution would bring into reality the consolidated global boycott Germany had feared, the avoidance of which was a prime motive in the Reich's cooperation with Palestine.

In short, there could be no Zionist solution to the German Jewish question, there could be no transfer, and there could be no Jewish State in the foreseeable future if the resolution creating a global boycott entity was implemented. The members of the resolutions committee were all good Jews, all good Zionists. The Zionist movement was in fact a major impetus in the formation of the World Jewish Congress. These men and women had never expected to have to choose between being good Jews and being good Zionists. But a choice was necessary.

41. The Final Moment

AT NOON on Friday, September 8, 1933, the delegates and reporters gathered at the Salle Centrale. Divisive conflicts, painful delays, and Jewish communal chaos had preceded this moment. For six months, Stephen Wise had battled and baffled every boycott leader from Samuel Untermyer to Lord Melchett—always on the basis of the superior, decisive boycott organization that would emerge from this Geneva conference. All of Wise's organizational brinkmanship had been devoted to the achievement of this one moment.

The delegates and the world knew what to expect. Wise had thrilled the convention and the press in his keynote speech with promises to "organize, *organize*, ORGANIZE." He had lectured on the inadvisability and uselessness of a "spontaneous" boycott. He had identified international structure as the missing ingredient needed to make the anti-Hitler boycott triumphant. Now came the moment when the global boycott entity was to be announced.

Nahum Goldmann opened the session, announcing to the crowded hall that the various committees of the conference had formulated resolutions divided into two parts. He added, "It is no secret that the resolution about the boycott was preceded by long negotiation. In the end, we agreed, however. And I believe this text can be unanimously approved."[1] Goldmann then announced, "I will read the [non-boycott] resolutions first, because they are the least controversial." He then read the resolutions calling for elections in Jewish communities throughout the world to create the World Jewish Congress as a democratic representative body to fight for Jewish rights. The enthusiastic crowd shouted their approval, and Goldmann proclaimed that the resolution was adopted by acclamation.[2]

"I am now asking Dr. Wise to read the boycott resolution."[3] Wise stepped up to the lectern to read the six sentences divided into two paragraphs that the Jewish world and indeed all foes of Hitler had awaited. The last sentence was the pivotal one. It would explain the shift from a spontaneous boycott to an organized boycott under the coordination of a Central Jewish Committee.

Wise began reading: "The World Jewish Conference notes with deepest satisfaction that from the beginning of the Hitler regime, and its anti-Jewish laws and acts, the Jewish people instinctively and spontaneously resorted to the one immediately accessible weapon of self-defense: the moral and economic boycott. In the spirit of individual and collective self-respect, the Jewish people through the boycott affirms that Jews cannot hold any economic or other relation with the Nazi government of the Third Reich"—this was the reference to Zionist deals with Germany—"and believes that its boycott must continue to be shared by millions of non-Jews in all lands, who understand and sympathize with the Jewish people's abhorrence of the Nazi anti-Jewish precept and practice."[4]

Wise went on: "When the Jewish boycott of German goods and wares is to be ended depends not upon the Jewish people but upon the Nazi government. This instrumentality of moral and economic pressure Jews have been compelled reluctantly to adopt and utilize. But they will not lay this down until such time as the great wrong inflicted upon the German Jews is undone and the German Jews once again be placed in the status and position which were rightly their own before the accession of the Hitler government."[5]

The final sentence was to ordain the Central Jewish Committee to enforce the ban on Jewish relations with the Reich—which would end the Transfer Agreement, and coordinate the spontaneous boycott. Wise read the words: "The conference solemnly calls upon the Jewish people loyally to continue in their legitimate, honorable, and peaceable resistance against the war waged by Hitlerism upon the German Jews and upon the whole Jewish people."[6]

But where was it? Where was the enforcement clause? Where was the Central Jewish Committee? Where was the promise to be organized? This resolution merely called for the continuation of the *spontaneous* boycott, the "unorganized" boycott.

They had backed down. It is unknown exactly when. Sometime after the reporters left late on the night of September 7, perhaps in the middle of the night, perhaps at dawn, perhaps just before noon. But sometime before the September 8 closing ceremony, the boycott resolution of the Second World Jewish Conference was changed.[7] The decisive moment had come, but Wise, Goldmann, and the others on the resolutions committee could not carry through. Not if it meant war with Zionism, and subversion of what increasingly seemed to be the pivotal opportunity to redeem the Jewish nation. Israel was at stake. The Jewish people were at stake.

It was a choice, and perhaps since Prague they all knew what choice they would make no matter how hard they protested and resisted. Those who understood even a fraction of the power the Transfer Agreement held knew in their hearts that the Jewish State would rise out of the anguish and ashes of German Jewry—and indeed German Jewry would be only the first wave. Nazism would reach out to all Europe. Whole branches of the Jewish people may wither, but the trunk remains. Wise, Goldmann, and the others saw the branches going down and grabbed for the trunk with a sense of desperation and destiny.

Wise had probably known it deep inside for days as he grasped the true meaning of the Transfer Agreement. Torn between the instinct to fight and the need for establishing a Jewish national home, Wise himself acted out the fundamental Jewish conflict between the call of Zion and the urge to achieve equality in the Diaspora. Two days before, on September 6, Stephen Wise had injected an unexpected and strangely melancholy passage into a speech before the conference. Essentially, he conceded the destruction of European Jewry as a sacrificial warning to the world of the coming Hitler danger. He said this: "Once again the Jewish people seems called upon to play a great role in history, perhaps the greatest role in all the ages of its tragic history. Once again the Jewish people are called upon to suffer, for we are the suffering servants of humanity. We are called upon to suffer that humanity and civilization may survive and may endure. We have suffered before. We are the eternal suffering servants of God, of that world history which is world judgment.

"We do not rebel against the tragic role we must play if only the nations of the earth may achieve some gain, may profit as a result of our sufferings, and may realize in time the enormity of the danger they face in that common enemy of mankind which has no other aim than to conquer and destroy. We are ready if only the precious and the beautiful things of life may survive. This is once again the mission of the Jews."[8]

It was in this same speech that Wise suddenly switched topics and lashed out at Zionist commercial ties with Nazi Germany.

What went through Wise's mind on September 8 as he read the resolution that reneged on his international promise to organize the anti-Nazi boycott no one will ever know. The conference audience, however, was unaware of the subtle change, unaware that the construction of Dr. Wise's well-elocuted words specifically deleted the coordinating authority he had promised. When the sixth and final sentence of the boycott resolution was read, they all cheered and applauded. Goldmann took the opportunity to say, "I note that the resolution has been accepted unanimously." Even more applause followed.[9]

Wise even followed up with a stern denunciation of Palestinian commercial relations with Germany. He called it "the new Golden Calf—the Golden Orange," and told a cheering crowd, "I think I speak the mind of Jews everywhere when I say we hold in abhorrence any Jew, whether in or out of Palestine, who undertakes to make commercial arrangements with the Nazi government for any reason whatsoever." He added the obligatory qualifications that hopefully such rumors were not true.[10]

After the boycott resolution, Goldmann introduced Leo Motzkin, who read a special third resolution, this one on the German Jewish question. The eloquent five-point declaration condemned Nazi persecution and called for a program under League of Nations auspices to finance the emigration of German Jews to Palestine. The conference's resolution on the German Jewish question, except for its condemnatory language, was almost identical to the one passed at Prague. Goldmann then announced that this third resolution was also unanimously adopted.[11]

He added that a special decision had been made to turn over "the political affairs" of the Second World Jewish Conference to the Paris-based Committee of Jewish Delegations until international elections created a viable World Jewish Congress. The Committee of Jewish Delegations was a Zionist-sponsored Jewish defense body that, like the Zionist Organization, was recognized by the League of Nations. The president of the Committee of Jewish Delegations was Leo Motzkin. The Committee would manage the Geneva conference's "political affairs" in joint tenancy with a panel of ten eminent Jewish and Zionist leaders, including Nahum Goldmann and Victor Jacobson, a member of the Zionist Executive.[12]

While the "political affairs" of the conference mainly embraced the special resolution calling for organized emigration to Palestine, they also included the spontaneous boycott. As such, leadership of the worldwide boycott was being consigned to Zionist officials and Zionist organizations. This was the fate of the international boycott so painstakingly nurtured by the Jews of the world. The boycott would be led by leaders who in fact opposed it.

Once again, after reading the text of the decision, Goldmann announced adoption by acclamation.[13]

Stephen Wise then rose to deliver his final comments. It must have been a difficult speech. He could not boast of triumph in finally organizing the Jewish people. Instead, he had to pretend the Geneva conference was not a fiasco for the boycott movement. Wise rambled a bit and contradicted himself. In fact, his first two sentences were: "We have just adopted a most important [boycott] resolution. It is true that in that resolution we have said nothing new to the Jewish people, but we dare believe that we have fulfilled its wish and . . . have given our approval to that which the masses of the people have instinctively done from the beginning and demanded of us— namely, moved forward to the boycott."[14]

Wise once more felt obligated to explain: "We have postponed action . . . for half a year in the hope that a change might come over the situation. Alas, the situation grows graver from day to day, and it is now nothing more but instinctive preservation which moves us to resort to . . . the only weapon which is accessible to us, namely the moral and material boycott. . . . We do not declare war against Germany, but . . . we are prepared to defend ourselves against the will of Hitler Germany to destroy. We must defend ourselves because we are a people which lives and wishes to live."[15]

In a dramatic flourish, he declared to the crowd, "My last word that I wish to speak to you is this—Our people lives—*Am Yisrael chai!*"[16]

Wild applause erupted as the audience cheered the emotional moment,[17] never comprehending that it was an ovation for failure. The object of the conference—creation of a world boycott infrastructure—was never achieved, was in fact abandoned.

A few minutes later, Nahum Goldmann formally declared the Second World Jewish Conference to be over. Even before he did, the delegates were streaming for the doors, confident that an organized boycott was to be triumphantly led by conference leaders. A dramatic confrontation in the aisle only reinforced that view. The Munich correspondent for Hitler's personal newspaper, *Volkischer Beobachter*, was seated in the press gallery. He was about to leave when he was suddenly confronted by Stephen Wise. As a crowd drew around, Wise told the Nazi in perfect German: "I cannot help wondering what would have been my fate . . . if I had come to Nuremberg. . . . The representative of *Volkischer Beobachter* can remain quietly here. He is secure among us and all that we ask of him is that he reports the truth. There is nothing secret in our councils, and we wish above all that the Germany of Hitler learn the truth . . . concerning our feelings and attitudes."[18]

Drama, applause, speechmaking, plenty of promises, eloquent resolutions, and defiant confrontation made the Second World Jewish Conference an elaborate show that pleased its audience. But when the boycott resolution was finally studied, revealing an obvious absence of any move to organize the anti-Hitler movement, it quickly became clear that the Geneva conference simply did not advance the boycott cause.

A syndicated column in the St. Louis Jewish weekly *Modern View* reported, "After considerable debate and argument, the resolution committee of the World Jewish Conference . . . brought in a report which failed to proclaim a world Jewish boycott against Germany, but which endorsed the 'instinctive and spontaneous resort to boycott' which already exists." London's *Jewish Chronicle* said the resolutions "opened no new avenues and would be approved by any Jewish gathering." Many other newspapers chose to merely report the Geneva resolution matter-of-factly, emphasizing that the conference called for the continuation of the "spontaneous" boycott, with the word "spontaneous" always in quotes. And of course, Stephen Wise himself told the delegates in Salle Centrale, "It is true that in that resolution we have said nothing new to the Jewish people." [19]

In many ways, Geneva was the crossroads, more than New York, Jerusalem, London, Amsterdam, or Prague—or at least Geneva was the final crossroads. An awesome choice was made. Stephen Wise and the other Jewish leaders made the choice. They chose the road to Palestine.

42. After Geneva

THE SECOND WORLD JEWISH CONFERENCE occupied Stephen Wise's thoughts as the train headed north from Geneva to Paris. Decisions had been made that only God could judge, only history could vindicate. During the several-hour train ride, a shy and obviously fearful seventeen-year-old German girl kept glancing furtively at Wise and his party. Wise could not help but notice, and in fact became preoccupied with the girl. Several times he tried to speak with her, but she would only stare in silence. Finally, near Paris she gathered the courage to ask, "Are you coming from the World Jewish Conference in Geneva?" [1]

"Yes," Stephen Wise answered. "Why do you ask?" The young girl would not respond. Wise repeatedly tried to break her silence, but she would not speak until just before her stop. She was a German Jewish refugee, without family, now working as a maid in a French village. In Germany, she had lived in a nice house with her family. One night the Nazis came and abducted her brother. The next day he was returned in a coffin marked "NOT TO BE OPENED—SHOT IN FLIGHT."[2]

Wise asked the terrified girl, "Was the coffin opened?" She answered, "Yes, but don't ask me." Yet, in a moment more, the girl relived the discovery that her brother's face had been shot away.[3]

The girl's tragic story and the girl herself couldn't help but move Stephen Wise. He bluntly asked whether she thought the Geneva Conference had helped or done damage. The girl looked at him and answered, *"Es muss sein, es muss sein"*—(What must be, must be.)[4] She then left the train, but her last remark haunted Wise. For several weeks, he could not help but recall in his private and public conversations that unclear instant when the innocent young refugee spoke those few words: "What must be, must be."[5]

On Friday, September 15, Rabbi Wise arrived in New York. Unlike the return of Samuel Untermyer, there were no welcoming committees, no fanfare, no national radio broadcasts. After resting on the Sabbath, Wise called a small press conference in his study at the Free Synagogue.[6]

In a dramatic session marked by Wise's barely controllable emotional outbursts, Wise tried to explain his activities abroad to reporters. He emphasized that the situation for Jews in Germany was graver than anyone could imagine. Only international pressure, hopefully by the League of Nations, coupled with the anti-Nazi boycott could "bring about the end of the Hitler regime." But, he added, the world must also be prepared to organize an emigration out of Germany. One reporter asked why Wise had wavered so long on the boycott question, and whether the Geneva resolution was not merely a repetition of the boycott voted some months earlier by Untermyer's World Jewish Economic Federation in Amsterdam.[7]

Wise replied emotionally and defensively, "You ask . . . what has led me to change my mind? I have from the beginning believed that the boycott was a natural, inevitable weapon in the hands of individual Jews against Hitlerism. . . . My position from the beginning has been that a world Jewish boycott could only be declared against Germany by a world body of Jews. I have never changed my position with regard to that. If boycott there was to be, I insisted all the time that representatives of the world must assemble and declare such a boycott. This was finally done under the auspices of the World Jewish Conference . . . and it was I who introduced and urged its unanimous adoption."[8]

Unable to restrain his bitterness about Untermyer's triumph, Wise added, "I do not know anything about the World Economic Federation, if there is such a body. I believe there was a conference of one dozen or fifteen people in Amsterdam, which called itself the World Jewish Economic Federation. I refuse to discuss anything that may have been said or done by the so-called World Jewish Economic Federation, or its head [Samuel Untermyer]. My battle is against Hitlerism. We Jews are engaged in a war of self-defense which will tax every atom of energy of Jews everywhere. There may be Jews who are so little concerned about the peril to world Jewry as to be prepared to engage in the divertissement of Jewish quarrel and strife. I refuse to be diverted. One war at a time.[9]

"For the same reason, I refuse to permit any celebration of my homecoming by the American Jewish Congress." This referred to the fanfare for Untermyer upon his return from Amsterdam. "There is no occasion, as far as I can see, for celebrations or banquets or thanksgivings, nor will there be any in Jewish life until after the Hitler regime shall have ended."[10]

Wise castigated America as being alone in refusing any sizable number of refugees. He praised "countries like England, Spain, Portugal, France, Belgium, Holland, Switzerland, Czechoslovakia, Poland, Denmark, and Austria in extending their hospitality to refugee Jews. Up to this time, the only great country which has failed to offer such hospitality is our own."[11]

However, there was hope, Wise explained, because Palestine would be able to absorb 50,000 to 100,000 German Jews within the next decade. "Such a possibility is rendered likelier because for reasons . . . difficult to understand, Germany permits Jews to leave the country for Palestine and to take . . . £1000 of their possessions, which is not true in the case of refugees fleeing to other lands." This comment raised the issue of pacts between Germany and Zionist bodies, including the Transfer Agreement.[12]

Wise answered that there was still great confusion over whether the Transfer Agreement actually existed, although he was unalterably opposed to an arrangement allowing emigration with assets via a merchandise sale. "I, for my part, felt and feel that of all places on earth, Palestine must be above suspicion, and that nothing could be worse than that the Jewish boycott against Germany should be breached by Palestine or those wishing to go to Palestine."[13] Wise was angry. He wanted to fight. Yet he knew whatever fight ensued could not be victorious.

For several more minutes, Wise rambled between different postures on the boycott, what the Geneva conference had actually accomplished, and whether the boycott would or would not be successful. At the end he suddenly broke into a telling of the incident on the train, recounting how he had met a young refugee girl whose brother's face had been shot away. "This is a sample of the horrors to which my people are being subjected in Germany!" he cried.[14]

The press conference that morning was less a presentation of fact than an unwitting statement of confusion about what organized Jewry had done and was intending to do about the Hitler question. Few reporters published any mention of Dr. Wise's statements.

One week later, on September 23, at 9:00 P.M., Dr. Wise went to the offices of the American Jewish Congress to explain his activities in Europe to several dozen members of the Congress' Administrative Committee. They wanted answers about whatever had happened to the *organized* boycott, why it was necessary to sabotage Untermyer's work, and what were the facts about the Transfer Agreement. This time Wise's audience was composed of people who knew many of the ins and outs of protest politics over the summer, people with the power to turn the Congress away from Wise at this moment of accountability.

After a few words of introduction, Wise began speaking: "I think the best thing to do would be to give a chronological story, a story which will be more or less chronological in its character. My work already began on the steamer going to Europe." Wise stopped. "If I am to speak frankly tonight, it must be with the understanding that you [Bernard Deutsch], as chairman, will guarantee that nothing I say will be reported in the press. I cannot begin to talk of the things which I am going to say . . . unless, ladies and gentlemen, I have the feeling that nothing will be repeated." Having received the assurance he needed, Wise proceeded.[15]

He tried to make them understand what immeasurable good he had contributed to the worldwide protest movement. "There was no action, there was no *thought* of action in Europe until . . . Deutsch and I . . . sent those cables to Poland, Rumania, and Czechoslovakia [calling for a worldwide day of protest focusing on the March 27 Madison Square Garden rally]. The whole great European protest movement was undertaken as a result of our inspiration and suggestion. . . . It was not until the twenty-third or twenty-fourth of March that the agitation throughout Europe and Palestine began, not one day sooner. . . . Up to our last day in Europe, I never met anyone . . . who did not feel that things would have been infinitely worse in Germany if it had not been for the agitation led by America—infinitely worse."[16]

A moment later, Wise found himself again talking about the girl on the train. "I asked that girl if she thought we had helped or done damage," related Wise. "Her answer was '*Es muss sein, es muss sein*,' It has to be." His very next words were, "I want you to know, for your satisfaction, that I hesitated, I faltered just as much as anyone did. I knew the terrible responsibility. But I got the impression, I want you to know it, that our agitation was enormously helpful. All German Jews, whose judgment is worthwhile, think so."[17]

He returned to a chronological account explaining intrigue-filled meetings in London as he bargained with the Board of Deputies to support the Geneva conference. He repeatedly denied responsibility for canceling Untermyer's London boycott gathering, but admitted he opposed it because the World Economic Conference was convening in London at the same time. Wise recounted the serpentine development at the Eighteenth Zionist Congress, its failure even to vote on the Revisionist boycott resolution, and the confusion over the Transfer Agreement. "Labor [Mapai] must accept the responsibility . . . Labor had a virtual majority; Labor controlled the Congress; Labor said absolutely nothing must be said about the boycott." Wise then told of his repeated but unavailing efforts to force revocation of the Transfer Agreement and indeed all relations between Zionist bodies and the Third Reich.[18]

Rabbi Wise tried to cast the best light possible upon the Second World Jewish Conference held in Geneva. Although he extolled its show of unity, he was in the end forced to confront the fact that the boycott had not been organized, that Geneva had failed in its prime mission. The boycott, asserted Wise, "is a weapon, but it is not *the* weapon. . . . The president of the United States and the prime minister of England can do more than a hundred boycotts." [19]

Wise spoke for some time to the Administrative Committee, alone and without interruption, offering sharp analysis, defensive explanations, rambling insights, emotional observations, and desperate denials. He had tried to explain his motives, his achievements, his contributions, his failures, his disappointments. To both critics and supporters alike, Wise summed up his efforts with these emotional words: "I gave my best, I gave the uttermost of my devotion, and such strength as I have, to the American Jewish Congress and the World Jewish Conference. In return, I think I have the right to ask for the loyal, faithful cooperation of the members of the Administrative Committee in the days that are coming. I would like to feel that, whether the members . . . always agree with me or not—after all, I am not an arbiter, I am not a tyrant, I do not try to impose my will upon this body—I may have made a mistake in the boycott, I don't believe I did." [20]

The very first to speak after Wise's apologia was Mrs. Goldie Myerson, an Administrative Committee member and prominent Mapai leader in America. She declared Wise could not expect Mapai people to sit by quietly in the face of his remarks about the Zionist Congress. Others tried to steer the conversation to pragmatic questions of cooperation with Untermyer's movement and whether Wise's report was acceptable. Mrs. Myerson interrupted and demanded that some of Dr. Wise's comments about Mapai be stricken from the record.[21] Mrs. Goldie Myerson was later to change her name to Golda Meir and become one of Israel's most memorable prime ministers.

Mrs. Myerson's objections were finally overruled, and the ensuing debate revolved around whether Stephen Wise had properly explained himself. In one inadvertent but telling remark, Bernard Deutsch, Wise's most loyal associate, declared that Dr. Wise had satisfactorily answered what he had "been charged with" doing in Europe. Stephen Wise immediately stood to reject this unintentionally accusatory language. Wise denied that the vituperations of his critics, such as Untermyer, were valid charges, and he asked that Deutsch's comments be expunged from the record.[22]

Then Joseph Tenenbaum, a leading boycott advocate, rose to second a motion of confidence, adding these comments: "Dr. Wise was the first to raise the question of a boycott, but a silent boycott. It is not due to him that the silent boycott on our part was not put into action. . . . Dr. Wise was not opposed to the [boycott] resolution, only postponement. We got his . . . [pro-boycott] opinion in Prague when it was announced throughout the world. . . . I therefore rise not only to endorse the action of Dr. Wise, but to assure him that our loyalty is steadfast . . . and that we are happy to greet him here and to thank him for his noble work in Europe as well as here."[23]

Those dissatisfied with Wise's statement, especially Mr. Zelig Tygel, who had become an Untermyer organizer, pressed for a debate with an eye toward forcing Wise to cooperate with Untermyer.[24] But Wise's supporters outnumbered the critics. His supporters could not abandon the man who had devoted his entire life's energies to the defense and advancement of the Jewish community. And they could not abandon him because Stephen Wise *was* the Congress. Yes, there were hundreds of thousands of federated members, with branch offices and constituent organizations in dozens of cities; there were committees and commissions and special panels and an array of vice-presidents and functioning and titular officials. But all that notwithstanding, Stephen Wise *was* the Congress. And they could not and would not abandon him.

Nor did Stephen Wise want to be abandoned. For Wise, there was no existence outside his devotion to the cause of Jewish dignity and rights. Jewish leadership was his air, his salt, his bread.

In a moment of choice, his supporters stood to demand a resolution of full confidence for Stephen Wise. Finally, even his detractors could not abstain. The resolution was carried unanimously.[25]

The next day, September 24, at a Congress press conference, Wise announced the immediate pursuit of German Jewish emigration, with a special provision whereby emigrants to Palestine could take part of their capital, along the lines of the Ruppin plan introduced at the Eighteenth Zionist Congress.[26]

As for the boycott, Wise was confronted by acerbic questions from reporters about cooperation with Untermyer, Wise's sabotage of the London boycott conference, and Wise's stance on the boycott altogether. Wise answered that he would cooperate with Untermyer's League for the Defense of Jewish Rights (American alter ego of Untermyer's Federation) if Untermyer would cooperate with the American Jewish Congress. "The boycott began long before the American League for the Defense of Jewish Rights was dreamed of," Wise said. "When I was pressed to declare a boycott, my position was this: A boycott, yes, by all means, the stiffest, sternest kind of boycott against German wares, products and goods, but there were . . . considerations that moved me, and I am not in the last ashamed of having been governed by them.[27]

"Some of you [reporters] may not have thought it important . . . but in March and April, a rather well-known citizen of the United States whose name is Franklin Delano Roosevelt was preparing to convene . , . a World Economic Conference. . . . I confess that I felt as an American that I did not wish to . . . [facilitate] a conference to be called in London for a boycott against Germany . . . at a time and in a place at which . . . the president of the United States had summoned a World Economic Conference."[28] With his customary flair, Wise defiantly told them, "Whether that was an error of judgment will be decided, not by you, ladies and gentlemen, but by the times that are to be."[29]

Fall was approaching and the Reich was unsure whether they had broken the boycott. The Eighteenth Zionist Congress had adjourned on September 4 with a guarantee that the boycott would be smothered, but the ensuing days revealed a continued drama of major boycott developments. On September 6, the 600,000-member Federation of Swedish Trade Unions adopted the boycott—as their British and Dutch counterparts had in prior weeks. Sweden was among Germany's most vital customers, and because the Stockholm government openly endorsed the action, the move was seen as semi-official. In America, Untermyer was proving unstoppable as he began constructing a nationwide boycott infrastructure to snuff out Germany's last large markets in the United States. Since so many prominent Zionists were at Geneva when Stephen Wise's conference promulgated its "spontaneous" boycott resolution, the Reich again wondered if the Zionists were not playing a duplicitous game.[30]

On September 13, 1933, Hitler's news organ, *Volkischer Beobachter*, published a threatening notice. "It is clear that the Zionists are responsible for the boycott resolution presented to Geneva. With Rabbi Wise and other Geneva boycott leaders being directly drawn from the Zionist Organization, it could not be otherwise. . . . Boycott of this sort would be equivalent to a declaration of war! . . . The Board of Deputies is playing a double game with Germany. With one hand it is holding in check the boycott movement and with the other it is inciting the British government to act against Germany."[31]

Nazi Germany could take no chances. They would have to be ready for the worst. On September 13, Chancellor Hitler and Propaganda Minister Goebbels entered a Berlin reception room where the foreign and domestic press was waiting. As Hitler appeared, an honor cadre of tall, muscular black-shirted guards snapped to attention with a forceful click of heels, a powerful raised-arm salute, and a unison shout of "Heil Hitler." Der Führer, dressed in a dark blue double-breasted suit, acknowledged the ritual with his customary return gesture—arm casually bent at the elbow, palm facing forward.[32]

Goebbels walked to the front and announced a comprehensive Winter

Relief program to keep starvation from the German people during the coming bitter months. Beginning at once, all Germans would be expected to make the Sunday midday meal—traditionally the elaborate family meal—a one-pot affair costing no more than fifty pfennigs. This cost limit would restrict the fare to varieties of puddings, porridge, stew, and soup. The savings was to be donated to Winter Relief to feed the unemployed. National meatless days were to be observed once weekly, with fish being recommended to help the ailing fish industries. All public restaurants, hotels, and railway dining cars would be expected to serve model one-pot meals as an example to the rest of the country.[33]

Farmers would be required to donate foodstuffs. Retailers were to contribute warm clothing. Fuel companies were to donate coal and oil. Relief goods would reach the smallest dorf via an immense distribution network manned by transport employees, the army, police, fire brigades, and Nazi volunteers. The railroads would carry all goods free of charge, the bus companies would provide vehicles. The hardest-hit towns and rural areas were to be "adopted" by more fortunate locales.[34]

A second phase of Winter Relief revolved around a fund-raising effort that Goebbels termed "unparalleled" and "grandiose." A house-to-house donation drive was to canvass every urban and rural dwelling. Any German with an active bank account was instructed to make an immediate deduction. Workmen were to donate one hour's wages each month. All those donating once for the month would receive a special tag or home plaque making them immune from street collectors. Special donations were encouraged from all commercial concerns and individuals, especially Jews and foreign-relief organizations if they expected to keep Jews from starvation that winter. Arrangements were made for exemplary large contributions: RM 100,000 from NSDAP headquarters in Munich and *Volkischer Beobachter*; various banks and manufacturing firms donated RM 30,000 to RM 50,000 each; I. G. Farben outdid them all with a RM 1 million contribution.[35]

The fact that Hitler appeared in person for Goebbels' announcement and the fact that the foreign press was invited was significant. This was to be the first big, decisive battle, the battle for survival. Would Germany crack that winter? Adolf Hitler was boldly telling the world his answer: *nein*!

The one man who most embodied the potential death blow to Germany was Samuel Untermyer. Upon learning of the Transfer Agreement and the Eighteenth Zionist Congress' refusal to join the boycott, Untermyer dispatched organizers throughout America to commence a massive fund-raising campaign for his new boycott organization. By the time the shock of Geneva's inaction registered, Untermyer's American League for the Defense of Jewish Rights had called an emergency meeting of 250 national civic, business, and interfaith leaders.[36]

On September 10, standing before his boycott leaders at New York's

Hotel Astor, Untermyer issued a warning to Hitler: "The day of reckoning is at hand!" In a matter of hours, a national strategy had been formulated. The United States was divided into twelve boycott zones. Nonsectarian coordination committees would work on an industry-by-industry basis to replace German products with substitutes of equal quality, preferably American products. Boycott offices were to act as clearinghouses to "reduce imports from Germany to the vanishing point."[37]

Much of the appeal would be "strictly business," involving entrepreneurs whose sole interest was ousting their German competitors. Shielded from publicity, a great numer of major U.S. corporations could then quietly take a leading role in the boycott. The movement would be brought into every neighborhood via posters, plaques, filmstrips, and radio talk shows, all of it dovetailing with the National Recovery Act, making it a patriotic duty to switch to American goods. An international liaison office would coordinate with the commercial attachés and trade sections of foreign embassies and consulates, introduce foreign chambers of commerce to American sources, and publish weekly trade bulletins.[38]

Women, the greatest commercial power in America, would be the front line of offense. In addition to organizing consumers, women by the thousands were to go from store to store, identifying remnant German stock and convincing merchants to return or withdraw them.[39]

Leading the war alongside Untermyer would be a "committee of 100" located in all major cities. The top fifteen of this committee would function as the decision-making body. The assembled delegates expeditiously elected J. George Fredman of the Jewish War Veterans; Elias Ginsburg, America's top-ranking Revisionist; outspoken Zionist leader Rabbi Abba Hillel Silver of Cleveland; Max Korshak of Chicago; Philadelphia publisher J. David Stern, and ten others.[40]

To blanket the nation with boycott required half a million dollars at once. An inaugural dinner was held that night, September 10, to launch the fundraising campaign. Over 1,500 guests were encouraged by former U.S. Ambassador to Germany James W. Gerard, former secretary of state Bainbridge Colby, and former New York governor Al Smith. The major speeches congratulating Untermyer and advocating boycott were once again broadcast live on national radio. And newspapers devoted prominent coverage to the new boycott organization.[41]

During the days and weeks to follow, Untermyer's hundred disciples set off to bring the nation to boycott. Donations poured in. Offices opened. Printing presses began rolling. Women took to the avenues with their banners and their clipboards.[42]

Industrial experts were tapped to identify alternate sources for the 7,000 German products still sold in America. The boycott had been well received in the more populated East, the North, and the West, but remained relatively undeveloped in the South and the Southwest. For instance, 25 percent of the sugar beets used by southern sugar-beet refineries came from German farms in Westphalia. But swift action was seen when by September 16, the Kansas City boycott committee enlisted the cooperation of sixteen regional food wholesalers in gathering the signatures of 8,000 retail grocers demanding southern beet refineries replace German beet sugar with crops grown in America and elsewhere.[43]

A whirlwind tour by the seventy-five-year-old Untermyer was scheduled at once for Philadelphia, Hartford, Chicago, St. Louis, San Francisco and other cities.[44]

And he built a national organization, or at least the skeleton of one. It took several months, but there were official district offices throughout the country, and informal grass-roots offices in dozens of cities. Hundreds of thousands of dollars had been raised nationally to pay for the trains and cabs, the posters and stamps, the telephones and telegrams, the rents and the little miscellaneous things like coffee and doughnuts for the December picket lines.

But it was too late. It was just too late. It had all taken too long. By the time Untermyer's organized boycott was skeletally in place, winter had arrived. Too much time had been lost. The crucial late-summer, fall, and early-winter German exports had not been sufficiently disrupted to have an impact during the brunt of the cold winter months. Untermyer's people tried. But they just couldn't do it in time. Many had perceived the coming defeat even before the final campaign began on September 10. But they had to try. They were ultimately forced to accept the awesome reality: Germany did not crack that winter.

Epilogue: The Transfer Years

Germany did not crack that winter, but the anti-Nazi boycott continued. Month after month, and indeed year after year, Samuel Untermyer tirelessly worked toward the economic downfall of the Third Reich. There were periodic showdowns with major department stores, with American industries buying German commodities, and even with the U.S. Postal Service, which awarded lucrative transatlantic contracts to German shipping lines. The Reich was able to regularly foil the boycott's full effectiveness by exporting via third countries and by mislabeling German merchandise as "Made in Switzerland," "Made in Saxony," or "Made in Austria."

The American and world masses grew tired of incessant boycott pleas, key workers became too ill to continue, and funds dried up. Thus, vital boycott bastions often crumbled from apathy or neglect. Constant vigilance was required to rebuild the breaches. Boycotting became a *cause célèbre* among a dedicated core of volunteers, who were often a few hours too late to stop a German delivery, or a few dollars too short to achieve a regional victory.

For Germany, the boycott was a constant harassment, denying the Nazis the economic recovery they sought. Each autumn, the Reich would announce a Winter Relief program to undo the economic damage of the previous spring and summer. Winter Relief became institutional and the Nazis turned it into a gala patriotic season of struggle. The hated one-pot meals were popularized by a gamut of gimmicks—from circus elephants lugging one-pot posters through town squares, to staged extravaganzas featuring Germany's finest chefs, bedecked in white uniforms, each with his gourmet rendering of a fifty-pfennig, one-pot meal. Door-to-door relief collections became a celebrity affair, with Hermann Goering and Magda Goebbels jingling their tin collection boxes on street corners along with the rank and file. Even when Winter Relief was only marginally necessary, the Reich maintained it to keep morale high.

The indefatigable work of Untermyer and the other champions of boycott kept recovery out of Hitler's reach. It forced the Third Reich to vigilantly restrain anti-Jewish violence in Germany, since each incident helped intensify the anti-Nazi movement. In its first years, the boycott also helped prevent Hitler from carrying out his vow to conquer Europe. Plagued by boycott and antagonistic trade barriers, and continually denied foreign exchange, the Reich was for years unable to acquire the raw materials needed to rebuild its war machine. Hitler was repeatedly forced to push back his war timetables. Hjalmar Schacht, charged with creating the war economy, devised the only alternative. It was the so-called New Plan, begun in late 1934, whereby Germany would withdraw from Western commerce, execute bilateral barter agreements with Eastern and underdeveloped countries rich in raw materials, and achieve a high level of economic self-sufficiency. In this way, the war machine could be built despite the scarcity of foreign currency.

In the meantime, Jewish existence in Germany underwent a rapid dismantling. Jewish communities in many provincial districts and towns essentially disappeared. The Jewish niche in many economic sectors vanished as industries and professions cleansed themselves of Jewish participation. Jewish cultural contributions were banned. Jewish scholarship in universities ended almost entirely, with few opportunities for Jewish youth to advance beyond secondary school.

The more repressive conditions in the provinces forced Jews to migrate to the large cities, such as Berlin, Hamburg, Frankfurt, and Munich, where Jewish communities were allowed—in condensed form—to maintain a special subculture of religious, cultural, and athletic activities, a revival of Hebrew, and a rapid integration with the Zionist movement. The Nazis delighted in the Jewish subculture and demanded that it thrive. Indeed, every Jewish gathering was approved and attended by the Gestapo. For Aryans, an active Jewish subculture provided reinforcement that Jews were an alien people who had no place in Germany. In 1935, Jewish existence continued to contract as fewer Jewish people could even survive in the Reich. Getting out was the only alternative to inevitable starvation.

As Jewish existence was dismantling in Germany, however, it was reconstructing in Jewish Palestine. The Haavara brought in many of the fundamentals: coal, iron, cement, fertilizer, seed, hammers, saws, and cultivators. Haavara also brought in the capital: cash, loans, mortgages, deposits, and credits. All this produced an economic explosion in Jewish Palestine, requiring companies to be formed, investments to be made, and most of all, jobs to be filled.

Palestine's economic absorptiveness tripled, perhaps quadrupled, within a year or so of the Transfer Agreement. Economic opportunity translated into a dramatic increase in immigration certificates under the twice-yearly "worker quota." Most of these certificates were awarded to Mapai's halutzim, the young pioneers eager to plant the seed, dig the ditches, and trowel the cement. As more buildings were erected, more kibbutzim established, and more small factories founded, ever more job openings were created for halutzim. The spiral of economic expansion increased the flow of worker immigrants from just a few thousand yearly before the Transfer Agreement to more than 50,000 during the two years following. Most were Mapai halutzim, and only about 20 percent of them were from Germany.

Jewish Palestine's rapidly expanding economy brought more than worker and commercial opportunities. There also developed a need for more doctors, lawyers, engineers, teachers, hoteliers, restaurateurs, and entrepreneurs. Many of these niches were filled by the several thousand German Jews who came over on unlimited capitalist certificates by virtue of Haavara.

By 1935, Palestine's need to sell German merchandise to offset Jewish deposits in transfer accounts became greater than anyone expected. The Palestinian market was becoming saturated. So the Zionist Organization established another transfer corporation, this one called the Near and Middle East Commercial Corporation, assigned the acronym NEMICO. NEMICO operated a regional sales network in Iraq, Egypt, Syria, Cyprus, and elsewhere in the region, coordinating mainly through Bank Zilkha of Beirut. Mideast markets were opened for a vast array of key German exports, from Volkswagens to municipal bridgeworks. This worked in tandem with

Hjalmar Schacht's New Plan of exchanging German goods for the raw materials of underdeveloped nations.

As NEMICO was opening new markets to German commerce, so too was the Palestinian citrus industry. Year after year, growers were increasingly compelled to become purveyors of German goods to guarantee vital Reich purchases of orange and grapefruit crops. Most of Palestine's commercial relationships with Nazi Germany remained a secret from the Jewish world, but several deals came to light. Trade statistics published by the British could not hide the unparalleled increase in German exports to Palestine. The Third World Jewish Conference held in Geneva in 1934 finally passed a resolution condemning Palestinian-German trade and demanding the Zionist Organization terminate all such contacts. Pressure within the Zionist world to disavow the Transfer Agreement and its complex of collateral undertakings became so intense by mid-1935 that the Anglo-Palestine Bank announced it was no longer willing to front for the Zionist Organization.

The question of abandoning the Haavara was debated during a period of escalated anti-Jewish persecution. The Third Reich was unhappy with the slow pace of Jewish exits from Germany. Life was therefore made progressively more unbearable. The list of Jewish prohibitions became more and more all-encompassing. Jews were not even allowed to enter many towns. The announcement in mid-1935 that racial laws would be decreed at the NSDAP's fall convention in Nuremberg presaged a turning point in the Reich's anti-Semitic campaign. The laws would deprive all Jews of their German citizenship and almost all legal rights. Moreover, the Nuremberg Laws would define exactly who was "Jewish," and were expected to include anyone with Jewish grandparents. This would extend the political pogrom to tens of thousands of German Jews who had previously felt somewhat safe in their niche on the periphery of the Jewish community.

As Nazi persecutions heightened in 1935, the world, saturated with approximately 100,000 penniless refugees, began closing its doors. Palestine was becoming the only haven available. As many Jews as possible had to be brought over from Germany as fast as possible—not to save their culture, not to save their wealth, but to save their lives.

A showdown over the Transfer Agreement occurred in late 1935 during the Nineteenth Zionist Congress held in Lucerne, Switzerland. The German Zionists were this time allowed to attend, with Adolf Eichmann monitoring from afar the delegation's every move. Mindful of Eichmann's distant scrutiny, the German delegates were the principal opponents of any boycott attempts. After great debate, the Congress finally declared that the Zionist Organization would openly take control of the Transfer Agreement from the Anglo-Palestine Bank. The bank complied by transferring its stock in Haavara Ltd. to the Jewish Agency. Just days later, the promised Nuremberg laws were published. The place for Jews in Germany was officially dissolved. The place for Jews in Palestine was all that was left.

Just two years before, Palestine had been a sparsely populated, mostly barren region inhabited by 800,000 Arabs, some in villages and towns, but most in rocky rural settings. These Arabs coexisted uneasily with approximately 200,000 religious Jews and Zionist pioneers, 80,000 of whom were in Jerusalem, the remainder living in a collection of unconnected settlement enclaves. From January to December of 1935, more than 53,000 European Jews, including almost 9,000 Germans, entered Palestine through worker and capitalist schedules, most of them by virtue of the new economy created by Haavara. By 1936, the Jewish population had doubled and those enclaves had begun growing and connecting. Town settlements and kibutzim had been planted up and down the coastal plain along the Mediterranean Sea between Tel Aviv and Haifa. The town of Haifa had itself grown into a bustling German immigrant city. More kibbutzim were appearing throughout the western Galilee. Palestine was on its way to a Jewish majority, on its way to Jewish statehood.

The Arabs revolted. Led by the virulently anti-Semitic pro-Nazi Mufti of Jerusalem, Arab activists in April 1936 began a six-month campaign of bombings, assassinations, ambushes, sabotage, and general strikes. Their target was all that was Jewish or British in Palestine, from synagogues to post offices. Only a rigorous crackdown by Great Britain restored a façade of order. However, Arab violence prompted the British to now talk openly of a permanent political solution in Palestine, creating two sovereign mini-states, one Arab, one Jewish. For the first time, the international community was seriously discussing establishing not a Jewish colony, not a Jewish homeland, not an autonomous Jewish canton, but a sovereign Jewish State. The Nazis were shocked.

For years Nazi leaders had cooperated with the Zionists, not out of sympathy with Jewish nationalism, but to effect the removal of Jews from Germany and to break the anti-Hitler boycott. Throughout it all, leading Nazis would regularly declare the need for a Jewish State. But Aryan concepts of Jewish inferiority never permitted them to really believe that the Jews could actually assemble a state. Yet in mid-1937, a British government commission formalized the recommendation: Disputed Palestine should be divided into sovereign Arab and Jewish states.

The Nazi hierarchy broke into two distinct schools of thought. The first wanted to expand the Haavara to concentrate as many Jews as possible in distant Palestine. The Jews would then be isolated from Germany's enemies, such as France and Great Britain. Later, when Germany was ready, perhaps it could still tackle the "Jewish menace" while Jews were concentrated and prone in one remote setting. The second school of thought, led by Eichmann, believed the Jews could and would create a state, that the Third Reich had been duped through Haavara into supplying the men and materials, and that once established, that state would become a "Jewish Vatican" devoted to Germany's destruction. Eichmann's answer was mass dispersion of utterly destitute Jews throughout the remote regions of South America and Africa, where local populations would rise up against them and wipe them out.

In the fall of 1937, after several months of uncertainty, der Führer finally decided in favor of Haavara; the government added its insistence that Jews be expelled not only from Germany but from all of Europe. Hitler's final attempt to prepare for war—the so-called Four Year Plan—was already under way. He wholly expected to begin his conquest of Europe in late 1939. Germany did not want yet another Jewish problem waiting when the Reich took over neighboring lands.

By 1937, Germany was no longer a powerless aggressor in Europe. The Nazi regime was partially armed and fully dangerous. No one in Europe wanted to provoke Germany by maintaining a Jewish presence. Since Palestine was the only open door for ousted Jews, Germany's neighbors began concluding transfer agreements with the Jewish Agency.

The first was Poland, which in late 1937 authorized a transfer company named Halifin Ltd. What Haavara had done for German Jewry and their assets, Halifin (Hebrew for "exchange") began doing for Polish Jewry and their assets, although on a far smaller scale.

The building of Palestine and the emigration of Jews literally became a matter of life or death. Every acre, every certificate, every seat on a ship bound for Haifa was yet another Jew saved from extinction in Germany. As the whole world knew, the rest of Europe was not far behind. Hitler's surrogates throughout Europe had successfully legitimized the persecution and expulsion of Jews. By the end of 1937, violent Nazi factions and their allies throughout Central and Eastern Europe were tired of waiting. Four years had passed since Hitler had assumed power, and the Jews had not yet been eradicated. Local pogroms became commonplace, not only in Germany but in Poland, Hungary, Rumania, Yugoslavia, Lithuania, and Austria.

Time was running out. Yet Palestine was far from ready to receive the hundreds of thousands needing to flee Europe. At the same time, British authorities had virtually closed Palestine to Jewish refugees in order to placate Arab opposition. Worker immigration quotas previously geared to economic absorptiveness were artificially stunted, allowing just several hundred desperate Jews into Palestine each month. The only way to continue the transfer and rescue was to bring over large groups of so-called capitalist emigrants possessing £1,000 each. Capitalist emigrants could bypass the quota system. But the impoverished German Jewish community was now almost out of assets to deposit and transfer, and the cash-strapped Reichsbank would no longer provide the required foreign currency.

It was now up to Haavara to acquire the foreign currency needed to bring Jews to safety. Working with the Reich Economics Ministry and the international consortium of creditor banks known as the Standstill Committee, which governed various aspects of Germany's foreign exchange, yet another transfer company was formed. This one was called the International Trade and Investment Agency Ltd., assigned the acronym INTRIA. INTRIA was permitted to intercept all relief donations intended for German Jews and divert them to Palestine. A special "relief mark" was introduced by the Reich and sold at banks around the world. By purchasing these relief marks, people in America or France could send charity dollars to their destitute loved ones still in Germany. An American donor, for example, would purchase $100 in relief marks from the American Express office in New York. American Express would credit the INTRIA account in London. INTRIA, however, would not send the money to the intended recipient in Germany. Instead, the money would be credited to a Zionist bureau in Palestine. INTRIA would then send a notice to Haavara's Berlin office, instructing it to pay the German recipient the *equivalent* of $100 in reichmarks from the blocked pool of Jewish deposits that had still not been transferred. In this way 71,000 donations from around the world, totaling almost $900,000, were diverted to Palestine and infused into the effort to build the Jewish home. Once in Palestine, the money was rewoven into various financial instruments and provided to desperate emigrants, enabling them to enter Palestine.

And still, the pace was not fast enough for Nazi Germany. No matter how much the Zionists expanded the economic structure of Palestine, the British did all in their power to obstruct the entry of Jews. With war imminent, Britain was worried about oil and strategic cooperation from Moslem groups in Iraq, Egypt, and India who opposed Jewish entry into Palestine even under these most dire circumstances. In mid-1938, an intergovernmental conference was held at Evian in an attempt to solve the crisis of both the refugees and the Jews still remaining in Germany. The Jewish Agency presented a plan for a worldwide German merchandise sale to finance the rescue of the remaining Jews of Germany and other European countries and their transfer to Palestine—the only haven available. But no action on a global transfer plan was taken. Few refugees were helped.

Nazi Germany was outraged. The world would not cooperate in the expulsion of Jews from Germany. In early November 1938, as a clear warning shot, Nazi officials staged a spectacular national pogrom. In a single night, thousands of Jews were dragged into concentration camps; roving bands filled the streets, beating and killing any Jews they could find; nearly every synagogue in Germany was set aflame; thousands of Jewish-owned store windows were broken in a ritual of hatred and sadism that became known to history as the Night of the Broken Glass—*Kristallnacht.*

By the summer of 1939, Austria had been "absorbed" by Germany; Czechoslovakia had been dismemberd under a Hitler *Diktat.* The question haunting the world was not whether war would come, but *when.* And still the British refused to reopen Palestine to admit the Jews frantic to leave Europe before the promised bloodbath. In desperation, Haavara officials shuttled from European capital to capital to negotiate transfer agreements.

One haavara was established with remnant Czechoslovakia pegged to the Jewish purchase of Czechoslovakian National Bank debentures. Rumania agreed to a haavara financing a fleet of freighters. Hungary, Italy, and several other nations under Fascist influence also signed agreements. By late summer of 1939, transfer agreements existed in at least six European countries.

Palestine was not quite ready, but it would suffice. European Jews were facing utter annihilation, and Zionism, through the dispassionate mobilization of money and malice, was now ready to rescue, ready to receive, ready for redemption.

And then, in September 1939, Germany invaded Poland. The Second World War had begun. Great Britain's mandated territory Palestine was forced to break all relations with Germany. The upheaval in Europe also forced the rupture of the other transfer agreements, most of them even before they began. Germany rolled through Europe, conquering or establishing puppet states with little difficulty. Its first order of business after every conquest was to ghettoize the Jews and then deport them to concentration camps where they were worked as slaves, often until death. At some point, too many Jews came under German jurisdiction. They could not be efficiently transported, housed, and worked in labor camps. Efforts were made to send them to Palestine via underground Zionist rescue routes. The Gestapo, working with elite Zionist rescue units known as Mossad, dispatched Jews in trucks, rickety ships, and on foot via Turkey, Bulgaria, and Rumania. When Britain would accept no more and the Zionist solution was no longer viable, a new solution was needed. In vast killing factories the Jews would be gassed and cremated. The names Auschwitz and Treblinka were added to the memory of man. This would be the Final Solution.

Six thousand per day went to Auschwitz alone. Some were fooled. Most knew. The world outside began to suspect. Newspapers reported the existence of the killing camps, front-page cartoons depicted the Angel of Death standing over the Jews of Europe, and the clouds over the world darkened with the smoke of incinerated human beings.

The struggle for a Jewish Homeland now entered a new and ever more painful phase. Without the transfer machinery, Zionist rescue committees were forced to pick and choose who would live and who would die. They could not save everyone in every place. Emphasis was placed on the young and the strong, who could survive the taxing journey to Palestine, often in the bottoms of leaky barges, squeezed between a cold, slimy wall and a grim, hungry comrade. They were also chosen for their ability to survive in a beloved but hostile land, wracked by desert heats, Arab enemies, and British masters. Last but not least, they were chosen to become a new breed of Jew that would never stand before a pit waiting for the bullet to arrive, never stand in a line waiting for a man with white gloves to send some to the left and some to the right—they would never stand and wait for destruction. They would fight first.

In the period between late 1933 and 1941, over $30 million had been transferred directly via Haavara. Perhaps another $70 million had flowed into Palestine via corollary German commercial agreements and special international banking transactions, this during a period when the average Palestinian Jew earned a dollar a day. Some of Israel's major industrial enterprises were founded with those monies, including Mekoroth, the national waterworks; Lodzia, a leading textile firm; and Rassco, a major land developer. And vast quantities of material were stockpiled, including coal, irrigation pipes, iron and metal products for companies and enterprises not yet in existence.

From 1933 to 1941, approximately one-hundred immigrant settlements were established along strategic corridors in western Galilee, the coastal plan, and in the northern Negev. About sixty of these settlements were established between 1936 and 1940. Most were possible only because Haavara or Haavara-related funds flowed to Zionist agencies for land purchase and development. And the settlements were made possible in large part because the Haavara economy had expanded the worker immigrant quota, allowing the influx of halutzim and German settlers. In 1948, the outline of these strategic settlements approximated the borders of the new Jewish State, for each settlement was not only a demarcation of Jewish life, each was an outpost of Jewish defense where battles were fought and a boundary line was ultimately drawn.

Between 1933 and 1941, 20,000 German Jews directly transferred to Palestine via Haavra. Many of them never collected their money, and often when they did, it was only partially in cash and mostly in mandatory stocks and mortgages. Another 40,000 German Jews emigrated to Palestine during this period via the indirect and corollary aspects of transfer. Many of these people, especially in the late 1930s, were allowed to transfer actual replicas of their homes and factories—indeed rough replicas of their very existences.

And something intangible also transferred with the German Jews during those years. It had nothing to do with concrete or cash accounts and had everything to do with culture. A German fondness for music, for art, for spotless homes, for cafés with chocolate tortes, for philosophy, for antiquities, for theater, for the finer things that struggling Palestine had never stopped to develop. These intangibles were transferred like everything else.

After World War II, when hundreds of thousands of Jews from a dozen different nations wandered through Europe stateless and displaced, each Jew a remnant of a family, a town or a ghetto, all ravaged survivors without homes and without lives to return to, after the Holocaust, when the moment of the in-gathering of the exiles was at hand, Israel was ready. A nation was waiting.

Fifteen years earlier, it hadn't existed. Fifteen years earlier few could have visualized what was to come, what was to be. But a small group of men did. They foresaw it all. That's why nothing would stop them; no force was too great to overcome. These men were the creators of Israel. And in order to do so, each had to touch his hand to the most controversial undertaking in Jewish history—the Transfer Agreement. It made a state. Was it madness, or was it genius?

Afterword
by Abraham H. Foxman

For years, students of the Holocaust have struggled over whether the Zionists did right or wrong in negotiating the Transfer Agreement with the Hitler regime. This arrangement transferred some 60,000 Jews and $100 million from Germany to Palestine during the pre-War years. To do so necessitated protracted commercial dealing with the Nazis and flew in the face of the global Jewish-led anti-Nazi boycott striving to topple the Hitler regime in its first years. The debate back in the thirties briefly tore the Jewish world apart before being relegated to the realm of a hushed necessity. In the aftermath of the Holocaust, the whole subject of the Haavara, or Transfer, was reduced to an obscure footnote. Despite the enormity of its economic and human importance to the Jews of Europe and the development of Palestine, the entire subject is conspicuously absent from almost all standard histories of the period.

But the debate was rekindled in 1984 when Edwin Black's book *The Transfer Agreement* appeared and told the full story for the first time, vividly describing in tense style the minute-to-minute negotiations as Zionists rushed to save what could be saved in the face of a darkening future.

People are still debating the Transfer Agreement, often just as acrimoniously as its proponents and opponents did in 1933. But what the men and women of those dark years slowly grew to understand and painfully accept has eluded the comfortable among us. Why? Because those who look back were not there, and did not live through the terrifying hours of the twelve-year Reich.

I was born in Poland. I was hidden in Vilna by my Polish Catholic nursemaid who baptized me, and I was reunited with my parents only after the War. That is why I am alive today.

I have spent all of my adult life in the organized defense of Jewish rights and dignity. That is why I live today.

Desperate situations, hard choices, agonizing possibilities and the debates between rescue and relief have filled my world since infancy. So I have an understanding of the heartbreaking decisions that must be made by leadership, just as I understand the throbbing compulsion by all people to confront those decisions.

In my mind, the Transfer Agreement's most important and indispensable element was the rescue of people. The rescue of assets comes second. But clearly, if the Zionists could rescue people only if they had assets and once rescued, assets were needed to maintain those people in Palestine, it was the Zionists' duty to deal in assets. The cruel reality was that the price of salvaging these lives and assets was widespread trafficking in German goods.

Unquestionably, without the Transfer Agreement, German Jewry's property— and the people it sustained—would have been completely liquidated by the Nazis. Today's headlines are filled with tales of pilfered Jewish gold, Jewish art, Jewish insurance, Jewish property, and Jewish slave labor. Of course, the ultimate and most inestimable pilferage was the theft of Jewish life and culture that can never be replaced. The Transfer Agreement played a role for some 60,000 Jews who were allowed to live and transfer a modicum of their possessions to the only place in the world that would accept them—Palestine.

The potential for the subsequent transfer agreements negotiated in other countries, such as Czechoslovakia and Hungary, boggles the mind. Had the other Haavara agreements been implemented in the other European countries, we can only imagine how many more hundreds of thousands of Jews could have been saved. Unfortunately, the war broke out before these transfer organizations could make any meaningful progress.

The counterquestion is whether it was correct to deal with the Devil, and if the dealing itself strengthened that Devil. Decades later, it is easy to employ judgmental hindsight. Those who do so were not there but seem to think that books, records, and movies can adequately recreate the context. We are talking about the thirties—a very bad time for European Jews. But no one back then could imagine how bad things would actually become. Even Jabotinsky, who opposed the Haavara, and who had the vision to urge all Jews to leave Europe, could not imagine how much worse it would get. In light of the bitter reality of the Holocaust and the world's unwillingness to stop it, the decision to transfer Jews and their possessions to Palestine was a wise one.

Today, it is easy to display wisdom and perspective in retrospect. It is easy for us to judge in hindsight. But try as we might, there is no virtual reality button for Nazi Germany. We cannot recreate the emotion and context surrounding those dark days. We cannot fathom what was right and was wrong as much as the threatened communities themselves. True hindsight belongs not to pundits, but to history.

Jewish and Zionist leaders of the day confronted a history repeatedly marked by pogroms and expulsion. Each time we emerged from crisis, we hoped for the best. We always thought times had changed, that enlightenment had come, that things would get better. How could things be worse than the Middle Ages, worse than the Czar's oppression, we asked? How bad could it become in a cultured society such as Germany where Jews proudly displayed military medals and falsely felt completely integrated into society. But "How bad?" is indeed the central question Zionism has always posed . . . and always sought to preempt before learning the answer.

I remember a scene in the film *Ship of Fools.* The boat is sailing back to the Reich. German Jews are seated around the captain's table. A Jew cannot believe the dire consequences awaiting them. "What are they going to do," he asks incredulously, "kill a million Jews?" Many European Jews went to their death precisely because they couldn't imagine that such atrocities could occur.

Nor could anyone. Zionists negotiating the Transfer Agreement did not anticipate the concentration camps and gas chambers. No civilized person could. But those in Zionist leadership did understand one precept: it can always get worse. They understood that even their darkest nightmares could somehow become blacker in ways they could not predict—and indeed no one since has ever been able to explain. For this reason, statebuilding was the Zionist priority. Transfer was their mechanism. German goods was the hateful modality. As a result, lives were saved, property transferred, and an indispensable column of the human, economic, and physical infrastructure of the future state of Israel was erected.

Motivated by the desire to save both the threatened community and future communities, the Zionists had to coldly assume the distasteful, gun-to-temple responsibilities of standing up to the Devil in his own lair and negotiating a way out. That way was the Transfer Agreement.

Certainly, we have learned from the Haavara. Its legacy has been replayed in the rescue of Soviet, Ethiopian, Syrian, Iranian, and Yemenite Jewry. The mechanisms and methods have differed, but have always abided by the same imperative. At some point, when the effort for relief and defense yields to the rush to rescue, negotiations are needed. A mechanism is needed. It will be created.

The enemies of the Jewish people and the Jewish nation will always claim that Zionists undertook the Transfer just to promote emigration. Just to build their state. That's the easy cop-out for people who don't see red when Jewish blood spills. But we do. The people who were there know better. And thanks to Edwin Black's *The Transfer Agreement,* future generations can also know what the victims of that day ultimately and painfully understood.

Abraham H. Foxman is national director of the Bnai Brith's Anti-Defamation League. He resides in the New York area.

Notes

AJA	American Jewish Archives	Cincinnati
AJCm	American Jewish Committee	New York
AJCmA	American Jewish Committee Archives	New York
AJC	American Jewish Congress	New York
AJCAdCom	American Jewish Congress Administrative Committee	Waltham
AJHS	American Jewish Historical Society	Waltham
ALM	Beit Lessin/Archives of the Labor Movement	Tel Aviv
BDC	Berlin Documentation Center	Berlin
BERL	Bet Berl/Mapai Archives	Kfar Saba
BBA	B'nai B'rith Archives	Washington, D.C.
BDBJ-A	Board of Deputies of British Jews Archives	London
BPM	Brandeis Papers Microfilm* at AJA	Cincinnati
BA	Bundesarchiv	Koblenz
CAJP	Central Archives for the Jewish People	Tel Aviv
CZA	Central Zionist Archives	Jerusalem
DDF	*Documents Diplomatiques Francais*	Paris
DBFP	*Documents on British Foreign Policy*	London
DGFP	*Documents on German Foreign Policy*	London
18th ZC	18th Zionist Congress	Vienna
FA	Ford Archives	Dearborn
FRUS	*Foreign Relations of the United States*	Washington, D.C.
HAG	Hagana Archives	Tel Aviv
HS	*Hebrew Standard*	New York
HMSO	His/Her Majesty's Stationery Office	London
HIST	Histtadrut Archives	Tel Aviv
IfZ	Institut fer Zeitgeschichite	Munich
ICJ	Institute for Contemporary Jewry	Jerusalem
YIVO	Institute for Jewish Research	New York
ISA	Israel State Archives	Jerusalem
JABA	Jabotinsky Archives	Tel Aviv
JA Exec	Jewish Agency Exec Committee	Jerusalem
JC	Jewish Chronicle	London
JDB	*Jewish Daily Bulletin*	New York

JEF	Jewish Economic Forum	London
JLMA	Jewish Labor Movement Archives	New York
JPSA	Jewish Publication Society of America	Philadelphia
JWV	Jewish War Veterans Files	New York & Washington, D.C.
JBC	Joint Boycott Committee Archives at AJA	Cincinnati
JR	*Juedische Rundschau*	Berlin
LBI-A	Leo Baeck Institute Archives	New York
NA	National Archives	Washington, D.C.
NYPL	New York Public Library Manuscript Collection	New York
NYT	*New York Times*	New York
PA	*Politische Archiv/Auswartiges Amt*	Bonn
PSA	Prussian State Archives	Berlin
PRO-FO	Public Record Office/Foreign Office	London
SA	Sarnoff Archives	Princeton
SR	Sears Roebuck Archives	Chicago
SC	Spertus College Collection	Chicago
VB	Volkischer Beobachter	Munich
WA	Weizmann Archives	Rehovet
WWI	Weltwirtschafts Institut	Keil
WLB	*Wiener Library Bulletin*	London
YVA	Yad Vashem Archives	Jerusalem
ZA	Zionist Archives	New York
ZOE	Zionist Organization Executive	London
ZOA	Zionist Organization of America	New York

*Original Brandeis Papers at University of Louisville.

AUTHORS/TRANSLATORS

GB	George Bichunsky	VH	Varda Hirsch
YC	Yoni Cohen	DN	Dan Niederland
DD	Danuta Dombrowska	MS	Manfred Seigfried
EF	Egon Fain	SS	Shlomo Sela
HG	Hanna Gunther	NS	Nathan Synder
GG	Gali Gur	GW	Gabi Witzum
OH	Otto Hirsch	GZ	George Zinnemann

CHAPTER 1

1. Arthur D. Morse, *While Six Million Died: A Chronicle of American Apathy* (New York: Ace, 1968), 101; John Fox, "Great Britain and the Jews, 1933," *Wiener Library Bulletin* XXVI (nos. 1–2 [1972], n.s. nos. 26–27): 40–46; telegram, "The Secretary of State to the Chargé in Germany (Gordon)," *FRUS* (1933) II: 337; "Joint Statement by President Roosevelt and the German Representative (Schacht)," *FRUS* (1933) I: 505; see Cordell Hull, *The Memoirs of Cordell Hull* (New York: Macmillan, 1948), I: 231, 383; also see Hull, *Memoirs*, II: 978; see Naomi Cohen, *Not Free to Desist: The American Jewish Committee, 1906–1966* (Philadelphia: JPSA, 1972), 162; "Hull Obtains Consul's Data on Jews," *Chicago Sunday Tribune*, Mar. 26, 1933.

2. Nathan Schachner, *The Price of Liberty: A History of the American Jewish Committee* (New York: AJC, 1948), Eric E. Hirshler, "Jews From Germany in the United States," *Jews From Germany in the United States,* ed. Eric E. Hirshler (New York: Farrar, Straus and Cuddahy, 1955), 72–75; Moses Rischin, *The Promised City: New York's Jews, 1870–1914* (Cambridge, Mass.: Harvard, 1977), 95–98; *HS*, June 15, 1894, as quoted in Rischin, 97; Edward E. Grusb, *B'nai B'rith: The Story of a Covenant* (N.Y.: Appleton–Century, 1966), vii, 12–23, 89–90, 113, 125.

3. Edward E. Grusd, *B'nai B'rith: The Story of a Covenant* (New York: Appleton–Century, 1966), vii, 12–23, 89–90, 113, 125.

4. Cohen, *Not Free*, 15–17; Schachner, 25–26.

5. Letter, Jacob Schiff to Max Warburg, Nov. 5, 1915, cited in Cyrus Adler, *Jacob H. Schiff: His Life and Letters* (Garden City, New York: Doubleday, Doran, 1928), II:190–91; see letter, Jacob Schiff to Alfred Zimmermann, Nov. 9, 1914, cited in Isaiah Friedman, *Germany, Turkey and Zionism, 1897–1918* (Oxford: Clarendon, 1977), 205; see Adler, *Schiff*, II: 181–82; Cyrus Adler, *Jacob H. Schiff: His Life and Letters* (Garden City, N.Y.: Doubleday, Doran, 1928) II: 190–91.

6. Stephen Wise, *Challenging Years: The Autobiography of Stephen Wise* (New York: Putnam, 1949), 202–5; Rosenstock, 53–54; Frommer, 67, 528–529; Schachner, 28.

7. *Ibid.*, 205–6.

8. *Ibid.*, 207; Morton Rosenstock, *Louis Marshall, Defender of Jewish Rights* (Detroit: Wayne State, 1962), 52–53; see Cohen, *Not Free*, 102–19; also see letter, Jacob Schiff to Solomon Schechter, Sept. 22, 1907, and assorted writings of Jacob Schiff, 1915–1920, cited in Adler, *Schiff*, II: 166–69, 296–98, 307–20.

9. Rosenstock, 52–53; see Cohen, *Not Free*, 102–19; also see letter, Jacob Schiff to Solomon Schechter, Sep. 22, 1907, and assorted writings of Jacob Schiff, 1915–1920, cited in Adler, *Schiff*, II; 166–69, 296–98, 307–20.

10. Grusd, 185–86, 194–97; Schachner, 109–14; Morris Frommer, "The American Jewish Congress: A History, 1914–1950," (unpub. Ph.D. diss., Ohio State, 1978), 37, 58, 60, 322, 337–41; Cohen, *Not Free*, 5, 20–21, 155, 193; see Andre Manners, *Poor Cousins* (New York: Coward, McCann and Geoghegan, 1972), 275–77.

11. Palestine Royal Commission, *Report of the Palestine Royal Commission* (London: HMSO, 1937), 2–5; Esco Palestine Study Committee, *Palestine: A Study of Jewish, Arab and British Policies* (New Haven: Yale, 1947), I: 17–18, 54, 333, 338–40, 366–81; Esco, II: 686–90; "Israel," *Encyclopaedia Judaica* (Jerusalem: Keter, 1972) IX: 248.

12. Yehuda Chorin, *Citrus in Israel* (Tel Aviv: Israel Periodicals, 1966), 26–27; Sophie A. Udin, ed., *The Palestine Year Book 5706: Review of Events, July 1944 to July 1945,* I (Washington, D.C.: ZOA, 1945), 209 10; see "Minutes of Conversation on Jewish Labor in Offices of the Histadrut in T.A.," Jan. 4, 1933, BPM at AJA; Walter Laqueur, *A History of Zionism* (New York: Holt, Rinehart and Winston, 1972), 308, 315, 316.

13. See Nicholas Bethell, *The Palestine Triangle: The Struggle for the Holy Land, 1935–48* (New York: Putnam, 1979), 24; see "British Policy in Palestine, 1922," (Churchill White Paper), cited in Esco, I: 282–84; Esco, I: 256, 315–18; Esco, II: 645–48, 653–54; Great Britain Colonial Office, *Palestine and Trans-Jordan for the Year 1932* (London: HMSO, 1933), 24–27; see "Immigration to Palestine with Reference to German Jewish Refugees," PRO-FO 371/16767–1527, pp. 58–60.

CHAPTER 2

1. Letter, Alfred M. Cohen to Morris D. Waldman, Feb. 16, 1933, AJCmA; *Annual Report of the Executive Committee, 27th Annual Report* (New York, 1934), BBA, 36.

2. See Stephen Wise, *Challenging Years: The Autobiography of Stephen Wise* (New York: Putnam, 1949), 236–37; see *Annual Report of the Executive Committee,* BBA, 36; Moshe Gottlieb, "The Anti-Nazi Boycott Movement in the United States: An Ideological and Sociological Appreciation," *Jewish Social Studies* XXXV (July–Oct., 1973): 199, 211, 225; Edward E. Grusd, *B'nai B'rith: the Story of a Covenant* (New York: Appleton–Century, 1966),

201; Deborah Dash Moore, *B'nai B'rith and the Challenge of Ethnic Leadership* (Albany: State Univ. of New York, 1981), 176).

3. Gottlieb, "Anti-Nazi Boycott Movement," (article), 211.

4. "Victory for Hitler is Expected Today," *NYT*, Mar. 5, 1933; "Offices of Jews Raided," *NYT*, Mar. 6, 1933.

5. See F. Thelwell, "Memorandum on the German Economic Situation, April 1933," Apr. 26, 1933, PRO-FO 371/16695–1527, pp. 1–3, 7–10; Dr. Joseph Goebbels, *My Part in Germany's Fight,* trans. Dr. Kurt Fiedler (London: Hurst and Black-

ett, 1935), 227–29; see telegram, "The Counselor of Embassy in Germany (Gordon) to the Secretary of State," Mar. 23, 1933, *FRUS 1933* (Washington, D.C.: United States Government Printing Office, 1949), II: 328–29; "Reich Takes Over Rule of Hamburg," NYT, Mar. 5, 1933; "Nazi Bands Stir Up Strife in Germany," *NYT*, Mar. 9, 1933; "3 More Americans Attacked in Berlin as Raiding Goes On," *NYT*, Mar. 10, 1933; "German Fugitives Tell of Atrocities," *NYT*, Mar. 20, 1933; "Reports of German Atrocities Not Exaggerated, Declares Anglo–Jewish Doctor," *JDB*, Mar. 24, 1933.

6. "3 More Americans Attacked," *NYT*, Mar. 10, 1933.

7. "Protest Meeting at Madison Square Garden Decided on by American Jewish Congress," *JDB*, Mar. 14, 1933.

8. See "Protest Meeting at Madison Square Garden," *JDB*, Mar. 14, 1933.

9. Letter, M. D. Waldman to A. M. Cohen, Mar. 15, 1933, AJCmA.

10. *Ibid.*

11. *Ibid.*; See letter, S. S. Wise to L. D. Brandeis, Mar. 23, 1933, in Carl Hermann Voss, ed., *Stephen S. Wise: Servant of the People* (Philadelphia: JPSA, 1969), 180–81.

12. *Ibid.*; See "Speech of Hitler in Reischstag on His Policies for Germany," *NYT*, Mar. 24, 1933; William L. Shirer, *The Rise and Fall of the Third Reich: A History of Nazi Germany* (New York: Fawcett Crest, 1960), 191–92.

13. *Annual Report of the Executive Committee*, BBA, 37, 39; Stephen Birmingham, *"Our Crowd:" the Great Jewish Families of New York* (New York: Dell, 1967), 416–28; Wise, 219.

14. Letter, Waldman to Cohen, March 15, 1933, AJCmA.

15. Telegram, Harry Schneiderman to Alfred M. Cohen, Mar. 14, 1933, AJCmA.

16. Letter, Waldman to Cohen, Mar. 15, 1933, AJCmA; cable, Waldman to Cohen, Mar. 15, 1933, AJCmA.

17. Interview with Morris Mendelsohn by Moshe Gottlieb, July 20, 1965, author's transcript.

18. *Ibid.*

19. *Ibid.*; "Conference Called by the Jewish Congress Decides on Protest Demonstration," *JDB*, Mar. 21, 1933.

20. *Annual Report of the Executive Committee*, BBA, 37.

21. Letter, Werner Senator to Berl Locker, Mar. 19, 1933, CZA S49/381 (trans. GZ/EF).

22. Moshe Gottlieb, "The Anti-Nazi Boycott Movement in the American Jewish Community, 1933–1941," (unpub. Ph.D. diss., Near Eastern and Judaic studies, Brandeis, 1967), 20.

23. Goebbels, 236–37; "Reich is Worried Over Our Reaction," *NYT*, Mar. 23, 1933; also see "Herr Hitler's Nazis Hear an Echo of World Opinion," *NYT*, Mar. 26, 1933.

24. Statement, AJC, in Gottlieb, "Anti-Nazi Boycott Movement," (dissertation), 46.

25. "Nazi Foes Here Calmed by Police," *NYT*, Mar. 20, 1933.

26. *Ibid.*; "Conference Called by the Jewish Congress," *JDB*, Mar. 21, 1933; "American Jewry Protests," *JC*, Mar. 24, 1933.

27. "Nazi Foes Here Calmed by Police," *NYT*, Mar. 20, 1933; "Conference Called," *JDB*, Mar. 21, 1933; "American Jewry Protests," *JC*, Mar. 24, 1933.

28. See letter, John Haynes Holmes to Stephen Wise, Apr. 20, 1933, BPM at AJA; see "Christian Leaders Protest on Hitler," *NYT*, Mar. 22, 1933; also see press release, AJC, Sep. 16, 1933, BPM at AJA.

29. Interview with Morris Mendelsohn.

30. "Boycott Advocated to Curb Hitlerism," *NYT*, Mar. 21, 1933; interview with Morris Mendelsohn.

31. "Vast Protest Movement Throughout Poland: Jews, Non-Jews Join in Demonstration," *JDB*, Mar. 29, 1933; dispatch, British Embassy, Warsaw, to Sir John Simon, Mar. 29, 1933, PRO-FO 371/16721–1556; "Poland Antagonized," *JC*, Mar. 31, 1933; see telegram, "The Ambassador in Great Britain to the Foreign Minister," Mar. 8, 1933, *DGFP 1918–1945* (London: HMSO, 1957), ser. C, I: 124–25; telegram, "The Deputy of Department IV to the Consulate General at Danzig," Mar. 10, 1933, *DGFP*, 130; "The Minister in Poland to the Foreign Ministry," Apr. 19, 1933, and enclosed memorandum, Apr. 12, 1933, *DGFP*, 306–10; also see "In Europe's New Tenseness the 'Corridor' Looms Large," *NYT*, Mar. 19, 1933.

32. "Polish Jews Condemn Germany," *NYT*, Mar. 21, 1933; "Vast Protest Movement Throughout Poland," *JDB*, Mar. 29, 1933.

33. Carl Herman Voss, *Rabbi and Minister: The Friendship of Stephen S. Wise and John Haynes Holmes* (Buffalo, New York: Prometheus, 1980), 275–76.

34. Letter, S. Wise to J. W. Mack, Mar. 8, 1933, in Voss, ed., *Servant*, 180.

35. "Jews Here Demand Washington Action," *NYT*, Mar. 21, 1933; "Protest on Hitler Growing in Nation," *NYT*, Mar. 23, 1933.

36. Letter, S. Wise to L. D. Brandeis, Mar. 23, 1933, in Voss, ed., *Servant*, 180–81; Wise, 218.

37. Morris Frommer, "The American Jewish Congress: A History, 1914–1950," (unpub. Ph.D. diss., history, Ohio State, 1978), 376–77; letter, Max J. Kohler to Cordell Hull, Aug. 28, 1933, AJCmA.

38. Gottlieb, "Anti-Nazi Boycott Movement," (dissertation), 453, n. 5.

39. *Ibid.*, 49; see telegram, "The Secretary of State to the Chargé in Germany (Gordon)," Mar. 24, 1933, *FRUS*, 330–31.

40. Martin Rosenbluth, *Go Forth and Serve: Early Years and Public Life* (New York: Herzl, 1961), 253; see *VB*, Apr. 1, 1933; "Roosevelt Under Jewish Influence, Nazis Charge," *JDB*, May 19, 1933; "Nazis Get Pick of Jobs," *NYT*, July 20, 1933.

41. "Reich is Worried Over Our Reaction," *NYT*, Mar. 23, 1933.

42. *Ibid.*; see "Memorandum of Press Conference of the Secretary of State," Mar. 22, 1933, *FRUS*, 327–28.

43. Nathan Schachner, *The Price of Liberty: A History of the American Jewish Committee* (New York: AJC, 1948), 113. Naomi W. Cohen, *Not Free to Desist: The American Jewish Committee, 1906–1966* (Philadelphia: JPSA, 1972), 162; see "Hull Obtains Consul's Data on Jews' Cases," *Chicago Sunday Tribune*, Mar. 26, 1933; see telegram, "The Secretary of State to the Chargé in Germany (Gordon)," Mar. 24, 1933, *FRUS*, 330–31.

44. See "Jews Here Demand Washington Action," *NYT*, Mar. 21, 1933.

45. *Ibid.*

46. Telegram, "The Secretary of State to the Chargé in Germany (Gordon)," Mar. 24, 1933, *FRUS*, 330–31; telegram, "The Secretary of State to the Chargé in Germany (Gordon)," Mar. 26, 1933,

FRUS, 333–34.

47. Cohen, 338; see Frederick Aaron Lazin, "The Reaction of American Jewry to Hitler's Anti-Jewish Policies 1933–1939 (unpub. Master's thesis, political science, Univ. of Chicago, 1968), 22; see "Jews Here Demand Washington Action," *NYT*, Mar. 21, 1933.

48. Telegram, "The Secretary of State to the Chargé in Germany (Gordon)," Mar. 24, 1933, *FRUS*, 330–31.

49. Telegram, "The Chargé in Germany (Gordon) to the Secretary of State," Mar. 25, 1933, *FRUS*, 331.

50. Telegram, "The Chargé in Germany (Gordon) to the Secretary of State," Mar. 26, 1933, *FRUS*, 334.

CHAPTER 3

1. "Protest on Hitler Growing in Nation," *NYT*, Mar. 23, 1933.

2. *Ibid.*

3. "Boycott Advocated to Curb Hitlerism," *NYT*, Mar. 21, 1933; see Morris Frommer, "The American Jewish Congress: A History, 1914–1950" (unpub. Ph.D. diss., history, Ohio State, 1978), 315–16, also see 314, n. 29.

4. Interview with Morris Mendelsohn by Moshe Gottlieb, July 20, 1965, author's transcript.

5. "O'Brien Reviews 4,000 Hitler Foes," *NYT*, Mar. 24, 1933; "Protest on Hitler Growing in Nation," *NYT*, Mar. 23, 1933.

6. See Dr. Joseph Goebbels, *My Part in Germany's Fight*, trans. Dr. Kurt Fiedler (London: Hurst and Blackett, 1935), 236–37, 269–70; see "Reich is Worried Over Our Reaction," *NYT*, Mar. 24, 1933; "Reich Warns Correspondents Not to Send Atrocity Reports," *NYT*, Mar. 24, 1933; see *VB*, Mar. 30, 1933 and Mar. 31, 1933; see Lucy S. Dawidowicz, *The War Against the Jews, 1933–1945* (Toronto: Bantam, 1976), 70–71.

7. William L. Shirer, *The Rise and Fall of the Third Reich: A History of Nazi Germany* (New York: Fawcett Crest, 1960), 54; Nora Levin, *The Holocaust: The Destruction of European Jewry 1933–1945* (New York: Schocken, 1973), 23 25, 35; Isaiah Friedman, *Germany, Turkey and Zionism, 1897–1918* (Oxford: Clarendon, 1977), 317; Francis R. J. Nicosia, "Germany and the Palestine Question, 1933–1939" (unpub. Ph.D. diss., history, McGill, 1977), 62.

8. James Pool and Suzanne Pool, *Who Financed Hitler: The Secret Funding of Hitler's Rise to Power, 1919–1933* (New York: Dial, 1978), 246.

9. See Shirer, 167, 192; Nicosia, 72–73.

10. Pool and Pool, 248, 413–14.

11. Report, F. Thelwell, "The Economic Situation in Germany, February, 1933," PRO-FO 371/16694–1527.

12. *Ibid.*; Shirer, 240–41.

13. Thelwell, "Economic Situation," PRO-FO 371/16694–1527.

14. *Ibid.*, 7–8.

15. Dawidowicz, 24 28, 47, 68–69; see George L. Mosse, *The Crisis of German Ideology: The Intellectual Origins of the Third Reich* ("The Universal Library"; New York: Grosset & Dunlap, 1971), 242–43; see Shirer, 586.

16. Thelwell, "Economic Situation," PRO-FO 371/16694–1527; Pool and Pool, 246; see Shirer, 357.

17. See Dawidowicz, 68–71; see "Reich is Worried Over Our Reaction," *NYT*, Mar. 23, 1933; see Goebbels, 236–39.

18. Dawidowicz, 43; Moshe Gottlieb, "The Anti-Nazi Boycott Movement in the American Jewish Community, 1933–1941" (unpub. Ph.D. diss., Near Eastern and Judaic studies, Brandeis, 1967), 13–14; see Marvin Lowenthal, *The Jews of Germany: A Story of Sixteen Centuries* (New York: Longmans, Green, 1936), 277.

19. See Levin, 43–44, 72–73; Lowenthal, 369–71; see Stephen Wise, *Challenging Years: The Autobiography of Stephen Wise* (New York: G. P. Putnam, 1949), 247; see Sidney Bolkosky, *The Distorted Image: German Jewish Perceptions of Germans and Germany, 1918–1935* (New York: Elsevier, 1975), 169–70.

20. See Carol Gelderman, *Henry Ford: The Wayward Capitalist* (New York: Dial, 1981), 218–21, Albert Lee, *Henry Ford and the Jews* (New York: Stein and Day, 1980), 25–28.

21. Pool and Pool, 86–87, 95, 101–2; Morton Rosenstock, *Louis Marshall, Defender of Jewish Rights* (Detroit: Wayne State, 1965), 128–41.

22. Lee, 42; Rosenstock, 145–47; David Lewis, *The Public Image of Henry Ford: An American Folk Hero and His Company* (Detroit: Wayne State, 1976), pp. 142–43.

23. Lewis, 143; Norman Cohn, *Warrant for Genocide: The Myth of the Jewish World Conspiracy and the Protocols of the Elders of Zion* (New York: Harper and Row, 1967), 138.

24. Pool and Pool, 90–91; " 'Heinrich' Ford Idol of Bavaria Fascisti Chief," *Chicago Tribune*, Mar. 8, 1923.

25. Pool and Pool, 91; *Detroit News*, Dec. 31,

1931, cited in Lee, 46; see Lee, p. 51.

26. Lewis, 140; Rosenstock, 149–50, 169–70, 183–84.

27. Lewis, 140; Lee, 34, 38.

28. Rosenstock, 170.

29. See Lee, 38; Rosenstock, 188–89.

30. Lee, 38–39; 43–44; Rosenstock, 188–89. See Lewis, 140.

31. Lee, p. 39; Lewis, p. 140.

32. Rosenstock, 189–91.

33. Rosenstock, 190–92; Lee, 84–85; Lewis, 145.

34. Rosenstock, 191.

35. *Ibid.*

36. Rosenstock, pp. 197–98; Lewis, 147.

37. Gelderman, 235.

38. Lewis, 143; Adolf Hitler, *Mein Kampf,* trans. Ralph Manheim (Boston: Houghton–Mifflin, 1943), 639.

39. Hitler, 639, n. 1.

40. Rosenstock, 193; Lee, 84–85.

41. Salo W. Baron, *The Russian Jew Under Tsars and Soviets* (New York: Macmillan, 1976), 44–49.

42. Eric Hirshler, "Jews from Germany in the United States," in Eric Hirshler, ed., *Jews from Germany in the United States* (New York: Farrar, Straus and Cudahy, 1955), 62–64, 75–76; see Cyrus Adler, *Jacob H. Schiff: His Life and Letters* (Garden City, New York: Doubleday, Doran, 1929), I: 42–154, and II: 117–38, 296–97; see Hirshler, "Jews from Germany," in Hirshler, pp. 96–98; 72–76; Moses

Rischin, *The Promised City: New York's Jews, 1870–1914* (Cambridge, Mass.: Harvard, 1977), 95–98.

43. Adler, *Schiff,* II, pp. 120–138.

44. Marvin Tokayer and Mary Swartz, *The Fugu Plan: The Untold Story of the Japanese and the Jews During World War II* (New York: Paddington, 1979), 46; Memorandum, Takahashi, in Adler, *Schiff,* I: 215–26; Stephen Birmingham, *"Our Crowd:" The Great Jewish Families of New York* (New York: Dell, 1967), 335.

45. Tokayer and Swartz, 46; memorandum, Takahashi, in Adler, *Schiff,* I: 216, 228.

46. Nathan Schachner, *The Price of Liberty: A History of the American Jewish Committee* (New York: AJC, 1948), 7–8, 37–42; Adler, *Schiff,* II: 160–61.

47. Naomi W. Cohen, "The Abrogation of the Russo–American Treaty of 1832," *Jewish Social Studies,* XXV (Jan. 1963): 21; Rosenstock, p. 75; Adler, *Schiff,* II, pp. 150–151.

48. Cohen, "Abrogation," 22–28, 35; Cyrus Adler and Aaron M. Margalith, *With Firmness in the Right; American Diplomatic Action Affecting Jews, 1840–1945* (N.Y.: AJC, 1946), 285–289.

49. Cohen, *Not Free,* 89–90.

50. Cable, J. Schiff to Count Witte, in Adler, *Schiff,* II: 135, 138.

51. Letter, Schiff to President Taft, February 20, 1933, in Adler, *Schiff,* II: 148.

52. Adler, *Schiff,* I: vii, ix.

CHAPTER 4

1. See Adolf Hitler, *Mein Kampf,* trans. Ralph Manheim (Boston: Houghton Mifflin, 1943), 454–55, 458–60, 638–40; see speeches, Adolf Hitler, July 28, 1922 and Apr. 10, 1923, in Norman H. Baynes, ed., *The Speeches of Adolf Hitler,* (London: Oxford, 1942), I: 26, 42, 43.

2. "250,000 Jews Here to Protest Today," *NYT,* Mar. 27, 1933; "55,000 Here Stage Protest on Hitler Attacks on Jews," *NYT,* Mar. 28, 1933.

3. "Polish Jews Condemn Germany," *NYT,* Mar. 21, 1933; "Protest Demonstration in Warsaw Forbidden on Grounds of Public Safety," and "Warsaw Bourse Closed in Sympathy with Protest," *JDB,* Mar. 28, 1933; "Vast Protest Movement Throughout Poland: Jews, Non-Jews Join in Demonstrations," and "Mercantile Organizations in Poland Declare German Boycott," *JDB,* Mar. 29, 1933; dispatch, British Embassy, Warsaw, to Sir John Simon, Mar. 29, 1933, PRO-FO 371/16721–1556; see "Boycott of German Goods by Morrocan Jewry," *JDB,* Mar. 31, 1933; "World Reactions; An Outcry of Horror Everywhere," *JC,* Mar. 31, 1933; "Move for Boycott Gaining in London," *NYT,* Mar. 25, 1933; letter, British Legation, Kovno, to British Legation, Riga, Mar. 28, 1933, PRO-FO 371/17184–1556; "The Kolo Supports Boycott," *JC,* Apr. 28, 1933.

4. "German Ships Affected," *NYT,* Mar. 24, 1933; minutes, Cabinet meeting of the German Government, Mar. 31, 1933, NA T-120 roll 1712,

D792238/9 (trans. GZ); "Nazi Attacks Stir British Catholics," *NYT,* Mar. 24, 1933.

5. "Speech of Hitler in Reichstag on His Policies for Germany," *NYT,* Mar. 24, 1933; "Reich Warns Correspondents Not to Send Atrocity Reports," *NYT,* Mar. 24, 1933.

6. "Nazi Attacks Stir British Catholics," *NYT,* Mar. 24, 1933; "Move for Boycott Gaining in London," *NYT,* Mar. 25, 1933.

7. "Hitler Debt Talk Points to Revisionism," *NYT,* Mar. 25, 1933; "Decreasing Surplus of German Exports," NYT, Mar. 20, 1933.

8. Martin Rosenbluth, *Go Forth and Serve; Early Years and Public Life* (New York: Herzl, 1961), 250–51.

9. Hitler, 308–21; speech, Adolf Hitler, "Free State or Slavery," July 28, 1922, in Baynes, 21–41; Francis R. J. Nicosia, "Germany and the Palestine Question, 1933–1939" (unpub. Ph.D. diss., history, McGill, 1977), 57–64.

10. See Ludwig Pinner, *In Two Worlds: Siegfried Moses, On His Seventy-Fifth Birthday* trans. EF (Tel Aviv: Publisher Bitaon Ltd., 1962); interview with Dr. Dolf Michaelis by author, Sep. 1, 1980; Donald L. Niewyk, *The Jews in Weimar Germany* (Baton Rouge: Louisiana State Univ. 1980), 125.

11.–21. Rosenbluth, 250–54.

22. *Ibid.,* 253.

23. "Jews in Reich Deny Atrocities by Nazis," *NYT,* Mar. 25, 1933; "250,000 Jews Here to Protest

Today," *NYT*, Mar. 27, 1933; see Dawidowicz, 70.

24. Cable, Bertling, Amerika Institute, to M. D. Waldman, Mar. 25, 1933, AJCmA.

25. Cable, Dr. Brund, National Association of German–American Chamber of Commerce, to Dr. Degener, German–American Board of Trade, Mar. 24, 1933, AJCmA; see "Jews in Reich Deny Atrocities by Nazis," *NYT*, Mar. 25, 1933.

26. "250,000 Jews Here to Protest Today," *NYT*, Mar. 27, 1933.

27. "Jews in Reich Deny Atrocities by Nazis," *NYT*, Mar. 25, 1933.

28. Stephen Wise, *Challenging Years: the Autobiography of Stephen Wise* (New York: Putnam, 1949), 240–41.

29. "250,000 Jews Here to Protest Today," *NYT*, Mar. 27, 1933.

30. " 'We Ask Only for the Right,' Says Wise," *NYT*, Mar. 28, 1933.

31. Wise, 234–35; Nahum Goldmann, *The Autobiography of Nahum Goldmann: Sixty Years of Jewish Life*, trans. Helen Sebba (New York: Holt, Rinehart and Winston, 1969), 124–27; Morris Frommer, "The American Jewish Congress: A History, 1914–1950," (unpub. Ph.D. diss., history, Ohio State, 1978), 467; see letter, Stephen Wise to Julian Mack, Mar. 29, 1933, in Carl Hermann Voss, ed., *Stepen S. Wise: Servant of the People* (Philadelphia: JPA, 1969), 181–82.

32. Letter, S. Wise to L. D. Brandeis, Mar. 23, 1933, in Voss, ed., *Servant*, 180–81; Moshe Gottlieb, "The Anti-Nazi Boycott Movement in the American Jewish Community, 1933–1941," (un-

pub. Ph.D. diss. Near Eastern and Judaic studies, Brandeis, 1967), 38, 43.

33. Letter, S. Wise to William Rosenau, Apr. 19, 1933, in Voss, ed., *Servant*, 185–86.

34. "Nazis End Attacks on Jews in Reich, Our Embassy Finds," *NYT*, Mar. 27, 1933.

35. Telegram, "The Secretary of State to the Chargé in Germany (Gordon)," Mar. 24, 1933, *FRUS* II: 330–31.

36. Telegram, "The Chargé in Germany (Gordon) to the Secretary of State," Mar. 25, 1933, *FRUS* 331–33.

37. "Nazis End Attacks," *NYT*, Mar. 27, 1933; telegram, Stephen S. Wise and Bernard S. Deutsch to Cordell Hull, Mar. 26, 1933, NA 862.4016/136-GC.

38. Wise, 244–45.

39. Rosenbluth, 257–58; see letter, S. Wise to J. H. Holmes, Apr. 3, 1933, in Voss, ed., *Servant*, 182–83.

40. Wise, xi–xiv, 23–26, 29, 31–34.

41. Carl Hermann Voss, *Rabbi and Minister: The Friendship of Stephen S. Wise and John Haynes Holmes* (Buffalo: Prometheus, 1980), 46–49.

42. Wise, 82–103; Voss, *Rabbi and Minister*, 101–9.

43. Wise, 161–81, 194–98; Voss, *Rabbi and Minister*, 182–83.

44. Wise, 202–9.

45. Voss, ed., *Servant*, xix, 128, 132–34, see 134, 149.

46. Wise, 245; letter, S. Wise to L. D. Brandeis, Sept. 19, 1933, BPM at AJA.

CHAPTER 5

1.–3. "35,000 Jam Streets Outside the Garden," *NYT*, Mar. 28, 1933.

4. *Ibid.*; "55,000 Here Stage Protest on Hitler Attacks on Jews," *NYT*, Mar. 28, 1933.

5. *Ibid.*; "250,000 Jews Here to Protest Today," *NYT*, Mar. 27, 1933; "Chicago Jews Demand U.S. Act to Curb Nazis," *Chicago Daily Tribune*, Mar. 28, 1933.

6. Stephen Wise, *Challenging Years: The Autobiography of Stephen Wise* (New York: Putnam, 1949), 250; "Jews Fast in Poland," *NYT*, Mar. 28, 1933.

7. "55,000 Here Stage Protest," *NYT*, Mar. 28, 1933.

8. "Smith Calls for a World-Wide Fight on Religious Bigotry," *NYT*, Mar. 28, 1933.

9. "55,000 Here Stage Protest," *NYT*, Mar. 28, 1933.

10. *Ibid.*; "250,000 Jews Here to Protest," *NYT*, Mar. 27, 1933.

11. "55,000 Here Stage Protest," *NYT*, Mar. 28, 1933.

12. *Ibid.*: "Leaders of Nations Send in Protest," *NYT*, Mar. 28, 1933.

13. " 'We Ask Only for the Right,' Says Wise," *NYT*, Mar. 28, 1933; letter, S. Wise to J. Mack, Mar. 29, 1933, in Carl Hermann Voss, ed., *Stephen S. Wise: Servant of the People* (Philadelphia: JPSA, 1969), 181–82; see interview with Rabbi David Polish by author, Oct. 18, 1981; see interview with Justine Wise Polier by author, Oct. 21, 1981.

14. " 'We Ask Only for the Right,' " *NYT*, Mar. 28, 1933; see letter, S. Wise to J. Mack, Mar. 29, 1933, in Voss, ed., *Servant*, 181–82.

15. " 'We Ask Only for the Right,' " *NYT*, Mar. 28, 1933; see interview, Justine Wise Polier by author, Oct. 21, 1981.

16.–18. " 'We Ask Only for the Right,' " *NYT*, Mar. 28, 1933.

19. "250,000 Jews Here to Protest Today," *NYT*, Mar. 27, 1933; "50,000 Here Stage Protest," *NYT*, Mar. 25, 1933.

CHAPTER 6

1. "Anti-Nazi Protest March Through New York Voted by American Jewish Congress," *JDB*, Mar. 21, 1933; see letter, Stephen Wise to Ruth Mack Brunswick, Apr. 6, 1933, in Carl Hermann Voss,

ed., *Stephen S. Wise: Servant of the People* (Philadelphia: JPSA, 1969), 183.

2. Associated Press (A.P.) dispatch, *NYT*, Mar. 27, 1933; see dispatch, British Embassy, Warsaw, to

Sir John Simon, Mar. 29, 1933, PRO-FO 371/
16721-1556.

3. "Move for Boycott Gaining in London," *NYT*,
Mar. 25, 1933; "Jews In England Boycott German
Goods and Cafes," *Chicago Sunday Tribune*, Mar. 26,
1933; "Equality for Jews in Reich Demanded," *NYT*
, Mar. 27, 1933.

4. "Christian Leaders Protest on Hitler," *NYT*,
Mar. 22, 1933; "Boycott Movement in Full Swing,"
JC, Mar. 24, 1933; "Press German Boycott," *NYT*,
Mar. 25, 1933.

5. Martin Rosenbluth, *Go Forth and Serve; Early
Years and Public Life* (New York: Herzl, 1961), 253;
see "Extract from Minutes of the Conference of Min-
isters," Apr. 7, 1933, *DGFP 1918-1945* (London:
HMSO, 1957), ser. C, I: 256-62; "55,000 Here
Stage Protest on Hitler Attacks on Jews," *NYT*,
Mar. 28, 1933; see "Boycott Spreads in Reich but
Hitler Bans Violent Acts," *NYT*, Mar. 30, 1933.

6. Dr. Joseph Goebbels, *My Part in Germany's
Fight*, trans. Dr. Kurt Fiedler (London: Hurst and
Blackett, 1935), 237; "55,000 Here Stage Protest,"
NYT, Mar. 28, 1933.

7. Goebbels, 237.

8. Goebbels, 237-38; "Goebbels Warns of Action," and "55,000 Here Stage Protest," *NYT*, Mar.
28, 1933.

9. "55,000 Here Stage Protest," *NYT*, Mar. 28,
1933; "Hitlerites Order Boycott Against Jews in
Business, Professions and Schools," *NYT*, Mar. 29,
1933.

10. "Hitlerites Order Boycott," *NYT*, March 29,
1933; "55,000 Here Stage Protest," *NYT*, Mar. 28,
1933.

11. "Hitlerites Order Boycott," *NYT*, Mar. 29,
1933; "Boycott Spreads in Reich but Hitler Bans
Violent Acts," *NYT*, Mar. 30, 1933; see "Facts Give
Hitler the Lie," *JC*, Mar. 31, 1933.

12. "Boycott Manifesto Includes 11 Orders," and
"Hitlerites Order Boycott," *NYT*, Mar. 29, 1933.

13. "Boycott Spreads in Reich," *NYT*, Mar. 30,
1933; see Lucy S. Dawidowicz, *The War Against the
Jews, 1933-1945* (Toronto: Bantam, 1976), 71; see
"Boycott of Jews in Germany," London *Times*, Mar.
31, 1933; see minutes, Cabinet Meeting of the German Government, Mar. 31, 1933, NA T-120 roll
1712, D792205 *et seq.*; see letter, "M. Francois
Poncet, French Ambassador in Berlin, to M. Paul-
Boncour, Minister of Foreign Affairs," Apr. 5, 1933,
DDF 1932-1939 (Paris: Imprimerie Nationale,
1967); lst ser., III: 144.

14. Cable, Eric Warburg to Frieda/Felix Warburg, Mar. 29, 1933, AJCmA.

15. Letter and enclosure, Cyrus Adler to Mr.
Waldman, Mar. 29, 1933, AJCmA.

16. "Suggested Statement of Dr. Adler," Mar. 29,
1933, AJCmA; see "Boycott Warning Sent from
Berlin," *NYT*, Mar. 31, 1933.

17. Cable, Felix Warburg to Eric Warburg, Mar.
29, 1933, AJCmA.

18. Poster, cited in "Nazis Lay Boycott to 'Lies'
of Jews," *NYT*, Apr. 1, 1933.

19. "Brooklyn Jews Protest," "Staten Islanders
Add Protest," and "Urge Inquiry in Nazi Raids,"
NYT, Mar. 29, 1933; "6,000 Gather in Protest,"

NYT, Mar. 31, 1933, see Werner E. Braatz, "German Commercial Interests in Palestine: Zionism and
the Boycott of German Goods, 1933-1934,"
European Studies Review (SAGE, London and Beverly Hills), IX (1979): 486; "Chicago Jews Demand
U.S. Act to Curb Nazis," *Chicago Daily Tribune*,
Mar. 28, 1933; see "Wave of Protest Against Persecutions in Germany throughout United States,"
JDB, Mar. 24, 1933.

20. "Jews In Greece Start Boycott," *NYT*, Mar.
30, 1933; "Boycott German Goods!" and "World
Reaction; An Outcry of Horror Everywhere," *JC*,
Mar. 31, 1933; Braatz, 485, 495; see "Belgian Gov-
ernment's Indignation," and "The Kolo Supports
Boycott," *JC*, Apr. 28, 1933.

21. "German Business Protests Boycott," *NYT*,
Mar. 31, 1933; see Braatz, 486-87; also see letters,
Apr., 1933, NA T-120 roll 4956, L370262/371913
(trans. GZ).

22. *Frankfurter Zeitung*, Mar. 30, 1933, 1st
morning edition (trans. MS); see "Boycott Manifesto
Includes 11 Orders," *NYT*, Mar. 29, 1933; "Boycott
Spreads in Reich," and "Says Nazis Want Jobs,"
NYT, Mar. 30, 1933.

23. "German Business Protests Boycott," *NYT*,
Mar. 31, 1933.

24. See John L. Heineman, *Hitler's First Foreign
Minister; Constantin Freiherr von Neurath, Diplomat
and Statesman* (Berkeley: Univ. of California, 1979),
275, n. 41; see minutes, Cabinet Meeting of the German Government, Mar. 29, 1933, NA T-120 roll
1712, D792205 *et seq.* (trans. GZ); see letter, "M.
Francois-Poncet French Ambassador in Berlin, to
M. Paul-Boncour, Minister of Foreign Affairs," Apr.
5, 1933, *DDF*, p. 155.

25. See minutes, Cabinet Meeting of the German
Government, Mar. 29, 1933, NAT-120 roll 1712,
D792205 *et seq.* (trans. GZ); "Boycott Spreads in
Reich," *NYT*, Mar. 30, 1933.

26. Minutes, Cabinet Meeting of the German
Government, Mar. 29, 1933, NA T-120 roll 1712,
D792205 *et seq.* (trans. GZ).

27. "Boycott Spreads in Reich," and "Says Nazis
Want Jobs," *NYT*, Mar. 30, 1933; telegram, "The
Chargé in Germany (Gordon) to the Secretary of
State," Mar. 30, 1933, *FRUS*, 1933 (Washington,
D.C.: United States Government Printing Office,
1949); II: 335-36; letter, "The Chargé in Germany
(Gordon) to the Secretary of State," April 2, 1933,
FRUS, 347-50.

28. Letters, "M. Francois-Poncet, French Am-
bassador in Berlin, to M. Paul-Boncour, Minister of
Foreign Affairs," Apr. 5 and Apr. 7, 1933, *DDF*,
155, 185; telegram, "Sir H. Rumbold (Berlin) to Sir
J. Simon," Apr. 1, 1933, *DBFP*, *1919-1939*
(London: HMSO, 1956) 2nd. ser., V: 14-15;
Heineman, 81.

29. "German Business Protests Boycott," *NYT*,
Mar. 31, 1933; see "Nazis Cut Boycott to Day,"
NYT, Apr. 1, 1933.

30. "German Business Protests Boycott," *NYT*,
Mar. 31, 1933.

31. "Washington Urged to Block Boycott," and
"Will Use Influence Quietly," *NYT*, Mar. 31, 1933;
telegram, "The Chargé in Germany (Gordon) to the

Secretary of State," Mar. 30, 1933, *FRUS*, 335–36; see telegram, "The Chargé in Germany (Gordon) to the Secretary of State," Mar. 29, 1933, *FRUS*, 334–35.

32. Telegram, "The Chargé in Germany (Gordon) to the Secretary of State," Mar. 30, 1933, *FRUS*, 335–37.

33. See letter, S. Wise to J. H. Holmes, Apr. 3, 1933, in Voss, ed., *Servant*, 182.

34. Letter, S. Wise to J. Mack, Mar. 29, 1933, in Voss, ed., *Servant*, 181–82.

35. *Ibid.*

36. "Washington Urged to Block Boycott," *NYT*, Mar. 31, 1933; see "Jews Here Demand Washington Action," *NYT*, Mar. 21, 1933.

37. Telegram, "The Secretary of State to the Chargé in Germany (Gordon)," Mar. 30, 1933, *FRUS*, 337.

38. *Ibid.*; see Cordell Hull, *The Memoirs of Cordell Hull* (New York: Macmillan, 1948), I: 81, 85; "Hull Obtains Consul's Data on Jews' Cases," *Chicago Sunday Tribune*, Mar. 26, 1933.

39. "Lords Cheer Plea for Jews in Reich," *NYT*, Mar. 31, 1933; see telegram, "Sir J. Simon to Sir H. Rumbold (Berlin), Mar. 2, 1933, *DBFP*, 2nd ser., IV: 436; also see "Aid for Jews Urged in Spirit of Balfour," *NYT*, Apr. 2, 1933; also see "The House of Commons and German Jewry," *JC*, Aug. 4, 1933.

40. "Sir J. Simon to Sir H. Rumbold (Berlin)," Mar. 30, 1933, *DBFP*, V: 9.

41. "Lords Cheer Plea for Jews in Reich," *NYT*, Mar. 31, 1933; see "House of Lords," *JC*, Apr. 7, 1933; Rosenbluth, 259–60.

42. Braatz, 486–87.Francis R. J. Nicosia, "Germany and the Palestine Question, 1933–1939" (unpub. Ph.D. diss. history, McGill, 1977), 81–82.

43. Braatz, 486–87.

44. *VB*, Mar. 30, 1933; *Der Angriff*, Mar. 30, 1933, in "Nazis, Warned, Set on Plan of Boycott," *Washington Post*, Mar. 31, 1933.

45. William L. Shirer, *The Rise and Fall of the Third Reich: A History of Nazi Germany* (New York: Fawcett Crest, 1960), 204–05, 265–66, see 284, 358–59; see Hjalmar Horace Greeley Schacht, *Confessions of "The Old Wizard": The Autobiography of Hjalmar Horace Greeley Schacht*, trans. Diana Pyke (Boston: Houghton Mifflin, 1956), 2, 6, 14.

46. Letter, "M. Francois-Poncet, French Ambassador in Berlin, to M. Paul-Boncour, Minister of Foreign Affairs," Apr. 5, 1933, *DDF*, 155–56 (trans. GZ).

47. Telegram, "The Chargé in Germany (Gordon) to the Secretary of State," Mar. 30, 1933, *FRUS*, pp. 335–36; letter, "The Chargé in Germany (Gordon) to the Secretary of State," April 2, 1933, *FRUS*, 347–50; "Boycott Spreads in Reich," *NYT*, Mar. 30, 1933; "Jews' Jobs sought for Nazi Backers," *NYT*, Mar. 31, 1933.

48. Telegram, "Sir H. Rumbold (Berlin) to Sir J. Simon," Apr. 1, 1933, *DBFP*, 2nd ser., V: 14–15; letter, "Sir H. Rumbold (Berlin) to Sir J. Simon," Apr. 5, 1933, *DBFP*, 2nd ser., V; 25; see letter, "Chancellor Hitler to President Hindenburg," Apr. 5, 1933, *DGFP*, 253–55.

49. *Leipziger Tagezeitung*, Mar. 21, 1933, in Gott-

lieb, "Anti-Nazi Boycott Movement" (dissertation), 31.

50. See Letter, "M. Francois-Poncet, French Ambassador in Berlin, to M. Paul-Boncour, Minister of Foreign Affairs," Apr. 5, 1933, *DDF*, 160; see "Rule by Aryans Decreed," *NYT*, Apr. 9, 1933; see "1,500 Jewish Physicians Expelled from Sick Funds in Berlin; 6,000 in Reich," *JDB*, July 7, 1933.

51. See "Geneva Sees Ground for Appeal on Jews," *NYT*, Apr. 1, 1933; see "In Europe's New Tenseness the 'Corridor' Looms Large," *NYT*, Mar. 19, 1933; see "Polish Jews Condemn Germany," *NYT*, Apr. 21, 1933; see "Vast Protest Movement Throughout Poland," *JDB*, Mar. 29, 1933; see memorandum, Apr. 12, 1933, in report, "The Minister in Poland to the Foreign Ministry," *DGFP*, 307–10.

52. Minutes, Cabinet Meeting of the German Government, Mar. 31, 1933, NA T-120 roll 1712, D792205 *et seq.* (trans. GZ); see letter, "The Chargé in Germany (Gordon) to the Secretary of State," Apr. 2, 1933, *FRUS*, 347–48; see letter, "M. Francois-Poncet, French Ambassador in Berlin, to M. Paul-Boncour, Minister of Foreign Affairs," Apr. 5, 1933, *DDF*, 155; see letter, "Sir H. Rumbold to Sir J. Simon," Apr. 5, 1933, *DBFP*, 2nd ser., V: 24–25; see "Nazis Try to Rule on Foreign Policy," *NYT*, Apr. 2, 1933; see "Boycott at an End, Germany Believes; Cabinet Against it," *NYT*, Apr. 3, 1933.

53. "Close Woolworth Shops," *NYT*, Mar. 29, 1933; see "Boycott Spreads in Reich," *NYT*, Mar. 30, 1933; "German Business Protests Boycott," *NYT*, Mar. 31, 1933; "Nazi Rifles Close Stores in Munich," *NYT*, Apr. 1, 1933.

54. Letter, "The Chargé in Germany (Gordon) to the Secretary of State," Apr. 2, 1933, *FRUS*, 347–48; "Memorandum of Trans-Atlantic Telephone Conversation," Phillips/Gordon, Apr. 2, 1933, *FRUS*, 345; see telegram, "M. Francois-Poncet, French Ambassador in Berlin, to M. Paul-Boncour, Minister of Foreign Affairs," Apr. 1, 1933, *DDF*, 127–28; see "Nazis Try to Rule on Foreign Policy," *NYT*, Apr. 2, 1933; "Boycott at an End," *NYT*, Apr. 3, 1933; see Heineman, 81.

55. Letter, "Chargé in Germany (Gordon) to the Secretary of State," Apr. 2, 1933, *FRUS*, 348; "Memorandum of Trans-Atlantic Telephone Conversation," Phillips/Gordon, Apr. 2, 1933, *FRUS*, 345; Heineman, 3–4, 71, 81.

56. Heineman, 4–6, 71, 81; letter, "Chargé in Germany (Gordon) to the Secretary of State," Apr. 2, 1933, *FRUS*, 348; telegram, "M. Francois-Poncet, French Ambassador in Berlin, to M. Paul-Boncour, Foreign Minister," Apr. 1, 1933, *DDF*, 127–28 (trans. GZ); telegram, "M. Francois-Poncet, French Ambassador in Berlin to M. Paul-Boncour, Foreign Minister," Apr. 7, 1933, *DDF*, 185 (trans. GZ).

57. Minutes, Cabinet Meeting of the German Government, Mar. 31, 1933, NA T-120 roll 1712, D792205 *et seq.* (trans. GZ); telegram, "Sir H. Rumbold (Berlin) to Sir J. Simon," Apr. 1, 1933, *DBFP*, 2nd ser., V: 14–15; Heineman, 81.

58. Minutes, Cabinet Meeting of the German Government, Mar. 31, 1933, NA T-120 roll 1712,

D792205 *et seq.* (trans. GZ); telegram, "M. Francois-Poncet, French Ambassador in Berlin, to M. Paul-Boncour, Minister of Foreign Affairs," Apr. 7, 1933, *DDF*, 185; Heineman, 81.

59. Braatz, 487; see telegram, "The Secretary of State to the Chargé in Germany (Gordon)," Mar. 30, 1933, *FRUS*, 337.

60. "Memorandum of Trans-Atlantic Telephone Conversation," Phillips/Gordon, Mar. 31, 1933, *FRUS*, 342; see "Memorandum of Trans-Atlantic Telephone Conversation," Phillips/Gordon, Mar. 31, 1933, *FRUS*, 343.

61. See telegram, "Sir H. Rumbold (Berlin) to Sir J. Simon," Apr. 1, 1933, *DBFP*, 2nd ser., V: 14–15; "Memorandum of Trans-Atlantic Telephone Conversation," Phillips/Gordon, Mar. 31, 1933, *FRUS*, 342; Heineman, 81.

62. "French Prepare to Boycott German Goods in Sympathy With Jewish Victims of Nazis," *NYT*, Apr. 1, 1933.

63. "Over 2,000 Attend Fur Trade Protest," and "Boycott German Goods!" *JC*, Mar. 31, 1933; see "Reich Merchants Appeal," *NYT*, Apr. 2, 1933; "Lists Big German Loss," *NYT*, Apr. 16, 1933.

64. "Toscanini Heads Protest to Hitler," "Nazis Hold 1-Day Boycott," "Little Violence in Reich," and "Reich Merchants Appeal," *NYT*, Apr. 2, 1933.

65. "Boycott of Jews in Germany," London *Times*, Mar. 31, 1933.

66. "Threat to Foreign 'Campaign,' " London *Times*, Apr. 1, 1933; "Nazis Lay Boycott to 'Lies' of Jews," *NYT*, Mar. 31, 1933.

67. Goebbels, 239.

68. Meir Michaelis, *Mussolini and the Jews; German–Italian Relations and the Jewish Question in Italy, 1922–1945* (Oxford: Clarendon, 1978), 10–11, 14–15, 24–25, 30, 58–65.

69. Hitler, 681; Shirer, 97.

70. Michaelis, 49, 58–59; telegram, "Sir H. Rumbold (Berlin) to Sir J. Simon," Mar. 30, 1933, *DBFP*, 2nd ser., V: 8.

71. Michaelis, 59; John Toland, *Adolf Hitler* (New York: Ballantine, 1976), 424; Elizabeth Wiskemann, *The Rome–Berlin Axis: A Study of the Relations Between Hitler and Mussolini* (London: Fontana Library, 1966), 44–45.

72. Telegram, "Sir H. Rumbold (Berlin) to Sir J. Simon," Apr. 1, 1933, *DBFP*, 2nd ser., V: 14–15, see n. 4.

73. Wise, 248–50.

74. Telegram, Oscar Wasserman to Cyrus Adler, Mar. 30, 1933, AJCmA; see "Boycott Warning Sent from Berlin," *NYT*, Mar. 31, 1933.

75. "Boycott Warning Sent from Berlin," *NYT*, Mar. 31, 1933.

76. Telegram, "Sir H. Rumbold (Berlin) to Sir J. Simon," Apr. 1, 1933, *DGFP*, 2nd ser., V: 14–15.

77. "Memorandum of Trans-Atlantic Telephone Conversation," Phillips/Gordon, Mar. 31, 1933, *FRUS*, 343; see "Memorandum of Trans-Atlantic Telephone Conversation," Phillips/Gordon, Apr. 2, 1933, *FRUS*, 345.

78. See letter, "The Chargé in Germany (Gordon) to the Secretary of State," Apr. 2, 1933, *FRUS*,

348; "Nazis Try to Rule on Foreign Policy," *NYT*, Apr. 2, 1933; "Boycott At An End, Germany Believes," *NYT*, Apr. 3, 1933.

79. "Memorandum of Trans-Atlantic Telephone Conversation," Phillips/Gordon, Mar. 31, 1933, *FRUS*, 342.

80.–82. *Ibid.*

83. Letter, "The Chargé in Germany (Gordon) to the Secretary of State," Apr. 2, 1933, *FRUS*, 347–50; see "Boycott Spreads in Reich but Hitler Bans Violent Acts," *NYT*, Mar. 30, 1933; see letter, "Chancellor Hitler to President Hindenburg," Apr. 5, 1933, *DGFP*, 253–55; see Dawidowicz, 77; see "Nazis Cut Boycott to Day," *NYT*, Apr. 1, 1933.

84. Goebbels, 239; "Nazis Cut Boycott to Day," *NYT*, Apr. 1, 1933.

85. Goebbels, 239; "Memorandum of Trans-Atlantic Telephone Conversation," Phillips/Gordon, Mar. 31, 1933, *FRUS*, 343; "Nazis Cut Boycott to Day," *NYT*, Apr. 1, 1933.

86. "Memorandum of Trans-Atlantic Telephone Conversation," Phillips/Gordon, Mar. 31, 1933, *FRUS*, 343.

87. *Ibid.*; "Nazis Cut Boycott to Day," *NYT*, Apr. 1, 1933.

88. "Nazis Cut Boycott to Day," *NYT*, Apr. 1, 1933; see letter, "The Chargé in Germany (Gordon) to the Secretary of State," Apr. 2, 1933, *FRUS*, 347–50.

89. "Nazis Cut Boycott to Day," and "Whips Crowd Into Frenzy," *NYT*, Apr. 1, 1933.

90. "Whips Crowd Into Frenzy," *NYT*, Apr. 1, 1933.

91. "Memorandum of Trans-Atlantic Telephone Conversation," Phillips/Gordon, Mar. 31, 1933, *FRUS*, 343–44.

92. Wise, 247–50.

93. "Nazis Hold 1-Day Boycott," *NYT*, Apr. 2, 1933; "Speedy Collapse of Boycott," *JC*, Apr. 7, 1933; see "Boycott Spreads Throughout Reich," *NYT*, Mar. 30, 1933; see "German Business Protests Boycott," *NYT*, Mar. 31, 1933; see "Facts Give Hitler the Lie," *JC*, Mar. 31, 1933.

94. See "Boycott Spreads in Reich," and "Reich Warns Window-Breaking Hits Insurance Firms, Not Jews," *NYT*, Mar. 30, 1933; "Nazis to Photograph Persons Who Try to Enter Jews' Stores," *NYT*, Mar. 31, 1933; see "Nazis and Jews," London *Times*, Mar. 29, 1933; see "Nazis Cut Boycott to Day," *NYT*, Apr. 1, 1933.

95. Andre-Francois-Poncet, *The Fateful Years*, trans. Jacques LeClerq (New York: Harcourt, 1949), 78; see "In Darkest Germany," *JC*, Mar. 31, 1933; see "Jewish Camp Set Saturday by Nazi Chiefs," *Washington Post*, Mar. 29, 1933.

96. "Nazis Hold 1 Day Boycott," *NYT*, Apr. 2, 1933; "Jewish Lawyer Lynched," *JC*, Apr. 7, 1933.

97. See "Nazis Cut Boycott to Day," *NYT*, Apr. 1, 1933; "Threat to Foreign Campaign," London *Times*, Apr. 1, 1933; see A.P. photograph, *NYT*, Mar. 30, 1933; see "The Consul General at Berlin (Messersmith) to the Secretary of State," Mar. 31, 1933, *FRUS*, 338–41; see "Memorandum of Trans-Atlantic Telephone Conversation," Phillips/Gordon,

Apr. 2, 1933, *FRUS*, 345; see telegram, "Sir H. Rumbold (Berlin) to Sir J. Simon," Apr. 1, 1933, *DBFP*, 2nd ser., V: 16.

98. Wise, 245–47, 249–51; see " 'We Ask Only

For the Right,' Says Wise," *NYT*, Mar. 28, 1933.

99. Photograph, *VB*, Apr. 1, 1933; Goebbels, 239; see Rosenbluth, 253.

CHAPTER 7

1. "Many Jews Flee Reich," *NYT*, Apr. 2, 1933.

2. "Refugee Jews Tax Paris Charity Funds," *NYT*, Apr. 3, 1933; "20 German Refugees Smuggle Themselves into Belgium," *JDB*, Apr. 6, 1933; *Haaretz*, Apr. 6 and Apr. 9, 1933 (trans. G.G.); "German Ban Halts Tide of Refugees," *NYT*, Apr. 6, 1933; "3,000 Jewish Refugees Cross Swiss Border," *JDB*, Apr. 7, 1933; "Jewish Refugees in Holland," *JC*, Apr. 7, 1933; "10,000 Jews Flee Nazi Persecution," *NYT*, Apr. 15, 1933; "Sir John Simon Replies," *JC*, Apr. 21, 1933.

3. "10,000 Jews Flee Nazi Persecution," *NYT*, Apr. 15, 1933.

4. Salo W. Baron, *The Russian Jew Under the Tsars and Soviets* (New York: Macmillan, 1976), 44–46, 56–58, 182–85; Abram Leon Sachar, *Sufferance is the Badge* (New York: Knopf, 1939), 229–34.

5. Theodor Herzl, *The Jewish State: An Attempt at a Modern Solution of the Jewish Question*, trans. Sylvie D'Avigdor (London: Central Office of the Zionist Organization, 1936); see Alex Bein, *Theodore Herzl: A Biography*, trans. Maurice Samuel (Philadelphia: JPSA, 1942), 114–16, 173–75.

6.–13. Herzl, 14–77.

14. Bein, 201–3, 225, 238–42, 251–54, 269–70, 319; Jessie E. Sampter, ed., *A Guide to Palestine* (New York: ZOA, 1920), 60; Bernard A. Rosenblatt, "The Jewish National Fund and the Jewish Colonial Trust," in Sampter, *Guide*, 64–65.

15. Ben Halpern, *The Idea of the Jewish State* (Cambridge: Harvard, 1969), 28–31, 152–153; Anna and Maxa Nordau, *Max Nordau: A Biography* (New York: Nordau Committee, 1943), 169–72; see Bernard A. Rosenblatt and Jessie Sampter, "Factions and Tendencies in Zionism," in Sampter, ed., *Guide*, 101–7.

16. Chaim Weizmann, *Trial and Error: The Auto-biography of Chaim Weizmann* (New York: Harper, 1949), 200–8.

17. Walter Laqueur, *A History of Zionism* (New York: Holt, Rinehart and Winston, 1972), 204–5, 251; see Halpern, 31–32, 303–5, 313–15, 330; also see Susan Lee Hattis, *The Bi-National Idea in Palestine During Mandatory Times* (Haifa: Shikmona, 1970), 38–40, 83–84.

18. See Bein, 156–57, 238–39; see Anna and Maxa Nordau, 182; see Max Nordau, "Address at the Tenth Zionist Congress," Aug. 9, 1911, in Max Nordau, *Max Nordau to his People* (New York: Scopus, 1941), 195–97; see "Zionism," *Encyclopaedia Judaica* (Jerusalem: Keter, 1972), XVI: 1055–56.

19. See Max Nordau, "Le Travail Immediat" and "Hier, Aujourd'hui, Demain," *Le Peuple Juif*, Nov. 5 and 26, 1920; see Weizmann, 47; see Joseph Schechtman, *Fighter and Prophet: The Vladimir Ja-*

botinsky Story, the Last Years (New York: Thomas Yoseloff, 1961), 350–51.

20. Halpern, 184–85; Schechtman, *Fighter*, 350–51; Weizmann, 47; see Anna and Maxa Nordau, 281.

21. Joseph Schechtman, *Rebel and Statesman: The Vladimir Jabotinsky Story, the Early Years* (New York: Thomas Yoseloff, 1956), 350–51, 399–415; Schechtman, *Fighter*, 350–51; see Laqueur, 341–45.

22. Recha Freier, *Let the Children Come: The Early History of Youth Aliyah* (London: Weidenfeld and Nicolson, 1961), 10–21.

23. George Warburg, *Six Years of Hitler: The Jews Under the Nazi Regime* (London: George Allen & Unwin, 1939), 129–31, 135–45; see "East Prussia Ends Mail Delivery to Jews; Children are Forced Out of School," *JDB*, Aug. 17, 1933; see "Teaching Racial Madness" and "Too Terrible for Words," *JC*, Sept. 22, 1933; see "Guardian Describes Tortures Inflicted on Jewish Children in Schools in Upper Silesia," *JDB*, Oct. 10, 1933.

24. Stephen Wise, *Challenging Years: The Auto-biography of Stephen Wise* (New York: Putnam, 1949), 237; letter, Stephen Wise to L. D. Brandeis, Sept. 19, 1933, BPM at AJA.

25. Letter, Dr. Franz Kahn to "Fellow Believers," Mar. 5, 1933, CZA. S25/9703 (trans. GZ); see letter, W. Senator to B. Locker, Mar. 19, 1933, CZA S49/419 (trans. EF).

26. Martin Rosenbluth, *Go Forth and Serve: Early Years and Public Life* (New York: Herzl, 1961), 254–55.

27. *Ibid.*

28. *Ibid.* 256–58; see Laqueur, 400.

29. Rosenbluth, 258–60.

30. *Ibid.* 259–60; see "Lords Cheer Plea for Jews in Reich," *NYT*, Mar. 31, 1933.

31. Rosenbluth, 260–61.

32. *Ibid.*, 261; see telegram, Chaim Weizmann to Israel M. Sieff, Apr. 16, 1933, in Camillo Dresner, ed., *The Letters and Papers of Chaim Weizmann*, XV, ser. A, Oct. 1930–June 1933 (New Brunswick, New Jersey: Transaction, 1978), letter no. 363, pp. 402–3.

33. Letter, B. Locker to S. Wise, Apr. 4, 1933, BPM at AJA.

34. Shaul Esh, *Studies in the Holocaust and Contemporary Jewry* (Jerusalem: ICJ 1973), 54; Letter, Berl Locker to Stephen Wise, Apr. 4, 1933, BPM at AJA; letter, Emanuel Neumann to S. Wise, May 9, 1933, BPM at AJA.

35. Esh, 54; Letter, B. Locker to S. Wise, Apr. 4, 1933, BPM at AJA; letter, E. Neumann to S. Wise, May 9, 1933, BPM at AJA.

36. Telegram, Zionist Organization and National Council of Palestine Jews to Reich Chancellor's Of-

fice, Mar. 31, 1933, NA T-120 roll 4887, L318927 (trans. GZ); telegram, Chaim Arlosoroff to the Zionist Organization, Apr. 2, 1933, CZA S25/9757, in Esh, 55, n. 33.

37. *Haaretz* and *Doar Hayom*, Apr. 2, 1933, in Esh, 55, n. 32; see "Anti-German Boycott Will Stop if Nazi Boycott is Discontinued, says Vaad Leumi," *JDB*, Apr. 2, 1933.

38. See Nora Levin, *The Holocaust: The Destruc-*

tion of European Jewry, 1933–1945 (New York: Thomas Y. Crowell, 1968), 82; see "Unfinished Business Prolongs Sessions of Zionist Congress," *JDB*, Aug. 31, 1933.

39. Halpern, 179–80; see protocol, *JA* Exec. Session, Apr. 14, 1933, CZA S25/794 (trans. GB); see protocol, JA Exec. Session, Apr. 16, 1933; CZA S25/794 (author's trans. pp. 3–4); see letter, E. Neumann to S. Wise, May 9, 1933, BPM at AJA.

CHAPTER 8

1. Letter, Werner Senator to Berl Locker, Mar. 19, 1933, CZA S49/381 (trans. GZ).

2. Letter, W. Senator to B. Locker, Mar. 19, 1933, CZA S49/381 (trans. GZ); see letter, G. Landauer to W. Senator, Mar. 3, 1933, CZA S49/381; see "Nazis Bands Stir Up Strife in Germany," *NYT*, Mar. 9, 1933; see Shaul Esh, *Studies in the Holocaust and Contemporary Jewry* (Jerusalem: ICJ, 1973), 38, n. 26; see Karl A. Schleunes, *The Twisted Road to Auschwitz: Nazi Policy Toward German Jews, 1933–1939* (Urbana: Univ. of Illinois, 1970), 195.

3.–6. Letter, Senator to Locker, Mar. 19, 1933, CZA S49/381 (trans. GZ).

7. Arthur Schweitzer, *Big Business in the Third Reich* (Bloomington: Indiana Univ., 1964), 413–17; see Gustav Stolper, *German Economy 1870–1940: Issues and Trends* (New York: Reynal and Hitchcock, 1940), 191–92.

8. Protocol, Jewish Agency Executive Session, Apr. 9, 1933, CZA S25/794 (trans. GB).

9. Interview with Esther Aharony by Gali Gur, Jan. 31, 1981; interview with David Cohen by Gali Gur, Mar. 26, 1981.

10. Attested copy, the Kaiser-German Police President in Warsaw, Nov. 17, 1915, CZA K11/180–1 (trans. DD).

11. Letter, Dr. Jacob Thon to Mr. Sam Cohen, Nov. 23, 1933, CZA K11/180–1 (trans. DD).

12. Interview with Dr. Nahum Goldmann, *Haaretz*, May 16, 1927; interview with David Cohen by Gail Gur, Mar. 26, 1981.

13. Interview with Esther Aharony; interview with Ovid Ben Ami by Gali Gur, Jan. 25, 1981.

14. Letter, G. Landauer to Sam Cohen, Mar. 31, 1932 (misdated), CZA K11/180–1 (trans. DD); interview with Esther Aharony; see Ernst Marcus, "The German Foreign Office and the Palestine Question in the Period 1933–1939," in Shaul Esh, ed., *Yad Vashem Studies in the European Jewish Catastrophe and Resistance*, II (Jerusalem: Yad Vashem, 1958): 182; see letter, Landauer to Jacobsohn, June 9, 1933, CZA S7/92 (trans. DD/GZ); see letter, Sam Cohen to Dr. Eberl, Aug. 1, 1933, NA T-120 roll 4954, L369093/5.

15. Esh, *Studies in the Holocaust*, 45–46; Marcus, 181–83; see letter, Landauer to Jacobsohn, June 9, 1933, CZA S7/92.

16. See letter, Landauer to Cohen, March 31, 1932 (misdated), CZA K-11/180–1; see cable, S. Brodetsky to Arlosoroff, Apr. 13, 1933, CZA S25/9706; letter, Landauer to Brodetsky, undated (Apr. 15–18, 1933), CZA S25/9706; see minutes,

JA Exec. Session, Apr. 9, 1933, CZA S25/794 (trans. GB); memorandum, G. Landauer, May 12, 1933, CZA S25/9707 (trans. EF); see report, "Some Theses to the Question of the Liquidation Bank," Chaim Arlosoroff, May 19, 1933, CZA S25/9706 (trans. DD); see letter, H. Fleiss to Arlosoroff, June 10, 1933, CZA S25/9706 (trans. DD).

17.–18. Esh, *Studies in the Holocaust*, 45–46; see Marcus, 181–82.

19. Esh, *Studies in the Holocaust*, 46.

20. Letter, G. Landauer to S. Cohen, Mar. 31, 1932 (misdated), CZA K-11/180–1 (trans. DD).

21. See letter, M. Achi-Felix (Martin Rosenbluth) to Arlosoroff, Apr. 6, 1933, CZA S25/794 (trans. DD); letter to "Lieber Franz," unsigned, Apr. 4, 1933, CZA S25/794; letter, unsigned (Arlosoroff) to Chaim Weizmann, Apr. 4, 1933, CZA S25/794; letter, unsigned (Berl Locker) to Franz Kahn, Apr. 5, 1933, CZA S25/794; letter, G. Landauer to Prof. Brodetsky, undated (Apr., 1933), CZA S25/9706; letters, unsigned (Martin Rosenbluth) to G. Landauer, May 19 and June 7, 1933, CZA L-13/138/II.

22. Cable, Brodetsky to Arlosoroff, Apr. 13, 1933, CZA S25/9706 (trans. GB).

23. Cable 613, Jewish Agency to Zionistburo London, Apr. 4, 1933, CZA S25/9809 (trans. GB).

24. Letter, Central Department, British Foreign Office to the Chancery, British Embassy, Berlin, Apr. 27, 1933, PRO-FO 371/16721-1556; letter, A.C.C. Parkinson, Colonial Office, to Prof. Brodetsky, Apr. 8, 1933, PRO-FO 371/16721–1556.

25. Letters, Central Department to the Chancery, Apr. 17, 1933, and Parkinson to Prof. Brodetsky, Apr. 8, 1933, PRO-FO 371/16721–1556; Schweitzer, 192–93; Schleunes, 139.

26. Werner Feilchenfeld, Dolf Michaelis and Ludwig Pinner, *Haavara-Transfer Nach Palestina Und Einwanderung Deutscher Juden, 1933–1939* (Tubingen: Mohr Verlag, 1972), 21.

27. Letters, Central Department to the Chancery, Apr. 17, 1933, and Parkinson to Brodetsky, Apr. 8, 1933, PRO-FO 371/16721–1556.

28. *Ibid.*; letter, A.C.C. Parkinson to Brodetsky, Apr. 15, 1933, and note, R.M.A. Hantke, Apr. 18, 1933, PRO-FO 371/16721–1556.

29. Letter, Brodetsky to Parkinson, Apr. 13, 1933, PRO-FO 371/16721–1556.

30. Letter, Parkinson to Brodetsky, Apr. 15, 1933, and notes, R.M.A. Hankey, Apr. 18, and J. C. Stendale-Bennett, Apr. 22, 1933, PRO-FO 371/16721–1556.

31. Cable, Brodetsky to Arlosoroff, Apr. 13, 1933, CZA S25/9706; letter, Landauer to Bro-

detsky, undated (Apr., 1933), CZA S25/9706; see cable 613, Jewish Agency to Zionistburo, Apr. 4, 1933, CZA S25/9809; see protocol, JA Exec. Session, Apr. 9, 1933, CZA S25/794 (trans. GB); also see memorandum, Chaim Arlosoroff, May 19, 1933, CZA S25/9706 (trans. DD).

32. Letter, Landauer to Brodetsky, undated (Apr., 1933), CZA S25/9706 (trans. GZ).
33. See Dr. Werner Feilchenfeld, *Five Years of Jewish Immigration From Germany and Haavara-Transfer, 1933–1938* (Tel Aviv: Trust and Transfer Office "Haavara" Ltd., 1938), 5–10.

CHAPTER 9

1. Report, Berl Locker, Apr. 10, 1933, CZA S25/9809 (trans. EF); letter, B. Locker to Arlosoroff, Apr. 8, 1933, CZA S25/794.
2. Letter, B. Locker to Arlosoroff, Apr. 8, 1933, CZA S25/794; report, B. Locker, Apr. 10, 1933, CZA S25/9809.
3. "Drive Opened Here to Aid Reich Jews," and "Canadians Protest," *NYT*, Apr. 3, 1933.
4. See Mark Wischnitzer, *To Dwell in Safety: The Story of Jewish Migration Since 1800* (Philadelphia: JPSA, 1949), 122, 141–42, 145–46; Herbert Agar, *The Saving Remnant: An Account of Jewish Survival Since 1914* (London: Rupert Hart-Davis, 1960), 25, 30, 51–54, 64–69; "10,000 Jews Flee Nazi Persecution," *NYT*, Apr. 15, 1933.
5. See report, B. Locker, Apr. 10, 1933, CZA S25/9809; letter, M. Achi-Felix (Martin Rosenbluth) to Arlosoroff, Apr. 6, 1933, and Locker to Arlosoroff, Apr. 8, 1933, CZA S25/794; see protocol, JA Exec. Sessions, Apr. 9, 14 and 23, 1933, CZA S25/794.
6. See "We Must Enlarge the Yishub," *New Palestine*, Jan. 20, 1933; see "Dinner to Straus to Open New York Drive," *New Palestine*, Mar. 3, 1933; see Great Britain Colonial Office, *Palestine and Trans-Jordan for the Year 1932* (London: HMSO, 1933), 21; see letter, E. Neumann to R. Szold, Apr. 27, 1933, and attached "Exhibit C," BPM at AJA.
7. Protocol of the 19th Zionist Congress, p. 78, cited in Yoab Gelber, *Hamediniut Hazionit Veheskem Ha-Haavara, 1933–1935* (Tadpis Mitoch: "Yalkut Moreschet," Hoveret 17), 99.
8. See "Sharp Jewish Labor Shortage in Palestine, Histadruth Appeals for New Chalutzim," *JDB*, Feb. 24, 1933; see "Jewish Labor Shortage in Palestine," *New Palestine*, Mar. 3, 1933; "Pupils of Jewish Schools and Colleges Mobilized to Relieve Labor Shortage in Palestine," *JDB*, Mar. 9, 1933.
9. Letter, B. Locker to Chaim Weizmann, Apr. 4, 1933, CZA S25/794.
10. Letter, W. Senator to Bernard Kahn, Apr. 6, 1933, CZA S49/381 (trans. EF).
11. *Ibid.*: see Esco Foundation for Palestine, Inc., *Palestine: A Study of Jewish, Arab and British Policies* (New Haven: Yale, 1947), I: 316–19; see Great Britain Colonial Office, *Palestine and Trans-Jordan for the Year 1930* (London: HMSO, 1931), 35–36, 41; see Great Britain Colonial Office, *Palestine and Trans-Jordan for the Year 1931* (London: HMSO, 1932), 17–18, 23; see Great Britain Colonial Office, *Palestine and Trans-Jordan for the Year 1932* (London: HMSO, 1933), 21, 26, 28.
12. Letter, Senator to Kahn, Apr. 6, 1933, CZA S49/381 (trans. EF).
13. Protocol, JA Exec. Session, Apr. 9, 1933, CZA S25/794 (author's trans. 12; trans. GB).
14.–16. *Ibid.* (author's trans. 3–12).
17. *Ibid.* (author's trans. 11–14); see protocol, JA Exec. Session, Apr. 16, 1933, CZA S25/794 (author's trans. 6).
18.–19. Protocol, JA Exec. Session, Apr. 9, 1933, CZA S25/794 (see author's trans. 1–2).
20. Walter Laqueur, *A History of Zionism* (New York: Holt, Rinehart and Winston, 1972), 476–77; see Golda Meir, *My Life* (New York: Dell, 1975), 138–39; see Chaim Weizmann, *Trial and Error: The Autobiography of Chaim Weizmann* (New York: Harper, 1949), 300.
21. Protocol, JA Exec. Session, Apr. 9, 1933, CZA S25/794 (author's trans. 4–5).
22.–25. *Ibid.* (author's trans. 4–15).
26. *Ibid.* (author's trans. 16); see letter, Neumann to Szold, Apr. 27, 1933, BPM at AJA.
27. Extract from minutes, meeting of the Executive of the JA, Mar. 23, 1933, BPM at AJA; letters, Maurice Hexter to Julius Simon and Nahum Sokolow, Mar. 24, 1933, BPM at AJA.
28. See "Daily Report of the Activities of Emanuel Neumann, March 11 to March 17, 1933," and "Daily Activities of Emanuel Neumann, Mar. 19 to March 28, 1933," BPM at AJA.

CHAPTER 10

1. See letter, Arlosoroff to "Members of the Executive," Apr. 7, 1933, BPM at AJHS; letter, E. Neumann to R. Szold, Apr. 27, 1933, BPM at AJA, 1–4; see "Mizarchi Asks Removal of Dr. Arlosoroff Over Transjordan Negotiations," *JDB*, Apr. 27, 1933.
2. Letter, Neumann to Szold, Apr. 27, 1933, BPM at AJA; "Transjordan Chiefs Entertained," London *JC*, Apr. 21, 1933; "Dr. Weizmann and the Sheikhs," *Palestine Post*, Apr. 10, 1933.
3. "Dr. Weizmann and the Sheikhs," *Palestine Post*, Apr. 10, 1933.
4. Susan Lee Hattis, *The Bi-National Idea in Palestine During Mandatory Times* (Haifa: Shikmona, 1970), 19–21, 24–30, 43–45, 59–60, 64–67, 86–92, 115–16; see Jacob Boas, "The Jews of Germany: Self-Perceptions in the Nazi Era As Reflected in the German Jewish Press, 1933–1938" (unpub. Ph.D. diss., history, Univ. of California, Riverside, 1977), 13–14.

5. Hattis, 84–86, 95–96, 101–2; Walter La-queur, *A History of Zionism* (New York: Holt, Rinehart and Winston, 1972), 258–59.

6. Letter, Neumann to Szold, Apr. 27, 1933, BPM at AJA.

7. Letter, B. Locker to Arlosoroff, Apr. 8, 1933, CZA S-25/794.

8. Letter, "M. Achi-Felix" (Martin Rosenbluth) to Arlosoroff, Apr. 6, 1933, CZA S-25/794 (trans. DD).

9. Lucy S. Dawidowicz, *The War Against the Jews, 1933–1945* (Toronto: Bantam, 1976), 77–78; see Dr. Joseph Goebbels, *My Part in Germany's Fight*, trans. Dr. Kurt Fiedler (London: Hurst and Blackett, 1935), 236–37; see letter, "M. Francois-Poncet, French Ambassador to Germany, to M. Paul-Boncour, Foreign Minister," Apr. 5, 1933, *DDF 1932–1939*, 1st ser., III (Paris: Imprimerie Nationale, 1967): 155; see minutes, cabinet meeting of the German government, March 31, 1933, NA T-120 roll 1712, D792205 *et seq.*; also see Raul Hilberg, *The Destruction of the European Jews* (New York: Harper Colophon, 1979), 21; see report, Chaim Arlosoroff, May 19, 1933, CZA S25/9706; see letter, Jacob Billikopf to Herbert Lehman, Sep. 1, 1933, BPM at AJA, 9–10.

10. "Nazis See Victory in their Boycott," *NYT*, Apr. 4, 1933; "German Ban Halts Tide of Refugees," *NYT*, Apr. 6, 1933; "20 German Refugees Smuggle Themselves into Belgium," *JDB*, Apr. 6, 1933; wireless to *NYT*, Apr. 7, 1933; "Boycott of Jews in Germany," London *Times*, Mar. 31, 1933.

11. Protocol, JA Exec. Session, Apr. 14, 1933, CZA S-25/794 (trans. GB).

12. Letter, Weizmann to Israel M. Sieff, Apr. 23, 1933, n. 2, in Camillo Dresner, ed., *The Letters and Papers of Chaim Weizmann* (New Brunswick, New Jersey: Transaction, 1978), XV, ser. A, Oct. 1930–June 1933, letter no. 364, p. 403; see protocol, JA Exec. Session, Apr. 23, 1933, CZA S25/794 (trans. GB; author's trans. 3).

13. Elias M. Epstein, "The Redemption of the Land," in Jessie Sampter, ed., *Modern Palestine: A Symposium* (New York: Hadassah, 1933), 91–92; see Great Britain Colonial Office, *Palestine and Transjordan for the Year 1933* (London: HMSO, 1934), 27.

14. Letter, Weizmann to Sieff, Apr. 23, 1933, in Dresner, Letter no. 364, p. 403, n. 2; protocol, JA Exec. Session, Apr. 23, 1933, CZA S25/794.

15. Protocol, JA Exec. Session, Apr. 14, 1933, CZA S25/794 (trans. GB; author's trans. 2).

16.–17. *Ibid.* (author's trans. 2–4).

18. Protocol, JA Exec. Session, Apr. 16, 1933, CZA S25/794 (author's trans. 3–4); see protocol, JA

Exec. Session, Apr. 23, 1933, CZA S25/794; see letter, Neumann to Szold, Apr. 27, 1933, BPM at AJA, 1.

19. Protocol, JA Exec. Session, Apr. 16, 1933, CZA S25/794 (author's trans. 3–4).

20.–21. *Ibid.* (author's trans. 4–8).

22. *Ibid.* (author's trans. 8); see cable 620, JA to Zionistburo, Apr. 18, 1933 (misdated), CZA S25/9809; see cable 620, Arlosoroff to Zionistburo, undated, CZA S25/9809; see letter, Neumann to Szold, Apr. 27, 1933, BPM at AJA, 1.

23. Letter, Neuman to Szold, Apr. 27, 1933, BPM at AJA, 1–2; see letter, Weizmann to Sieff, Apr. 23, 1933, in Dresner, letter no. 364, p. 403, see n. 2.

24. Letter, Neumann to Szold, Apr. 27, 1933, BPM at AJA.

25. See protocol, JA Exec. Session, Apr. 19, 1933, first session (author's trans. 5), and protocol, JA Exec. Session, Apr. 25, 1933, CZA S25/794.

26. Cable 622, Arlosoroff to Zionistburo, London, CZA S25/9809.

27. Protocol, JA Exec. Session, Apr. 19, 1933, second session, CZA S25/794.

28. Protocol, JA Exec. Session, Apr. 23, 1933, CZA S25/794 (author's trans. 6).

29. See Hilberg, 19–20, see 19, n. 5; see Dawidowicz, 71–72, 77–78.

30. See protocol, JA Exec. Session, Apr. 23, 1933 (author's trans. 1) and protocol, JA Exec. Session, April 9, 1933 (author's trans. pp. 1–2), CZA S25/794.

31. Protocol, JA Exec. Session, Apr. 23, 1933, CZA S25/794 (author's trans. 1–6, 12).

32.–34. *Ibid.* (author's trans. 1–14).

35. Letter, Arlosoroff to Consul Wolff, Apr. 23, 1933, CZA S25/9809, in Yoab Gelber, *Hamediniut Hazionit Veheskem Ha-Haavara, 1933–1935* (Tadpis Mitoch: "Yalkut Moreshet," Hoveret 17), 107 (author's trans. 12–13); letter, Wolff to Mr. Pruefer, Apr. 24, 1933, CZA A-44/14 (trans. GZ).

36. Protocol, JA Exec. Session, Apr. 25, 1933, CZA S25/794 (author's trans. 1–3).

37.–38. *Ibid.* (author's trans. 2–4).

39. See report, Consul Wolff, Apr. 24, 1933, NA T-120 roll 4954, L368911 (trans. GZ).

40. *Ibid.*; see report, Alexander Sloan, American Consulate, Jerusalem, "Proposed Settlement of Arab Villagers on Household Plots Provided by Jewish Auspices," May 1, 1933, NA 867N.00/174.

41.–42. Report, Wolff, Apr. 25, 1933, NA T-120 roll 4954, L368911 (trans. GZ).

43. Gelber, 108 (author's trans. 13); Shaul Esh, *Studies in the Holocaust and Contemporary Jewry* (Jerusalem: ICJ, 1973), 42 (author's trans. 8).

CHAPTER II

1. "Paris Boycott is Started," and "Jews in Istanbul Urge Boycott," *NYT*, Apr. 2, 1933.

2. "Canadians Protest," and "Refugee Jews Tax Paris Charity Funds," *NYT*, Apr. 3, 1933.

3. "Clash at Jewish Protest in Greece," *NYT*,

Apr. 5, 1933; "Jews in Panama Boycott Germany," and "French Jews Press Boycott Till Reich Ends Discrimination," *NYT*, Apr. 4, 1933.

4. "Foreign Reactions: Hitler Brings the World About His Ears," *JC*, Apr. 7, 1933.

5. "15,000 Reds Cheer Attacks on Hitler," *NYT*, Apr. 6, 1933.

6. "Berlin Asks Curb on Silesia Terror," *NYT*, Apr. 7, 1933; "Attack German Buildings," *NYT*, Apr. 10, 1933; "Poles Burn German Papers," *NYT*, Apr. 12, 1933; political report, "The Minister in Poland to the Foreign Ministry," Apr. 19, 1933, and enclosed memorandum, Apr. 12, 1933, *DGFP 1918–1945* (London: HMSO, 1957), ser. C, I: 306–310.

7. "2 British Cities Ban Anti-German Signs," *NYT*, Apr. 10, 1933; "London Lifts Ban on Anti-German Posters; Cabinet Permits Jewish Boycott of Goods," *NYT*, Apr. 11, 1933.

8. "Lists Big German Losses," *NYT*, Apr. 16, 1933.

9. "Rumanian Jews Boycott Germans," *NYT*, Apr. 14, 1933.

10. "Antwerp Jews Boycott Germany," *NYT*, Apr. 18, 1933.

11. "Croatian Nationalists Start Boycott Against Boycotters," *JDB*, Apr. 20, 1933.

12. See "Nazis Begin to Dodge Anti-Semitic Boomerang," *NYT*, Apr. 9, 1933; *Haaretz*, Apr. 6, 1933 (trans. GG); "Hitler's Boomerang Policy," *JC*, Apr. 7, 1933.

13. *Haaretz*, Apr. 6, 1933 (trans. GG).

14. "Centre of Interest at Basle," *NYT*, Apr. 10, 1933; see "Extract from the Minutes of the Conference of Ministers," Apr. 7, 1933, *DGFP*, 261–262.

15. "Hitler Policy Hits German Business," *NYT*, Apr. 10, 1933.

16. "More Moderation is Shown by Nazis," *NYT*, Apr. 12, 1933; see letter, "Chancellor Hitler to President Hindenburg," Apr. 5, 1933, *DGFP*, 253–55; "Hitler to Clarify Policy on Jews," *NYT*, Apr. 19, 1933.

17. "Trade Groups Deny German Export Rise," *NYT*, Apr. 24, 1933.

18. F. Thelwell, "Memorandum on the German Situation, April 1933," Apr. 26, 1933, PRO-FO 371/16695–1527.

19. Letter, unsigned (B. Locker) to Franz Kahn, Apr. 5, 1933, CZA S25/794 (trans. DD).

20. Letter, B. Locker to the Jewish Agency Executive, Apr. 4, 1933, Weizmann Archive; see letter, Locker to Weizmann, Apr. 4, 1933, WA (trans. NS).

21.–23. Letter, "Lionel" to Cyrus Adler, Apr. 3, 1933, AJCmA.

24. Telegram, Cyrus Adler and Alfred Cohen to Secretary of State Cordell Hull, Apr. 6, 1933, AJCmA.

25. *Ibid.*; telegram, Cordell Hull, Secretary of State, to Cyrus Adler, Apr. 7, 1933, AJCmA.

26. "Drive Opened Here to Aid Reich Jews," *NYT*, Apr. 3, 1933.

27. Letter, G. Fredman to Cyrus Adler, Apr. 14, 1933, AJCmA; letter, Cyrus Adler to J. George Fredman, Apr. 19, 1933, AJCmA.

28. Editorial, *Der Tog*, Apr. 29, 1933, cited in "Jewish 'Day' Scores Anti-Parade Stand," *JDB*, May 1, 1933.

CHAPTER 12

1. See Werner E. Braatz, "German Commercial Interests in Palestine; Zionism and the Boycott of German Goods, 1933–1934," *European Studies Review* (SAGE, London and Beverly Hills), IX: 490–491; see letter, John Wanamaker Co., Apr. 21, 1933; letter, Finland, Apr. 17, 1933; letter, Brussels Leather Merchants Syndicate, Apr. 3, 1933; boycott handbill, forwarded by the German representative in Egypt, undated; reports, from North Africa, London, Denmark, Romania, Norway, Ireland, and the United States, all transmitted by the German Foreign Office to other agencies, all in NA, T-120 roll 4956, L370262/371913 (trans. GZ).

2. Letter, Chamber of Commerce, Muenster, Apr. 19, 1933, and letter, Chamber of Commerce, Offenbach, May 9, 1933, NA T-120 roll 4956, L370262 *et seq.* (trans. GZ).

3. Telegram, "The Consul-General at Danzig to the Foreign Minister," Mar. 7, 1933, *DGFP 1918–1945* (London: HMSO, 1957), ser. C, I:

111–12, see n. 2; see telegram, "The Deputy Director of Department IV to the Consulate General at Danzig," *DGFP*, 130; see "In Europe's new Tenseness the 'Corridor' Looms Large," *NYT*, Mar. 19, 1933.

4.–9. "Extract from the Minutes of the Conference of Ministers," Apr. 27, 1933, *DGFP*, 250–62.

10. Memorandum by Moltke, Apr. 12, 1933, in "The Minister in Poland to the Foreign Ministry," Apr. 19, 1933, *DGFP*, 307–10.

11. Telegram, "The Ambassador in Italy to the Foreign Ministry," Apr. 22, 1933, *DGFP*, 325, see n. 1.

12.–13. Political report, "The Minister in Poland to the Foreign Ministry," *DGFP*, 328–33.

14.–16. Telegram, "The Minister in Czechoslovakia to the Foreign Ministry," Apr. 25, 1933, *DGFP*, 343, see no. 2.

CHAPTER 13

1. "Boycott Chief's View," *NYT*, Apr. 4, 1933.

2. "Sweep of Officials is Decreed in Reich," *NYT*, Apr. 13, 1933; see letter, "The Chargé in Germany (Gordon) to the Secretary of State," *FRUS, 1933*,

(Washington, D.C.: U.S. Government Printing Office, 1949), II: 347–350.

3. "Demand New Move to Aid Reich Jews," *NYT*, Apr. 20, 1933; "Anti-Nazi Protest March

Through New York Voted by American Jewish Congress," *JDB*, Apr. 21, 1933.

4. See letter, Wise to Ruth Mack Brunswick, Apr. 6, 1933, in Carl Hermann Voss, ed., *Stephen S. Wise: Servant of the People* (Philadelphia: JPSA, 1969), 183; letter, J. H. Holmes to Wise, Apr. 20, 1933, BPM at AJA; see cablegram, Wise to Mr. Deutsch, in minutes, AJCAdCom., Aug. 17, 1933, AJHS, 1–2; "Dr. Wise's Report on his Activities in Europe," in minutes, AJCAd, AJHS, 13; see press release, AJC, Sep. 25, 1933, BPM at AJA, 4–5.

5. "Anti-Nazi Protest March Through New York Voted," *JDB*, Apr. 21, 1933.

6. *Ibid.*; "Demand New Move to Aid Reich Jews," *NYT*, Apr. 21, 1933; "Protest Parade on Nazi Book Burning Day to Be Largest Ever Staged Here," *JDB*, May 5, 1933.

7. "Call 2,000,000 Jews to March in Protest," *NYT*, Apr. 21, 1933; "Protest Parade on Nazi Book Burning to be Largest Ever Staged Here," *JDB*, May 5, 1933; "Colby to be Speaker at Hitler Protest," *NYT*, May 9, 1933; "Jews of World Join in Great Demonstration Against Hitler Persecutions," *JDB*, May 12, 1933.

8. "Frown on Parades as Hitler Protest," *NYT*, Apr. 28, 1933.

9. "A Universal Verdict," *NYT*, Apr. 29, 1933.

10. "250,000 to Protest," *NYT*, May 4, 1933.

11.–12. "Schacht Aroused by Dispatch to The Times; Challenges Account of Nazi Rally Plans," *NYT*, May 5, 1933.

13. Telegram, "The President of the Reichsbank to the Foreign Ministry," May 6, 1933, *DGFP, 1918–1945* (London, HMSO, 1957), ser. C. I: 390–391; Hjalmar Horace Greely Schacht, *Confessions of "The Old Wizard": The Autobiography of Hjalmar Horace Greeley Schacht*, trans. Diana Pyke (Boston: Houghton Mifflin, 1956), 282.

14. Telegram, "The President of the Reichsbank to the Foreign Ministry," May 6, 1933, *DGFP*, 392; Schacht, 282.

15.–16. Telegram, "The President of the Reichsbank to the Foreign Ministry," May 6, 1933, *DGFP*, 390–93.

17. "German Dye Trust Hit by Reprisals," and "Untermyer Urges German Boycott," *NYT*, May 8, 1933; see "Extract from the Minutes of the Conference of Ministers," Apr. 7, 1933, *DGFP*, 262.

18. "Jews Invite Schacht," *NYT*, May 8, 1933.

19. See letter, Wise to Albert Einstein, May 9, 1933, in Voss, 188.

20. "Boycott of Reich Verified in Munich," *NYT*, May 9, 1933.

21. Schacht, 283; Cordell Hull, *The Memoirs of Cordell Hull* (New York: Macmillan, 1948), I: 237.

22. Hull, 236–38.

23. William E. Dodd, Jr., and Martha Dodd, *Ambassador Dodd's Diary, 1933–1938* (New York: Harcourt, Brace, 1941), 4–5; Schacht, 283–84;

Hull, 237–38.

24. Hull, 237–38; Schacht, 283–84.

25. Hull, 238.

26. Letter, Wise to Einstein, May 9, 1933, in Voss, 187.

27. "Schacht Will Measure Cost of Anti-Semitism," *NYT*, May 7, 1933.

28. "Untermyer Urges German Boycott," *NYT*, May 8, 1933.

29. "100,000 March Here in 6-Hour Protest Over Nazi Policies," *NYT*, May 11, 1933; "Jews of World Join in Great Demonstration Against Hitler Persecutions in Germany," *JDB*, May 12, 1933; see photograph, "Anti-Nazi Demonstration Organized by the American Jewish Congress in New York, May 10, 1933," in "United States," *Encyclopaedia Judaica* (Jerusalem: Keter, 1972), XV: 1629–30.

30. "100,000 March Here," *NYT*, May 11, 1933; "Jews of World Join in Great Demonstration," *JDB*, May 12, 1933.

31. "100,000 March Here," *NYT*, May 11, 1933; "Jews of World Join in Great Demonstration," *JDB*, May 12, 1933; see Justine Wise Polier and James Waterman Wise, ed., *The Personal Letters of Stephen Wise* (Boston: Beacon, 1965), 9–10.

32. "100,000 March Here," *NYT*, May 11, 1933; "Jews of World Join in Great Demonstration," *JDB*, May 12, 1933: "50,000 Jews Unite in Chicago Protest," *NYT*, May 11, 1933; see "Paris Joins Protest," "Protest Goebbels Appointment," and "20,000 in Philadelphia Parade," *JDB*, May 12, 1933.

33. Schacht, 284–85; see telegram, "The President of the Reichsbank to the Foreign Ministry," May 15, 1933, *DGFP*, 423; see letter, Wise to Einstein, May 9, 1933, in Voss, 188; see confidential memo, L.D.B. (Brandeis) to S.S.W (Wise), May 11, 1933, BPM at AJA.

34. "Private and Confidential Bulletin," J.T.A., undated, BPM at AJA; see letter/diary, James G. McDonald to the Foreign Policy Association, Apr. 3, 1933, BPM at AJA,, 2–4; see letters, Wise to George Alexander Kohut, Apr. 26, 1933, and Wise to Einstein, May 9, 1933, in Voss, 186–87; Confidential memo, L.D.B. (Brandeis) to S.S.W. (Wise), May 11, 1933, BPM at AJA; letter, Wise to L.D.B. (Brandeis), May 12, 1933, BPM at AJA; see letter, Joe Comming to Wise, May 10, 1933, BPM at AJA: see Naomi W. Cohen, *Not Free to Desist: The American Jewish Committee, 1906–1966* (Philadelphia: JPSA, 1972), 162; Schact 284–85.

35. Schacht, 285; see telegram, "The President of the Reichsbank to the Foreign Ministry," May 15, 1933, *DGFP*, 423.

36. Telegram, "The President of the Reichsbank to the Foreign Ministry," May 15, 1933, *DGFP*, 423–24; see Schacht, 284.

37. Telegram, "The President of the Reichsbank to the Foreign Ministry," May 15, 1933, *DGFP*, 423–24.

CHAPTER 14

1. Isaiah Friedman, *Germany, Turkey and Zionism, 1897–1918* (Oxford: Clarendon, 1977), 3–6, 59–66, 73–90; H. G. Adler, *The Jews in Germany* *from the Enlightenment to National Socialism*, (Notre Dame: University of Notre Dame Press, 1969), 104.

2. Friedman, 80, 197–201, 211–27, 339–41;

see Great Britain Arab Office, *The Future of Palestine* (Geneva, Switzerland: "Imprimerie Centrale," 1947), 96–104.

3. Dickram Boyajian, *Armenia: The Case for a Forgotten Genocide* (Westwood, New Jersey: Educational Book Crafters, 1972), 15, 145, see 192–36.

4. Friedman, 400–2, 406; Francis R. J. Nocosia, "Germany and the Palestine Question, 1933–1939" (unpub. Ph.D. diss., history, McGill, 1977), 23–27, 47–48, see appendix no. 8, p. 356.

5. "Is Palestine in Need of German Goods?" *Haaretz*, Aug. 16, 1933, in report, American Consulate General in Jerusalem, Aug. 30, 1933, NA ADT-667N.6212/6; see letter, Wolff to RFM, July 3, 1933, NA T-120 roll 4954, L368972/77; see "Palestine as a German Export Market," *JR*, July 25, 1933 (trans. GZ); see Nicosia, 30–32, see appendixes nos. 6 and 7, pp. 354–55.

6. *Doar Hayom*, Mar. 27, 1933, in Werner E. Braatz, "German Commercial Interests in Palestine: Zionism and the Boycott of German Goods, 1933–1934," *European Studies Review* (SAGE, London and Beverly Hills), IX (1979): 494–85.

7. *Haaretz*, Apr. 3, 1933 (trans. GG); see confidential minutes, American Economic Committee for Palestine Executive Committee, May 15, 1933, BPM at AJA; see editorial, *Kol Israel*, May 18, 1933, NA T-120 roll 4028, L015469/72; see letters, Wolff to the RFM, Mar. 28, 30, and telegram, Mar. 31, NA T-120 roll 4028, L015398/406 (trans. GZ); see report, "Jewish Boycott of German Goods and Opportunities for American Exporters," American Consulate General in Jerusalem to the Secretary of State, July 7, 1933, NA ADT 667N.6212/2.

8. Joseph Schechtman, *Fighter and Prophet: The Vladimir Jabotinsky Story, The Last Years* (New York: Thomas Yoseloff, 1962), 139–40, 158–59, 164–72, see 214–16; see Walter Laqueur, *A History of Zionism* (New York: Holt, Rinehart and Winston, 1972), 343–59.

9. *Hazit Haam*, Apr. 22, 1933, in JABA (trans. GG); see report, "Boycott of German Goods Expanding," American Consulate General in Jerusalem to the Secretary of State, Apr. 5, 1933, NA ADT 667N.6212/1; see report, "Continued Boycott of German Goods," American Consulate General in Jerusalem to the Secretary of State, Aug. 26, 1933, NA ADT 667N. 6212/7.

10. Letter, Wolff to RFM, May 8, 1933, NA T-120 roll 4887, L319007/013 (trans. GZ); see Braatz, 490–92.

11. Letter, Chancery, British Embassy, Berlin, to the Central Department, Foreign Office, May 6, 1933, PRO-FO 371/16723–1556; "Difficulties for Palestine Emigrants Made Despite Nazi Promise to Britain," *JDB*, May 5, 1933.

12. See letter, G. Landauer to Prof. Brodetsky, undated (mid-Apr., 1933), CZA S25/9706 (trans. GZ).

13. Notes, R.M.A. Hankey, Apr. 18, 1933, and J. C. Stendale-Bennett, Apr. 22, and confidential letter, A.C.C. Parkinson to Brodetsky, Apr. 15, 1933, in "Foreign Office Minute: Position of Jews in Germany," PRO-FO 371/16721–1556.

14. Letter, I. H. Wallace to R.M.A. Hankey, Apr.

21, 1933, and letter, Central Department to the Chancery, British Embassy, Berlin, Apr. 27, 1933, PRO FO 371/16721–1556.

15. "Moses, Sigfried," *Encyclopaedia Judaica* (Jerusalem: Keter, 1972), XII: 415–16; see "Note Concerning the Transfer Agreement," Sam Cohen, Oct. 9, 1933, CZA Z4/3434.

16. "Note Concerning the Transfer Agreement," Sam Cohen, Oct. 9, 1933, CZA Z4/3434.

17. See letter, Wolff to RFM, Apr. 25, 1933, NA T-120 roll 4954, L368911 (trans. GZ); see note, "Permission for Emigrants to Palestine to Deposit Monies on the Sperrkonto of the Firm Hanotaiah," Dr. Reichhardt for the Ministry of Economics to Hanotaiah, May 19, 1933, CZA K-11/180–2 (trans. GZ).

18. Karl A. Schleunes, *The Twisted Road to Auschwitz: Nazi Policy Toward German Jews, 1933–1939* (Urbana: Univ. of Illinois, 1970), 195–96; see Werner Fellchenfeld, Dolf Michaelis, and Ludwig Pinner, *Haavara-Transfer nach Palestina und Einwanderung deutscher Juden 1933–1939* (Tuebingen, 1972), 21 (author's trans. 7); see interview, Dr. Dolf Michaelis with the author, Sep. 1, 1981, author's transcript 4–7, 61.

19. Interview with Dr. Michaelis, Sep. 1, 1981, author's transcript 61–68.

20. Note, "Permission for Emigrants to Palestine to Deposit Monies," Dr. Reichhardt for the Ministry of Economics to Hanotaiah, May 19, 1933, CZA K-11/180–2 (trans. GZ); see interview, Dr. Michaelis, Sep. 1, 1981, author's transcript 12–14; also see letters, Landauer to Jacobsohn, June 9, 1933, and Landauer to Pinner, July 3, 1933, CZA S7/92 (trans. GZ); see Histadrut minutes, "Protocol on the Situation of Jews in Germany," Bellinson and Julius Berger, July 14, 1933, ALM (trans. GG); also see letter, Wolff to the RFM, July 27, 1933, NA T-120 roll 4954, L369010/20 (trans. GZ); also see letter, Herman Ellern to Schmidt-Roelke, July 27, 1933, NA T-120 roll 4954, L369051/2.

21. See Theodor Herzl, *The Jewish State: An Attempt at a Modern Solution of the Jewish Question*, trans. Sylvie D'Avigdor (London: Central Office of ZO, 1936), 34; see note, "Permission for Emigrants to Palestine to Deposit Monies," Dr. Reichhardt for the Ministry of Economics to Hanotaiah, May 19, 1933, CZA K-11/180–2 (trans. GZ); see letter, Herman Ellern to Schmidt-Roelke, July 27, 1933, NA T-120 roll 4954, L369051/2; see interview, Dr. Michaelis, Sep. 1, 1981, author's transcript 13–14.

22.–25. Confidential report, "Sir H. Rumbold to Sir John Simon," May 11, 1933, PRO-FO 371/16751–1556, pp. 1–2.

26. *Ibid.*; see memorandum, "Sir E. Phipps (Berlin) to Sir J. Simon," Oct. 24, 1933, *DGFP, 1918–1945* (London: HMSO, 1957), ser. C, I: 713.

27.–30. Confidential report, "Sir H. Rumbold to Sir J. Simon," May 11, 1933, PRO-FO 371/16751–1556, pp. 2–3.

31. Schleunes, 140; "Jewish Reaction on Reich," *NYT*, May 15, 1933.

32. "Jews Here Decree Boycott on Reich," *NYT*, May 15, 1933.

33. "Jewish Reaction on Reich," *NYT*, May 15,

1933; "Stores Find 'Made in Germany' a Handicap; Importers are Looking Elsewhere for Goods," *NYT*, May 16, 1933.

34. "Reich Exports Cut by 10% in April," *NYT*, 5/17/33; "Reich Prices Rise; Nazis Are Worried," *NYT*, 5/22/33; see Richard Grunberger, *The 12-Year Reich; A Social History of Nazi Germany, 1933–1945* (New York: Holt, Rinehart and Winston, 1971), 4.

35. See "The Reich Minister of Food and Agriculture to the Reich Chancellor," Apr. 12, 1933, *DGFP*, 287–88; see "The Minister in Poland to the Foreign Ministry," Apr. 19, 1933, and enclosed "Memorandum," Apr. 12, 1933, *DGFP*, 306–10; see political report, "The Minister in Poland to the Foreign Ministry," Apr. 23, 1933, *DGFP*, 328–33; letter, "Minister Moltke to State Secretary Bulow," Apr. 26, 1933, *DGFP*, 351–53; see telegram, "The Ambassador in Italy to the Foreign Ministry," Apr. 22, 1933, *DGFP*, 325; strictly confidential telegram, "The Minister in Czechoslovakia to the Foreign Ministry," Apr. 25, 1933, *DGFP*, 343, see n. 2; letter, "Sir H. Rumbold (Berlin) to Sir J. Simon," May 5, 1933, *DBFP* (London: HMSO, 1956), *1919–1939*, ser. 2, V (1933): 200–2.

36. Letter, "Sir R. Graham (Rome) to Sir J. Simon," Apr. 14, 1933, *DBFP*, 143; telegram, "The President of the Reichsbank to the Foreign Ministry," May 15, 1933, *DGFP*, 423–24; "Minute by an Official of Department II," May 2, 1933, *DGFP*, 369–72; "Memorandum by the Reichswehr Minister," May 15, 1933, *DGFP*, 435–36.

37. Telegram, Moses, Berlin, to Mazurka, Lodz, May 13, 1933, CZA K-11/180–1 (trans. DD).

38. Letters, Landauer to Jacobsohn, 6/9/33, and Landauer to Pinner, 7/3/33, CZA S7/92; memorandum, Landauer to Arlosoroff, 5/12/33, CZA S-25/9707 (trans. EF); see interview with Chaim Arlosoroff, "What Does Palestine Have to Offer the German Jews?" *JR*, no. 41, 5/23/33 (trans. GZ).

39. See letter, Chaim Arlosoroff to Sima Arlosoroff, May 21, 1933, in *The Writings of Chaim Arlosoroff*, Tel Aviv University (trans. GG); Sima Arlosoroff, in *Chaim Arlosoroff: A Selection of His Writings and Biographical Chapters*, 52 (trans. GG); see Hans-Otto Meissner, *Magda Goebbels; The First Lady of the Third Reich*, trans. Gwendolin Mary Keeble (New York: Dial, 1980), 13–14.

40. See memorandum, Landauer to Arlosoroff, May 12, 1933, CZA S-25/9707 (trans. EF); see top secret memorandum, "Some Thesis to the Question of the Liquidations Bank," Chaim Arlosoroff, May 19, 1933, CZA S-25/9706.

41. "Leipzig Fur Auction Fails," *NYT*, 5/13/33.

42. Confidential report, "Sir H. Rumbold to Sir John Simon," May 11, 1933, PRO-FO 371/16751–1556; see speech, Adolf Hitler to the Doctor's Union, Apr. 1933, in Norman H. Baynes, ed. and trans., *The Speeches of Adolf Hitler*, I (London: Oxford, 1942), 728–29; interview, Adolf Hitler by Bernard Ridder and William J. Margreve, *Staats-Zeitung* and *Herald*, in "Hitler, 'Man With a Holy Mission' Explains Jewish Stand to Ridder," *JDB*, May 24, 1933; see interview, Adolf Hitler by Anne O'Hare McCormick, "Hitler Seeks Jobs for All Germans," *NYT*, July 10, 1933; see speech, Adolf Hitler, Oct. 24, 1933, in Baynes, 729–30.

43.–44. Interview with Adolf Hitler by Ridder and Margreve, in "Hitler 'Man With a Holy Mission,' Explains Jewish Stand," *JDB*, May 24, 1933.

45. Memorandum, Landauer to Arlosoroff, May 12, 1933, CZA S25/9707; also see letter, Landauer to Pinner, July 3, 1933, CZA S-7/92, (trans. GZ/DD); telegram, Moses, Berlin, to Mazurka, Lodz, May 13, 1933, CZA K-11/180–1.

46. Telegram, Moses, Berlin, to Mazurka, Lodz, May 13, 1933, CZA K-11/180-1.

47. Note, "Permission for Emigrants to Palestine to Deposit Monies," Dr. Reichardt for the Ministry of Economies to Hanotaiah, May 19, 1933, CZA K-11/180–2 (trans. GZ).

CHAPTER 15

1. Telegram, Moses, Berlin, to Mazurka, Lodz, May 13, 1933, CZA K-11/180–1 (trans. DD).

2. Letter, Landauer to Jacobsohn, June 9, 1933, CZA S7/92 (trans. DD/GZ).

3. See statement, RFM, in letter, Chancery, British Embassy, Berlin, to the Central Department, May 23, 1933, PRO-FO 371/16724–1723.

4. Letters, Landauer to Jacobsohn, June 9, 1933, and Landauer to Pinner, July 3, 1933, CZA S7/92; see letters, President of the State Finance Office/Office of Foreign Currency to prospective emigrants to Palestine, June 2, 7, and 12, 1933, CZA S7/92.

5. Letters, Landauer to Jacobsohn, June 9, 1933, and Landauer to Pinner, July 3, 1933, CZA S7/92; see letter, no signature (Martin Rosenbluth) to Landauer, May 19, 1933, CZA L-13/138-II (trans. DD).

6. Letter, Landauer to Jacobsohn, June 9, 1933, CZA S7/92 (trans. GZ/DD); see "Note About the Transfer Agreement," Sam Cohen, Oct. 9, 1933,

CZA Z4/3434; see "Highly Confidential" report, "Some Theses to the Question of the Liquidation Bank," Chaim Arlosoroff, May 19, 1933, CZA S25/9706 (trans. DD).

7.–9. "Highly Confidential" report, "Some Theses to the Question of the Liquidation Bank," Chaim Arlosoroff, May 19, 1933, CZA S25/9706; also see letter, H. Fleiss to Chaim Arlosoroff, June 10, 1933, CZA S25/9706 (trans. DD).

10.–11. "Highly Confidential" report, "Some Theses to the Question of the Liquidation Bank," Chaim Arlosoroff, May 19, 1933, CZA S-25/9706.

12. *Ibid.*; see Theodor Herzl, *The Jewish State; An Attempt at a Modern Solution of the Jewish Question*, trans. Sylvie D'Avigdor (London: Central Office of ZO, 1936), 18, 29.

13. Letter, no signature (Martin Rosenbluth) to Landauer, May 19, 1933, CZA L-13/138-II (trans. DD); see report, "Some Theses to the Question of the Liquidation Bank," Chaim Arlosoroff, May 19, 1933, CZA S-25/9706; interview with Chaim

Arlosoroff, "What Does Palestine Have to Offer the German Jews?" *JR*, no 41, May 23, 1933, 214 (trans. GZ); see speech, "Palestine and the Present Jewish Emergency," Chaim Arlosoroff, *Selbstwehr*, no. 21, May 26, 1933 (trans. HG).

14. Interview with Dr. Chaim Arlosoroff, "What Does Palestine Have to Offer the German Jews?" *JR*, no. 41, May 23, 1933, 214 (trans. GZ); see Shaul Esh, *Studies in the Holocaust and Contemporary Jewry* (Jerusalem: ICJ, 1973), 42, no. 9 (author's trans. 63).

15.–16. Interview with Dr. Chaim Arlosoroff, "What Does Palestine Have to Offer the German Jews?" *JR*, no. 41, May 23, 1933, 214 (trans. GZ).

17. "Report From Germany," in protocol, ZO Exec. Session, June 1, 1933, CZA L-13/138-I (trans. DD).

18.–20. Statement, RFM, in dispatch, Chancery, British Embassy, Berlin, to the Central Department, May 23, 1933, PRO-FO 371/16724–1723.

21. Speech, Chaim Arlosoroff, "Palestine and the Present Jewish Emergency," *Selbstwehr*, no. 21, May 26, 1933 (trans. HG); see "Transportation of Jewish Capital from Germany to Palestine," *Haaretz*, July 20, 1933 (trans. GZ).

22. Letter, no signature (Martin Rosenbluth) to Landauer, May 19, 1933, CZA L-13/138-II (trans. DD).

23. Letter, Zionist Central Office to Sam Cohen, May 30, 1933, NA T-120 roll 4887, L015521 or L319146 (trans. GZ).

24.–26. "Report from Germany," in protocol, ZO Exec. Session, June 1, 1933, CZA L-13/138-I (trans. DD).

27. *Ibid.*; telegram, ZO, London, to the Jewish Agency, Jerusalem, June 9, 1933, CZA L-9/441.

28. "Report from Germany," in protocol, ZO Exec. Session, June 1, 1983, CZA L-13/138-I (trans. DD); telegram, ZO, London, to Jewish Agency, Jerusalem, June 9, 1933, CZA L-9/441.

29.–31. "Minutes of a Conversation with the Colonial Secretary," S. Brodetsky, June 1, 1933, CZA S25/9706 (trans YC)

32. Telegram, Arlosoroff/Cohen to Hanotaiah, June 4, 1933, NA T-120 roll 4007, L31914/ (trans. GZ).

33. Letter, A. M. Hyamson, Government of Palestine Dep. of Immigration, to the Jewish Agency Executive, May 19, 1933, WA.

34. See Letters, President of the State Finance Office/Office of Foreign Currency Control, to prospective emigrants to Palestine, June 2, 7, and 12, 1933, CZA S7/92.

35. Letter, Landauer to Jacobsohn, June 9, 1933, CZA S7/92 (trans. DD/GZ).

36. See Joseph Schechtman, *Fighter and Prophet: The Vladimir Jabotinsky Story, the Last Years* (New York: Thomas Yoseloff, 1961), 164–66.

37. See Walter Laqueur, *A History of Zionism* (New York: Holt, Rinehart and Winston, 1972), 281, 318, 326–27, 332–33; Esco Foundation, *Palestine: A Study of Jewish, Arab and British Policies*, (New Haven: Yale, 1947), I: 349–51, 359–63: see editorial, M. Smilansky, "The Happy Isle," *Boustani*,

Feb. 8, 1933, in confidential minutes, Executive Committee of the American Economic Committee for Palestine, Mar. 20, 1933, BPM at AJA.

38. Laqueur, 351–53; see Schechtman, 231–37; Esco, II: 749, 1135, no. 64.

39. Schechtman, 158.

40. Laqueur, 318, 359–62; see "The Facts About Revisionism," *JC*, July 14, 1933, 28; *Davar* and *Doar Hayom*, Apr. 18, 1933, in "Confidential Review of the Press," Alexander Sloan, American Consul in Jerusalem, June 19, 1933, NA 867N. 9111/100.

41. See Esco, II: 749; Schechtman, 235, 248; see "Make Palestine a Land of Fulfillment," *JDB*, Aug. 22, 1933, 4; see "Unfinished Business Prolongs Session of Zionist Congress," *JDB*, Aug. 31, 1933, 4.

42. Laqueur, 318–19; Esco, I: 362–63; see Schechtman, 237.

43. Imperial and Foreign News: "Latvia," *JC*, May 5, 1933, 34; see Schechtman, 248.

44. Schechtman, 214.

45. *Haaretz*, May 12, 1933, in Esh, 58, 74; letter, Wolff to RFM, May 16, 1933, NA T-120 roll 4887, L319035 (trans. GZ).

46. Letter, Wolff to RFM, "Jewish Boycott and How to Fight It," May 17, 1933, NA T-120 roll 4887, L015493 (trans. GZ).

47. Editorial, *Kol Israel*, no. 31 (549), May 18, 1933, NA T-120 roll 4028, L015546 (trans. GZ); Werner E. Braatz, "German Commercial Interests in Palestine: Zionism and the Boycott of German Goods, 1933–1934," *European Studies Review* (SAGE, London and Beverly Hills), IX (1979): 497.

48. See Susan Lee Hattis, *The Bi-National Idea in Palestine During Mandatory Times* (Haifa: Shikmona, 1970) 64, 86–98; Christopher Sykes, *Crossroads to Israel* (Cleveland: World, 1965), 122–24, 126; see *Falastin* and *Al Jamia Al Arabia*, Apr. 22, 1933, in "Confidential Review of the Press," Sloan, American Consul in Jerusalem, June 19, 1933, NA 867N. 9111/100.

49 Hattis, 90–91, 117; see "Mizrachi Asks Removal of Dr. Arlosoroff Over Transjordan Negotiations," *JDB*, Apr. 27, 1933.

50. Letter, Brodetsky to A.C.C. Parkinson, Feb. 14, 1933, PRO-FO 371/E963/257/31–1933, in Hattis, 122.

51. *Falastin* and *Al Jamia Al Arabia*, Apr. 22, 1933, in "Confidential Review of the Press," Sloan, American Consul in Jerusalem, June 19, 1933, NA 867N. 9111/100.

52. "Mizrachi Asks Removal of Dr. Arlosoroff Over Transjordan Negotiations," *JDB*, Apr. 27, 1933; *Palestine Post*, Apr. 29, 1933, in "Confidential Review of the Press," Sloan, American Consul in Jerusalem, June 19, 1933, NA 867N. 9111/100.

53. Minutes, Actions Committee of ZO, first session, Aug. 17, 1933, CZA Z4/287/1 (trans. GB); also see Edwin Viscount Samuel, *A Lifetime in Jerusalem* (London: Abelard Schuman, 1970), 137–38.

54. *Haaretz*, Apr. 27, 1933, in "Confidential Review of the Press," Sloan, American Consulate in

Jerusalem, June 19, 1933, NA 867N. 9111/100; see letter, Neumann to Szold, Apr. 27, 1933, BPM at AJA, 2–3.

55. Confidential report, "Proposed Settlement of Arab Villagers on Household Plots Provided by Jewish Auspices," Alexander Sloan, American Consul, Jerusalem, May 1, 1933, NA 867N.00/174.

56. "Transjordan Leaders Invite Jewish Agency to Buy Land Here," *JDB*, May 26, 1933; see *Haaretz*, May 24, 1933 (trans. GB).

57. "Transjordan Leaders Invite Jewish Agency to Buy Land Here," *JDB*, May 26, 1933; see "Pro-Zionism in Trans-Jordan," *Palestine Post*, May 26, 1933.

58.–62. "Strictly Secret-Confidential Minute of a Conversation between Mr. W. J. Johnson and Mr. Emanuel Neumann on May 24, 1933," in letter, Neumann to Szold, May 25, 1933, BPM at AJA.

63. Pamphlet, Defense Committee of the Revisionists Arrested in Palestine, *I Can't Keep Quiet!* (New York, 1933), 11; see Schechtman, 158.

64. Laqueur, 362–63; see Schechtman, 216; see "Sicarii," *Encyclopaedia Judaica* (Jerusalem: Keter, 1972), XIV: 1491–92.

65. Chaim Arlosoroff, *Writings in Six Volumes*, I:5; see Hattis, 84–85.

66. Chaim Arlosoroff, *Jerusalem Diary* (MAPAI Publications, 1948), 334, 341, in Hattis, 101–2.

67. See *Haaretz*, May 24, 1933 (trans GZ); "Two Forces in Transjordan are Continually Fighting Between Themselves," *Doar Hayom*, May 25, 1933; "Pro-Zionism in Transjordan," *Palestine Post*, May 26, 1933; "A Plan for Helping German Jewry," *Palestine Post*, June 12, 1933; see "The Stalin–Ben-Gurion–Hitler Alliance," *Hazit Haam*, June 16,

1933 (trans. GB); Die Welt (Poland), June 9, 1933, in Teveth, chap. 5 (trans. GB); *Hazit Haam*, June 9, 1933, in Teveth, chap. 5 (trans. GB).

68. Sima Arlosoroff, in *Chaim Arlosoroff: A Selection of His Writings and Biographical Chapters*; Teveth, chap. 6 (trans. GB).

69.–70. Teveth, chap 4.

71. *Ibid.*; interview, Shaul Arlosoroff with the author, Jan. 1982.

72. Teveth, chap. 4.

73. *Ibid.*; "Rewards Are Posted for Capture of the Slayers of Dr. Arlosoroff," *JDB*, June 19, 1933.

74. "The Stalin–Ben-Gurion–Hitler Alliance," *Hazit Haam*, June 16, 1933 (trans. GB); see "100,000 At Funeral of Dr. Arlosoroff," *Palestine Post*, June 16, 1933; Teveth, chap. 5.

75. Samuel, 137–38; Teveth, chap. 5.

76. Teveth, chap. 8; "Attention Focused on Jaffa As Evidence Mounts Against Arlosoroff Suspects," *JDB*, Aug. 11, 1933, 2.

77. Teveth, chap. 8; "Attention Focused on Jaffa," *JDB*, Aug. 11, 1933; Sima Arlosoroff, in *Chaim Arlosoroff: A Selection of His Writings and Biographical Chapters* (trans. GG).

78. Teveth, chap. 8.

79. *Ibid.*; "Rewards Are Posted," *JDB*, June 19, 1933.

80. Teveth, chap. 8; "Attention Focused on Jaffa," *JDB*, Aug. 11, 1933, 2.

81. Teveth, chap. 8; "Attention Focused on Jaffa," *JDB*, Aug. 11, 1933, 2; "100,000 At Funeral of Dr. Arlosoroff, *Palestine Post*, June 16, 1933.

82.–83. Teveth, chap. 8.

84. *Ibid.*; interview with Shaul Arlosoroff on Israeli television, Jan., 1981.

CHAPTER 16

1. "Rewards Are Posted for the Capture of the Slayers of Dr. Arlosoroff," and "British House of Commons to Make Issue of Murder of Dr. Chaim Arlosoroff," *JDB*, June 19, 1933; "100,00 at Funeral of Dr. Arlosoroff," *New Palestine*, June 16, 1933; "Warsaw in Mourning," and "Funeral at Tel Aviv," *JDB*, June 20, 1933.

2. "Revisionist Held in Arlosoroff Murder," *JDB*, June 21, 1933; see "The Stalin–Ben-Gurion–Hitler Alliance," *Hazit Haam*, June 16, 1933 (trans. GB).

3. "Revisionist Held in Arlosoroff Murder," *JDB*, June 21, 1933; "Two Revisionists Charged With Stavsky in Murder Conspiracy," *JDB*, Aug. 4, 1933; "Resume Arlosoroff Murder Trial," *JDB*, Aug. 25, 1933; Joseph Schechtman, *Fighter and Prophet: The Vladimir Jabotinsky Story, the Later Years* (New York: Thomas Yoseloff, 1961), 184–85.

4. See "Jaffa Police to Ask to hold Stavsky at Arraignment," *JDB*, July 6, 1933; see Letters to Editor, Yosef Ahimeir and Dr. Dov Joseph, "The Arlosoroff Affair," *Jerusalem Post*, June 17, 1979.

5. See "Arlosoroff Assassin Escaped to Lebanon, Arab Paper Reports," *JDB*, June 28, 1933; see "Sephardic Jew's Arrest Leads to Rumor He Has Clue to Murder of Arlosoroff," *JDB*, July 5, 1933; "Net for Dr. Arlosoroff Slayer is Spread Wide," *JDB*,

July 10, 1933; report, American Consulate General, Jerusalem, to the Secretary of State, "The Legacy of Dr. Arlosoroff," June 29, 1934, NA 867N. 00/197; report, American Consulate General, Jerusalem, to the Secretary of State, "Aquittal of Stavsky in Conclusion of Arlosoroff Murder Trial," Aug. 7, 1934, NA 867N. 00/203; see Schechtman, 197–205.

6. See "Was Arlosoroff Murdered by the British?" Canadian *Daily Hebrew Journal*, June 27, 1958; see Schechtman, note on 202–3; see Letters to the Editor, Yosef Ahimeir and Dr. Dov Joseph, "The Arlosoroff Affair," *Jerusalem Post*, June 17, 1979; see Hesi Carmel and Jaques Derogy, *The Untold History of Israel* (New York: Grove, 1979), 44–49; "Official Probe Into Arlosoroff Affair," *Jerusalem Post*, Mar. 15, 1982; see "People Who Remember," and Menachem Begin, "Anatomy of Incitement," *Jerusalem Post*, Mar. 19, 1982.

7. Schechtman, 185.

8. *Ibid.*; Our Voice, July 1934, and *Die Welt*, Nov. 16, 1933, in Schechtman, 186.

9. Kaunas, Lithuania *Yiddische Stimme*, no 1418, in Schechtman, 189.

10. See "Zionists and Laborites Mourn Dr. Arlosoroff Memorial Meeting," and "Tension in Poland," *JDB*, June 23, 1933; Schechtman, 189–90.

11. Schechtman, 190; Eitan Haber, *Menachem Begin: The Legend and the Man* (New York: Dell, 1978), 71.

12. Haber, 71–72.

13. Shaul Esh, *Studies in the Holocaust and Contemporary Jewry* (Jerusalem: ICJ 1973), 75 (author's trans. 32); "To Aid German Immigrants," *Doar Hayom*, July 19, 1933 (trans. GB); minutes, meeting of Conference of Representatives of Institutions, July 2, 1933, CZA S-25/9706 (trans. YC).

14. Minutes, meeting of Conference of Representatives of Institutions, July 2, 1933, CZA S-25/9706 (trans. YC).

15. Letter, Wolff to RFM, June 15, 1933, NA T-120 roll 4954, L368939 *et seq.* (trans. GZ).

16. *Ibid.*; see report, American Consulate General, Jerusalem, to the Secretary of State, "Suspension of the Newspaper 'Doar Hayom,'" Jan. 29, 1931, and enclosed "Memorandum on the Suspension of the Doar Hayom," NA 867N. 918 DOAR HAYOM/11.

17. Letter, Wolff to RFM, June 15, 1933, NA T-120 roll 4954, L368939 *et seq.* (trans. GZ).

18. See letter, Moses A. Leavitt to Justice Brandeis, May 24, 1933, BPM at AJA; *Industrie & Handel*, June 19, 1933, NA T-120 roll 4956, L370302/3 (trans. GZ); see Great Britain Colonial Office, *Palestine and Trans-Jordan for the Year 1932* (London: HMSO, 1933), 165, 167.

19.–27. Letter, Wolff to RFM, June 15, NA T-120 roll 4954, L368939 *et seq.* (trans. GZ).

28. *Ibid.*; Francis R. J. Nicosia, "Germany and the Palestine Question, 1933–1939" (unpub. Ph.D. diss., Dept. history, McGill, 1977), 87–88, see n. 2 on 88; Ernst Marcus, "The German Foreign Office and the Palestine Question in the Period 1933–1939," *Yad Washem Studies on the European Jewish Catastrophe and Resistance*, II (Jerusalem:

Yad Washem, 1958): 181, 183–84; see *JDB*, July 5, 1933, 4.

29. Telegram, ZO London, to Jewish Agency, Jerusalem, June 9, 1933, CZA L-9/441.

30. Letter, Landauer to Jacobsohn, June 9, 1933, CZA S7/92 (trans. GZ/DD).

31. Letter and enclosed memorandum, Landauer to the Ministry of Economics, June 20, 1933, CZA K-11/180-2 (trans. DD).

32. See letter, Wolff to RFM, June 15, 1933, marked "received June 20," NA T-120 roll 4954, L368939 (trans. GZ).

33.–34. Sam Cohen, "Note Concerning the Transfer Agreement," Oct. 9, 1933, CZA Z4/3434 (trans. DD).

35. Sam Cohen, "Note Concerning the Transfer Agreement," Oct. 9, 1933, CZA Z4/3434 (trans. DD).

36. *Ibid.*; letter, Landauer to L. Pinner, July 3, 1933, CZA S7/92 (trans. GZ/DD); see telegram, Ulrich to Wolff, July 24, 1933, NA T-120 roll 4954, L369000/01 (trans. GZ).

37.–39. Letter, Landauer to Pinner, July 3, 1933, CZA S7/92 (trans. GZ/DD).

40. Letter, Wolff to RFM, June 24, 1933, NA T-20 roll 4954, L368959 *et seq.* (trans. GZ); letter, Ussischkin to Sam Cohen, June 25, 1933, NA T-120 roll 4028, Lo15518/19 (trans. GZ).

41. Letter, Ussischkin to Sam Cohen, June 25, 1933, NA T-120 roll 4028, Lo15518/19 (trans. GZ).

42. Letter, Ussischkin to Jewish National Fund, Berlin, June 25, 1933, NA T-120 roll 4028, Lo15520 (also in CZA K-11/180-1; trans. GZ/DD).

43.–47. Letter, "Urgent," Wolff to RFM, June 24, 1933, NA T-120 roll 4954, NA T-120 roll 4954, L368959 *et seq.* (trans. GZ).

CHAPTER 17

1. Marvin Lowenthal, *The Jews of Germany: A Story of Sixteen Centuries* (New York: Longmans, Green, 1936), 224–26, 234, 242–48; Jehuda Reinharz, *Fatherland or Promised Land: The Dilemma of the German Jew, 1893–1914* (Ann Arbor: Univ. of Michigan, 1975), 8.

2. Donald L. Niewyk, *The Jews in Weimar Germany* (Baton Rouge: Louisiana State Univ., 1980), 98–103.

3.–4. Reinharz, 172–176.

5. Reinharz, 102–5, 210–17; see Jacob Boas, "The Jews of Germany: Self-Perceptions in the Nazi Era as Reflected in the German Jewish Press, 1933–1938" (unpub. Ph.D. diss. history, Univ. of California, Riverside, 1977), 142.

6. Lowenthal, 285; Isaiah Friedman, *Germany, Turkey and Zionism, 1897–1918* (Oxford: Clarendon, 1977), 340, 343–44; Niewyk, 152–57; see Francis R. J. Nicosia, "Germany and the Palestine Question, 1933–1939" (unpub. Ph.D. diss., history, McGill, 1977), 62–63.

7. Reinharz, 141–42; Niewyk, 149, 156; "Zion-

ism," *Encyclopaedia Judaica* (Jerusalem: Keter, 1971), XVI: 1116.

8. Friedman, 347–53, see 212–27.

9. See Martin Luther, "That Jesus Christ Was Born A Jew," trans. Walther I. Brandt, *Luther's Works*, vol. 45, "The Christian in Society," II, ed. Walther I. Brandt (Philadelphia: Muhlenberg, 1962): 199; see Louis Israel Newman, *Jewish Influence on Christian Reform Movements* (New York: Columbia, 1925), 619–21, 625–27.

10. Martin Luther, "On the Jews and Their Lies," trans. Martin H. Gertram, *Luther's Works*, vol. 47, "The Christian in Society," ed. Franklin Sherman (Philadelphia: Fortress, 1971): 157, 172, 264.

11. *Ibid.* 266.

12. *Ibid.*, 276.

13. *Ibid.*, 265, 288.

14. *Ibid.*, 268–269, 288.

15. *Ibid.*, 269–270, 272.

16. *Ibid.*, 272.

17. *Ibid.*, 292.

18. Roland H. Bainton, *Here I Stand: A Life of*

Martin Luther (New York: Abingdon–Cokesbury 1940), 324–25, 373.

19. Uriel Tal, *Christians and Jews in Germany: Religion, Politics, and Ideology in the Second Reich, 1870–1914*, trans. Noah Jonathan Jacobs (Ithaca: Cornell, 1975), 248–52, 258; Richard Gutteridge, *Open Thy Mouth for the Dumb! The German Evangelical Church and the Jews, 1879–1950* (Oxford: Basil Blackwell, 1976), 4–6; see Luther, "On the Jews," *Luther's Works*, vol. 47: 265, 275.

20. Gutteridge, 17–18.

21. William L. Shirer, *The Rise and Fall of the Third Reich: A History of Nazi Germany* (New York: Fawcett Crest, 1960), 155–59; Gutteridge, 341–42.

22. Gutteridge, 26–27.

23. *Ibid.*, 37–41.

24. Raul Hilberg, *The Destruction of the European Jews* (New York: Harper Colophon, 1979), 8–10; Shirer, 326–27; see interview with Eberhard Bethge by Beryl Satter, Dec. 14, 1981; interview with Ruth Zerner by Beryl Satter, Dec. 14, 1981.

25. "Hitler, 'Man With a Holy Mission,' Explains Jewish Stand to Ridder," *JDB*, May 24, 1933.

26. Luther, "On the Jews," *Luther's Works*, vol. 47: 264–265.

27. Gutteridge, 17.

28. Testimony by Streicher, *Trial of the Major War Criminals*, XII: 335.

29. *Ibid.*, 318.

30. Nicosia, 67–68.

31. *Ibid.*, 58; Joseph Schechtman, *Rebel and Statesman: The Vladimir Jabotinsky Story, the Early Years* (New York: Thomas Yoseloff, 1956), 399.

32. Nicosia, 70.

33. Alfred Rosenberg, *Die Spier*, 153, in Nicosia, 65.

34. See letter, Dr. Franz Kahn to "Fellow Believers," Mar. 5, 1933, CZA S-25/9703; see letter, "M. Achi-Felix" (Martin Rosenbluth) to Arlosoroff, Apr. 6, 1933, CZA S-25/794; see Boas, 93–94.

35. Boas, 93; *JR*, May 12, 1933 (trans. GZ).

36. Alfred Rosenberg, *Der Staatsfeindliche Zionismus* (Hamburg: Deutschvillkfache Verlag-

sanstalt, 1922), 63, in Nicosia, 65 (trans. GZ).

37. See letter, Dr. Franz Kahn to "Fellow Believers," Mar. 5, 1933, CZA S/25, 9703; Martin Rosenbluth, *Go Forth and Serve: Early Years and Public Life* (New York: Herzl, 1961), 247–50.

38. *JR*, Apr. 7, 1933, in Boas, 111.

39. Speech, Kurt Tuchler, "Experiences and Observations During the First Four Years of the Hitler Regime," no date, YVA, 01/24 (trans. GZ); see series, "Ein Nazi Faehrt Nach Palestina," *Der Angriff*, Sept. 26–Oct. 9, 1934.

40. Jacob Boas, "A Nazi Travels to Palestine," *History Today* (Jan. 1980), 38; Hannah Arendt, *Eichmann in Jerusalem: A Report on the Banality of Evil* (New York: Viking, 1964), 40; Nora Levin, *The Holocaust: The Destruction of European Jewry, 1933–1945* (New York: Thomas Y. Crowell, 1968), 105, 290–91, 295–96.

41. Boas, "Jews of Germany," 11, 21–23; "Report from Germany," in protocol, ZO Exec. Session, June 1, 1933, CZA L-13/138-I (trans. DD).

42. Boas, "Jews of Germany," 25, 37, n. 67.

43. Boas, "Jews Of Germany," 21–26.

44. Marcus, 220, 276, 293; Boas, "Jews of Germany," 89: Nicosia, 118.

45. Policy statement by ZVfD, June 21, 1933, in Klaus J. Herrmann, *Das Dritte Reich und die Deutschjeudischen Organisationen 1933–1934* (Munich: 1969), 16 (trans. GZ); same document, in Boas, "Jews of Germany," 112–13.

46. Policy statement by ZVfD, June 21, 1933, in Herrmann, 16 (trans. GZ).

47.–53. "Wear It With Pride, the Yellow Spot!" *JR*, Apr. 4, 1933 (trans. GZ).

54. See Lowenthal, 371–72, see 414; see Bolkosky, 15, 17, 172–73; Niewyk, 164; Ludwig Pinner, "Vermoegenstransfer nach Palestina 1933–1939," In *Zwei Welten; Siegfried Moses Zum Funfundsiebzigsten Geburtstag* (Tel Aviv: Verlag Bitaon, 1962), 133–38 (trans. EF); see interview with Dr. Dolf Michaelis by the author, Sep. 1, 1980, author's transcript 3.

CHAPTER 18

1. " 'Horribly Mutilated': The Terror That Still Goes on," *JC*, May 19, 1933, 15; "Report Another Example of Nazi Torture Methods," *JDB*, May 11, 1933.

2. "Refugees Reach Warsaw," *JC*, June 9, 1933, 16.

3. "The Terror Receives New Impetus," *JC*, June 30, 1933, 18.

4. "Murdered Jews Ordered Buried in Non-Jewish Cemetaries in Future," *JDB*, May 5, 1933; "Report Another Example of Nazi Torture Methods," *JDB*, May 11, 1933; "More Suicides," *JC*, May 19, 1933, 14.

5. "Refugees Reach Warsaw," *JC*, June 9, 1933, 16; see "Frommer Returns Home from Investigation of Reports of Persecution," *NYT*, Aug. 13, 1933.

6. See *JC*, June 23, 1933, 22; "The Terror Re-

ceives New Impetus," *JC*, June 30, 1933, 18; see letter/diary, James McDonald to the Foreign Policy Association, Apr. 3, 1933, BPM at AJA; letter, "The Chargé in Germany (Gordon) to the Acting Secretary of State," July 8, 1933, *FRUS, 1933* (Washington, D.C.: United States Government Printing Office, 1949) II: 354–56; see "Persecution Stories True, Southern Minister Says," *JDB*, Aug. 15, 1933.

7. "Hitler Compares His Curbs to Ours," *NYT*, June 23, 1933.

8. "To Kill All German Jews if War Occurs, Nazi Warns," and "Danzig Nazis Promise Final Punishment of Jews," *JDB*, June 2, 1933.

9. "Should Sterilize Jews, Nazi Doctor Advises," *JDB*, June 2, 1933.

10. "Not Quite Siegfried," *NYT*, June 20, 1933.

11. "Australia Raises a Fund," "Polish Jewry

Unites," and "Manchester's Gigantic Protest," *JC*, May 5, 1933; "The Wearside Protests," "No Uncertain Voice," "A Civic Demonstration," "Leeds Youth Protest Meeting," "An Appeal by Dr. Barnes," and "Great Demonstration in Queen's Hall," *JC*, May 19, 1933; "German Jews in France," *JC*, June 9, 1933, 18.

12. *JC*, May 5, 1933.

13. "London May Bar German Film; Jews are Reported Boycotting all Reich Liners," *JDB*, May 22, 1933.

14. "The Argentine Boycott" and "The Boycott in France Goes on," *JC*, May 19, 1933, 16, 18.

15. "Anti-Nazi Stamps Shown," *NYT*, May 24, 1933; Werner E. Braatz, "German Commercial Interests in Palestine; Zionism and the Boycott of German Goods, 1933–1934," *European Studies Review* (SAGE, London and Beverly Hills), IX (1979): 494; "Boycott Stamps Issued," *NYT*, May 22, 1933.

16. "Intensifying the Boycott" and "Textile Trade's Meeting," *JC*, May 26, 1933, 30.

17. Report, "Movement in the Netherlands to Boycott German Goods," Roberts to Simon, May 18, 1933, PRO-FO 371/17405–1556.

18. Francis R. J. Nicosia, "Germany and the Palestine Question, 1933–1939" (unpub. Ph.D. diss., history, McGill, 1977), 76–77.

19. "The Anti-German Boycott Works," *JC*, May 19, 1933, 14.

20. Letter, Chamber of Commerce, Velbert, June 6, 1933, NA T-120 roll 4954, L370296 (trans. GZ); "Egypt's Organized Protest," *JC*, June 2, 1933, 12.

21. "Silent Boycott Goes On," *JC*, June 23, 1933, 22.

22. "Foreign Trade Up for Reich in May," *NYT*, June 17, 1933.

23. "Diamond-Cutting Trade in Antwerp Booms Because Jews Won't Send Gems to Reich," *NYT*, June 2, 1933; see "Diamond Merchants' Vigorous Boycott," *JC*, July 28, 1933, 14, 26.

24.–26. Letter, "Directorate of the Reichsbank to the Reich Chancellor," June 6, 1933, *DGFP, 1918–1945* (London: HMSO, 1957), ser. C, I: 528–530.

27. "Memorandum by the Foreign Minister," June 7, 1933, *DGFP*, 531–32.

28.–29. Letter, "John Foster Dulles to Hjalmar Schacht," June 3, 1933, and enclosed aid-memoire, *DGFP*, 538–542.

30. "Berlin Counters Boycott in Latvia," *NYT*, June 11, 1933.

31. "German Embassy to Sue Anti-Nazi Students," *JDB*, May 24, 1933; "Rip Swastika Off German Ship," and "Latvian Jews Proclaim Boycott," *JDB*, June 6, 1933; "Berlin Counters Boycott in Latvia," *NYT*, June 11, 1933; "Reich and Latvia Agree," *NYT*, June 17, 1933; "Latvia Combats Jewish Boycott of German Goods," *JDB*, June 19, 1933; see "World Jewish Economic Conference," *JC*, June 30, 1933, 38.

32. "Intensifying the Boycott," *JC*, May 26, 1933, 21, 30; see "The 'Silent Boycott' Goes On," *JC*, June 23, 1933, 22; see "Nazis Evolve New Sign," *NYT*, June 25, 1933.

33. "Intensifying the Boycott," *JC*, May 26, 1933, 21, 30; "Big Boycott to Start July 1st," *JC*, June 9, 1933, 19; "Captain Webber at the Cenotaph," *JC*, June 16, 1933, 32; "Captain Webber's Boycott Certificate," *JC*, July 14, 1933, 32, see 19; "Anglo–Jewry Closes It's Ranks," *JC*, July 28, 1933, 26; "Anti-Nazi Ban Enforced," *NYT*, July 23, 1933.

CHAPTER 19

1. "Nazis to Tolerate Fund to Aid Jews," *NYT*, May 21, 1933; "Nazis Block Payment of Jewish Relief Funds in Virtual Confiscation," *JDB*, July 13, 1933; "Bulletin," *JDB*, July 18, 1933.

2. "Importers to Use 'Blocked' Mark Balances," *NYT*, May 20, 1933.

3. "Nazi Government Aids Crippled Film Industry," *JDB*, June 7, 1933.

4. "London May Bar German Film," *JDB*, May 22, 1933; see "Tel Aviv Boycotts German Film," *JDB*, June 5, 1933; see "London Theatre Withdraws Expensive German Film; Disorders Mar Premiere," *JDB*, July 20, 1933.

5. See "Rumania Retaliates on Reich by Tariff and Curb on Imports," *NYT*, March 23, 1933.

6. "Memorandum on the German Economic Situation for the Week Ending 16th May, 1933," F. Thelwell, PRO-FO 371/16695-1527, pp. 4–6.

7. See Raul Hilberg, *The Destruction of the European Jews* (New York: Harper Colophon, 1979), 93.

8. "Nazis to Tolerate Fund to Aid Jews," *NYT*, May 21, 1933; see "Nazi Interference Imperils Business," *NYT*, Apr. 26, 1933.

9. Letter, "Sir H. Rumbold (Berlin) to Sir J. Simon," June 14, 1933, *DBFP, 1919–1939* (London:

HMSO, 1956) ser. 2, V: 1933: 351–52; see "American Jewish Congress Endorses Boycott, Move to Adopt German Jewish Children Here," *JDB*, Aug. 22, 1933.

10. Letter, "Sir H. Rumbold (Berlin) to Sir J. Simon," June 30, 1933, *DBFP*, 384–90, see 390.

11. See "Boycott on Reich Extended Here," *NYT*, May 16, 1933; see "Plans Being Made for World Parley to Boycott Reich," *JDB*, June 5, 1933; "World Boycott Issue Up at Jewish Groups Parley," *JDB*, June 12, 1933.

12. "Extract from the Minutes of the Conference of Ministers," June 23, 1933, *DGFP, 1918–1945* (London: HMSO, 1957), ser. C, I: 598–99.

13. "Untermyer Celebrates 75th Birthday, Plans to Attend Boycott Parley," *JDB*, June 7, 1933; "World Boycott Issue Up at Jewish Groups Parley," *JDB*, June 12, 1933.

14. "World Jews Plan to Widen Boycott," *NYT*, July 19, 1933; "World Jews Push Boycott of Reich for 'Inhuman' Acts," *NYT*, July 21, 1933; "Untermyer Assails Wise as Preliminary Boycott Meeting is Opened in Amsterdam," *JDB*, July 21, 1933.

15. "Parley in London Put Off by Jews," *NYT*, July 15, 1933.

16.–18. Letter, Wolff to RFM, June 24, 1933, NA T-120 roll 4954, L368959 *et seq.* (trans. GZ).

19. Letter, Reich Economics Ministry, June 24, 1933, cited in R. J. Nicosia, "Germany and the Palestine Question, 1933–1939," (unpub. Ph.D. Diss., history, McGill, 1977), 96 (trans. GZ).

20. Letter, Wolff to Prufer, June 27, 1933, in Nicosia, 95 (trans. GZ); same letter, in Shaul Esh, *Studies in the Holocaust and Contemporary Jewry* (Jerusalem: ICJ, 1973), 65 (author's trans. 25) and footnote 24 (author's trans. 78).

21. Minutes, meeting of the Conference of Representatives of Institutions, July 2, 1933, CZA S-25/9706 (trans. YC).

22.–26. Letter, Wolff to RFM, July 3, 1933, NA T-120 roll 4954, L368972/77 (trans. GZ).

27. John P. Fox, "Great Britain and the German Jews, 1933," *WLB* XXVI (1972, no. 1–2, n.s. 26–27): 40–45; "Wise Hails British for Scoring Nazis," *NYT*, July 21, 1933; see "Lead on the Boycott," *JC*, July 21, 1933, 28.

28. "London Jews Hold Anti-Nazi Parade," *NYT*, July 21, 1933; see "British Board of Deputies in Secret Session Decides Against Boycott Sponsorship," *JDB*, July 25, 1933; see "Move for Boycott Gaining in London," *NYT*, Mar. 25, 1933.

29. Bernard Wasserstein, *Britain and the Jews of Europe, 1939–1945* (Oxford: Clarendon, 1979), 38; Colin Holmes, *Anti-Semitism in British Society, 1876–1939* (New York: Holmes & Meier, 1979), 200; Walter Laqueur, *A History of Zionism* (New York: Holt, Rinehart and Winston, 1972), 184, 193–94, 400; see "Jews in Hiding," *JC*, July 14, 1933, 11; see "London Jews Hold Anti-Nazi Parade," *NYT*, July 21, 1933; see "Lead on the Boycott," *JC*, July 21, 1933, 28; also see letter, Wise to the American Jewish Congress Administrative Committee, July 28, 1933, attached to minutes,

AJCAdCom, June 29, 1933, *AJHS*, 3; see "Our Leaders; A Mockery of Democracy," *JC*, July 28, 1933, 16.

30. Letter to the Editor, *Manchester Guardian*, July 1, 1933; "English Jewry Against Boycott," *Frankfurter Zeitung*, July 5, 1933; see minutes, Joint Foreign Committee, June 30, 1933, BDBJ-A; see "Frankfurter Zeitung on the Boycott in England," JEF, July 7, 1933.

31. See JEF, June 30, 1933; "World Boycott Issue Up at Jewish Groups Parley," *JDB*, June 12, 1933; "The Conference," *JEF*, July 7, 1933.

32. Minutes, Joint Foreign Committee, July 12, 1933, BDBJ-A; Wasserstein, 38; "Jewry in Great Britain Moves for United Action," *JDB*, July 17, 1933.

33. Minutes, Joint Foreign Committee, July 12, 1933, BDBJ-A; "Sudden Crisis At the Deputies," *JC*, July 14, 1933, 7; "Jewish Unity," JEF, July 14, 1933; "Jewry in Great Britain Moves for United Action," *JDB*, July 17, 1933.

34. Minutes, Joint Foreign Committee, July 12, 1933, BDBJ-A; "Sudden Crisis at the Deputies," *JC*, July 14, 1933, 7; see "Jewry in Great Britain Moves for United Action," *JDB*, July 17, 1933.

35. "World Jewry to Deliberate," *JC*, July 21, 1933, 7; "British Board of Deputies Accepts Proposal to Enlarge Joint Foreign Committee," *JDB*, July 21, 1933.

36. "Sudden Crisis at the Deputies," *JC*, July 14, 1933, 7; "World Jewry to Deliberate" and "Federation of Synogogues," *JC*, July 21, 1933, 7, 26; see "Jewry in Great Britain Moves for United Action," *JDB*, July 17, 1933; see "London Confirms Report," *JDB*, July 13, 1933.

37. "London Confirms Report," *JDB*, July 13, 1933.

CHAPTER 20

1. See Paul Seabury, *The Wilhelmstrasse: A Study of German Diplomats under the Nazi Regime* (Berkeley: Univ. of California, 1954).

2. Letter, Landauer to Hoofien, July 19, 1933, CZA S-25/9706 (trans. GB); see Sam Cohen, "Note About the Transfer Agreement," Oct. 9, 1933, CZA Z4/3434 (trans. EF).

3. Letter, Landauer to Hoofien, July 19, 1933, CZA S25/9706 (trans. GB).

4. Note, Dr. Reichhardt for the Minister of Economics, to Sam Cohen, July 18, 1933, CZA Z4/3434 (trans. DD); see letter, Wolff to RFM, June 24, 1933, NA T-120 roll 4954, L368959 *et seq.* (trans. GZ); see letters, Landauer to Hoofien, July 19 and July 21, 1933, CZA S-25/9706 (trans. GB).

5. Note, Dr. Reichhardt for the Minister of Economics, to Sam Cohen, July 18, 1933, CZA Z4/3434 (trans. DD).

6. Letter, Landauer to Hoofien, July 19, 1933, CZA S-25/9706; see minutes, Political Committee of the 18th ZC, 5th meeting, Aug. 29, 1933, CZA Z4/232/4 (trans. GB).

7. Letter, Landauer to Hoofien, July 19, 1933, CZA S-25/9706 (trans. GB); note, Dr. Reichhardt

for the Minister of Economics to Sam Cohen, July 18, 1933, CZA Z4/3434 (trans. DD).

8. Letter, Landauer to Hoofien, July 19, 1933, CZA S25/9706 (trans. GB); Memorandum, Landauer to the REM, "Transfer of the Capital of Jewish Immigrants from Germany to Palestine Through Export of Goods," July 19, 1933, NA T-120 roll 4954, L369080 (trans. GZ); see letter and enclosed memorandum, Landauer to the REM, June 20, 1933, CZA K-11/180-2 (trans. DD).

9. Letter, Landauer to Hoofien, July 19, 1933, CZA S-25/9706 (trans. GB); memorandum, Landauer to the REM, "Transfer of the Capital of Jewish Emigrants," July 19, 1933, NA T-120 roll 4954, L369080.

10. Letter, Landauer to Hartenstein, July 14, 1933, NA T-120 roll 4954, L369009 (trans. GZ); letter, Landauer to Hoofien, July 19, 1933, CZA S25/9706 (trans. GB); memorandum, Landauer to the REM, "Transfer of the Capital of Jewish Emigrants," July 19, 1933, NA T-120 roll 4954, L369080 (trans. GZ).

11. Letter, Landauer to Hoofien, July 19, 1933, CZA S25/9706 (trans. GB); memorandum, Land-

auer to the REM, "Transfer of the Capital of Jewish Emigrants," July 19, 1933, NA T-120 roll 4954, L369080.

12. See letters, Landauer to Jacobsohn, June 9, 1933, and Landauer to Pinner, July 3, 1933, CZA S7/92 (trans. GZ); see letter, Wolff to RFM, July 27, 1933, NA T-120 roll 4954, L369010/20 (trans. GZ); letter, Margulies to Hoofien, July 27, 1933, CZA S-25/9706 (trans. DD); letter, Hermann Ellern to Schmidt-Roelke, July 27, 1933, NA T-120 roll 4954, L369051/2 (trans. GZ).

13. Letter, Landauer to Hartenstein, July 14, 1933, NA T-120 roll 4954, L369009 (trans. GZ); letter, Landauer to Hoofien, July 19, 1933, CZA S-25/9706 (trans. GB); see memorandum, Landauer to the REM, "Transfer of the Capital of Jewish Emigrants," July 19, 1933, NA T-120 roll 4954, L369080 (trans. GZ).

14. Karl A. Schleunes, *The Twisted Road to Auschwitz: Nazi Policy Toward German Jews, 1933–1939* (Urbana: Univ. of Illinois, 1970), 188; see Werner Rosenstock, "Exodus 1933–1939: A Survey of Jewish Emigration from Germany," *Middle Eastern Studies* (Oct., 1969), 379, see 380 n. 6; Jacob Boas, "The Jews of Germany: Self-Perceptions in the Nazi Era as Reflected in the German Jewish Press, 1933–1938" (unpub. Ph.D. diss. history, Univ. of California, Riverside, 1977), 84–85; see "Merchants Lured Back to Germany," London *JC*, July 14, 1933, 30; see letter, "Ambassador in Germany (Dodd) to the Acting Secretary of State," July 28, 1933, *FRUS, 1933* (Washington, D.C.: United States Government Printing Office, 1949), II: 248–49; see "Jewish Telegraphic Agency Closed," *JC*, July 28, 1933, 14.

CHAPTER 21

1. "About Ourselves," *JEF*, June 2, 1933.

2. Minutes, Joint Foreign Committee, July 14, 1933, BDBJ-A; see "Sudden Crisis at the Deputies," *JC*, July 14, 1933.

3. Minutes, Joint Foreign Committee, July 12 and July 14, 1933, BDBJ-A.

4. "Jewish Unity," *JEF*, July 14, 1933; see *JEF*, July 21, 1933.

5. "Jewry in Great Britain Moves for United Action," *JDB*, July 17, 1933.

6. See "Textile Trades Meeting," *JC*, May 26, 1933, 30; letter, Henry (Melchett) to Chaim Weizmann, May 29, 1933, WA; see *JEF*, June 2, 1933.

7. See "Lord Melchett Becomes a Jew," *Manchester Guardian*, July 17, 1933; "World Jews Plan to Widen Boycott," *NYT*, July 19, 1933; see "The Road Back," *JC*, July 28, 1933, 9; see "Imperial and Foreign News," *JC*, Aug. 11, 1933, 22.

8. See letter to the editor, *Manchester Guardian*, dated June 30, 1933, in minutes, Joint Foreign Committee, June 30, 1933, BDBJ-A; see minutes, Joint Foreign Committee, June 30, 1933, BDBJ-A.

9. Martin Rosenbluth, *Go Forth and Serve: Early Years and Public Life* (New York: Herzl, 1961), 267–68.

10. See "Federation of Polish Jews," *JC*, July 21, 1933, 12.

11. See minutes, Joint Foreign Committee, July 26, 1933, BDBJ-A; see minutes, Political Committee of the 18th ZC, 6th meeting, Aug. 30, 1933, CZA Z4/232/4, pp. 32–34 (trans. GB).

12. "World Jewish Economic Conference," *JC*, July 21, 1933, 30.

13. "Bulletin," *JDB*, July 6, 1933; Minutes, AJCAdCom, Sep. 23, 1933, AJHS, 5; press release, AJC, Sep. 25, 1933, BPM at AJA, 5–6.

14. Letter, Wise to the AJCAdCom, July 28, 1933, AJHS, 3; "Dr. Wise's Report on His Activities in Europe, Verbatim Record," in minutes, AJCAdCom, Sep. 23, 1933, AJHS, 4–6.

15. "World Boycott Issue Lit Up at Jewish Groups Parley," *JDB*, June 12, 1933.

16. Letter, Wise to the AJCAdCom, July 28, 1933, AJHS, 1–2; "Dr. Wise's Report," in minutes, AJCAdCom, Sep. 23, 1933, AJHS, 4–5; press release, AJC, Sep. 25, 1933, BPM at AJA, 5–6.

17. Letter, Wise to the AJCAdCom, July 28, 1933, AJHS, 3; "Dr. Wise's Report," in minutes, AJCAdCom, Sep. 23, 1933, 5–6, 13.

18. "Polish Boycott Group Prepares for World Parley," *JDB*, July 14, 1933.

19. "Anglo-Jewish, German Embassy Pact, Press Asserts; Hits Failure to Uphold It," *JDB*, July 13, 1933; see " 'Frankfurter Zeitung' on the Boycott in England," *JEF*, July 7, 1933; see "English Jewry Against Boycott," *Frankfurter Zeitung*, July 5, 1933, p. 3.

20. "London Confirms Report," *JDB*, July 13, 1933.

21.–22. "Economic Conference Postponement: Continental Rumours of 'Pressure,' " *JC*, July 21, 1933, 30.

23. "World Jewry to Deliberate," and "Federation of Synogogues," *JC*, July 21, 1933, 7, 26; see minutes, Joint Foreign Committee, July 12 and July 14, 1933, BDBJ-A; also see "Dr. Wise's Report," in minutes, AJCAdCom, Sep. 23, 1933, AJHS, 5.

24. "World Jewish Economic Conference: Mr. Untermyer's Preliminary Plans," *JC*, July 21, 1933, 30; "World Jews Plan to Widen Boycott," *NYT*, July 19, 1933.

25.–26. "World Jews Plan to Widen Boycott," *NYT*, July 19, 1933.

27. *Ibid.*; see Walter Laqueur, *A History of Zionism* (New York: Holt, Rinehart and Winston, 1972), 355, 359.

28. "World Jews Plan to Widen Boycott," *NYT*, July 19, 1933; "World Jewish Economic Conference: Mr. Untermyer's Preliminary Plan," *JC*, July 21, 1933, 30.

29. See "Untermyer Assails Wise as Preliminary Boycott Meeting is Opened in Amsterdam," *JDB*, July 21, 1933; see "World Jews Push for Boycott of Reich for 'Inhuman' Acts," *NYT*, July 21, 1933; see "Boycott Exceeds Untermyer's Hope," *NYT*, Aug. 1, 1933; see "Reception Planned Sunday for Untermyer Returning From Boycott Conference," *JDB*,

Aug. 3, 1933; see "Untermyer Back, Greeted in Harbor," and "Text of Untermyer's Address," *NYT*, Aug. 7, 1933; minutes, AJCAdCom, Aug. 3, 1933; AJHS, 3–8; see "The Boycott in America: Public Demands a Lead," *JC*, July 28, 1933, 14; see "American Jewish Congress to Consider Boycott Action," *JDB*, Aug. 16, 1933.

30.–34. Letter, Wise to the AJCAdCom, July 28, 1933, AJHS, 1–4.

35. "World Jewish Economic Conference Meets: The Boycott 'Reaffirmed,' " *JC*, July 28, 1933, 27; "World Jews Push Boycott of Reich for 'Inhuman' Acts," *NYT*, July 21, 1933.

36. "World Jewish Economic Conference Meets," *JC*, July 28, 1933, 27; "World Jews to Push Boycott," *NYT*, July 21, 1933.

37. See "World Jews Plan to Widen Boycott," *NYT*, July 19, 1933; see "World Jews Push Boycott of Reich," *NYT*, July 21, 1933.

38.–40. "World Jews Push Boycott of Reich," *NYT*, July 21, 1933.

41. "World Jews Plan to Widen Boycott," *NYT*, July 19, 1933.

42. "World Jews Push Boycott of Reich," *NYT*, July 21, 1933.

43. *Ibid.*; "World Jewish Economic Conference Meets: The Boycott 'Reaffirmed,' " *JC*, July 28, 1933, 27.

44. "Ecomomic Conference Postponement: Continental Rumours of 'Pressure,' " *JC*, July 21, 1933, 30; see "Likewise—Contrariwise!," *JC*, July 28, 1933, 27; "World Jews Push Boycott of Reich," *NYT*, July 21, 1933.

45. "Likewise—Contrariwise!," *JC*, July 28, 1933, 27; "World Jews Push Boycott," *NYT*, July 21, 1933.

46. "Likewise—Contrariwise!," *JC*, July 28, 1933, 27; "World Jews Push Boycott," *NYT*, July 21, 1933.

47. Minutes, AJCAdCom, Aug. 3 and 17, 1933, AJHS; see "Dr. Wise's Report," in minutes, AJCAdCom, Sep. 23, 1933, AJHS; see "Enthusiastic Crowds Greet Untermyer Who Urges Boycott Spread in Broadcast," *JDB*, Aug. 8, 1933; see "Text of Untermyer's Address," *NYT*, Aug. 7, 1933; see "Rabbi Wise Breaks Silence on Boycott: Calls It Duty of All Self-Respecting Jews," *JDB*, Aug. 15, 1933; see "Rabbi Wise Backs Boycott on Nazis," *NYT*, Aug. 15, 1933.

CHAPTER 22

1. "London Jews Hold Anti-Nazi Parade," *NYT*, July 21, 1933; see "30,000 March in London," *JDB*, July 21, 1933; see "The March Through London" and "Our Leaders; 'A Mockery of Democracy,' " *JC*, July 28, 1933, 6, 16.

2. "London Jews Hold Anti-Nazi Parade," *NYT*, July 21, 1933; "Monster Jewish Protest Demonstration," *JC*, July 21, 1933, 10; "The Great Protest Demonstration," *JC*, July 28, 1933, 20; "30,000 March in London," *JDB*, July 21, 1933.

3. "London Jews Hold Anti-Nazi Parade," *NYT*, July 21, 1933; see "30,000 March in London," *JDB*, July 21, 1933; see "The March Through London" and "Our Leaders; 'A Mockery of Democracy,' " *JC*, July 28, 1933, 6, 16.

4. "British Labor Orders Boycott of Germany; Seeks to Make Her People Repudiate Hitler," *NYT*, July 20, 1933.

5. See Werner Senator, "Strictly Confidential Memorandum on the Transfer of Jewish Capital From Germany," July 24, 1933, CZA S-25/9706; also see "The Deputies: Boycott Discussed *In Camera*," *JC*, July 28, 1933, 15.

6. Minutes, Joint Foreign Committee, July 19, 1933, and statement, Joint Foreign Committee, July 20, 1933, BDBJ-A.

7.–9. Minutes, Joint Foreign Committee, July 19, BDBF-A.

10. Minutes, Joint Foreign Committee, July 12, 1933, and "Draft Heads of Proposals," July 13, 1933, BDBJ-A; minutes, Joint Foreign Committee, July 14, 1933, and "Confidential Statement of the Joint Foreign Committee," July 14, 1933, BDBJ-A; letter, Wise to the AJCAdCom, July 28, 1933, AJHS, 3.

11. Statement, Joint Foreign Committee, July 20, 1933, BDBJ-A.

12. Minutes, Joint Foreign Committee, July 26, 1933, BDBJ-A; JEF, July 21, 1933.

13. "The Deputies; Boycott Discussed *In Camera*," and "Our Leaders; 'A Mockery of Democracy,' " *JC*, July 28, 1933, 15, 16; see "Wasting Time at Deputies' Meeting," *JC*, Nov. 11, 1933, 16.

14. "The Deputies; Boycott Discussed," *JC*, July 28, 1933, 15; minutes, Board of Deputies of British Jews Board Meeting, July 23, 1933, BDBJ-A.

15. "The Deputies; Boycott Discussed," *JC*, July 28, 1933, 15; minutes, Board of Deputies of British Jews Board Meeting, July 23, 1933, BDBJ-A.

16.–18. "The Deputies; Boycott Discussed," *JC*, July 28, 1933, 15.

19. *Ibid.*, 15–16; see minutes, of Board of Deputies of British Jews Board Meeting, July 23, 1933, BDBJ-A, 2–3.

20. Letter, Neville Laski to Sir Robert Vansittart, July 25, 1933, PRO-FO 371/16727–1527; see minutes, Joint Foreign Committee, July 19, 1933, BDBJ-A, 2; "The Deputies; Boycott Discussed," *JC*, July 28, 1933, 16.

21. Letter, Laski to Vansittart, July 25, 1933, PRO-FO 371/16727-1527; "The Deputies; Boycott Discussed," *JC*, July 28, 1933, 16; "The Deputies and the Official Boycott; 'Farcical Proceedings,' " *JC*, Aug. 4, 1933.

22. Minutes, Board of Deputies of British Jews Board Meeting, July 23, 1933, BDBJ-A; "The Deputies; Boycott Discussed," *JC*, July 28, 1933, 16.

23. Letter, Dr. Nahum Goldmann to Sam Cohen, July 25, 1933, Esther Aharony Private File (trans. GZ).

CHAPTER 23

1. "Oust Jewish Traders From Market Places," *JDB*, June 2, 1933; "Jewish Trade at a Standstill," *JC*, June 30, 1933, 19; "All Jews to Be Dismissed," *JC*, June 16, 1933, 14; see "The 'Silent Boycott' Goes On," *JC*, June 23, 1933, 22; "Dismiss Jews from Chemical Trust," "Other Jewish Dismissals," and "Jews Can't Advertise in Berlin Phone Book," *JDB*, June 22, 1933; see letter, "The Chargé in Germany (Gordon) to the Acting Secretary of State," July 8, 1933, *FRUS 1933* (Washington, D.C.: United States Government Printing Office, 1949), II: 354–56.

2. "Frankfurt Disturbances," *JDB*, June 28, 1933; "Nazis Arrest Scores for 'Economic Sabotage," *JDB*, June 27, 1933.

3. "Map of Berlin Torture Centers," *Sunday Referee*, reproduced in *JC*, June 16, 1933, 18.

4. Letter, "Mr. Newton (Berlin) to Sir J. Simon," July 11, 1933, *DBFP, 1919–1939*, ser. 2, V: 1933, 409–14; letter, "The Chargé in Germany (Gordon) to the Acting Secretary of State," July 8, 1933, *FRUS*, 276–277; "Nazis Arrest Scores," and "Jews Moving Business are Traitors, Say Nazis," *JDB*, June 27, 1933.

5. Letter, "The Chargé in Germany (Gordon) to the Acting Secretary of State," June 24, 1933, *FRUS*, 236–39; letter, "The Chargé in Germany (Gordon) to the Acting Secretary of State," June 30, 1933, *FRUS*, 239–44; letter, "The Chargé in Germany (Gordon) to the Acting Secretary of State," July 10, 1933, *FRUS*, 244–45.

6. "War on Jews to Go On, Goebbels Assures Nazis: 'Worse Still in Store,' " *JDB*, June 26, 1933.

7. Letter, "The Chargé in Germany (Gordon) to the Acting Secretary of State," July 10, 1933, *FRUS*, 245–46.

8. "Checking the Nazi Revolution," London *Times*, July 15, 1933.

9. See letter, "Sir H. Rumbold (Berlin) to Sir J. Simon," June 30, 1933, *DBFP*, 384–87; Arthur Schweitzer, *Big Business in the Third Reich* (Bloomington: Indiana Univ., 1964), 120–25; "Hitler Threatens the Nazi Radicals," *NYT*, July 12, 1933; "Check to Nazi Extremism," and "Nazis and Department Stores," London *Times*, July 12, 1933; "Mr. Newton (Berlin) to Sir J. Simon," July 11, 1933, *DGFP*, 409–14; letter, "The Chargé in Germany (Gordon) to the Acting Secretary of State," July 10, 1933, *FRUS*, 245–47.

10. Letter, "Sir H. Rumbold (Berlin) to Sir J. Simon," June 30, 1933, *DBFP*, 386–89.

11. Letter, "Mr. Newton (Berlin) to Sir J. Simon," July 11, 1933, *DBFP*, 409–14; letter, "Chargé in Germany (Gordon) to the Acting Secretary of State," July 10, 1933, *FRUS*, 246.

12. Letter, "Chargé in Germany (Gordon) to the Acting Secretary of State," July 10, 1933, *FRUS*, 246; letter, "Mr. Newton (Berlin) to Sir J. Simon," July 11, 1933, *DBFP*, 411.

13.–14. Letter, "Mr. Newton (Berlin) to Sir J. Simon," July 11, 1933, *DBFP*, 413.

15. Letter, "The Chargé in Germany (Gordon) to the Acting Secretary of State, July 8, 1933, *FRUS*

, 354–56; "Jewish Merchants Liquidate Businesses in Face of Nazi Drive," *JDB*, July 12, 1933; "Anti-Jewish Boycott Intensified," *JC*, July 14, 1933, 14–15; "New Assault on Jewish Workers," *JC*, July 21, 1933, 14.

16. Helmet Genschel, *Die Verdragung der Juden aus der Wirtschaft im Dritten Reich* (Berlin: Musterschmidt-Verlag), 115 (trans. GZ); Heinrich Uhlig, *Die Warenhauser im Dritten Reich* (Koln-Opladen, 1956), 115 (trans. GZ); " 'Coordinated' Tietz Firm Gets Nazi Gov't Subsidy," *JDB*, Aug. 1, 1933.

17. Letter, "The Chargé in Germany (Gordon) to the Acting Secretary of State," July 10, 1933, *FRUS*, 246–47; Adolf Hitler, speech, delivered in the Reich Chancery to the Reich Commissioners, July 6, 1933, in Norman H. Baynes, trans. and ed., *The Speeches of Adolf Hitler* (London: Oxford, 1942), I: 865.

18. Letter, "The Chargé in Germany (Gordon) to the Acting Secretary of State," July 10, 1933, *FRUS*, 245–47.

19. Order, Dr. Frick to the Statthalter, State Governments, the Premier of Prussia and the Prussian Minister of the Interior, in "Check to Nazi Extremism," London *Times*, July 12, 1933; see letter, "The Ambassador in Germany (Dodd) to the Acting Secretary of State," July 17, 1933, *FRUS*, 277–78.

20. Communique, Rudolf Hess, in "Nazis and Department Stores," London *Times*, July 12, 1933.

21. Schweitzer, 120–24; see James Pool and Suzanne Pool, *Who Financed Hitler: The Secret Funding of Hitler's Rise to Power, 1919–1933* (New York: Dial, 1979), 354–55; see William L. Shirer, *The Rise and Fall of the Third Reich: A History of Nazi Germany* (New York: Fawcett Crest, 1960), 265–66.

22. Schweitzer, 124–25; "Hitler Invokes Aid of Business Heads," *NYT*, July 16, 1933; "The Ambassador in Germany (Dodd) to the Acting Secretary of State," July 17, 1933, *FRUS*, 279.

23.–24. Schweitzer, 117–19, 124–27, 136–37.

25. *Ibid.*, 249; Adolf Hitler, speech, July 13, 1933, in Baynes, 484–85, see 867–68.

26. See Schweitzer, 134–38.

27. Letter, "The Ambassador in Germany (Dodd) to the Acting Secretary of State," July 28, 1933, *FRUS*, 248–49; see Erika Martens, *The Phenomenology of the Press in a Totalitarian Regime* (Cologne, 1972), 19 (trans. GZ).

28. Letter, "The Ambassador in Germany (Dodd) to the Acting Secretary of State," July 28, 1933, *FRUS*, 1933, 248.

29. *Ibid.*; letter, "The Ambassador in Germany (Dodd) to the Acting Secretary of State," July 17, 1933, *FRUS*, 279–80.

30.–31. "Hitler Invokes Aid of Business Heads," *NYT*, July 16, 1933.

32. Letter, "The Ambassador in Germany (Dodd) to the Acting Secretary of State," July 17, 1933, *FRUS*, 277–80.

33. Letter, "The Ambassador in Germany (Dodd) to the Acting Secretary of State," July 28, 1933, *FRUS*, 248–49; see letter, "The Ambassador

in Germany (Dodd) to the Secretary of State," August 12, 1933, *FRUS*, 252–53.

34. Letter, "The Ambassador in Germany (Dodd) to the Acting Secretary of State," July 28, 1933, *FRUS*, 248–50.

35. "No Cessation of Physical Violence," and "Cold Pogrom a Frost?," *JC*, July 28, 1933, 13; "Nazis Round Up 300 Jews in Nuremberg: Businessmen are Paraded Through City," *NYT*, July 21, 1933; "160 Nuremberg Jews Freed by Nazis After Mass Arrest," *JDB*, July 25, 1933.

36. See letter, "Mr. Newton (Berlin) to Sir J. Simon," July 11, 1933, *DBFP*, 413.

37. Letter, "Ambassador in Germany (Dodd) to the Acting Secretary of State," July 28, 1933, *FRUS*, 250.

CHAPTER 24

1. Jessie Sampter, "Jewish Colonization Before 1917," in Jessie Sampter, ed., *Modern Palestine: A Symposium* (New York: Hadassah, 1933), 96; Eliezer S. Hoofien, "Currency, Banking and Insurance in Palestine," in Sampter, *Modern Palestine*, 252; Bernard A. Rosenblatt, "The Jewish National Fund and the Jewish Colonial Trust," in Jessie Sampter, ed., *A Guide to Zionism* (New York: ZOA, 1920), 68–70.

2. See "Growing With the State," *Jerusalem Post International Edition*, Bank Leumi supplement, Mar. 30–Apr. 5, 1980.

3. Letters, G. Landauer to Hartenstein and Schmidt-Roelke, July 14, 1933, NA T-120 roll 4954, L369009 (trans. GZ).

4. Letter, Landauer to Hartenstein, July 14, 1933, NA T-120 roll 4954, L369009 (trans. GZ).

5. *Ibid.*; Shaul Esh, *Studies in the Holocaust and Contemporary Jewry* (Jerusalem: ICJ, 1973), 69, n. 40 (author's trans. 81).

6. See letter, Wolff to RFM, July 3, 1933, NA T-120 roll 4954, L368972 (trans. GZ); letter, Landauer to Pinner, July 3, 1933, CZA S7/92; Esh, 67 (author's trans. 26); Sam Cohen, "Note Concerning the Transfer Agreement," Oct. 9, 1933, CZA Z4/3434 (trans. DD).

7. "Protocol on the Situation of the Jews in Germany," Beilinson and Julius Berger, July 14, 1933, Histadrut protocols, ALM; protocol, meeting of the Histadrut, July 31, 1933, ALM (trans. GG).

8. Memo, Landauer to the REM "Transfer of the Capital of Jewish Emigrants From Germany to Palestine Through Export of Goods," July 19, 1933, NA T-120 roll 4954, L369080 (trans. GZ); letter, Landauer to Schmidt-Roelke, July 20, 1933, NA T-120 roll 4954, L369080 (trans. GZ).

9.–10. Letter, Landauer to Hoofien, July 19, 1933, CZA S25/9706 (trans. GB).

11. See Werner Senator, "Strictly Confidential Memorandum on the Transfer of Jewish Capital from Germany," July 24, 1933, CZA S-25/9706.

12. Mr. Williams (Colonial Office) to Mr. Rendel, "Proposed facilities for Dr. W. Senator," July 25, 1933, PRO-FO 371/16927–1556.

13. Letter, Landauer to Hoofien, July 21, 1933, CZA S-25/9706 (trans. GB); letter, Ellern to RFM, July 21, 1933, NAT-120 roll 4954, 1369041 *et seq.* (trans. GZ).

14. Letter, Landauer to Hoofien, July 21, 1933, CZA S-25/9706 (trans. GB); note, Minister of Economics to Hanotaiah, July 18, 1933, CZA Z-4/3434 (trans. DD/EF); see "Minister of Economics to Hanotaiah, Ltd., Tel Aviv," July 18, 1933, *DGFP, 1918–1945* (London: HMSO, 1957): ser. C, I: 661–62.

15. Note, Minister of Economics to Hanotaiah, July 18, 1933, CZA Z4/3434 (trans. DD/EF).

16. *Ibid.*; letter, Landauer to Hoofien, July 21, 1933, CZA S-25/9706.

17.–19. Note, Minister of Economics to Hanotaiah, July 18, 1933, CZA Z4/3434 (trans. DD/EF).

20.–23. Letter, Landauer to Hoofien, July 21, 1933, CZA S25/9706 (trans. GB).

24. Letter, Ellern to RFM, July 21, 1933, NA T-120 roll 4954, L369041 *et seq.* (trans. GZ).

25.–26. Letter, Landauer to Hoofien, July 21, 1933, CZA S-25/9706 (trans. GB).

27.–31. Letter, Ellern to RFM, July 21, 1933, NA T-120 roll 4954, L369042 *et seq.* (trans. GZ).

32.–33. Letter, Hartenstein to Schmidt-Roelke, July 22, 1933, NA T-120 roll 4954, L368997 (trans. GZ).

34. Telegram to Wolff, signed "Ulrich," July 24, 1933, NA T-120 roll 4954, L369000/01 (trans. GZ).

CHAPTER 25

1. Letter, Heinrich Margulies to E. S. Hoofien (signed Landauer), July 27, 1933, CZA S-25/9706 (trans. DD).

2. Letter, Wolff to RFM, July 27, 1933, NA T-120 roll 4954, L369010 *et seq.* (trans. GZ).

3.–9. Letter, Margulies to Hoofien, July 27, 1933, CZA S-25/9706, (trans. DD).

10. Letter, Ellern to Schmidt-Roelke, July 27, 1933, NA T-120 roll 4954, L369041/2 (trans. GZ).

11.–15. Letter, Margulies to Hoofien, July 27, 1933, CZA S-25/9706.

16. *Ibid.*, pt. 24, see pt. 1; see telegram, Margulies to Hoofien, July 27, 1933, CZA S-25/9706 (trans. YC).

17.–21. Letter, Wolff to RFM, July 27, 1933, NA T-120 roll 4954, L369010/20 (trans. GZ).

22. Telegram, Margulies to Hoofien, July 27, 1933, and letter, Margulies to Hoofien, July 28, 1933, pts. 3, 4, 5, CZA S-25/9706 (trans. GZ/YC).

23. Letter, Margulies to Hoofien, July 28, 1933, CZA S-25/9706, pts. 7, 8.

24. Telegram, Margulies to Hoofien, July 27, 1933, CZA S-25/9706 (trans. YC).

25. Telegram, Hoofien to Margulies, no date, CZA S-25/9706 (trans. YC).

26. Letter, Chamber of Commerce to the Jewish Agency, July 17, 1933, CZA S-25/9706 (trans. YC).

27. Letter, Margulies to Hoofien, July 28, 1933, CZA S-25/9706, pts. 1, 2 (trans. GZ); see letter, Margulies to the Consul-General in Jerusalem (Wolff), July 28, 1933, CZA S-25/9706 (trans. GB).

28. Cover letter, Margulies to the German Consul General, July 28, 1933, CZA S-25/9706 (trans. GB).

29.–32. Letter, Margulies to the Consul General in Jerusalem, July 28, 1933, CZA S-25/9706 (trans. GB).

33.–36. Letter, E. S. Hoofien to Landauer, July 28, 1933, NA T-120 roll 4954, L369085/88 (trans. GZ).

37. Cover letter, Landauer to Schmidt-Roelke, July 31, 1933, and letter, Hoofien to Landauer, July 28, 1933, NA T-120 roll 4954, L369084/88 (trans. GZ).

38.–45. Letter, Hoofien to Landauer, July 28, 1933, NA T-120 roll 4954, L369085/88 (trans. GZ).

46. Cover letter, Landauer to Schmidt-Roelke, July 31, 1933, NA T-120 roll 4954, L369084.

47.–56. Letter, Sam Cohen to Dr. Eberl, Aug. 1, 1933, NA T-120 roll 4954, L369093/5 (trans. GZ).

CHAPTER 26

1. "The Ministry of Economics to the Foreign Ministry," Aug. 10, 1933, and enclosure, "The Minister of Economics to Herr S. Hoofien," *DGFP, 1918–1945* ser. C, I (London: HMSO, 1957): 732–36; see handwritten notes, E. S. Hoofien, no date, CZA A-95/19; Alex Bein, ed., *Arthur Ruppin: Memoirs, Diaries, Letters* (London: Weidenfeld and Nicolson, 1971), 264; see minutes, Political Committee of the 18th ZC, 5th meeting, Aug. 29, 1933, CZA Z4/232/4, 30 (trans. GB).

2. See letter, Sam Cohen to Dr. Eberl, Aug. 1, 1933, NA T-120 roll 4954, L369093/5 (trans. GZ); see "Ministry of Economics to the Foreign Ministry," Aug. 10, 1933, *DGFP*, 733; also see photograph, Sam Cohen, author's file.

3. "Ministry of Economics to the Foreign Ministry" and enclosure, "The Minister of Economics to Herr S. Hoofien," Aug. 10, 1933, *DGFP*, 732–36.

4. *Ibid.*, 734; see letter, Landauer to Hoofien, July 20, 1933, CZA S-25/9706 (trans. GB).

5. See Werner Senator, "Strictly Confidential Memorandum on the Transfer of Jewish Capital from Germany," July 24, 1933, CZA S-25/9706.

6. See letter, Sam Cohen to Dr. Eberl, Aug. 1, 1933, NA T-120 roll 4954, L369093/5; also see letter, Margulies to Hoofien, July 27, 1933, CZA S-25/9706.

7. See letter, Hoofien to Landauer, July 28, 1933, NA T-120 roll 4954, L369085/88 (trans. GZ).

8. "The Ministry of Economics to the Foreign Ministry," Aug. 10, 1933, *DGFP*, 734; letter, Landauer to Hoofien, July 21, 1933, CZA S-25/9706; letter, Hartenstein to Schmidt-Roelke, July 22, 1933, NA T-120 roll 4954, L368997.

9. Telegram, Wolff to the RFM, Aug. 7, 1933, NA T-120 roll 4954, L369064/5.

10. *Ibid.*; see "The Ministry of Economics to the Foreign Ministry," Aug. 10, 1933, *DGFP*, 734.

11. "The Ministry of Economics to the Foreign Ministry," Aug. 10, 1933, *DGFP*, 734.

12. See Ernst Marcus, "The German Foreign Office and the Palestine Question in the Period 1933–1939," in Shaul Esh, ed., *Yad Vashem Studies in the European Jewish Catastrophe and Resistance*, II (Jerusalem: Yad Vashem, 1958): 181; see Francis R. J. Nicosia, "Germany and the Palestine Question,

1933–1939" (unpub. Ph.D. diss. history, McGill, 1977), 110.

13.–14. Telegram, Wolff to the RFM, Aug. 7, 1933, NA T-120 roll 4954, L369064/5.

15. *Ibid.*; see "The Ministry of Economics to the Foreign Ministry," Aug. 10, 1933, *DGFP*, 733; also see Shaul Esh, *Studies in the Holocaust and Contemporary Jewry* (Jerusalem: ICJ, 1973), 77 (author's trans. 34).

16. Esh, *Studies in the Holocaust*, 77; see telegram, Wolff to the RFM, Aug. 7, 1933, NA T-120 roll 4954, L369064/5; see "The Ministry of Economics to the Foreign Ministry," Aug. 10, 1933, *DGFP*, 735; also see letter, Hartenstein to Schmidt-Roelke, July 22, 1933, NA T-120 roll 4954, L368997.

17. "The Ministry of Economics to the Foreign Ministry," and enclosure, "The Minister of Economics to Herr S. Hoofien," Aug. 10, 1933, *DGFP*, 732–36.

18. *Ibid.*, 735–36; see circular no. 54/33, Ministry of Economics, Aug. 28, 1933, in "Financial Arrangements Between German Government and Certain Organizations in Palestine for the Promotion of the Emigration of German Jews to Palestine," Sep. 14, 1933, PRO-FO 371/16757-1527; see Dolf Michaelis, "The Economic and Political Development of the Emigration and Transfer Question in National-Socialist Germany," in Werner Feilchenfeld, Dolf Michaelis and Ludwig Pinner, *Haavara-Transfer Nach Palestina Und Einwanderung Deutscher Juden, 1933–1939* (Tubingen: Mohr Verlag, 1972), 27 (author's trans. 14); also see Dr. Werner Feilchenfeld, *Five Years of Jewish Immigration from Germany and the Haavara-Transfer, 1933–1938* (Tel Aviv: "Haavara" Ltd., n.d.), 5, 16–18.

19.–20. "The Ministry of Economics to Herr S. Hoofien," Aug. 10, 1933, *DGFP*, 735.

21. *Ibid.*, 736, see n. 8; see letter, Economics Ministry (Scheuerl) to the Foreign Office, Aug. 25, 1933, NA T-120 roll 4954, L369117 (trans. GZ); see circular no. 54/33, Economics Ministry, Aug. 28, 1933, in "Financial Arrangements Between German Government and Certain Organizations in Palestine," Sep. 14, 1933, PRO-FO 371/16757-1527.

CHAPTER 27

1. Werner Senator, "Strictly Confidential Memorandum on the Transfer of Jewish Capital from Germany," July 24, 1933, CZA S-25/9706, 2, pt. 6.

2. *Ibid.*, pts. 8, 9.

3. Ludwig Pinner, "The Meaning of the Immigration from Germany for Palestine," in Werner Feilchenfeld, Dolf Michaelis and Ludwig Pinner, *Haavara-Transfer Nach Palestina Und Einwanderung Deutscher Juden, 1933–1939* (Tubingen: Mohr Verlag, 1972), 100–2 (author's trans. 61–62).

4. Senator, "Strictly Confidential Memorandum on the Transfer of Jewish Capital," July 24, 1933, CZA S-25/9706, 2, pts. 13, 14.

5. *Ibid.*, pt. 16.

6. *Ibid.*, 3, pts, 17, 18.

7. *Ibid.*, pt. 20.

8. *Ibid.*, 3–5, pt. 21.

9. Leo Motzkin, memorandum, July 27, 1933, CZA L9/441, 1.

10. *Ibid.*, 7.

11.–14. Motzkin, memorandum, July 27, 1933, CZA L9/441, 8–10.

15. Paltreu to the Economics Ministry, Mr. von Heinz, Aug. 30, 1933, CZA S/97 (trans. NS); see letter, Marcus to Marguelies, Sep. 18, 1933, CZA S-7/84 (trans. YC).

16. Shaul Esh, *Studies in the Holocaust and Contemporary Jewry* (Jerusalem: ICJ, 1973), 104, n. 36 (author's trans. 99).

17. Confidential minutes, meeting of the Acting Executive Committee of the American Economic Committee for Palestine, Sep. 11, 1933, BPM at AJA, 3.

18.–19. Protocol of the Histadrut, July 31, 1933, ALM (trans. GG).

20.–22. Letter, Landauer to Hartenstein, August 17, 1933, CZA S-7/84 (trans. EF).

23.–24. Dr. Chaim Weizmann, "The German–Jewish Tragedy and Palestine," *Palestine Post*, July 5, 1933.

25. "Australian Gov't Considers German Jewish Settlement to Check Japanese Influx," *JDB*, July 13, 1933; "A Refugee Colony in North Australia," London *JC*, July 21, 1933, 18.

26. "Crimea, Ukraine Settlement Carried Out for Year, Bureya Fails of Quota," *JDB*, July 18, 1933.

27. "Zionists Rejected Manchuria as Jewish Refuge in 1933," *Jerusalem Post International Edition*, Jan. 24–30, 1982; also see letter, Maurice William to Justice Brandeis, Oct. 23, 1933, BPM at AJA; see Marvin Tokayer and Mary Swartz, *The Fugu Plan: The Untold Story of the Japanese and the Jews During World War II* (New York: Paddington, 1979), 9–10, 53, 63–64, 68–69.

CHAPTER 28

1. "Limiting of Jews in Trades and Professions Divides Austrian Press," *JDB*, July 24, 1933; "Nazi Terror Continues in Austrian Province," *JDB*, Aug. 3, 1933; "Silent Boycott Against Jews Revealed in Vienna," *JDB*, Aug. 15, 1933.

2. "Nazi Boycott Protest Reported Winning Backing of Mexican Government," *JDB*, July 27, 1933; "Mexican Anti-Semitism Takes Nationalistic Tinge as it Revives in Interior," *JDB*, Aug. 23, 1933, 6.

3. "Nazis Boo Appointment of Kelsen to Prague Post," *JDB*, June 2, 1933.

4. "Dutch Bar Uniformed Nazis," *NYT*, Aug. 24, 1933.

5. "Demand Swastika Fly on World Fair Building Repulsed by Germans," *JDB*, July 30, 1933; "Investigate Nazi Leaflets 'Bombing' of N.J. Meeting," *JDB*, Aug. 10, 1933.

6. "Ban Roumanian Paper for Criticism of Cuzists," *JDB*, June 22, 1933; "Roumanian Official Denies Anti-Semitic Numerus Clausus Plan," *JDB*, Aug. 16, 1933.

7. "Huge Sign Barring Jews Arouses Ire in Hamilton," *JDB*, July 12, 1933; "Swastika At Ball Game Provokes Toronto Riot with 8,000 Participating," *JDB*, Aug. 18, 1933.

8. "Budapest Curbs Nazis," *NYT*, Aug. 29, 1933.

9. "30,000 March in London Anti-Hitler Protest Parade; Police Balk Fascist Disorder," *JDB*, July 21, 1933; "Accuse Mosley of Conducting Raid on Rival Fascist Outfit," *JDB*, July 24, 1933; "Hitler and Nazi Regime Acclaimed in British Press, Goebbels' Attack Reprinted," *JDB*, Aug. 1, 1933; "Lord Rothermere Swallows Hitler Whole," *JC*, July 14, 1933, 8.

10. "Anonymous Appeal Calls on Brazilians to Create a Fascist Fatherland," *JDB*, Aug. 10, 1933.

11. Telegram, Wolff to RFM, Mar. 31, 1933, in Francis R. J. Nicosia, "Germany and the Palestine Question, 1933–1939" (unpub. Ph.D. diss., history, McGill, 1977), 162 (trans. GZ); "Templars as Nazis," *Palestine Post*, June 5, 1933.

12. "Brown Shirt Disorders in Poland," *JDB*, Aug. 16, 1933; "Jail Polish Anti-Semites for Attacks on Jews," *JDB*, Aug. 22, 1933.

13. "Iraq Disorders Involve Anti-Jewish Campaign, London Paper Reports," *JDB*, Aug. 24, 1933.

14. "Reports Huge Nazi Drive," *NYT*, June 11, 1933; "Nazis Active in Sweden," *NYT*, Aug. 22, 1933.

15. "Aryan World Congress Urged by Nazi Press," *JDB*, June 22, 1933.

16. "Jews Throughout Germany Dismissed Wholesale, Bank Head Flees to Switzerland," *JDB*, July 5, 1933.

17. Letter, Wise to the AJCAdCom, July 28, 1933, AJHS, 2; minutes, AJCAdCom, Aug. 3, 1933, AJHS, 3; see letter, Wise to Mack, July 19, 1933, BPM at AJA.

18. See letter, Wise to Mack, Aug. 20, 1933, in Carl Hermann Voss, ed., *Stephen S. Wise: Servant of the People* (Philadelphia: JPSA, 1969), 192–93.

CHAPTER 29

1. "Philadelphia Record Points Out Effects of Spontaneous Boycott Against Germany," *JDB*, July 30, 1933; "Germany; 'Blindfolded,'" *Time* magazine, Aug. 7, 1933.

2. "Philadelphia Record Points Out Effects of Spontaneous Boycott," *JDB*, July 30, 1933.

3. "German Trade Languishing; The Price of Barbarism," London *JC*, Aug. 4, 1933; "German Steel Gains in Domestic Market," *NYT*, Aug. 14, 1933.

4. "Correspondent Hails Genius of Hitler as Wrecking Crew Boss," *JDB*, Sep. 5, 1933.

5. "Hitler Invokes Aid of Business Heads," *NYT*, July 16, 1933; "German Exports Drop," *NYT*, Aug. 14, 1933; "Reich Loses Again on Trade Balance," *NYT*, Aug. 16, 1933; "Reich Fails to Gain Under Nazi Rule," *NYT*, Aug. 21, 1933.

6.–7. "Nazi Rule Menace to Wine Growers," *NYT*, Aug. 24, 1933.

8. "Nazis Oust Jewish Metallurgists, Then Name Them as Advisors," *JDB*, July 12, 1933; "Nazification of Jewish Firms," *JC*, July 21, 1933, 14.

9.–10. "Germans Squealing at the Boycott," *JC*, July 21, 1933, 30.

11. "Hitler Hard Up," *JC*, Aug. 11, 1933.

12.–13. Letter, "The Consul General at Berlin (Messersmith) to the Secretary of State," Sep. 1, 1933 *FRUS 1933*, (Washington, D.C.: United States Government Printing Office, 1949), II: 448–50.

14. Letter, "The Ambassador in Germany (Dodd) to the Secretary of State," Sep. 14, 1933, *FRUS*, 450–51.

15. "German Ship Lines Protest New Ban" and "Freight Restrictions Reported," *NYT*, Aug. 16, 1933.

16. "Reich Fails to Gain Under Nazis' Rule," *NYT*, Aug. 21, 1933; "Germany's Cotton Business Improves," *Wall Street Journal*, Aug. 23, 1933.

17.–18. "Minute by an Official of the Economic Department," Sep. 5, 1933, *DGFP, 1918–1945*, ser. C, (London: HMSO), 1957 I: 777–78.

19. "Minute by an Official of the Economic Department: Supplement to Today's Memorandum on a German–Rumanian Compensation Transaction," Sep. 5, 1933, *DGFP*, 779.

20. Memorandum, Davidson, "Meeting of the Reich Chancellor with the Americans Mann and Behn," Aug. 2, 1933, NA T-120 roll 5689, L495447 (trans. GZ).

21. "German Trade Languishing; The Price of Barbarism," *JC*, Aug. 4, 1933.

22. "The Success of the Boycott; Dr. Goebbels' Admission," *JC*, Sep. 8, 1933, 14.

23. "Reich Fails to Gain under Nazis' Rule," *NYT*, Aug. 21, 1933; "Germany Reports Big Cut in Jobless," *NYT*, Aug. 24, 1933.

24. "Reich Fails to Gain," *NYT*, Aug. 21, 1933; "Germany Reports Big Cut in Jobless," *NYT*, Aug. 24, 1933.

25. "Germany Reports Big Cut in Jobless," *NYT*, Aug. 24, 1933.

26. *Ibid.*; "Reich Fails to Gain," *NYT*, Aug. 21, 1933.

27. Report, "Mr. Newton (Berlin) to Sir J. Simon," July 11, 1933, *DBFP, 1919–1939*, 2nd ser., V: 1933 (London: HMSO, 1956), 413–14.

28. "Reich Fails to Gain Under Nazi Rule," *NYT*, Aug. 21, 1933.

29.–30. Report, "Mr. Newton (Berlin) to Sir J. Simon," July 11, 1933, *DBFP*, 413.

31. "Reich Fails to Gain," *NYT*, Aug. 21, 1933.

32. "Germany Reports Big Cut in Jobless," *NYT*, Aug. 24, 1933.

33. "Report Schacht Escapes Death by Assassins," *Chicago Daily News*, Aug. 24, 1933.

CHAPTER 30

1. See letter, Samuel Untermyer to B. Dubovsky, May 11, 1939, AJA, folder 8, JBC; letter, Lipsky to Weizmann, Sep. 24, 1933, CZA L-13/150.

2. See "Coordinating World Boycott," London *JC*, Aug. 4, 1933; see "Zionist Leadership," *JC*, Aug. 11, 1933.

3. See "Untermyer Back, Greeted in Harbor," and "Text of Untermyer's Address," *NYT*, Aug. 7, 1933; see "World Boycott of German Goods," *JC*, Aug. 4, 1933; see minutes, AJCAdCom, Aug. 3, 1933, AJHS; see "Samuel Untermyer: A Character Sketch," *Chicago Sentinal*, Sep. 28, 1933.

4. "Boycott Exceeds Untermyer's Hope," *NYT*, Aug. 1, 1933; "World Boycott of German Goods," *JC*, Aug. 4, 1933.

5. "Untermyer Back, Greeted in Harbor," and "Text of Untermyer's Address," *NYT*, Aug. 7, 1933; see "World Boycott of German Goods," *JC*, Aug. 4, 1933; see "Boycott of German Products Launched at N.Y. Conference," Boston *Jewish Advocate*, Sep. 12, 1933.

6. "German Exports Drop," *NYT*, Aug. 14, 1933.

7. "Text of Untermyer's Address," *NYT*, Aug. 7, 1933.

8. "Boycott Exceeds Untermyer's Hope," *NYT*, Aug. 1, 1933.

9.–20. Minutes, AJCAdCom, Aug. 3, 1933, 1–14.

21. "Untermyer Back, Greeted in Harbor," *NYT*, Aug. 7, 1933; "Enthusiastic Crowds Greet Untermyer Who Urges Boycott Spread in Broadcast," *JDB*, Aug. 8, 1933.

22. "Untermyer Back," *NYT*, Aug. 7, 1933.

23.–24. "Enthusiastic Crowds Greet Untermyer," *JDB*, Aug. 8, 1933.

25.–31. "Text of Untermyer's Address," *NYT*, Aug. 7, 1933.

32. Minutes, AJCAdCom, Aug. 17, 1933, AJHS, 1; see "American Jewish Congress to Consider Boycott Action," *JDB*, Aug. 16, 1933.

33.–34. Minutes, AJCAdCom, Aug. 17, 1933, AJHS, 1.

35. Cablegram, Wise to Deutsch, in minutes, AJCAdCom, Aug. 17, 1933, AJHS. 1–2.

36. "Rabbi Wise Breaks Silence on Boycott; Calls it Duty of All Self-Respecting Jews," *JDB*, Aug. 15, 1933; "Rabbi Wise Backs Boycott on Nazis," *NYT*, Aug. 15, 1933.

37. "Rabbi Wise Breaks Silence," *JDB*, Aug. 15, 1933; "Rabbi Wise Backs Boycott," *NYT*, Aug. 15, 1933.

38.–40. See minutes, AJCAdCom, Aug. 17, 1933, AJHS, 2–3.

41. Moshe Gottlieb, "The Anti-Nazi Boycott Movement in the American Jewish Community, 1933–1941" (unpub. Ph.D. diss., Near Eastern and Judaic studies, Brandeis, 1967), 103.

42. Press release, AJC, Aug. 21, 1933, BPM at AJA; see "Jews Here to Push Boycott on Hitler," *NYT*, Aug. 21, 1933.

43. "American Jewish Congress Endorses Boycott, Move to Adopt German Jewish Children Here," *JDB*, Aug. 22, 1933; "Resolution on Boycott Presented by Dr. Joseph Tenenbaum," Aug. 20,

1933, Tenenbaum Collection, folder 19, YIVO; press release, AJC, Aug. 21, 1933, BPM at AJA; see letters, Wise to Mack, Apr. 15 and July 14, 1933, in Carl Hermann Voss, ed., *Stephen S. Wise: Servant of the People* (Philadelphia: JPSA, 1969), 184–85, 191–92; see Morris Frommer, "The American Jewish Congress: A History, 1914–1950" (unpub. Ph.D. diss., history, Ohio State, 1978), 324–26; see Gottlieb, 99.

44.–50. Press release, AJC, Aug. 21, 1933, BPM at AJA, 2–9.

51.–53. "Samuel Untermyer Salutes American Jewish Congress Upon (its) Joining the Boycott Movement," *Der Morgan Journal*, Aug. 21, 1933 (trans. N. Stampfer and B. Nadel).

54.–56. "Exerpts from Address by Rabbi Jacob Sonderling at the National Executive Committee," Aug. 20, 1933, BPM at AJA.

57. "Samuel Untermyer Salutes," *Der Morgan Journal*, Aug. 21, 1933 (trans. B. Nadel); "American Jewish Congress Endorses Boycott," *JDB*, Aug. 22, 1933; press release, AJC, Aug. 21, 1933, BPM at AJA, 13.

58. "Samuel Untermyer Salutes," *Der Morgan Journal*, Aug. 21, 1933 (trans. B. Nadel); "American Jewish Congress Endorses Boycott," *JDB*, Aug. 22, 1933; "Jews Here Push Boycott of Reich," *NYT*, Aug. 21, 1933; press release, AJC, Aug. 21, 1933, BPM at AJA, 13.

CHAPTER 31

1. See "Zionist Convention Ratifies Hadassah Share in Naming Prague Delegates," *JDB*, July 7, 1933; also see letters, Wise to Mack, July 13 and 21, 1933, BPM at AJA.

2. Joseph Schechtman, *Fighter and Prophet: The Vladimir Jabotinsky Story, the Last years* (New York: Thomas Yoseloff, 1961), 215; also see "Make Palestine a Land of Fufillment, Sokolow Urges," *JDB*, Aug. 22, 1933, 4.

3. See "Revisionist Split Complete," *JC*, Aug. 11, 1933; see "Laborites Demand Voice in Actions Committee in Proportion to Strength," *JDB*, Aug. 16, 1933; see "Make Palestine Land of Fufillment," *JDB*, Aug. 22, 1933, 2.

4. See *Stenographisches Protokoll der Verhandlungen Des XVIII Zionistenkongresses Und Der Dritten Tagung Des Council Der Jewish Agency Für Palästina* (Wien: Fiba-Verlag, 1934) 23 (trans. GZ); also see Walter Laqueur, *A History of Zionism* (New York: Holt, Rinehart and Winston, 1972), 318; Schechtman, 191.

5. Schechtman, 191–92; see "General Zionists Protest Actions Committee Delay on Laborite Demands," *JDB*, Aug. 17, 1933; "Zionist Congress Awaits Weizmann," *NYT*, Aug. 29, 1933; "Laborites Renew Drive on Revisionists," *JDB*, Aug. 29, 1933, 4.

6. See *Selbstwehr*, Aug. 18, 1933, no. 33, p. 3 (trans. HG); see letter, Wise to Mack, Aug. 18, 1933, in Carl Hermann Voss, ed., *Stephen S. Wise: Servant of the People* (Philadelphia: JPSA, 1969), 192; see "Weizmann Neither Denies Nor Confirms

Reports He'll Attend Zionist Congress," *JDB*, Aug. 25, 1933; Schechtman, 194.

7. "New Yorkers Cable Prague to Recall Dr. Weizmann," *JDB*, Aug. 24, 1933.

8. Letter, Wolff to RFM, July 3, 1933, NA T-120 roll 4954, L368972/77 (trans. GZ).

9. Letter, Landauer, Leibenstein, Sereni and Skolnik, Aug. 4, 1933, CZA L-8/441 (trans. EF).

10. See "German Zionists Plead for Restraint, Practical Measures at Congress," *JDB*, Aug. 17, 1933.

11. Letter, "The Ministry of Economics to the Foreign Ministry," Aug. 10, 1933, *DGFP, 1918–1945*, ser. C, I (London: HMSO, 1957): 733.

12. Cordell Hull, *The Memoirs of Cordell Hull* (New York: Macmillan, 1948), I: 240; "Memorandum by the Secretary of State of a Conversation with the German Chargé (Luther)," Aug. 11, 1933, *FRUS 1933* (Washington, D.C.: United States Government Printing Office, 1949), II: 357.

13. See "Zionists Attacked," *JC*, July 21, 1933, 15; "German Zionists Plead for Restraint," *JDB*, Aug. 17, 1933.

14. "Hitlerites Bar German Zionists From Attending Congress," St. Louis *Modern View*, Aug. 24, 1933; "Refusal to Grant Visa to Jabotinsky Stirs Zionist Congress Circles," *JDB*, Aug. 16, 1933; see "Zionist Leader's Appeal to League," *JDB*, Aug. 23, 1933, 5, 7; "World Jewish Plea Urged on Zionists," *NYT*, Aug. 22, 1933; Martin Rosenbluth, *Go Forth and Serve: Early Years and Public Life* (New York: Herzl, 1961), 269.

15. "Reprisals Against German Zionists for Congress Acts Threatened by Rosenberg," *JDB*, Aug. 18, 1933; "Germany Watches Zionist Congress," *NYT*, Aug. 20, 1933.

16.–17. "Germany Watches Zionist Congress," *NYT*, Aug. 20, 1933.

18. "German Zionist Paper Banned After Answering Attack by Rosenberg," *JDB*, Aug. 21, 1933.

19. "Laborites Want Coalition for Zionist Organization Excluding Revisionists," *JDB*, Aug. 9, 1933.

20. "Refusal to Grant Visa to Jabotinsky Stirs Zionist Congress Circles," *JDB*, Aug. 16, 1933; "Grant Visa to Jabotinsky to Attend Prague Congress," *JDB*, Aug. 18, 1933; see "General Zionists Protest Actions Committee Delay on Laborite Demands," *JDB*, Aug. 17, 1933.

21. "Refusal to Grant Visa to Jabotinsky Stirs Zionist Congress Circles," and "Laborites Demand Voice in Actions Committee in Proportion to Strength," *JDB*, Aug. 16, 1933; see "Laborites Want Coalition for Zionist Organization Excluding Revisionists," *JDB*, Aug. 9, 1933.

22. "General Zionists Protest," *JDB*, Aug. 17, 1933.

23. "Actions Committee Reaches Compromise with Labor," *JDB*, Aug. 18, 1933; minutes, Actions Committee of ZO, first session, Aug. 17, 1933, CZA Z4/287/1 (trans. GB); see "Zionists Act to Aid 250,000 Reich Jews," *NYT*, Aug. 21, 1933; see "Reich Believed Ready to Allow Jews Seeking Homes in Palestine to Export Goods and Thousand Pounds in Capital," *JDB*, Aug. 24, 1933, 4.

24. Minutes, Actions Committee of ZO, first session, Aug. 17, 1933, CZA Z4/287/1, 9 (trans. GB); letter, Wise to Mack, Aug. 18, 1933, in Voss, 192.

25.–27. Minutes, Actions Committee of the ZO, first session, Aug. 17, 1933, CZA Z4/287/1, 11–13 (trans. GB).

28. Letter, Wise to Mack, Aug. 18, 1933, in Voss, 192.

29.–30. Minutes, Actions Committee of ZO, first session, Aug. 17, 1933, CZA Z4/287/1, 13–14 (trans. GB).

31. Letter, Wise to Mack, August 18, in Voss, 192.

32. *Selbstwehr*, Aug. 18, 1933, no. 33, 3 (trans. HG); see "Make Palestine Land of Fufillment," *JDB*, Aug. 22, 1933, 4.

33. See "Congress—and After," *JC*, Sep. 8, 1933, 7; see letter, Wise to Brandeis, Sep. 19, 1933, BPM at AJA; see "Observations of Jacob de Haas," Sep. 25, 1933, BPM AJA; see Schechtman, 197.

34. "Congress and the German Jews," and "Dr. Ruppin's Address," *JC*, Sep. 1, 1933, 7, 20; Arthur Ruppin, "Settling German Jews in Palestine," in Aruthur Ruppin, *Building Israel: Selected Essays, 1907–1935* (New York: Schocken, 1949), 269–82.

35. Ruppin, 278; also see letter, Landauer to Hartenstein, Aug. 17, 1933, CZA S-7/84 (trans. EF).

36. See "Make Palestine Land of Fufillment," *JDB*, Aug. 22, 1933, 2; Schechtman, 214–18; see "Zionist Congress Ends with World Appeal for Palestine Upbuilding," *JDB*, Sep. 6, 1933, 3; 18th ZC, 505 (trans. EF).

37. "18th World Zionist Congress Opens Today," *JDB*, Aug. 21, 1933.

38. *Der Morgen Journal*, Aug. 21, 1933, in Moshe Gottlieb, "The Anti-Nazi Boycott Movement in the American Jewish Community, 1933–1941" (unpub. Ph.D. diss. Near Eastern and Judaic studies, Brandeis, 1967), 116–17; see "Urges Congress Boycott Nazis," *JDB*, Aug. 22, 1933.

39.–40. *Der Morgen Journal*, Aug. 21, 1933, in Gottlieb, 116–17.

41. "Zionist Leader's Appeal to League," *JDB*, Aug. 23, 1933, 3.

CHAPTER 32

1. Joseph Wechsberg, *Prague: The Mystical City* (New York: Macmillan, 1971), 29, 50–53; Hans Kohn, "Before 1918 in Historic Lands," in *The Jews of Czechoslovakia: Historical Studies and Surveys* (Philadelphia: JPSA, 1968), I: 14.

2. Felix Weltsch, "Masaryk and Zionism," in *Thomas G. Masaryk and the Jews: A Collection of Essays*, trans. Benjamin R. Epstein (New York: B. Pollak, 1945), 82–83; see Weschberg, 14–15; see "President Masaryk and the German Jews," *JC*, Sep. 1, 1933.

3. "The Jewish Olympiad," *JC*, Sep. 1, 1933; "Prague Mayor Greets World Zionist Women," *JDB*, Aug. 14, 1933; "German Tongue Unused as Signs in 6 Languages Greet Congress Delegates," *JDB*, Aug. 15, 1933.

4. "18th Zionist Congress Opens—Mr. Sokolow's Address," *JC*, Aug. 25, 1933; photograph, "World Zionist Conference (sic)," *Boston Post*, Sep. 4, 1933, 13; "End Jewish Problem by Making Palestine Land of Fufillment Instead of Promise," *JDB*, Aug. 23, 1933.

5. See confidential report, Mr. Gurney to Sir John Simon, Sep. 21, 1933, PRO-FO 371/16927–1556; "End Jewish Problem by Making Palestine Land of Fufillment," *JDB*, Aug. 23, 1933.

6. "End Jewish Problem," *JDB*, Aug. 23, 1933, 2; "Grant Visa to Jabotinsky to Attend Prague Congress," *JDB*, Aug. 18, 1933.

7. "End Jewish Problem," *JDB*, Aug. 23, 1933; "Day to Day Story of the Congress," *New Palestine*, Sep. 20, 1933, 3; confidential report, Mr. Gurney to Sir John Simon, Sep. 21, 1933, PRO-FO 371/16927–1556.

8. "End Jewish Problem," *JDB*, Aug. 23, 1933, 2, 4, 8; "18th Zionist Congress Opens," *JC*, Aug. 25, 1933; "Day to Day Story of the Congress," *New Palestine*, Sep. 20, 1933.

9. "End Jewish Problem," *JDB*, Aug. 23, 1933.

2; see confidential report, Mr. Gurney to Sir John Simon, Sep. 21, 1933, PRO-FO 371/16927–1556.
10. "The Opening Speech," *JC*, Aug. 25, 1933; "End Jewish Problem," *JDB*, Aug. 23, 1933.
11. "End Jewish Problem," *JDB*, Aug. 23, 1933, 2.
12. "The Opening Speech," *JC*, Aug. 25, 1933; "End Jewish Problem," *JDB*, Aug. 23, 1933, 4;

"World Jewish Plea Urged on Zionists," *NYT*, Aug. 22, 1933.
13. "The Opening Speech," *JC*, Aug. 25, 1933; "End Jewish Problem," *JDB*, Aug. 23, 1933, 4.
14. "The Opening Speech," *JC*, Aug. 25, 1933; "End Jewish Problem," *JDB*, Aug. 23, 1933.
15. "End Jewish Problem," *JDB*, Aug. 23, 1933, 4.

CHAPTER 33

1.–2. "Make Palestine Land of Fufillment," *JDB*, Aug. 22, 1933, 2.
3. *Ibid.*; "World Jewish Plea Urged on Zionists," *NYT*, Aug. 22, 1933.
4. "Make Palestine Land of Fufillment," *JDB*, Aug. 22, 1933, 4.
5. "End Jewish Problem by Making Palestine Land of Fufillment Instead of Promise," *JDB*, Aug. 23, 1933, 8; "18th Zionist Congress Opens," *JC*, Aug. 25, 1933, 17.
6. "Reich Believed Ready to Allow Jews Seeking Homes in Palestine to Export Goods and Thousand Pounds in Capital," *JDB*, Aug. 24, 1933, 4; "Zionist Leader's Appeal to League," *JDB*, Aug. 23, 1933, 3.
7. "Zionist Leader's Appeal," *JDB*, Aug. 23, 1933, 1, 3; "Professor Brodetsky's Political Report," *JC*, Aug. 25, 1933, 17.
8. "Professor Brodetsky's Political Report," *JC*, Aug. 25, 1933, 17; "Zionist Leader's Appeal," *JDB*, Aug. 23, 1933, 3.
9. "Zionist Leader's Appeal," *JDB*, Aug. 23, 1933, 3.
10. *Ibid.*, 3, 5, 7; "Jewish Claims in Palestine," London *Times*, Aug. 23, 1933.
11. "Zionist Leader's Appeal," *JDB*, Aug. 23, 1933, 5.
12. *Vossische Zeitung*, Aug. 23, 1933 (trans. GZ).
13. "Reich Believed Ready to Allow Jews Seeking Homes in Palestine to Export Goods," *JDB*, Aug. 24, 1933, 2; "Presidium Elected," *JC*, Aug. 25, 1933, 17.
14. "Reich Names Bank as Trustee for Funds of Jews It May Allow to Migrate to Palestine," *JDB*,

Aug. 24, 1933; *Vossische Zeitung*, Aug. 23, 1933 (trans. GZ).
15.–16. "Reich Believed Ready," *JDB*, Aug. 24, 1933, 2.
17. "Reich Names Bank," *JDB*, Aug. 24, 1933.
18. "Accord With Reich Reported," *NYT*, Aug. 24, 1933; "Reich Believed Ready," *JDB*, Aug. 24, 1933; "Zion Congress Plans New Palestine Colony," *Chicago Daily News*, Aug. 24, 1933.
19. "Accord with Reich Reported," *NYT*, Aug. 24, 1933; "Reich Believed Ready," and "Reich Names Bank," *JDB*, Aug. 24, 1933; "Zion Congress Plans New Palestine Colony," *Chicago Daily News*, Aug. 24, 1933; "Agreement with Germany for Taking Out of Jewish Property to Palestine," *Haaretz*, Aug. 24, 1933 (trans. GB).
20.–22. "Mr. Sokolow Reviews World Jewry," *JC*, Aug. 25, 1933, 17; "Zionist Urges U.S. Administration Open Doors to German Jewish Exiles," *JDB*, Aug. 25, 1933, 2–3.
23. Arthur Ruppin, "Settling German Jews in Palestine," in Arthur Ruppin, *Building Israel: Selected Essays, 1907–1935* (New York: Schocken, 1949), 269.
24. *Ibid.*, 269–80; "Dr. Ruppin's Address," *JC*, Sep. 1, 1933, 20.
25.–26. Ruppin, 278.
27. *Stenographisches Protokoll Der Verhandlungen Des XVIII Zionistenkongresses Und Der Dritten Tagung Des Council Der Jewish Agency Für Palästina* (Wien: Fiba-Verlag, 1934), 190 (trans. GZ).
28. "Zionist Urges U.S. Administration Open Doors," *JDB*, Aug. 25, 1933, 1, 2.
29. See "Speech by Ruppin," 18th ZC, LBI and compare Ruppin, 269–82.

CHAPTER 34

1. "Zionists Reject Boycott of Reich," *NYT*, Aug. 25, 1933.
2. "Day to Day Story of the Congress," *New Palestine*, Sep. 20, 1933, 4.
3. "Resolution on the Persecution of the Jews in Germany," PRO-FO 371/16927–1556; "The Resolutions on Germany," *JC*, Sep. 1, 1933.
4.–5. "Resolution on the Persecution of the Jews in Germany," PRO-FO 371/16927–1556.
6. *Stenographisches Protokoll Der Verhandlungen Des XVIII Zionistenkongresses Und Der Dritten Tagung Des Council Der Jewish Agency Für Palästina* (Wien: Fiba-Verlag, 1934), 198–99 (trans. GZ).
7. *Ibid.*, 200–1; "The Resolutions on Germany," *JC*, Sep. 1, 1933.

8. Joseph Schechtman, *Fighter and Prophet: The Vladimir Jabotinsky Story, The Last Years* (New York: Thomas Yoseloff, 1961), 194; "Zionists Reject Boycott of Reich," *NYT*, Aug. 25, 1933.
9. *Rasswyet*, Sep. 2, 1933, in Schechtman, 194; *XVIII Zionistenkongresses*, 202.
10. *XVIII Zionistenkongresses*, 202 (trans. GZ); "Zionists Reject Boycott of Reich," *NYT*, Aug. 25, 1933.
11. *XVIII Zionistenkongresses*, 202 (trans. GZ).
12. "Zionists Reject Boycott of Reich," *NYT*, Aug. 25, 1933; "Zionist Assails Pact with Reich," *NYT*, Aug. 26, 1933; "Wife of Leader Shoved; 2 Zionist Factions Scrap," *Chicago Daily Tribune*, Aug. 25, 1933; Schechtman, 196–97.

CHAPTER 35

1. "Runschau Will Reappear After Official Shutdown," *JDB*, Aug. 25, 1933; "The Congress' Germany Resolution," *JR*, Aug. 29, 1933 (trans. GZ).

2. *Der Deutsche*, Aug. 25, 1933, in "Germans Favor Emigration," *NYT*, Aug. 26, 1933; "Nazis in Agreement With Zionists That Jews Must Give Up Homeland," *Chicago Daily News*, Aug. 26, 1933.

3. "The Transfer of Capital Belonging to Jewish German Citizens to Palestine," *Deutsche Allgemeine Zeitung*, Aug. 25, 1933 (trans. GZ); see "Transfer of Jewish Property to Palestine," *Selbstwehr*, Aug. 25, 1933, XXVII, nr. 35 (trans. EF); *Haaretz*, Aug. 27, 1933 (trans. GB); "German Capital for Palestine," *Palestine Post*, Aug. 25, 1933.

4. Telegram, Peirre Dreyfus and Max Klang for the Defense Committee for Persecuted German Jews, Aug. 25, 1933, CZA L-9/101 (trans. DD).

5. Telegram, Central Union of Merchants, Central Union of Jewish Craftsmen, Central Union of Retail Dealers, Aug. 26, 1933, CZA L-9/101 (trans. DD).

6. Telegram, Untermyer, Aug. 26, 1933, CZA L-9/101.

7. "General Debate Opens," London *JC*, Sep. 1, 1933, 21.

8. Walter Laqueur, *A History of Zionism* (New York: Holt, Rinehart and Winston, 1972), 326–28, see 335, 487.

9. See Chaim Arlosoroff, "Report From Germany," in minutes, Executive Session of ZO, June 1, 1933, CZA L-13/138-1 (trans. DD).

10. Arthur Ruppin, "Settling German Jews in Palestine," in Arthur Ruppin, *Building Israel: Se-*lected Essays, *1907–1935* (New York: Schocken, 1949), 278.

11. "The General Debate Opens," *JC*, Sep. 1, 1933, 21.

12.–14. *Stenographisches Protokoll Der Verhandlungen Des XVIII Zionistenkongresses Und Der Dritten Tagung Des Council Der Jewish Agency Für Palästina* (Wien: Fiba-Verlag, 1934), 244 (trans. GZ).

15. "General Debate Opens," *JC*, Sep. 1, 1933, 21.

16. "Mr. Jabotinsky's Statement," *JC*, Sep. 1, 1933, 25; Joseph Schechtman, *Fighter and Prophet: The Vladimir Jabotinsky Story, the Last Years* (New York: Thomas Yoseloff, 1961), 194–95.

17. "Mr. Jabotinsky's Statement," *JC*, Sep. 1, 1933; Schechtman, 194–95, 218–19.

18.–22. *XVIII Zionistenkongresses*, 248 (trans. GZ).

23. "Day by Day Account," *New Palestine*, Sep. 20, 1933, 4–5; "Possible Composition of the Executive," *JC*, Sep. 1, 1933, 22; "Scene at the Zionist Congress," *Palestine Post*, Aug. 28, 1933.

24. "Possible Composition of the Executive," *JC*, Sep. 1, 1933, 22; "Scene at the Zionist Congress," *Palestine Post*, Aug. 28, 1933.

25. "The Labor-Revisionist Fight," *JC*, Sep. 1, 1933, 22; see Schechtman, 196.

26. Schechtman, 196; see "The Labor-Revisionist Fight," *JC*, Sep. 1, 1933, 22.

27. Schechtman, 196.

28. Ibid.; "Laborites Renew Drive on Revisionists," *JDB*, Aug. 29, 1933.

CHAPTER 36

1. "Zionists' Resolution on Germany Riles Beobachter," *JDB*, Aug. 28, 1933; Joseph Schechtman, *Fighter and Prophet: The Vladimir Jabotinsky Story, the Last Years* (N.Y.: Thomas Yoseloff, 1961), 217.

2. "Congress Dawdles," London *JC*, Sep. 1, 1933, 25; see Schechtman, 218–19; see memo, Jabotinsky to all Central Committees of Revisionist-Zionists, Oct. 30, 1933, JABA, filc 2/23/2, H-14 (trans. SS).

3. Schechtman, 218; letter, Jabotinsky to Elias Ginsberg, Sep. 8, 1933, in Schechtman, 218.

4.–8. "Untermyer Urges B'nai B'rith Join Boycott; Criticizes Zionist Congress for Nazi Deal," *JDB*, Aug. 29, 1933.

9. See *Financial News of Palestine*, no. 10, June 5, 1933, BPM at AJA; see Great Britain Colonial Office, *Palestine and Trans-Jordan for the Year 1932* (London: HMSO, 1933), 166–67; see Great Britain Colonial Office, *Palestine and Trans-Jordan for the Year 1933* (London: HMSO, 1934), 197, 203.

10. *Financial News of Palestine*, no. 10, June 5, 1933, BPM at AJA; see Great Britain Colonial Office, *Palestine, 1932*, 166; Great Britain Colonial Office, *Palestine, 1933*, 197–98.

11. "The Future of Citrus," *Palestine Post*, July 7, 1933; see minutes, American Economic Committee for Palestine, Oct. 9, 1933, BPM at AJA, 15–16; "New Season, What of the Citrus Crop?" *Palestine Post*, Sep. 28, 1933; see "Reich Facilitates Exodus to Palestine," *NYT*, Sep. 1, 1933.

12. See "Palestine Trade With the Nazis," *Palestine Post*, Aug. 30, 1933; see handwritten statement, Herr Erwin Schuster, no date (early Sep. 1933), CZA S-25/9706 (trans. EF); see cable, Hoofien, Sep. 8, 1933, CZA S-25/9706 (trans. EF/YC).

13. See "British, Palestine Govt's, Zionists Deny Reports as Nazis Reveal Orange Deal," *JDB*, Aug. 29, 1933; see "The Labour-Revisionist Fight," *JC*, Sep. 1, 1933; see "Nazis Report Deal With Palestine," *NYT*, Aug. 29, 1933.

14. "British, Palestine Govt's, Zionists Deny Reports," *JDB*, Aug. 29, 1933; "Labor-Revisionist Fight," *JC*, Sep. 1, 1933; "Nazis Report Deal With Palestine," *NYT*, Aug. 29, 1933.

15. "British, Palestine Govt's, Zionists Deny Reports," *JDB*, Aug. 29, 1933; "Nazis Report Deal with Palestine," *NYT*, Aug. 29, 1933.

16. "Boycott Chief Doubts Barter," *NYT*, Aug. 29, 1933.

17. "The Zionist Congress," London *Times*, Aug. 29, 1933; "Loan to Settle German Jews in

Palestine Urged," *Chicago Daily Tribune*, Aug. 29, 1933; "Wise Attacks Weizmann," *JC*, Sep. 1, 1933.

18. "Nazis Report Deal With Palestine," *NYT*, Aug. 29, 1933.

19. "Palestine Trade With The Nazis," *Palestine Post*, Aug. 30, 1933.

20. "British, Palestine Govt's, Zionists Deny Reports," *JDB*, Aug. 29, 1933.

21. "On the Question of the Agreement for an Orange Shipment to Germany," *Haaretz*, Aug. 29, 1933.

22.–25. "Untermyer, Rabbi Silver Denounce Deals Reported Negotiated with Germany," *JDB*, Aug. 30, 1933.

26. *Ibid.*; see "Untermyer Urges B'nai B'rith Join Boycott," *JDB*, Aug. 29, 1933.

27. "New Yorkers Cable Prague to Recall Dr. Weizmann," *JDB*, Aug. 24, 1933.

28. See "Congress News Item," *JC*, Sep. 1, 1933; see letters, Louis Lipsky to Weizmann, Sep. 12 and 24, 1933, CZA L-13/150.

29. See "Wise Attacks Laborites, Weizmann, Urges Zionist Congress to Elect Leaders Who Will Carry On Fight for Jewish State," *JDB*, Aug. 30, 1933; see "Weizmann Neither Denies Nor Confirms

Reports He'll Attend Zionist Congress," *JDB*, Aug. 25, 1933; see letter, Wise to AJCAdCom, July 28, 1933, AJHS; see "Congress—and After," *JC*, Sep. 8, 1933, 7; see "Dr. Wise's Report on His Activities in Europe, Verbatim Record," in minutes, AJCAdCom, Sep. 23, 1933, AJHS, 8–9.

30. "Wise Attacks Laborites," *JDB*, Aug. 30, 1933; "Wise Attacks Weizmann," *JC*, Sep. 1, 1933, 25.

31. *Stenographisches Protokoll Der Verhandlungen Des XVIII Zionistenkongresses Und Der Dritten Tagung Des Council Der Jewish Agency Für Palästina* (Wien: Fiba-Verlag, 1934), 314–19 (trans. GZ); see "Wise Attacks Laborites," *JDB*, Aug. 30, 1933; "Wise Attacks Weizmann," *JC*, Sep. 1, 1933, 25; see "Unfinished Business Prolongs Session of Zionist Congress," *JDB*, Aug. 31, 1933, 2, 4.

32. *XVIII Zionistenkongresses*, 314–19 (trans. GZ); see "Wise Attacks Laborites," *JDB*, Aug. 30, 1933; see "Unfinished Business Prolongs Session of Zionist Congress," *JDB*, Aug. 31, 1933.

33.–40. *XVIII Zionistenkongresses*, 322–24 (trans. GZ).

41. *Ibid.*; see "Wise Attacks Laborites," *JDB*, Aug. 30, 1933, 2.

CHAPTER 37

1. "Hoofien, Eliezer Siegfried," *Encyclopaedia Judaica* (Jerusalem: Keter, 1972), VIII: 968–69.

2. Letter, Hoofien to Motzkin, Aug. 24, 1933, CZA L-9/101 (trans. GB/DD).

3.–12. Handwritten notes, E. S. Hoofien, no date, CZA A-95/19 (trans. DD/GZ).

13. *Ibid.*; see minutes, Political Committee of the 18th ZC, 5th meeting, Aug. 29, 1933, CZA Z-4/232/4 (trans. GB).

14. Minutes, Political Committee of the 18th ZC, 5th meeting, Aug. 29, 1933, CZA Z-4/232/4, 26–27 (trans. GB).

15. *Ibid.*, 27–28; see handwritten notes, Hoofien, CZA A-95/19 (trans. GZ/DD); see "Dr. Wise's Report on His Activities in Europe, Verbatim Record," in minutes, AJCAdCom, Sep. 23, 1933, AJHS, 9–10.

16. Minutes, Political Committee of the 18th ZC, 5th Meeting, Aug. 29, 1933, CZA Z-4/232/4, 28 (trans. GB); "Wise Repudiated; The 'Three Million Mark' Agreement," *JC*, Sep. 1, 1933, 26.

17.–19. Minutes, Political Committee of the 18th ZC, 5th meeting, Aug. 29, 1933, CZA Z-4/232/4, 29 (trans. GB).

20. *Ibid.* "Wise Repudiated," *JC*, Sep. 1, 1933, 26.

21.–22. Handwritten notes, E. S. Hoofien, CZA A-95/19 (trans. DD/GZ).

23. "Unfinished Business Prolongs Sessions of Zionist Congress," *JDB*, Aug. 31, 1933.

24.–25. *Stenographisches Protokoll Der Verhandlungen Des XVIII Zionistenkongresses Und Der Dritten Tagung Des Council Der Jewish Agency Für Palästina* (Wien: Fiba-Verlag, 1934), 329–36, see 334–338 (trans. EF).

26. *Ibid.*, 342; "Unfinished Business Prolongs Session," *JDB*, Aug. 31, 1933, 4.

27. *XVIII Zionistenkongresses*, 342; "Unfinished Business Prolongs Session," *JDB*, Aug. 31, 1933, 4.

28.–31. *XVIII Zionistenkongresses*, 350–52 (trans. EF).

32. Minutes, meeting of the Political Committee of the 18th ZC, 6th meeting, Aug. 30, 1933, CZA Z-4/232/4, 32–35 (trans. GB).

33. See "Zionist Congress Vote Inquiry Commission for Palestine Terrorist Group," *JDB*, Sep. 1, 1933, 4.

34. *Ibid.*; "Dr. Wise's Report on His Activities in Europe, Verbatim Record," in minutes, AJCAdCom, Sep. 23, 1933, AJHS, 10.

35. "Zionist Congress Votes Inquiry Commission," *JDB*, Sep. 1, 1933, 4.

36.–38. *XVIII Zionistenkongresses*, 382–83 (trans. EF).

39. "Plea for Unity at Congress," *Palestine Post*, Sep. 1, 1933.

CHAPTER 38

1. "Zionist Congress Votes Inquiry Commission for a Palestine Terrorist Group," *JDB*, Sep. 1, 1933.

2. *Ibid.*; "Actions Committee Resolution Adopted," *JC*, Sep. 8, 1933, 20; *Stenographisches Protokoll Der Verhandlungen Des XVIII Zionisten-*

kongresses Und Der Dritten Tagung Des Council Der Jewish Agency Für Palästina (Wien: Fiba-Verlag, 1934), 397–98 (trans GZ/EF).

3. "Zionist Congress Votes Inquiry," *JDB*, Sep. 1, 1933; "Actions Committee Resolution Adopted,"

JC, Sep. 8, 1933, 20; *XVIII Zionistenkongresses*, 397–98; Joseph Schechtman, *Fighter and Prophet: The Vladimir Jabotinsky Story, the Last Years* (New York: Thomas Yoseloff, 1961), 195–96.

4. "Zionist Congress Votes Inquiry," *JDB*, Sep. 1, 1933; "Actions Committee Resolution Adopted," *JC*, Sep. 8, 1933; "Zionists Will Sift Palestine 'Terror,' " *NYT*, Sep. 1, 1933; "World Zionists to Probe Alleged 'Terror,' " *Chicago Daily Tribune*, Sep. 1, 1933; *XVIII Zionistenkongresses*, 402.

5. See "Jewish Oranges for Germany," *JC*, Sep. 1, 1933; see "British, Palestine Govt's, Zionists Deny Reports," *JDB*, Aug. 29, 1933; "Nazis Report Deal with Palestine, *NYT*, Aug. 29, 1933.

6. "The Ambassador in Germany (Dodd) to the Secretary of State," Sep. 7, 1933 *FRUS: 1933*, (Washington, D.C.: United States Government Printing Office, 1949), II: 356–58; see report, Mr. Newton, Berlin, "Financial Arrangement Between German Government and Certain Organizations in Palestine," Sep. 14, 1933, PRO-FO 371/16757–1527.

7. See "Reich Facilitates Exodus to Palestine," *NYT*, Sep. 1, 1933; see "German Jews' Emigration to Palestine," London *Times*, Sep. 2, 1933; "Palestine–German Agreement," *Palestine Post*, Sep. 3, 1933.

8. See "The Palestine–German Orange Agreement," *Palestine Post*, Sep. 2, 1933; "Reich Facilitates Exodus to Palestine," *NYT*, Sep. 1, 1933.

9. "Warsaw Community Protests Palestine–German Agreement," and "U.S. Jewish War Veterans Condemn Nazi–Palestine Deal," *JDB*, Sep. 1, 1933.

10. "The Emigration Agreement," *JC*, Sep. 8, 1933, 15–16.

11. Minutes, Political Committee of the 18th ZC, 9th meeting, Sep. 2, 1933, CZA Z-4/232/4, 39–40 (trans. GB).

12. *Ibid.*; see "Dr. Wise's Report on his Activities in Europe, Verbatim Record," in minutes, AJCAdCom, Sep. 23, 1933, AJHS, 10.

13. Minutes, Political Committee of the 18th ZC, 9th meeting, Sep. 2, 1933, CZA Z-4/232/4, 40 (trans. GB).

14. *Ibid.*, 40–41; see "Dr. Wise's Report," in minutes, AJCAdCom, Sep. 23, 1933, AJHS, 10.

15. Minutes, Political Committee of the 18th ZC, 9th meeting, Sep. 2, 1933, CZA Z-4/232/4, 41

(trans. GB); "Re-Election of Dr. Nahum Sokolow Looms As World Zionist Congress Draws to a Close," *JDB*, Sep. 5, 1933.

16.–20. Minutes, Political Committee of the 18th ZC, 9th meeting, Sep. 2, 1933, CZA Z-4/232/4, 41.

21. *Ibid.*; "Dr. Wise's Report," in minutes, AJCAdCom, Sep. 23, 1933, AJHS, 10; *XVIII Zionistenkongresses*, 505 (trans. EF); see "Zionist Congress Ends," *JDB*, Sep. 6, 1933, 3.

22. Minutes, Political Committee of the 18th ZC, 9th meeting, Sep. 2, 1933, CZA Z-4/232/4, 43 (trans. GB).

23. "Political Resolutions of the 18th Zionist Congress," PRO-FO 371/16927–1556.

24. See Comite Executif de Congres Juif Mondial, ed., *Protocole de la IIe Conference Juif Mondiale* (Geneva), 82–87, see 83 (trans. GZ).

25. "Getting Down to Work," *JC*, Sep. 8, 1933, 20–21; "Zionist Congress Ends With World Appeal for Palestine Upbuilding," *JDB*, Sep. 6, 1933, 4; *XVIII Zionistenkongresses*, 435–39.

26. "Getting Down to Work," *JC*, Sep. 8, 1933, 20–21; "Zionist Congress Ends," *JDB*, Sep. 6, 1933, 4; *XVIII Zionistenkongresses*, 435–39.

27. "The Final Proceedings," *JC*, Sep. 8, 1933, 21; see "Zionist Congress Ends," *JDB*, Sep. 6, 1933; *XVIII Zionistenkongresses*, 440 et seq.

28. *Ibid.*, 1; see "Weizmann as Leader?" *JC*, Sep. 1, 1933, 25; "The End In Sight," *JC*, Sep. 8, 1933, 21; see protocol, conference in Moran, Sep. 19, 1933, CZA S-25/9809.

29. "Zionist Congress Ends," *JDB*, Sep. 6, 1933, 1.

30. See "Rothenberg and Lipsky Back from Prague Tell of Zionist Congress and German Situation," *New Palestine*, Sep. 20, 1933.

31. *XVIII Zionistenkongresses*, 505 (trans. EF/GZ); see "Political Resolutions of the 18th ZC," PRO-FO 371/16927–1556.

32. *XVIII Zionistenkongresses*, 505 (trans. GZ/EF); "Zionist Congress Ends," *JDB*, Sep. 6, 1933, 3.

33. *XVIII Zionistenkongresses*, 505; "Zionist Congress Ends," *JDB*, Sep. 6, 1933, 3.

34.–39. *XVIII Zionistenkongresses*, p. 505–7.

40. "Zionist Congress Ends," *JDB*, Sep. 6, 1933, 3; "The Final Proceedings," *JC*, Sep. 8, 1933, 22; *XVIII Zionistenkongresses*, 517–18.

CHAPTER 39

1. See "Those German Trading Agreements," *JC*, Oct. 10, 1933, 8; see "Rothenberg and Lipsky Back from Prague, Tell of Zionist Congress and German Situation," *New Palestine*, Sep. 20, 1933; see press conference with Stephen Wise, in press release, *AJC*, Sep. 16, 1933, BPM at AJA; see "Lipsky Back from Prague," *JDB*, Sep. 25, 1933; also see "The Nazi–Palestine Deal," New Orleans *Jewish Ledger*, Sep. 8, 1933.

2. "Those German Trading Agreements," *JC*, Oct. 13, 1933, 8.

3. "The Congress Must Speak Out," St. Louis *Modern View*, Sep. 14, 1933.

4. Press conference with Stephen Wise, in press release, *AJC*, Sep. 16, 1933, BPM at AJA, 4.

5. "Rothenberg and Lipsky Back from Prague," *New Palestine*, Sep. 20, 1933.

6. "Storm in Zionist Actions Committee as Factions Charge Plot on Inquiry," *JDB*, Sep. 6, 1933.

7. "Those German Trading Agreements," *JC*, Oct. 13, 1933, 8.

8. Comite Executif de Congres Juif Mondial,

ed., *Protocole de la IIe Conference Juive Mondiale* (Geneva), 5–7.
9. "World Jewry and Herr Hitler," London *Times*, Sep. 6, 1933.
10. Congres Jiuf Mondial, 9–20.
11.–15. *Ibid.*, 23–24.
16. See "The Anti-Nazi Boycott," St. Louis *Modern View*, Sep. 7, 1933; see "Palestine Oranges and Germany," Omaha, Nebraska *Jewish Press*, Sep. 8, 1933; see telegram, Central Organization of Academicians in Poland to the 18th ZC, Sep. 1, 1933, CZA L-9/101 (trans. DD); see "Boycott in Toronto," *JDB*, Sep. 5, 1933; "Texas Young Judeans Join Boycott," and "Chicago Boycott Leader Gets Threatening Letter," *JDB*, Sep. 7, 1933; "Boycott of German Goods," London *Times*, Sep. 7, 1933.

17. See Jacob Katz, *Tradition and Crisis: Jewish Society at the End of the Middle Ages* (Glencoe: Free Press of Glencoe, 1961), 99–101.
18.–21. "Orthodox Rabbis Pronounce Excommunication," *JDB*, Sep. 7, 1933; "Orthodox Rabbis Vote Boycott," *NYT*, Sep. 7, 1933; "Orthodox Jews Boycott 'All Things German,' " *Chicago Daily Tribune*, Sep. 7, 1933.
22. See Congres Juif Mondial, 31–39 (trans, GZ); "League of Nations Ready to Defend Jews," *JDB*, Sep. 7, 1933, 2.
23. See Congres Juif Mondial, 37; "League of Nations Ready," *JDB*, Sep. 7, 1933.
24. See Congres Juif Mondial, 37.
25. *Ibid.*, 41–50, see 50 (trans. GZ).
26.–28. *Ibid.*, 60–63.

CHAPTER 40

1. Comite Executif du Congres Juif Mondial, ed., *Protocole de la IIe Conference Juive Mondiale* (Geneva), 67–68 (trans. GZ); see "Geneva Conference Delegates Protest Nazi Deals, Criticize Zionists for Entering Them," *JDB*, Sep. 8, 1933.
2. Congres Juif Mondial, 68; "Geneva Conference Delegates Protest," *JDB*, Sep. 8, 1933.
3.–7. Congres Juif Mondial, 68–69.
8. *Ibid.*, 72–75; see Walter Laqueur, *A History of Zionism* (New York: Holt, Rinehart and Winston, 1972), 318–19; see Joseph Schechtman, *Fighter and Prophet: The Vladimir Jabotinsky Story, the Last Years* (New York: Thomas Yoseloff, 1961), 237.
9.–12. Congres Juif Mondial, 75–77.
13. "The Zionist Congress," London *Times*, Sep. 7, 1933; "Jewish Delegates Back Nazi Boycott," *NYT*, Sep. 8, 1933; "World Jewish Conference Votes to Support Anti-German Boycott," St. Louis

Modern View, Sep. 14, 1933; also see "Jewish Delegates at Geneva Back Nazi Boycott," Philadelphia *Jewish Exponent*, Sep. 15, 1933.
14. "Jewish Delegates Back Nazi Boycott," *NYT*, Sep. 8, 1933; "Jewish Delegates At Geneva Back Nazi Boycott," Philadelphia *Jewish Exponent*, Sep. 15, 1933; "World Jewish Conference Votes to Support Anti-German Boycott," St. Louis *Modern View*, Sep. 14, 1933.
15. Report, American Consulate in Geneva to the Secretary of State, "Second World Jewish Conference," Sep. 22, 1933, NA 540 .16 JEWISH CONFERENCES/1, 3–4; see Congres Juif Mondial, 89; "Jewish Delegates Back Nazi Boycott," *NYT*, Sep. 8, 1933; see "Official Boycott on German Goods," *Boston Post*, Sep. 8, 1933.
16.–18. Congres Juif Mondial, 82–87 (trans. GZ).

CHAPTER 41

1. Comite Executif du Congres Juif Mondial, *Protocole de la IIe Conference Juive Mondiale* (Geveva), 89–90 (trans. GZ).
2. *Ibid.*, 89–92.
3. Congres Juif Mondial, 92–93.
4.–6. Congres Juif Mondial, 93.
7. See "Jewish Delegates Back Nazi Boycott," *NYT*, Sep. 8, 1933; see "League Aid Asked for German Jews," *NYT*, Sep. 9, 1933.
8. Congres Juif Mondial, 62.
9. *Ibid.*, 94.
10. "League Aid Asked for German Jews," *NYT*, Sep. 9, 1933.
11. Congres Juif Mondial, 94–101.
12. *Ibid.*, 101–2; see Louis Lipsky, *Memoirs in*

Profile (Philadelphia: JPSA, 1975), 140–44; see Oscar I. Janowsky, *The Jews and Minority Rights, 1898–1919* (New York: Columbia, 1933), 309–18.
13.–17. Congres Juif Mondial, 101–2.
18. *Ibid.*, 102–103; "League Aid Asked for German Jews," *NYT*, Sep. 9, 1933.
19. "World Jewish Conference Votes to Support Anti-German Boycott," St. Louis *Modern View*, Sep. 14, 1933; "How Many Voices," *JC*, Sep. 15, 1933, 8; see "Jewish Delegates at Geneva Back Boycott," Philadelphia *Jewish Exponent*, Sep. 15, 1933; "League Aid Asked for German Jews," *NYT*, Sep. 9, 1933; "World Jewry and Hitlerism," London *Times*, Sep. 9, 1933; see Congres Juif Mondial, 102.

CHAPTER 42

1.–4. "Dr. Wise's Report on His Activities in Europe, Verbatim Record," in minutes, AJCAdCom, Sep. 23, 1933, AJHS, 4.
5. *Ibid.*; press conference with Dr. Wise, in press release, AJC, Sep. 16, 1933, BPM at AJA.
6. "Dr. Stephen S. Wise Says League Will Re-

view Hitler Menace to World," Philadelphia *Jewish Exponent*, Sep. 15, 1933; press conference with Stephen Wise, in press release, AJC, Sep. 16, 1933, BPM at AJA.
7. "Dr. Stephen S. Wise Says League Will Review Hitler Menace," Philadelphia *Jewish Exponent*,

Sep. 15, 1933; press conference with Stephen Wise, in press release, AJC, Sep. 16, 1933, BPM at AJA; "Nazi Threat to Jews More Grave Than World Knows, Says Wise on Return," *JDB*, Sep. 18, 1933.

8.–13. Press conference with Stephen Wise, in press release, AJC, Sep. 16, 1933, BPM at AJA, 2–4.

14. *Ibid.*, 7.

15.–20. "Dr. Wise's Report on His Activities in Europe, Verbatim Record," in minutes, AJCAdCom, Sep. 23, 1933, BPM at AJA, 1–13.

21.–25. Minutes, AJCAdCom, Sep. 23, 1933, BPM at AJA, 14–16.

26. Press release, AJC, Sep. 25, 1933, BPM at AJA, 3.

27.–29. *Ibid.*, 5.

30. "Swedish Trade Unions Order German Boycott," *NYT*, Sep. 7, 1933; "$500,000 Sought for Nazi Boycott," *NYT*, Sep. 11, 1933; see "Nazi Press Lashes Einstein, Laski, Zionists; Warns Britain Against Boycott," *JDB*, Sep. 13, 1933.

31. "Nazi Press Lashes Einstein," *JDB*, Sep. 13, 1933.

32. "Hitler and Goebbels Plead for Winter Relief Move," *Chicago Daily News*, Sep. 13, 1933.

33. *Ibid.*; "Unemployed in Germany," London *Times*, Sep. 14, 1933; "German Winter Relief," London *Times*, Sep. 15, 1933.

34. "Hitler and Goebbels Plead," *Chicago Daily News*, Sep. 13, 1933; "Unemployed in Germany," London *Times*, Sep. 14, 1933; "German Winter Relief," London *Times*, Sep. 15, 1933.

35. "Unemployed in Germany," London *Times*, Sep. 14, 1933; see "Winter Relief for Jews," *JC*, Nov. 10, 1933, 12.

36. "$500,000 Sought for Nazi Boycott," *NYT*, Sep. 11, 1933.

37. *Ibid.*; "1,500 Honor Untermyer at Testimonial Dinner; Boycott Conference Organizes for Work," *JDB*, Sep. 12, 1933; "Boycott Movement Against the Nazis," Boston *Jewish Advocate*, Sep. 12, 1933; "American Jewish Bodies Move to Strengthen Boycott, Curb Nazi Activities Here," Boston *Jewish Advocate*, Sep. 26, 1933.

38. "$500,000 Sought for Nazi Boycott," *NYT*, Sep. 11, 1933.

39. "The Boycott Movement Against the Nazis," Boston *Jewish Advocate*, Sep. 12, 1933; "American Jewish Bodies Move to Strengthen Boycott," Boston *Jewish Advocate*, Sep. 26, 1933.

40. "1,500 Honor Untermyer," *JDB*, Sep. 12, 1933.

41. "Smith Denounces Nazis as 'Stupid,' " "Smith's Talk at Untermyer Dinner," and "$500,000 Sought for Nazi Boycott," *NYT*, Sep. 11, 1933; "1,500 Honor Untermyer," *JDB*, Sep. 12, 1933; see "To Raise $500,000 Fund for Boycott," Philadelphia *Jewish Exponent*, Sep. 15, 1933; see "Untermyer to Take Helm of Boycott Movement," Omaha *Jewish Press*, Sep. 15, 1933; "Boycott of German Products Launched at N.Y. Conference," Boston *Jewish Advocate*, Sep. 12, 1933; "Anti-Nazi Boycott in America," *Palestine Post*, Sep. 11, 1933.

42. See "German-Made Goods Listed for Boycott," *NYT*, Sep. 12, 1933; see "Nazi Boycott Plans Widen," *NYT*, Sep. 18, 1933; see "American Jewish Bodies Move to Strengthen Boycott," Boston *Jewish Advocate*, Sep. 26, 1933.

43. "Chicagoans Press Anti-Nazi Boycott," *NYT*, Sep. 16, 1933.

44. "Anti-Nazi Boycott Plans Widen," *NYT*, Sep. 18, 1933; "Untermyer Will Address Hartford Anti-Nazi Rally," Boston *Jewish Advocate*, Sep. 26, 1933.

Index